MAGILL'S
CINEMA
ANNUAL

MAGILL'S CINEMA ANNUAL

1987

A Survey of the Films of 1986

Edited by

FRANK N. MAGILL

SALEM PRESS

Pasadena, California   Englewood Cliffs, New Jersey

LIBRARY OF CONGRESS CATALOG CARD No. 83-644357
ISBN 0-89356-406-0
ISSN 0739-2141

First Printing

PRINTED IN THE UNITED STATES OF AMERICA

PUBLISHER'S NOTE

Magill's Cinema Annual, 1987, is the sixth annual volume in a series that developed from the thirteen-volume core set, *Magill's Survey of Cinema*. Each annual covers the preceding year and follows a similar format in reviewing the films of the year. This format consists of five general sections: essays of general interest, the films of 1986, retrospective films, lists of obituaries and awards, and the indexes.

In the first section, the first article reviews the career and accomplishments of the recipient of the Life Achievement Award, which is presented by the American Film Institute. In 1986, this award was given to the distinguished director-screenwriter-producer Billy Wilder. Following this initial essay, the reader will find interviews with several industry notables. This year there are four interviews with the following: producer Pandro S. Berman, actor Willem Dafoe, director-screenwriter Jim Jarmusch, and screenwriter Catherine Turney. The next essay lists selected film books published in 1986. Briefly annotated, the list provides a valuable guide to the current literature about the film industry and its leaders.

The largest section of the annual, "Selected Films of 1986," is devoted to essay-reviews of eighty-seven significant films released in the United States in 1986. The reviews are arranged alphabetically by the title under which the film was released in the United States. Original and alternate titles are cross-referenced to the American-release title in the Title Index.

Each article begins with selected credits for the film. Credit categories include: Production, Direction, Screenplay, Cinematography, Editing, Art direction, and Music. Also included are the MPAA rating, the running time, and a list of the principal characters with the corresponding actors. This introductory information on a film not released originally in the United States also includes the country of origin and the year the film was released there. If the information for any of the standard categories was unavailable, the heading is followed by the phrase "no listing." Additional headings such as Special effects, Costume design, and Song have been included in an article's introductory top matter when appropriate. Also, the symbol (AA) in the top matter identifies those artists who have received an Academy Award for their contribution to a film from the Academy of Motion Picture Arts and Sciences.

The section of the annual labeled "More Films of 1986" supplies the reader with an alphabetical listing of an additional 239 feature films released in the United States during the year. Included are brief credits and short descriptions of the films. These films can be located, along with any cross-references, in the indexes.

Following "More Films of 1986" are essays on thirteen retrospective films. These essay-reviews follow exactly the same format as the articles in the "Selected Films of 1986" section, and in each instance, the original release date is also provided. Because the Motion Picture Association of America (MPAA) was established in 1956, any film released prior to that year will not have an MPAA rating.

Two further lists conclude the text of the volume. The first of these is the Obituaries, which provides useful information about the careers of motion-picture professionals who died in 1986. The second list is of the awards presented by ten different international associations, from the Academy of Motion Picture Arts and Sciences to the Cannes International Film Festival and the British Academy Awards.

The final section of this volume includes nine indexes that cover the films reviewed in *Magill's Cinema Annual*, 1987. Arranged in the order established in the introductory matter of the essay-reviews, the indexes are as follows: Title Index, Director Index, Screenwriter Index, Cinematographer Index, Editor Index, Art Director Index, Music Index, and Performer Index. A Subject Index is also provided. To assist the reader further, pseudonyms, foreign titles, and alternate titles are all cross-referenced. Titles of foreign films and retrospective films are followed by the year, in brackets, of their original release.

The Title Index includes all the titles of films covered in individual articles, in "More Films of 1986," and also those discussed at some length in the general essays and interviews. The next seven indexes are arranged according to artists, each of whose names is followed by a list of the films on which they worked and the titles of the essays (such as "Interview with Jim Jarmusch, An") in which they are mentioned at length. The final listing is the Subject Index, in which any one film can be categorized under several headings. Thus, a reader can effectively use all these indexes to approach a film from any one of several directions, including not only its credits but also its subject matter.

CONTRIBUTING REVIEWERS

Michael Adams
Freelance Reviewer

Terry L. Andrews
Freelance Reviewer

James Baird
North Texas State University

Dan Barnett
Freelance Reviewer

Rebecca Bell-Metereau
Southwest Texas State University

Mira Reym Binford
Quinnipiac College

Raymond Carney
Stanford Humanities Center

Norman Carson
Geneva College

Hubert Cohen
University of Michigan

Paul Cremo
Pennsylvania State University

David Desser
University of Illinois

Susan Doll
Freelance Reviewer

Thomas L. Erskine
Salisbury State College

Joan Esposito
Nassau Community College

John L. Fell
Emeritus, San Francisco State University

Jeffrey L. Fenner
Freelance Reviewer

Gabrielle J. Forman
Freelance Reviewer

Jordon Fox
Freelance Reviewer

Sidney Gottlieb
Sacred Heart University

Laura Gwinn
Columbia University

Ann Harris
University of Connecticut at Stamford

John Hartzog
California State University, Northridge

Dorn Hetzel
Pennsylvania State University

Annette Insdorf
Columbia University and *Yale University*

Andrew Jefchak
Aquinas College

Richard B. Jewell
University of Southern California

John Robert Kelly
Boston University

Ira Konigsberg
University of Michigan

Leon Lewis
Appalachian State University

Janet E. Lorenz
Freelance Reviewer

Blake Lucas
Freelance Reviewer

Mary Lou McNichol
Freelance Reviewer

Marc Mancini
Loyola Marymount University

Roger Manvell
Boston University

Cono Robert Marcazzo
Upsala College

Bill-Dale Marcinko
Freelance Reviewer

Harriet Margolis
Florida Atlantic University

Joss Marsh
Freelance Reviewer

John Martin
West Virginia University

Karl Michalak
Columbia University

CONTENTS

CONTENTS

xi

MAGILL'S
CINEMA
ANNUAL

Life Achievement Award
BILLY WILDER

Sophisticated without being pretentious, Billy Wilder has long been one of the most potent creative spirits in cinema, and, happily, the luster of his body of work has grown ever brighter with the passing of years. By the time he became the fourteenth winner of the American Film Institute Life Achievement Award in 1986, this prodigious director-screenwriter-producer enjoyed the appreciation of industry professionals, critics of all schools, and general filmgoers in equal measure. It would be difficult today to find any lover of film who has not been entranced, delighted, or deeply moved by some film shaped and guided by Wilder.

Wilder earned this universal regard through conscientious effort as well as talent. Not only did he know how to capitalize on his innate gifts, especially his wry sense of humor, but also he ultimately transcended his limitations— he was not naturally a distinctive stylist—to become fluent and expressive in his approach to the medium. Always personal in his ideas, he constantly sought opportunities to broaden his range, quickly becoming as confident with dramatic subjects as with comedy. From the beginning, there was a humorous side to his darker films and seriousness in the lighter ones, and, in his most mature work, he mixed moods so artfully that stinging satire could in a moment give way to wistful romanticism and grave introspection could intrude into an atmosphere of broad playfulness. Though he courted popular acceptance, his vision of the world seems sincere and totally his own. The accessibility of his work now seems to be one of his supreme virtues. Unlike many prestigious successes of the past, his most famous films—notably *Double Indemnity* (1944), *Sunset Boulevard* (1950), *Some Like It Hot* (1959), and *The Apartment* (1960)—generally deserve their reputations as classics. At the same time, others of his films—among them *Ace in the Hole* (also known as *The Big Carnival*, 1951), *Love in the Afternoon* (1957), *The Private Life of Sherlock Holmes* (1970), and even the much-maligned *Kiss Me, Stupid* (1964; reviewed in this volume)—which may not have been as fashionable when first released, wear equally well. So any reassessment of his career cannot fail both to confirm his reputation and enhance it.

Wilder established himself as a screenwriter in Germany in the early 1930's, made his Hollywood directorial debut in the 1940's, and became a producer in the 1950's. His skill as a writer in all phases of his career (he coauthored the scripts of all his own films, as well as those of numerous earlier productions) has never been disputed, for he was always quick with witty dialogue, flavorful characterizations, and inventive narrative twists and turns. As a director, however, he did in the past have detractors who considered his approach to cinema conventional on some levels. His compositions, camerawork, and editing—though striking when the material encouraged it—were essentially functional; and illustration of scripts, however brilliant the illustration, can seem like a prosaic accomplishment in comparison with the formal boldness so strongly in evidence in the work of many great directors. Also, Wilder's treatment of his own stories could seem glib, his penetrating insights and provocative observations undermined by a complacent allegiance to Hollywood formulas and soft, undisturbing resolutions. These strictures now seem undiscerning, if not completely ludicrous. Among uncompromisingly astringent portrayals of society, *Ace in the Hole* is arguably the harshest film in the history of the American cinema, and even if his other films are gentler, he typically does not so much soften as transform the rueful pessimism that sets them in motion; it is his acerbic wit that would seem glib if it were not tempered with the sensitivity and compassion he projects so eloquently. Aesthetically, too, the director is in fact extremely refined. His style, better described as traditional than conventional, was always distinguished at the least by a classical clarity and precision which aptly reflected his sensibility, and as it evolved it became increasingly rich in nuance, subtlety, and an appreciation of atmosphere.

Now looking like the last romantic, Wilder was long considered the most cynical of filmmakers. A closer look at his work will show that he has always been both cynical and romantic; tear off one layer of his personality and the opposite tendency will reveal itself, while other layers will still lie submerged, echoing the pattern. Callous self-interest is a leading theme in his work, but so is the more positive one of learning to be open and honest and to act from one's heart, however painful such a process may be. At his best, Wilder finds a tone in which cynicism and romanticism coexist in fruitful tension, notably in *The Apartment*, in which the hero's ignoble plan for success and the heroine's demeaning affair with a married man are portrayed realistically but are also set against the wider human dimensions of both characters, who are poignant in their vulnerability and ultimately able to transcend their weaknesses. Similarly, *Kiss Me, Stupid* savagely satirizes the moral apathy of its small-town characters but warmly validates the inherent dignity of marriage in the midst of the satire. *The Private Life of Sherlock Holmes* amusingly strips away the myth of its famous hero's infallibility and makes him, on one level, naïve and foolish; but at the same time, it reveals, with wonderful delicacy, reserves of tenderness and sensitivity which even Sir Arthur Conan Doyle did not imagine. Even *Double Indemnity*, superficially a cold-blooded study of a pair of heartless murderers, is tempered by unexpected flashes of feeling—both in Wilder's realization and in the characters themselves—that give the squalid events a touch of tragic dignity. Wilder characteristically walks a rather narrow path between meanspiritedness and sentimentality, poised and graceful enough to avoid both. His humor can be strained and crude, but such instances are surprisingly infrequent in the face of constant treatments of sexual ambiguity and insecurity. Masquerades, deceptions, and grotesque schemes abound in his work, but he is too affectionate toward his characters ever to make them completely pathetic or ridiculous. Mostly, he simply enjoys letting his men and women be at once quirkily individual and representative of humanity in a bizarre world. Appreciative of the complexities of life, he is a moralist without severity. His principal goal is to entertain—not in a forgettable, superficial way but in a personal manner that will remain evocative of elemental human concerns. In this, he has been uncommonly successful. At least half of the films he has directed (to consider only those for which he is most responsible) are not only enjoyable and absorbing but are also totally coherent within their specific intentions, while his lesser works are often engaging, lively at the least, and never without some flash of inspiration.

While stamping his films with his own personality, Wilder has also collaborated well on every level of filmmaking. He has enjoyed two long, fruitful writing partnerships, first with Charles Brackett and later with I. A. L. Diamond (and worked with numerous other excellent writers, too). Among the superb cinematographers who have worked with him, John F. Seitz, Charles B. Lang, Jr., and Joseph LaShelle each shot four Wilder films. Art director Alexander Trauner was an especially vital contributor on most of Wilder's films from 1957 on, and other creative associations have also spanned numerous films. Invariably, Wilder's films are beautifully crafted and technically impeccable, and they are also extremely well acted. Wilder generally used stars and knew how to exploit their personalities to best advantage, while sometimes also exposing aspects of those personalities not seen before. His favorite actor, Jack Lemmon, has thrived in his seven Wilder films, exhibiting as nowhere else his full gifts as a comedian as well as his down-to-earth soulfulness. Wilder made a star of longtime supporting player Walter Matthau in *The Fortune Cookie* (1966) by creating a role especially for that matchlessly sardonic actor. Within a space of half-a-dozen years (1944 to 1950), he transformed no fewer than three light leading men—Fred MacMurray, Ray Milland, and William Holden—into compelling dramatic presences by using the charm and affability of their established screen personalities in counterpoint to the callousness, selfishness, and moral weakness of characters few would have expected them to play so persuasively. They all worked with him more than once, as did, among others, Marlene Dietrich, demystified but as charismatic as ever in *A Foreign Affair* (1948) and *Witness for the Prosecution* (1958); Marilyn Monroe, honing her comedic skill in *The Seven Year Itch* (1955) and *Some Like It Hot*; Audrey Hepburn, blossoming as an inimitable modern Cinderella in *Sabrina* (1954) and *Love in the Afternoon*; and Shirley MacLaine, capitalizing on her early captivating blend of worldliness and guileless openheartedness in *The Apartment* and *Irma la Douce* (1963). No less impressive are the many actors and actresses who appeared only once for Wilder. Among the first-rate players whose performances in his films rank among their best are Barbara Stanwyck, Ginger Rogers, Kim Novak, Jan Sterling, Kirk Douglas, Edward G. Robinson, Maurice Chevalier, Tony Curtis, and Dean Martin. Then there is the most memorable of all Wilder characterizations, that of Gloria Swanson—emerging from the shadows of silent screen legend to play her darker Pirandellian counterpart, Norma Desmond, in *Sunset Boulevard*. In harmony with his associates on both sides of the camera, Wilder made his films shine with professionalism and glow with behavioral beauty.

Born Samuel Wilder on June 22, 1906, in Austria, the future filmmaker began his working life as a reporter in Vienna, moving to Berlin in 1926 and continuing as a newspaperman while trying to break into screenwriting. In 1929, he began his film career, working on the famous film *Menschen am Sonntag* (*People on Sunday*), a comic/dramatic account of flirtation and romance that boasted a still lovely, open-air style of poetic realism very much against the grain of the German Expressionism that had prevailed throughout the decade. The film owes its reputation at least partly to the participation of no fewer than four men—credited director Robert Siodmak, Edgar G. Ulmer, and Fred Zinnemann, in addition to Wilder—who would eventually make their mark as American directors. It is intriguing that none of them would gravitate to a style that owed much to this film—as creatively intense as each may have been about it at the time—and the contribution that still stands out as especially personal is that of celebrated cinematographer Eugen Schüfftan. Once established, Wilder went on to write or collaborate on the scripts of about a dozen more German films, of which one, *Emil und die Detektive* (1931; *Emil and the Detectives*), a charming story of a group of street urchins, is well remembered even though it plays a bit heavily today. Like many other brilliant artists in the German film industry of the period, the Jewish Wilder fled Nazism in 1933 and would wind up in the United States (and like Otto Preminger, Fritz Lang, and the others, he took from the experience a sharp social and cultural perspective—no rose-colored glasses for these émigrés). During the ten months he stayed in Paris, he collaborated with Alexander Esway on the direction of *Mauvaise graine* (1933; *Bad Seed*, from Wilder's original story), a light but reasonably polished street romance about small-time thievery, with young and vivacious Danielle Darrieux portraying a heroine very much in the mold of later Wilder women.

Wilder's first writing assignments in Hollywood were not auspicious and he endured some economically difficult years, but in 1938 at Paramount, he was teamed with another gifted screenwriter, Charles Brackett, and the two men came into their own together. Of the seven Brackett-Wilder collaborations before the latter's American directorial debut, only *What a Life* (1939) is today regarded as routine. The other six films are classy comedies and romantic dramas directed by Ernst Lubitsch, Mitchell Leisen, and Howard

Hawks—each already established and still recognized today as a major cinematic talent. The first of these films, Lubitsch's *Bluebeard's Eighth Wife* (1938), boasts a classic opening scene involving the first meeting of the hero (Gary Cooper) and heroine (Claudette Colbert) as they try jointly to purchase a single pair of pajamas, but the playful romantic reversals that make up most of the film—incensed that he has been married seven times, she becomes a cunning adversary whose machinations finally drive him to a nervous breakdown before the happy ending—are sometimes sour even if they are consistently amusing.

More sparkling, *Ninotchka* (1939) remains one of Lubitsch's best-loved films; Wilder and Brackett (collaborating with Walter Reisch) here had the opportunity to write a rare comic role for Greta Garbo—that of the apparently cold and forbidding Soviet agent who melts under the spell of Paris and romance with an American (Melvyn Douglas). Lubitsch was Wilder's mentor and always remained his favorite director, and the influence of this older Berlin émigré is discernible in Wilder's work many years later. Intriguingly, though, the three films Wilder and Brackett wrote for Leisen are arguably even more beguiling than the two for Lubitsch. The marvelous *Midnight* (1939) is an enchanting Paris-set contemporary comedy that ingeniously throws a gold-digging Cinderella (Colbert at her most beautiful) into an elaborate masquerade involving an aristocrat (John Barrymore, who at one point imitates a little girl over the telephone), his faithless wife (Mary Astor), and a clever Hungarian taxi driver (Don Ameche). *Arise, My Love* (1940) neatly synthesizes melodrama, comedy, romantic elegance, and social awareness in its story of two Americans, a reporter (Colbert yet again) and a flyer (Ray Milland), who meet in a bizarre fashion in the midst of the Spanish Civil War. The tender, affecting *Hold Back the Dawn* (1941) artfully recasts some of Wilder's personal experiences in the character of the displaced European (Charles Boyer) who romances a shy American schoolteacher (Olivia de Havilland) in order to cross the Mexican border into the United States by the expedient means of marriage. (In Berlin, Wilder too had once been a gigolo, and, again like the hero, he later had to stop anxiously in a cheap Mexican hotel while waiting for a United States visa.) Leisen's visual elegance and warm treatment brought out all the sensitivity and poised comedy of these screenplays, among the best ever to fall into his hands. Finally, Wilder and Brackett wrote *Ball of Fire* (1941) for the great Howard Hawks, once again finding a sexy modern comedy in a variation on an old fairy tale (this time, the model is *Snow White and the Seven Dwarfs*), as yet another of Wilder's deceivers, a seductive gangster's mistress (Barbara Stanwyck), is romantically undone by her own machinations, falling in love with the youngest and most attractive of seven cloistered professors (Gary Cooper). Most of the screwball spontaneity one would expect from the director of the earlier comedy classics *Twentieth Century* (1935), *Bring-*

ing Up Baby (1938), and *His Girl Friday* (1940) is here provided by Stanwyck; overall, Hawks responds to the gentle charm that pervades this script by emphasizing it, an impressive tribute to the writers.

Wilder graduated to directing with *The Major and the Minor* (1942), the kind of the delightful comedy he knew that he and Brackett could do well— an appealing adult woman (Ginger Rogers) masquerades as a young girl, leading to romantic complications with a solicitous army officer (Ray Milland). Modest in its ambition, perhaps, the film is nevertheless a total success, realized with as much finesse as Lubitsch, Hawks, and Leisen had brought to the previous films. Even if Wilder did not yet display as much stylistic individuality as those directors, he did come into his own with his subtle handling of the offbeat sexual undercurrents and in the remarkable intimacy of a climactic reunion/revelation scene. *The Major and the Minor* also strengthened the position of the Wilder-Brackett team at Paramount, thanks to solid commercial and critical success, and on the next film, Brackett became the producer of their joint efforts, and Wilder was able to demonstrate his versatility by directing a World War II drama set in North Africa. *Five Graves to Cairo* (1943) is basically a conventional wartime effort—relying on familiar suspense, heroics, romance, and patriotic sentiments—but it is enlivened by some idiosyncratic wit and interesting photography by John F. Seitz, and it gave Wilder the opportunity to work with Erich von Stroheim (playing Erwin Rommel), who as a director had been, with Lubitsch, one of his two most important formative influences.

The film that really begins to suggest Wilder's admirable range is his next one, the extraordinary *Double Indemnity*. The year 1944 saw the first full flowering of the *film noir* cycle (although the *noir* style had been emerging for several years), and Wilder's adaptation of James M. Cain's novella is— even more than Siodmak's *Phantom Lady* and *Christmas Holiday* or Preminger's *Laura*—astonishing in its thorough presentation of seedily romantic *film noir* ambiance. As casually immoral insurance salesman Walter Neff (Fred MacMurray) and seductive Phyllis Dietrichson (Barbara Stanwyck) meet, ignite with passion, plot cold-blooded murder, and betray each other, the full weight of the nightmarish oppressiveness of a world plunging into cynical despair is felt at every turn of the narrative and in every aspect of the realization. There is the wisecracking yet fatalistic narration of the doomed Neff, the low-key, black-and-white lighting of Seitz, the darkly romantic music of Miklos Rozsa, the evocation of a stucco-and-venetian blind 1940's Los Angeles—all synthesized in a brisk, punchy piece of storytelling that never falters. Cain was easily the best writer Wilder ever adapted, and it is worth remembering that *Double Indemnity* is the one cinematic treatment of a Cain work that not only equals but even surpasses its source, as Cain himself always observed. The character of dogged insurance investigator Keyes (Edward G. Robinson) is built up and his relationship with Neff made fascinating and ultimately poignant, the intimations of failed romanticism are made more resonant and haunting by a story change that throws Neff and Phyllis into a half-sincere embrace as he responds to her treachery by killing her, and the hard-edged dialogue is steadily enriched by Wilder's bracing humor. Wilder's insight into the material is also commendable because at the time—in the absence of an accepted *film noir* tradition—the story was widely considered unsavory, even by his partner Brackett, who neither produced nor coscripted (the director enlisted Raymond Chandler— whose excellent modern detective novels suggested affinities with Cain—to collaborate on the screenplay). Both MacMurray and Stanwyck were nervous about playing killers, but Wilder's flair for casting and knowing direction made them both *noir* prototypes in the end.

Melodrama of a different kind surfaced in *The Lost Weekend* (1945), which Wilder and Brackett adapted from Charles Jackson's novel about an alcoholic writer on a binge. As he had done with MacMurray, Wilder cast personable Ray Milland against his image as the obsessively self-destructive Don Birnam, while using that image to promote empathy and, characteristically, to infuse unexpected humor into certain scenes. Milland is totally convincing, and superb location photography in New York (again by Seitz) enhances the film's realism. Forceful enough to win several Academy Awards (among them, Best Picture and Best Director), *The Lost Weekend* holds up as one of the most striking portraits of alcoholism in the cinema— often harrowing and bleak in its surface detail—but a hopeful resolution (not really one of the film's imperfections, as it is part of Wilder's wisdom to see life's most difficult struggles and challenging experiences as preparation for enlightenment and transformation) is only the last of a number of contrivances that make it seem too comfortably schematic to be one of Wilder's finest works. More memorable than the whole are scenes—Birnam's eloquent description of the way drinking changes his mood as he breaks his dry spell in the calm daylight atmosphere of a local bar, his futile walk with his typewriter down Third Avenue as he vainly looks for an open pawnshop on a holiday, his frustrating search for a bottle he has hidden too cleverly.

Wilder did a complete turnabout with his next film, *The Emperor Waltz* (1948), a musical comedy in the Lubitsch tradition, with Bing Crosby as an American phonograph salesman gauchely intruding into the splendors of old Austria. Wilder's touch with the frivolous material is sometimes heavy, and the film is commonly regarded as one of his most insignificant works. Yet although it is admittedly minor, it boasts some pleasing qualities. While most of Wilder's early films are tightly scripted, this one relies more on stylistic imagination; long after its inane plot is forgotten, the bold use of Technicolor (all of Wilder's other films before 1955 are in black and white) and marginal scenes such as the impromptu dance by members of a hotel staff may be recalled with great pleasure. Though more substantial, *A Foreign*

Affair, a comedy set in the ruins of postwar Berlin which Wilder and Brackett wrote with Richard L. Breen, is largely bereft of the mellowness and warmheartedness of its predecessor. The harsher side of Wilder's nature informs his treatment of a righteous Iowa congresswoman (Jean Arthur) who suffers cruel lies and humiliation before her status as heroine allows her to reveal a sweet inner nature and romantic vulnerability. As the heroine's unprincipled German rival, Marlene Dietrich is a glamorous and soulful figure throughout, especially when she sings three dramatic Frederick Hollander songs in a beautifully visualized back street nightclub, and only so naturally appealing an actress as Arthur could hope to win ultimate sympathy in the face of the contrast between the two characters. The strength of this film is its audacity. For Wilder, even this sad setting of poverty and moral breakdown can be a background for life-affirming romantic comedy, and the juxtaposition provides a fascinating context for his perceptions.

Wilder's Hollywood melodrama, *Sunset Boulevard*, has many bizarre elements—what can be said of a film in which the story is narrated by a dead man and Cecil B. De Mille is the most compassionate character? Returning to a "noirish" atmosphere, ripe with intimations of decay, Wilder has also created a vividly immediate Hollywood of 1950 that seems real years later, much as Norma Desmond's world of silent screen glory must be, in her mind, barely a moment away from the present. Without descending into madness while dreaming of a comeback, as Norma, Gloria Swanson can nevertheless persuasively validate her assertion of ageless cinematic life ("I *am* big; it's the pictures that got small") simply by incarnating her with undiminished presence and authority. Wilder might have seen a little of himself in cynical screenwriter Joe Gillis (William Holden, here totally dismantling the callow boy-next-door *persona* from which he had tried unsuccessfully to break away for years), and the attempted car repossession that throws Gillis into the lap of Norma Desmond in the film's crackling early scenes was in fact drawn from Wilder's own experience in his down-and-out early days in Hollywood. A strange thing happens, though, as the film progresses: Gillis wins no sympathy even though Norma has killed him. The more his dispassionate narration describes her and her life as grotesque, the more she becomes an awesome romantic figure, and that aura of romanticism extends to the pitiable Max von Mayerling (Erich von Stroheim, like the character a forgotten great director of the past) and to everything about Hollywood illusion that Gillis treats with contempt. Even the love of a nice, bright fellow professional (Nancy Olson) cannot redeem Gillis, and the film's final power comes from the broken focus in the final image, an inspired moment that marks Norma's entry into oneness with her dreams.

After *Sunset Boulevard*, one of the peaks of their creative partnership, Wilder and Brackett went their separate ways—Brackett became a writer and producer at Fox, while Wilder produced as well as directed the last three of his Paramount films. Walter Newman and Lesser Samuels collaborated with Wilder on the screenplay of *Ace in the Hole*, in which hard-boiled reporter Chuck Tatum (Kirk Douglas) tries to recover his reputation in New Mexico by building up the plight of cave-in victim Leo Minosa (Richard Benedict) while carrying on an affair with the latter's burnt-out wife (Jan Sterling). As scorching as acid in its pessimistic treatment of all levels of society—journalism, once Wilder's own vocation, is presented as an especially callous profession—the film today seems thoroughly realistic and not at all overstated as it builds with admirable deliberation toward a dark but moral resolution. In 1951, however, Wilder's lucidity about man's potential for inhumanity met with distaste, and even a new title, *The Big Carnival*, could not save it commercially. Wilder bounced back to popularity, though, with the excellent *Stalag 17* (1953; cowritten with Edwin Blum), a solidly suspenseful and brilliantly constructed World War II prison-camp drama with some well-integrated drag comedy that anticipates *Some Like It Hot*. The clever, self-interested Sefton (William Holden)—who becomes a hero after being wrongly suspected of treachery by his fellow prisoners—is a character who seems especially close to Wilder's heart; in Holden's knowing, Oscar-winning performance, he seems to be a spiritual stand-in for the director, toughly cynical to all appearances but warm and honest at the core. *Sabrina*, Wilder's hit 1954 adaptation of a Samuel Taylor play (coscripted by Ernest Lehman and Taylor himself), is a feathery romantic comedy given a lilt by adorable Audrey Hepburn as the awkward daughter of a chauffeur who becomes a swan and gets to choose between two attractive brothers (Humphrey Bogart and Holden); enhanced by Charles Lang's lovely lighting and Edith Head's stunning costumes, Hepburn brings a needed freshness and poignancy to what is, for Wilder, a fairly conventional work.

Free-lancing after leaving Paramount, Wilder is erratically inspired in the five films that make up the rest of his work in the 1950's, only the best two of which he produced himself. *The Seven Year Itch* (which Wilder adapted with George Axelrod from the latter's play) is an overrated comedy, often theatrical and heavy-handed in its depiction of the fantasies and realities of contemplated infidelity. *The Spirit of St. Louis* (1957; cowritten with Wendell Mayes) is very uncharacteristic—an inspirational dramatic account of Charles Lindbergh's famous flight across the Atlantic—but flawed only by Wilder's reliance on flashbacks that needlessly intrude on the pure line of the lonely aerial odyssey. (James Stewart, who plays Lindbergh, could certainly have sustained this lengthy stretch of narrative by himself, as many beautifully realized sequences demonstrate.) *Love in the Afternoon* (the first Wilder-Diamond collaboration) is one of the peaks of Wilder-style comedy—a glowingly romantic and unerringly delightful variation on the theme of liberation through benevolent deception, as Ariane (Audrey Hepburn), the wholesome but adventurous daughter of a sweet-natured Parisian detective (Maurice Chevalier), masquerades as a sophisticate to be with the American Lothario she loves (Gary Cooper) and ultimately wins his complete devotion. With its wonderfully amusing quartet of gypsy musicians endlessly playing "Fascination," its scenes of bittersweet intimacy, and its heartrending train-station climax, this is the film that shows Wilder sailing into a mellow maturity. On the other hand, *Witness for the Prosecution*, an Agatha Christie courtroom mystery that Wilder adapted with Harry Kurnitz, is essentially a well-handled but relatively impersonal genre piece. Although Wilder's humorous touches and storytelling skill make it the best cinematic adaptation of Christie, the film depends more on dramatic twists and turns than emotional resonance. Finally, there is the hilarious *Some Like It Hot* (cowritten by Diamond), with Tony Curtis and Jack Lemmon as Prohibition-era musicians masquerading as women in an all-girl band after witnessing a gangland killing. The impersonation that propels this breezy farce provides a context for a liberating exploration of sexual ambiguity as well as gracefully executed scenes of pure comic delirium. When Joe/ Josephine (Curtis), in drag, kisses vulnerable vocalist Sugar Kane (Marilyn Monroe) to affirm their true love, it is a moment that elicits surprising emotions, while the intoxication of Jerry/Daphne (Lemmon) in the face of romantic attentions from a millionaire (Joe E. Brown) is as weirdly exhilarating as it is funny. Justly cherished as cinema's funniest closing line, Brown's deadpan "Well, nobody's perfect" (after Jerry reveals that he is a man) arouses laughter partly because it is so startling but also because it is so audaciously provocative.

Wilder's richest period is signaled by the forging of professional relationships on *Love in the Afternoon* and *Some Like It Hot* (both of which he produced) that would remain stimulating in the years ahead. Diamond has been Wilder's writing partner on all of his subsequent films, and the two men's sensibilities and talents are uncommonly harmonious and complementary, while Jack Lemmon became the ideal Wilder protagonist. It is difficult to evoke Lemmon's uniquely plaintive but uproarious delivery of a line such as, "That's the way it crumbles, cookie-wise" (in *The Apartment*), or his special kind of graceful physical expressiveness. Most fortuitously, Wilder's feeling for the aesthetics of cinema was immeasurably deepened by the contributions to his films of art director Alexander Trauner, whose expressive sets were not only beautiful in their own right but seemed to encourage the director to seek a more intimate feeling. Though Wilder's films had always been well designed, only melodramas such as *Double Indemnity* and *Sunset Boulevard* had been especially notable for their visual texture and stylistic suppleness. Yet his later films—mostly comedies, in form if not in every emotional detail—all abound in lovely and dramatically resonant imagery. The characters do not simply enact the scripts but become one with imaginatively constructed worlds, and as a result, long, superbly written dialogue scenes play with a new fluency and deepened appreciation of mood. Beginning with *Love in the Afternoon*—a film that takes place almost entirely in the modest apartment Ariane and her father share and in an elegant hotel suite—Trauner created a remarkably diverse group of settings for Wilder. Especially memorable are the cold and cavernous office, humble apartment, and Manhattan nightclub of *The Apartment*; the colorful Parisian red-light district of *Irma la Douce*; the seedy desert town of *Kiss Me, Stupid*; and the elegant Victorian London of *The Private Life of Sherlock Holmes*.

The Apartment displays the Wilder-Diamond-Lemmon-Trauner creative interplay at its peak. Telling the story of likeable but ambitious accountant C. C. Baxter (Lemmon), who allows his apartment to be used for his bosses' trysts in order to get ahead until the girl with whom he is in love, Fran Kubelik (Shirley MacLaine), attempts suicide there, Wilder makes his most affecting statement about values and relationships. Abundant comic invention is seamlessly interlaced with powerfully dramatic scenes (such as the one in which Fran's married lover, played by Fred MacMurray, gives her a one-hundred-dollar bill as a Christmas present), and the end of the 1950's—when traditional moral and social structures were starting to disintegrate—is passionately and heartbreakingly evoked. Myriad masterful touches—such as Fran's cracked compact mirror, which shocks Baxter into awareness when he looks at his own broken reflection—add to the artistic density of a film that holds up as Wilder's greatest achievement, both thoroughly of its own time and ageless. Academy Awards (Best Picture, Best Director, Best Screenplay, Best Art Direction, and Best Editing) have seldom been more merited.

Inexplicably, Wilder's next film, *One, Two, Three* (1961), a strained, Cold War satire set in Berlin—has only visual aptness, a few very funny jokes, and James Cagney's unflagging energy to recommend it; but this low point of the director's career is followed by a decade of outstanding works that are both masterly in execution and shot through with the complexities of the Wilder personality. *Irma la Douce* (1963), his most commercially successful motion picture, reunites Lemmon and MacLaine in the story of a gendarme who falls in love with a prostitute; retaining none of the songs of the source musical play, Wilder fills this charming work with behavioral beauty, comic insight, and captivating color imagery. (The cinematographer, Joseph LaShelle, was also responsible for the dazzling wide-screen black-and-white lighting of *The Apartment*, *The Fortune Cookie*, and *Kiss Me, Stupid*.) The Catholic Legion of Decency condemned the inspired *Kiss Me, Stupid*—in which an aspiring songwriter (superbly played by Ray Walston) tries to escape his hellish existence in Climax, Nevada, by passing off a prostitute (Kim Novak) as his wife in order to sell a song to a stranded singer (Dean Martin). Yet the unforeseen double infidelity toward which the film pirouettes is at once tonic and compassionately delineated (as sensitive and thoughtful an observer as Joan Didion was only one of the earliest of the film's many articulate defenders). Again both caustic and humane in *The Fortune Cookie*, Wilder undercuts a masterful portrait of malevolence—the unscrupulous lawyer (Walter Matthau) who coaxes his essentially decent brother-in-law (Jack Lemmon) into a fraudulent insurance claim—by brilliantly placing well-judged elements of pathos (the guilt-ridden football star played by Ron Rich is a wholly original creation) in the midst of the hard-edged comic action. Wilder's dream project, *The Private Life of Sherlock Holmes* was regrettably cut by almost an hour before its release but still holds together as one of cinema's most ruefully romantic works. The Holmes (Robert Stephens) and Watson (Colin Blakely) whom Wilder and Diamond throw into a cleverly plotted, amusing adventure are freshly perceived; the ambivalent love between Holmes and a beautiful German spy (Genevieve Page) is fraught with melancholy; and the tragic coda—in which the great detective, no longer aloof to his own emotions and visibly shattered, retreats to his room to still his tenderness with cocaine—provides what is surely Wilder's most haunting moment. Here, as never before, Wilder reveals that his cleverness and cynicism—like Holmes's—exist to protect a pure, idealistic heart. Though scene after scene is blessed with the wry wit one would expect, Wilder builds a feeling of emotional yearning throughout, especially through his use of Miklos Rozsa's sublime music. At Wilder's suggestion, the great composer (who had years earlier contributed so impressively to *Double Indemnity* and *The Lost Weekend*) based his score on his own celebrated violin concerto. The warm spirit of this magnificent testament film also pervades *Avanti!* (1972), as two modern neurotics (Jack Lemmon and Juliet Mills) melt in the golden glow of the Mediterranean and become magically transformed into lovers filled with new hope.

Avanti!, a film of euphoric romanticism released in a coldly unromantic age, was initially underrated, but retrospectively, this film and *Love in the Afternoon* have come into their own as romantic comedies worthy of Wilder's mentor, Lubitsch. In full artistic maturity, Wilder is indeed worthy of the comparison—and not only in the two films cited. For example, while *The Apartment* and Lubitsch's equally great *The Shop Around the Corner* (1940) are superficially very different, they have deep affinities in their perceptions of love and attraction. Lubitsch may be more gentle and he may direct with a lighter hand, but the Wilder film has more dark, piercing moments. The differences reflect some divergences in sensibility but are also accounted for by the more pronounced harshness of modern life, which Wilder faithfully illuminates. Unlike Lubitsch, whose films are usually Continental both in subject and attitude, Wilder has drawn much of his inspiration from the landscape and character of America. In this, he is at one with other masters of American comedy such as Frank Capra, Leo McCarey,

Preston Sturges, Vincente Minnelli, and George Cukor. So when a film such as *Kiss Me, Stupid* provocatively echoes one such as Lubitsch's classic *The Marriage Circle* (1924), it places both the themes and inherent tastefulness of the model in a bold new context; virtue becomes more eroded and therefore even more precious. When Wilder is accused of being vulgar, it may be because the postwar world is actually more puritanical than Lubitsch's. Wilder could do a very Lubitsch-like moment—the camera tracking slowly away from the closed door of a hotel room as Ariane begins her affair in *Love in the Afternoon*—but the inflections are totally Wilder's own; the mood is graver and sadder. That kind of mood—discernible in key scenes of all Wilder's best comedies from *The Major and the Minor* to *Avanti!*—is a distinguishing feature of his art. For all of their masquerades and deceptions, his characters ultimately wear their hearts on their sleeves. It is easy to remember countless Lubitsch characters concealing the most profound melancholy beneath an elegant pose, but difficult to imagine in any of his films a scene comparable to the one in *The Fortune Cookie* in which Lemmon's hapless hero wistfully reminisces about the wife who has deserted him.

Wilder produced his films with a free hand for the Mirisch Company from 1959 (*Some Like It Hot*) until 1972 (*Avanti!*). During that time he became unfashionable, though paradoxically more respected for his overall achievement than ever before. It may have been disillusioning to go from great popular success to frequent commercial failure in such a relatively short time, especially as the director was at the height of his powers and more personal than ever. Whatever the cause, Wilder's last three films (followed by what appears to be involuntary retirement) are not among his best—though well made, they do not display the same stretching of his talent as their predecessors. He played it safe with two more Lemmon-Matthau teamings, *The Front Page* (1974) and *Buddy Buddy* (1981), comedies which have flashes of brilliance but are a long way from being thorough revitalizations of their sources (rather old in the case of *The Front Page*), notwithstanding the wonderful acting of the two stars. The most interesting film of the three is *Fedora* (1978), a melodrama about film stars and filmmaking that superficially recalls *Sunset Boulevard*—Holden plays an aging director cynical about the new Hollywood (much like Wilder himself in these years), while the past of the mysterious central character, a legendary film star, weighs heavily on the present. Thomas Tryon's novella posed tricky problems of adaptation, and Wilder and Diamond do not avoid a midpoint revelation that Fedora (Hildegarde Knef) has passed on her identity to her daughter (Marthe Keller) with tragic results; but intriguingly, it is at just this point that the film starts to become meaningful and emotionally penetrating. Faced with the spectacle of Fedora's total selfishness in sustaining her myth, Wilder is perversely but touchingly compassionate—in the face of such a pessimistic depiction of a mother/daughter symbiosis, this striking attitude underscores his profound humanism.

Billy Wilder likes to think of himself as a composer of waltzes in an age of disco. Such a description reflects both his cynicism and his romanticism, and the man is in fact much like his films; he is spontaneously witty and can induce laughter as readily with a casual comment as with a carefully deliberated line of dialogue. It is fortunate that his sense of humor has not deserted him for, sadly, his perspective on his art is correct. The philosophical and aesthetic currents of his timelessly pleasing work run against the tide of a postclassical American cinema that is too often flashy and empty. Ironically, the sense of beauty and purpose in his films has become increasingly evident as contemporary taste has deserted him. As Wilder himself has shown us so often, however, life is bittersweet.

Blake Lucas

An Interview with
PANDRO S. BERMAN

"I wanted to be a picture producer when I was ten years old. It never entered my mind to do anything else. I had no talent for directing or writing, and I certainly was a bad businessman. If I couldn't have produced pictures, I couldn't have earned a living."

Born in 1905 in Pittsburgh, Pennsylvania, Pandro S. Berman came from pioneering picture people. "My father was a film salesman who worked in towns like Pittsburgh, Kansas City, and Cincinnati. I used to accompany him on these nocturnal visits to exhibitors. I was quite young at the time, but that's where I got interested in the business.

"Eventually, my father found his way to New York, working for Universal Pictures, but in those days the exhibiting end was not very lucrative. I had five or six cousins and uncles who all sold film and they never earned anything. They all told me not to follow in their footsteps, but to go to California where I could make some money."

Berman's father wanted him to go to business college, but Berman told him, "Give me the money you're going to spend on my tuition and let me take a train to California."

In 1923, Pandro Berman got his first job in Hollywood at a company his father had helped to form, FBO studios (Film Booking Offices of America, which later became RKO Pictures Corporation). "Those of us who began in the business during that period were a little luckier than young people are today. We didn't have quite as many obstacles to overcome to get a job. A guy could go into a studio, take a job at twenty-five dollars a week . . . and work his way up.

"The very first job I ever had was called *The Telephone Girl*; it was a series of two-reelers. Darryl Zanuck was the writer. He was a dynamo, a rather fierce young man. Very argumentative. Very strong-minded. It was inevitable that he would go up the ladder, because he was going to get there no matter what happened.

"In the first three or four years, I had six different kinds of jobs. I started as a gofer helping an assistant director, then I became an assistant director, then I got a job cutting and eventually ran the department.

"I learned the most through my experience as a cutter. The actual experience of putting film together with your hands, learning what could be used and what had to be sacrificed, gave me an understanding of the construction of a script that I would never have had from any other educational source.

"During the silent era, editing was a little more freewheeling. We had title cards instead of spoken dialogue. We were free to transpose film when things didn't work. We'd even rewrite the titles and change the story."

When Berman looks back on the studio system, he also sees the disadvantages of the "freewheeling" early days. "When I was a kid of eighteen, you worked a six-day week instead of a five-day week. When Saturday night came around, instead of going home, you got your. . . heavy clothes on and carried your camera outdoors and shot the night stuff. The studio kept you out working till the sun rose, and you'd go home having done a seven-day week. Not a penny of overtime, for anything, and my salary was twenty-five dollars a week. I call that exploitation, practically slavery! That's where the unions were a godsend to people."

In 1928, after five years at FBO, which by then had merged with RKO, Berman went to work for Columbia Pictures as head of the editing department. "I got along well with Harry Cohn for the one week we worked together! Actually, I was there for about two or three months. It was his brother, Jack Cohn, who fired me. I had a one-year contract, and he gave me sixteen hundred dollars to get the hell out of the studio. So, I went back to RKO."

Between 1928 and 1929, Berman worked as the editorial assistant to RKO studio executive William LeBaron. "That was how I happened to stumble into producing, which had always been my desire. I didn't anticipate getting the chance at that time. It came as a kind of a 'break.'"

In the style of a good Hollywood legend, LeBaron gave Berman an opportunity to step in at the last minute when a producer quit a film that was ready to go into production. "*The Gay Diplomat* [1931] was a terrible picture but at least I got my feet wet. Then he allowed me to make a couple of very cheap little pictures."

When LeBaron left the company, his successor, David Selznick, offered Berman his old job as editorial assistant. "So, the process started all over again, and a year later I was able to get Selznick to let me make a picture." By 1932, Pandro Berman was earning credits on "A" pictures, and the popularity of *What Price Hollywood?* (1932) established him as one of RKO's top talents.

As Berman's status at the studio rose, the role of the producer was evolving as well. "In the very early days of the film business, before 1925, the director was king and there were no supervisors, as we originally were called. There were no producers except the man who ran the studio. That all changed when Louis Mayer brought in the supervisor/producer system at MGM under Irving Thalberg. And the director status went downhill for many years and the producer status rose.

"We were in from beginning to end. A producer was the man who developed the screenplay. He may never have written a line of dialogue, but he certainly had to be there to help construct the screenplay. He also selected the material, hired the director and the cast, and edited the final picture. Our main job was to get a better script, a better movie, by virtue of constant reworking, rewriting, and recutting."

Once a film was in production, "I saw dailies every night with the director, and I gave him my comments then, alone with him in the projection room, not while he was shooting.

"The director always did the first cut, never a final cut. You let him do the first cut and preview it—give him the pleasure and give yourself the advantage of going out to an audience with his version. But, then, if something had to be done, and sometimes plenty had to be done, we'd go and do it. You never released a first cut, even your own, because the audience always showed you where you could do something better.

"It was pretty simple, in those days. If you were making a comedy, did they laugh? If you were making a drama, did they cry? And when they came out of the theater, would they spit on you or congratulate you?"

Berman made a variety of films at RKO, such as *Morning Glory* (1933), *Of Human Bondage* (1934), *Stage Door* (1937), *Room Service* (1938), and *Gunga Din* (1939). Among the best remembered, however, are a series of musicals starring Fred Astaire and Ginger Rogers. "The series was a result of a picture which I had nothing to do with called *Flying Down to Rio* [1933]. Astaire and Rogers did a couple of dance numbers and stole the picture from the stars, Delores Del Rio and Gene Raymond."

Berman saw the potential of starring Astaire and Rogers in their own film and approached the producer of *Flying Down to Rio*, Lou Brock, with the idea of buying a play called *The Gay Divorcée* as a vehicle for them. Brock read it and hated it. "He said he could blow a better script out of his nose!"

So, Berman took it upon himself to convince the studio to buy *The Gay Divorcée* (1934) and *Roberta* (1935) and ended up producing eight Astaire and Rogers pictures. "We were only interested in keeping them light and frothy and not following the backstage formula of Warner and MGM musicals. We just let people dance and sing without having to get up on a stage to do it. We didn't take the stories too seriously, but tried to use them as a basis for comedy and dance numbers.

"After the first picture, Fred didn't want to work with Ginger. Not that he didn't like her. He adored her. It was really a matter of self-preservation. Fred had been a member of a team with his sister, and, when Adele got married, he found himself unable to get employment. He vowed he'd never be a member of a team again.

"It became a constant struggle to get him to work with her in subsequent films. So, RKO gave him a contract that gave him 10 percent of the profits to the pictures. On every picture he refused to work with her for a while, but as the grosses kept coming in from previous films, and he got his checks, he decided he'd better take the money while he could get it.

"Of course, she didn't like making these pictures too well either. In her opinion, she was a star in her own right and she wanted to do dramas and pictures without Fred Astaire."

In 1933-1934 and again in 1938-1939, in addition to producing individual films, Berman acted as RKO's executive producer, the actual studio head. "I found it frustrating to be an executive, but they had nobody else at the time. If you're a producer who loves to make pictures, you don't want to be an executive! You were too far removed from the actual script—from the daily work with the writer.

"It used to annoy me to have to get involved in the work that other producers were doing. I preferred to be concentrating on a few pictures of my own. I used to get so sore at some of the producers that I'd go to their previews hoping the film wouldn't look good because they didn't do what I wanted them to do.

"At RKO we had to struggle all the time. When I took charge, we were already in Chapter Eleven bankruptcy proceedings. It was always hand-to-mouth. We didn't have a big stock company, although we did develop Katharine Hepburn, Astaire, Rogers, and Irene Dunne. We didn't own any big properties. We couldn't afford to compete with Metro and Warner and Fox.

"We found ways of making pictures in our own way that were sometimes better than theirs and sometimes not. It gave us opportunities with a lot of talented people that the big studios were passing up. For example, John Ford tried for years to make *The Informer* [1935]. Nobody'd touch it. We let him make it. It didn't cost much and it was a good picture."

When George Schaefer took over in 1939 and began to reorganize the studio, Berman left to go to work at Metro-Goldwyn-Mayer. A few years earlier, Louis B. Mayer had offered Berman a job at MGM just after he had signed a new three-year contract with RKO. When Berman explained that he was not free, Mayer responded, "I'll take you when you're ready." So, in 1940, Berman took him up on his offer. "I gave up my percent of the profits and took a flat salary to go to Metro because I thought the time had come when I needed the opportunity to use those personalities they had under contract.

"Mayer, with all his faults, was a brilliant executive, and he had something very few other men had in that job. He had long-range vision. He also believed in buying the best people in the market in every job and letting them do their job. I found him a reasonable man. He even let me make pictures that he didn't want me to make!

"I went to work on Mayer's assumption that I was going to make musicals because he liked the ones I did at RKO. But when I got there, I found out they *had* three good musical producers—Arthur Freed, Joe Pasternak, and Jack Cummings—and it would have been insane for them to have a fourth. They couldn't make that many musicals! Besides, I had gotten a little miffed because some critic said I could only make musicals, and I made up my mind never to make any more!"

Despite Berman's vow, his first film was a musical, *Ziegfeld Girl* (1941). It was the beginning of twenty-seven years at the studio, producing a wide variety of the studio's best productions with their top stars and directors, including such films as *National Velvet* (1944), *The Three Musketeers* (1948), *Father of the Bride* (1950), *The Prisoner of Zenda* (1952), *Tea and Sympathy* (1957), *Butterfield 8* (1960), *Sweet Bird of Youth* (1962), and *A Patch of Blue* (1965).

"Being at Metro was a delight. Metro was lush and lavish in everything it did. It even extended to the commissary! Everything was on a different scale entirely. They had everything under the sun to work with. They had a fixed stable of stars, a tremendous group of fine character actors, and a lot of directors and writers under contract.

"In some cases, we the producers were the guiding factor of the picture and in some cases the directors were. At MGM, the director was very often allowed to spend only a limited period of time on the picture before shooting started and was off the minute it ended. They were anxious to squeeze a lot of pictures out of each director.

"With directors like George Stevens, Mark Sandrich, Vincente Minnelli, and George Cukor, it became a collaboration, a matter of give-and-take. But there were also times when I was glad to get a guy who would take the script I gave him and shoot it without asking any questions. Take the cast. Make it fast. Make it under budget. *Ivanhoe* [1952; directed by Richard Thorpe] was made that way."

Berman was paired over and over again with such diverse personalities as George Stevens (*Alice Adams*, 1935; *Swing Time*, 1936; *Vivacious Lady*, 1938; and *Gunga Din*), Vincente Minnelli (*Madame Bovary*, 1949; *Father of the Bride*, and *Tea and Sympathy*), and Richard Brooks (*The Blackboard Jungle*, 1955; *The Brothers Karamazov*, 1958; and *Cat on a Hot Tin Roof*, 1958), each with his own special talents.

"I never would have dreamed of giving Richard Brooks a comedy. Now, he might have been great at it, but the thought never would have entered my mind. On the other hand, you'd give George Cukor a comedy instantly. Vincente Minnelli was at his best with musicals, but he could do comedy and drama. George Stevens could do anything: break your heart or make you laugh. So, there were no rules. You've got to learn about each fellow."

For example, "Richard Brooks was an explosive sort, loved to rant and rave, but he didn't mean any of it. When you knew him, you liked him. He was a very hard worker and a very capable writer. He was painstaking to the degree that I don't think he ever made a picture until he had written seven versions of the script. He was economical. He was good with actors. Good with crew."

On the other hand, "George Cukor was the best director of women I've ever seen. He had that feminine quality about him that made him understand how women would react in situations. Give him a great stage play and a good actress and he would do a great job. And I know he'd hate me for saying it, but he was also a damned good director of men.

"He never really learned the technique of motion pictures; he could never master anything mechanical. For the first ten or twelve pictures, he always had a fellow on the set with him, whom you might call a production designer. He would set up the camera for George and tell the cameraman what George wanted."

In addition to the constraints of talent, there were always the censors to satisfy. "The Breen Office didn't affect me very much. I found them arbitrary. Usually I'd get a letter where I was asked to change two or three lines of dialogue. I didn't have any problems with them because I reconciled myself to the fact that it had to be their way and that was that. We were trying to stay within the Code but at the same time to win a few victories over it."

One of the battles Berman regrets losing was over the ending of *Bachelor Mother* (1939), the story of a working girl (Ginger Rogers) who cannot convince her employer (David Niven) that she is not the mother of a foundling. "At the preview, the picture had a magnificent concluding line. David Niven has fallen in love with Ginger and is going to marry her despite the fact that he *knows* that's her bastard child. So, when she asks, 'You still think I'm the mother of that baby?' he says, 'Of course I do.' And she responds, 'Boy, have I got a surprise for you!'

"The audience laughed for three or four minutes, but I was forced by Joseph Breen to take it out!"

Additionally, at Metro, "There was a studio policy (which really emanated from New York) about the things you *could not do*. Nothing controversial. You couldn't make a picture about Congress that might insult them. So when *Born Yesterday* [1950] came along and I tried to buy it, thumbs down. You couldn't make a picture about the navy that the navy wouldn't love. So you couldn't make *The Caine Mutiny* [1954]. You couldn't make one about the army. So, Columbia made *From Here to Eternity* [1953]."

Still, Pandro Berman managed to produce an occasional controversial film. When he proposed *The Blackboard Jungle*, a picture about high-school juvenile delinquents, "The New York office went crazy. They thought it was anti-American propaganda. All of them! The publicity department. The sales department. Nick Schenck sent for me, and I had to go back there and sell them all on it. But Dore Schary (then the head of the studio) was great, he stood behind us."

In 1965, when Berman completed *A Patch of Blue*, the story of the affection of a black man (Sidney Poitier) for a blind, white girl (Elizabeth Hartman), he found MGM president Robert O'Brien less cooperative. "He tried to hide it from the public. He was afraid of repercussions in theaters.

He was afraid it would create riots. He was afraid it would be a flop.

"I tried to get him on the phone innumerable times, and he would always duck me. About six months after the original release date, he called me. He told me that they had tried out the picture in Atlanta, Georgia (of all places), that it was a smash hit, and everybody loved it.

"I said, 'You . . . , I don't even want to talk to you!' And I never talked to him again. That's why I left Metro when I did in 1967."

In the 1950's, it was Pandro Berman who convinced MGM to broaden its concept of film stars to include television personalities Lucille Ball and Desi Arnaz in *The Long, Long Trailer* (1954; reviewed in this volume), directed by Vincente Minnelli. The studio argued that no one would pay to watch what they could see "every Friday night for free." The grosses proved Berman right.

Again he fought the studio brass when he produced Elvis Presley's third film, *Jailhouse Rock* (1957). "My wife, Kathryn Hereford, was a Presley fan long before I heard anyone else mention his name. So, she was the associate producer, and I let her do all the work." It was Berman, however, who had to convince MGM to release the final product. "I couldn't have let Metro tamper with it, I'd have lost my home!

"They had never made anything like that. They didn't know rock and roll. To them, it was just ridiculous. I didn't like it myself, but I thought it was going to be a big hit. He was introducing a kind of music that was going to sweep the country."

So when Berman was asked what he wanted to do with the film, he said, " 'Nothing. Just send it out.' Well, we did a tremendous gross. The critics even went for it."

Diversity was the key to Berman's success. "There was no pattern. I made a lot of pictures because I loved them and I wanted to make them and I could make them at a reasonable price and they were not necessarily box-office pictures. *Of Human Bondage. Alice Adams. Winterset* [RKO, 1936]. *The Seventh Cross* [MGM, 1944].

"Some pictures you made just because you thought they would do business. *Gunga Din. The Hunchback of Notre Dame* [RKO, 1939]. *Ivanhoe* [MGM]. And then there were those that you should never have made. If I had it to do over again, out of 115 films, I wouldn't have made two-thirds of them."

While Berman was producing at RKO, the studio was releasing forty films a year. "You were scrambling to make pictures. They wanted one a week for the RKO theater circuit. They changed the bill once a week in those days. I made pictures I shouldn't have made because they needed pictures.

"I think the secret of making pictures of a variety is having the people who are great at that type of picture on them. I liked making musicals, but after I left RKO, I didn't want to make any more. I liked making what we used to call society comedies or sophisticated comedies, an occasional drama and some of the spectacles. I never made a Western. I never cared for horseback riding. I think when you're a Jew brought up on the pavements of New York you don't become a Western addict.

"I liked making women's pictures most of all. I guess I had more fun and made more pictures with girls than I did with men. Katharine Hepburn. Ginger Rogers. Lucille Ball. Liz Taylor. Myrna Loy. Joan Fontaine. Irene Dunne. Ann Harding. And Carole Lombard, who was my favorite woman of all time in the picture business. She was a wonderful woman, a wonderful person."

After 1957, Berman regained the percentage deal he had lost when he went to work for MGM. He organized several production companies, but he always worked under the protective umbrella of the studio system. "I was born to be an employee. I was always a pessimist. I never thought any picture would ever make money. I was always surprised if I got a dime out of a movie.

"I wouldn't want to be in the business today. It's a young man's business, and you'd better do it while you're young. I always used to say that when a man was fifty they should throw him out of the studio. I let them keep me till I was sixty-five, and then I threw myself out. I stayed two years too long as it was. . . .

"The last couple of years, I had a miserable time. Forty-seven years in the film business had taken its toll, and I didn't enjoy it anymore. That's about all there was to it. I went over to Fox to make four pictures, but by the time I got there old man Zanuck was already crazy. I made two bad pictures [*Justine*, 1969, and *Move*, 1970] and said to myself, 'I'm not going to make the other two.' So, I tore up the contract and went home, and I was so glad I did. You work for two studios in your lifetime—seventeen and twenty-seven years—you can't start at sixty-five somewhere else!"

The memory of the last two failures faded quickly, however, and in 1977, Pandro Berman was given the Academy of Motion Picture Arts and Sciences' prestigious Irving G. Thalberg Memorial Award, for a lifetime of outstanding achievements as a producer. "It was the biggest surprise I ever had in my life. I always wanted that more than anything else, and I'd hoped that I'd be considered for it as far back as 1939. I had a very good year, and when I didn't get it, I gave up hope. I never dreamed it would come."

Joanne L. Yeck
Richard B. Jewell

An Interview with
WILLEM DAFOE

Willem Dafoe received the Oscar nomination for Best Supporting Actor in 1986 for his role as Sergeant Elias in *Platoon* (1986; reviewed in this volume). His portrayal of the compassionate but war-hardened squad leader has been recognized for its poignancy and pathos. The image of Dafoe as Elias, arms outstretched in agony toward the sky, served as the film's trademark in all the print publicity and on select cinema marquees.

For ten years, Dafoe has been at the center of New York City's experimental theater scene, as a founding member of SoHo's highly praised, frequently controversial Wooster Group. His initial film appearances were in *Heaven's Gate* (1980) and *The Hunger* (1983).

His first starring role, in *The Loveless* (1983), cast him as a jaded, taciturn motorcycle-gang leader in the 1950's. In *Roadhouse 66* (1984), he played a drifter who hitchhikes into a small town. For Walter Hill's *Streets of Fire* (1984), Dafoe again played a biker/gang leader, though the character was more violent than the previous role in *The Loveless*. In William Friedkin's *To Live and Die in L. A.* (1986), Dafoe portrayed an antiheroic forger who is no less guilty (and possibly more sympathetic) than the police detectives pursuing him.

Although Dafoe was in danger of becoming typecast as a classic villain, his most significant roles prior to *Platoon* (in *The Loveless* and *To Live and Die in L. A.*) actually dealt with more complex characters whose lives interweaved good and evil. His portrayal of the sympathetic Sergeant Elias in *Platoon* was less a matter of Dafoe breaking type, and more an opportunity for him to display his broader dramatic capabilities.

Dafoe's first acting experience was with Theater X in Milwaukee, Wisconsin. This satirical improvisation group toured the college circuit in the United States and in Europe. In 1977, he moved to Manhattan and joined the company which would evolve into the Wooster Group. Dafoe also became romantically involved with the company's director, Elizabeth LeCompte. Dafoe (now thirty-one) and LeCompte still live and work together, and they have a six-year-old son, Jack.

For this interview, we met in Dafoe's Manhattan loft. Son Jack, nearby on the rug, was quietly absorbed in playing with his new erector set, while LeCompte was busy with a telephone interview.

Louis A. Morra

Q: How were you cast for *Platoon*?
Dafoe: Oliver Stone initially asked me to read for every role other than

the black parts. He told me that he saw possibilities but couldn't decide where to place me. In the process, he watched a trailer for my previous film, *To Live and Die in L. A.* That was when something clicked. He said that he saw something in my character there which connected to the real-life officer he had known, who was the basis for my character Sergeant Elias in *Platoon.*

Q: That must have placed a heavy responsibility on you as an actor in creating the role of Sergeant Elias.

Dafoe: We all knew that Oliver Stone's script was in some way autobiographical. We were aware that we were going to be telling his story, and that it was very important to him that this story be told. Out of respect for his vision of the film, and the message he wanted to get across, all of us developed some degree of personal involvement and responsibility.

Now as for what went into developing the *persona* of Sergeant Elias, *Platoon* was absolutely unique as film work, because the entire cast underwent an intensive field-training program for several weeks before we started shooting. This training was utterly crucial to the making of *Platoon.* It set the whole atmosphere for doing the film, for how we were going to be asked to perform as actors.

The training was done on location in the Philippines. It was actual jungle training, not boot camp where you do push-ups and jog through an obstacle course. We were under the supervision of Marine advisers who were Vietnam vets. Retired Marine Captain Dale Dye, former editor of *Soldier of Fortune* magazine, was the man actually in charge. He took the job of training us on an extremely serious level.

The idea was to parallel the actual life of a grunt. Every day we took long hikes. We received training in how to do an ambush, air navigation, how to move tactically in the jungle, to live in holes that we had to dig ourselves. We got very little sleep, and we were constantly asked to perform tasks in situations where we were completely out of our element.

The marines who were training us would then attack us at night. At night, mind you! We had to sit up all night in shifts. You would get so tired you started to imagine that you heard movement in the brush, or saw something. Certainly we weren't going to be killed, but the experience of the training was real enough.

As in a real combat situation, you unavoidably encountered tests of your character, your courage. When you didn't measure up, you had to face the other actors, and the marines who were training you. We all became engaged in the soldier's survival mentality. It totally cured me of any romantic, John Wayne-style images I might've had of military life. The jungle is a stinking swamp filled with snakes and insects, and if it's not raining, then it's pouring cats and dogs.

So as I say, the experience of jungle training set the tone for how we were going to perform in *Platoon*. As an initiation rite, we earned the respect and authority of our military advisers. And I think that in turn we also felt that we had earned Oliver Stone's respect. We now were capable of telling his story faithfully and truthfully.

Q: How do you relate personally to the role of Sergeant Elias?

Dafoe: I have never been able to talk about my roles, either in films or on the stage. When someone talks to me about one of my characters, I clam up. Sergeant Elias the character, the role I played out in this film called *Platoon*, actually means nothing to me. Sergeant Elias was who I was during three months in the Philippines, under a very special set of ground rules, including the jungle training. My belief is that all characters live in you. With the help of a film or a play, you frame them, you provide them with the circumstances that will allow them to come alive.

But to look at the matter less from an acting perspective, I saw Sergeant Elias as the hero, the conscience of the platoon. You have the classic situation of the good guy Elias, the bad guy Sergeant Barnes [Tom Berenger], and the young kid who is being initiated into warfare, the narrator Chris [Charlie Sheen]. He starts from ground zero with those two sides influencing him. *Platoon* is the story of how a man/boy would deal with this nightmarish situation. Not just the war, but the moral conflicts. So Sergeant Elias is the good guy, but what he stands for only takes on meaning in relationship to the other characters, and to whatever the theme or moral or political messages of *Platoon* may be.

Q: Would you care to talk about those issues? *Platoon* has already become a symbol of the Vietnam War in the mind of the American public.

Dafoe: Vietnam is still such a touchy subject. It's impossible to approach the horror, or to express the truth, concerning an experience you haven't actually had. People died, and other people's lives were decimated by it. It's true that playing a role in a value-charged film such as *Platoon* creates additional responsibilities for an actor, which do not ordinarily come into play.

All you want to do ultimately is to be in good faith as an actor. I spoke earlier about the responsibility we developed toward Oliver Stone in helping him to bring his story into reality as a film. That set the tone, and we all worked hard. None of the actors was a Vietnam vet. In fact, most of us, myself included, were really too young to have had a political stance while the war was going on.

Q: What about Elias as a Christ figure? In his final scene in *Platoon*, he is pursued by Vietcong as the other soldiers watch helplessly from a helicopter that has already left the evacuation area. As he is shot and dies, he stretches his arms upward toward the sky, in a gesture that is reminiscent of the Crucifixion.

Dafoe: I realize that a lot of people have picked up on this and interpreted specific things into the film as a result. Elias is a moral character, but

Christ on the Cross was probably the furthest image from my mind at that moment. The gesture seemed to fit what was happening in the film, namely Elias' death under those circumstances. That doesn't mean that people viewing the film after it's been shot shouldn't read in whatever associations or projections it may provoke.

Q: In your previous starring roles in *The Loveless* and *To Live and Die in L. A.*, you played the bad guy. The *New York Times* review of the latter film praised you for being an archetypal villain in the Richard Widmark tradition. How does it feel to break type in the good-guy Elias role in *Platoon*?

Dafoe: It doesn't feel terribly different. Externally it may seem like a major role change, to go from playing a villainous biker as in *The Loveless* or *Streets of Fire*, to being the moral conscience of a platoon fighting for its survival in Vietnam. But internally, the characters don't feel all that different to me. My approach to acting remains the same.

People have talked to me about typecasting, and I've been aware of it. You notice that directors take a malicious sneer for granted and depend on you to provide it. It's true that *Platoon* has changed that and that now more possibilities exist.

When you are typecast into playing one sort of role, it can bolster your presence on the screen with a mythic strength. Then, in every film you make, people see your face and relive or remember every other time they have seen you in a similar part. That can be a great strength for an actor. However, every time I get an opportunity not to have to function as the heavy, not to have to create a certain effect against the hero, it's an increase in the range of what I can do.

Actually, what's interesting, in my previous films such as *The Loveless* and *To Live and Die in L. A.*, is that it's really somewhat the set-up, the plot line, that makes the character evil. It's his function in the story. It came very close in *To Live and Die in L. A.*, because many of the supposedly good characters, such as the police, were despicable and unethical.

What's important is that you do your job well. You see, in a strange way, I really do believe that I am the one who is going through all of these roles. It's not that I become the other person. It's more that I happen to be that other person in that particular circumstance.

Q: Could you elaborate on that?

Dafoe: I always maintain that I can't be anything other than myself. I borrow from my own life history and adjust it. I match up my fantasies with what the character is required to do. As an actor, I have no definite techniques which carry me regardless of the role I'm creating. It's always something specific to the situation. If there's any sort of transformation when I take on a role, it's still me, but me in radically different life circumstances, which call up dormant, or hidden, or unused, parts of my self. The character I portray is who I might be if I had had his life history.

Q: Does this approach to acting relate to your long-standing involvement with Off-Off Broadway theater in New York City?

Dafoe: Absolutely. I have worked with the Wooster Group for ten years now, and incidentally, I first got to do work in films from people seeing me perform our pieces.

The Wooster Group represents an unusual approach to theatrical performance. Our work is not about someone sitting down to write a play which is intended to communicate a single theme or set of ideas. The pieces are all group-developed under the guidance of our director, Elizabeth LeCompte.

What this means, in terms of our group working process, is that we collect things. We collect texts, objects, ideas, theatrical conventions, and we begin to experiment with what they mean, how they interact. These things have a life to them, which, broadly speaking, is their meaning or significance as cultural icons.

In early 1987, we presented a retrospective of three plays which form a trilogy entitled *The Road to Immortality.* Now for instance, one of the theatrical conventions which was the basis for the creation of the first play, *Route 1 & 9,* was blackface, the blackface routines which were popularized by someone like Al Jolson.

Theater critics have applied the theoretical term deconstruction to some of our work. We may not completely accept it, and certainly it wasn't ever a conscious decision that we were going to take apart and analyze other literary works. But it is true that *Route 1 & 9* places long passages of Thornton Wilder's classic play *Our Town* in an unusual context. The second part of this trilogy, *Just the High Points,* initially was derived from Arthur Miller's *The Crucible.* Part three, *Frank Dell's Saint Antony,* bears some relationship to the novel *The Temptation of Saint Anthony,* by French author Gustave Flaubert. But so much other material is layered around these works.

Q: How does film acting differ from performing with the Wooster Group?

Dafoe: Most people think of acting as something with a primarily psychological message. But the Wooster Group mixes "performance" and acting, and as I've explained, most of what we do is not in the form of traditional play structures. This creates an incredibly open personal space for experimenting with personas. You can also work on the level of pure action and dance. The immediate sense of freedom and self-expression on stage, even within the structures that we do define, is obviously rather different from how a film is shot.

But there's no way you can read a film script and have the director immediately exclaim, "Okay, keep it like that." Everything changes as the work proceeds. Not unlike with the Wooster Group, you are feeling your way along.

Also, a lot of actors like to improvise, and sometimes I like to, but essentially I like it laid out.

Q: Have you ever collaborated with film directors?

Dafoe: I recently worked on a video project with the writer Burt Barr, based on his short story, "The Red Cloud." The video was shot by James Benning and is called *O Panama.* I read the short story, then we filmed me doing various actions, not to illustrate the story but to parallel it. I was like the object of a portrait. They built a world and I inhabited it. Emotions ranging from fear and sorrow to boredom are invoked through atmosphere and my facial expressions.

The Wooster Group always tapes the stage performances. We made a sixteen millimeter film with Ken Kobland, entitled *Flaubert Dreams of Travel.* And our pieces often include videotapes of us acting, to parallel and interface with what's happening live on the stage, projected through several television monitors mounted in various places as part of the theatrical environment. We expect to be doing more film work in the future.

If you are referring to feature films, obviously the situation is vastly different. But when we started shooting the climax of *To Live and Die in L.A.,* William Friedkin came up to me and said, this is just too common, like a cop show. As the script was originally written, my character, the artist-turned-forger, is sitting in the burning warehouse. He tries to escape when the cop arrives, but, just by the physics of gunplay, the cop gets the drop on him and blows him away.

Friedkin and I talked, and we came up with the ending as it now exists, in which my character is seen to be waiting, very passively. He demonstrates this odd kind of passivity in regard to the cop's arrival, which takes the viewer by surprise. It's as though he is waiting for the cop to come and take control, in order to complete the game they're both playing.

It's weird but it fits, because all throughout, the forger has shown something like a twisted spiritual side. He has a death wish that he's always flirting with. He knows he's in trouble at the end, and the fact that he's sitting in the warehouse on fire makes it quite clear that he has a hand in his own death. And since that's his choice, the moment is not entirely sad. It's kind of a glorious death. So because of his antihero status, that passivity toward dying fit. It strengthened the character.

Also, Friedkin wanted the actors to be comfortable, so as far as dialogue went, if we had an idea for something that felt like it would come out of our mouths more smoothly, he thought it was just fine. He'd use it.

Q: Your first feature film, *The Loveless,* was billed as an homage to *The Wild One* (1954).

Dafoe: I was pretty central to the project, and nobody told me it was an homage to *The Wild One.* That misrepresents the film somewhat, and creates expectations that it wasn't meant to satisfy. It's a very different kind of film. Some of the story elements are similar, since we're dealing with bikers, but the point of view is altogether different. Certainly I wasn't trying to emulate Brando.

Q: What is your next film project?

Dafoe: The film is titled *Saigon.* It's directed by Christopher Crowe, and Gregory Hines and myself are the costars. It's a murder mystery set against the backdrop of the Vietnam War, in which I play an M.P. who is investigating the murder of several prostitutes. We'll be shooting in Thailand.

Q: Your Oscar nomination for Best Supporting Actor in *Platoon* confirms you as a Hollywood film actor. How will this impact on your future work with the Wooster Group?

Dafoe: There's no conflict, if that's what you mean. I feel rooted in the Wooster Group, and they are my friends. If I go off to make a film, it only takes three months.

Being a film actor may carry that aura of success, but in the reality of my life, the Wooster Group is also very important. It's a little schizophrenic at times, being high-profile with the film work and low-profile with the Wooster Group, but that can be pleasurable in itself. I prefer keeping myself a little off-balance as an actor; you stay more alert for what's around the next corner.

An Interview with
JIM JARMUSCH

When *The New York Times* film critic Vincent Canby published his Ten
Best List of 1986, he called *Down by Law* (1986; reviewed in this volume)
"the most original, most bold, most organically cinematic film of the year."
This capped a year in which Jim Jarmusch's quirky and independently made
film premiered at the Cannes Film Festival and was the opening night selection of the New York Film Festival. This was quite an achievement for a
thirty-three-year-old director's third feature, made far from Hollywood
conventions, stars, budgets, or concerns.

Down by Law, shot in New Orleans in rich tones of black and white, follows the intertwining tales of an unlikely trio. Jack (musician John Lurie,
who made an impressive debut in *Stranger than Paradise*, 1984) is a talkative pimp; Zack (singer Tom Waits) is a taciturn disc jockey. Each has been
framed and arrested, and they meet in a prison cell, where they immediately
dislike each other. Soon they are joined by Roberto (Italian comedian
Roberto Benigni), whose halting English provides a touching and often
hilarious gap between himself and the American convicts. They eventually
escape from the prison, only to wander aimlessly through the Louisiana
swamps. The plot of *Down by Law*, however, is ultimately secondary to the
tone created by the offbeat characters, situations, rhythms, and textures, as
well as the haunting music composed by Lurie and Waits.

Jarmusch is a tall and lanky New Yorker whose white hair and perennially
black or gray clothes suggest that his films are not in technicolor. Born in
Akron, Ohio, he majored in English literature at Columbia University and
did some graduate work in New York University's Film School. For this
soft-spoken director who likes to maintain his privacy, the Cannes brouhaha
was a bit much, and he consented to an interview only after returning to the
United States.

"The weirdest thing for me," he confessed in a downtown Manhattan restaurant, "was that while I was making *Down by Law*, I never thought about
the fact that the people who liked *Stranger than Paradise* would be waiting
to see what I followed it up with. Then I arrived in Cannes and realized,
'these people have expectations!' It kind of flipped me out.

"I knew I couldn't handle publicity," he continued, "so I went to Cannes
for only four or five days. I saw no films there because I had no time! I refused about a hundred interviews but still did so many that I was exhausted.
I look at publicity as propaganda. I don't like being made into a product."

Although Jarmusch does not like to talk about himself, he grew visibly
animated in discussing how *Down by Law* took shape. In particular, the
deep friendship that developed between the director and his actors remains
a source of gratification for him. "I was working on another script and was

sort of blocked," he recalled, "and was writing a little sketch of something for Tom [Waits] and John [Lurie]. Then I went to Italy and met Roberto Benigni. As a result of hanging around with him, I got the idea for the rest of the story because he's the central character. I showed him a treatment in Rome, and he said he'd like to do it."

Jarmusch had never seen Benigni's work and did not even know that he was Italy's most popular comic performer of his generation. "He's the funniest person I've ever met," Jarmusch exclaimed. "I didn't want to see any of his other work until after I finished the script. When I finally did see it, I realized that his acting style in the Italian films is completely different from what he does in *Down by Law*. Roberto is known in Italy for his machine-gun-fire use of language; that's his weapon, as in *Tuttobenigni* [1986], a concert film of Roberto directed by Giuseppe Bertolucci. It's interesting to have this intellectual character who, in *Down by Law*, is not equipped with the most essential means of communication, language. But he can communicate with the guys in a very deep way. He's the angel of the film."

Here, one might recall another stranger to America, Eva (Eszter Balint) in *Stranger than Paradise*. Watching John Lurie eat his TV dinners, she conveyed a fascination with *homo americanus* similar to what one sees in Roberto. "I'm concerned with people being in cultures that are alien to them," Jarmusch acknowledged, "misinterpreting things and therefore having a different perspective on them. I wasn't trying to repeat the same story or theme, but all three of my films are about America [including his debut, *Permanent Vacation*, 1982]. It's important to me to travel for this reason: I like misinterpreting things because it makes my imagination open up. When I was an undergraduate at Columbia University, I wanted to be a writer and studied with David Shapiro and Kenneth Koch. They'd have us translate poetry from languages we did not speak or read. Through misinterpretation, your imagination starts to work. I feel very happy when I don't have to know if what I've done is correct."

An example of this "misinterpretation" can be found in the film's title. *Down by Law* is a slang term, which Jarmusch traced back to the 1920's when blacks came from the South to Northern cities. "Once they knew their way around, it was said they were down by law—in control of themselves. The term has stayed in use mostly in prisons and with blacks, till the late 1970's when it emerged from prison slang. Initially, it meant a very fraternal thing, like a gang. The term means an outsider can be trusted; now, it has become diluted to meaning simply, 'you're cool with us.' I like the fraternal sense of these three guys in the film, and the literal sense of being oppressed by law, which the term implies. But it really means the opposite. You could say it's cultural vampirism on my part to steal it, but that's what slang is all about. I like slang because it makes language a living thing."

Curiously enough, it was in Italy that Jarmusch wrote his pungent American lines. Lighting a cigarette, he explained, "Since it was a prison escape, a lot of images of New Orleans and Louisiana were in my head from crime fiction, Tennessee Williams, films of the thirties and forties, pop music, especially the New Orleans rhythm 'n' blues scene from the late fifties to early sixties. I'd never been there before, but I knew there were swamps. The way New Orleans is depicted in the film is pretty abstract. I like minimalizing things so that what we see has a stronger impression. If you fill everything up with too many details, you have a weaker sense of atmosphere."

To this end, Jarmusch chose once again to work in black and white. He insisted that it is a different kind of black and white from *Stranger than Paradise*, "a finer grain with more gray tones, very tactile and sensual. Black and white can be as varied as color, which gives you more information: I didn't think it was appropriate for this story. *Down by Law* alludes to genres, like *film noir* and prison escapes, so I always saw it in black and white. The script I was writing before was in color. But some distributors said they'd give me more money if I shot *Down by Law* in color. That made me more adamant to do it in black and white."

He was fortunate that one of the world's most respected cinematographers saw things the same way as Jarmusch and wanted to work with him. Robby Muller, known primarily for his collaboration with Wim Wenders, was excited by the prospect of shooting in black and white—which he had not done since *Kings of the Road* (1976) more than ten years previously. According to Jarmusch, the film's visual strategy was "no point-of-view shots or inserts. There's never anything that cuts away—which made the film difficult to edit but interesting to shoot. We talked about how Westerns are always horizontally composed because of the landscape, whereas *film noir* or crime films are always vertically composed because of the urban landscape. We wanted to find something that was neither, something with its own sense of composition that could be maintained through all the film's different landscapes—prison interior, New Orleans exterior, and the swamp.

"We also tried to allow characters to push the edges of the frame," he continued. "Robby worked very hard to get as deep a focus as he could. Especially in the scenes with the women, the male character is always in the shot along with the female—another aesthetic choice of how to compose things. The women are telling them exactly what their weaknesses are—fairly lucid critiques that the men aren't really aware of." Along with the deep focus and wide angles, Jarmusch opted for long takes, about which he explained, "We wanted to invent our shots *in* the location. It's intuitive: I like to let things go past the point of the expected dramatic pinnacle of the scene. I'm trying to find unexpected ways of doing things, but on a simple level."

Before directing *Down by Law*, Jarmusch had just made a music video for Talking Heads, "The Lady Don't Mind," which is also mostly in black and white. His producer had been Alan Kleinberg, a major figure in the music-video world. Although Kleinberg had never produced a feature, Jarmusch asked him if he would be interested in assuming that responsibility for *Down by Law*. The answer was yes, and Jarmusch now credits his young producer with keeping the budget to just over a million dollars.

The director's tendency to work with musicians and people from the music industry is exemplified by his casting of Lurie and Waits, both of whom also wrote the film's score. Waits, the award-winning singer-composer who wrote the sound track for Francis Coppola's *One from the Heart* (1982), had already acted in a few films. Jarmusch had been listening to Waits's music when he went location-scouting in Louisiana, and he recalled, "His songs were so much in my head that I used them for inspiration, thinking about the rhythm of the shots. It's not that he composed songs for the ideas the film already captured: My ideas were influenced by his songs." Lurie, on the other hand, composed the music after shooting was completed. "He was free to do what he wanted, but we discussed it a lot," said Jarmusch. According to Lurie—whose album, *Lounge Lizards Live in Tokyo*, was subsequently released by Island Records—"I had the idea for the music while we were in the swamp. I had this specific feel for what the sound should be. Now I think the sound track really encapsulates the film."

Along with Benigni, they constitute one of the most idiosyncratic examples of creative casting. Jarmusch calls it "semiconscious. I have a real thing about the number three. Both films are three-part, with *Stranger than Paradise* obviously marked as three sections. If you have two characters, they can agree or disagree. I like the idea of three characters because you can have more play with point of view: There can be one central character and two antithetical ones. Or," he said with a smile, "three is the infinite perspective."

When asked about the film's ending—in which each character goes his separate way, although Roberto finds and stays with a lovely Italian woman (Nicoletta Braschi)—Jarmusch replied, "Roberto's persistent optimism is a different way of looking at things from the two American guys, and it influences them. But the film doesn't end with a little moral—'yes, these guys learned from him and are going to employ what they learned.' We don't know what's going to happen. We observe them being affected by this angelic guy, but there's no little payoff like 'they lived happily ever after.' I don't like films where the curtain comes down. I like stories that continue—that you don't really want to end: Those characters are still alive when the credits come up."

Annette Insdorf

An Interview with
CATHERINE TURNEY

Catherine Turney is at heart a playwright, but since the 1930's she has become accomplished in virtually every dramatic form. She has enjoyed a series of careers writing for radio, motion pictures, and television, in an era when few women matched her success. In more recent years, she has concentrated on writing prose, publishing both novels and nonfiction. Yet, despite her long and varied career, few people associate Turney's name with her most well-respected and best remembered film, *Mildred Pierce* (1945).

"It was 1944," Miss Turney remembers, "and my agent, Alvin Manuel, wanted to renegotiate my contract with Warner Bros. and ask for a raise in salary. That was pretty hard to do during the war because salaries were frozen. The studio was willing, but they never wanted to raise anybody's salary if they could avoid it."

At that time, Turney had earned a series of solo credits, and Manuel was convinced that their case would be stronger if she did not take any cocredits. "So, like a damn fool," Turney says, "I listened to my agent and took my name off *Mildred Pierce!*"

Producer Jerry Wald was "flabbergasted." Prints of the film had already gone out with Catherine Turney's name on them, sharing a credit with Ranald MacDougall, who had replaced her on the project when she began work on her next film, *A Stolen Life* (1946; reviewed in this volume). While she clearly deserved credit for her contribution, the recent memories of creative differences with Wald undoubtedly made it easier for her to follow her agent's advice.

In the early stages of development, Wald approved of her adaptation, but he had a change of heart when he saw what director Billy Wilder had achieved with another novel by James Cain. "Jerry and I had been working a straight-line story for *Mildred Pierce*, when he saw *Double Indemnity* [Paramount Pictures, 1944] and immediately decided that he was never going to do another picture that wasn't in flashback form!

"Michael Curtiz was set to direct, and he, too, wanted to add a flashback and a murder. I argued with them, but they were determined. In *Double Indemnity*, it was the *raison d'etre* of the whole story, but I felt there was no reason for it in *Mildred Pierce*. I did add the murder, but it was a matter of having to please Wald as the producer. I didn't want to include it."

Turney respected Cain's novel about a divorced mother of two trying to make her own way in the world, and she was doing her best to write a screen version which was true to the original. "I saw *Mildred Pierce* as a serious middle-class study about a woman caught up in a typical middle-class situation and her efforts to cope with it. I thought James Cain was very sympathetic to the woman's problem. He wrote it truthfully. But Curtiz didn't understand the story. He couldn't believe anyone cared about a Glendale housewife who baked pies. . . ."

Film scholars have since rectified Turney's "mistake" and have reestablished her contribution to *Mildred Pierce*. Yet the film that exists—the dark murder mystery that won for Joan Crawford an Academy Award—is not the film that Turney wrote. Hers was more reflective of her own background: her knowledge of Pasadena society, of the musical world, and of the struggles of a talented woman trying to make her way in a man's world.

Turney was born in Chicago, but at the age of six months, her family moved to Rome, New York. "I really feel that that's my hometown. Then we moved to California in 1922 and I went, practically off the train, to an Episcopalian college preparatory school in La Jolla while my parents found a house in Pasadena."

Following three years at the Bishop's School, "I went back East to the Columbia School of Journalism. I took playwriting and stage work and a course in short story writing." After six months, Turney became ill and returned to Pasadena, where she started classes again at the University of California, Southern Branch. In the summer of 1928, however, she started to work at the Pasadena Community Playhouse.

"It was love at first sight. I never went back to the college. I did everything there, and soon became the director of the Workshop, directing plays. I learned what makes a play tick. It rubs off on you. I also worked as the production manager of the Main Stage shows, and then I got to be Gilmore Brown's assistant on Eugene O'Neill's *Lazarus Laughed*. In 1930, when the School of Theater was started, I was a member of the first class.

"The first job I ever had in Hollywood was through Jeane Wood, director Sam Wood's daughter. She was a great friend of mine from the Playhouse. I wrote dialogue for Wood at Eddie Small's studio, Reliance Pictures." (During the 1930's, Small produced some very successful independent productions, *The Count of Monte Cristo*, 1934, and *The Last of the Mohicans*, 1936.)

Wood quit the picture and went back to Metro-Goldwyn-Mayer. "Later, I was hired by Small to work on the screenplay for *The Melody Lingers On* [1935]. Lillian Hellman had written the first script, but it didn't come off. This is nothing against Hellman—she wrote magnificent plays—but the story was obviously not her métier. Hellman's approach was entirely different from what they wanted. They were looking for *Madame X*. In the end, they practically stole it!

"I only stayed six weeks. I was completely naïve—a fugitive from the Playhouse—and had had no dealings whatsoever with the motion-picture business. Eddie Small and I didn't mesh at all. Of course, he meshed with very few people, particularly writers."

Like many of the Hollywood pioneers, Small had a native feel for making pictures. "Small would make these strange remarks; they had a sort of gut showmanship. For instance, in one case there was a letter that was important in the story and they showed an insert of the letter. Small's response was, 'I don't like a story where a woman is believing in inserts!' He was right, of course."

It was E. Barrington's *The Glorious Apollo* (1925), a fictionalized version of the life of Lord Byron, that provided Turney with her next step. "I was entranced with this book. I fell so in love with Byron that I decided I was going to write a play about him. It was about his love affair with his sister and his disastrous marriage, which resulted in his self-imposed exile from England."

Turney's first play was a critical success. Initially produced by the Arts Theatre, London, in 1936 and then by Gilbert Miller and Daniel Mayer in London's West End at the St. Martin's Theatre, *Bitter Harvest* starred Eric Portman. "It was the start of his brilliant acting career and was the springboard for how I got back to Hollywood. It was clear that talking pictures were here to stay, and the studios were still importing anyone who could write plays or dialogue. So, Metro-Goldwyn-Mayer hired me sight unseen."

At Metro-Goldwyn-Mayer Turney worked on *The Bride Wore Red* (1937) with another new writer named Waldo Salt and later on *A Yank at Oxford* (1938). Although she and Salt were given an Academy credit on *The Bride Wore Red*, Turney never earned a screen credit.

She was at Metro-Goldwyn-Mayer for a year, but her option was not renewed. So, she returned to dramatic writing and collaborated with Jerry Horwin on a comedy, *One More Genius*. It was performed at the Pasadena Playhouse and in summer stock. "On the strength of that, Jerry and I decided that we would try another play." The result was *My Dear Children*, which would become John Barrymore's sensational comeback in 1939.

"It was all about a matinee idol who is on the skids—a womanizer who runs off with the girlfriend of a rich industrialist. . . . Contrary to what people thought, we did not write it for Barrymore. We were thinking in terms of Lowell Sherman, who was also a matinee idol at the time.

"Elaine Barrie, then Barrymore's wife, was trying to find a play that was suitable for her. . . to go back to New York, with Barrymore as her leading man! They were deluged with scripts and ours was on the top of the pile. It was a fluke that the Barrymores even read it."

The play was an enormous success, and in 1940, "Darry Zanuck decided to make a film based on the shenanigans that went on with the production of *My Dear Children*. It was called *The Great Profile*. I was portrayed by Mary Beth Hughs. I was supposed to be the author who vamped the old man into doing her play.

"After *My Dear Children*, I went back to New York and lived there for a few years. I was living off of my royalties and getting ready to write another play." But before she could complete her next play, she returned to California.

In 1943, "James Geller, the story editor at Warner Bros., hired me while Jack Warner was out of town. I slipped in through the back door. Warner wasn't much for hiring women writers, but it was World War II, many of the writers were in the service, and they needed people to write pictures."

Her first assignment was *Of Human Bondage* (1946), a remake of the 1934 version, starring Bette Davis and Leslie Howard. It was produced by Henry Blanke and directed by Edmund Goulding. "Goulding was certainly considered a women's director, but he was awfully hard to work with. He just rode roughshod over everybody. He was a charming man, but he took your script and rewrote every line.

"He eliminated what Blanke and I had tried so hard to put in, which was to make it the *whole* story of Philip Carey, not just the story of Philip and Mildred."

The film had a disastrous preview, but when an edited sequence was restored, the film was salvaged. "Goulding was a good director, but not for *Of Human Bondage*. Well, it wasn't exactly his fault. We had no one to play Philip. I think Eleanor Parker was pretty good as Mildred—the part that Bette Davis created. But Paul Henreid wasn't good as Philip, Leslie Howard had made the role his. Anyway, you couldn't think of Henreid as a crippled man that no woman would give a second thought to. . . ."

Of Human Bondage was followed by *My Reputation* (1946), a women's picture based on the novel *Instruct My Sorrows*, which Barbara Stanwyck brought to the studio's attention. Produced by Blanke and directed by Curtis Bernhardt, *My Reputation* was set in Lake Forest, Illinois, in an atmosphere Turney understood. "Because I'd been in Chicago for a year and a half when I was doing *My Dear Children*, I got to know several people living in Lake Forest."

Stanwyck herself was uncomfortable playing the role of a sexually and emotionally repressed, affluent woman, but, "Curt Bernhardt got a wonderful performance out of her, even though he never really grasped the character. He couldn't understand why this grown woman was so prissy about men—after all, she was a widow, with two children. I said that she was a lady, and to me this explained everything . . . but to a European it didn't!

"Henry and Curt worked very closely with me on *My Reputation*. They would come to my office, start out in a rather peaceable manner, and end up screaming at each other in German. People would stand around outside the door wondering what was going on! Then it would be time for lunch and, suddenly, they would stop and say, 'Okay, ve go to lunch.' And off they'd go arm and arm.

"*My Reputation* was quite popular at Warners. Even Jack Warner was crazy about it. It was kind of a departure from the ordinary run of Warner pictures—particularly Barbara Stanwyck pictures—and everybody was very admiring of Curt Bernhardt's direction."

The success of *My Reputation* led to a second film with Bernhardt, *A Stolen Life*, starring Bette Davis. "It was because of *My Reputation* that Bette wanted us for *A Stolen Life*. Curt and I got along well. He wasn't easy to work with, but we seemed to mesh as far as our thoughts on pictures."

Jack Chertok, fresh from Metro-Goldwyn-Mayer, started out on the picture as the producer but during preproduction was fired from the studio, and Bette Davis took over as producer. Like other highly paid stars, Davis had formed a production company to cut down on heavy taxes. "Bette Davis was not at all reluctant to express her opinions. In fact, most of those stars knew what was right for them. They looked very closely at things; they were good businesswomen."

For all practical purposes, Bernhardt functioned as both director and producer, but Davis took her title seriously. "When the studio gave her the job as producer, they should have known that she would react exactly as she did. Her attitude was, if I'm the producer, I'm going to act like a producer!"

The story was based on a British picture, *Stolen Life* (1939), which starred Elizabeth Bergner. It was another woman's picture, the story of twins—the good sister takes the bad one's identity when she is accidentally killed.

In the Bergner film, the interesting character had been the "bad" sister. "It was a story without much substance, and the good sister was a nothing—very drab. In our version, the good sister is the main character. We had to start from scratch and build up a second act so that the audience has some sympathy for this girl's desire to take her sister's place."

By the time *A Stolen Life* was finished, Turney was typed as a "women's writer," specializing in tearful women's stories. "When we were writing these pictures, we were just writing about *a* woman in a certain set of circumstances. They used to call them three-handkerchief pictures.

"They were supposed to appeal to women. They dealt with women's problems, and were generally hard to write at that period of time, because there were very few women's problems that were not involved with men or sex. It took a great deal of ingenuity to get around the censors. . . .

"Other studios made pictures about noble women, *Madam Curie* [Metro-Goldwyn-Mayer, 1943] or *Sister Kenny* [RKO, 1946] . . . but in most cases Warner Bros. didn't go in much for that. They wanted stories about women in relationship to men. They figured, and rightly so, that this was what would interest the audience. That's all they were trying to do. They didn't have any idea of any message. And the last thing in Jack Warner's mind would have been a 'women's lib' picture!

"In fact, I think one of the reasons women's lib was formed was because the movies have had such an effect on people. For so many years, they dealt entirely with women as sex objects. They still do today, but in a different way. In my time you could have no more done a film like *Dressed to Kill* [1980] than you could have flown to the moon!"

In 1946, Turney's name was on four very successful films. Like *Of Human Bondage, My Reputation* was also held for release until 1946. Warner Bros. was rushing out topical products for the wartime audience, saving its general interest pictures and period films, such as *Saratoga Trunk* (1943) and *Devotion* (1944), for after the war. "That year I got to be a 'box-office champion.' I was in very good company as a matter of fact, with Charles Brackett and Billy Wilder and Charlie Hoffman.

"*My Reputation* set me off," she remembers. "I acquired a kind of reputation of my own for being a troubleshooter." She quickly became the top woman writer on the lot. "To some extent, I took Lenore Coffee's place; she worked at home and no longer came to the studio. There were only two or three other women there, including Harriet Frank, Jr., and Margaret Buell Wilder."

More than once, Turney was asked to assist new women writers, who were inexperienced at screenwriting. "I was assigned to Louise Randall Pierson, who came to write the screenplay of her autobiography, *Roughly Speaking* [1943]. She was a very dominating woman.

"The only other woman I can think of who was there at the time was Ayn Rand. Before they decided to bring her out, they gave me *The Fountainhead* [1943] to read. Frankly, I couldn't stand it. It seemed to me that it had such phony premises, and the character of the woman didn't ring true to me. If she loved this man so much, why was she bent on destroying him?"

To Turney's relief, she never started on the script. "Once Rand came out, the film was her baby. From her point of view, nobody else was going to touch it. She was a very strange woman, although, I must say, she did have a certain power in her work."

It was not only Turney's talent that earned for her a privileged place among Warner Bros.' screenwriters but also her special working relationship with Bernhardt which resulted in exceptional opportunities. "I was able to sit in on everything connected with *My Reputation* and *A Stolen Life*. So, as a result, I got a marvelous training at Warner Bros. I was very, very lucky.

"In those days, the studio expected the script to be ready to shoot. In fact, they had very strict rules that no part of the script would be changed without permission once it went into production. But, of course, nobody ever paid any attention to that. . . .

"Curt was constantly calling me down on the set. He didn't make any pretense about being able to write dialogue. In Europe, where he began his career, they worked as a group, but that wasn't the custom in Hollywood. Here you were working for a studio, and they wanted to keep you busy writing new material. At Warner Bros., particularly, they were great for that."

The vast majority of Turney's screenplays were based on novels or plays, each one presenting its own adaptation problems. *"The Man I Love* [1946] had kind of a curious history. The book, *Night Shift*, was enormously long with hundreds of characters. It sat on the shelf a long time; everybody had turned it down. Then, they gave it to Arnold Albert to produce, Ida Lupino agreed to play the lead, and Raoul Walsh was assigned to direct it.

"Walsh was an old-fashioned director, who didn't pretend he was a writer. It was a nice association. I liked him. We had to change the leading man's story completely because censorship would never have permitted it. It was a little bit on the order of the William Faulkner's *Sanctuary* [1931]. . . . Now it's being revived as an example of *film noir!"*

Although Turney continued to specialize in women's pictures, her breadth expanded with films such as *Cry Wolf* (1947), a suspense film starring Barbara Stanwyck and Errol Flynn. "Again, Barbara was the one who brought *Cry Wolf* to the studio, although it was really the man's story. . . ."

Flynn was nominally the film's producer, but unlike Bette Davis, "he didn't give a hoot! He just wanted to take the money." Flynn's concerns were about the relative importance of his character in the story. "He thought it was a fascinating part, but was worried because the woman's part was also very important. In other words, he realized he was playing the leading man to Barbara Stanwyck! It turned out to be a pretty good picture, although I hated working with the director, Peter Godfrey."

Godfrey also directed *One More Tomorrow* (1946), a remake of *The Animal Kingdom* (RKO, 1932), starring Ann Sheridan, Alexis Smith, and Dennis Morgan, on which Turney shared the screenwriting credit with Charles Hoffman. Additional dialogue was provided by two other top Warner Bros. writers, Philip and Julius Epstein. "I thought it was a mistake to make that picture. It was so good the first time. It went out and made a lot of money, but there was no comparison between it and the original with Ann Harding, Leslie Howard, and Myrna Loy."

Turney's last film at Warner Bros., *Winter Meeting* (1948), started out promisingly; it was a sensitive story about a spinster poet (Bette Davis) who falls in love with a war hero (Jim Davis). In the end, it turned out to be a dismal failure which seriously affected several careers.

"It was a very difficult story, but Bette decided it would be a good part for her. . . . Henry Blanke and I worked very closely on the adaptation. Everybody loved that script, but we realized it was much too long and very talky, so we cut it. Then the director, Bretaigne Windust, who had never directed a motion picture (although he had a considerable name on Broadway), came out and put all those lines back. . . .

"Every kind of thing seemed to go wrong, and yet at the time we weren't aware of it. The studio wanted a Warner contract player to play the leading man, and there wasn't anybody suitable. This was a very sensitive part. Richard Widmark came through with a wonderful test, but Jim Davis was under contract . . . so, they cast him, despite a poor screen test.

"Well, the first ten days' rushes were unqualified disasters and, in fact, Lew Wasserman, who was Bette's agent at the time, implored the studio to scrap it and get rid of Jim. But, the front office looked at the amount of money they had already spent on the picture and got cold feet.

"So, when Windust said, 'I'll make him act!' they fell for it, and once we were committed to Jim Davis, it was constant disaster.

"When we went to the sneak preview, the audience laughed. Between Bette's smoking and Jim's awkwardness, the audience didn't get together with us until the scene where he confesses he'd always wanted to be a priest. This really shocked them, or at least, startled them."

Despite the film's failure in 1949, *Winter Meeting* has played more successfully on television. "I think," reflects Turney, "it is precisely because it was a talky, static picture and because it had ideas. In those days, audiences didn't want to spend too much time with ideas.

"That picture was a very painful experience for all concerned. It got a bad review, and everybody suffered from it. After the debacle, my contract was coming up for quite a hike in salary. It was going to be one thousand dollars a week. Well, I went on layoff for the first time in the five years and when I came back, another screenwriter, Danny Fuchs, was in my office. They had taken everything out of my desk. All my scripts and things—they'd all vanished. I still remember how angry I was. . . ."

There was another significant contributing factor to Turney's unceremonious dismissal, one with far-reaching implications—the decline of the studio system itself. "They let a lot of us go, at that time. Many of the big women stars that the studio had wanted women writers for were already gone. Rosalind Russell had left. Barbara Stanwyck had left. And even Bette was failing at the box office. . . .

"It was a combination of things; the whole studio concept was beginning to change and fade. It was the wind[ing] down of the heyday years at Warner Bros. They didn't want to sign any new seven-year contracts, particularly with writers. And don't forget, I came in through the back door. Yes, I established myself, became accepted, and was eventually sought after as a writer, but it was always there—that slight prejudice against women writers. There's no doubt about it.

"After I left Warners, I signed a one-picture contract with Paramount to write a script based on the book *I Married a Dead Man* by Cornell George Hopley-Woolrich [written under the pseudonym William Irish]." It was yet another women's film, starring Barbara Stanwyck as a woman who takes a stranger's identity to provide a name for her soon-to-be born illegitimate child.

Initially, the studio hired Sally Benson to adapt the Woolrich novel. Paramount had paid her a high salary and was now stuck with a script they couldn't use. "Woolrich was pretty good at writing dramatic form. By simply adding 'fade-in/fade-out' his novel could have turned into a screenplay. . . but Sally had to fiddle around with things.

"I think they hired me largely because of the story's similarity to *A Stolen Life*, but later I thought, 'I don't want to spend the rest of my life writing about people who are taking each other's lives . . . twins or not!'"

On the production, "Everyone was in fear and trembling because the director, Mitchell Leisen, had a terrible reputation of being very hard to work with, but was deceptively charming. When I first started working with him, I thought, 'What's so hard about working with this delightful man?' Well, I found out.

"By slow degrees he began to infiltrate the script. He was always taking it home and rewriting . . . and there wasn't much I could do about it, and actually they weren't bad changes. . . ."

Everything was "all very polite," according to Turney, until the producers decided to give Benson a screenwriting credit, "even though they weren't using anything of her script.

"I had a right to fight it, but the producer, Richard Maybaum, explained that Leisen was waiting for a chance to take credit on the basis of all the finagling he did and that, if I did fight it, I might be aced-out completely."

Eventually, Turney requested an arbitration at the Screen Writer's Guild, and the result was a shared credit with Benson. Leisen, who tried to seize the opportunity to establish himself as a writer/director, "demanded an appeal and raised hell when he lost it. He immediately dropped his membership in the Guild, and went around telling everybody that he had been discriminated against. It was a very unpleasant situation."

Following *No Man of Her Own*, Turney's credits include *Japanese War Bride* (Twentieth Century-Fox, 1952), directed by King Vidor, and an adaptation of one of her own novels (*The Other One*), called *Back from the Dead* (Twentieth Century-Fox-Regal). She then moved into writing for television, and eventually turned to working exclusively on novels.

Looking back over her long career, Turney believes that "of all the forms, I liked playwriting the best. But now, it's getting harder and harder to get a well-made play produced. I'm so conditioned to that that I don't know whether I could break out of that mold.

"I think I was pretty good as a screenwriter, but that's only because it was dialogue. It was really an extension of playwriting. Television was my least favorite, but radio was interesting because there you had to readjust all your sights, literally! You had to be constantly aware that this was an 'ear' medium. . . .

"Of course, now I love the idea of writing well. As a prose writer, I want to write well. And, I'm making an effort to perfect my style." Today, the author of the biography *Byron's Daughter* (1977) and the novel *Surrender the Seasons* (1981) is concentrating on her ability to combine serious historical research with her keen sense of structure and character.

She draws upon years of rich experience as she writes at the Huntington Library, in San Marino, California, where she works among world-famous scholars who respect her past accomplishments. It is evident that, although she may have "slipped in through the back door," Catherine Turney stayed in Hollywood long enough to prove both her value and her talent.

Joanne L. Yeck

SELECTED FILM BOOKS OF 1986

Allen, Don. *Finally Truffaut: A Film-by-Film Guide to the Master Film-maker's Legacy.* New York: Beaufort Books, 1986. Allen updates his 1974 study, *François Truffaut,* analyzing each of the director's films and relating it to the others in Truffaut's canon.

Alpert, Hollis. *Burton.* New York: G. P. Putnam's Sons, 1986. This behind-the-scenes biography of the late Richard Burton is aimed at the popular audience and concentrates on Burton's stormy love life.

——————. *Fellini: A Life.* New York: Atheneum Publishers, 1986. There is no shortage of books about the films of Italian director Federico Fellini. Alpert concentrates on Fellini's life and succeeds in sorting out some of the myths surrounding the celebrated filmmaker.

Antonioni, Michelangelo. *That Bowling Alley on the Tiber: Tales of a Director.* New York: Oxford University Press, 1986. The Italian director tells thirty-three anecdotes about his life and travels, each of which contributes to the reader's insights on Antonioni's creative processes.

Aros, Andrew A. *A Title Guide to the Talkies, 1975 Through 1984.* Metuchen, New Jersey: Scarecrow Press, 1986. This third volume of the *Title Guide to the Talkies* series completes the set, with total coverage extending from 1928 to 1984. Films are listed alphabetically by title, and each entry is supplemented with information on the film's director, writer, release date, and MPAA rating. Finally, an abbreviated list of review sources is provided.

Basinger, Jeanine. *The* It's a Wonderful Life *Book.* New York: Alfred A. Knopf, 1986. Everything anyone could want to know about Frank Capra's beloved classic is packed into this book, including the complete script, production stills, behind-the-scenes photographs, and interviews with key figures involved with the film.

——————. *The World War II Combat Film: Anatomy of a Genre.* New York: Columbia University Press, 1986. Arguing that the World War II combat film exists in such numbers that it is more than merely a subgenre of the war film, Basinger outlines the history and evolution of this newly defined genre. She suggests that its conventions have spread to other genres as well, especially Westerns and combat films about Korea and Vietnam.

Beath, Warren Newton. *The Death of James Dean.* New York: Grove Press, 1986. More than three decades after his untimely death, Dean continues to inspire both reverence and controversy. Beath suggests that there was a conspiracy to conceal the facts regarding Dean's death in an automobile crash in 1955.

Benayoun, Robert. *The Films of Woody Allen.* New York: Harmony Books, 1986. French film critic Benayoun reviews Allen's career through *Hannah and Her Sisters* (1986). The text is accompanied by numerous photographs.

Berrigan, Daniel. The Mission: *A Film Journal.* New York: Harper and Row, Publishers, 1986. Radical activist-priest Daniel Berrigan was an adviser for *The Mission* (1986). This journal records his philosophical ruminations regarding religion, poverty, and cinema while on location in South America.

Betrock, Alan. *The I Was a Teenage Juvenile Delinquent Rock 'n Roll Horror Beach Party Movie Book.* New York: St. Martin's Press, 1986. Despite the book's campy title, Betrock has produced a well-researched and well-written account of films produced to exploit the teenage audience. Concentrating on films produced between 1954 and 1969, Betrock provides an annotated filmography and copious illustrations of his subject.

Bonderoff, Jason. *Mary Tyler Moore: A Biography.* New York: St. Martin's Press, 1986. This biography of the popular television and film actress is aimed at fans rather than scholars.

Bresson, Robert. *Notes on the Cinematographer.* London: Quartet Books, 1986. This book consists of brief memos—a sentence or two at most—that the great French director wrote to himself, providing insight into the mind of an important filmmaker.

Burnett, Carol. *One More Time.* New York: Random House, 1986. The popular television and film actress writes movingly of her childhood, which was complicated by poverty and the alcoholism of her father. The account ends with Burnett achieving success as a television comedienne in 1960.

Burton, Julianne, ed. *Cinema and Social Change in Latin America.* Austin: University of Texas Press, 1986. Burton's compilation contains twenty interviews (which span three decades) with Latin American filmmakers regarding the influence of social ferment on the cinema of the region.

Carney, Raymond. *American Vision: The Films of Frank Capra.* London: Cambridge University Press, 1986. Carney's scholarly study of Capra's work argues that what some critics have dismissed as sentimentality is actually rooted firmly in the tradition of American romanticism.

Ciment, Michel. *John Boorman.* London: Faber and Faber, 1986. The French critic provides the most detailed study so far of Boorman's career, from *Catch Us if You Can* (1965) through his celebrated *The Emerald Forest* (1985). The book includes numerous still photographs, as well as interviews with Boorman and others who have worked with him.

Cowie, Peter, ed. *International Film Guide 1986.* London: The Tantivy Press, 1986. This twenty-third annual survey of world cinema contains essays summarizing filmmaking in each country that produces films. It is especially useful for monitoring films produced in Third World countries.

Culhane, Shamus. *Talking Animals and Other People.* New York: St. Martin's Press, 1986. This history of animation in cinema and television was written by an animator who worked for the Walter Lantz and Disney studios. Culhane's book is especially useful for its biographical sketches of important animators from the 1920's through the 1970's.

Dale, R. C. *The Films of René Clair*. Metuchen, New Jersey: Scarecrow Press, 1986. This two-volume work contains a scholarly examination of the work of the prominent French director, from his films in the silent era through 1965. The first volume is devoted to analysis of the films, while the second volume contains detailed reconstructions of each film.

Deutelbaum, Marshall, and Leland Poague, eds. *A Hitchcock Reader*. Ames: Iowa State University Press, 1986. Deutelbaum and Poague have collected several essays on the films of Alfred Hitchcock. Although most of the essays are reprinted from other sources, the editors have performed a useful service to the student of Hitchcock's films by publishing them in a single volume.

Dixon, Wheeler, ed. *Producers Releasing Corporation: A Comprehensive Filmography and History*. Jefferson, North Carolina: McFarland and Company, 1986. Producers Releasing Corporation was an important minor studio in the 1940's, creating such popular series as the *Charlie Chan* and *Bowery Boys* films. This compilation of essays, interviews, and filmographies chronicles the history of the studio.

Dmytryk, Edward. *On Filmmaking*. Boston: Focal Press, 1986. Dmytryk takes the reader on a step-by-step tour through the filmmaking process, from the screenplay through the final edit. This volume collects and expands upon information previously published by Dmytryk in his series of books on acting, directing, and editing.

Drew, William M. *D. W. Griffith's* Intolerance: *Its Genesis and Its Vision*. Jefferson, North Carolina: McFarland and Company, 1986. Drew's book is a detailed study of Griffith's epochal film. He analyzes the artistic and social forces that led Griffith to make the film, along with the impact of *Intolerance* on contemporary audiences.

Faulkner, Christopher. *The Social Cinema of Jean Renoir*. Princeton, New Jersey: Princeton University Press, 1986. Faulkner traces the development of Renoir's conception of the function of art and the artist from the 1930's to the 1950's, arguing that the director's later work was idealistic rather than political.

Fisher, Kim N. *On the Screen: A Film, Television, and Video Research Guide*. Littleton, Colorado: Libraries Unlimited, 1986. An annotated bibliography of reference books and related materials on the subject of film and television has been compiled here.

Friedrich, Otto. *City of Nets: A Portrait of Hollywood in the 1940's*. New York: Harper and Row, Publishers, 1986. This fascinating, readable book chronicles the studio system during its heyday and demise.

Gado, Frank. *The Passion of Ingmar Bergman.* Durham, North Carolina: Duke University Press, 1986. This book offers a scholarly study of the interconnection between the life and works of the great Swedish film-maker.

Gallagher, Tag. *John Ford: The Man and His Films.* Berkeley: University of California Press, 1986. This critical biography is the most extensive study to appear of the great director—and certainly one of the best. Gallagher divides Ford's work into four periods: introspection, idealism, myth, and mortality. He argues that these periods mirrored stages in Ford's personal life.

Gehring, Wes D. *Screwball Comedy: A Genre of Madcap Romance.* New York: Greenwood Press, 1986. Gehring examines the screwball comedy, arguing that this genre provided the forum for the popularization of the antihero—the easily befuddled and less than fully competent male pro-tagonist.

Gianetti, Louis, and Scott Eyman. *Flashback: A Brief History of Film.* Englewood Cliffs, New Jersey: Prentice-Hall, 1986. Gianetti and Eyman offer a decade-by-decade summary of cinema history, from the silent era through the early 1980's. Gianetti and Eyman break no new ground here, but their book serves as a useful general introduction to the study of film.

Goldman, Louis. *Lights, Camera, Action.* New York: Harry N. Abrams, 1986. This book consists primarily of black-and-white photographs from twenty years of American and European films. The photographs illustrate the extensive preparation that goes on behind the scenes before a film is shot.

Gomery, Douglas. *The Hollywood Studio System.* London: Macmillan Publishing Company, 1986. Gomery analyzes the economic workings of the seven major Hollywood studios at the height of their power, from 1930 to 1949. He concludes that these studios formed an oligopoly, maximizing their own and one another's profits while effectively neutralizing would-be competitors.

Guerif, Francois. *Clint Eastwood.* New York: St. Martin's Press, 1986. The French critic defends Eastwood against charges of misogyny and excessive violence and provides a detailed filmography of the actor's film and television career.

Guinness, Alec. *Blessings in Disguise.* New York: Alfred A. Knopf, 1986. The great English actor recalls his career in film and theater in this discursive but well-written autobiography.

Hanson, Patricia King, and Stephen L. Hanson. *Film Review Index, Vol. I: 1882-1949.* Phoenix, Arizona: Oryx Press, 1986. This reference book is an important index to reviews of films from the silent era through the end of the 1940's. Films are listed alphabetically, followed by review sources in major newspapers and periodicals.

Hayes, R. M. *Trick Cinematography.* Jefferson, North Carolina: McFarland and Company, 1986. Hayes's work contains extensive information on the cast and credits of all films that won or were nominated for an Academy Award for special effects and related technical awards. In addition, he offers brief critical comments on the merits of each contender.

Hemming, Roy. *The Melody Lingers On: The Great Songwriters and Their Movie Musicals.* New York: Newmarket Press, 1986. Hemming analyzes the cinematic contributions of ten important songwriters of the Tin Pan Alley era, such as Irving Berlin, Jerome Kern, and Richard Rodgers. The book includes illustrations and extensive filmographies for each of its subjects.

Herrman, Dorothy. *S. J. Perelman: A Life.* New York: G. P. Putnam's Sons, 1986. Best known as a writer of witty short pieces for *The New Yorker*, Perelman wrote the screenplays for such films as *Around the World in 80 Days* (1956) and the Marx Brothers' *Animal Crackers* (1930) and *Horse Feathers* (1932). Herrman has produced a creditable biography of this important figure.

Higham, Charles. *Lucy: The Life of Lucille Ball.* New York: St. Martin's Press, 1986. Higham's account of the life of the successful film and television comedienne is aimed at the popular audience.

Hillier, Jim, ed. *Cahiers du Cinema: 1960-1968.* Cambridge, Massachusetts: Harvard University Press, 1986. This compilation of articles from the French cinema journal is the second of four projected volumes. In the 1960's, *Cahiers du Cinema* was in the forefront of film theory and criticism, introducing the concept of auteurism and examining previously neglected directors. This publication makes those seminal articles available in English translation and is an important contribution to film scholarship.

Hogan, David J. *Dark Romance: Sexuality in the Horror Film.* Jefferson, North Carolina: McFarland and Company, 1986. Covering films from the silent era to the 1980's, Hogan examines the role of sex and eroticism in the horror-film genre.

Hollis, Richard. *Walt Disney's Mickey Mouse: His Life and Times.* New York: Harper and Row, Publishers, 1986. Hollis has written a "biography" of Disney's most famous cartoon character, documenting Mickey's development from a minor character to an internationally recognizable symbol of the Disney empire.

Holloway, Ronald. *The Bulgarian Cinema.* Rutherford, New Jersey: Fairleigh Dickinson University Press, 1986. Holloway has written the first English-language book-length study of the Bulgarian cinema. He concentrates on the historical development of its film industry, placing each film in its cultural context.

Houseman, John. *Entertainers and the Entertained: Essays on Theater, Film and Television.* New York: Simon and Schuster, 1986. This collection of essays, speeches, and book reviews chronicles Houseman's participation in the entertaiment industry over the course of five decades.

Hudson, Rock, and Sara Davidson. *Rock Hudson: His Story*. New York: William Morrow and Company, 1986. Oddly enough, of the two books published on the heels of Rock Hudson's untimely death from AIDS, the one containing the most titillating gossip is this authorized biography. Hudson worked briefly with Davidson during the terminal stages of his illness, allowing her full access to those with knowledge of his secret life as a homosexual, which is the primary focus of this book.

Jackson, Kathy Merlock. *Images of Children in American Film: A Sociocultural Analysis*. Metuchen, New Jersey: Scarecrow Press, 1986. This scholarly study examines the changing cultural image of children in American films from the silent era through the early 1980's. Jackson finds that prior to World War II children symbolized innocence; thereafter, they increasingly came to be used in negative, even nightmarish ways.

Junor, Penny. *Burton: The Man Behind the Myth*. New York: St. Martin's Press, 1986. In this better than average look at an oft-examined actor, Junor portrays Richard Burton as a gifted actor who wasted his talents in mediocre films.

Kahn, Roger. *Joe and Marilyn: A Memory of Love*. New York: William Morrow and Company, 1986. Kahn, noted for his books on baseball, examines the complex relationship between Marilyn Monroe and Joe DiMaggio, the New York Yankee great.

Keller, Marjorie. *The Untutored Eye: Childhood in the Films of Cocteau, Cornell, and Brakhage*. Rutherford, New Jersey: Fairleigh Dickinson University Press, 1986. This scholarly study examines the treatment of children and childhood in the films of three experimental filmmakers.

Kelley, Kitty. *His Way: The Unauthorized Biography of Frank Sinatra*. New York: Bantam Books, 1986. Kelley's exhaustive chronicle of Sinatra's personal life collects in a single volume all the gossip that the singer-actor has inspired over the decades. The resulting best-seller may or may not capture the essence of the man, but it fails to convey the essence of his talent.

Kinnard, Roy, and R. J. Vitone. *The American Films of Michael J. Curtiz*. Metuchen, New Jersey: Scarecrow Press, 1986. Curtiz was born in Hungary and began making films in Europe. He came to the United States in 1926 to work for Warner Bros., for which he directed such films as *Yankee Doodle Dandy* (1942) and *Casablanca* (1943). This volume offers analyses of his important films, along with shorter discussions of his other American films.

Kirkpatrick, Sidney D. *A Cast of Killers*. New York: E. P. Dutton, 1986. Director William Desmond Taylor was murdered in 1922; the case remained unsolved until 1966, when King Vidor, researching the incident for a film, unearthed the identity of the killer. Kirkpatrick, Vidor's biographer, reconstructs the case from Vidor's notes in this fascinating account of crime and corruption in the Hollywood of the 1920's.

Kobal, John, ed. *Clark Gable*. Boston: Little, Brown and Company, 1986. Kobal continues his "Legends" series with a pictorial survey of Gable's career, accompanied by a brief commentary by James Card.

_____. *Joan Crawford*. Boston: Little, Brown and Company, 1986. Another in the "Legends" series, this volume features publicity photographs and production stills of Crawford's screen career and is accompanied by Anna Raeburn's commentary.

Landy, Marcia. *Fascism in Film: The Italian Commercial Cinema, 1931-1943*. Princeton, New Jersey: Princeton University Press, 1986. Landy's book is a scholarly study of the cultural milieu which influenced Italian film during the Mussolini years, examining the predominant themes of the era.

Leamer, Laurence. *As Time Goes By: The Life of Ingrid Bergman*. New York: Harper and Row, Publishers, 1986. Leamer used Bergman's own autobiography and extensive interviews with her associates, including her husbands and children, to compile this well-written biography of the late actress.

Levy, Alan. *Forever, Sophia*. New York: St. Martin's Press, 1986. This starstruck biography of Italian actress Sophia Loren is aimed at the popular audience. Levy, a longtime friend of his subject, adds little to already-available knowledge of Loren's life, although he does bring previous biographies up to date by a few years.

Linet, Beverly. *Star-Crossed: The Story of Robert Walker and Jennifer Jones*. New York: G. P. Putnam's Sons, 1986. This detailed account of the failed marriage between Walker and Jones is written with more sympathy for Walker.

Litwak, Mark. *Reel Power: The Struggle for Influence and Success in the New Hollywood*. New York: William Morrow and Company, 1986. Litwak is a former associate of Ralph Nader who sought his fortune as a Hollywood screenwriter. Unsurprisingly, he discovered that profit was more important than art to most studios. This book chronicles the behind-the-scenes wheeling and dealing that Litwak found so frustrating.

McGilligan, Pat, ed. *Backstory: Interviews with Screenwriters of Hollywood's Golden Age*. Berkeley: University of California Press, 1986. Fourteen screenwriters, active in film from the 1920's to the 1950's, discuss their craft in this collection of interviews.

McKay, Keith. *Mel Gibson*. Garden City, New York: Dolphin Books, 1986. A fan surveys the Australian actor's film career, including the *Mad Max* trilogy as well as his more serious work.

_____. *Robert De Niro: The Hero Behind the Masks*. New York: St.

Martin's Press, 1986. McKay's work, the most extensive study of De Niro thus far, concentrates on the actor's career and leaves his personal life in the background. This is a creditable attempt to analyze the work of one of cinema's best contemporary actors.

Macpherson, Don, and Louise Brody. *Leading Ladies*. New York: St. Martin's Press, 1986. This handsome volume consists of publicity photos of Hollywood actresses from the 1920's through the 1980's. The photographs are accompanied by brief biographical sketches which provide surveys of the stars' careers.

Malkiewicz, Kris. *Film Lighting*. New York: Prentice Hall Press, 1986. This useful book on a rather specialized subject, film lighting, consists of interviews with gaffers (chief electricians) and cinematographers.

Mancini, Elaine. *Luchino Visconti: A Guide to References and Resources*. Boston: G. K. Hall, 1986. This book consists of brief surveys of Visconti's life and career (including a complete filmography), followed by an extensive bibliography of writings by and about the Italian filmmaker.

Medved, Harry, and Michael Medved. *Son of Golden Turkey Awards: The Best of the Worst from Hollywood*. This sequel to the original *Golden Turkey Awards* (1980) is consistently amusing, illustrating the depths of inadvertent bad taste in American filmmaking.

Morella, Joe, and Edward Z. Epstein. *Loretta Young: An Extraordinary Life*. New York: Delacorte Press, 1986. Morella and Epstein contrast Young's scandal-prone personal life with her saintly screen image in a rather standard Hollywood biography of the film and television actress.

Mott, Donald R., and Cheryl McAllister Saunders. *Steven Spielberg*. Boston: Twayne, 1986. The most detailed and scholarly study to appear of the prolific and vastly popular filmmaker begins with *Duel* (1971) and ends with *The Color Purple* (1985).

Munn, Michael. *Charlton Heston*. New York: St. Martin's Press, 1986. Munn argues that Heston's good looks often overshadow his considerable acting abilities. This well-written biography provides a useful supplement to Heston's own *The Actor's Life* (1978).

Neibaur, John. *Movie Comedians: The Complete Guide*. Jefferson, North Carolina: McFarland and Company, 1986. Neibaur's book contains brief (and often highly opinionated) analyses of the careers of sixteen major and twenty-five minor screen comedians and comic teams, along with abbreviated filmographies for those actors whom he considers major. More and better information is available elsewhere for the important comedians, although the book is a useful source of information on the more obscure actors cited.

Nickens, Christopher. *Natalie Wood: A Biography in Photographs*. Garden City, New York: Doubleday and Company, 1986. Nickens does not attempt an in-depth analysis of Wood's life; he simply uses photographs, accompanied only by captions, to survey her career from her days as a child star to her adult acting career.

Okuda, Ted, and Edward Watz. *The Columbia Comedy Shorts*. Jefferson, North Carolina: McFarland and Company, 1986. This book is an inventory and analysis of the two-reel comedies produced by Columbia Pictures between 1933 and 1958 (of which the Three Stooges films were the most popular). The book also includes brief biographical sketches of the studio's directors and actors.

Olivier, Laurence. *On Acting*. New York: Simon and Schuster, 1986. One of the premier actors of the twentieth century discusses his most important films and theatrical roles, including his definitive work as a Shakespearean hero.

Oppenheimer, Jerry, and Jack Vitek. *Idol: Rock Hudson, the True Story of an American Film Hero*. New York, Villard Books, 1986. Although Oppenheimer and Vitek do not avoid the more sensational aspects of Hudson's life, their sympathetic account of Hudson's life and career is balanced.

Ott, Frederick W. *The Great German Films*. Secaucus, New Jersey: Citadel Press, 1986. In this illustrated overview of German cinema from 1895 through the early 1980's, Ott analyzes each era, primarily by focusing on important and/or characteristic films of the period.

Oumano, Ellen. *Sam Shepard: The Life and Work of an American Dreamer*. New York: St. Martin's Press, 1986. This book is a brief but useful critical analysis of the life and work of the multitalented actor and screenwriter.

Pastos, Spero. *Pin-up: The Tragedy of Betty Grable*. New York: G. P. Putnam's Sons, 1986. Despite its tabloid-sounding subtitle, Pastos' book is a creditable account of Grable's life, recording her successes along with her failures.

Perry, Ted, and Rene Prieto. *Michelangelo Antonioni: A Guide to References and Resources*. Boston: G. K. Hall, 1986. This book briefly surveys Antonioni's life and career (including a complete filmography), and it is followed by an extensive bibliography of writings by and about the Italian filmmaker.

Phillips, Gene D. *Fiction, Film, and F. Scott Fitzgerald*. Chicago: Loyola University Press, 1986. Phillips' scholarly study is divided into three parts: an examination of Fitzgerald's work as a screenwriter; an analysis of the films made from his novels; and a study of the films made from his shorter fiction.

Quinlan, David. *The Illustrated Encyclopedia of Movie Character Actors*. New York: Harmony Books, 1986. This useful reference tool offers an alphabetical list of 850 character actors, from the silent era through the 1980's. Entries include a brief description of acting specialties and a filmography.

Quirk, Lawrence J. *Lauren Bacall: Her Films and Career.* Secaucus, New Jersey: Citadel Press, 1986. Like Quirk's many other contributions to "The Films of" series, this volume is a copiously illustrated biographical sketch of Bacall, which is accompanied by a film-by-film synopsis of her work.

Schacter, Susan, and Don Shewey. *Caught in the Act: New York Actors Face to Face.* New York: New American Library, 1986. Schacter's photographs illustrate this series of interviews with fifty-four New York based actors (both stage and film) who discuss their craft.

Schwartz, Ronald. *Spanish Film Directors (1950-1985): Twenty-one Profiles.* Metuchen, New Jersey: Scarecrow Press, 1986. This book is a useful collection of short critical biographies of twenty-one postwar Spanish directors, most of whom have received little previous English-language criticism.

Sennett, Ted. *Great Movie Directors.* New York: Abrams, 1986. Sennett has produced a rather pedestrian survey of the careers of more than two hundred directors, not all of whom could reasonably be categorized as great. The book is profusely illustrated, and its primary usefulness is that it offers biographical sketches of lesser-known filmmakers.

Slide, Anthony. *The American Film Industry: A Historical Dictionary.* New York: Greenwood Press, 1986. This useful and important reference work is an excellent, comprehensive dictionary of film terms as well as names of production companies, film series, studios, and so forth.

Smith, Ronald Lande. *The Stars of Stand-up Comedy: A Biographical Encyclopedia.* New York: Garland, 1986. The subjects of these biographical sketches include many comics (such as Abbott and Costello, Richard Pryor) who appeared in films. For many of these comedians, this book provides the most extensive biographical information available.

Smith, Thomas G. *Industrial Light and Magic: The Art of Special Effects.* New York: Ballantine Books, 1986. Smith, a former employee of Industrial Light and Magic, uses his knowledge of the company's techniques to explain the special effects that it produced for the films of George Lucas and Steven Spielberg. The lavishly illustrated volume is designed to appeal to the science-fiction film fan rather than to the scholar.

Spiegel, Penina. *McQueen: The Untold Story of a Bad Boy in Hollywood.* Garden City, New York: Doubleday & Company, 1986. Of the two books on the late Steve McQueen published in 1986, Spiegel's is the most detailed, providing a look at the seamier aspects of his private life. The actor is portrayed as a drug addict and a compulsive womanizer. His screen career is treated as a backdrop to his scandalous behavior.

Steinem, Gloria. *Marilyn.* New York: Henry Holt, 1986. Feminist Gloria Steinem attempts to counter what she regards as the generally sexist biographies of Marilyn Monroe. Her biographical essay is illustrated with photographs by George Barris.

Stowell, Peter. *John Ford.* Boston: Twayne, 1986. Concentrating on fourteen films spanning the years 1933 to 1962, Stowell examines Ford's contributions to the popular image of the American West. He argues that Ford was a conscientious mythmaker and that the common thread which runs through his best films is the romantic quest for the American dream.

Sultanic, Aaron. *Film: A Modern Art.* New York: Cornwall Books, 1986. This scholarly survey concentrates on placing cinema in its proper context in modern culture. The author studies the development of film through an examination of its various genres, including the epic, comedy, and documentary.

Toffel, Neile McQueen. *My Husband, My Friend.* New York: Atheneum Publishers, 1986. Neile Toffel was actor Steve McQueen's first wife. She describes their relationship, flaws and all, in this anecdotal narrative.

Vadim, Roger. *Bardot Deneuve Fonda: My Life with the Three Most Beautiful Women in the World.* New York: Simon and Schuster, 1986. Vadim chooses to reveal as little as possible about himself, instead concentrating on relating an abundance of information about the three famous actresses with whom he lived (and in Bardot's case, married).

Warren, Bill. *Keep Watching the Skies: American Science Fiction Movies of the Fifties, Vol. II, 1958-1962.* Jefferson, North Carolina: McFarland and Company, 1986. Warren provides cast and credit information, along with lengthy synopses and critical analyses, for American science-fiction films released between 1958 and 1962. Volume I, covering the years 1950 through 1957, was published in 1982.

Waters, John. *Crackpot: The Obsessions of John Waters.* New York: Macmillan Publishing Company, 1986. Waters is the underground filmmaker responsible for such camp classics as *Pink Flamingos* (1978). This collection of essays is a humorous celebration of bad taste.

Watson, Thomas J., and Bill Chapman. *Judy: Portrait of an American Legend.* New York: McGraw-Hill Book Company, 1986. This relatively brief text by Watson and some rare photographs from Chapman's collection highlight this celebration of the life and career of Judy Garland.

Webb, Michael, ed. *Hollywood: Legend and Reality.* Boston: Little, Brown and Company, 1986. This handsome exhibition catalog commemorates a Smithsonian touring exhibit which features photographs, drawings, and other artifacts that illuminate the filmmaking process.

White, Tony. *The Animator's Handbook.* New York: Watson-Guptill, 1986. Although White's book is aimed at working animators, the techniques he describes provide useful information for those simply interested in learning something about the animation process.

Wiley, Mason, and Damien Bona. *Inside Oscar.* New York: Ballantine Books, 1986. This informative and entertaining book stands as the definitive work on the Academy Awards. In addition to a list of all nominees and winners in every category from 1927 to 1984, Wiley and Bona provide information on performers, masters of ceremonies, and presenters for each year, along with anecdotes and other miscellaneous information on the proceedings.

Willis, John. *Screen World 1986*. New York: Crown Publishers, 1986. This thirty-seventh annual volume covers the films, both foreign and domestic, which were released in 1985, providing production and cast credits.

Wood, Robin. *Hollywood from Vietnam to Reagan*. New York: Columbia University Press, 1986. This book is a series of interconnected essays on Hollywood films of the 1970-1984 period, focusing on how these films have reflected society's changing perspectives regarding sexual politics.

Wright, William. *Lillian Hellman: The Image, the Woman*. New York: Simon and Schuster, 1986. Hellman has been a controversial figure since the days of the Hollywood blacklist. Wright strips away the legends in this biography of an important writer.

Zeffirelli, Franco. *Zeffirelli: An Autobiography*. New York: Weidenfeld and Nicolson, 1986. The Italian director offers an anecdotal account of his life, including encounters with Richard Burton, Maria Callas, Gina Lollobrigida, and Luchino Visconti.

Zorina, Vera. *Zorina*. New York: Farrar, Straus and Giroux, 1986. Zorina is a German-born dancer and actress who was married for eight years to George Balanchine. This autobiography ends in 1946, with her divorce from the impresario.

SELECTED
FILMS
OF
1986

"ABOUT LAST NIGHT..."

Production: Jason Brett and Stuart Oken for Tri-Star Pictures and Delphi
IV and V; released by Tri-Star Pictures
Direction: Edward Zwick
Screenplay: Tim Kazurinsky and Denise DeClue; based on the play *Sexual
Perversity in Chicago* by David Mamet
Cinematography: Andrew Dintenfass
Editing: Harry Keramidas
Art direction: Ida Random; set decoration, Chris Butler and Jean Alan
Special effects: Darrell Pritchett
Makeup: Robert Ryan and Brian Kossman
Costume design: Deborah L. Scott
Music: Miles Goodman
MPAA rating: R
Running time: 113 minutes

> *Principal characters:*
> Dan Martin .... Rob Lowe
> Debbie Sullivan .... Demi Moore
> Bernie Litko........................ James Belushi
> Joan........................... Elizabeth Perkins
> Mr. Favio...................... George DiCenzo
> Mother Malone .... Michael Alldredge
> Steve Carlson .... Robin Thomas
> Gary............................ Robert Neches
> Gus................................Joe Greco

"About Last Night..." is based loosely on *Sexual Perversity in Chicago*,
the play by David Mamet which was first produced in 1974. The film appropriates from the play its focus on the interaction of four single characters
who live, work, and play in Chicago. Dan Martin (Rob Lowe) and Bernie
Litko (James Belushi) are friends who work at the same restaurant-supply
company. Early in the film, at a baseball game in which the two men are
involved, Dan exchanges a few remarks with Debbie Sullivan (Demi
Moore), who is sharing evaluations of the players' bodies with a group of
women which includes Joan (Elizabeth Perkins), Debbie's closest friend and
roommate. At a postgame celebration, Dan and Debbie make eye contact,
exchange a few brief remarks and, in an abrupt transitional cut, are next
seen together in Dan's apartment, engaging in foreplay.

As subsequent scenes that illustrate the evolution of their relationship
make clear, the couple fail to move beyond a mutual sexual attraction. Even
after Debbie moves in with Dan, their relationship remains problematic,

and Dan in particular is reluctant to communicate openly or to make a full commitment. Ironically, their relationship reaches a crisis point during a New Year's Eve celebration. Equally ironic is the fact that Dan only realizes how much he loves Debbie after their relationship has dissolved. Debbie rebuffs a series of attempts that Dan undertakes to reestablish contact with her and urges him to get on with his life. Belatedly taking her advice, Dan quits his job and reopens a restaurant in partnership with Gus (Joe Greco), the former owner of the establishment. At the end of the film, Dan and Debbie meet again at a baseball game in which Bernie and Dan are involved. The ending is doubly circular in that it not only returns to a setting from the beginning of the film but also reinitiates the relationship between Dan and Debbie, implying that they will begin again on a more solid footing.

Whereas Mamet's play is unflinchingly mordant in its investigation of the dynamics of sexual and social interaction, the film attempts an uneasy balance between social commentary and Hollywood romance. The film's ambiguous tone can be traced back to the opening scenes. While the transitional cut from baseball to bedroom provides an ironic comment on how sexual intercourse has preceded social intercourse for the couple, the song on the sound track during the foreplay scene contributes to a romantic aura which seems intended to make the scene alluringly sensual. A few shots later, as Debbie unsuccessfully attempts to leave without waking Dan, the embarrassment and awkwardness of the couple again emphasizes the fact that they are literally intimate strangers.

As it charts the course of the relationship between Dan and Debbie, the film continues to send mixed messages. On the one hand, the way in which the film demonstrates that they continue to be strangers even after Debbie moves in with Dan suggests that the couple needs to develop beyond a merely sexual relationship and communicate on other levels. Yet, a montage intended to summarize the couple's initiation into domesticity highlights sexual scenes between them which are again given an alluring quality by the accompanying music. Similarly, the notion that the couple must transcend physical appearances in their relationship is counteracted throughout the film by the way in which the camera celebrates the physical magnetism of Rob Lowe and Demi Moore. Indeed, at one point, the manner in which the camera peers at the lovemaking couple through a window inadvertently exemplifies the fact that the viewer is all too often encouraged to exercise a passive voyeurism. Equally problematic is the characterization of Bernie, whose preoccupation with female anatomy and casual sex is not made the object of censure in the film but is apparently intended as primarily comic. One suspects, however, that few feminist viewers would find Bernie's wisecracks very amusing.

"*About Last Night . . .*" is perhaps most effective when it is exploiting the potential of the film medium for a serious investigation of relationships. An effective use of visual symbolism occurs in a scene immediately after Debbie moves in with Dan. In the heat of an argument, Dan spills his tea and begins to wipe it up with a cloth that turns out to be a keepsake for which Debbie has a strong sentimental attachment. The cloth thereby becomes an apt token of how little Dan knows about Debbie. Later in the film, as Debbie is moving out, Dan gingerly hands her the cloth, but she violently rips it in half. Her gesture not only suggests that the relationship is being rent asunder but also reminds the audience that the inability of the couple to get to know each other has been their main problem. After Debbie has vacated the apartment and denuded it of her belongings, there is a shot of Dan which is enhanced by the creative use of *mise en scène*. As he enters the apartment, Dan is shown in a medium-long shot, and the emptiness which surrounds him is a visual correlate for the emptiness of his own life. Prominent in the background of this shot is a stuffed bear that had been highlighted in an earlier scene of tenderness between the couple.

In a few specific instances, the film achieves a sense of caustic irony reminiscent of Mamet's play. For example, during their encounter on the night following their first sexual tryst, Debbie's resolve that the previous night's sexual activities will not be repeated is ironically undermined by a sudden cut to the couple in bed. Editing is used in a similarly creative way later in the film. On the verge of having sex with a boyfriend who is also her boss, Steve Carlson (Robin Thomas), Debbie suddenly realizes that even though she has not heard from Dan for several days, she has strong feelings for him which she is betraying by seeing Steve. Debbie formally breaks off her relationship with Steve, and in the next scene she visits Dan, who apologizes for not calling and who urges her to come in. Although the previous scene involving Debbie and Steve had made it obvious that Debbie has emotional ties to Dan, she is reluctant to appear vulnerable and declines his invitation. An instant after she rejects his offer, however, the film quickly cuts to the couple hurtling onto a couch, and their sexual passions triumph over the mind games they have been attempting to play with each other. A final example of irony in the film involves the implicit connection between two separate scenes. After an argument with Dan, Debbie takes refuge at Joan's apartment. While there, she meets Joan's lover, Gary (Robert Neches), who, in an attempt to console Debbie, admits that men can be abominable sometimes. The audience's temptation to applaud Gary's generosity is undercut later in the film. During a New Year's Eve celebration, Gary decides to tell Joan that he is moving back in with his wife. When one learns that Gary had not told Joan that he was married in the first place, one realizes that Gary's earlier observation to Debbie applies forcefully to himself.

To a great extent the film is organized in terms of a series of parallels. The grouping of the four characters into two men and two women allows for some investigation of male attitudes versus female attitudes and gives rise to some comparison between Dan's friendship with Bernie and Debbie's friendship with Joan. Moreover, an implicit comparison is made between Bernie and Joan. Admittedly, they are different in many ways, and one of the film's running gags involves the animosity between them. Despite the fact that both characters project themselves as worldly, somewhat cynical individuals, however, both on occasion betray vulnerability and sensitivity. Bernie and Joan also share a disinclination to encourage the relationship between Dan and Debbie. When Debbie informs Joan that she is moving in with Dan, Joan's terse response is "I give you two months." Bernie's suspicious and disapproving attitude regarding Dan's relationship with Debbie is summed up by his habitual reference to Debbie as "What's 'er name." The film fails to explore why Bernie and Joan share this negative outlook, however, and the audience is left to wonder whether they are motivated by jealousy or by a deep pessimism concerning male-female relationships.

Also implicitly paralleled in the film are scenes in which the four main characters are encumbered by oppressive work situations. Dan and Bernie are plagued by a belligerent, dictatorial boss; Joan complains about her job as a kindergarten teacher; and Debbie's work situation is complicated by the sexual relationship she has had with her boss. That the film is attempting to explore the characters' working lives is also suggested by the fact that Dan's relationship to his job is highlighted in several scenes. For example, when he is ordered by his boss, Mr. Favio (George DiCenzo), to cut off Gus's credit, Dan is furious, but his inability to confide in Debbie about this exemplifies his general reluctance to share his deeper feelings with her. Toward the end of the film, as Dan labors with Gus to fix up their restaurant, Bernie unexpectedly drops by. In one of the film's closest approaches to a poignant scene, Bernie simultaneously rebukes Dan for not contacting him and offers him a huge supply of exotic restaurant items. Such a scene provides an intimation of how substantially the film would have profited by a more extensive investigation of the theme of friendship. The scene also gives the audience some idea of the kind of emotional depth that the film might have achieved had it not diluted its serious side with easy laughs and romantic clichés.

Paul Salmon

Reviews
Commonweal. CXIII, August 15, 1986, p. 435.
Films in Review. XXXVII, October, 1986, p. 479.
Los Angeles Times. July 1, 1986, VI, p. 1.
Macleans. XCIX, July 28, 1986, p. 40.

The New Republic. CXCV, August 4, 1986, p. 24.
The New York Times. CXXXV, July 1, 1986, p. C12.
The New Yorker. LXII, July 14, 1986, p. 64.
Newsweek. CVIII, July 14, 1986, p. 69.
Time. CXXVIII, July 14, 1986, p. 62.
Variety. CCCXXIII, July 2, 1986, p. 13.
The Wall Street Journal. CCVIII, July 3, 1986, p. 15.

ALIENS

Production: Gale Anne Hurd for Brandywine Productions; released by Twentieth Century-Fox
Direction: James Cameron
Screenplay: James Cameron; based on a story by James Cameron, David Giler, and Walter Hill
Cinematography: Adrian Biddle
Editing: Ray Lovejoy
Production design: Peter Lamont
Art direction: Bert Davey, Fred Hole, Michael Lamont, and Ken Court; set decoration, Crispian Sallis
Special effects: John Richardson, Robert Skotak, Stan Winston, and Suzanne Benson (AA)
Makeup: Peter Robb-King
Costume design: Emma Porteous
Sound: Don Sharpe (AA)
Music: James Horner
MPAA rating: R
Running time: 137 minutes

Principal characters:
Ripley	Sigourney Weaver
Newt	Carrie Henn
Hicks	Michael Biehn
Burke	Paul Reiser
Bishop	Lance Henriksen
Hudson	Bill Paxton
Vasquez	Jenette Goldstein

Rare is the sequel that lives up to expectations. Yet *Aliens*, which returns to the distressing, forbidding world of the 1979 film, *Alien*, does so with boldness and brilliance. *Newsweek*'s David Ansen labeled it "a spectacular sequel." *Time*'s Richard Schickel characterized it as "the summer's inescapable movie." Audiences concurred. The film drew more than $13 million its first five days of release.

The seven-year road from Ridley Scott's original classic to James Cameron's sequel was a bumpy one, though, as unpredictable as the film's narrative structure itself. *Alien* had been a major financial success for Twentieth Century-Fox. Made for $18 million, the film eventually garnered more than $100 million in worldwide ticket sales. The company's fiscal unsteadiness at the time, however, and a rash of well-publicized lawsuits over the film's profit distribution delayed any notion of a sequel.

Thereafter, the executive producers of the original film chanced upon an impressive science-fiction script called *The Terminator*, by then unknown James Cameron (*The Terminator* would become an unexpected hit in 1984). In the fall of 1983, they commissioned a treatment from Cameron for the *Alien* sequel; within three days Cameron had typed out a forty-two-page story. This first draft, though, apparently lacked the depth of characters for which the producers had hoped. The project languished for another year.

With a new head of production at Twentieth Century-Fox, Larry Gordon, the *Aliens* project was revived. By this time *The Terminator* had made Cameron a director in demand. Again the project was buffeted by complications: Could it be made within a reasonable budget? Was Gale Hurd, Cameron's girlfriend, an acceptable producer? Should Sigourney Weaver reprise her role as the sole survivor of an encounter with a deadly extraterrestrial? By the spring of 1985, the answer to all questions was yes. The studio gave its blessing to Cameron.

In turn, the director wisely fashioned a sequel that drew its strength equally from *Alien* and his own debut work, *The Terminator*. Ridley Scott's smoky, strobing images remain, as well as minimalist dialogue, a phobia-laden story line, and the disorienting organic sets of Swiss surrealist H. R. Giger. At the same time, Cameron replaces the original's pause-and-shock structure with his own restless, relentless pacing. Indeed, Cameron and his editor, Ray Lovejoy, fuse editing and movement in such a way that each shot is a synergism of energy. They achieved this in part by eschewing conventional, static storyboard drawings in favor of short video practice sequences which served as a rough draft for the film to come. *Aliens*, moreover, is not merely an empty exercise in visual flair, for Cameron has also filled its core with compelling characters, offbeat relationships, and provocative concerns, all held together by a taut plot.

The film opens with Ripley (Sigourney Weaver) deep in cryogenic sleep and presumably safe from the vile, invasive alien she had battled in the original film. This peaceful tableau is quickly disrupted by a robotlike creature that makes its way into Ripley's spaceship. The film's tone, suddenly made distressing, shifts quickly again as the viewer discovers that the strange machine is the tool of a team there to rescue Ripley.

The film cuts from Ripley's face in repose to a shot of the Earth outside a window: She has been brought to an orbiting hospital to recuperate from fifty-seven years of aimless space drifting. Once again, however, the film tacks unpredictably: The young woman begins to scream, her stomach begins to heave, and those who have seen *Alien* fear that a monster is once again about to erupt from the stomach of a character. It turns out to be a dream, a clichéd narrative trick, in fact, but it nevertheless introduces the viewer to Cameron's aptitude for shock, surprise, and mercurial narrative structure.

A neatly compact expository sequence follows, in which Ripley attends a meeting where the original film's events are recapped and updated: Seventy families have since colonized the planet LV426, engineers have begun to adapt the hostile planet to a more Earth-like environment, and, in twenty years, not one encounter has occurred with an alien creature such as Ripley has described. Not, perhaps, until now. For Earth has lost contact with its colony, and a platoon of space marines will soon depart for the planet. Ripley, as an expert on the potential dangers, is urged to accompany them.

At first she finds the notion horrifying, and understandably so, but her concern for the colonists and indignation against the alien creatures prevail. She joins a diverse though surprisingly undisciplined crew: Hudson (Bill Paxton), a swaggering marine; Vasquez (Jenette Goldstein), an aggressive soldier with a chip on her shoulder; Bishop (Lance Henriksen), an android whom Ripley scorns (an android went berserk during her original mission); Burke (Paul Reiser), a civilian adviser who represents an all-powerful "Company"; and Hicks (Michael Biehn), a cool, quiet warrior in a role close to that which he played in *The Terminator*.

As the marines prepare to descend to the planet ("We're on an express elevator to hell," says one), Cameron dwells on their formidable weaponry and strutting behavior. It is familiar territory—Cameron coauthored the screenplay to *Rambo: First Blood Part II* (1985). When, however, the squadron finally does encounter the swarm of relentless, acid-blooded, insectlike aliens that have annihilated the colony, these swaggering marine heroes, the inheritors of a muscle-bound mythology, stumble badly. Cameron thus intentionally deflates the "Ramboism" he himself helped to popularize and that here, in the future, has reached its illogical limits.

First, though, the director delays the viewer's initial encounter with the alien horde in an excruciating fashion, conjuring all the while an impressive, oppressive sense of doom: The slimy ceilings and floors suggest that something entirely strange infests the processing plant, unrecognizable forms seem to lurk in every corner, gaping holes and doors welded shut allude to dramatic battles that humans have clearly not won, water drips irritatingly from beams and pipes (a reprise of one of the original film's most effective sound effects), Adrian Biddle's nearly monochromatic cinematography shifts from a chilling blue to a sickening green, and James Horner's clanging, driving music mutes into disquieting silence.

Suddenly, radar blips indicate that something is converging on the marines from every direction. The creatures erupt from walls, floors, and ceilings. Though the soldiers have been warned not to use heavy ammunition—the explosives could spray the alien's acid blood in every direction and even set off a nuclear chain reaction in the plant—they do not hold back. Nothing works, including an erratic television camera that transmits jumpy, snowy video images of the battle to Ripley in the command center. Along with its abrupt, disorienting editing, this poor television picture makes the viewer feel quite viscerally Ripley's frustration as the creatures—seen only in near-subliminal blurs—once again decimate a crew of humans.

With a ferocity that outstrips her behavior during the first encounter with one of these creatures, Ripley takes charge. She plows the command vehicle into the plant and rescues Hicks, Vasquez, and Hudson, among others. Any hope of quick escape from the planet dissipates, however, when their shuttle crashes. It will be seventeen days until those in the mother ship realize that something is wrong.

Ripley, in the meantime, has become the de facto group leader; whatever professionalism, cohesiveness, or good sense the crew once had has vanished. Hudson has become a sniveler. Vasquez, though heroic, sees through a haze of bravado and revenge. Burke's motives have become increasingly slippery; one wonders, justly, on whose side he is fighting. Ripley rallies her few useful allies, including the android Bishop, whose good sense and bravery finally elicit her confidence, and Hicks, who emerges from the background of characters as the one soldier worthy of Ripley's total trust. Indeed, it is a textbook example of how character transformations can help energize a conventional genre story line.

A little girl, Newt (Carrie Henn), whom the crew has rescued after spotting her on another television screen, likewise proves to be a source of inspiration to Ripley, both for the child's resilience in evading the aliens (she, like Ripley, is a survivor) and for the protective, nurturing emotions that she stirs. In one of the film's calm moments, in a scene bathed in uncharacteristically warm, orange light, Ripley promises the little girl that all will turn out right. Says Newt as she clutches a headless doll, "My mommy said there are no monsters, no real monsters, but there are."

The mayhem returns, this time with a vengeance. The group is now in a lab a few miles from the planet. Several crablike alien specimens break out and attack Newt and Ripley. Burke, who secretly perceives the creatures as weapons useful to his company, freed them in order to forestall efforts to defeat the aliens. (This earthman thus inherits the callous motives of the original film's deadly, soulless android and, more universally, personifies the monstrous greed of overly pragmatic thinking.) The fully grown creatures themselves soon arrive, this time on a crest of complications: The lights dim, the ammunition runs out, the processing plant will explode within four hours, and Bishop must crawl down a cramped culvert toward a radio dish in order to contact a second shuttle. Meanwhile, creatures are popping out from everywhere, killing just about everyone in their path. Burke himself pays for his treachery; an alien rips him apart terribly.

Of the crew, only Ripley, Hicks, and Bishop survive. The creatures have abducted and possibly killed Newt. Ripley manages to rescue the child, but not before a dramatic and pivotal encounter in an egg chamber with the aliens' giant queen. For a moment Ripley pauses, almost out of respect, certainly to think out her options. She finally flames the eggs, escapes the pursuing, enraged queen mother, and rockets off the planet, a nuclear detonation behind her.

It has been a thoroughly exhausting sequence for the viewer, with strobing lights, thumping sounds, a preexplosion countdown, and Horner's furious music to heighten the tension. This action proves to be a false climax, however, and the short denouement that follows it is a spurious one. For, unknown to the crew or to the viewer, the queen mother climbed aboard the ship before its departure. A new, unexpected round of havoc will soon be unleashed. This bit of plot trickery, which also marked both *Alien* and *The Terminator*, is, in this case, doubly effective, since the film has already run the conventional two hours and therefore seems as if it should be over.

There now follows a fight between the immense spidery creature and Ripley, clad in a huge, power-assisted suit. This climactic scene plays upon events that are wildly improbable, even for this film: Ripley survives a near vacuum as the several-ton alien hangs onto her foot; Newt survives as a nearly dismembered Bishop grabs her just before she is sucked out into space. Yet despite its implausibility, the sequence works, for the film has become so relentless, so draining an experience that it numbs logic. Finally the creature careens into space. In a series of lap dissolves, Ripley, Newt, and Hicks, a "family" forged by necessity, slide into peaceful, unthreatened hibernation.

Though derivative, *Aliens* stands several of its genre conventions on end: Faced with a threat, Howard Hawks-like camaraderie unravels; attacked by monsters, comic-book heroes prove to be altogether inadequate; awakened by the princelike Burke, Ripley eventually discovers him to be a toad. Other traditions survive intact: the gothic shadows of dank, howling places; the single-named, single-minded protagonists of combat films; the final shootouts of Westerns (the female protagonists of *Johnny Guitar*, 1954, come to mind); the claustrophobic environments of horror films and certain war pictures (Cameron often cites the confined, monochromatic spaces of *Das Boot*, 1981, as a key influence).

If *Aliens* is more than a well-wrought sequel, however, it is because of the intriguingly motivated nature of its central character and the presence which Sigourney Weaver brings to that role. In the original film, Ripley was a laconic, no-nonsense loner who, surrounded by symbolic rapes, obscene parodies of birth, and murderous alien reproductive impulses, tapped into the "male" side of her personality to survive. This quasi-feminist perspective, a novel one within the often sexist horror genre, suited the 1970's. In *Aliens*, however, Ripley's motivations have shifted from herself to others, from a sense of independence and survival to a parentlike commitment. Ripley may once again be a woman of action, but now her behavior flows from maternal, protective instincts.

Indeed, Ripley is given good reason to act. The alien creatures have decimated an entire colony of parents and children, deprived Ripley of any remaining family roots (after a forced fifty-seven-year hibernation no close relatives could possibly remain), and kidnapped her surrogate daughter, Newt. Moreover, Ripley is a single mother, for the men who surround her are all either cowardly or broken. Thus, *Aliens*' vision is that of a 1980's "supermom," who must reconcile conflicting impulses toward nurturing and self-sufficiency.

Yet, although the aliens repeatedly violate human families, they do so to assure the success of their own inhuman reproductive structures. Parallel instincts do indeed motivate their queen. This is what causes Ripley to pause when she first meets the alien mother, a bloated, fearsome parody of the maternal, protective rage that Ripley herself feels. So, when these two engage in their final battle, it becomes an archetypal confrontation between the noble and dark sides of the same emotion, a cat fight played operatically. It is also the film's most clever irony, one delivered perhaps mischievously and tongue in cheek. Yet a measure of James Cameron's success is that although *Aliens* ultimately teeters on the brink of B-movie parody, its central conceit of resolute maternalism, in the end, rings altogether true.

Marc Mancini

Reviews
American Film. X, July, 1986, p. 81.
Film Comment. XXII, July, 1986, p. 4.
Films and Filming. Number 383, August, 1986, p. 34.
The Nation. CCXLIII, September 20, 1986, p. 257.
The New York Times. CXXXV, July 18, 1986, p. C11.
The New Yorker. LXII, August 11, 1986, p. 78.
Newsweek. CVIII, July 21, 1986, p. 64.
Time. CXXVIII, July 28, 1986, p. 54.
Variety. CCCXXIII, July 9, 1986, p. 15.
The Wall Street Journal. CCVIII, July 17, 1986, p. 22.

AN AMERICAN TAIL

Production: Don Bluth, John Pomeroy, and Gary Goldman; and Steven
Spielberg, David Kirschner, Kathleen Kennedy, and Frank Marshall
(executive producers) for Amblin Entertainment; released by Universal
Direction: Don Bluth
Screenplay: Judy Freudberg and Tony Geiss; based on a story by David
Kirschner, Judy Freudberg, and Tony Geiss
Editing: Dan Molina
Design and storyboarding: Don Bluth
Directing animators: John Pomeroy, Dan Kuenster, and Linda Miller
Special effects directing animator: Dorse A. Lanpher
Music: James Horner
Songs: Cynthia Weil, James Horner, and Barry Mann, "Somewhere Out
There"
MPAA rating: G
Running time: 89 minutes

> *Voices of principal characters:*
> Bridget . . . . Cathianne Blore
> Tiger . . . . Dom DeLuise
> Warren T. Rat . . . . John Finnegan
> Fievel Mousekewitz . . . . Phillip Glasser
> Tanya Mousekewitz . . . . Amy Green
> Gussie Mausheimer . . . . Madeline Kahn
> Tony Toponi . . . . Pat Musick
> Papa Mousekewitz . . . . Nehemiah Persoff
> Henri . . . . Christopher Plummer
> Honest John . . . . Neil Ross
> Digit . . . . Will Ryan
> Mama Mousekewitz. . . . . Erica Yohn

Publicized widely as the first animated film to be presented with the im-
primatur of Steven Spielberg (*Jaws,* 1975; *Close Encounters of the Third
Kind,* 1977; *Raiders of the Lost Ark,* 1981; *The Color Purple,* 1985), *An
American Tail* more tellingly represented the second full-length feature by
former Disney studio animator Don Bluth (*The Secret of NIMH,* 1982). A
throwback to the style of classic animation characterized by such features as
lush, detailed visuals, winning, lovable characters, and rich, ambitious nar-
ratives which tap the fears and wonders of childhood, the Bluth-Spielberg
collaboration dramatizes the arrival on American shores of an immigrant
Jewish mouse who has fled czarist Russia in 1885 and depicts his heartwarming, picaresque struggle to reunite with the family from whom he

has become separated during the arduous ocean voyage. With its child-in-jeopardy protagonist set against a background of vaguely familiar New World history—the film's release was timed to coincide with the centennial of the Statue of Liberty, an icon which figures prominently in the narrative—the film had a built-in appeal to the full family-film market, the coveted "audiences of all ages."

At the time of the film's release, the theatrical feature-length animation field seemed dominated by the kind of limited animation familiar from television, characterized by minimal detail, skimpy backgrounds, unimaginative scripting, and ubiquitous tie-ins with the toy industry. The Disney studio had provided a recent alternative with such releases as *The Black Cauldron* (1985) and *The Great Mouse Detective* (1986; reviewed in this volume), the handsome results of its aggressive recruiting program in the nation's art schools in an effort to resuscitate an expiring art form.

During production, Bluth staged a simple demonstration of the difference between classical, full-fledged screen animation and the inferior product which has largely supplanted it. The director had his staff collect exactly two minutes' worth of cels (individual celluloid paintings which are overlaid to create the final frame) from the film and stack them in a pile next to a stack of cels necessary for a two-minute segment of a typical Saturday-morning television program. It is not surprising that the collection of cels from *An American Tail* dwarfed the other pile. By the time *An American Tail* was finished—two years and nine million dollars later—more than one million drawings, one hundred thousand hand-painted cels, and eight hundred background paintings had been committed to celluloid. Still, what gives the film its impact is not the project's immensity but the combination of state-of-the-art technique, complex and meticulous movements, enthralling imagery, a sense of depth, and—perhaps most important of all—inspired storytelling.

Bluth, who also designed, created the storyboards, and coproduced the film, worked with Walt Disney Pictures for many years, contributing to such animated films as *The Sleeping Beauty* (1959), *The Sword in the Stone* (1963), *Robin Hood* (1973), and *Pete's Dragon* (1977). Along with John Pomeroy and Gary Goldman, his coproducers on this film, Bluth left the Disney fold in 1979 in protest of Disney's seeming abandonment of high-standard animated features. Their first independent feature-length release was *The Secret of NIMH*, a feature about mice and rats which received critical praise, sputtered at the theatrical box office, prospered in the video market, and attracted the attention of an admiring Spielberg.

Spielberg, the director and/or producer of seven of the twenty top-grossing films ever made, had long harbored a desire to bring an animated film to his young, responsive, and appreciative live-action audience. *The Secret of NIMH* reminded him of the classic, animated Disney features of his youth and motivated him to try to revive the public's appetite for the foundering art form by undertaking a project to which no live-action techniques, however sophisticated, could do cinematic justice. With his Amblin Entertainment production company colleagues, Spielberg approached Bluth, promising him acceptable artistic freedom and proposing a project the hero of which would be a mouse named Fievel (after Spielberg's Russian-immigrant grandfather) who would travel an adventurous path similar to that traveled by Spielberg's grandparents and many of their generation. The story would be a mouse's-eye view of persecuted characters giving up their homes and possessions, undertaking a difficult journey to America, struggling to assimilate and start over again, overcoming seemingly insurmountable obstacles, and emerging triumphant. At first afraid that he would be repeating himself with yet another project featuring a mouse protagonist, Bluth overcame his reservations by assigning the central character the kind of childlike traits—mischievousness, curiosity, vulnerability, resourcefulness, and pluck—which would gain the affection of the adult audience and the identification of viewing children.

The narrative begins with a modest Hanukkah celebration at the humble Russian home of Fievel Mousekewitz, his sister, and his parents, whose abode is then destroyed by marauding, mouse-hating cats. Believing that freedom from pogroms and other such atrocities is possible only in America, where "there are no cats and the streets are paved with cheese," the Mousekewitzes embark on the long voyage westward to the New World. The over-curious and under-obedient Fievel is washed overboard en route to the United States, completing his trip in a bottle and washing ashore in a New York harbor. Alone and desperate to find his family, who have also landed in New York but presume that he has drowned, Fievel (now called Philly) meets a succession of characters—some friends, some foes—as he continues his search for the other Mousekewitzes and comes to the sad but bracing realization that there are more cats and less cheese than the optimistic immigrants had been led to believe.

Initially befriended and transported around the city by Henri, a French pigeon literally overseeing the construction of the Statue of Liberty, Fievel soon meets and is assisted by teenage Italian mouse Tony Toponi and his inamorata, Irish mouse Bridget. He must, however, overcome the machinations of con artist Warren T. Rat, his devious henchman, the cockroach Digit, and corrupt political mouse Honest John. With the further help of wealthy anticat activist Gussie Mausheimer and New York's only friendly, compassionate, mouse-loving cat, Tiger, Fievel is able not only to lead a successful scheme to rid the city of cruel, murderous cats, but also to reunite with his beloved family.

One of *An American Tail*'s achievements is its admirable success in seamlessly meshing several appropriate themes without undermining its leisurely but compelling narrative. The immigrants' myth of the American Dream is explored, as is the melting-pot mix of ethnic American citizens with similar ambitions and problems at the turn of the century. Most effective, however, is the tapping of the universal childhood fear of abandonment, addressed through Fievel's separation from his parents—the central plot thrust and one intended purposefully to grip and scare youngsters, then deliver them cathartically from its grasp.

In the standard tradition, the dialogue of the film was recorded before the animation was done so that the movements and facial expressions could be drawn to match the aural intent and flavor of the actors' voices, translating the emotions and moods of individual scenes into expressive visuals. For some complicated sequences, videotaped live action was used as a model that could be adapted to the drawing board. Multiple camera shots (that is, multiple passes of various cels in front of the camera to add depth and dimension)—more than in any film since Disney's *Bambi* (1942)—are on plentiful display throughout the film, as are painstaking special effects (fire, rain, shadows, and reflections), and colors (more than six hundred of them).

Memorable music, always an important ingredient in a good animated film, is here the contribution of James Horner, who conducted the London Symphony Orchestra in the recording of his original score. Horner also wrote the music, along with Barry Mann, to go with Cynthia Weil's lyrics for the film's four songs, each performed by on-screen characters—"There Are No Cats in America," "Never Say Never," "A Duo," and "Somewhere Out There." The latter is Fievel's plaintive but hopeful plea that his parents will eventually turn up and is the film's signature song, which is reprised over the closing credits and which earned an Academy Award nomination as Best Song.

Undoubtedly bolstered by the commercial marketing connections with such heavily advertising institutions as Sears and McDonald's, both of which used characters from the film in promotions aired during the film's initial release, *An American Tail* set animated-film box-office records during its first run. Nor did the objections of the Anti-Defamation League of B'nai Brith to the use of the Jewish Fievel character in McDonald's Christmas commercials—an official complaint which led to a discontinuation of the television spots—retard the film's commercial momentum. Moreover, the success of the film validated the producers' hopes for a long life of video rentals, seasonal re-releases, repeat viewings, and perhaps even a rebirth of labor-of-love animation.

Bill Wine

Reviews
Chicago Tribune. November 21, 1986, VII, p. 53.
Los Angeles. XXXI, December, 1986, p. 277.
Los Angeles Times. November 22, 1986, VI, p. 8.
Macleans. XCIX, December 1, 1986, p. 68.
New York. XIX, December 1, 1986, p. 132.
The New York Times. November 7, 1986, p. C8.
People Weekly. XXVI, December 15, 1986, p. 12.
Time. CXXVIII, November 24, 1986, p. 98.
Variety. CCCXXV, November 19, 1986, p. 18.
The Wall Street Journal. November 20, 1986, p. 24.
The Washington Post. November 22, 1986, p. G1.

EL AMOR BRUJO
(LOVE, THE MAGICIAN)

Origin: Spain
Released: 1986
Released in U.S.: 1986
Production: Emiliano Piedra; released by Orion Classics
Direction: Carlos Saura
Screenplay: Carlos Saura and Antonio Gades; based on the ballet of the
   same name by Manuel de Falla
Cinematography: Teo Escamilla
Editing: Pedro Del Rey
Production design: Emiliano Otegui
Art direction: Gerardo Vera
Costume design: Gerardo Vera
Choreography: Carlos Saura and Antonio Gades
Sound: Daniel Goldstein
Music direction: Jesús López Cobos
Music: Manuel De Falla
Song interpretations: Rocío Jurado
MPAA rating: PG
Running time: 100 minutes

> *Principal characters:*
> Carmelo . . . . Antonio Gades
> Candela . . . . Cristina Hoyos
> Lucía . . . . Laura Del Sol
> José . . . . Juan Antonio Jiménez
> Aunt Rosario . . . . Emma Penella
> José's father . . . . Enrique Ortega
> Candela's father . . . . Diego Pantoja
> Chulo . . . . Candy Roman

Carlos Saura's films are among some of the most distinctively stylized
works in the history of cinema. His touch as a director is always a very personal one; his recurring subjects include the world of childhood, the importance of memory, and the role of passion. Whereas Saura was once regarded
as a political filmmaker, criticizing Francisco Franco and Fascism through
such works as *La Prima Angelica* (*Cousin Angelica,* 1973) and *Cria cuervos*
(*Raise Ravens,* 1976), he now celebrates Spain's rich cultural heritage, focusing his lens on the world of dance. *El amor brujo* (*Love, the Magician*) is
the final entry in a trilogy of dance films that began with *Bodas de sangre*
(*Blood Wedding,* 1981) and *Carmen* (1983). Like its predecessors, *El amor*

brujo is a tribute to flamenco, Spanish music, and romance.

In all Saura's works, there are certain stylistic elements that recur frequently. The camera does not merely record the action but almost always plays a narrative role as it swirls around like an invisible dance partner. Music is crucial to Saura's films. Manuel de Falla's original score is the inspiration for *El amor brujo*. It is idiosyncratic, characteristically Spanish, and gives the film its backbone much as Hector Berlioz's score and Federico García Lorca's play set the stage for *Blood Wedding* and *Carmen*. Finally, Saura has a penchant for placing films within the context of films. He wants to make the audience aware of the act of performing and the conscious leap of imagination involved in this process. To Saura, reality pales in comparison with the fantastic world of the imagination which sets the stage for *El amor brujo*.

The film opens against a blue background. De Falla's music swells ominously as a garage door silently rises (much like a stage curtain) to reveal a large, skeletal film set. As the camera sweeps over the monolithic structure, it zooms down on a town below, an arid, dusty place where gypsies live.

Two swarthy middle-aged men are drinking companionably. One of them (Diego Pantoja) glances at his wiry young daughter Candela, who is jumping rope with friends. After a moment, he speaks to his friend (Enrique Ortega), promising him that Candela will one day marry his friend's son José. They summon the children to inform them of the plans for the arranged marriage while they seal their pact by pouring a drink over their clenched hands. Candela and José look cautiously at each other, while from the shadows, a gypsy boy, Carmelo, stares longingly at Candela.

The camera dissolves slowly on young Carmelo, while a husky, mournful voice is heard on the sound track, singing about the cyclical patterns of love, jealousy, and tragedy. Carmelo's image is transformed into that of a man, and when the action starts again he moves in front of a mirror, carefully adjusting his outfit. Today, everyone in the town square is celebrating the marriage of José (Juan Antonio Jiménez) and Candela (Cristina Hoyos). As the two leave the church, dancing breaks out in the streets.

Carmelo (Antonio Gades) seeks out Candela, his eyes still expressing a longing for her, while José joins his lover, the fiery-eyed Lucía (Laura Del Sol), who shuns his advances, telling him that she is not interested in married men. After a moment, the crowd hoists Candela and José into the air, singing a folk song about love.

After the dancing stops, Candela and José return to their bedroom. Before embracing, they methodically remove their clothing item by item, hesitating before each other. After a beat, they embrace, but it is clear that they married only out of respect to their fathers' wishes and not because of a passion they might share for each other. The camera then cuts to Carmelo, who is weeping silently alone in his room.

A few months later, the townspeople congregate to celebrate the Christmas season. At first, José sits obediently by his wife, but after a few moments he slips away in search of Lucía. He goes to a garbage heap where Carmelo, Lucía, and other gypsies are drinking and dancing. Lucía savors her reputation as the town's bad girl, as it soothes the pangs of José's rejection. When she first sees José again, she is angry, but she quickly weakens, and soon they are dancing and laughing together. Candela notices her husband's absence and goes off in search of him. A fight breaks out as an outsider tries to steal Lucía from José. Saura films the fight as a dramatic ballet scene, where movement suggests conflict instead of actual physical violence. Just as Candela arrives, José crumples to the ground, a knife thrust in his back. The police sirens sound, and innocent Carmelo is framed for the murder.

Four years pass. Every evening, Candela reenacts a strange ritual as José's ghost beckons to her. In a dreamlike trance, she puts on the clothes she wore when José was murdered, which are still streaked with his blood. She goes to the scene of his murder, calling to him. After a moment, José appears, and the two dance together until his ghost vanishes in the mist.

Finally, Carmelo returns from prison to the village. He stops to see his Aunt Rosario (Emma Penella) and visits his cousin Chulo (Candy Roman), who irons his clothes and gives him the news of the past four years—including an account of Candela's nocturnal ritual. Carmelo spends the afternoon in town, where the gypsies play cards, teach young boys how to fight, and dance, in the same way that generation after generation has passed the time. A group of women, including Candela, Lucía, and Chulo, leave the square to wash laundry. After a few minutes of friendly banter sprinkled with sexual innuendo, the women sing and dance to a song full of double entendres about the differences between men and women. This is one of the film's strongest scenes, where all the elements of drama, music, and dance combine to create a memorable impression.

The sky darkens and is filled with thunder and lightning. All the women leave, and Carmelo seeks out Candela.

The two stand transfixed, and then they begin to dance slowly and sensuously together. When a lightning bolt strikes, José's image appears to Candela, and she runs home horrified. Once in her bedroom, she looks out and sees Carmelo alone on his bed. She walks through the rain to be with him. As the two fall on the bed to make love, Carmelo once again appears to be José. Candela weeps out of frustration, saying that José's ghost is too strong for her to fight.

The lovers decide to consult Aunt Rosario, who tells them how to purge José's memory from Candela's mind. That evening, all the townspeople gather in the square and perform a ritualistic fire dance which chases away spirits. As the dancers weave around the fire, images of José's and Candela's life together flash briefly in bursts of flame. When José again appears to Candela, it is evident that his ghost did not succumb to magic. Carmelo again consults his aunt, who can only think of one other solution: to rejoin Lucía with José, who will then leave Candela alone.

Later that day, Carmelo teaches some flamenco moves to Lucía when the seductive young woman begins to kiss him. Although he expresses his attraction for her, he declares his love for Candela. Lucía expresses her scorn for the woman who has taken every man she ever loved. After a moment, Carmelo cautiously tells her of Candela's night visits and asks her if she would like to be reunited with José. Lucía enthusiastically agrees.

That evening Carmelo, Candela, and Lucía go to the spot where José appears. After Candela summons his ghost, José dances into view. The two couples circle each other cautiously, making very deliberate moves. After dancing with Candela, Lucía and José dance together. After a moment, he whisks Lucía off into the mist with him, and they both disappear. Candela, no longer possessed by José's spirit, is finally free to be with Carmelo. As the sun rises on the gypsy town, a folk song announcing a new day plays in the background. After the camera moves in on the two ecstatic lovers, it pulls away at a dizzying speed, zooming up in the air above the film set, leaving the story and the gypsies behind.

El amor brujo is the third cinematic collaboration between Carlos Saura and Antonio Gades. The partnership has been rewarding for both, as Saura's unique directorial style and Gades' interpretive choreography complement each other. The same leading actors and actresses, namely Hoyos, Del Sol, and Jiménez have starred in all three of Saura's dance films. While *El amor brujo* soars with energy and passion in the dance numbers, the clichéd love story detracts from the suggestive mood the film exudes.

Structurally, *El amor brujo*'s complicated love triangle seems overly calculated and plodding. Hoyos and Gades are masters of flamenco, but neither is convincing as a dramatic lead, while Del Sol is such a strong screen presence that she overpowers Hoyos, although she plays a much smaller role. *El amor brujo* would have been a much more compelling film if the drama and irony unfolded more through the dance scenes, as they did in *Blood Wedding,* and less through dramatic sequences.

Shot on the huge set which American producer Samuel Bronfman constructed during the shooting of *Fifty-five Days to Peking, El amor brujo* is very satisfying stylistically. The combination of flamenco, De Falla's haunting music, and Rocío Jurado's strange, throaty love songs creates an intensely moody atmosphere. Teo Escamilla's artistic cinematography captures the passion of dance, as well as the power of the surreal, and plays a vital role in giving the film its point of departure.

While *El amor brujo* is a well-crafted film, critics noted its dramatic flatness. The opening moments make the viewer aware that he is watching a staged production and not real life unfolding, but this idea is not explored further. The play-within-the-play motif took viewers behind the scenes of *Blood Wedding* as they watched the arithmetic involved in performing a flamenco ballet. In *Carmen,* the drama that unfolded behind the dance rehearsals enhanced the presentation of the mythical story. In *El amor brujo*, however, the deliberate violation of the dramatic illusion does not heighten the viewer's perception of the story.

Saura had all the right elements at his disposal in creating *El amor brujo*, and the film is worthwhile for its imaginative score and fiery dance numbers. Nevertheless, the world of fantasy and imagination that Saura can evoke so powerfully is not fully realized in this film, which relies on cinematic style rather than on narrative substance.

Laura Gwinn

Reviews
Dance Magazine. LX, December, 1986, p. 55.
Los Angeles. XXXII, February, 1987, p. 214.
The New York Times. CXXXVI, December 23, 1986, p. C17.
Philadelphia Magazine. LXXVIII, March, 1987, p. 61.
The Village Voice. December 30, 1986, p. 77.

THE ASSAULT
(DE AANSLAG)

Origin: The Netherlands
Released: 1986
Released in U.S.: 1986
Production: Fons Rademakers (AA); released by Cannon Films
Direction: Fons Rademakers
Screenplay: Gerard Soeteman; based on the novel of the same name by Harry Mulisch
Cinematography: Theo van der Sande
Editing: Kees Linthorst
Art direction: Dorus van der Linden; set decoration, Allard Bekker
Special effects: Harry Wiesenhaan
Makeup: Ulli Ulrich
Costume design: Anne-Marie van Beverwijk
Music: Jurriaan Andriessen
MPAA rating: PG
Running time: 149 minutes

> *Principal characters:*
> Anton Steenwijk.................Derek de Lint
> Anton (as a boy)...............Marc van Uchelen
> Truus Coster/Saskia de Graaf...Monique van de Ven
> Cor Takes ....John Kraaykamp
> Fake Ploeg/his father.........Huub van der Lubbe
> Mrs. Beumer......................Elly Weller
> Karin Korteweg................Ina van der Molen
> Father Steenwijk ....Frans Vorstman
> Mother Steenwijk..................Edda Barends
> Peter Steenwijk ....Caspar de Boer
> Mr. Korteweg.....................Wim de Haas
> Fake Ploeg (as a boy)...............Mike Bendig
> Karin (as a young girl)........Hiske van der Linden
> Mr. Beumer ....Piet de Wijn
> Elisabeth ....Mies de Heer

Fons Rademakers' film *The Assault*, drawn from the 1983 novel of the same name by Harry Mulisch, offers multiple insights into the wartime experiences and postwar remembrances of both director and author. Rademakers, an actor by profession who was serving in the Dutch army when Germany occupied his country, was instantly drawn to Mulisch's story of pain and memory rooted in the limbo that was the Netherlands during the closing years of World War II. Like Rademakers, Mulisch was marked by the war; his Jewish mother's family perished in the concentration camps, and his father was imprisoned as a Nazi collaborator.

Rademakers himself was jailed by the German SS in 1943. He was released, however, in a move indicative of the character of authority in the occupied Netherlands: The town leader, sympathetic to the theater, could not abide the closing of the play in which Rademakers had the lead. This notion of ambiguous power pervades the opening section of *The Assault* and provides the film's protagonist with a complex set of memories which surface at intervals throughout the years after the war.

The film opens with a shot of a field of snow, punctuated by twigs and sparse vegetation. The scale of the shot is not apparent until a boy's mittened hand reaches in to brush away the thin snow cover and reveal the earth. A spade plunges into the patch of dirt, removes a chunk, and is replaced in the hole. After tapping the spade handle, the boy, Anton Steenwijk (Marc van Uchelen), reaches into the disturbed dirt and extracts earthworms, which he places in a glass jar and delivers to a neighbor who keeps lizards and toads in terraria. These caged creatures are eating better than their human counterparts, who are suffering through the Dutch "Hunger Winter." It is January, 1945, and the residents of Haarlem, a small city west of Amsterdam, are eking out an existence under German oppression, anticipating the close of the war.

The scene in Haarlem is desolate: Corpses are wheeled by on carts, children scraping the dregs out of soup pots are scolded and shooed away by authorities, and an off-duty nurse, Anton's neighbor Karin Korteweg (Hiske van der Linden), must don her identifying white scarf to obtain preferential treatment in the food line for herself, Anton, and Mrs. Beumer (Elly Weller), another neighbor who accompanies them for fear of losing her food to thieves. Back at home, Anton's father (Frans Vorstman) burns the pages of an encyclopedia for fuel as twelve-year-old Anton peruses them and tears them out for the stove.

With darkness rapidly encroaching, Anton, his mother (Edda Barends), brother Peter (Caspar de Boer), and father consume their one-course dinner, then set up a board game for some small entertainment before curfew. As Anton is about to make the first roll, however, gunshots are heard from the street. From the windows the family spies a body prone in the street before the Kortewegs' house. Peter investigates, and while he is explaining to the family that the dead man was Fake Ploeg (Huub van der Lubbe), Haarlem's most notorious collaborator, they notice Karin Korteweg and her father (Wim de Haas) emerging from their house to place the dead man and the bicycle he was riding in front of the Steenwijks', thereby avoiding guilt by association.

The retribution resulting from this association is swift and cruel. Nazis storm the Steenwijk house and remove the family. Anton is separated from his parents and watches from a truck while his house is torched and his parents, along with a group of Dutch prisoners, are machine-gunned in the hot glare of his burning home. Shaking with cold and terror, Anton is hustled away to a Dutch jail while the Germans decide his fate.

By accident he is placed in a cell with Truus Coster (Monique van de Ven), a woman who, as Anton later learns, was involved in shooting the collaborator. Illumined only by sparse moonlight, her face is not fully visible. Still, Anton watches her lips and her silhouette as she draws him near for warmth and to whisper stories to assuage his fears. She is a powerful influence on Anton. Her warmth and compassion soothe him, and her mystery, enlarged by the stories of lost love she relates in the cell's darkness, has a dual effect: She offers Anton both his first exposure to alluring femininity and the unconscious incentive to unravel his own mysteries later. Before they are separated, she instructs him to remember always that the Germans alone were responsible for the death of his family. As his captors take him away, Anton glimpses her face in a flash of light—too quick for detailed inspection, but long enough for unconscious memory.

The Germans shuffle Anton from district headquarters to Amsterdam (after dressing him in a helmet and hastily tailored soldier's overcoat for the journey), where he is consigned to an uncle. Upon leaving the army office Anton opens a clenched hand to reveal the die he had been about to cast at the moment fate intervened with its own tragic destiny. The repercussions from this moment of ghastly upheaval form a set of conditions which Anton must confront, willingly or not, through the course of the film.

Anton does not return to Haarlem until seven years after the liberation. He wanders off from a garden party where his friends are debating the current ramifications of Communism in Korea and finds himself back on his old street, directly in front of an overgrown rubble pile which was his house. Visibly shaken, he clings to a tree; Mrs. Beumer, who still lives next door with her now-infirm husband, calls him out of his daze and asks him inside. During their discussion of the assault and the years following, Anton (now played by Derek de Lint) undergoes his first flashback, recalling his brother's anger at the Kortewegs for moving the body. Mrs. Beumer urges him to visit the memorial to the victims of that night; he does, but remains impassive while reading the names of his family. He strolls away from the monument and away from Haarlem, not to return until years later when his daughter asks to be guided through her family history.

Anton, studying medicine, takes up residence in Amsterdam. There, during the anti-Communist protests of 1956, he is literally thrown together with another witness to the past—Fake Ploeg (Huub van der Lubbe), the son and namesake of the murdered collaborator and Anton's former classmate. Fake, now in trade school and involved in the protests, is chased off the street by riot police into Anton's building just as Anton opens his door. Fake, earthy and crass in contrast to the refined Anton, attacks the student in a diatribe about guilt and responsibility, both historical (comparing the actions of both their families during the Hunger Winter) and contemporary (accepting or denying Communism). In a rage, spurred in part by Anton's persistent equanimity, Fake brandishes the brick he carried into the apartment and, seeking a target, spots himself in a mirror. The image of his face, distorted by anger, shatters as the brick finds its mark. Confronted with such a drastically different, and vehemently held, view of the traumatic episode in his past, Anton begins to intuit that he must resolve the facts for himself.

Resolution, however, finds itself sublimated by his studies, then the practice of his profession as an anesthesiologist. In 1960, he takes Easter vacation in London. There, in Westminster Abbey, he is startled by a woman speaking Dutch behind him. Turning to respond, he sees her face, backlit and shadowed except for her mouth; he immediately recalls Truus, the woman in the dark cell. Naturally, he is attracted to Saskia (also played by Monique van de Ven), and they are married a year later.

In 1966, they attend a funeral service for a member of the Dutch Resistance who was a friend of Saskia's father. The funeral provides the occasion for Anton's most acute and provocative confrontation with the past. Sitting with the mourners in a bar following the service, Anton overhears a man describing the murder of a traitor one night in Haarlem. Questioning the man, Cor Takes (John Kraaycamp), Anton realizes that he was responsible for the death which led to the extermination of Anton's family and the prisoners. Anton, however, expresses no hostility toward the man; he is characterized by an existential indifference to his history. As the two men relate their memories of the night in 1945, each realizes that the other holds valuable keys to the past. For Anton, Cor provides a link to and a possible elucidation of that night, while for Cor the encounter is significant because Anton had the last contact with his accomplice Truus Coster, the jailed woman. Cor reveals that he was in love with her, above and beyond their shared distaste for the Nazis, and was never sure, before she died, if the love was mutual.

Anton, deeply disturbed by this encounter and sympathetic to Cor's own desire for resolution, forces himself for the first time to re-create the details of the assault and his encounter with Truus. There is an alarming scene in which Anton, swimming in the ocean while Saskia watches from shore, undergoes the first pangs of an emotional breakdown, flounders in the waves, and struggles back to the beach and her warmth. He then visits Cor's apartment, which opens this reservoir of suppressed memories. A back room of the apartment serves as a time capsule for Cor's mementoes—a photo of Truus, her gun and bicycle, and a map of Europe, stuck with strategic pins and imprinted with a lipstick kiss in the North Sea of the Netherlands. Seeing these, and hearing Cor repeat a story she told Anton, he confirms that it was Truus in the cell, to Cor's partial relief; the question of her feelings for him remains unresolved.

Having cleared up the mystery surrounding the woman in the cell, Anton undergoes a diminishment of his connection to Saskia. They part amicably in 1967, and Anton soon remarries. With his new wife Elisabeth (Mies de Heer), who bears no resemblance to Truus/Saskia, Anton fathers a son whom they name after Anton's dead brother Peter—thereby affording Peter's spirit some tribute. Anton's demons, however, are not yet fully exorcised; he suffers from periodic emotional breakdowns, which he ultimately conquers by force of will. There remains, too, one unanswered question—why did the dead man's body end up in front of his family's house?

The question does not plague Anton, but its resolution would bring peace to his soul. Another demonstration, this time in the early 1980's, and another coincidental meeting conspire to provide the answer. At a demonstration against nuclear arms (which Anton was coerced into attending as payment for emergency dental care), he encounters the severely aged Karin Korteweg (Ina van der Molen). Aware that she can provide the final elucidation, Anton challenges her outright. She reveals that her father was initially motivated to move Ploeg out of concern for his lizards, which were inconceivably precious to him. (Karin explains that they signified immortality and eternity to her father.) She also explains that the reason they moved the body right to the Steenwijks' rather than left to the Aartses' was that Mr. and Mrs. Aarts were hiding a Jewish family in their basement. (This revelation resolves an auxiliary mystery—why the Aartses had always been so taciturn around their neighbors, always providing the gossipy Mrs. Beumer with something about which to complain.) The guilt and sorrow which followed Korteweg and Karin as they exiled themselves to New Zealand exacted a greater vengeance upon them than Anton ever could have, if he had been so inclined.

Freed of his psychic burden after nearly forty years, Anton drifts deliriously away from Karin amid the teeming mass of demonstrators. A moment of panic ensues when he realizes that he has lost track of his son in the throng, but Peter promptly grabs his hand and is hefted up by Anton. The film closes on the pair becoming increasingly smaller in an overhead crane shot; Anton's reunion with his son is mingled with his rejoining the ranks of those unencumbered by ghosts of the past and concerned in the present for the welfare and protection of days to come.

The Assault ends with a scene vastly different from the film's opening. The demonstration is replete with life and color, and is of immense scale, in contrast to the barren square-yard of snow seen at the outset. Anton's life has undergone a similar transformation: The tabula rasa of a twelve-year-old has broadened and elaborated beyond measure. Anton himself, however, can claim little responsibility for his experiences; he has lived his life in a passive mode. Considering the trauma which scarred his childhood, one would assume that Anton might have made an effort to relieve himself of the pain. He seems impervious to it, however, wanting to believe that pain will dissipate if ignored.

Nevertheless, his past persists, manifesting itself periodically to remind him of his responsibility to his family, to others (such as Cor Takes), and to himself. As Father Steenwijk said while Anton consigned the encyclopedia to the stove and Peter struggled over his Greek translations, knowledge of the past contributes to an understanding of the present. Confronting his past is difficult for Anton—he became an anesthesiologist to help others avoid pain in the same mechanical way that he sublimates his own—but it is apparent when he presses Karin Korteweg for the truth that finally he desires to eradicate the mystery.

Rademakers has created, in *The Assault*, a strikingly original treatment of a much-explored theme. Compared to other films which take for their subject the postwar experiences of survivors, *The Assault* is an anomaly; Anton prefers to ignore all references to his war-born tragedy rather than seek them out and resolve them. The success of Rademakers' film derives from its ability to maintain the tension between knowing and not knowing, participating and remaining passive—Anton draws sympathy from the viewer as he progresses along those lines. The story of his progress is fascinating, and *The Assault*, winner of the Academy Award for Best Foreign-Language Film, enthralls both in form and content.

George Slade

Reviews
Los Angeles Times. January 16, 1987, VI, p. 10.
New York. XX, February 16, 1987, p. 77.
The New York Times. February 6, 1987, p. C8.
The New York Times. April 12, 1987, p. B11.

AT CLOSE RANGE

Production: Elliot Lewitt and Don Guest; released by Orion Pictures and
Hemdale Film Corporation
Direction: James Foley
Screenplay: Nicholas Kazan; based on a story by Elliot Lewitt and Nicholas
Kazan, which was inspired by a series of articles in the *Philadelphia In-
quirer* by Julia Cass
Cinematography: Juan Ruiz-Anchia
Editing: Howard Smith
Production design: Peter Jamison
Art direction: Chuck Roseberry; set decoration, R. Chris Westlund
Sound: Ron Clark
Music: Patrick Leonard
Song: Patrick Leonard and Madonna, "Live to Tell"
MPAA rating: R
Running time: 115 minutes

> *Principal characters:*
> Brad Whitewood, Jr. . . . . Sean Penn
> Brad Whitewood, Sr. . . . . Christopher Walken
> Terry . . . . Mary Stuart Masterson
> Tommy . . . . Christopher Penn
> Julie . . . . Millie Perkins
> Grandma . . . . Eileen Ryan
> Mary Sue . . . . Candy Clark
> Ernie . . . . Alan Autry
> Lucas . . . . Crispin Glover

In 1978, reporter Julia Cass, through a series of *Philadelphia Inquirer*
articles, traced the sordid, shocking activities of Bruce Johnston, a professional criminal who placed a fifteen-thousand-dollar bounty on the head of
his own son, Bruce Jr., and his son's fourteen-year-old girlfriend, Robin
Miller. Johnston's two brothers ambushed the young couple; the girl died,
but Bruce Jr. miraculously survived eight gunshot wounds.

The report of this bizarre, unsettling crime touched millions of readers,
including James Foley, then a film student at the University of Southern
California; Elliot Lewitt, an East Coast documentary filmmaker; Nicholas
Kazan, a novelist-playwright and the son of director Elia Kazan; and Sean
Penn, a fledgling actor. Little did they know at the time that their paths
would eventually converge on a film project, *At Close Range,* that would
depict the complex events leading to Johnston's crime. Kazan would script,
Lewitt coproduce, Foley direct, and Penn star as the son-victim.

Kazan and Lewitt found that their bleak, disturbing, downbeat script hardly fit Hollywood's partiality for fizzy entertainment. The project received a boost, however, from another article, Stephen Rebello's 1983 piece for *American Film,* "One in a Million," which documented Hollywood's finest unproduced screenplays. *At Close Range* was at the top of Rebello's list.

The *American Film* article provoked much discussion among Hollywood producers. This and Penn's clout created momentum, and Hemdale Film Corporation finally agreed to finance the $6.5 million project. Foley, who had impressed many with his stylish first feature, *Reckless* (1984), and who was a close friend of Penn (for a time they were roommates), became the film's director.

Though the story took place in Pennsylvania's Brandywine River Valley area, the producers decided to set up production in the rural countryside outside Nashville, Tennessee. The forty-eight-day shoot was not without controversy. The arrest of Penn for throwing rocks at two English journalists was widely reported. Producer Lewitt complained that the project was turning out to be a "much-diluted version of the film that I hoped would result," and several reporters misjudged Foley's easy, earnest rapport with Penn as a case of the tail wagging the dog.

Though the film that resulted is far from flawless, it is nevertheless a courageous, disturbing, and emotionally turbulent work, a film that challenges its audience and testifies to the considerable talent and commitment of its makers.

The film opens at a town square; it is nighttime, and a passing tractor suggests the story's small-town, agricultural setting. Brad Whitewood, Jr. (Sean Penn), surveys a group of teenage girls who idle close by. He then catches up with several friends, one of whom, Tommy, proves to be Brad's brother. (He is played by Penn's real-life sibling, Christopher.) Tommy explains that a man has taken five dollars from them to buy liquor and now refuses to hand over the purchase or the money. Brad Jr. calmly but firmly asks for the money; when the man ignores him and drives off, Brad jumps onto the windshield and hangs on as the adult tries to swerve him off. The driver gives up, returning both a bottle of gin and a five-dollar bill. With bravado but without violence, Brad Jr. has won a victory. Flush with this small success, he walks off with Terry (Mary Stuart Masterson), one of the girls he had eyed earlier.

This opening sequence testifies to Foley and Kazan's ability to condense complex exposition through imagery. The dark, rain-slicked streets, underscored by foreboding but romantic music, foreshadow the drama to come. Brad Jr.'s point of view is conveyed through languorous slow motion; here is a young man whose slow-paced life magnifies even the smallest moments of drama. These opening scenes likewise provide a quick shortcut to Brad Jr.'s personality. His defense of Tommy indicates the importance he gives to family ties and to fair play. Significantly, he shuns violence, though he appears physically quite capable of it. (Penn was able to convey the controlled power of his character because he worked out for months in preparation for the part.) Nevertheless, he is indeed an adventuresome thrill-seeker: He offers Terry some unidentified pills ("they make things stronger"), and while on the man's windshield he places a wiper-blade, piratelike, between his teeth.

Brad Jr.'s home contrasts starkly with the setting that opened the film. Peter Jamison's set design is appropriately tacky and disarrayed; a flickering television provides a window onto a realm of exotic self-indulgence that is far removed from Brad's world, protected as it is by his mother, Julie (Millie Perkins), and his grandmother (Eileen Ryan, Sean Penn's real-life mother). Though the two women have good intentions, it is also clear that Brad Jr. has a compelling need for greater excitement and, above all, a father figure. (Julie's surly boyfriend, played by Alan Autry, is an unsympathetic, soon-to-leave substitute.)

Into this matriarchal tableau walks Brad Sr., played with cool, seductive malevolence by Christopher Walken. Cinematographer Juan Ruiz-Anchia immediately signals the shot's moral implications: The father is framed by a dark, muddy background, the son by a bright, glowing one. Penn's face will also consistently be shot half-dark, half-light, a visual allusion to the conflicting impulses that duel within him.

"I heard you were a thief," remarks Brad Jr. to his father. Brad Sr.'s response is to invite his son to a gathering of his own makeshift family, which includes his girlfriend Mary Sue (Candy Clark) and brother Patch (Tracey Walter), an erratic, dissolute simpleton. Brad Jr. later learns that this surrogate family is in reality a well-organized, highly successful band of burglars.

Brad Jr.'s allegiance is soon divided between his girlfriend Terry and his father. Terry's world is represented by poetic, Wyeth-like panoramas (the film's rising crane shots are breathtaking), Brad Sr.'s by fireworklike sparks as his gang welds through a safe. Both characters, though they embody widely dissimilar values, are seen from Brad Jr.'s romanticizing perspective.

The father's diabolic influence is powerfully evident when he invites his two sons to a diner; there he plays with a gun and threatens a pathetic former gang member, Lester (Jake Dengel). For the first time, Christopher Walken is lit from below, his character a grinning Mephistopheles who dominates his son-converts who sit, uneasily, in soft, dark light. Inspired by his father's example, Brad Jr. decides to burglarize on his own. With his gang of thrill-seeking friends, he goes out on a stealing spree, ostensibly to have enough money to buy a necklace for his girlfriend, in fact to impress the model for his behavior, his father. It works. Brad Sr. accepts his son into the gang. They go out on their first caper, celebrate their success in what must be the area's fanciest restaurant, and cap the evening by drowning Lester, who has become a police informant.

This scene is the film's pivotal and perhaps most disturbing moment. For the first time, Brad Jr. sees someone get hurt, and he finally realizes that his father is a cold-blooded killer. (Icy-blue light underscores Brad Sr.'s inhumanity throughout the sequence.) The dispassionate killing of Lester culminates in a moment of quiet but ferocious impact: There is a slight flicker in the darkness as one of the gang's henchmen casually lights a cigarette while holding down the drowning victim's head; Brad Sr. then turns to the camera (the scene is shot from Brad Jr.'s point of view), puts his finger over his lips, and says "Shh . . . ." Foley's ability to punctuate such critical sequences proves itself repeatedly in this film. In this particular scene, the effect is devastating.

Brad Jr. decides to break from his father, to become a mechanic. "It's a steady job," he explains, "nobody gets killed." When his father asks him to take part in another robbery, Brad says no. Brad Sr., miffed by this sudden turn, appeals to his son's insecurities about money, manhood, and future. "I thought you were like me," he says.

A residual attraction to his father's life-style, however, remains in Brad Jr. It is hard for him to shake the memory of his father's warehouse of stolen goods; it is surely the most prosperous operation in town. Misguidedly, he organizes his friends into a tractor-stealing caper. They are caught; Brad Jr. is jailed. Terry appeals to Brad's father for help. Instead, Brad Sr. gets the young girl drunk, takes her to a motel room, forces a pill down her throat, and, warning her never to see his son again, rips off her clothes; her screams echo through a dusky, decaying, autumn countryside, and the viewer is left to assume that Brad Sr. has raped his own son's girlfriend.

In the meantime, Brad Jr.'s code of family honor prevents him from confessing to the police, who are investigating his father. (Director Foley, in a cameo role, plays an assistant district attorney.) Meanwhile, Brad Sr. is driving madly around a dusty field. As the camera descends into the swirling dust storm that Brad Sr. has created, his eyes look up. This small, dramatic moment signals that from his angry turmoil Brad Sr. has coldly resolved to take some action.

That action turns out to be the slaying of those who know too much: his two sons and their friends. During what looks like a vile version of the Last Supper, the gang enthusiastically discusses ways to dispose of their victims. They settle on taking each youngster to the top of a hill for execution; so calculatingly planned is the operation that the victims tumble into predug graves. Brad Jr., however, is still in jail and thus protected. When he learns what his father has done, he tells all. While Brad Sr. carouses in a bar, Brad Jr. and his girlfriend prepare to get away. Unexpectedly, shots tear into their car. Terry is dead, Brad Jr. badly wounded.

The sound track goes completely silent as the youth gets out. His actions—tearing off clothes, washing off blood—are a ritualistic cleansing of the horror that he has experienced. All of this is shown in close-ups, with a shot of Brad's face kept to last, his expression that of anguish, pain, and determination.

Brad Jr. enters his father's house. Brad Sr. is clearly surprised that his son is alive (the shot places them symbolically at far ends of the screen). In the film's most powerful sequence, Brad Jr. at first pretends that nothing has happened. He then draws a gun on his father. Angry, almost crying and barely conscious, he presses the gun barrel into his father's face but refuses to pull the trigger: "No, I ain't you." The police arrive, taking Brad Sr. into custody. As if returning from the dead, Brad Jr. arrives at his father's trial, a coat shroudlike over his head. Initially nervous and soft-spoken on the stand, he starts crying, pulls himself together, and identifies the defendant: "He's my father. . . ."

Critical support for *At Close Range* was often impassioned: Critics admired the film's exploration of a complex father-son relationship and its engagement with such serious themes as the sinister glamour of evil and the perils of small-town naïveté. Indeed, *At Close Range* was at the leading edge of a wave of similarly themed films, including *Blood Simple* (1984), *Something Wild* (1986; reviewed in this volume), *Blue Velvet* (1986; reviewed in this volume), and *River's Edge* (1987), which all examined the dark subconscious of rural America.

The principal criticism leveled against *At Close Range* is that its style is overly self-conscious and theatrical. The scene in which the informant is drowned, for example, as effective as it may be, draws undue attention to lighting; the viewer cannot help but puzzle over the lighting sources in such an isolated locale. Other equally mannered images, however, support rather than undermine the narrative content. One shot is especially meaning-filled: Father and son, standing in a doorway, discuss crime with a bright countryside behind them; at the same time, they are framed by the dark border of the building's interior, the items half-perceived there presumably stolen. Another conversation, this one between Terry and Brad Jr., is presented in a montage of theaterlike blackouts; brash as it may be, the procedure, rather than drawing attention to itself, suggests the foreboding nature of their exchange. Foley also borrows from several classic films: An outing at a local swimming hole alludes to *Olympia* (1936) and *Breaking Away* (1979), while the hilltop execution scene, with actors outlined against the sky, pays homage to the final sequence of Ingmar Bergman's *The Seventh Seal* (1956).

Such resonant, meaning-laden imagery suggests expressionistic intentions. At the same time, director and screenwriter prevent the film from escaping believability altogether through considerable realistic ballast: the untraditional attractiveness of Penn and Masterson; the awkward, pause-filled cadence of much of the film's dialogue; the casting of Penn's real-life brother and mother; the cluttered appearance of the characters' home; the deliberate pace of their lives.

Several commentators have noted that the development of some of the film's secondary characters and emotional undercurrents is stunted: One wonders about the motives of Mary Sue, and certainly about those of Lucas (Crispin Glover), Brad Jr.'s decadent friend. Such truncated characters, however, are more than offset by Walken's performance as Brad Sr., intoxicated with evil, getting by through slippery but persuasive mumblings and aging boyish charm. Penn shines, too; his controlled, tenacious presence makes Brad Jr.'s shifting behavior altogether believable. When he confronts his father, his character struggling to hold on to consciousness after being shot, Penn's face turns from bright red to bluish white—a mark of the intense physicality with which the actor inhabited his role.

At Close Range enjoyed only modest box-office success, though its sound track did spawn a major hit record, Madonna's "Live to Tell." Orion Pictures, its distributor, appeared to be thoroughly confused about how to market such a disturbing film. Hollywood, however, seemed not at all confused about Foley's talent to paint powerful images and, at the same time, to extract powerful performances from his actors. Despite *At Close Range*'s lackluster box-office performance, Foley was immediately signed by Warner Bros. to direct a major feature, *Who's That Girl?*

Marc Mancini

Reviews
American Film. XI, April 1986, p. 20.
American Film. XII, March, 1987, p. 46.
Film Comment. XXII, March–April, 1986, p. 16.
Glamour. LXXXIV, July, 1986, p. 111.
Los Angeles Times. April 18, 1986, V, p. 1.
Mademoiselle. XCII, September, 1986, p. 108.
New York. XIX, June 9, 1986, p. 131.
The New York Times. May 30, 1986, p. C10.
Newsweek. CVII, June 9, 1986, p. 79.
Time. CXXVII, April 28, 1986, p. 70.
Variety. CCCXXII, February 26, 1986, p. 16.
Video. X, December, 1986, p. 102.
The Wall Street Journal. June 5, 1986, p. 24.
The Washington Post. June 20, 1986, p. D1.

BACK TO SCHOOL

Production: Chuck Russell; released by Orion Pictures
Direction: Alan Metter
Screenplay: Steven Kampmann, Will Porter, Peter Torokvei, and Harold Ramis; based on a story by Rodney Dangerfield, Greg Fields, and Dennis Snee
Cinematography: Thomas E. Ackerman
Editing: David Rawlins
Art direction: David Snyder; set decoration, Edmund Silksitis
Sound: William Nelson
Music: Danny Elfman
MPAA rating: PG-13
Running time: 96 minutes

Principal characters:
Thornton Melon . . . . Rodney Dangerfield
Diane . . . . Sally Kellerman
Lou . . . . Burt Young
Jason Melon . . . . Keith Gordon
Derek . . . . Robert Downey, Jr.
Philip Barbay . . . . Paxton Whitehead
Valerie . . . . Terry Farrell
Coach Turnbull . . . . M. Emmet Walsh
Vanessa . . . . Adrienne Barbeau
Chas . . . . William Zabka
Dean Martin . . . . Ned Beatty
Dr. Barazini . . . . Severn Darden
Professor Terguson . . . . Sam Kinison
Giorgio . . . . Robert Picardo
Kurt Vonnegut, Jr. . . . . Kurt Vonnegut, Jr.
Marge . . . . Edie McClurg

Every season Hollywood cranks out a batch of films often discussed under the rubric of "teen movie." In 1963, the modest *Beach Party*, featuring swimsuited former Mouseketeers, succeeded at the box office in a way that inspired countless sequels and imitators. The hit musical *Grease* (1978) revived producers' faith in the adolescent market, while darker hues of the horror genre expanded possibilities for teenage films in such hits as *Halloween* (1978) and *Friday the Thirteenth* (1980). Filmmakers exploited the lucrative potential of youthful preoccupation with sexuality in *Porky's* (1982), *Fast Times at Ridgemont High* (1982), and *Risky Business* (1983).

In *Back to School*, Rodney Dangerfield creates what at first appears to be merely another teenage comedy, playing on the comedian's popularity with younger viewers. On closer inspection, however, this film appears to speak at least as much to personal concerns of the aging comedian as to fantasies of the film's target audience. The very fact that it had strong box-office draw indicates that mutual elements may exist in the dreams of young and old. Both long for a sense of connection between generations, a theme almost totally absent in other school films, such as *The Breakfast Club* (1985) or *Pretty in Pink* (1986; reviewed in this volume). The popularity of *Back to School* and its star indicates the mood of a nation, revealing a desire for cohesion that cuts across boundaries of age, economics, or politics.

In its opening, *Back to School* captures the nostalgic spirit of the 1940's with a youth scrabbling to get ahead and stay out of trouble as he shows a failing report card to his father. In an easily identifiable gesture, pulling at his collar with a bug-eyed grimace of discomfort, the boy establishes his identity as the nascent Dangerfield *persona* who gets "no respect." In the next scene, an adult Dangerfield speaks directly into the camera, a favored self-reflexive technique of comedy, but the speech turns out to be a television advertisement for protagonist Thornton Melon's Tall and Fat stores.

As a savvy businessman, Thornton Melon gets respect at Tall and Fat board meetings, where he hosts an oddball assortment of world-class eaters, sniveling flunkies, and homely creators of the "Melon Patch" doll. In contrast, his home life plays on a common Dangerfield motif, the long-suffering husband battling his faithless wife. Adrienne Barbeau plays Vanessa, a spouse who accuses Thornton of having no taste, to which he replies, "You're right. I married you." Melon is a common man, who wants a simple beer and a huge sandwich instead of the martinis, champagne, and "small food" the caterers serve. After finding Vanessa in the pantry making love with another man, Thornton files for divorce. Determined to start a new life, he takes off to visit his son Jason, whom he has assumed to be a successful college athlete, fraternity member, and scholar.

When he arrives, Thornton learns that his son, far from being a campus success, is ready to drop out of school. In one of the few jokes allowed him, Jason (Keith Gordon) describes himself as having only one friend, a blue-haired punk named Derek (Robert Downey, Jr.), who has no friends. Downey, of television's *Saturday Night Live*, lends interesting hints of fey and unconventional intimacy to the young men's relationship, in a performance more subtle and light-handed than any others in the film, while Keith Gordon plays the part of an unspectacular son with an appropriate lack of gusto. Just as actor Rodney Dangerfield refuses to let any of the other actors control the action, father Thornton steamrollers over Jason's wishes by declaring that if his son will stay in school, Thornton himself will join him and get a degree.

Thornton approaches college life with the same relaxed enthusiasm and pragmatic unself-consciousness that has made him a success in the business world. His easygoing nature shines through in scenes in which he declares during a barroom brawl, "I'm not a fighter, I'm a lover." When history teacher Professor Terguson (Sam Kinison) screams maniacally into the face of a fellow student, Thornton comments that he is a good teacher: "He really seems to care—about what I have no idea." Dangerfield delivers such lines with the perfect timing of an experienced stand-up professional.

An endearing quality of both film and star is a combination of nervousness and ease. The audience senses that at any moment the protagonist may make a terrible gaffe, and indeed he does, at regular intervals. For example, so taken is he with an erotic recitation of Molly Bloom's soliloquy by a literature instructor (Sally Kellerman) that he jumps up in the middle of a huge lecture hall and cries out, "Yes, yes," much to his son's chagrin. Later, as he cheats his way through his courses, hiring Kurt Vonnegut, Jr., for advice on his literature essay and the Rand Corporation for help on his economics assignment, his son's anxiety and embarrassment echo that of the audience. With complete aplomb, Thornton sails through exams, barely passing, largely oblivious to Jason's disapproval of his dishonest methods.

While Thornton Melon may appear uncritical to the point of idiocy in certain scenes, his aggressiveness and perspicacity appear in a variety of arenas. He embarrasses his economics professor by suggesting the necessity of bribes in land development, and he irritates the literature instructor's boyfriend (Paxton Whitehead) by seducing an "A" as well as amorous attentions from her. He pulls the diving team out of defeat by performing his famed "triple Lindy," accompanied by slow-motion camera and majestic music, in parody of *Chariots of Fire* (1981).

Dangerfield's film may draw criticism on a number of scores, from threadbare plot to corny jokes. While the film obviously aims at adolescents, not all of its humor is appropriate to teenagers. Word games, such as naming the school administrator Dean Martin, will probably float past some younger viewers. Some of the film's risqué humor may offend parents while eluding the youngsters whose innocence these adults wish to protect. In an early scene, for example, a party guest standing before a painting says that the wife has shown them her Klimt, to which Dangerfield replies, "You too, huh?" Later at a college party, he asks a curvaceous female to help him straighten out his Longfellow. Many of the jokes are old ones, and feminist critics may attack the film for its misogyny, while ideologues may view its subtext as an anti-intellectual invitation to materialism and expediency. Even if one accepts the film as harmless entertainment, *Back to School* is pure Dangerfield, and viewers who do not care for his mugging and vaudeville humor may find little to appreciate in the film.

A look at comedian Dangerfield's own career shows to what extent the film is autobiographical—if not in its particulars, then in the general outline of a self-made man who rises from a poor background, achieving success and becoming popular with the kind of youths who ignored him when he himself was young. Born into a poor family as Jacob Cohen, Dangerfield at one point changed his name to Jack Roy. The last part of this stage name came from a father whose own vaudeville career and unhappy marriage kept him frequently away from home.

Like the boy in *Back to School*, Dangerfield spent most of his youth working. He claims to have entered show business as a way to attain love, and, ironically, love for his first wife was the motivation for abandoning the entertainment field for twelve years. After a rocky marriage and divorce, Jack Roy returned to the nightclub circuit, this time as Rodney Dangerfield. Just as Melon succeeds at starting life over at a rather ripe age, so Dangerfield made an astounding rebound into a career that featured him in nightclubs, commercials, television specials, and films including *The Projectionist* (1970), *Caddyshack* (1980), and *Easy Money* (1983). Despite Dangerfield's successful entry into films, he still keeps his comedic hand in through club bookings, where he can interact with audiences and feel the pressure of live performance. Like the character he plays in *Back to School*, Dangerfield's own life seems tinged with sadness, perennially unfulfilled.

Perhaps more important than the comedian's personal connection with the film is society's attachment to Dangerfield. The longing for a bond with the past is part of the *Zeitgeist* of the 1980's, as reflected in a swing toward political conservatism and youthful idolizing of older, more traditional media figures, all the way from typical heroes such as John Wayne or Ronald Reagan to baggy-pants comedians such as Rodney Dangerfield. The psychological appeal of a character such as Dangerfield resides in his most famous line, "I get no respect." This sentiment appeals to parents trapped by memories of childhood poverty, to young people ferociously entreated to grow up and become respectable, and to children constantly reprimanded to follow unilateral rules of respect for adults.

Something in Dangerfield's paradoxical mélange of anxiousness, offhandedness, and unaccountable success strikes a chord deep within the American psyche. The top-grossing summer films of 1986, along with *Back to School*, were *Ferris Bueller's Day Off*, *Top Gun*, and *Cobra* (all reviewed in this volume). This peculiar juxtaposition of militarism and schoolboy humor as the most popular film subjects suggests strong ambivalence within the society. Audiences long for violent action as an antidote to frustration, yet at the same time they wish to escape to a period of innocence when such solutions were unnecessary. Through Rodney Dangerfield's comedies, viewers draw tremendous satisfaction from seeing happy endings for the sad clown, in whose mournful face people see the reflection of their own private failures and their silent longing for recognition, for respect.

Rebecca Bell-Metereau

Reviews

Chicago Tribune. June 13, 1986, p. CT 7.
Films in Review. XXXVII, October, 1986, p. 480.
Los Angeles Times. June 12, 1986, VI, p. 1.
New York. XIX, July 14, 1986, p. 55.
The New York Times. CXXXV, July 6, 1986, II, p. 15.
The New Yorker. LXII, July 28, 1986, p. 79.
Time. CXXVII, June 30, 1986, p. 87.
Variety. CCCXXIII, June 11, 1986, p. 14.
The Washington Post. June 13, 1986, p. D1.

THE BEST OF TIMES

Production: Gordon Carroll for Universal
Direction: Roger Spottiswoode
Screenplay: Ron Shelton
Cinematography: Charles F. Wheeler
Editing: Garth Craven
Art direction: Anthony Brokliss; set decoration, Marc E. Meyer, Jr.
Sound: James Dehr
Music: Arthur B. Rubinstein
MPAA rating: PG-13
Running time: 104 minutes

   Principal characters:
   Jack Dundee . . . . Robin Williams
   Reno Hightower . . . . Kurt Russell
   Gigi Hightower . . . . Pamela Reed
   Elly Dundee . . . . Holly Palance
   The Colonel . . . . Donald Moffat
   Darla . . . . Margaret Whitton
   Charlie . . . . M. Emmet Walsh

The Best of Times is a comic redemption fable set in a small California desert town, Taft, where losers are transformed into winners and the town is put back on the map. This transformation occurs through the unlikely device of replaying a high school football game which occurred thirteen years before, when Taft lost its one chance to beat its big-city rival, Bakersfield. The culprit in this defeat, Jack Dundee (Robin Williams), who dropped a winning touchdown pass in the final seconds of play, is also the instigator of the rematch, as he tries to erase his unforgivable flop. Whether Jack, given a second chance, will catch the ball and reverse history, however, is not the center of the story. Instead, the story involves the effect of Jack's crazy scheme, which he carries out against all obstacles, on the friends, family, and townspeople around him, all of whom have lost in some way the initiative to change their lives because of the overwhelming resistance of the past.

A clever opening montage details the accumulated disasters and defeats in Taft's history. Taft's oil wells have fizzled out, its location lay not along the freeway but along the fault line, and its one local hero walked away head down into obscurity after losing a boxing match for the title. This résumé of misfortune culminates the night Jack misses the catch, and Taft misses another potential moment of glory. Thirteen years later, both Taft and Jack are still missing something.

While Jack's desire to replay history is the central motivating factor in the story, the emotional center belongs to Reno Hightower (Kurt Russell), the star quarterback who ruined his knee in the same game and on the same play that Jack wants to exorcise. Reno had the ability to leave Taft and play football in college and maybe professionally, but that future disappeared when injury intervened. Reno, like Jack, is inevitably tied to the past, but in a very different way. Reno's memories are of success, not failure, and he is uncertain if he wants to risk these in Jack's rematch. No second chance can erase what happened to Reno or give him back the career he lost.

Both Jack and Reno have stayed in Taft where the lack of change has resulted in a sharpened sense of the past. Jack, whose high school fumble still causes irritation among the Taft football faithful, is the president of the local branch bank. Reno, whose high school glories grow in popular memory each passing year, owns a body shop and paints classical pastiches on the sides of vans. Reno has outwardly accepted his life and tells himself that he neither wants nor needs more. Jack, however, is a volcano of discontent. He owes his position at the bank to his father-in-law and nemesis, the Colonel (Donald Moffat), who is the head of Bakersfield's football booster club and a firm believer that Jack will never make anything of himself any more than he would ever catch a winning touchdown pass if given a hundred chances.

The tensions felt by Jack and Reno are also present in different degrees within their wives. Reno is married to former cheerleader Gigi (Pamela Reed). Every weekend she sings old songs at the local Safari Room, and, as with Reno, the past has a strong hold on her. Unlike Reno, however, she is not content with life as it is and regularly threatens to walk away from her disillusions. Short and nearsighted Jack is happily married to tall and elegant Elly (Holly Palance), but she feels threatened by his dissatisfaction with the job and the future he owes indirectly to her. This forces Jack each week to visit circuitously the local hooker Darla (Margaret Whitton), a former attendant in the homecoming queen's court, who listens while he replays aloud the horrible mistake that has sent his life down the wrong path. It is Darla who, tired of Jack's continual complaining, gives him the straightforward if not immediately obvious advice to replay the game for real.

Jack becomes obsessed with the idea that he can replay the game and thereby remake history. When he presents the idea to the local townspeople, represented by the loony Caribou lodge, they are skeptical, seeing it instead as another disaster looming on the horizon. Nevertheless, Jack fast-talks the Colonel into setting up a rematch. Then he proceeds to trick Reno and the others into accepting the challenge by masquerading as the Bakersfield mascot and vandalizing the Taft lodge. With Taft united, Jack and Reno round up former football players and start to whip them into shape, while everyone else rejuvenates the town and celebrates with a parade. Elly and Gigi, however, do not understand this obsession with the past. Elly sees it as Jack's final break with a comfortable and secure life with her, and Gigi sees it as Reno's final irresponsibility. The two women stand together and send Jack and Reno packing. When the girls invite the boys over for a trial dinner, the recourtship goes well until Jack blunders by trying to watch Monday night football behind the girls' backs. Each couple needs to put the past behind them in order to revitalize their marriage, but they must first relive the past. Thus, they are returned to a courting relationship, as if they were back in high school on the eve of the big game.

When the big game comes, for all Jack has done, the outcome rests with Reno. He is the only true athlete for Taft, and without him they are nothing. Reno, however, has retreated into anonymity and does not want to be a leader anymore. While Jack is acting out a fantasy, Reno is living a real game and only wants to get through it without embarrassing himself.

After the first half of the game, however, Reno is embarrassed and mad, both at himself and at Jack, whose deceptions have brought about the crazy game. Then Reno resolves to win the game. In an action both simple and pure, he puts on the white shoes he wore in high school, which set him apart from and above all the other players, and goes out to test himself against the memory of what he once was. A sudden and providential rainstorm turns the playing field into an equalizing mudfield, and by Reno's command the clock is turned back, history reversed, and Jack redeemed.

The Best of Times is a fresh approach to standard Hollywood material. The initial plot device concerning Jack's struggle with the memory of his missed catch gradually recedes over the course of the film, and by the end, it quietly dissolves. In its place emerge a number of small, unexpected revelations about people whose hopes for something better are actually a nostalgia for a past that holds them down. Ron Shelton, who previously worked with Roger Spottiswoode on the bold adventure-romance *Under Fire* (1983), has constructed an insightful group of attracted opposites, who are tied together in a tenuous web of emotion and memory. Spottiswoode, who was editor of Sam Peckinpah's *Straw Dogs* (1971) and *Pat Garrett and Billy the Kid* (1973), turns from action fare to a gentle comedy, directing crisply and clearly and avoiding the clichés that cripple most underdog success stories.

Above all, however, the appeal of *The Best of Times* lies in the vivid performances, which bend to the will of comic fable but do not lose touch with reality. Kurt Russell, a former professional athlete himself, gives a restrained performance which illuminates the fear of losing that lies closer to a winner than any success. In contrast, Robin Williams gives a fireball performance which combines physical humor and barely repressed verbal explosions underneath a rigorously bland exterior. Holly Palance and Pamela

Reed, though given less material with which to work, are both emotionally believable and complex.

Nevertheless, while all the elements in *The Best of Times* deserve individual praise, still it is questionable whether a successful combination is achieved. The pace of the film is slow, appropriate for a Capraesque fable, but not for the mad antics of Williams' Jack, which occasionally send the film reeling. In addition, the focus of the story continually shifts from Jack's conflict to Reno's conflict with a resultant dramatic disruption. Even though the problems of the two dramatic centers are parallel, they never merge or find clear resolution. In similar fashion, while the stories of the wives and of the town are recognizably connected to the main plot, they always seem like digressions. Spottiswoode's inability to find the right tone that would harmonize the elements so well realized individually resulted in mixed reviews and mediocre box office receipts.

If *The Best of Times* never fully integrates the conflicting pulls of small-town fable, wacky comedy, and gentle romance, the film as a whole nevertheless has a thematic unity that keeps the dramatic parts from toppling each to its own side. With comic grace, Jack and Reno, Elly and Gigi confront the past held within them and pass through it to a future they can all live together freely.

Terry Nixon

Reviews
Films in Review. XXXVII, May, 1986, p. 305.
Los Angeles Times. January 30, 1986, VI, p. 1.
Macleans. XCIX, February 17, 1986, p. 48.
The New York Times. CXXXV, January 31, 1986, p. C20.
The New Yorker. LXII, February 24, 1986, p. 89.
Newsweek. CVII, February 17, 1986, p. 68.
Time. CXXVII, February 24, 1986, p. 71.
Variety. January 29, 1986, p. 3.
Variety. CCCXXII, February 5, 1986, p. 29.

BETTY BLUE
(37, 2 LE MATIN)

Origin: France
Released: 1986
Released in U.S.: 1986
Production: Claudie Ossard and Jean-Jacques Beineix for Gaumont; released by Alive Films
Direction: Jean-Jacques Beineix
Screenplay: Jean-Jacques Beineix; based on the novel *37, 2 Le Matin* by Philippe Djian
Cinematography: Jean-François Robin
Editing: Monique Prim
Production design: Kim Doan
Art direction: Carlos Conti; set decoration, Jacques Leguillon
Special effects: Jean-François Cousson; special fire effects, George Demetreau
Makeup: Judith Gayo
Costume design: Elisabeth Tavernier
Sound: Pierre Befve
Music: Gabriel Yared
MPAA rating: no listing
Running time: 120 minutes

Principal characters:
Betty............................Béatrice Dalle
Zorg......................Jean-Hugues Anglade
Lisa ....Consuelo de Haviland
Eddy ....Gérard Darmon
Annie.......................Clémentine Celarie
Bob ....Jacques Mathou
Owner.......................Claude Confortes
Gyneco publisher ....Philippe Laudenbach
Policeman Richard................Vincent Lindon
Old policeman ....Raoul Billeray
Doctor........................Claude Aufaure

Betty Blue takes the theme of obsessive, tragic love—long a favorite of French filmmakers—in refreshingly naturalistic directions. Although the film has its share of histrionic moments and an overwrought, predictable climax, for the most part director-screenwriter Jean-Jacques Beineix eschews the genre's usual melodrama and facile psychology. Instead, he builds his characters simply by displaying their emotional responses to a specific series of everyday situations and imbues the form's story conventions with fresh, unobtrusively allegorical insights. Beineix also employs a visual plan rich with earth tones, point-of-view camera work, and extensive frontal nudity; the high artifice design strategies that informed every frame of his first two efforts, *Diva* (1980) and *The Moon in the Gutter* (1983), are used here sparingly, almost as punctuation. Thus, *Betty Blue* is the first Beineix film to be more concerned with people than with style.

Opening with a slow track-in on Zorg (Jean-Hugues Anglade) and Betty (Béatrice Dalle) making ardent love in his seaside bungalow, Beineix instantly establishes the thematic motifs that will run throughout the rest of the film: unbridled passion, the primacy of sensual and emotional experience over thoughtful analysis, and the impossibility of one human being ever fully understanding the mind of another. In voice-over narration, Zorg reads a passage from Philippe Djian's novel on which the film is based, *37, 2 Le Matin*, which informs the viewer that Zorg has known Betty for a week, they make love every night, and the forecast calls for stormy weather.

Betty moves in with Zorg the following day. An aimless, unassertive drifter in his early thirties, Zorg works as a maintenance man at the multi-unit resort community where he lives. Betty cheerfully helps him paint fifty of the cottages pink with blue trim, although she cannot tolerate Zorg's submissive attitude toward the complex's owner (Claude Confortes) and does not hesitate to show it. One night, in a fit of pique, Betty starts hurling Zorg's things out the window but stops when she finds a box containing a manuscript—a novel Zorg had handwritten a few years earlier. Intrigued, she reads through the night and into the next day. Convinced upon finishing that Zorg is a literary genius, the nineteen-year-old woman determines that her lover should stop wasting his talent doing menial jobs. To this end, Betty pushes the owner off the bungalow's veranda, packs a few belongings and the manuscript, and burns down the structure.

Betty and Zorg hitchhike to Paris, where they move into a small, non-operating hotel which is owned by Betty's widowed best friend, Lisa (Consuelo de Haviland). Here, Betty painstakingly types Zorg's story into submittable form, while Zorg himself tries to write something new (he burns the results). They both become good friends with Lisa's new lover, a hard-drinking, fun-loving restaurateur named Eddy (Gérard Darmon), who gives them jobs at his pizza parlor.

When the publishers respond to Zorg's work, they are uniformly discouraging; indeed, most editors seem insulted that the talentless Zorg tainted their desks with his rotten prose. Disappointed, Betty exhibits increasingly unstable behavior, going to one snide publisher's apartment and slashing his face with a metal comb and stabbing an abusive restaurant patron's arm with a fork. Mortified by both incidents, Zorg can only slap and shake Betty until she calms down.

Eddy's mother dies, and his three friends accompany him to the provincial town where she lived. After the funeral, Eddy asks Zorg and Betty to stay on in his unoccupied family home and run his mother's piano store. The couple eagerly accept the offer, set about remodeling the house to their taste, and appear well on their way toward domestic bliss. Even when Annie (Clémentine Celarie), the neighborhood grocer's attractive, frustrated wife, tries to seduce Zorg, he rejects her out of fidelity to his adored Betty.

Unaccountably upset one evening, Betty shoves her fist through a window, then runs out, hysterical, into the street. In a sustained, subjective steadicam shot, Zorg pursues her to the steps of a church, where two suspicious, bickering policemen (Vincent Lindon and Raoul Billeray) stop and question them, then cheerfully offer them a ride upon learning that they are friends of Eddy. Some days later, Betty announces that a home-pregnancy test has yielded positive results. Both she and Zorg are elated and deeper in love than ever before.

Zorg discovers that Betty has been taking tranquilizers. Though she claims that they are only for occasional sleeplessness, her overall energy level has dropped. One evening, she falls asleep without making love, a new situation that annoys and disorients Zorg. He goes to the kitchen and begins to write until a white cat comes in through the window. He then follows it up to their bedroom, where the cat perches itself on the bed beside Betty, so close that it seems an extension of the woman herself.

A medical examination contradicts the home-pregnancy test results, sending Betty into schizophrenic depression. Convinced that anything she wants will always be denied her, she sulks constantly, breaks into crying fits, and, late at night, hears imaginary voices. Finally, she plucks out one of her eyes.

The next morning, a publisher calls from Paris to tell Zorg that he wants to publish his book. Zorg rushes to the hospital with the good news but finds Betty strapped to her bed and sedated into a nearly catatonic state. A doctor (Claude Aufaure) informs Zorg that Betty is totally insane, but there is a chance drug therapy may help her recover. Remembering the tranquilizers, Zorg assaults the doctor, blaming drugs for her mental state. Zorg is forcibly ejected from the premises and told not to come back.

That night, disguised as a woman, Zorg slips back into the hospital. Alone with the uncomprehending Betty, he tells her that he hears her voice every night and that they are going away together to a place where no one can ever part them again. Zorg then tightens the straps on Betty's bed and smothers her with a pillow.

The following evening, Zorg sits with pen and paper at the dining-room table. The cat jumps up and, in Betty's voice, asks him if he is writing. Zorg says no; he is only thinking.

Somewhat understandably, *Betty Blue* generated a fair amount of ire among some feminist critics. The film's frequent, explicit sex scenes and nudity (although as much of Anglade is seen as of Dalle), coupled with Betty's self-consuming devotion to Zorg and the equating of her voracious sex drive with insanity (while the equally randy Zorg remains level-headed throughout), do give the sexism charges some basis.

Nevertheless, Zorg and Betty's is far from a male-dominated relationship. She is the assertive one: It is she who burns down the bungalow, markets Zorg's novel, and takes the initiative in rearranging Eddy's mother's house. Indeed, Zorg passively follows her lead in every significant decision that affects their lives; he even refuses to accept Eddy's offer to stay and manage the house and piano store unless Betty approves. Except for his reluctant physical attempts to bring her out of her hysterical fits, Zorg is unfailingly tender, appreciative, and thoughtful toward Betty. He may never understand her, but he genuinely wants to feel what she feels. After Betty receives the gynecologist's report that she is not pregnant, her face is metamorphosed into a ghastly clown mask of tear-smeared makeup, and in commiseration, Zorg rubs sausages and red sauce over his own face, then, crying himself, embraces her. In their last scene together, Zorg, unable to share her soul, tries at least to take on her form by dressing as a woman.

While on one level Betty may be a male fantasy figure—a combination beauty queen/great cook/dedicated secretary/insatiable sex partner, and crazy enough always to be exciting and in need of protection—to Zorg she is obviously much more. Allegorically, Betty is the artist's muse, nurturing, encouraging, pushing, and inspiring him on to faith in his own talent and further creative achievement. Beineix displays a complex, ambivalent attitude toward this side of Betty's *persona*; though it is clearly her enthusiasm and dedication that resuscitates the repressed author inside Zorg, the sensual satisfaction she also provides distracts him from the actual creative act. He does not write anything worth keeping, for example, until the first night that they do not make love. Not coincidentally, this is when the white cat first appears and settles itself beside the sleeping Betty. It can be argued that the cat here represents a purer form of Betty's inspirational spirit, freed from her maddeningly diverting flesh. This possibility is buttressed by the final scene: Having destroyed the gorgeous but impure body (so, as he said, they can never again be parted), Zorg is writing again and gaining the full benefit of the muse's loving help. Considering the genuine affection both partners express for each other throughout the film, that, and not some critics' vulgar assumptions that Beineix reduced Betty to all he ever fundamentally perceived her as—a sex object—seems the more accurate interpretation of the film's conclusion.

As previously noted, *Betty Blue* is not without some of Beineix's trademark stylistic flourishes: More scenes than necessary are bathed in iridescent blue light; the haunting piano and harmonica theme song, like the music in *Diva*, is so often repeated that it takes on the dimensions of a supporting character; and the camera is often showily peripatetic. The story's extreme, somewhat adolescent romanticism is typical of Beineix as well. What is so unexpected about *Betty Blue*, however, is the visceral authenticity of the emotions which Beineix and his two leads (Dalle is remarkably assured in her acting debut) have drawn from a project seemingly more suited to the humanist sensibilities of a François Truffaut or Jean Renoir. These filmmakers and many like them long ago mined the vein of *amour fou* to near depletion; it took Beineix—the essential French stylist—to find new life in the old genre conventions and to make them both sparkle and resonate.

Robert H. Strauss

Reviews

Films and Filming. September, 1986, Number 384, p. 31.
Los Angeles Times. November 7, 1986, VI, p. 1.
National Review. XXXVIII, December 19, 1986, p. 57.
The New Republic. CXCV, November 24, 1986, p. 30.
New Statesman. CXII, September 12, 1986, p. 23.
The New York Times. CXXXVI, November 7, 1986, p. C19.
Newsweek. CVIII, November 10, 1986, p. 86.
Time. CXXIX, January 19, 1987, p. 72.
Variety. CCCXXI, December 4, 1985, p. 5.
The Wall Street Journal. CCVIII, November 13, 1986, p. 30.

BLISS

Origin: Australia
Released: 1985
Released in U.S.: 1986
Production: Anthony Buckley for Window III and New South Wales Film Corporation; released by New World Pictures
Direction: Ray Lawrence
Screenplay: Peter Carey and Ray Lawrence; based on the novel of the same name by Carey
Cinematography: Paul Murphy
Editing: Wayne Le Clos
Art direction: Owen Paterson
Special effects: Bob McCarron
Costume design: Helen Hooper
Music: Peter Best
MPAA rating: R
Running time: 110 minutes

> *Principal characters:*
> Harry Joy..............................Barry Otto
> Bettina Joy ....Lynette Curran
> Honey Barbara......................Helen Jones
> Lucy Joy............................Gia Carides
> David Joy ....Miles Buchanan
> Joel ....Jeff Truman
> Alex Duval........................Tim Robertson
> Adrian Clunes....................Bryan Marshall
> Aldo ....Jon Ewing
> Alice Dalton.......................Kerry Walker
> The Reverend Desmond Pearce.........Paul Chubb
> Patricia Joy ....Sarah de Teliga
> Harry's daughter ....Saski Post
> Vance Joy ....George Whaley
> Damian ....Robert Menzies
> Ken McLaren.....................Nique Needles
> Dwarf.........................Marco Colombani
> De Vere...........................Tommy Dysart
> Paul Bees ....Les Foxcroft
> Nurse.............................Alexander Hay
> Bettina's father.....................Allan Penny
> Hastings ....Rob Steele
> Box ....Paul Kean

Bliss opens on its protagonist, forty-year-old Harry Joy (Barry Otto), characteristically telling a story to entertain family and friends gathered to celebrate his birthday. Another narrator's voice begins, Harry steps outside his beautiful home to stretch in his luxurious garden, and he is struck by a heart attack. For nine minutes, Harry Joy experiences death. His spirit floats above his body until, as the narrator would have it, he "found his way back" to life or, more prosaically, the rescue squad revives him. Either way, he returns to Earth, where a life once lived in Paradise has turned into veritable Hell.

While recovering, Harry gradually sees what he had ignored before: His wife and business partner betray him routinely; his daughter sells herself to her fascistically inclined pusher brother for drugs; and his successful advertising agency prospers by promoting carcinogenic commodities. His unexpected reactions to these discoveries prompt his daughter to quip that the surgeon operated on Harry's brain rather than his heart. His son arranges Harry's admission to a mental institution for the dangerously idealistic, headed by a nightmarishly exaggerated caricature of British Prime Minister Margaret Thatcher, who runs the establishment on a for-profit-only basis.

Harry decides that to atone for the horror of his life he must escape and be very, very good. Leaving his family to their own destruction, he forsakes his entire life-style and finds salvation in a hippie named Honey Barbara (Helen Jones), a prostitute who accepts payment by credit card while expressing her contempt for modern life and her determination to leave the city for the outback. In pursuit of Honey Barbara's love, Harry regains the innocence that he enjoyed before his experience with death. He follows her to the outback, where he patiently cultivates trees, with the design in mind to seduce Honey Barbara through the intermediary of her beloved bees. It takes eight years, but one spring he succeeds: His trees flower. Honey Barbara's bees bring home good honey, and she forgives him for his past errors.

By tending his garden, Harry regains his sense of balance and well-being. He returns to an earlier era of living in harmony with nature, known to him from his childhood when his mother's prayers could end droughts by evoking miraculous floods. The story of the floods, which Harry is retelling when the film opens, originated as a bedtime story in which Harry's father explained the Vision Splendid, or how he fell in love with Harry's mother when he saw her in the bow of a boat holding a cross as the floodwaters ending the drought passed through town. There is no return at the end of *Bliss* to this particular story; there is, however, a return to its evocation of a serene and mystical union with nature.

A religious tale of Everyman faced by Good and Evil, a satire on modern life, an ecological warning—*Bliss* is all this and more. In many ways, though, *Bliss* seems a rambling collection of tenuously related stories tied together through bravado and style. *Bliss* is based on Peter Carey's prize-winning first novel; he had previously published two successful collections of short stories, two of which he and *Bliss* coscenarist Ray Lawrence have adapted for film. Carey once also worked in advertising (he supported his early work with a stint in an agency not unlike his protagonist's), which may explain the flamboyant nerve with which *Bliss* serves up so many situations, characters, and issues.

Yet the film's visual appearance alone undercuts its attempts at deadpan humor and belies its message of a forthcoming apocalypse. Its bright, crowded images—outdoor scenes lit by brilliant sunshine and indoor scenes that take place in airy, windowed rooms filled with luxuriant, exotic blossoms—compete with the wealth of stories narrated by an excess of full-blooded characters. This unwieldy mixture brought the film such intense reactions of both criticism and praise at its Cannes Film Festival screening that Carey and producer Anthony Buckley reedited and reduced the film to a more manageable affair.

Although streamlined from its original, the commercially released version of *Bliss* remains cluttered with characters and surrealistic details. Consider, for example, the maitre d' and the little red car: One day during Harry's hospital stay, his wife and partner have lunch at his favorite restaurant, and the maitre d' begins narrating Harry's story. While the two lovers fornicate on a restaurant table unnoticed by the other guests, the maitre d' dryly comments on their perfidy, complaining that he would never have given them Harry's table if he had known Harry was so ill. Upon Harry's recovery, the same maitre d', high on marijuana he now smokes to counteract chemotherapy side effects, happily joins in the laughter when a circus worker reports that an elephant has sat on Harry's little red car. The car and Harry now both look peculiar, and when he drives off, he is stopped by some disgruntled traffic police. Only another of Harry's wonderful stories rescues him from their wrath; this episode, however, was radically excised from the final version, leaving a curious gap in a film already suffering from lack of continuity.

If *Bliss* seems unlike contemporary Australian and American film productions, it finds its place in a galaxy of literary and cinematic works, represented by such authors as Jorge Luis Borges and Gabriel García Márquez and by filmmakers such as Federico Fellini and Luis Buñuel. In fact, its closest cinematic forebear is the work of Buñuel (minus his cutting attacks on Catholicism). In images recalling Buñuel's *Un Chien andalou* (1928), both Harry Joy and his daughter (the latter in one of Harry's nightmares) seem to have cockroaches crawling out of long scars on their chests. In addition to her opening appearance as the Vision Splendid, with its Arthurian overtones added to religious symbolism, Harry's mother appears in other scenes which emphasize the incongruity of her luminous presence in mundane, worldly surroundings.

Where *Bliss* differs from the works of such twentieth century artists, though, is its belief in clearly definable concepts of Good and Evil, which in turn leads, perhaps inevitably, to a reduced if not simplistic view of Harry's situation. Fundamentally, *Bliss* is an Everyman story. Haunted by the biblical warning that it is harder for a rich man to enter the kingdom of God than for a camel to pass through the eye of a needle, Harry sets out, like John Bunyan's pilgrim, for the Heavenly City. On the way, *Bliss*'s surrealistic aura gradually cedes to a quiet lyricism. The beauty of its closing images, however, cannot quite hide the fact that *Bliss* has skimmed over philosophical and social difficulties to suggest that bliss lies in joining a rustic commune.

Fortunately, *Bliss* suffers from no saccharine oversentimentality or stiff religious fervor; to the contrary, it is always irreverent and gently mocking. At the hospital, Harry wants to discuss the nature of God and Hell with a minister who is more comfortable talking about mismatched socks. Later, Harry tries to believe that he is mad rather than admit that his family is evil.

If in many ways *Bliss* reflects the fact that it is a first effort by its writers, director, and cinematographer, the resultant flaws are balanced by a compensatory freshness and energy. The cast, all relatively unknown if not themselves newcomers, bring a robust, earthy quality to their roles. They all physically suit their parts very well: Barry Otto's balding, mustachioed face and lanky physique embody Harry Joy's amiable if bungling charms. Helen Jones captures Honey Barbara's odd combination of mysticism and practicality, while Gia Carides as Harry's daughter Lucy and Lynette Curran as his wife, Bettina, ooze a slightly tacky, overripe decadence. Owen Paterson's art direction deserves special mention, and Bob McCarron's special effects should be noted for their restraint, although certain scenes (those involving heart surgery and cockroaches, for example) are too graphic.

Like British director Terry Gilliam's *Brazil* (1985), *Bliss* is apocalyptic fantasy on a grand scale. Despite their resemblances, though, *Bliss* ultimately is more successful. Gently funny, whimsical rather than grandiose, *Bliss* never takes itself too seriously—part of the lesson Harry Joy eventually learns.

Harriet Margolis

Reviews
Film Comment. XXI, December, 1985, p. 64.
Los Angeles Times. February 21, 1986, VI, p. 6.
The New York Times. CXXXV, October 4, 1985, p. C11.
Time. CXXVII, March 17, 1986, p. 78.
Variety. CCCXIX, July 17, 1985, p. 14.

BLUE VELVET

Production: Fred Caruso; released by De Laurentiis Entertainment Group
Direction: David Lynch
Screenplay: David Lynch
Cinematography: Frederick Elmes
Editing: Duwayne Dunham
Art direction: Patricia Norris
Sound: Alan Splet
Music: Angelo Badalamenti
Song: Lee Morris and Bernie Wayne, "Blue Velvet"
MPAA rating: R
Running time: 120 minutes

Principal characters:
Jeffrey Beaumont . . . . Kyle MacLachlan
Dorothy Vallens . . . . Isabella Rossellini
Frank Booth . . . . Dennis Hopper
Sandy Williams . . . . Laura Dern
Mrs. Williams . . . . Hopé Lange
Ben . . . . Dean Stockwell
Detective Williams . . . . George Dickerson
Mrs. Beaumont . . . . Priscilla Pointer
Aunt Barbara . . . . Frances Bay
Mr. Beaumont. . . . . Jack Harvey

In a year that witnessed few digressions from the Hollywood mainstream, David Lynch's brilliant and disturbing *Blue Velvet* provided filmgoers with a compelling glimpse at a daring alternative vision of the American suburban landscape. This cinematic aptitude was already evident in Lynch's first feature, *Eraserhead* (1977), a cult classic which wedded an affectionate homage to the trashy, lowbrow, monochromatic science-fiction films of the 1950's with a trenchant cultural critique of a postapocalyptic society. *Blue Velvet* also marked the return of director Lynch to critical form after the lackluster reception accorded his previous feature, *Dune* (1984), an ambitious science-fiction epic that challenged Lynch's acclaimed visual sensibility but suffered from the artistic compromises attendant to any cinematic adaptation of literary material of such populist notoriety. While *Blue Velvet* was nearly universally praised as a contemporary masterpiece, the vivid depiction of aberrant sexual behavior stirred some lively debate, especially within the feminist community.

Blue Velvet represents both an artistic redemption for Lynch and a shockingly original version of the conventional themes in an American teenager's rite of passage. The proliferation of coming-of-age films in recent years has created a virtual minigenre populated by predictable cardboard cutouts of feckless innocents and roguish hedonists in an atmosphere dully leavened with fanciful optimism and sexual high jinks. Lynch challenges these stereotypes with a satirist's pen and the palette of a surrealist, and he fashions a scenario which is at once as hauntingly alluring as a romantic ballad and as dangerous and frightening as an animate nightmare. *Blue Velvet* opens with a sequence that captures the essence of Lynch's narrative method: To the strains of Bobby Vinton's rendition of "Blue Velvet," the camera tilts down from a nearly cloudless blue sky to highlight a white picket fence with a perfect bed of red roses and yellow tulips in the foreground. A fire truck glides in slow motion down a suburban street, children pass a crosswalk before a uniformed matron's watchful eye, and Mr. Beaumont (Jack Harvey), the local hardware retailer, effortlessly waters his lawn. Suddenly, the garden hose tangles in the shrubbery, and, while disengaging it, Beaumont has a stroke. The hose phallically coils between the legs of the now supine, yet suggestively spasmodic Beaumont, while a dog ferociously drinks from the spurting tube. The sound track angrily echoes this canine fury as the camera travels rapidly at ground level until finally resting on a close-up shot that fills the entire wide screen of a beetle locked in combat, and it amplifies the roar of pain from the insect's prey. Lynch's deconstruction of the peaceful suburban environment is skillfully modeled in this initial sequence. The sleepy town of Lumberton, which celebrates its major industry, logging, by cheerfully incorporating the sound of chain saws and falling timber into its radio station identifications, hides real danger and mystery behind its bucolic façade. Lynch skillfully juxtaposes an idiosyncratic blend of sanguine settings, macabre humor, and startling visual and aural dexterity to create a film experience that challenges the classic Hollywood narrative formulas. The ferocity of the tone and the unusual conjunction of abnormal sexuality, of sadism and masochism, contained within this conventional environment destroys the bond of pleasurable identification that is typically proffered to the viewer during the expository scenes of a film.

The hero of the story, Jeffrey Beaumont (Kyle MacLachlan), returns home from college to manage the family hardware business while his father recovers from his stroke. While returning from visiting his father at the hospital, Jeffrey discovers a severed human ear in the wooded area behind his home, and he promptly delivers it to his neighbor, Detective Williams (George Dickerson), for forensic investigation. The police can offer no explanation for his discovery, but Williams' daughter Sandy (Laura Dern), a high school student who eavesdrops on her father's police affairs, suggests to Jeffrey that the mystery involves a local cabaret singer, Dorothy Vallens (Isabella Rossellini). Jeffrey devises a plan to hide himself in Dorothy's apartment and place her under surveillance, and, abetted by Sandy and an exterminator's uniform, he successfully gains entry. The reception of information through hearing, repeated throughout the film, is underscored by both the visual motif of the ear, through which the camera travels in an extreme close-up, and the extraordinary aural impact of the sound design by veteran Lynch collaborator Alan Splet. The sound track combines industrial effects, primarily piston-driven machinery, with distorted noises and rumbles to create a cacophonous counterpoint to the lush melancholy of the title song.

While hidden in Dorothy's apartment closet, Jeffrey learns that she is indeed involved in his mystery—the ear has been severed from her kidnapped husband, Don, to force her to comply with the sexual desires of a gangster, Frank Booth (Dennis Hopper). When Jeffrey is discovered by Dorothy, he enters a world of depravity and obsession that contradicts the mores of the culture through which he and Sandy conduct their innocent romance. Jeffrey is forced at knife point to submit to the advances of Dorothy and, later the same evening, surreptitiously views Frank sadistically abusing Dorothy. Rossellini depicts Dorothy's complexity in a performance that alternates from masochistically encouraging Dorothy's physical and psychological humiliation to a fearful acknowledgment of her status as a tragic victim with a courage and energy that belie her lack of experience. Frank exhibits a virtual catalog of deviant psychological mannerisms, including regressive and infantile behavior, episodes of homicidal rage, paranoia, and an addiction to a gas he carries in a portable tank and periodically inhales to heighten his sexual excitement. In addition, Frank has a fixation on the song "Blue Velvet," a fetish that extends to Dorothy's blue-velvet bathrobe, from which he cuts a totemic swatch to carry about and utilize during sexual encounters. Dennis Hopper attacks the role with a manic ferocity, intelligently investing the character with a serpentine bravado, which allows the audience an occasional glimpse at the inner torture that motivates Booth.

Despite ominous warnings from Sandy, the naïve and chivalrous Jeffrey descends into this maelstrom intent on rescuing Dorothy from her malevolent tormentor, but under her enthusiastic tutelage he soon begins to imitate Frank's sadistic sexual practices. Although shocked by his behavior, Jeffrey is unable and ultimately unwilling to quench the flames of sadism ignited by his mentor. Lynch links Frank and Jeffrey with a sonic signature, the ominous roar first emitted by the beetle in the opening sequence, and the visual motif of a flame. Jeffrey's budding relationship with the innocent Sandy blossoms in counterpoint to the casual degradation of women that emanates from the ethos of this mysterious middle-American underworld. In the Hardy Boys tradition, this adolescent amateur sleuth uncovers the mystery, which now includes murder, police corruption, and a drug ring—activities that Jeffrey documents with a hidden camera. The Lumberton police, however, appear oblivious to the danger to the community posed by Frank and his criminal minions. Sandy, no Nancy Drew, also remains distanced from the corruption, though she relates a prescient dream to Jeffrey, promising that these troubling events will cease when the robins return to Lumberton. In these difficult roles, both Kyle MacLachlan and Laura Dern prove to be winning actors, assaying their often improbably jejune dialogue with an admirably understated conviction. Dern is especially impressive and assured as the quiveringly sensitive, oftentimes comically insipid Sandy.

When Jeffrey is discovered by Frank at Dorothy's apartment, the youth is taken on a harrowing joyride through the criminal underworld that finishes at a transparently titled house of prostitution identified by the neon sign "this is it." Ben (Dean Stockwell), the effete proprietor of the enterprise, is a small-town satyr complete with a gaudy tuxedo, a cigarette holder, and heavy makeup, which only serves to accentuate the ravages of time— affectations that Frank deems, without a soupçon of irony, as "suave." Stockwell, a former child actor of some reknown, is chillingly effective in this cameo performance as a preening libertine of ambiguous sexual orientation. While Ben regales Frank with a tour-de-force lip sync of Roy Orbison's "In Dreams," a plaintive paean to an imaginary lover, Frank writhes in paroxysms of pleasure that mercurially turn to grimaces of pain. Frank later emphatically repeats these lyrics as he paints himself with lipstick and transfers this adornment to Jeffrey's face while repeatedly kissing him. This homoerotic initiation ceremony links mentor to pupil, a transference which explicitly suggests a *doppelgänger* relationship, and ends as Frank severely beats Jeffrey and leaves him amid the detritus of a deserted factory.

Jeffrey finally shares his photographic evidence of Frank's activities with Detective Williams, who recognizes that his partner is implicated in murder and illicit drug trafficking. That same evening Sandy and Jeffrey, after declaring their love, discover a naked and battered Dorothy waiting for Jeffrey at his home. Though nearly incoherent, Dorothy manages to betray her secret relationship with Jeffrey to the distraught Sandy. Jeffrey returns to Dorothy's apartment after she has been taken away in an ambulance and finds two brutally murdered bodies in her living room—her husband, Don, and the corrupt policeman. Jeffrey hides in the same closet in which he initially eavesdropped while Frank frantically searches for him; when he is eventually found, Jeffrey shoots Frank through the forehead. Lynch neatly parallels the beginning of the mystery by slowly traveling out of an ear canal to reveal Jeffrey sleeping in a chaise lounge. After awakening, Jeffrey signals a greeting to his now recovered father and Detective Williams and meets Sandy in the kitchen, where they watch a robin on the window ledge and Sandy reminds him of her dream while repeating the oft-spoken motto of the film: "It's a strange world."

It is indeed: The robin has a distinctly mechanical mobility that betrays its human manufacture, and it holds a beetle in its beak, an ironic coda to the opening sequence. In fact, much of the ending is composed of exact shots from the beginning, creating a bookend effect that circumscribes the fictional landscape. Despite the harshness of the subject matter, Lynch manages to convey a macabre humor in his skillful juxtaposition of the deadpan satire of the middle-class mores of the Lumberton community, including improbably artless dialogue, with the sexual violence generated by the malefic Frank Booth. The filmmaker revels in the artificiality of the fictional environment, using strategies not unlike those employed in some of Alan Rudolph's films, and the potential in the material substance of the celluloid apparatus. While the story itself is a deceptively simple tale, Lynch's means of organizing the plastic elements are idiosyncratic. Lynch employs daring experimental techniques, both visually and aurally, to manipulate the audience's reception of this complex narrative. There is a disquieting tension in the oneiric passages that bespeaks a tortured subconscious lurking within the placid Jeffrey and that aligns his hidden passions with those of the more overtly obsessive Frank. Even more troubling, especially to those critics who read Lynch most literally, is the masochism of Dorothy Vallens, who appears to exhibit an active desire for corporal punishment. The primary tone of the film, however, is surreally comic, intent on puncturing the mystery-suspense genre while satirizing and deconstructing itself as well. The director undercuts the potential for misreading the film by successfully treading the dangerously thin line between artistic judgment and moral recklessness. As the spectators travel metaphorically "in one ear and out the other," Lynch explores the inner psyche, a terrain that he depicts with an honesty and bemusement rarely encountered in American films.

The skill and integrity of David Lynch were recognized by the members of the National Society of Film Critics, who named *Blue Velvet* best film of the year and Lynch best director. In addition, the award for best supporting actor went to Dennis Hopper, and Frederick Elmes was honored as best cinematographer.

John Robert Kelly

Reviews
Films in Review. XXXVII, December, 1986, p. 622.
Los Angeles Times. October 12, 1986, p. C28.
Macleans. XCIX, September 29, 1986, p. 57.
The Nation. CCXLIII, October 18, 1986, p. 383.
National Review. XXXVIII, November 7, 1986, p. 54.
The New York Times. CXXXVI, September 19, 1986, p. C12.
The New Yorker. LXII, September 22, 1986, p. 99.
Newsweek. CVIII, September 15, 1986, p. 69.

Rolling Stone. October 23, 1986, p. 383.
Time. CXXVIII, September 22, 1986, p. 86.
Variety. CCCXXIV, September 3, 1986, p. 16.
The Wall Street Journal. CCVIII, September 18, 1986, p. 30.

BRIGHTON BEACH MEMOIRS

Production: Ray Stark; released by Universal MCA
Direction: Gene Saks
Screenplay: Neil Simon; based on his play of the same name
Cinematography: John Bailey
Editing: Carol Littleton
Production design: Stuart Wurtzel
Art direction: Paul Eads; set decoration, George DeTitta, Jr., and Gary
    Jones
Makeup: Allen Weisinger and Mickey Scoff
Costume design: Joseph G. Aulisi
Sound: Chris Newman
Music: Michael Small
MPAA rating: PG-13
Running time: 117 minutes

> *Principal characters:*
> Eugene .... Jonathan Silverman
> Kate .... Blythe Danner
> Jack .... Bob Dishy
> Stanley .... Brian Drillinger
> Blanche .... Judith Ivey
> Nora .... Lisa Waltz
> Laurie .... Stacey Glick
> Frank Murphy..................... James Handy

Prior to its translation to the screen, *Brighton Beach Memoirs*, the first part of Neil Simon's planned semiautobiographical trilogy, was an extremely successful work on the stage—successful not only commercially (it ran for three years on Broadway) but also critically (it won several prizes and was widely praised by critics as a far deeper, more serious work than Simon had created previously).

Brighton Beach Memoirs is the story of the Jerome family of Brooklyn, New York, as narrated by their adolescent son Eugene (Jonathan Silverman), whose main ambition in life, next to seeing a naked woman, is to be a writer. The year is 1937, and Eugene lives in a working-class neighborhood with his parents Kate (Blythe Danner) and Jack (Bob Dishy), and with his eighteen-year-old brother, Stanley (Brian Drillinger). The Jeromes share their brownstone home with Kate's widowed younger sister, Blanche Morton (Judith Ivey), and her two daughters, sixteen-year-old Nora (Lisa Waltz), who is the frequent object of Eugene's fantasies, and Laurie (Stacey Glick), a pampered, sickly, younger child who has a "flutter" in her heart.

Blanche and her two daughters have been living with the Jeromes since Blanche's husband died unexpectedly of a heart attack at age thirty-six. With this added family to support, Jack, a cutter in a clothing factory, has been forced to take on a second job, selling party favors to nightclubs. The second job enables the family to get by, but it has taken a toll on Jack's health.

One fall day, several things happen to cause family tensions to mount. First, Nora, who is still in high school, comes home from her dance class elated, bringing news that a Broadway producer has invited her to audition for his new musical. The response from her mother and her Aunt Kate is less than enthusiastic. Nora sees it as the chance of a lifetime and demands an immediate decision from her mother as to whether she will be allowed to audition. Blanche, characteristically refusing to make a decision on her own, infuriates her daughter by telling her to wait until her Uncle Jack gets home.

Next, Stanley comes home from work with a dilemma: He faces the threat of being fired for having confronted his boss to protest the unfair treatment of one of his coworkers. He has until nine o'clock in the morning to hand in a letter of apology. Stanley's salary helps to support the rest of the household, so its loss would mean hardship for the family.

To make matters worse, Jack comes home, worn out, with his own bad news. He confides in Kate that the party-favor company has gone bankrupt without warning. His second job and the extra twenty-five dollars a week it brought in are a thing of the past. He wonders aloud to Kate if Blanche will ever remarry and move out.

After dinner that night, Stanley comes to his father for advice. Jack, clearly worried by the possible loss of another paycheck in the family, is initially angered by Stanley's predicament, but as he calms down, his tone changes, and he expresses pride in his son for having the courage to stand up for his principles—his only question is whether, given the times, the Jerome family can afford to have principles. Stanley, satisfied that at least he has his father's support, decides to write the letter and keep the job, for a while anyway.

Several days later, Jack, who has taken another night job driving a cab, suffers a minor heart attack and is confined to bed. Stanley, in a misguided attempt to try and make up for his father's lost earnings, turn to gambling, but he instead loses his entire paycheck.

Back at home, Blanche is getting ready for her first date since her husband's death. She is to have dinner with Frank Murphy (James Handy), an Irishman who lives across the street and of whom Kate strenuously disapproves.

Kate, needing carfare for Blanche (in case, she explains, Frank should get drunk on their date), goes to get Stanley's pay envelope. Stanley tells her that the money is gone and, after considerable pressure, confesses how he lost it. Kate keeps the news to herself, fearing the effect it would have on Jack.

Meanwhile, Blanche gets word that Mrs. Murphy (Bette Henritze) wants to see her. When Blanche goes to her, she learns that Frank, driving while intoxicated, is in the hospital and that the Murphys will soon be moving to be near a clinic to help with Frank's alcohol problem. Blanche returns home, her hopes for the romantic attachment dashed (as are Kate's and Jack's hopes for having Blanche move).

Kate, by now overwrought from dealing with other people's problems, reaches her limit when Blanche expresses sympathy for the Murphys and suggests that Kate might try to be a bit more charitable toward them. As Kate's suppressed resentment comes spilling out, she shouts that she has done enough in her life for other people—especially for Blanche—that it was the need to make more money to support Blanche and her two daughters that has ruined Jack's health. The venomous argument ends with Blanche announcing that she will move out first thing in the morning.

Eugene, who has been eavesdropping on the two women, runs upstairs to tell Stanley. The room, however, is empty except for a note. Eugene reads the note and then runs full speed to the subway station where he catches his brother about to board the train. Stanley, unable to tell his father either the truth or a lie, has decided to join the army. Eugene is unable to talk him out of it, and, as he watches his brother leave, he feels his childhood ending.

The next morning everything is calmer. The rift between Blanche and Kate is on the mend; they have jointly decided that Blanche will move out but not until she finds a job. Stanley, having had second thoughts at the recruiting center, returns home, deciding that his father needs him more than the army does. He gives Eugene a present—a French picture postcard of a completely naked woman. Eugene is in ecstasy.

As the film ends, the entire family (except for Eugene, who is otherwise engaged upstairs with his new gift) is gathered around the kitchen table as Jack reads a letter bringing word of relatives who have escaped from Poland and are setting sail for New York. Excitedly, the family makes plans to take in the soon-to-arrive immigrants.

Any summary of the film's plot makes it clear that the film has been amply supplied with moments of authentic emotion, or what should be moments of authentic emotion. Yet, for some reason, these events are treated as if they are not really of central importance. It is less a matter of the screen time they are given, than that they are lent so little emotional weight in the film. It is as if they had been dropped into the body of this essentially light comedy to give the film a patina of earnestness and seriousness it could not otherwise have earned.

Indeed, there is little in the work as a whole that would convince the viewer that its main character is really a writer other than his scribbling in a notebook. There is in Simon's script no attempt to show how everyday events are filtered, refined, laboriously and carefully transposed into the stuff of art.

Simon has once again entrusted the filming of his play to director Gene Saks, who not only directed the original stage version of *Brighton Beach Memoirs* but also has been the main screen interpreter of Simon for two decades, starting with *Barefoot in the Park* (1967) and *The Odd Couple* (1968). The problem with this is that Saks is primarily a theatrical director, with little sense of the imaginative re-envisioning a stage work requires for the demands of the screen. In a motion picture that has to struggle even in its best moments for the willing suspension of disbelief, Saks's decision to have Eugene deliver commentary directly to the camera distracts from whatever involvement has been created. Unfortunately, most of the information which these asides impart to the audience could have been worked into the scenes themselves; the action could have been trusted to speak for itself. To be fair, Saks's problem is that if Eugene were not given these commentaries to deliver, having almost nothing else active to do in the film, he would all the more speedily be revealed as the passively observing nonparticipant that he is.

Saks has never really mastered, or seemingly even understood, the complex interplay required between camera and actor: the art of microstaging of action for the selectively controlled eye of the camera as opposed to the broad sweep of the proscenium arch. His selection of camera angles, perspectives, and movements is at best only serviceable; at worst, it actually undercuts the emotive power or dramatic thrust of a scene.

Saks has done little to open up the film from the confines of its stage setting. The film rarely gets outside of the family apartment except for a walk to and from the store or subway stop, or a short scene at work. When it does, it remains so narrowly framed that one barely notices; the world, it seems, is merely background. It is hard to recall a film where sense of place has played so small a part. The result is that the drama is deprived of the very sense of particularized ethnic life that could have so memorably flavored a film about growing up in New York neighborhoods in the 1930's.

The skills of the director of photography, John Bailey, unfortunately go unchallenged here, bringing little visual style to the film. He is certainly capable of evoking the feel of a film's exterior and interior landscapes, even an environment as sanitized and familiar as the middle-class suburban Chicago he created in *Ordinary People* (1980). He seems not to have been pushed to give any texture to this nostalgic portrait of the idealized past. (In one instance, he imaginatively shoots a street hockey game with a backlit telephoto at ankle height through a maze of scurrying roller skates; the unexpected appearance of a creatively designed visual image is welcome.)

Reviews were mixed, with most applauding Simon's attempt at something deeper than his usual fare. Much of the favorable criticism was reserved for the performances by the cast's more seasoned players, especially Danner, who, cast against type, gives an exceptionally intelligent, well-thought-out performance. Those who remember Danner's impeccable portrayal of the quintessential suburban, WASP, wife and and mother in the dramatization of the John Updike "Maple" stories, *Too Far To Go* (1979), will be impressed by her range and willingness to risk herself as an actress here.

Dishy also deserves mention for his brave attempt to humanize the role of Eugene's father. In a gentle, understated performance, Dishy uses the little screen time he has to make the viewer believe in this man who, despite his bad heart, struggles to hold down jobs day and night to sustain his family. Constantly exhausted, he manages, with patience and perspective, to deal with the family's daily crises.

Finally, Silverman does a capable, straightforward job with the role of the film's main character: The fact that he is unable to make the character come fully alive can largely be attributed to the character's conception on the page. This portrait, as written, of Eugene as an ordinary, wisecracking Jewish kid, is handled by Silverman with intelligence and good humor, especially the self-conscious awkwardness of that torturous time of life. A problem arises because the audience is aware that this is not simply an ordinary wisecracking Jewish kid: He is an ordinary wisecracking Jewish kid who is going to grow up to be the single most popular writer in the American theater. Was there really nothing, one keeps thinking, that set the young Neil Simon, even at that age, apart? Even if one is not expecting Stephen Dedalus transported to Brooklyn, there is no sense of a young writer's necessary loneliness or isolation; no hint of scars inflicted, the healing of which required the balm of art; no sense of a unique vision being formed, of previously unnoticed life illumined; no sense of an anger, or a sorrow, or a guilt, that drove a vision to be shared.

Regrettably, *Brighton Beach Memoirs* is a film that, unlike Simon's best work, gives no shock of recognition in its laughter and exposes no nerves in its tears. At no point in this work does one doubt that everything will come out all right in the end.

As sympathetic as one wants to be to Eugene, essentially one is left with a main character who, when surrounded—in the wake of the Great Depression—by the real, human problems of those who love him the most, has as his overriding concerns seeing women without clothes and being clever.

For all the nostalgia and good humor, the film paints a disturbing portrait of Eugene's self-absorption, becoming all the more disturbing when one recalls that this is a portrait of an artist as a young man. Either the author of *Brighton Beach Memoirs* is unconsciously suggesting that the facile repartee of egocentric self-absorption constitutes the chief quality responsible for eventually rendering his hero the most successful playwright of his time, or Neil Simon deserves a more sensitive biographer.

Dorn Hetzel
Mary Lou McNichol

Reviews
Films in Review. XXXVIII, March, 1987, p. 172.
Los Angeles Times. December 25, 1986, V, p. 1.
Macleans. C, January 5, 1987, p. 20.
The New Republic. CXCVI, January 26, 1987, p. 26.
New York. XX, January 19, 1987, p. 77.
The New York Times. December 25, 1986, II, p. 20.
The New Yorker. LXII, January 26, 1987, p. 24.
Variety. CCCXXV, December 17, 1986, p. 18.
The Wall Street Journal. December 23, 1986, p. 18.
The Washington Post. December 25, 1986, p. C1.

CHILDREN OF A LESSER GOD

Production: Burt Sugarman and Patrick Palmer; released by Paramount
Pictures
Direction: Randa Haines
Screenplay: Hesper Anderson and Mark Medoff; based on the play of the
same name by Medoff
Cinematography: John Seale
Editing: Lisa Fruchtman
Production design: Gene Callahan
Art direction: Barbara Matis; set decoration, Rose Marie McSherry
Makeup: Ann Brodie
Costume design: Renee April
Choreography: Dan Siretta
Sound: Richard Lightstone
Music: Michael Convertino
MPAA rating: R
Running time: 119 minutes

Principal characters:

James Leeds	William Hurt
Sarah Norman	Marlee Matlin (AA)
Mrs. Norman	Piper Laurie
Dr. Curtis Franklin	Philip Bosco
Lydia	Allison Gompf
Johnny	John F. Cleary
Glen	Philip Holmes
Cheryl	Georgia Ann Cline
Danny	William D. Byrd
Tony	Frank Carter, Jr.
William	John Limnidis

If the destiny of the film version of *Children of a Lesser God* were to have
been simply to open quietly and close quickly, certainly no one would have
been astonished. The project did, after all, have more than the usual number of production minefields through which its creators had to tiptoe. True,
its marquees could boast the featuring of male lead William Hurt in his first
outing since his Academy Award-winning performance in *Kiss of the Spider
Woman* (1985). On the other hand, here was a substantially altered adaptation of an award-winning Broadway play, under the supervision of a first-
time feature-film director, with a newcomer in the pivotal female lead,
backed up by a cast of supporting actors and extras drawn largely from a
community of hearing-impaired nonprofessionals, featuring an extensive

amount of signing by one character while another character provides a simultaneous translation for the audience. Despite all this, the film went on to gain five Academy Award nominations including Best Picture, Best Actor (William Hurt), Best Actress (Marlee Matlin, the eventual winner), Best Supporting Actress (Piper Laurie), and Best Adapted Screenplay (Hesper Anderson and Mark Medoff).

This adaptation of Mark Medoff's play *Children of a Lesser God* takes as its inspiration the particular communication problems related to deafness, a subject that has been treated before on film. The film, however, is unique among similarly themed efforts—which include *Johnny Belinda* (1948), *The Miracle Worker* (1962), and *The Heart Is a Lonely Hunter* (1968)—in that only hearing-impaired artists were employed to portray hearing-impaired characters, and sign language was used integrally and extensively throughout the film. In addition, many of the prints released to theaters were captioned—that is, subtitled in English—in an effort to accommodate hearing-impaired viewers, a target audience which in the United States alone totaled more than fifteen million at the time of the film's initial release. Yet, the film steers clear of well-intentioned parochialism by universalizing the subject in a way that allows the conflicts dramatized to do double duty—both as consciousness-raising commentaries on the particular problems inherent in any relationship involving a hearing-impaired person and as insights into the general barriers encountered in all intimate relationships. In so doing, Burt Sugarman and Patrick Palmer have fashioned an unabashedly romantic, liberatingly sexual, and deeply moving melodrama about the love affair between a hearing teacher of the deaf and a deaf young woman, a couple whose battle for control within their relationship stands metaphorically for all such counterproductive confrontations.

The play on which the film is based was conceived in the mid-1970's, written by playwright Medoff for Phyllis Frelich, a deaf actress who had performed for the National Theatre of the Deaf. Frelich starred in the play on Broadway opposite John Rubinstein, and both won Tony Awards, as did the play itself. Burt Sugarman, who secured the motion-picture rights to the property, was joined by Patrick Palmer, who had produced two other stage-play adaptations for the screen—*A Soldier's Story* (1984) and *Agnes of God* (1985). The final choice for director of the property, which had been passing from producer to producer, director to director, screenwriter to screenwriter, and actor to actor for several years, was Randa Haines, an experienced television director (episodes of *Hill Street Blues*, the incest-themed telefilm *Something About Amelia*, 1984) with no feature films to her credit.

Haines decided as her first priority to translate Medoff's screenplay into one that would work cinematically. Although the film is a relatively seamless cinematization of the play, it eschews one of the play's thematic thrusts, one serviced onstage by a political subplot dealing with fair-employment rights of the hearing impaired. Haines jettisoned this component—to Medoff's apparent dismay—to protect the film's romantic, emotional spine. Thus, Medoff and Haines did not find it possible to collaborate, abandoning the attempt after one meeting.

Another major obstacle facing Haines was the fact that the central character, Sarah, never speaks, using American Sign Language (ASL) throughout the film. Thus James, the teacher, must not only speak his own lines but also must translate hers from sign language to speech so that the hearing audience can understand what is being said.

Still another problem was how to shoot the film: As the film centers on a relationship between two people only one of whom speaks, the director and cinematographer were confronted with a unique problem in that the camera could focus in only one direction at a time—if the film were to be anything more intimate than a monotonously static medium two-shot of Sarah and James, who must always be in eye contact, conversing. Thus *Children of a Lesser God* is shot largely from the perspective of a hearing-impaired person, relying primarily on full-face close-ups of speakers speaking their lines and medium shots of characters signing, their hands fully in the frame. The film also has atypically frequent patches of what might be called intense quiet, conveying the contrast between sounds and silence. In addition, related technical problems in matching and editing sequences were more acute than in the typical film—for both actors and technicians—because of the need for synchronizing signing and oral translation.

The latter responsibility fell squarely on Hurt's performance as James Leeds, in which he spends much of the film reciting both parts of a dialogue between two talkative characters. Thanks to Hurt's naturalness and the early exposition, the device works with almost miraculous effectiveness and unself-consciousness—so seamlessly is it woven into the tapestry of the film and so immediately is it accepted by the audience.

With the maritime province of New Brunswick, Canada, standing in for the coast of Maine, where the narrative is set, the film's credits appear over picturesque shots of a fog-enshrouded, seagull-escorted river crossing. Leeds, here to teach deaf students speech and language skills, has arrived at the Governor Kittridge School for the Deaf.

In his initial interview with the school supervisor, Dr. Curtis Franklin (Philip Bosco), Leeds is warned not to try to "change the world." Still, he attempts immediately to convey to his students his philosophy that everyone—even the totally deaf—should attempt to speak. He also espouses this view in his attempt to break through to Sarah Norman (Marlee Matlin), a striking graduate of the school who has stayed on campus to work as a cleaning woman. The combination of Sarah's physical attractiveness with her refusal to learn to speak or even read lips compels James to pursue her in headlong, headstrong fashion. Before long, they consummate their relationship and soon thereafter move in together, and as the relationship deepens, so do the inevitable conflicts, as each tries to dictate the style of communication within the bond.

The film's extraordinary emotional resonance is greatly enhanced by the effectiveness of young veteran Hurt and newcomer Matlin in their individual roles as well as the palpable sexual chemistry between them. The fact that actors Hurt and Matlin found themselves falling in love in well-publicized life-imitating-art fashion during filming surely did nothing to damage the film's verisimilitude or its marketing.

Children of a Lesser God provided the stage-trained Hurt with his seventh feature-film role. Haines pursued Hurt for the part, despite his reputation for being difficult, because of the complex technical demands of the project and the likelihood that his stage training would enable him to handle the nonstop flow of Leeds's dialogue. (As Leeds says at one point, he became a speech teacher because he likes to hear himself talk.) The skillful Hurt manages the difficult task of performing the dialogue of several major characters by varying his delivery in ways that maintain total clarity, using his newly learned sign language throughout the film, and never for an instant trying the audience's patience despite his onscreen dominance.

The Oscar-winning Matlin in her film debut is the film's most spectacular "find." Nearly totally deaf since the age of eighteen months, Matlin began acting in a deaf theater troupe at age eight. Unlike Sarah, the character she plays, the actress hears marginally with the help of a hearing aid and speaks relatively well. The producers spent six months searching for the right actress to play the feisty, sensuous Sarah. After contacting institutions for the deaf in the United States, Canada, the United Kingdom, and Sweden, and rejecting thousands of photographs—including one of Matlin—the producers saw a videotape of a Chicago stage production of *Children of a Lesser God* in which Matlin appeared as Lydia, Leeds's most enthusiastic pupil.

As an unfamiliar screen presence, Matlin is no less than a revelation. Combining unself-conscious beauty, riveting intensity, and boundless sensual energy, she lights up the screen without a sound. Sarah's vigorous, urgent signing, in counterpoint to the languid, rhythmic, exhilarating swimming she does in an early scene in the film, beckons the viewer so that he finds himself responding to her just as does Leeds.

If the film's other characters remain peripheral and undeveloped, if the original play's political text fails to emerge onscreen, if the denouement seems formulaic, all such aesthetic compromises or oversights spring from the same impulse. That is, the filmmakers' wish to buttress and highlight the film's central relationship between a hearing person and a deaf person, two people in love who must find a livable plateau somewhere between signing and lip-reading—by learning how to listen.

Bill Wine

Reviews

Commonweal. CXIII, September 26, 1986, p. 500.
Films in Review. XXXVII, December, 1986, p. 619.
Glamour. LXXXIV, November, 1986, p. 207.
Los Angeles Times. October 3, 1986, VI, p. 1.
Macleans. XCIX, October 20, 1986, p. 74.
The New York Times. CXXXI, October 3, 1986, p. C5.
Newsweek. CVIII, October 20, 1986, p. 77.
Time. CXXVIII, October 20, 1986, p. 95.
Variety. CCCXXIV, September 24, 1986, p. 13.
The Wall Street Journal. CCVIII, October 9, 1986, p. 32.

COBRA

Production: Menahem Golan and Yoram Globus; released by Warner Bros.
Direction: George P. Cosmatos
Screenplay: Sylvester Stallone; based on the novel *Fair Game*, by Paula Gosling
Cinematography: Ric Waite
Editing: Don Zimmerman
Production design: Bill Kenney
Art direction: William Skinner and Adrian H. Gorton; set decoration, Robert Gould
Makeup: Leonard Engelman and Steve Abrums
Costume design: Tom Bronson
Sound: Michael Evje
Music: Sylvester Levay
MPAA rating: R
Running time: 87 minutes

> *Principal characters:*
> Marion (the Cobra) Cobretti ...... Sylvester Stallone
> Ingrid .... Brigitte Nielsen
> Gonzales......................... Reni Santoni
> Detective Monte .... Andrew Robinson
> Captain Sears .... Art La Fleur
> Chief Halliwell .... Val Avery
> Commander Reddesdale .... Bert Williams
> Night Slasher.................... Brian Thompson
> Stalk .... Lee Garlington
> Supermarket killer .... Marco Rodriguez
> Cho .... John Herzfeld
> Television reporter................ Christine Craft
> Dan .... David Rasche

Cobra belongs to a group of motion pictures known as vigilante justice films, in which a larger-than-life protagonist single-handedly annihilates an enemy that threatens American ideals or the American way of life. Though films with this theme can be traced back to *Dirty Harry* (1971) and *Death Wish* (1974), a proliferation of such films were produced in the 1980's, including *Missing in Action* (1984), *Missing in Action 2* (1985), *Invasion U.S.A.* (1985), *Commando* (1985), *Rambo: First Blood Part II* (1985), *Delta Force* (1986; reviewed in this volume), and *Raw Deal* (1986). Most of these films originally focused on subjects involving the Vietnam War, but themes involving vigilante justice (a term that is essentially an oxymoron) have been adapted to other genres as well. *Cobra*, written by and starring Sylvester Stallone, follows the conventions of the police procedural tale, with some important differences.

Most of the vigilante films have been popular and financial successes, although not critical ones. Reviewers have attacked these films for their use of excessive violence to annihilate the enemy, who is usually depicted in a simplistic manner. *Cobra*, which was not made available to critics for advance screenings, was expected to be as popular with audiences as its predecessors—if not more so—because of its unprecedented 2,131-print launch by Warner Bros. and because opening weekend ticket sales grossed an impressive $15 million. Almost immediately, however, ticket sales plummeted, and, though the film did not lose money, it was not one of the summer's top box-office draws. In addition, critics were extremely harsh regarding the film's promotion of vigilante justice and violence as the answer to urban problems. Though there are undoubtedly a number of reasons that *Cobra* was not the smash success that was expected, part of the answer could lie in the the way in which the conventions of the police tale were altered somewhat to accommodate a vigilante justice theme. For audiences, the changes seem to have been particularly disturbing ones.

The narrative pattern of the police procedural tale is a straightforward one and is familiar to audiences from its frequent use on television. The story begins with a crime or series of crimes, of which the audience is often aware before the authorities are. This sets up a narrative device used throughout the story whereby the audience is privy to more information than are the police. The protagonist and his partner (sometimes police officers on the beat but more often detectives) are not assigned to the case at first and are either forbidden to get involved or are merely assigned to it by chance. The case quickly becomes more personal to the protagonist, as someone he knows, or will soon become involved with, is victimized by the antagonist; eventually, the detective begins to neglect his personal life. Often, the detective and/or his partner meet the antagonist halfway through the investigation but are unable either to apprehend him or hold him. At this point, the protagonist often receives a stern warning from his superiors. The warning can be either to work harder because there is pressure on the department to catch the criminal, to keep his working methods within the boundaries of the law, or to avoid becoming obsessed with the case. The protagonist continues to follow the trail, which eventually leads to a direct confrontation with the criminal leader, usually in an urban environment. The villain is then destroyed.

Cobra follows this narrative pattern fairly closely, with several significant variations. After a pretitle sequence in which Stallone recites some harrowing crime statistics, the film opens with a sniper (Marco Rodriguez) terrorizing shoppers in a supermarket in Los Angeles. After some deliberation, the authorities on the scene declare that this is a job for Marion Cobretti, also known as the Cobra (Stallone), of the Zombie Squad, a section of the Special Weapons and Tactics (SWAT) team that is assigned tasks too dangerous for most policemen. As Cobra rides to the scene in his 1950 Mercury coupe, shots of a large group of neo-Fascist urban terrorists chanting and waving their weapons imply to the audience that there is more going on than meets the eye. As more about the sniper is revealed, it becomes apparent that he is a member of this neo-Fascist group. Cobra enters the supermarket and, in a lengthy scene, does battle with the sniper, blasting him over the meat counter in one of the film's few clever—but gruesome—moments. As the sniper's lifeless body lies across the hamburger packages, the audience can see that he is literally "dead meat." This is a visual image that echoes Cobra's tough-sounding dialogue.

One of the leaders of this band of urban terrorists is a psychopath who has committed a series of brutal murders in the Los Angeles area. Thinking that he is a lone serial killer, the police have dubbed him the "Night Slasher" (Brian Thompson). After witnessing two more slayings of random victims, the audience is aware that he is not working alone. Another leader of this neo-Fascist group is a woman who exerts some control over the Slasher by goading him or spurring him on so that he will strike again. The audience soon learns that the woman is Officer Stalk (Lee Garlington), a policewoman with the Los Angeles Police Department. Her access to the police computers and inside information has helped keep the authorities completely off the trail. It is Cobra who first suggests that the Slasher is not working alone, but Detective Monte (Andrew Robinson), a more liberal police officer who despises Cobra's tactics, ridicules this suggestion and refuses to allow Cobra to become involved in the case.

After a beautiful young model named Ingrid (Brigitte Nielsen) witnesses the Slasher and three henchmen murdering a young woman, she herself is assaulted by the neo-Fascist group but survives the ordeal. Meanwhile, Cobra's superiors decide that with his knowledge of "all the sickos in town," Cobra and his partner, Detective Gonzales (Reni Santoni), should be assigned to the case, despite the objections of Detective Monte. Ingrid is attacked again in her hospital room, and Cobra, his partner, and Stalk are assigned to protect her. Cobra's involvement with the case becomes more personal, as he is attracted to Ingrid. After a third attempt on Ingrid's life, Cobra's superiors admonish him for failing to protect their only witness, not realizing that Stalk is responsible for revealing police information to the urban terrorists. Cobra decides that Ingrid would be safer away from Los Angeles, and he, Gonzales, and Stalk drive her north.

Stalk reveals their location to the terrorists, and the group follows them to a final confrontation in a small town upstate. After his partner is wounded, Cobra becomes a one-man army, single-handedly killing dozens of terrorists.

In an empty but fully operational steel foundry, Cobra fights one-on-one with the Slasher, finally hanging him on a rotating hook that sends him into a blast furnace to burn alive. The visual analogy is a simple one: Cobra, like God, has punished the evildoer and sent him straight to Hell.

A few plot deviations and variations in character types point out some differences between *Cobra* and the typical police procedural tale. For example, at some point the protagonist usually neglects his personal life to pursue the case, causing him to have feelings of doubt or anguish. Cobra, however, seems to have no personal life. Though some shots of his home are shown, it seems to be merely an extension of his office. A computer that is able to match fingerprints with criminal dossiers, plus a number of files, takes up much of the living space. The few times Cobra is shown at home, he is working on his computer or doing maintenance on his personal arsenal. By all indications, the character of Cobra exists only to fight crime. This idea is reinforced by the lack of personal information about Cobra, which is needed to explain why he is so ruthless, violent, and dispassionate.

Furthermore, though the character of Cobra shares a number of traits with the typical detective of the police drama, there are some important differences. Like the police detective, he is highly skilled in the use of weapons and equipment, but he is not highly intelligent. He is also a common man committed to maintaining the status quo, not a member of the higher classes who solves crimes for his own interest. Also, like many fictional policemen, he takes great delight in renouncing authority figures—judges, lawyers, other detectives, and some of his superiors. The typical police detective, however, is committed to the letter of the law, even when adhering to it prevents him from quickly apprehending the antagonist. Any deviation from the law either causes him personal anguish or gets him in trouble with his superiors. Cobra, on the other hand, frequently steps outside the boundaries of the law to destroy criminals—he sneers at their civil rights, employs brutal methods to stop them, and makes little effort to bring them in, assuming that he will have to stop them by killing them. Indeed, he has no qualms about violating the law, telling one criminal, "This is where the law stops, and I begin." While detectives in most police tales would be reprimanded for such behavior, Cobra's actions, for the most part, are commended by his superiors.

Another major difference in the narrative pattern of *Cobra* is that it is the criminals who are pursuing the protagonist. Usually it is the detective who follows a series of clues to trail the criminals. Cobra searches for few clues in the film and does no tracking of the terrorist group. He seems to be on the defensive throughout the narrative, acting as a protector of the public rather than as a detector of information. At the end, Cobra, his partner, and Ingrid are actually trying to escape from the terrorists as the neo-Fascist organization chases them north. The relentless pursuit of Ingrid by these urban terrorists suggests that crime and criminals are an evil force that exists for no rhyme or reason, an idea reinforced by the lack of details about the ultimate goal or purpose behind the group's reign of terror. The result is the presentation of the criminal as frighteningly insane and inhuman, which is supposed to justify Cobra's violent methods. Throughout, the film tries to suggest that all crime and criminals are a part of this inhuman evil force, from the opening shot where Stallone recites statistics involving day-to-day crimes such as robbery, rape, and murder to Cobra's speech to Ingrid about how judges (and the system) allow criminals to go free and that is why she is being pursued by these urban terrorists. The equation of common criminals and lawbreakers with a lunatic neo-Fascist group is a simple-minded view of crime and its causes.

Cobra has manipulated the conventions of the police procedural tale to accommodate a vigilante justice theme. By changing the character of the police detective into a ruthless one-man crime stopper, however, who has no personal life or family, and by altering the narrative pattern to suggest that criminals are part of an evil force in constant pursuit of the public, the film has taken the sympathy and humanity out of the genre. American genre films have always been used to express and externalize society's fears and concerns. Every era has found a type of film that expresses the conflicts peculiar to it: The trauma of the post–World War II era, for example, was externalized in the dark, pessimistic visuals of *film noir*, while the gangster films of the Depression years focused on the dark side of the American success story. The vigilante films of the 1980's offer a simplistic, cathartic solution to problems that seem uncontrollable to the general populace— whether the failure in Vietnam or the rising crime rate. *Cobra*'s story line and character types, however, have taken the vigilante justice theme to its disturbing extremes.

Susan Doll

Reviews
Films and Filming. September, 1986, Number 384, p. 32.
Films in Review. XXXVII, August, 1986, p. 429.
Los Angeles Times. May 24, 1986, V, p. 1.
The New Republic. CXCIV, June 23, 1986, p. 26.
The New York Times. CXXXV, May 24, 1986, p. 11.
Newsweek. CVII, June 9, 1986, p. 78.
Time. CXXVII, June 2, 1986, p. 80.
Variety. CCCXXIII, May 28, 1986, p. 17.
Video. X, January, 1987, p. 71, p. 71.
The Wall Street Journal. CCVIII, May 27, 1986, p. 24.
The Washington Post. May 24, 1986, p. C1.

THE COLOR OF MONEY

Production: Irving Axelrad and Barbara De Fina for Touchstone Films, in association with Silver Screen Partners II; released by Twentieth Century-Fox
Direction: Martin Scorcese
Screenplay: Richard Price; based on the novel of the same name by Walter Tevis
Cinematography: Michael Ballhaus
Editing: Thelma Schoonmaker
Art direction: Boris Leven; set decoration, Karen A. O'Hara
Makeup: Monty Westmore
Music: Robbie Robertson
Title design: Dan Perri
MPAA rating: R
Running time: 119 minutes

> *Principal characters:*
> "Fast" Eddie Felson .... Paul Newman
> Vincent .... Tom Cruise
> Carmen .... Mary Elizabeth Mastrantonio
> Janelle .... Helen Shaver
> Julian............................ John Turturro
> Orvis .... Bill Cobbs
> Grady Seasons.................... Keith McCready
> Earl .... Robert Agins
> Amos........................... Forest Whitaker
> Moselle .... Bruce A. Young

The Color of Money is a sequel to Robert Rossen's 1961 film *The Hustler*, a stylish treatment of the dark and smoky world of pool halls, cheap hotels, and bus-station coffee shops at dawn; it is a world of imminent violence populated by loners, losers, misfits, corrupt "big shots," and one smiling young pool hustler filled with hopes and dreams. These "mean streets" (in Raymond Chandler's now-famous phrase) are familiar turf to Martin Scorcese, who has achieved both fame and *auteur* status through his compelling depiction of such dark urban landscapes. *The Color of Money*, while it is a sequel which inherits characters, locales, and attitudes from the original, allows Scorcese to explore themes which have been central to much of his best work. From *Mean Streets* (1973) to *After Hours* (1985), Scorcese has been obsessed with the offbeat outsiders existing in urban subcultures. His themes are frequently violence, loneliness, frustrated hopes and dreams, and, above all, the need for some kind of salvation in a dark, corrupt world.

Scorcese's films often treat human actions in ritual terms, whether it be the rites of religion (*Mean Streets*), the boxing ring (*Raging Bull*, 1980), or the pool hall. *The Color of Money* examines the rituals of the pool game in a world which is vastly different from that of *The Hustler*. The rules of the game have changed, as have codes of behavior and concepts of honor.

    The Color of Money begins twenty-five years after the action of *The Hustler*. "Fast" Eddie Felson (Paul Newman in both films), having given up his hotshot career as a pool hustler for ethical reasons, has become a liquor salesman who puts morals aside for the fast dollar, peddling cheap liquor to be rebottled with pricey labels. During the opening sequence, there is a voice-over, spoken by Scorcese himself, about the relative virtues of the nine-ball game as opposed to straight pool. Nine-ball is the new game; it is quicker, easier, and allows luck to play a greater part in the outcome. Eddie watches a spunky young kid named Vincent (Tom Cruise) play the game with power and skill, but without the savvy to make money. Eddie experiences a kind of flashback to his own past in watching Vincent and quickly decides to become his manager. He first approaches Vincent's girlfriend, Carmen (Mary Elizabeth Mastrantonio); she is tough and streetwise in contrast to the naïveté of Vincent, whom she met while robbing his parents' home. In a series of short sequences, Eddie courts the favor of the young couple: He takes them to dinner, impressing them with his bejeweled hands, natty clothes, white Cadillac, and big bankroll; he offers to give Vincent his prized "Balabushka" (an expensive cue stick which in the world of pool is the equivalent of King Arthur's sword); and he even goes to see Vincent at his job at Child World. This location underlines Vincent's childlike nature— the overgrown kid who imagines that skill in playing video games can get him into West Point. Finally, at Vincent and Carmen's apartment, Eddie convinces them to join him on the road. He will stake Vincent, as they work their way through small-time pool halls to the big showdown in Atlantic City.

    The odyssey of this unlikely trio through a kind of lower-depths subculture of Midwestern pool halls allows Scorcese and cinematographer Michael Ballhaus to return to the tawdry *film noir* world of *The Hustler*. Implicit throughout this journey is the idea that things have drastically changed since Eddie inhabited this world more than two decades ago—a theme which is central to Walter Tevis' novel upon which the film is based and one of the few elements retained from it in the film. Their first stop is the Lincoln Room Tap, which Eddie remembers as a real classic but which has now become a warehouse. The image of old furniture piled high where the pool tables once stood, ironically juxtaposed to Eddie's excitement and expectancy, perfectly expresses the death of the world that he remembers. They move on to other dark and seedy pool halls in run-down, garbage-strewn neighborhoods until they arrive at Chalkies, a place where Eddie is known and remembered. All of these scenes, shot on location around Chicago, are evocative *film noir* atmospheres, with darkly muted browns and greens dominating in smoky rooms with only the low-hung ceiling lamps illuminating the spaces.

Each stop on the journey is a part of the process of Vincent's education and Eddie's own reeducation. Vincent must learn not to ease up on anyone when money is involved and also learn to lose judiciously to raise his odds. Vincent is at first an unwilling pupil; he cannot subdue his natural instincts and desire to show off, to win. Warned against beating Moselle, the best player at Chalkies, Vincent breaks into a spectacular game with dance moves and Samurai-like flourishes of the Balabushka between his perfect shots. (This set piece, with the song "Werewolves of London" in the background, is photographed like a rock video and exploits Cruise's vitality as a performer; it echoes his lip-synch performance in the earlier *Risky Business*, 1983.) Vincent learns that in winning he has actually lost, and from this point onward, he quickly moves from innocence to experience. In his next encounter with a top money player, Grady Seasons (Keith McCready), Vincent allows himself to suffer a humiliating defeat, but only after Carmen threatens to leave him if he does not "lay down." Throughout this sequence, which condenses several hours into a few minutes, the camera circles around, and slow dissolves overlap the faces of Vincent and Eddie. Eddie seems lost in a meditative trance, remembering his own joy in playing the game. In the following scene, Eddie returns alone to Goodie's to hustle, and the supreme hustler of the past gets hustled by a young black man named Amos (Forest Whitaker). Vincent and Carmen have joined him and witness the humiliating defeat. Profoundly embarrassed and self-doubting, Eddie tells them to continue alone, that there is nothing more that he can teach them. This emotional confrontation takes place, significantly, on the narrow stairwell of the pool hall; the stairway image underlines the crisscrossing patterns of Eddie's fall with Vincent's rise. From this point until the final reunion of the three principals in Atlantic City, the film's narrative focuses on Eddie's rejuvenation, his search for a new sense of integrity—his "redemption."

Time becomes radically compressed in the last quarter of the film, as Eddie prepares for his comeback. In a series of brief montages and jump-cuts, Eddie is seen practicing his game (realizing that perhaps faulty vision is an obstacle), swimming to tone his body, and finally being fitted for eyeglasses. One particular cut in this sequence clearly underscores Eddie's movement toward salvation and Scorcese's penchant for religious imagery. Eddie dives into a swimming pool and pushes up from the center to emerge triumphantly from the water as a close-up of his face is held in a freeze frame. The still shot of his face dissolves into a tightly framed shot of an optician's lens-testing apparatus. The striking juxtaposition of these images is not casual; the immersion in water becomes a new baptism, and the sight-testing apparatus suggests a new vision which is both physical and spiritual. The significance of this imagery is further emphasized by the ponderous classical music used at this point in the film: first an organ piece and then a selection from Giuseppe Verdi's *Nabucco*. Eddie now tests his new vision, his new spirit, in a series of money games with the best player at Chalkies. More than a dozen games are played in short scenes separated by dissolves. The passage of several days is indicated by the disappearance and reappearance of daylight outside the front windows. The exchange of money punctuates each of these scenes indicating the winner of the game, with Eddie finally winning more than losing. He is back and ready for the Nine-ball Tournament.

The vulgarly opulent milieu of Atlantic City's casinos is a fitting locale for the concluding actions of Scorsese's film. It is an atmosphere that reeks of materialism, of venality. The tournament room itself is a kind of cathedral to money. When Eddie first enters the empty tournament hall, it is seen from his point of view; the camera tilts slowly down from the vaulted, cathedral-like ceiling to the tables below to the accompaniment of church-like organ music. This shot is suggestive of Eddie's spiritual development. Later, Eddie reencounters Vincent and Carmen, who are involved in negotiating a bribe for Vincent to throw a game for fifteen hundred dollars. They have learned too well from their mentor; the innocent have been fully corrupted. Vincent knows how to go for the big money. Even his looks and clothes have changed: The boyish charm and vitality are gone. The narrative inevitably leads to a final confrontation between teacher and pupil, and when Eddie and Vincent must play each other in the tournament, Vincent loses. Shortiy thereafter, Carmen brings Eddie an envelope of money—his share of the take, since Vincent had "dumped" the game to raise his odds later. In a classic Frankenstein reversal, the monster created by Eddie has turned on his master. Eddie refuses the money and demands of Vincent his best game. The film ends as this final game begins, with another freeze-frame on Paul Newman's face—smiling in moral victory.

The Color of Money has been the most commercially successful film in director Martin Scorsese's checkered and always highly personal career. Doubtless, a major part of the success and appeal of the film lies in the performance of Paul Newman as Eddie, a performance which won for Newman his first Oscar as best actor after six previous nominations. The pairing of Newman (emblem of the old Hollywood) and Cruise (emblem of the new Hollywood) was not merely financially motivated. The very *personae* of the two actors lend depth and credence to the clash between worlds that Scorsese explores in the film. The youthful, dynamic, but easily corrupted character that Cruise plays, as well as the slick, fast game of nine-ball, in which only the last ball counts, can be seen as emblematic of commercial cinema generally; the last ball is the "bottom line." (It is significant that Scorcese himself reads the introductory passage relating the ascendancy of nine-ball.) The older and now unfashionable game of straight pool, in contrast, is variously described during the film as requiring greater skill and intelligence—the precision of a surgeon. Scorcese's film, in a sense, maintains a delicate balance between these two games, or two kinds of cinema.

Stylistically, the film has much in common with the slick rat-a-tat of the nine-ball game. Many of the pool-playing sequences are shot in a highly kinetic style, using fast montages, swirling camera moves, speeded-up film, tracking shots that follow the movement of balls across the table, and tricky dissolves and superimpositions. The techniques used in these sequences have the vitality of the rock-video form and certainly aim at a commercial youth-oriented appeal. Yet they also help to express the psychology of the players, the excitement of the game itself. The frequent ceiling shots of the pool table, and the speeded-up film effect, also emphasize the geometric patterns of the game and artfully abstract it. Much more of the film, however, is shot in a style more typical of Scorcese's work, with relatively long takes and languorous camera movement. This is especially true during the early scenes establishing the relationship between Eddie and the young couple and during their journey through run-down Midwestern pool halls.

The Color of Money is, admittedly, lighter and treads less dangerous ground than other more intensely personal films by Scorcese such as *Mean Streets*, *Taxi Driver* (1976), *Raging Bull*, or even *The King of Comedy* (1983) and *After Hours*, and it is his most commercially viable film as a star vehicle. Nevertheless, within the confines of a formula film and its sequel format, the film clearly displays Scorcese's personal stamp: his interest in ritualized behavior, ethical codes, and religious imagery, and the director's distinctive visual style. The screenplay by Richard Price, to which both Scorcese and Newman made contributions, improves on Tevis' own sequel in one respect. The introduction of the character of Vincent, absent in the novel, re-creates the older-manager/younger-hustler relationship at the center of the earlier film. While both films end with a sense of moral redemption, there is a significant difference between the two. Whereas in *The Hustler* it is the young man, "Fast" Eddie Felson, who finally leaves the corruption of the game and walks away from his depraved manager and easy money, in *The Color of Money* it is the now-older manager Eddie who is purified at the end. In Scorcese's more cynical conclusion it is the once-innocent young man, Vincent, who is finally corrupted, seduced by the materialism of the times—won over by the very color of money.

John Orlandello

Reviews

Films in Review. XXXVIII, January, 1987, p. 41.
Life. IX, November, 1986, p. 181.
Los Angeles Times. October 17, 1986, VI, p. 1.
The Nation. CCXLIII, October 25, 1986, p. 418.
New York. XIX, October 27, 1986, p. 128.
The New York Times. October 26, 1986, II, p. 19.
The New Yorker. LXII, November 3, 1986, p. 132.
Newsweek. CVIII, October 13, 1986, p. 68.
Sports Illustrated. LXV, November 3, 1986, p. 11.
Time. CXXVIII, October 20, 1986, p. 95.
Variety. CCCXXIV, October 8, 1986, p. 21.
The Washington Post. October 17, 1986, p. B1.

CRIMES OF THE HEART

Production: Freddie Fields; released by De Laurentiis Entertainment
Group
Direction: Bruce Beresford
Screenplay: Beth Henley; based on her play of the same name
Cinematography: Dante Spinotti
Editing: Anne Goursaud
Art direction: Ken Adam
Music: Georges Delerue
MPAA rating: PG-13
Running time: 105 minutes

> *Principal characters:*
> Lenny MaGrath.....................Diane Keaton
> Meg MaGrath......................Jessica Lange
> Babe MaGrath......................Sissy Spacek
> Doc Porter.........................Sam Shepard
> Chick Boyle.........................Tess Harper
> Barnette Lloyd..................David Carpenter
> Old Granddaddy...................Hurd Hatfield
> Zackery Botrelle ....Beeson Carroll
> Lucille Botrelle ....Jean Willard
> Uncle Watson ....Tom Mason
> Willy Jay.........................Gregory Travis
> Annie May Jenkins ....Annie McKnight

Beth Henley's plays have generally concentrated on the eccentricities of
character engendered by a Southern gothic milieu. In her less accomplished
work, the fey and the bizarre have tended to dominate, suggesting the now-
stereotyped stage Southerner of Tennessee Williams' less talented imitators,
but in *Crimes of the Heart*, familiar patterns of behavior are animated by a
wit and insight which recall the powerful psychic forces present at their origin. Using two of the most substantial—and universal—symbols of Southern mythology, the home and the family, Henley's play centers on three sisters who unite in a time of crisis to rediscover and share their mutual love
and individual strengths. The reunion is precipitated when Babe MaGrath
(Sissy Spacek) shoots her husband, Zackery Botrelle (Beeson Carroll),
ostensibly because she "doesn't like his stinking looks," but actually because
of his brutality, cruelty, and coldness. Meg MaGrath (Jessica Lange) returns
from Los Angeles to offer support but is driven home as much by her failure to find work as an actress as by her desire to help. Lenny MaGrath
(Diane Keaton) has never left home, being the victim of shyness, insecurity,

and suppressed desire. To compound the situation, Lenny's pet horse has just died after being hit by a bolt of lightning and the sisters' social-climbing harridan of a cousin, Chick Boyle (Tess Harper), has made claims on the MaGraths' ancestral home when the family patriarch, "Old Granddaddy" (Hurd Hatfield), suffers a stroke which will lead to his death.

The mixture of elements is reminiscent of many comically absurd stories about heartland rustics in which lovable characters display their oafish peculiarities for the amusement of a patronizing, supposedly sophisticated audience, but Henley has assumed the risks inherent in the material to show that the darkly comic behavior of her characters does not detract from their humanity. In addition, she is concerned with the indigenous American idea that idiosyncrasy is an important aspect of individuality and that nonconformity is often the only means of rebellion available to preserve the integrity of a person regarded as a misfit.

Each of the MaGrath sisters is defined by her relationship to her home (and her hometown) and by her responses to the invitations of romance to leave the apparent safety of home and family. Babe has denied her true instincts by marrying a powerful, ambitious lawyer, a pillar of the community who is interested only in the semblance of family respectability while he pursues his own pleasure. While this is a match sanctioned by society, it is totally wrong for Babe, a free-living sprite who must follow her whims or suffocate. It is not surprising that in a moment of despair, she tries to emulate her mother's suicide by smothering herself in an oven, underscoring the confinement of her spirit. Meg has bought the standard pop-culture fantasy that the most beautiful girl in town must fulfill her destiny in Hollywood and has left the true love of her youth, Doc Porter (Sam Shepard), in a futile quest for fulfillment in a strange, empty place. Lenny MaGrath has been misinformed by superstitious idiots that she is not fit for men because she has a "shrunken ovary," but in reality the only thing shrunken is her self-esteem. Surrounded by bric-a-brac, dusty fabric, and mildewed magazines, the pathetic detritus of her wasted life, she has parodied the true concept of home by turning her habitation from a refuge into a prison. Her withdrawal from the world is approaching irreversibility.

At the beginning of the narrative, all three sisters have ignored the wisdom of their heart and are following life patterns directed toward misery and desperation. Babe's defiant gesture shatters the pattern and brings the women back to the place of their initial departure into the world, where they try to reorganize their lives. The house where they gather is the central setting of the film (and the sole set of the play), and as they wander through its rooms and passages, reexamining their lives and themselves, history and memory are folded into the present, the living past intertwined with their failures in present time. Following the surge of excitement of their reunion, the three women begin to replay their interrelationship, recapitulating its development as they moved from a natural acceptance of one another in childhood to the competition, rivalry for attention, and destructive baiting of an emerging young womanhood. At first, Henley's determination to detail the petty bickering and emotional assaults the women employ tends to be irritating, but the strain and frenzy of their conversation are necessary for an understanding of their past failures to connect. As the women share experiences and disappointments, a new and more active support for one another emerges, based on a real understanding of each sister's needs and their genuine mutual affection. The warmth generated by their willingness to help one another through pain is earned as each of them transcends the prison of the self by recognizing how family can mean more than social status or an appeal to ancient glory.

Although the film concentrates on the interaction of the MaGraths, the motivating factor for each sister is her romantic desire to live fully in the world, a desire objectified by the men in their lives. These are not women who aspire to a genteel, withered spinsterhood of bogus respectability. The failure of their efforts, however, is based on the real crime they have committed—the denial of the heart's truth. Babe needs a man who will delight in her eccentricity, sweet decency, openness, and sharp if off-beat intelligence. Although her future remains uncertain, the possibility of such a relationship is glimpsed in her talks with the young, modest, but deceptively capable lawyer who defends her (David Carpenter). Meg's night of non-sexual rapture with her old flame, Doc Porter, is like a return to her true mate, thus a return to the promise of her beauty and honesty, although his marriage will probably prevent a permanent union. Nevertheless, one senses a kind of restoration of hope for both people. Lenny's plight is the most poignant because she has none of the outgoing exuberance of the other two. She desperately needs to be encouraged, and her one promising encounter with a man was ruined by her inability to extend the relationship. Even though the man seemed interested, she has been rendered incapable of recognizing when someone actually appreciates her camouflaged qualities. She is the "different" one, sensitive, poetic—whose "heart is a lonely hunter"— the girl who might write plays about her life but who will never be a cheerleader or prom queen and who cannot accept her own insight that such cheap popularity does not matter. In the region of the rural South where the play takes place, she is easily discouraged by conventional attitudes about beauty and desirability, and she substitutes being a good sport, caring for the house, and raising plants and animals for the things she really yearns for but feels she will never have. One of the film's best moments shows Lenny inspired to action through the urging, love, and good humor of her sisters.

Essentially, the strengths of the play are the strengths of the film. Additions to the script are mostly distracting or irrelevant (such as the flashback depicting Babe shooting her husband), and the action outside the house is primarily filler. Meg's night with Doc Porter is important, but the presentation of the scene seems ordinary and familiar. Bruce Beresford, the able director of such disparate films as *Breaker Morant* (1980) and *Tender Mercies* (1983), does not really have a special feel for the material. The camera work inside the house is fussy and uneven. Beresford has, however, done fine work with his players in his other films (Edward Woodward and Bryan Brown in *Breaker Morant* and Robert Duvall and Tess Harper in *Tender Mercies*), and in this case, he has some extraordinary players with which to work.

The decision to cast Spacek, Lange, and Keaton as the three sisters involved some risk since their star power might have overwhelmed the characterizations, but the film probably could not have been made without their box-office lure. Critical responses to their work in the film has been widely disparate, ranging from Vincent Canby's contention that they are "three individually splendid collectively lost actresses" to Pauline Kael's claim that their work is so good that it should qualify for the first collective Academy Award. While Canby is correct in noting that Beresford uses "larger-than-life close-ups" too often, all three actresses offer intelligent performances designed to emphasize one another's development of character in a kind of progressive mutual revelation of psychological reality. Because each sister's character is so distinct, familial connections must be established convincingly, especially since there is so little to suggest physically that the three actresses might be sisters. The manner in which Spacek, Lange, and Keaton accomplish this feat is both a testament to their craft and a demonstration of the kind of ensemble acting essential for a drama of this sort. They employ such basic techniques as a concentration on reaction to one another's speeches, a casual but significant physical rapport, a common sense of humor, secret signals hinting at a private language, and shared gestures that suggest their common origins. Their responses to one another are stronger than their responses to anyone outside the family, and by the conclusion of the film, their intimacy is authentic.

Individually, each part is also crucial to the film's success. Spacek is perfect as Babe, the part seemingly written with her in mind. Although she can do other things well, her gift for spontaneous action and her ability to make any act seem innocent and appropriate has never been used better. She is the incarnation of Babe's free-spirited, openhearted outlook. Lange also seems ideal as Meg. Her honest sexuality and forceful demeanor combine with a touching vulnerability to make her desires very appealing. Keaton has much the hardest time with her portrayal of Lenny, but she manages to suggest an inner-directed, worried woman who is more attractive than either she herself or the world is ready to acknowledge. Keaton's sharp-edged urban aura of other films is absent, and while her accent is not particularly

Southern, especially in contrast to the country tones of Lange and Spacek, it is not obviously non-Southern either, and this is sufficient.

The film is not an exceptional translation of the play, but it does permit the qualities of Henley's drama to emerge largely intact in cinematic form.

Leon Lewis

Reviews

Commonweal. CXIV, January 30, 1987, p. 55.

Films in Review. XXXVIII, March, 1987, p. 170.

Horizon. November, 1986, p. 33.

Los Angeles Times. December 12, 1986, VI, p. 1.

The New Republic. CXCVI, February 2, 1987, p. 26.

The New York Times. December 12, 1986, p. C17.

The New Yorker. LXII, December 15, 1986, p. 81.

Newsweek. CVIII, December 22, 1986, p. 75.

People. December 15, 1986, p. 12.

Time. CXXVIII, December 22, 1986, p. 70.

Variety. CCCXXV, December 10, 1986, p. 14.

The Washington Post. December 12, 1986, p. C11.

"CROCODILE" DUNDEE

Origin: Australia
Released: 1986
Released in U.S.: 1986
Production: John Cornell for Rimfire Films Limited; released by Paramount Pictures
Direction: Peter Faiman
Screenplay: Paul Hogan, Ken Shadie, and John Cornell
Cinematography: Russell Boyd
Editing: David Stiven
Art direction: Graham (Grace) Walker; set decoration, Martin O'Neill
Costume design: Norma Moriceau
Music: Peter Best
MPAA rating: PG-13
Running time: 105 minutes

> *Principal characters:*
> Michael J. (Mick) "Crocodile"
> Dundee . . . . Paul Hogan
> Sue Charlton . . . . Linda Kozlowski
> Walter Reilly . . . . John Meillon
> Richard Mason . . . . Mark Blum
> Sam Charlton . . . . Michael Lombard
> Con . . . . Ritchie Singer
> Donk . . . . Steve Rackman
> Nugget . . . . Gerry Skilton
> Duffy . . . . Terry Gill

This simple little comedy, as its makers call it, has not only wooed more audiences than any other film ever "down under," but it was also the industry's biggest fall hit in history (more than $100 million was earned by the end of the year) and the most profitable foreign film ever shown in the United States. *"Crocodile" Dundee*'s appeal in Australia is more immediately explicable: Star Paul Hogan is Australia's everyman, a working-class hero and top-rated television comic and commentator so trusted and so popular that Australia's prime minister trembles if Hogan's satirical cutting edge gets too sharp. One need not look too far from home, however, to explain the film's appeal to Americans.

First, there is the dearth of competing films that are witty, grown-up, sane, and reasonably subtle. A second factor is America's current love affair with Australia—a passion whose flames Hogan himself has fanned: His volunteered and unpaid 1984 commercials for the Australian Tourist Commission were the most successful tourist advertisements ever shown on American television. There is also America's own continual self reexamination, which helps partly to explain its fascination with the world's biggest island. On the one hand, *"Crocodile" Dundee* reworks one of the oldest possible ideas for a plot: Michael J. "Crocodile" Dundee (Paul Hogan), a bushman from the outback, is the innocent abroad, a country boy loose in slick, sophisticated New York, whose fresh and commonsensical observations create an anthropological anatomization of that strange creature, the American city dweller (subspecies New Yorker). Dundee's ancestors are Gulliver and Mark Twain's Connecticut Yankee as well as those the film itself acknowledges—Tarzan, Davy Crockett, and Jungle Jim. On the other hand, the outback itself is in a sense the new American frontier: It is not surprising that the Americanization of Australia should include appropriating its harsh empty spaces as new locales for old myths. Thus, Mick Dundee is also a descendant of the Western hero, the rough-diamond individualist at one with the savage land.

The story opens with journalist Sue Charlton (newcomer Linda Kozlowski) persuading her editor and fiancé, Richard Mason (Mark Blum), to let her prolong her Australian trip in the hope of tracking down a living legend of the Northern Territory—a man who wrestled a giant crocodile to death and, injured, survived a week of crawling through the bush to safety. Thus it is that Sue, a modern film heroine—that strange combination of brainy careerism and beautiful legs—who descends on Walkabout Creek (one notes the generic Australian name) to meet Dundee and retrace his dangerous journey through the bush. She awaits him at the hotel bar, where some unsavory specimens of Australian manhood named Con, Donk, Nugget, and Duffy (Ritchie Singer, Steve Rackman, Gerry Skilton, and Terry Gill) are demonstrating the local drinking and dueling rituals.

Into these aggressive revels strolls a man with a six-inch Bowie knife at his hip and a stuffed crocodile under his arm. In swift succession he sweeps Sue off her feet and into a dance, tricks beer-bellied Donk into dousing himself with Fosters lager, and knocks out a troublemaker. The journalist, visibly taken with his physical charms (a lithe, tanned body set off by "bush couture" clothes), asks about his name—"Crocodile" Dundee. Unabashed, he replies that it makes him more colorful for the tourist business—a line that underscores this opening sequence's self-conscious and self-critical edge.

"Crocodile" Dundee's charm, however, rests partly on the fact that it manages to poke fun at its own conventions. Having gained the audience's trust with these initial gestures toward some kind of realism and honesty, it next proceeds—though still always with tongue perceptibly in cheek—to present Mick Dundee as an archetypal hero, a natural man par excellence. This is a man who can nonchalantly kill a deadly snake whilst descanting poetically on the aborigines' relationship with the land, hypnotize a massive water buffalo, frighten off a gang of drunken "cowboy" kangaroo hunters (one kan-

garoo appears to shoot back—a comic surprise for both cowboys and audience), and, finally, rescue his companion from the jaws of death. This last escapade is a perfect example of how the film blends heroics with understated comedy (the latter makes the former that much more palatable). Understandably stung by Dundee's old-fashioned and sexist remarks about the outback as "man's country," Sue sets off for the next landmark alone. Not surprisingly, she soon needs help. Luckily, Dundee has secretly remained close to her to be able to render it chivalrously. She strips to a sexy swimsuit to cool herself in the creek—and, as Dundee creeps nearer to keep her in view (for both protective and voyeuristic purposes), he momentarily stuns himself on a low branch, disappearing from the frame with muffled four-letter imprecations. The next minute, however, he leaps to the rescue when a crocodile attacks. Underpinning this swift transition from comic to heroic is the audience's acceptance of yet another age-old convention: The strong hero becomes a fool under the influence of woman and of love.

It is this budding love that inspires Sue to ask Dundee to explore the urban jungle of New York and him to accept the offer. In this second, slightly longer half of the film, the cross-cultural gags are more subtle and more telling than one might expect—best of all is a chauffeur's conversion of the hood ornament of his limousine into a boomerang to help Dundee escape attackers—and some aspects of the plot are more ridiculous than one might have hoped: Sue's father (Michael Lombard) is a magnate who owns the newspaper for which she works, and his overdone stereotype functions as an entry route into upper-class society. Dundee's initial experiences of the city include fear of being eaten by an escalator, experimenting with an uncomfortable extra lavatory (a bidet, pronounced to rhyme with "g'day"), and arriving by a process of logical deduction to the idea that if so many people choose to live together they must be very, very friendly. The first blow to this theory comes when Mason and Sue take Dundee to an expensive Italian restaurant. The sneering and jealous city-bred editor attempts to humiliate his guest by asking that he order—in Italian. Dundee then does what most people would love to do in such a situation, were they not "civilized": He knocks his rival cold. As his tour of the city continues, Dundee dismisses other odd cultural behaviorisms with the same assured directness—he takes the quickest, frankest route to ascertaining whether an overdressed transvestite is or is not male, concludes that sniffing cocaine must feel like stuffing a blowfly up one's nose, and opines that only those who do not have "mates" need psychiatrists: In Walkabout Creek, he adds, if someone has a problem, he tells his mate Wally (John Meillon), then Wally tells everyone else, and that is how it gets out in the open. As such double-edged jokes suggest— city alienation is a self-induced problem, Wally and company are shameless small-town gossips—Dundee provides the audience with double delights.

As the innocent abroad, he lets one laugh at him; as the fast-learning, wise-cracking urban explorer, he makes one laugh with him.

"Crocodile" Dundee deftly weaves together romantic and comic threads: As Sue shows Dundee the city, he shows her more and more reasons to fall in love with him. At the film's completely unsurprising close, Sue has become sickened by the snobbish artificialities of Mason, the husband-to-be endorsed by her family. Meanwhile, however, Dundee has disappeared down the subway, intent on "going walkabout" to help himself forget her. The two are finally united in a scene wherein Manhattan inhabitants behave tribally. Separated by a dense crowd on a noisy subway platform, Sue and Dundee's declarations of love are entrusted to a variety of native bearers, who reword and reenact the messages as they pass them down the line.

This is a respectable scenario, then, but no more than that. Yet several factors make *"Crocodile" Dundee* a very satisfying and successful comedy-romance. One is technical: It features excellent cinematography. Hogan, his manager and producer John Cornell, and first-time director Peter Faiman, who among them have decades of collaboration in television work, but no experience in cinema, very wisely employed cinematographer Russell Boyd (*Picnic at Hanging Rock*, 1975, and *Gallipoli*, 1980). He both does justice to the light and landscapes of the outback and adds some witty touches of his own to the city scenes—reducing urban man to physical fragments, isolated hands, hurrying feet, and worried faces. Also, the film is much more than a vehicle for Hogan's talents. Its dialogue is sometimes razor sharp, its self-restraint unusual and admirable, its juggling with archetypes and conventions deft, and its structure well balanced, allowing for some mental input from audiences too often denied any cerebral pleasure. Thus, the audience is invited to compare and contrast aboriginal tribal dances with Manhattan parties, body paint with punk hairdos, and fried lizard with hot dogs (both taste vile but sustain life). Nor does the cerebral pleasure stop there. *"Crocodile" Dundee*'s social commentary has a cutting edge, evidence of its makers' long involvement with current-affairs broadcasting and journalism—Cornell, for example, was once the London editor of an Australian newspaper—and it touches on a surprising number of serious issues. The most important of these is perhaps the other side to the individualism coin: a lack of concern about the larger world. The only time Dundee protests anything is when he is thrown out of a pub. One laughs, but one might well also be inclined to agree with Sue that issues such as the arms race are everyone's business.

What above all has made *"Crocodile" Dundee* a hit is Hogan himself. He is both an original comic talent and a plausibly macho hero. Both these qualities have much to do with his working-class background: Hogan needed the muscles as a bridge rigger in Sydney, and his humor, like a stand-up comic's at a working-men's club, is by turns aggressively masculine and dryly self-deprecatory. What perhaps makes it most attractive to American audiences (reared on Woody Allen's angst and other comic neuroses) is its quality of uncomplicated certainty: He and God, Dundee asserts with disarming candor, would be "mates." *"Crocodile" Dundee* is a pleasant mixture—of the lightweight and the serious, the conventional and the original—and is probably unrepeatable. One hopes that Hogan will not succumb to the temptation to do a sequel—can one imagine a happily married Dundee? Having conquered this (American) New World, he should move on to others.

Joss Marsh

Reviews
Chicago Tribune. September 26, 1986, p. CT7.
Christian Herald. CIX, December, 1986, p. 36.
Films in Review. XXXVII, December, 1986, p. 622.
Los Angeles Times. September 25, 1986, VI, p. 1.
Macleans. XCIX, October 13, 1986, p. 60.
The New York Times. CXXXVI, September 26, 1986, p. C6.
Newsweek. CVIII, October 13, 1986, p. 91.
Philadelphia Magazine. LXXVIII, January, 1987, p. 51.
Time. CXXVIII, October 13, 1986, p. 107.
The Washington Post. September 26, 1986, p. 25.

CROSSROADS

Production: Mark Carliner for Columbia Pictures
Direction: Walter Hill
Screenplay: John Fusco
Cinematography: John Bailey
Editing: Freeman Davies
Production design: Jack T. Collis
Art direction: Albert Heschong; set decoration, Marvin March
Special effects: Larry Cavanaugh
Makeup: Michael Germain
Costume design: Dan Moore and Barbara Siebert-Bolticoff
Sound: Bonnie Koehler
Music: Ry Cooder
MPAA rating: R
Running time: 96 minutes

> *Principal characters:*
> Eugene Martone . . . . Ralph Macchio
> Willie Brown . . . . Joe Seneca
> Frances . . . . Jami Gertz
> Scratch . . . . Robert Judd
> Scratch's assistant . . . . Joe Morton
> Jack Butler . . . . Steve Vai
> Lloyd . . . . Dennis Lipscomb
> Bartender . . . . Harry Carey, Jr.
> Sheriff Tilford . . . . John Hancock
> Dr. Santis . . . . Allan Arbus
> Beautiful girl/dancer . . . . Gretchen Palmer
> Pawnbroker . . . . Al Fann
> O. Z. . . . . Wally Taylor
> Robert Johnson . . . . Tim Russ
> John McGraw . . . . Tex Donaldson
> Young Willie . . . . Guy Killum

Crossroads is a film about linkage: between youth and old age, North and South, black and white, urban and rural cultures, classical music and blues. The film, rich in background and textures, links a quest story of youthful ambition and a picaresque narrative of episodic adventures on the road. The road leads to the Mississippi Delta, taking the characters to the spiritual homeland of the blues.

The blues was born out of experience, reflecting the pain and hardships of rural blacks. The central character, Eugene Martone (Ralph Macchio), a music student from Long Island, is as far removed from that experience as a young man could be. He is a prodigy at the Juilliard School of Music who has mastered the techniques of classical guitar, but his ambition is to play blues guitar and to recover the music, the unknown thirtieth song, of legendary blues songwriter Robert Johnson.

The young man's quest begins with an old man named Willie Brown (Joe Seneca), who, Eugene suspects, played blues harmonica under the name Blind Dog Fulton and knew Robert Johnson at one time. Willie Brown is a security patient (said to have killed a man years before) at an old folks' home where Eugene works. At first Willie refuses to confirm his musical identity to the prying white boy, but eventually Willie strikes a deal with the young man: He will help Eugene discover the blues if Eugene will help him escape from the home. He claims to know about the mysterious song Eugene is seeking. A good-natured comic escape is therefore staged, bus tickets are purchased for Memphis, and their adventures on the road begin.

Eugene is able to bankroll a bus ride to Memphis, but from there onward, they have to make their way as best they can down the Mississippi Delta. Eventually, they link up with Frances (Jami Gertz), a teenage runaway headed for Los Angeles and a career in dance. Ultimately, however, Willie Brown cannot provide what Eugene is after: the lost song.

Willie's motive for escaping the nursing home is to get back to the Delta crossroads where, as a young man, he sold his soul to the devil, old Scratch (Robert Judd), in return for the talent to play the blues and the rewards of fame and success. After several comic encounters with redneck ruffians along the road, Willie gets to his destination. At the crossroads, another bargain is struck in which Willie's soul will be saved if "Lightnin' Boy" Martone can beat the devil's disciple Jack Butler (Steve Vai), a rock and roller, in a music contest. It is here that John Fusco's script, based in part on the writer's own experiences, becomes farfetched in its attempt to work a bizarre rock and roll variant on the Faust legend. In the play-off, Eugene's classical training and technique pay off, and he manages to save old Willie's soul. This final exploitive musical spectacle, set in an outlandishly satanic nightclub, in which authentic blues gives way to electric rock and roll in a manipulative fantasy, stretches plot logic and musical virtuosity to the outer limits.

The formula governing *Crossroads* vaguely resembles Ralph Macchio's earlier hit, *The Karate Kid* (1984), by teaming up a boy with an older man who represents a different culture and then putting the boy into the position of mastering a skill that belongs to that culture. Reviewers argued that the chemistry was better with Pat Morita in *The Karate Kid*, but Joe Seneca does make the character of Willie Brown seem authentic.

Up until the final metaphysical contest for Willie's soul, the film succeeds on its own terms. "Blues ain't nothin' but a good man feelin' bad," Willie tells Eugene, and the idea that a man cannot play the blues until he has lived them seems reasonable enough. Recording artist and folk music interpreter Ry Cooder coordinated the agreeable score and played the blues guitar, supported by Sonny Terry and John "Juke" Logan on blues harmonica. Cooder had previously worked with director Walter Hill on *The Long Riders* (1980), *Southern Comfort* (1981), and *Streets of Fire* (1984).

Cult director Walter Hill built his reputation on films that might best be described as teen fantasies and films set in the rural South. Hill's biggest hit to date, however, has been *48 HRS.* (1982), which earned more than one hundred million dollars. When Hill took chances with *48 HRS.*, he was clearly repaid with tremendous popular success. He again took chances with *Crossroads*, but in this instance, the experiment lacked a significant payoff. *Variety* argued that *Crossroads* was "too slick, contrived and faintly ridiculous," protesting that it was even potentially insulting to make a picture about the blues and black culture and then have the climax depend on a music contest between two white boys, one of them presumably trained in classical music.

Music, however, is the heart of the film. Joe Seneca began his career as a nightclub singer, who once toured with Pearl Bailey. In *Crossroads*, Seneca, who is also a songwriter, collaborated with Ry Cooder on "Willie Brown's Blues," performed with Frank Frost and The Wonders, a Delta Blues group from Greenville, Mississippi. The roadhouse blues provided by Frank Frost and his musicians is the most authentic component of the film, a kind of music, according to Ry Cooder, that "scarcely exists anywhere outside of central Mississippi." The musical progression is from classical guitar in the film's overture to the Delta Blues to the heavy metal rock of the musical finale. Most of the film was shot on location in and around several Mississippi towns, which adds to the atmosphere surrounding the music.

In his *Newsweek* review, David Ansen accurately described the script of *Crossroads* as an "uneasy hybrid." It is a musical odyssey and a Southern road picture, driven by teen ambition and seasoned by blues and rock and roll. The convolutions of the plot are bizarre, unexpected, and farfetched. It is somewhat surprising that Fusco's script could have won first place in the 1984 Nissan Focus Award competition, lacking, as it does, a logical ending, but this is compensated for by the fine plot line, which makes Willie Brown a tour leader through blues backroads, taking the boy into difficult situations that will over time teach him to understand the blues through exposure to hard times.

The strength of *Crossroads* is that it is loaded with talent and has more music to offer than a Bayou jukebox. The film was also praised for Ralph Macchio's simulations of guitar playing and for his acting in the first part of the film. Finally, Seneca's acting, the Deep South atmosphere, and Ry

Cooder's music create enough excitement to make the film an interesting experiment, if not a popularly successful one.

James M. Welsh

Reviews
Los Angeles Times. March 14, 1986, VI, p. 1.
Macleans. XCIX, March 17, 1986, p. 78.
The New York Times. CXXXV, March 14, 1986, p. C15.
The New Yorker. LXII, April 21, 1986, p. 100.
Newsweek. CVII, March 24, 1986, p. 77.
Teen. XXX, March, 1986, p. 48.
Variety. CCCXXII, March 12, 1986, p. 14.
The Wall Street Journal. CCVII, March 13, 1986, p. 28.
The Washington Post. March 24, 1986, p. C3.
Washingtonian. XXI, April, 1986, p. 69.

THE DECLINE OF THE AMERICAN EMPIRE
(LE DÉCLIN DE L'EMPIRE AMÉRICAIN)

Origin: Canada
Released: 1986
Released in U.S.: 1986
Production: René Malo and Roger Frappier for corporation Image M and M Ltée and the National Film Board of Canada; released by Cineplex Odeon Films
Direction: Denys Arcand
Screenplay: Denys Arcand
Cinematography: Guy Dufaux
Editing: Monique Fortier
Art direction: Gaudeline Sauriol; set decoration, Charles Bernier
Costume design: Denis Sperdouklis
Sound: Richard Besse
Music: Francois Dompierre
MPAA rating: no listing
Running time: 95 minutes

> *Principal characters:*
> Dominique . . . . Dominique Michel
> Louise . . . . Dorothée Berryman
> Diane . . . . Louise Portal
> Danielle . . . . Geneviève Rioux
> Pierre . . . . Pierre Curzi
> Rémy . . . . Rémy Girard
> Claude . . . . Yves Jacques
> Alain . . . . Daniel Brière
> Mario . . . . Gabriel Arcand

Denys Arcand's *The Decline of the American Empire* is a most unsettling piece of cinematic entertainment. No film in recent memory has explored the mechanics of sexual conquest in more feverish detail or displayed so little sympathy for the flawed human beings who are obsessed with and ultimately destroyed by the pursuit. The film examines the current sexual mores of a segment of the French-Canadian bourgeoisie, as represented by a group of academics who have gathered for a weekend at a pastoral lakeside cottage. These include a passel of men, most of whom are hurtling inexorably toward middle age, as well as their various wives, lovers, and friends. The unrelentingly bawdy talk springs from the fact that they have almost all had intimate relations with one another. This is the main source of the film's risqué humor; it also becomes the source of a massive amount of pain, anger, and recrimination—all of which emerges in the final reel. Praised by reviewers in the United States as a highly sophisticated sexual farce, *The Decline of the American Empire* received the Critics' Prize at the 1986 Cannes Film Festival, as well as the New York Film Critics' Award for Best Foreign Language Film. It also received an Academy Award nomination in the same category (losing to the Netherlands' *The Assault*; reviewed in this volume). Despite this critical acclaim, the film is, like its characters, ultimately debauched and debased. The characters' sexual exploits, which seem to cover every point on the spectrum of experience, are initially amusing in a naughty kind of way, reminiscent of *Tom Jones* (1963), but they become repellent as the characters' fundamental callousness, cynicism, and lack of regard for one another's feelings are made known. Indeed, in its relentless examination of the seedy underside of sexual freedom, the film is virulently anti-sex.

The film's grandiose title is derived from a book which has been written by one of the female characters. Called *The Changing Concepts of Happiness*, it describes the rampant pursuit of personal gratification as a major symptom of society's decline. There are two rather snide and self-serving notions at work here: The first is that the pursuit of sexual pleasure, in and of itself, should be considered a symptom of personal as well as societal degradation; the second is that the United States is a modern-day Babylon, leading the world in the ways of immorality and licentiousness and presumably dragging its Canadian neighbors into the maw of doom. Arcand's smug indictment of America as the root of all evil tends to deflect the viewer's attention from the truth of the matter, which is that the characters who appear in the film are largely to blame for their own misery.

The Decline of the American Empire is very much an ensemble piece. It is focused upon a group of intellectuals who are united by their shared academic concerns as well as by their obsession with sexual conquest. The first half of the film crosscuts rather neatly between the four men and the four women, each of whom has a salacious tale to tell. In a rather facile reversal of sexual stereotypes, the women are shown at a Montreal health club, pounding and pummeling themselves into shape, while the men cavort at home, bemoaning the sexual status quo as they prepare a sumptuous trout dinner. In these early scenes, Arcand demonstrates an unfailing sense of sexual equality, insofar as the women seem as jaded and fundamentally bored with sex as the men. The bawdy anecdotes are set forth at a breathless pace, as if to compensate for everyone's inward sense of satiety and unease.

Rémy (Rémy Girard), a rather jolly, rotund history professor, appears to be the kingpin of the men's side of this group: He talks more than anyone else and brags incessantly about his compulsive sexual interludes. Like the others, he tends to drape all this blather in supposedly profound intellectual observations ("Lying is the basis of all love affairs."). It is revealed, through the endless flow of conversation and a few well-placed flashbacks, that Rémy has enjoyed liaisons with most of the women in his immediate circle, as well as with a nearly endless parade of nubile young students. Pudgy and ridiculously self-important, he is nearly impossible to imagine as an irresistible figure, yet on and on he goes, describing in gratuitous detail the precise mechanics of sexual conquest—the most useful come-on lines, the agonies of seduction, and the nuisance that is caused by emotional attachments. The men around him take this all very seriously, since they are engaged in similar activities.

Pierre (Pierre Curzi) is also an erstwhile philanderer, but, unlike Rémy, he seems to derive no real pleasure from the experience. He operates from a hopelessly cynical point of view and is infinitely bored and self-pitying. Like a male version of the character played by Gunnel Lindblom in Ingmar Bergman's *The Silence* (1963), Pierre engages in sex as though it were a kind of psychic pain-killer. Alain (Daniel Brière) is a relatively innocent graduate student who still believes in the old ideals of romantic love and commitment. Appalled by his elders' lack of human sensitivity, he is ridiculed and chastised and soon made to imitate their behavior. Claude (Yves Jacques) is the token homosexual in this gathering. Depicted as being fundamentally passive and incapable of a lasting relationship, Claude derives his greatest thrill from participating in anonymous sex. He plays the rather thankless role of host and father confessor to this randy assemblage, tolerantly enduring their endless, self-congratulatory talk, while he himself remains an outsider with no perceptible romantic attachments. Vaguely admired by the other men because of his good looks and unbridled sex life, Claude is finally set up as a scapegoat figure and made to pay for his sexual transgressions in a way which the others are spared.

The women in this amazingly talkative group have their own tales to tell. Louise (Dorothée Berryman) is the most conventional of the four. She is married to Rémy, the philandering history professor, and spends much of her time working to maintain her trim figure. Outwardly, she is the most pleasant of the women, the least cynical and tormented, but this attitude results from the fact that she is unaware of her husband's assignations—his conquests include her two best friends. Conventional in her sexual tastes, Louise's only real exposure to the world of illicit sex consists of a middle-class orgy which she once attended with her husband. The event is revealed in flashback, and Louise's warmly self-deprecating account of the ridiculous event provides the film with one of its most engaging moments.

Louise is joined by Dominique (Dominique Michel), a feminist historian who has recently written the treatise from which the film's title is derived. Aging, embittered, and secretly vindictive, it is Dominique who destroys everyone else's illusions about the harmless nature of their sexual activities.

Diane (Louise Portal) has recently divested herself of a boorish husband and found true fulfillment in an unsettling, sadomasochistic relationship with Mario (Gabriel Arcand), a sullen, leather-jacketed drug dealer. Manifestly bored with more conventional forms of sex, Diane waxes ecstatic about her new fling, eagerly displaying the whip marks on her back and making such self-deluded pronouncements as,"The power of the victim is incredible." Rounding out this group is Danielle (Geneviève Rioux), a comely young graduate student who has been working part-time in a local massage parlor that allows illicit sexual activities. It is there that she first meets Pierre, engaging him in a dialogue on millennialism while she works. According to the standards of this motley group of philanderers, this amounts to an auspicious beginning.

There are a few genuinely humorous set pieces in the early stages of the film. The women's gleeful repartee reaches its height with Dominique's spontaneous proposal for a kind of Michelin guide to the male species, in which men are accorded stars for their phallic endowments and sexual performance. The women also revel in comparing the sexual attributes of men according to nationalities and ethnic groups. The men at the cottage are also most amusing when recounting the embarrassing difficulties of sexual seduction and conquest—the inanities of dance-floor conversation ("I love the films of Woody Allen!"), the anxieties of sexual performance. It is only later, after the characters' fundamental cynicism has been revealed, that the proceedings turn decidedly sour.

The foremost achievement of *The Decline of the American Empire* lies in its masterful use of dialogue to communicate ideas. Not since *My Dinner with André* (1981) has there been a film whose appeal rests so exclusively on an endless barrage of talk—and the talk here is admittedly intelligent and incisive, even though one is appalled by the characters' blighted view of the world. By contrast, Arcand sets little store by the conventions of dramatic structure: The film is rather like a cinematic variation on *La Ronde* (1950), in which the best and worst qualities of the characters are revealed as they recount their sexual exploits. The climax of the film consists of Dominique's gratuitous disclosure, at the height of the elegant dinner party, that she has had sex with Rémy, as have numerous other women. This revelation destroys Louise, who has consistently nurtured illusions of domestic bliss and mutual sexual contentment in the course of her fifteen-year marriage. Presumably bored by Louise's smug pronouncements concerning the lasting value of marriage and monogamy, Dominique deliberately chooses to obliterate her friend's happiness. Dominique's cruelty is shocking and insufficiently justified by the film's events, but her revelation assures that Louise— the only member of this circle who retains any illusions about the lasting nature of commitment—will quickly join the ranks of the cynical and the self-involved, thus becoming doomed to seek solace in a never-ending series of transient and unsatisfying sexual encounters.

It is consistent with Arcand's cynicism that Louise, who is the most conventional member of the group, should also be made to seem the most ridiculous and painfully self-deluded. According to Arcand's rather skewed moral schema, she becomes an emblem for the legions of women who willfully deceive themselves about their husbands' affairs. At the end of the long and lacerating evening, each member of the circle pairs off and retreats to the boudoir with his or her current flame, while Louise is left downstairs to cry. She is consoled by Claude, the long-suffering homosexual. The pairing of Louise and Claude is highly intriguing, since they presumably have the least to gain from the endless round of heterosexual conquest. It is here that Claude's position becomes most fully understood: He is that recurring, convenient, and disposable figure—the homosexual confidant. Reduced to a thankless role, Claude remains isolated and miserable. He becomes a kind of masochistic court jester to a group of heterosexual philanderers, the details of whose affairs could not interest him in the least.

Claude is quickly made distinct from the others, insofar as he seems to have no real friends of his own sexual persuasion or even a consistent sex partner. He is also the only member of the group whose sexual adventures result in perilous physical harm. At an early stage in the film, Claude is shown retreating to the bathroom, where he passes copious amounts of blood in his urine. This is presumably set forth by Arcand as an indication of acquired immune deficiency syndrome (AIDS)—though the presence of blood in the urine, in and of itself, is not a sign of the disease. It seems implausible, in this almost universally perilous age, that Claude should be the only member of the group for whom sexual activity has dangerous medical consequences.

Indeed, the characterization of Claude is the single most repellent aspect of Arcand's film. Passive, lonely, and self-isolated, Claude exists only to reassure the others that they are not so bad (they may be promiscuous adulterers and philanderers, but at least they are not gay). Claude's visual association with Louise—who becomes the film's other demoralized and powerless figure—reinforces this impression. The others may breathe a sigh of relief and cavort and carouse as much as they please, for Claude is ready and willing—and apparently doomed—to die for their sins.

It is this kind of exculpatory and simpleminded moralizing which undermines the appeal as well as the intellectual complexity of *The Decline of the American Empire*. Here is a film whose most reprehensible figures are allowed to get away with everything, while the relatively innocent are excoriated and exposed to ridicule. There is not much to complain about in regard to matters of performance or technical execution—the acting is genuinely fine, and the calm, pastoral compositions of cinematographer Guy Dufaux provide an excellent counterpoint to the moral chaos which pervades the scene inside the cottage—but these strengths do not compensate for the film's fundamentally nihilistic view of human relationships.

Plans are presently afoot to remake Arcand's film in the United States, retaining the basic premise of the original but using American actors and transplanting the action to an East Coast university setting (Paramount Pictures is originating the project; Arcand is being given the right of first refusal as director). It can only be hoped that the makers of the second incarnation will strive to create a film whose view of human relationships is not so mercenary. The worst aspects of Arcand's original—his ugly scapegoating of all of those who retain some illusion of belief in the ideals of romantic love and commitment, and his snide vilification of sexual outsiders—might be avoided or at least ameliorated in the American version. This is a doubtful prospect, however, since the kind of unrelieved cynicism which lies at the heart of *The Decline of the American Empire* presently seems remarkably in vogue among a vast segment of the American filmgoing public.

Karl Michalak

Reviews
Canadian Dimension. XX, December, 1986, p. 21.
Chicago Tribune. November 26, 1986, V, p. 3.
Los Angeles Times. November 21, 1986, VI, p. 1.
National Review. XXXIX, January 30, 1987, p. 61.
The New Republic. CXCV, December 8, 1986, p. 28.
The New York Times. September 27, 1986, p. 11.
The New Yorker. LXII, December 15, 1986, p. 85.
Newsweek. CVIII, November 17, 1986, p. 89.
Time. CXXIX, January 19, 1987, p. 70.
The Washington Post. December 25, 1986, p. C9.

THE DELTA FORCE

Production: Menahem Golan and Yoram Globus; released by The Cannon Group
Direction: Menahem Golan
Screenplay: James Bruner and Menahem Golan
Cinematography: David Gurfinkel
Editing: Alain Jakubowicz
Production design: Lucisano Spadoni
Art direction: Zviki Hen; set decoration, Ladi Wilheim
Special effects: John Gant
Makeup: Vitorio Biseo
Costume design: Tami Mor
Sound: Jerry Ross
Music direction: Paula Erickson
Music: Alan Silvestri
MPAA rating: R
Running time: 124 minutes

Principal characters:
Major Scott McCoy	Chuck Norris
Colonel Nick Alexander	Lee Marvin
Ben Kaplan	Martin Balsam
Edie Kaplan	Shelley Winters
Harry Goldman	Joey Bishop
Sylvia Goldman	Lainie Kazan
Father O'Malley	George Kennedy
Abdul	Robert Forster
Mustafa	David Menahem
Captain Campbell	Bo Svenson
Ingrid	Hanna Schygulla

The Delta Force is a docudrama about the real-life hijacking of a TWA plane in June, 1985. The plane was flown to Beirut, where the passengers were held for three weeks as secret negotiations took place to free them in return for 776 Palestinians held by Israel. During the ordeal, American viewers were treated to constant and sometimes surreal media coverage: The hijackers presented the hostages at press conferences and the pilot, Captain John Testrake, became something of a celebrity as he gave interviews from the cockpit.

The hijacking presented the first test of President Ronald Reagan's "get tough" rhetoric on terrorism. The news media wondered aloud whether Reagan would use the Delta Force, a classified army unit created under

President Jimmy Carter to rescue the American hostages in Iran. Yet such an operation was never possible: The hostages had been scattered throughout Beirut, United States intelligence in Lebanon was almost nonexistent, and, in any case, the Delta Force would have been grossly outnumbered in Beirut.

The Delta Force purports to give a fictionalized but accurate account of the hijacking, using captions throughout the film to effect a documentary style. *The Delta Force* begins with a precredit depiction of the disastrous Desert One mission to rescue the American hostages held in Iran during the last fifteen months of the Carter Administration. Major Scott McCoy (Chuck Norris) and Colonel Nick Alexander (Lee Marvin), who head the newly formed Delta Force, blame the disaster on the ill-conceived plans of the politicians in Washington, D.C. McCoy adds that he spent "five years in Vietnam watching them do the planning and us the dying," and promises to resign.

After the credits, the film jumps to Athens International Airport in 1985, where passengers wait to board the ill-fated flight. Two Jewish couples— Ben Kaplan (Martin Balsam), Edie Kaplan (Shelley Winters), Harry Goldman (Joey Bishop), and Sylvia Goldman (Lainie Kazan)—exchange pleasantries. When Father O'Malley (George Kennedy) passes in front of the Kaplans it is impossible not to recall Kennedy's role in the *Airport* films and Winters' role in *The Poseidon Adventure* (1972). In contemporary films, there is perhaps no more effective a way to make a viewer think "Don't get on that plane" than the sight of actors Kennedy and Winters waiting in line. After the parodic *Airplane!* (1980; reviewed in this volume) put an end to the disaster genre, however, one would also expect the well-known character actors to play against type. They do not.

Two Arabs, Abdul (Robert Forster) and Mustafa (David Menahem), also board the plane and hijack it just after takeoff. The film portrays the hijacking fairly accurately: The three United States Navy divers and the men with "Jewish sounding names" are separated, presenting a moral dilemma to the German purser, Ingrid (Hanna Schygulla), whom the hijackers force to help them. The plane flies to Beirut, then Algiers, and back to Beirut. One diver is shot and thrown to the tarmac. In Beirut, the male passengers are scattered throughout the city, while the pilots are kept on board. Other details evoke the TWA hijacking: Captain Campbell (Bo Svenson) bears a remarkable resemblance to his real-life counterpart, Captain Testrake; and the plane's logo, ATW, is a none-too-subtle variation of TWA.

After seventy minutes, the film rewrites history to show what would have happened if President Reagan had given the Delta Force free rein to attempt a rescue. The message is simple: Force and diplomacy can achieve the same results, with force being quicker and more glorious. The failure of Desert One is used here not to raise questions about the efficacy of force but instead, in conjunction with McCoy's reference to Vietnam, as an argument for military control over foreign policy. Thus far *The Delta Force* resembles *Airport* in its dramatization of the hijacking. Once the Delta Force packs its bags for the Middle East, the film begins to resemble *Missing in Action* (1984), a film also produced by Menahem Golan and Yoram Globus, cowritten by James Bruner, and starring and cowritten by Chuck Norris.

McCoy rejoins the Delta Force, which flies to Algiers before the hijacked plane can arrive there. The Delta Force is given the go-ahead after the women and children are released. The attack is stopped, however, after Ingrid informs Alexander that another six hijackers boarded the plane in Beirut. The Delta Force is then given carte blanche to mount a rescue mission from Israel. Using high-tech equipment, the Delta Force storms the two buildings where the hostages are being held.

Abdul and his troops escape the second building with the Jewish hostages, including a sympathetic Father O'Malley. Abdul plans to drive to Teheran, where the Ayatollah Ruhollah Khomeini has agreed to shelter them. McCoy chases after them on a motorcycle equipped with a machine gun and front- and back-firing missiles. In a scene that encodes McCoy as a mythic American hero, McCoy stops atop a hill just long enough to have the sun rise behind him. He then single-handedly stops the convoy, firing missiles at them until the other Delta Force members arrive. Abdul escapes in his white Mercedes-Benz to a nearby house, with McCoy promptly chasing after him and riding his motorcycle through a window and into the living room.

McCoy proceeds to exact revenge in a long, drawn-out, and exceedingly one-sided karate sequence. The fight sequence provides catharsis in two ways. First, Chuck Norris finally provides the payoff one expects from his films. Second, Abdul personifies the specter of international terrorism, which kept many Americans from traveling abroad in 1986. When McCoy fights hand-to-hand with Abdul, the audience has nothing less than a national revenge fantasy: America versus terrorism. Yet because the film never identifies the Arab hijackers as belonging to a specific political or religious faction within (presumably) Lebanon, the implication is that all Arabs are terrorists or terrorist sympathizers, an implication that denies the complexities of the Middle East. The tie-in with Khomeini, which did not happen in the real hijacking, adds to the dualism. The film, in portraying the rescue as one of force, also ignores the fact that the United States received help from Syria as well as Israel in freeing the hostages.

After McCoy kills Abdul, the Delta Force storms the plane, which they and the hostages then use to escape. The film ends with the hostages greeting their families, while the Delta Force members carry their one casualty to their plane and take off. Nondiegetic mournful music covers over the sound of the celebration. The focus is squarely on the Delta Force and not the hostages, and certainly not the consequences of a rescue that (unrealistically) decimates Beirut.

Director Golan also directed *Operation Thunderbolt* (1977), which depicts the famous Israeli raid on Entebbe airport and was nominated for an Oscar as Best Foreign Film. The actual events of the TWA hijacking strained relations between the United States and Israel and further undermined the government of Israeli Prime Minister Shimon Peres. Rather than address the issues and problems raised by the hijacking, Golan recast it as an American-style *Operation Thunderbolt*. At one point, Alexander tells an Israeli commando that "now it's our turn," making an oblique reference to the raid on Entebbe airport.

Paradoxically, *The Delta Force* derives its visual pleasure from covert actions that by their very nature are not to be seen or evaluated by the public. That these actions can be seen only in the form of entertainment further removes them from public debate. For example, the public is largely unaware that the Delta Force took part in the invasion of Grenada, failing in its mission and sustaining casualties, the number of which is classified. Also, since people tend to forget those events that are reported on the evening news, *The Delta Force* might easily pass for fact, perverting an already shaky sense of history.

Films such as *The Delta Force* relieve national frustrations and at the same time encourage support for covert government actions. Still, if it is true that terrorism relies on media coverage, then these films might also contribute to popular interest in hijackings and bombings, despite the fact that each year lightning kills four times as many Americans as do terrorist incidents. Professor of International Law Richard Falk writes that "terrorism as news and terrorism as entertainment are uncomfortably close. We are all terrorists to the extent that we receive pleasure from witnessing the pain and suffering of others." *The Delta Force* confuses news with propagandistic entertainment. In an age of colorization, *The Delta Force* renders black and white the recent events whose lessons should be remembered.

Chon Noriega

Reviews
Chicago Tribune. February 14, 1986, VII, p. F43.
Los Angeles Times. February 14, 1986, VI, p. 4.
The New York Times. CXXXV, February 14, 1986, III, p. 14.
The New York Times. CXXXV, February 23, 1986, VIII, p. 19.
People Weekly. XXV, March 17, 1986, p. 13.
San Francisco Chronicle. February 14, 1986, p. 82.
Variety. February 19, 1986, p. 12.
The Washington Post. February 14, 1986, IV, p. 3.

DESERT BLOOM

Production: Michael Hausman; released by Columbia Pictures
Direction: Eugene Corr
Screenplay: Eugene Corr; based on a story by Linda Remy and Eugene
  Corr
Cinematography: Reynaldo Villalobos
Editing: David Garfield, John Currin, and Cari Couglin
Narration: JoBeth Williams
Art direction: Lawrence Miller; set decoration, Bob Zilliox
Costume design: Hilary Rosenfeld
Music: Brad Fiedel
MPAA rating: PG
Running time: 103 minutes

> *Principal characters:*
> Jack Chismore........................Jon Voight
> Lily Chismore ....JoBeth Williams
> Aunt Starr ....Ellen Barkin
> Rose Chismore ....Annabeth Gish
> Barbara Jo Chismore..............Dusty Balcerzak
> Dee Ann Chismore................Desirée Joseph
> Robin...........................Jay Underwood
> Mr. Mosol ....Allen Garfield

Desert Bloom is a coming-of-age story that is unusual because, unlike recent Hollywood films that detail the maturation of an adolescent male, it recounts the experience of a young woman. Set against the backdrop of Las Vegas in the 1950's, the story is told in the form of a flashback, a memory of the fictional heroine, Rose Chismore (Annabeth Gish), who recalls a childhood which is glimpsed, not through rose-colored glasses, but in all its bittersweet ambivalences and emotional ambiguities.

The film opens with the adult Rose poring over her childhood keepsakes: dolls, dresses, photographs, even her first pair of eyeglasses. (The glasses will become an overarching metaphor for the character's perspective on her past.) A narrated flashback takes the audience back to the day on which thirteen-year-old Rose was fitted with the chic, upturned spectacles which she considered to be an important symbol of her passage into adulthood. An insecure, quiet girl, Rose can say simply that she loves films, books, Wonder Woman, and her grandmother.

In the first scene, Rose stops to visit with her stepfather, Jack Chismore (Jon Voight), at his gas station on the edge of the sprawling desert town of Las Vegas. The two exchange a joke; their lighthearted interchange and

Jack's fatherly pride in Rose's intelligence do not yet hint of the deeply troubled relationship between the two that will dominate the film. This does not indicate an inconsistency in the film's narrative but rather demonstrates how *Desert Bloom* refuses to consign its characters to easily established, broadly drawn stereotypes. Instead, the film carefully details the family's difficulties through authentically presented moments in which characters reveal their strengths as well as their weaknesses. *Desert Bloom* shows that it is still possible to make a small, carefully crafted film which depends upon convincing performances, sharply competent film technique, and a sense of the importance of character development. In drawing on the semiautobiographical novel of social scientist Linda Remy, the film chooses to build upon the audience's shared emotion in the drama rather than on special effects and thrill-provoking action.

Rose feels at odds with her family. Her stepfather, Jack, a veteran of World War II, is a hard worker and steady family man, but his secret drinking begins to surface as a recurring pattern that leads to family violence. Jack's alcoholism appears to be caused by panic attacks, by dreams and flashbacks of World War II, in which he was seriously wounded. Jack also is haunted by his acutely felt lack of control over events, past and present. He attempts to maintain a rather hollow military discipline in the household and condescendingly corrects his wife, Lily (JoBeth Williams), at the dinner table, even though his own range of knowledge is limited by his reading of *True Stories* and *The Great Thinker* series.

Jack desperately wants a child of his own, but tests indicate that he cannot father one. Ironically, his wife's nickname for him is "Daddy." In spite of his failings as a stepfather, his sister-in-law, Starr (Ellen Barkin), defends his efforts to rear the three daughters of another man. The psychiatrist at the sanatorium where Lily finally sends him to dry out tells him that he drinks because he is a perfectionist, a diagnosis which seems inadequate in the face of the family's complex dynamics and Jon Voight's own compelling, complex delineation of Jack.

Jack's retreat into alcohol is augmented by his all-consuming obsession with his shortwave radio. As Aunt Starr says when she arrives for a visit, you can always recognize the Chismore house because Jack inevitably has the largest antenna in town. Jack is convinced that something top secret is happening at the government installation in the desert. Lily quits her casino job to take a position as a secretary to a high-level official at the base. As rumors begin to circulate that the government will be conducting an aboveground A-bomb test, Jack becomes determined to protect his family from whatever might happen.

Rose does not understand Jack's paranoia, even though her school life is permeated by the sense of unease created by the bomb. She is given dog tags to wear. She calmly explains to her Aunt Starr that these are provided to identify her body in case something goes wrong with the test. At school, they test her blood, perhaps for radiation contamination. Her classes and recess are surrealistically punctuated by unannounced bomb drills.

Rose worries less about the meaning of the bomb than about her family life. She increasingly believes that Jack hates her. When Jack drinks, he goes berserk and takes his animosity out on Rose. One reviewer of the film speculated that this violence was sexually motivated, but the film implies that perhaps it is because they are more alike than different: Both are quiet, self-contained, and unsure. Rose's keen intelligence and her precociously observant manner may also threaten Jack's tenuous hold over his family. The Chismores are not a family which communicates about their problems, but there are allusions to past episodes which the family dares not discuss: Jack burned down their trailer in Barstow.

In spite of Jack's drinking, Lily attempts to keep up a front of utter middle-class normality. Rose realizes that her mother does not like to face reality, especially when it comes to Jack. Lily soothes over every mishap, every crisis with a carefully cultivated set of clichés that she appears to believe. "Every path has its puddle, Daddy," she tells Jack. Her daughters love her but recognize her limitations. In one of the film's best scenes, the girls giggle over Lily's inept cooking. The character of Lily is neither as complex as that of Jack nor as appealing as that of Aunt Starr, but JoBeth Williams, as an occasional critic recognized, offers a masterfully understated and believable performance in a role that wavers between evoking sympathy and derisive laughter.

It is clear that Rose wants the love of her mother and Jack, but home provides little emotional nurturance. While her stepfather is distant, her working mother seems to pay more attention to the two younger girls, Barbara Jo (Dusty Balcerzak) and Dee Ann (Desirée Joseph). Almost instinctively, Rose finds emotional support elsewhere. She is a member of a secret club of three friends who dub themselves the "The Pink Pinkie Club," and she finds a surrogate parent in Mr. Mosol (Allen Garfield), the father of her best girlfriend. Mr. Mosol takes the girls to school each morning and drills Rose in spelling. He enthusiastically praises her intelligence and is so sure that she will win the county spelling bee that he bets on her. Mr. Mosol, like Jack, is worried about the atomic testing. One day, he unexpectedly comes to the house to beg Lily to tell him when the atomic test will take place so he can send his wife and daughter to safety in Los Angeles.

Lily refuses to acknowledge Jack's drinking problems until he is obviously out of control. She admits to her sister Starr that in divorce-crazy Las Vegas, she could end her marriage in a short forty-two days, but, starting to cry, she declares that she loves him. Rose also admits that she was ambivalent about Jack's leaving for a hospital stay. She was happy that he was away but also afraid that he would not come back. His return is a classic set piece illustrating Lily's aspirations to middle-class life. The girls, dressed in matching homemade sailor suits, awkwardly welcome Jack home with a serenade accompanied by piano and violin.

Lily asks the girls to give Daddy another chance, but Jack and Rose are soon at odds again. Rose finally rebels on a family outing to the Hoover Dam. Her mother berates her for being insensitive to Jack's troubles. Encouraged by Aunt Starr, Jack and Rose attempt to resolve their differences, but, with the resumption of his nightmares, Jack is soon drinking again. He drunkenly accuses Rose of tampering with his radio, hits her, and forbids her to go out. Counter to Jack's orders, Starr helps Rose sneak out of the house to the Mosols' dance party.

Aunt Starr is a blonde bombshell whose dreams of Hollywood stardom have quickly paled. Starr comes to live with the family for the forty-two-day residence period required to secure a divorce. Not only does she encourage Rose's social life, but also she supports the girl's innocent romance with Robin (Jay Underwood), a boy from the trailer park across the street. Starr is experienced with men, but a failed romance with a Texas playboy leaves her distraught. Soon after, Rose finds Jack and Starr drunkenly embracing.

Although she is traumatized by her discovery of Starr and Jack's indiscretion, Rose wins the county spelling bee. She returns home to begin packing to go to her grandmother's. Lily demands to know why her little girl is leaving. Starr explains why Rose is upset. A family brawl erupts in a scene which melodramatically breaks the film's otherwise understated tone. The fight is stopped by the arrival of guests who have come to celebrate Rose's spelling bee victory.

In the confusion, Jack discovers that Rose has climbed out of her bedroom window. Wearing his World War II uniform, he follows her into the desert, where she has hitchhiked with Robin. He finds them after the army does. In an unexpected gesture of Jack's unexpressed love for Rose, he suddenly bolts into the darkness to retrieve her eyeglasses. She dropped them as she was being pursued by the soldiers assigned to guard the area, which had been declared out of bounds in anticipation of the bomb test.

It is clear from the ride back into town that Rose and Jack have found a common ground for understanding and reconciliation. In a voice-over, the grown-up Rose comments that the worst was over, even though Jack never had an easy time of it. The next morning, the family watches the A-bomb test from their porch. The sociopolitical meaning of the event is lost on them. Rose's little sister can only say, "It's beautiful," and, paradoxically, it is. A close-up of Rose's face ends the film as the local radio announcer greets Las Vegas "survivors" of the test. The family has survived the A-bomb, and Rose has survived her family.

In spite of remarkable performances from all the principal actors and the film's poignant evocation of a child's growth because of and in spite of her film's poignant evocation of a child's growth because of and in spite of her family, *Desert Bloom* failed to find an audience. It was delayed from release for almost a year, and its lackluster box-office returns seemed to confirm the contemporary audience's lack of interest in a small, carefully crafted production with honest virtues. Reviews were mixed, with many critics noting the excellent acting and convincing period ambience but also observing that documentary filmmaker Eugene Corr's first fiction feature film did not successfully integrate the domestic drama with the political implications of the 1950's backdrop.

The film is interesting also for its unique production history. *Desert Bloom* was the first film to emerge from Robert Redford's Sundance Institute development program. Screenwriter/director Corr participated in a script program that involved the mentorship of screenwriter Waldo Salt and a laboratory approach in which scenes of the evolving screenplay were first directed by other members of the institute. If *Desert Bloom* is any indication of the institute's potential, then there is at least a glimmer of hope that the adult drama has one promising forum for expression in contemporary American filmmaking.

Gaylyn Studlar

Reviews
American Cinematographer. January, 1986, p. 42.
The Christian Science Monitor. April 18, 1986, p. 23.
Commonweal. CXIII, May 23, 1986, p. 302.
Los Angeles Times. June 6, 1986, VI, p. 4.
Macleans. XCIX, July 14, 1986, p. 49.
Ms. XIV, June, 1986, p. 20.
National Review. XXXVIII, June 6, 1986, p. 59.
The New Republic. May 5, 1986, p. 26.
The New York Times. April 15, 1986, p. C15.
Variety. CCCXXII, February 5, 1986, p. 29.
The Wall Street Journal. April 17, 1986, p. 26.

DOÑA HERLINDA AND HER SON
(DOÑA HERLINDA Y SU HIJO)

Origin: Mexico
Released: 1985
Released in U.S.: 1986
Production: Manuel Barbachano Ponce; released by Cinevista
Direction: Jaime Humberto Hermosillo
Screenplay: Jaime Humberto Hermosillo; based on a novel by Jorge López Páez
Cinematography: Miguel Ehrenberg
Editing: Luis Kelly
Art direction: Daniel Varela
Music: no listing
MPAA rating: no listing
Running time: 90 minutes

> *Principal characters:*
> Doña Herlinda . . . . Guadalupe Del Toro
> Ramón . . . . Arturo Meza
> Rodolfo . . . . Marco Antonio Trevino
> Olga . . . . Leticia Lupersio

Jaime Humberto Hermosillo's *Doña Herlinda and Her Son* is a sun-drenched gay paean to the transcendent power of motherhood. Set in the languorous locales of Guadalajara, the film is most important as a satisfying depiction of a successful homosexual romance. It is also a kind of fable—a warmly funny tale of maternal accommodation.

Rodolfo (Marco Antonio Trevino) is a dashing pediatric surgeon. He is nearly as devoted to his medical practice as he is to his mother, a benevolent manipulator known as Doña Herlinda (Guadalupe Del Toro). The film's opening scenes quickly establish that there is a third object of Rodolfo's devotion—Ramón (Arturo Meza), an attractive but down-at-heel music student. Rodolfo and Ramón have difficulty finding adequate settings for their steamy trysts, as Rodolfo lives with his mother and Ramón occupies a room in a dismal boarding house, and Rodolfo soon resorts to hosting Ramón in the examination room of his medical office. When this arrangement proves untenable, it is left to Doña Herlinda to concoct a staggeringly forthright solution: She arranges for Ramón to move into her posh Guadalajara mansion ("Rodolfo has such a big bed," she says). Doña Herlinda engineers this move without the bat of an eyelash, as charming as a party hostess and as inscrutable as the Sphinx.

It remains uncertain whether Doña Herlinda is aware of her son's sexual proclivities, since the subject is never addressed openly by any of the parties concerned, but it is clear that nothing will stop her from getting what she wants, which is one big, happy family united under her domain. This premise is the source of most of the film's humor, as well as its dramatic tension. Hermosillo takes hold of a tired old myth—that a domineering mother is the cause of most male homosexual behavior—and turns it inside out, creating a scenario in which Mama manages to accommodate, knowingly or unknowingly, her son's homosexuality while also arranging events to suit her own plans. Far from being an imperious tyrant, Doña Herlinda is all sweetness and light, politely manipulating events by means of her considerable charm and sheer force of will.

Rodolfo is soon stunned to discover that Doña Herlinda's vision of a happy family leaves room for a wife and baby as well as her son and his lover. Even as Ramón takes up residence in Rodolfo's room and bed, Doña Herlinda encourages her son's courtship of Olga (Leticia Lupersio), a feminist student. Rodolfo passively complies with this arrangement, which allows Doña Herlinda to retain her respectability in the eyes of the world while allowing her son the male companionship he desires.

Rodolfo's initial dates with Olga are a comedy unto themselves. The festivities usually include the happy "heterosexual" couple as well as Doña Herlinda and Ramón. The mother smiles genially, while Ramón squirms and tries to puzzle out everything. These four-cornered affairs usually take place in a posh lakeside resort, to the decidedly unromantic strains of a thoroughly awful rock-and-roll band. (The film's musical motifs are a pointed source of humor. Doña Herlinda's provisions for Ramón are especially fortuitous, since he hopes to become a musician—a profession for which he is spectacularly unsuited. When the audience first sees him, Ramón is practicing the French horn, gamely mangling a section of *Tannhäuser und der Sängerkrieg auf Wartburg* by Richard Wagner.)

Rodolfo's eventual marriage to Olga results from Doña Herlinda's incessant manipulations, and the union is apparently a happy one. Rodolfo, whom his mother generously describes as "ambidextrous," artfully divides his time between Olga, who is soon pregnant, and Ramón, who remains a permanent fixture in the household even after the marriage. This quirky ménage à trois remains remarkably free of turbulence, thanks to Doña Herlinda's unswerving commitment to the sanctity of the home, her inexhaustible energy, and, possibly, her willful ignorance of Rodolfo's sexual preference. When Ramón's parents come for a visit, Doña Herlinda deftly steers them away from any discussion of sexual matters or Ramón's highly unusual living arrangement. (It is implied that Doña Herlinda succeeds in this elaborate deceit in part because of her considerable affluence as well as her adroit planning and unwavering resolve.) Months go by, the household thrives, and sexual satisfaction is apparently enjoyed by all: Even as Olga is

departing for the hospital, Rodolfo and Ramón are shown blissfully romp-
ing in bed. When the baby is born, Rodolfo comments to Ramón, "It's almost as if it were our child, isn't it?"

Such a declaration is not too farfetched, in the light of the strange and
wonderful intimacy which Doña Herlinda fosters on all sides. The characters seem genuinely to like one another, and Hermosillo displays a genuine tolerance of all forms of sexual expression. The film ends after the birth
of Rodolfo and Olga's baby with Olga's eventual departure for Germany,
where she plans to pursue graduate studies. At this juncture, Ramón is re-
cruited as a kind of surrogate mother—an arrangement which suits Doña
Herlinda very well.

One could argue that there is something rather unsettling about Doña
Herlinda's all-too-eager assimilation of Ramón into the luxurious and affluent household—it almost seems as though she intends to exert control over
her son's decidedly scandalous sexual urges by causing them to be subsumed
by the family unit, the preservation of which continues to be much more
important to Doña Herlinda than the desires of any one individual. Still, it
is amusing to watch Doña Herlinda as she asserts her supremacy, fulfilling
her own greatest desires as she works to satisfy everyone else's. Part of the
film's fascination lies in watching her slowly but inexorably work her way
toward center stage.

Doña Herlinda and Her Son is pleasing to watch, even though the film
consists of little more than a hyperextended comedy sketch. The characters
are likable but one-dimensional; this is especially true of Doña Herlinda
herself, who remains an enigma throughout. One also feels compelled to
question the role of Olga, who marries a man who feels no real passion for
her. She seems to exist solely as a function of the plot, and once she has ful-
filled this function—which includes having a baby and thus preserving the
respectability of the family—she is conveniently dispatched to Germany.
Rodolfo and Olga do have their share of sexual interludes—the best of
these are initiated by Olga, who seems to be clearly in charge of her own
sexuality—but it remains resoundingly clear that Rodolfo's heart belongs to
another.

This rather sunny, if incomplete, scenario is well served by Miguel Ehrenberg's cinematography, which is all bright, seemingly oversaturated colors,
and by the film's production values, which establish Doña Herlinda's elegant
home as the epitome of bourgeois comfort. The physical surroundings are
so ideal that the film takes on the tone of a Fauvist fairy tale, a dreamland
in which everyone's fairest wishes come true. One could quibble with the
fact that in this film, as in Arthur Hiller's well-meaning but grossly overrated
Making Love (1982), a pair of gay lovers seem able to have everything they
want, materially and sexually, precisely because of their elevated class status
and their ready access to money. Hermosillo's film might have been more

interesting had Rodolfo been compelled to adjust to Ramón's initially down-trodden surroundings, instead of the other way around—but this is asking perhaps too much from a film which seems to serve primarily as an example of gay cinematic wish fulfillment.

Doña Herlinda and Her Son is a small picture with few grandiose preten-sions and even fewer axes to grind. It lacks much in terms of dramatic con-flict—it seems especially implausible that nothing ever happens to disrupt Doña Herlinda's idyllic housing arrangement—but this is counterbalanced by the generosity with which the director treats his characters. Hermosillo refuses to lapse into banal pronouncements about morality and matters of sexual preference. For once, here is a film in which homosexuality is not equated with psychopathic or criminal behavior—as in William Friedkin's *Cruising* (1980)—or in which gay characters are merely silly and ineffectual, as in Edouard Molinaro's *La Cage aux folles* (1979). Because of its reso-lutely positive presentation of a homosexual relationship, Hermosillo's *Doña Herlinda and Her Son* bears something in common with Stephen Frears's recent success, *My Beautiful Laundrette* (1985; reviewed in this volume), as well as Bill Sherwood's *Parting Glances* (1986; reviewed in this volume) and Pedro Almodóvar's *Law of Desire* (1987). It is also significant that this film should come from Mexico, a seemingly conservative nation whose woefully underdeveloped and underfinanced film industry has nevertheless produced its share of little gems in recent years, including Arturo Ripstein's *El lugar sin límites* (*A Place Without Borders*, 1986), a poignant film concerning a transvestite and her macho lover.

Doña Herlinda and Her Son is most significant because it manages to rec-oncile two entities which have traditionally been considered to be vehe-mently antithetical to each other—the homosexual romantic couple and the traditional nuclear family. In some ways, the film addresses many gay peo-ple's desire to maintain family connections and pursue a sexual life without apology or fear of harassment. *Doña Herlinda and Her Son* is neither as ambitious nor as well crafted as it ought to be, but it is a relief to encounter a tale of gay romance which ends with an embrace rather than a bullet.

Karl Michalak

Reviews
Los Angeles Times. August 21, 1986, VI, p. 1.
The New Republic. CXCIV, May 12, 1986, p. 24.
New York. XIX, April 14, 1986, p. 94.
The New York Times. April 4, 1986, p. C14.
Variety. CCCXX, August 21, 1985, p. 20.

DOWN AND OUT IN BEVERLY HILLS

Production: Paul Mazursky; released by Buena Vista
Direction: Paul Mazursky
Screenplay: Paul Mazursky and Leon Capetanos; based on the play *Boudu sauvé des eaux* by René Fauchois
Cinematography: Donald McAlpine
Editing: Richard Halsey
Production design: Pato Guzman
Art direction: Todd Hallowell; set decoration, Jane Bogart
Costume design: Albert Wolsky
Music: Andy Summers
Song: Talking Heads, "Once in a Lifetime"
MPAA rating: R
Running time: 103 minutes

> *Principal characters:*
> Jerry Baskin..........................Nick Nolte
> Dave Whiteman.................Richard Dreyfuss
> Barbara Whiteman...................Bette Midler
> Orvis Goodnight....................Little Richard
> Jenny Whiteman....................Tracy Nelson
> Carmen..........................Elizabeth Peña
> Max Whiteman....................Evan Richards
> Matisse, the dog...........................Mike

Down and Out in Beverly Hills is not so much a homage to Jean Renoir's *Boudu Saved from Drowning* (1932) as it is a transformation and even rebuttal of this classic film. Paul Mazursky has made a Disney-like version of Renoir's occasionally disturbing and iconoclastic critique of bourgeois manners and morals. Renoir is initially sympathetic to the bookseller Lestingois, who after all is the only person willing to rescue a drowning man, but never loses sight of the fact that he is a hypocrite and a stuffed shirt. Boudu, the scruffy bum, is never charming but captures the viewer's interest because he is a constant source of disorder in an otherwise orderly household. Mazursky, on the other hand, seems far less critical of and much more fascinated by his rather well-off benefactor, and *Down and Out in Beverly Hills* is thus less a satire than a fable of integration: The unruly outsider is saved from drowning and taken in by a family that changes him nearly as much as he changes them.

The film opens and closes with the song "Once in a Lifetime" by the Talking Heads, as if to frame the vision of Beverly Hills with tension and barely controlled nervous hysteria, but this mood is rarely activated within the frame. It is an achievement of sorts that Mazursky is able to focus repeatedly on poverty, racism, anorexia, marital distress, infidelity, and guilt without managing to depress or frighten his audience. *Down and Out in Beverly Hills* is a comedy not because it is happy but because no one seems to suffer. Jerry Baskin (Nick Nolte) wanders the streets rummaging through garbage, befriended only by a mangy dog appropriately named Kerouac, but Baskin appears to be more numb than miserable. When Kerouac disappears, lured away by the offer of food from a well-to-do jogger, Baskin no longer has any reason to live. When he throws himself into the deep end of a pool, he is as immobile and unfeeling as the rocks he stuffs in his pockets.

The attempted suicide takes place in the backyard of the Whiteman family. Shots of the Whiteman family Thanksgiving dinner, a catered banquet, obviously contrast with Jerry's poverty, but the point is not to make any social commentary on the unfairness of it all but rather simply to introduce the various foibles and problems of the people who are only superficially well-off. David Whiteman (Richard Dreyfuss) is a financially successful but nervous self-made man, surrounded by material possessions that reinforce his feelings of guilt. He manufactures coat hangers, sleeps with his live-in maid, worries about his daughter, and is tormented by his dog, Matisse, whose actions provide a bizarre and comic commentary on much of what happens in the house throughout the film.

No one else in the family is any more content. Dave's wife, Barbara (Bette Midler), shuns him in bed and fills her life with Spanish lessons, shopping, and following the advice of her swami. In one scene, Mazursky shoots her reflected in a hallway of mirrors, coyly alluding to one of the most memorable shots in Orson Welles's *The Lady from Shanghai* (1948), but Barbara is not a mysterious, exciting femme fatale, only a typical woman from Beverly Hills: materialistic, hysterical, a little overweight, and more than a little tense. It is no surprise that the children of these parents are troubled. Jenny (Tracy Nelson) has an unresolved attachment to her father that makes her repressed, anorexic, and unable to choose a worthwhile love object. Max (Evan Richards) is not able to communicate directly with his father, so he uses videos to get his message across while he tries to "find himself" by playing a number of outrageous roles: a ballerina in a tutu, a tough guy, and a transvestite punk rocker, complete with lipstick. Even Matisse is in therapy, and the dog psychiatrist diagnoses his problem as "nipple anxiety." This is the family that comes to Jerry's rescue.

Specifically, it is Dave who pulls Jerry out from the pool. While his explanation "There but for the grace of God go you or I" is not completely convincing, Dave is basically, Mazursky would have one believe, a good-hearted man. Jerry is a reclamation project, dramatically transformed as he is rescued, fed, clothed, housed in the cabana, and escorted to the best shops and restaurants Beverly Hills has to offer. Moreover, he is also a se-cret sharer, a companion and confidant first to Dave but eventually to every-one in the family, and the ways in which he answers their needs and fulfills their fantasies is the focal point for much of the film.

From the beginning, Jerry is able to tell everyone exactly what he or she wants and needs to hear. He is not so much a liar as a charming and sincere masquerader and master of saving fictions. Just as Dave takes him into his world of affluence, Jerry more than returns the favor by taking Dave into the streets, and though this may only be a moment of slumming, Dave is un-usually buoyant as he tells Barbara of his return to his roots: "I ate garbage and loved it." Jerry's effect on the rest of the household is even more pro-found. He becomes the swami that Barbara never really had, and by using a combination of Balinese massage and sexual aura he "jangles" her into her first orgasm in nearly ten years. He also replaces Dave in the bed of the maid Carmen (Elizabeth Peña) and teaches her to express her resentment politically: She comes to see herself as an oppressed Third World nation serving a selfish capitalist master. (Dave thought that he was only having a harmless affair with her.) Jerry's power seems to be unfailing, in part be-cause he has boundless faith and a variety of techniques: He resolves Max's identity problems by simply telling him, "You gotta be what you gotta be," and he restores Matisse's appetite by carefully mixing up a special blend of dog food and sharing it with him from a bowl on the floor.

Jerry's interventions, however magical, are not always appreciated. He sweeps Jenny off her feet, gives her the physical love for which she was starving, and transforms her into a mature woman, no longer fixated on her father or fleeing from food and love. When Dave learns that Jerry has slept with not only his wife and maid but his daughter as well, he can no longer control himself: A party being given for visiting Chinese customers is com-pletely disrupted as Dave chases Jerry through the house, joined by all the guests. With Little Richard singing in his familiar hysterical manner, fire-works exploding, and the burglar alarm wailing, the film comes to a comic anti-climax: In the same pool from which he once rescued him, Dave tries to drown Jerry, who is dressed absurdly as Santa Claus.

The last scenes of the film threaten to return everything to the way things were at the beginning: Jerry walks away from the house and the family falls into their old habits—Dave scowls, Barbara becomes tense, Jenny refuses to eat, and Max picks up his camera. One can almost predict the rush of sentimentality, though, as the camera tracks in on Jerry, pans across the warm, smiling faces of the family, and then tracks back on them as Jerry is welcomed into the household once again. Only the slightest hint of an enig-matic smile on Dave's face suggests that this ending is as implausible as it is heartwarming.

An overall evaluation of *Down and Out in Beverly Hills* must take into account that the film does not aim for plausibility or profundity. It verges on satire, as any intelligent picture of Beverly Hills must, and there are a few troubling moments which break through the carefully established calm that normally prevails: For example, when Dave walks Jerry through his manufacturing plant, boasting of the company's health insurance plan, he reaches out to open the mouth of one worker to show his teeth as if he were a prized horse. Nevertheless, for the most part, this is a film without hard edges, scripted and shot by an insider enamored of his subject. At his toughest, Mazursky shows that the caricatured Beverly Hills way of life is ridiculous, filled with materialistic excess, insensitivity, and selfishness. This is unlikely to cause any weeping in greater Los Angeles, nor will it discourage anyone elsewhere in the United States from pursuing Beverly Hills dreams. The film pretends to offer the "strange wisdom" of an outsider entering into a world on the verge of collapse, but ultimately Jerry too proves to be only another insider, easily assimilated to a life of luxury, no matter what the price is. The fact that hero Jerry's philosophy is almost word for word the same as the phony swami's—the world is filled with universal oneness, and we all flow into one another—is an irony hidden at the heart of the film.

Mazursky is unquestionably a skilled craftsman, and this film, like nearly all of his others, is consistently interesting. The settings always make *Down and Out in Beverly Hills* visually attractive: The Whiteman house, from its pink master bedroom to its white-on-white living room, is a gaudy joy to look at, and the camera wanders freely through it. The acting is also extremely effective, especially from the three main performers: Nick Nolte gives a mysterious depth to the role of Jerry, creating the impression that he is simultaneously a complete faker and a man of wide and valuable experience; Richard Dreyfuss, with a balding head, compulsive nervous smile, and barely audible accent that betrays Dave's Brooklyn background, builds his character from equal parts of anxiety, ambition, and concern; and Bette Midler skillfully overplays the most outrageously stereotyped character in the entire film. Finally, Mazursky never lets the action go on for very long without distracting the audience with a laugh, and he runs the full gamut of comedy, from wit to near wit to broad humor. The constant bantering among the characters, each of whom is wise in his or her folly, is enjoyable but easily upstaged by the many moments of slapstick, most of which center on Matisse mugging for the camera. All of this accounts for the considerable charm of *Down and Out in Beverly Hills*, a successful blend of such films as *My Man Godfrey* (1936) and *The Shaggy Dog* (1959)—yet, ultimately, it remains disturbingly shallow. *Down and Out in Beverly Hills* might have been haunting; instead, it is only beguiling.

Sidney Gottlieb

Reviews
Christian Century. CIII, April 2, 1986, p. 330.
Commonweal. CXIII, April 11, 1986, p. 213.
Film Comment. XXII, January, 1986, p. 16.
Macleans. XCIX, February 17, 1986, p. 48.
The Nation. CCXLII, March 1, 1986, p. 251.
National Review. XXXVIII, March 28, 1986, p. 63.
The New Republic. CXCIV, February 24, 1986, p. 24.
New York. XIX, February 3, 1986, p. 82.
The New Yorker. LXI, February 10, 1986, p. 105.
Newsweek. CVII, February 3, 1986, p. 68.
Time. CXXVII, January 27, 1986, p. 64.
Variety. CCCXXI, January 15, 1986, p. 23.

DOWN BY LAW

Production: Alan Kleinberg; released by Island Pictures
Direction: Jim Jarmusch
Screenplay: Jim Jarmusch
Cinematography: Robby Muller
Editing: Melody London
Art direction: Roger Knight
Music: John Lurie
Songs: Tom Waits
MPAA rating: R
Running time: 107 minutes

Principal characters:
Jack.................................John Lurie
Zack ....Tom Waits
Roberto ....Roberto Benigni
Nicoletta ....Nicoletta Braschi
Bobbie..............................Billie Neal
Laurette ....Ellen Barkin

> Two roads diverged in a wood, and I
> I took the one less travelled by,
> and that has made all the difference.
> "Bob" Frost
> "The Road Not Taken"

In a central scene in *Down by Law*, the three fugitives—Jack the pimp (John Lurie), Zack the disc jockey (Tom Waits), and Roberto the foreigner (Roberto Benigni)—are hiding in a cabin in a swamp when suddenly Roberto recites in Italian the last stanza of "The Road Not Taken" by the poet he calls "Bob" Frost. Roberto's outburst has a wonderful, zany comic effect because it is so incongruous. *Down by Law* also ends with an elaborate visual joke which is a literal enactment of the central scene from "The Road Not Taken." Zack and Jack finish their reluctant journey together by coming to Frost's two roads and walking their separate ways out of the picture. This subtle use of Robert Frost is the perfect ending for this marvelously imaginative film that is one long visual and verbal double entendre—a series of deftly wrought literary and film allusions.

Frost's lines are a fitting epigraph not only for *Down by Law* but also for the filmmaker himself. Jim Jarmusch has chosen the road "less travelled by," which has indeed made all the artistic difference. A young American filmmaker (a Columbia University undergraduate literature major and a graduate of the New York University film school), whose low-budget *Stranger than Paradise* (1984) won international and national awards and even popular success, Jarmusch resisted multiple offers of directing in Hollywood, choosing to remain fiercely independent in writing, directing, and producing *Down by Law*. Jarmusch's films thus join the company of a growing number of recent American films, such as Alex Cox's *Repo Man* (1984), John Sayles's *The Brother from Another Planet* (1984), and Spike Lee's *She's Gotta Have It* (1986; reviewed in this volume) that have traveled their own independent routes across the American landscape. Consistent with his insistence on going his own way as filmmaker is Jarmusch's desire to present alternative American journeys. Both *Stranger than Paradise* and *Down by Law* are travel stories—but off-beat stories about marginal people who move around the edges of mainstream society, strangers to the American paradise.

Like *Stranger than Paradise*, *Down by Law* is a parody of conventional stories taken mostly from American films. The plot is deceptively simple. Two New Orleans fringe people, Jack, a second-rate pimp, and Zack, an itinerant disc jockey, are framed for crimes they did not commit—Jack as a child molester, Zack for a murder. They end up in an Orleans Parish Prison cell as reluctant companions. Jack and Zack spar with each other in bouts of noncommunication, until they are joined by a third prisoner—Roberto, an Italian immigrant who has, in spite of his innocent looks, actually killed a man in a pool-hall fight. With his zest for life, Roberto breaks through the barriers between Jack and Zack, creating some real camaraderie among the three of them. After Roberto discovers a way to escape, they break out of prison and are chased into the Louisiana swamp by hound dogs. After several days wandering lost in the swamp, they finally stumble onto a road to freedom. Following the road, they come to a roadside Italian restaurant in which Roberto discovers Nicoletta (Nicoletta Braschi), a beautiful Italian woman, who invites him to marry her and take over the restaurant. After Zack and Jack are well fed and outfitted, the two take off again. When they come to a fork in the road, the reluctant companions go off on their separate ways to freedom.

This plot summary reveals little about the film because the meaning resides primarily in the art of telling the story, not in what is told. *Down by Law* is pure artifice: Every scene parodies scenes from genre films, the speeches use the clichés of American film dialogue, and the film style self-consciously plays with conventional Hollywood genre styles. Three scenes in particular illustrate Jarmusch's subtle art of storytelling.

The opening sequence of *Down by Law* leading up to the introduction of the title and credits is an imaginative playing with film styles and techniques. Jarmusch parodies the film convention of establishing the setting and characters before the credits. He turns the standard introduction into a kind of shaggy-dog joke, making it inordinately long by using a series of lateral tracking shots of seedy sections of New Orleans. The first shot is a stationary shot of the rear end of a hearse in a cemetery. Rapid tracking shots begin as the camera travels from right to left through the city and out into a shabby countryside and back into the city, the images accompanied by the song "Jockey Full of Bourbon," written by Waits. Suddenly, the camera stops moving and cuts to a room where Jack is in bed with Bobbie (Billie Neal), a black woman. In perfect *film noir* style of high-contrast lighting, Jarmusch moves his camera in on the woman sleeping for a close-up which conventionally signals a dramatic moment. The woman suddenly opens her eyes. This gesture starts the music again, as the tracking shots of New Orleans reverse their direction across the screen. The camera travels again through town, ending up in a different room but the same situation, this time Zack and a woman in bed. The camera again moves in on the sleeping woman, Laurette (Ellen Barkin)—and her eyes open. The music starts as the traveling camera repeats its movement through town from right to left. Feigning *film noir* realism, Jarmusch makes the audience very aware of watching a film. Instead of the standard crosscutting to introduce parallel lives of characters, he uses the traveling shots to take the viewer through the city, first to one character and then to the other, who lives in another section of town. When the two women open their eyes, so does the audience.

Jarmusch is not finished mocking film conventions. The third trip with the camera through the city leads to the credits. The tracking shots stop, the credits move on, and the sound track changes to dogs barking and police sirens. Not content with visual jokes, Jarmusch adds a sound joke as he uses these clichéd sound effects from fugitive films to introduce his title. The barking and sirens get louder and louder until the title appears: *Down by Law*. The sounds slowly fade away as the credits roll on to their end and the film begins its story in Zack's room.

One of Jarmusch's artistic strengths is his sensitivity to language; he has a keen ear for clichés, especially the clichés of film dialogue. Much of the dialogue in *Down by Law* alludes to what countless stock characters have said in the same conventional situations—Jack and his prostitute, Zack and his girl, the confrontations with the cops, Jack's dreams about his future. The high point of Jarmusch's linguistic cleverness is the scene of Roberto, Zack, and Jack in jail. Roberto is the perfect vehicle for Jarmusch's language play because his knowledge of English is limited to a few stock expressions which he has heard and copied down in a precious notebook. His misuse of his small repertoire of partially understood expressions is the major source of humor in this scene and throughout the film. Anxious to get off on the right foot with his new cell mates, Roberto flips through his notebook until he finds just the right words: "If looks can kill I'ma dead now."

Jarmusch also carefully develops Roberto as the life force that resurrects his deadbeat cell mates. Bob, as he asks to be called, is a constant source of comic reversal of expectations. A small, inept-looking foreigner, Roberto reveals that he has killed a man in a pool hall with the eight ball; recites Walt Whitman's poetry in Italian; and animates the whole jail when he finds the meaning of "scream" in his notebook and begins the chant: "I scream, you scream, we all scream for ice cream." Jarmusch's deft comic touch makes Roberto, in spite of his limited language, the most articulate character. With his openhearted broken speech to his withdrawn cell mates, Roberto succeeds in creating a strange kind of friendship among them. The jail scene ends with a final reversal of expectation: Roberto discovers a way to escape which, as he tells Zack and Jack, he learned from watching American prison films. Jarmusch parodies the classic prison break by deliberately not showing how they did it, cutting to the conventional escape through the drainage pipe and flight into the woods. Pursued by the classic sound of hound dogs, Roberto says: "We have escaped like in the American movies."

A final scene illustrating Jarmusch's comic art is the one in which the three fugitives, exhausted from their flight through the swamp, finally stumble onto a road that leads them to a roadside café. Again mocking the conventions of fugitive films, Jarmusch has Zack and Jack send Bob into the restaurant to size up the situation while they hide in the bushes. When he does not come right back, they finally peer in the window to discover him eating, laughing, and speaking Italian with a beautiful woman. Here is another Jarmusch joke—an outlandish fairy tale ending for Roberto, who finds all he could wish for at the end of his flight from the law: the love of an Italian restaurant owner. Roberto calls Zack's and Jack's and the audience's attention to the fairy-tale allusion: "She has asked to me if I stay here to live together with her forever and ever like in a book for children." Jarmusch fittingly ends the scene with Roberto sending Jack and Zack off to their rendezvous with "Bob" Frost's two roads by proudly shouting two delightful clichés at the departing pair: "Don't forget to write" and "Wish you were here."

Down by Law is a complex work of comic art that does, finally, have a serious message. Early in the film, Zack is sitting drunk on a dingy street corner when suddenly Roberto enters the scene addressing Zack with words he thinks are a conventional American greeting: "It's a sad and beautiful world." Zack responds to Roberto by repeating his words and then telling him to buzz off. Roberto replies, "Thank you. Buzz off to you too." The world of *Down by Law* is indeed a sad and beautiful world, a sad and beautifully comic world.

John Hartzog

Reviews
The Christian Century. CIII, October 22, 1986, p. 920.
Commonweal. CXIII, October 10, 1986, p. 535.
Film Quarterly. XL, Winter, 1986, p. 11.
Films and Filming. January, 1987, Number 388, p. 33.
Los Angeles Times. October 3, 1986, VI, p. 1.
The New Republic. CXCV, September 29, 1986, p. 24.
The New York Times. September 19, 1986, p. C21.
The New Yorker. LXII, October 20, 1986, p. 115.
Newsweek. CVIII, September 22, 1986, p. 84.
Rolling Stone. November 6, 1986, p. 34.
Time. CXXVIII, November 3, 1986, p. 82.
The Wall Street Journal. September 18, 1986, p. 30.
The Washington Post. October 8, 1986, p. D7.

ECHO PARK

Production: Walter Shenson; released by Atlantic Releasing Corporation
Direction: Robert Dornhelm
Screenplay: Michael Ventura
Cinematography: Karl Kofler
Editing: Ingrid Kooler
Art direction: Bernt Capra
Music: David Rickets
MPAA rating: R
Running time: 93 minutes

Principal characters:
May .... Susan Dey
Jonathan .... Tom Hulce
August .... Michael Bowen
Henry .... Christopher Walker
Hugo .... John Paragon
Gloria .... Shirley Jo Feeney
Sid .... Richard ("Cheech") Marin

Echo Park is a "small" film from several perspectives. It is a low-budget production shot in Los Angeles, and, while the film features numerous fine acting performances, the narrative will be seen by many viewers as slight, predictable, and even somewhat pointless. Writer Michael Ventura and director Robert Dornhelm emphasize clever dialogue, the relationships between the major characters, May (Susan Dey), Jonathan (Tom Hulce), and August (Michael Bowen), and their encounters with several quirky representatives of the seamier side of the Los Angeles scene. Along the way, Ventura and Dornhelm do have something to say about certain versions of the pursuit of the American Dream.

May is an aspiring actress who lives in a seedy apartment in a Victorian house with her young son, Henry (Christopher Walker). The other inhabitants of the house include Gloria (Shirley Jo Feeney) and August, an Austrian immigrant whose abiding goal in life is to be as spectacularly successful as his hero, Arnold Schwarzenegger. August is a childishly naïve and good-hearted lad who spends most of his waking hours pumping iron. The comic dimension of his character develops, on the one hand, from his obsession with capitalizing on a crackpot muscle-energy scheme and, on the other, from the crazy double entendres which are produced by his uncertain command of the English language. May tries to support herself and her son by tending bar, but she is so short of cash that she advertises for a roommate in order to make ends meet. It is at this point that she really makes the acquaintance of August. May must ask him to restrain the grunts and groans that punctuate his workouts: The sounds can easily be heard in May's apartment, and they clearly resemble those of extraordinarily enthusiastic lovemaking.

May interviews a parade of bizarre prospective tenants. Jonathan, a would-be songwriter who works as a pizza deliveryman, shows up late one afternoon in his professional capacity, and May is so impressed with Jonathan's sincerity and gentle wit that she accepts him as her roommate. Soon a love triangle of sorts develops between May, August, and Jonathan. After a family-style cookout one evening, May and August bed down in drunken playfulness. While May looks upon sex with August as nothing more than casual satisfaction of a physical need, August conceives a kind of adolescent crush on May. Jonathan, too, has fallen for May, and he is deeply disappointed by what he sees between her and August, not only because he is jealous, but also because May's flippant morality offends him.

May, who has passed herself off in a trade-paper ad as "an experienced leading lady," receives a call for an audition. Gloria, already suspicious of what May might be getting herself into, drives May to a run-down loft in a not-so-chic section of the city. Indeed, Gloria's instinctual grasp of the setup has not been far from the mark: The audition turns out to be a tryout for a position as a "stripper-gram" girl. At first, May is disappointed, but when Hugo (John Paragon), the man in charge of the business, explains what he is looking for, her interest is piqued. Just as May is approaching the climax of a clumsy strip demonstration, the police raid the place. Despite the fiasco that ensues, May is hired.

Even though May's first real performance at a birthday party is aborted by her nervous modesty, eventually she warms to the task and becomes quite proficient at her job and enthusiastic about what she considers to be, after all, a kind of acting. Jonathan has more respect for May than the pragmatic girl has for herself, and he is embarrassed and disgusted when May gives a private performance at home for him, August, and Henry. Jonathan's moral conservatism surfaces at least partly on behalf of Henry, in whom he has taken genuine interest; after all, May is not what one would call a classic maternal figure.

From this point on in the narrative, the film presents crosscut installments of the stories of the three protagonists. May climbs the ladder of success as a stripper, but things do not go so well for Jonathan. He has the misfortune of delivering pizza to a gang of motorcycle thugs who beat and humiliate him. He is, however, avenged by August and some of his weight-lifter pals. August, meanwhile, has made a hit in "show business" by being cast in a ridiculous television commercial for Viking Spray deodorant. The viewer savors the absurdity of August's newly created media *persona*, but August worships posters of himself as a muscle-bound dragon slayer. Moreover, he sees his success in the commercial as a stepping stone to the marketing of his bodybuilding theories. Unfortunately, Sid (Richard "Cheech" Marin), the owner of a bodybuilding and weight-training facility, reneges on what August had presumed to be an agreement to bankroll his plans. The Austrian Viking goes berserk, wrecks Sid's "Muscle Heaven," and is subsequently arrested. To make matters worse, the police send word to August's father in Austria that his son is in jail.

As fate would have it, Jonathan and Henry (who has been affectionately named Hank by Jonathan) make a pizza delivery to a wild party where May has been doing her act. Things have gotten out of hand, and Jonathan and Henry see May being pawed by the honored host. The noble Jonathan leaps to May's defense and slugs the man who is menacing May, but it is too late: Henry has seen his mother in less than flattering circumstances. The little boy runs away, with Jonathan and May in hot pursuit through streets and alleys. When Henry is found, May at last understands the disillusionment which her child has experienced because of his mother's conduct. Jonathan, May, and Henry return home to find Hugo. Neither May nor Jonathan is happy to see him now, but it turns out that Hugo is the bearer of good news: The man whose party Jonathan ruined wants to audition May for a television commercial. All present rejoice at May's good fortune, but the last scene of the film features the sudden arrival of August's father. Father is definitely Old Country, working-class stock. (In fact, the film's first sequence is August's dream of his butcher father in a surreal setting.) He cannot abide the insult to family honor which his son has perpetrated by being arrested, and he greets August with a solid punch to the face. This freeze-frame is amusing, but it hardly contributes to a neat, tidy closure of the film.

Tom Hulce, Susan Dey, and Michael Bowen are the foundation upon which the appeal of *Echo Park* is built. Hulce's expressive countenance easily and touchingly registers Jonathan's fundamental goodness, vulnerability, and devotion to May and Henry. Dey successfully comes across very skillfully as jaded, sexy, ambitious, yet sensitive. Bowen provides notable comic relief, while striking a tender note with his naïve confidence that America is the land of every immigrant's dreams. (He even wears Stars and Stripes jockey shorts.)

From one point of view, the morals of the story of *Echo Park* are traditional and conservative: Sexual promiscuity is unwise and ugly; mothers should set positive examples for their children; one should not compromise one's dignity for material or professional gain; metropolitan America is a jungle, but one can always find solace and encouragement in good friends. On the other hand, *Echo Park* provides a discouraging but undoubtedly realistic rendering of the overwhelming odds against success which face starry-eyed young people in the glitter capitals of American culture. As Jonathan notes, Los Angeles is full of people who think that they are poets, song-writers, novelists, and actors, when in fact they are simply deluding them-selves—they are all, in a manner of speaking, just delivering pizza.

Gordon Walters

Reviews
Los Angeles. XXXI, May, 1986, p. 36.
Los Angeles Times. March 28, 1986, VI, p. 1.
The New York Times. CXXXV, April 25, 1986, p. C18.
Newsweek. CVII, May 19, 1986, p. 73.

ELIMINATORS

Production: Charles Band; released by Empire Pictures
Direction: Peter Manoogian
Screenplay: Danny Bilson and Paul De Meo
Cinematography: Mac Ahlberg
Editing: Andy Horvitch
Production design: Phillip Foreman
Art direction: Gumersindo Andres Lopez; set decoration, Juan Puerto
Special effects: Juan Ramon Molina
Makeup: John Buechler and Mechanical and Makeup Imageries, Inc.
Costume design: Jill Ohanneson
Fight choreography: Conan "Hutch" Lee
Sound: Antonio Bloch Rodriguez
Music direction: Dan Perry
Music: Richard Band
MPAA rating: PG
Running time: 96 minutes

> *Principal characters:*
> Mandroid......................Patrick Reynolds
> Abbott Reeves.....................Roy Dotrice
> Nora Hunter.....................Denise Crosby
> Harry Fontana....................Andrew Prine
> Kuji...............................Conan Lee
> Ray...............................Peter Schrum
> Bayou Betty......................Peggy Mannix
> Luis...............................Fausto Bara
> Takada............................Tad Horino
> Maurice ....Luis Lorenzo

Empire Pictures' *Eliminators* is a well-made exploitation film, not only in the technical sense, but also in terms of its tight and logical structure. Still, *Eliminators* cannot be considered a good film. Though the production values are high for a low-budget film, the plot is predictable and the acting mostly flat. That is exactly the point, however, behind the long tradition of B films: to be bad but entertaining, to mimic and parody the more expensive productions, and to make a fast buck and be discarded. Film criticism tends to miss the point about B pictures, generally denigrating them as if they were failed A pictures while elevating a few to cult status. *Eliminators* proclaims its position as a B picture, so that its exploitation of other films takes on a self-conscious quality that ranges from the bawdy to the subtle.
Eliminators draws heavily on *The African Queen* (1951) and *The Termina-*

tor (1984) to present both sexual equality and a negative view of technology unusual for the science fiction-horror-fantasy-action genre. At the same time, the film disclaims any pretentions to seriousness: Near the end, mercenary Harry Fontana (Andrew Prine) asks, "What is this anyway, some kind of . . . comic book? We got robots, we got cavemen, we got kung fu! This is all some kind of weird . . . science fiction thing, right?" Nora Hunter (Denise Crosby) replies with a straightforward, "Right." *Eliminators*, however, also demonstrates the power of the B picture to question the notion of classicism. Its numerous allusions to both high-culture and low-culture films emphasize the fact that all are commercial entertainment with the same price of admission.

Evil scientist and industrialist Abbott Reeves (Roy Dotrice) plans to travel back in time to Ancient Rome, where he will rule supreme. To that end, he has retrieved a young pilot, who was fatally injured when his plane crashed in the Mexican jungles near Reeves's compound, and transformed him into Mandroid (Patrick Reynolds). Mandroid is mostly machine, with detachable limbs, a bionic right eye and ear, and a computer replacing half his brain. Mandroid's mobile unit is one of the more innovative and visually striking special effects yet created in the genre. The mobile unit is a small tank that Mandroid can connect to his legless torso to look like a mechanical centaur. Since all the effects are done theatrically, *Eliminators* has a more tangible look to it than *The Terminator*, which makes extensive use of puppets and stop-motion photography.

Reeves uses Mandroid to test his bionics and time machine, and once they are perfected, he orders Mandroid dismantled. With the help of Reeves's sympathetic assistant, Takada (Tad Horino), Mandroid hooks up to his mobile unit and escapes. Takada is shot and dies, but not before he warns Mandroid to find Nora Hunter (Denise Crosby), a scientist at the robotics division of Reeves Space Research Center. Reeves, who has been presumed dead for the past five years, instead went to Mexico, where he kept himself alive through grafting and transplants. Hunter recognizes Mandroid's mechanical parts as her work put to evil ends and returns to Mexico with Mandroid to try to discover what Reeves is scheming. She brings her latest invention, S.P.O.T. (Search, Patrol, and Operational Tactician), a robot that looks like a miniature R2D2 from *Star Wars* (1977).

In Mexico, Hunter and Mandroid hire Fontana to take them upriver to Reeves's compound. The three are chased upriver by lesbian, gay, Cajun, and Mexican mercenaries; join forces with a Ninja named Kuji (Conan Lee), the son of Reeves's assistant Takada; are captured by a Neanderthal tribe (the result of Reeves's experiments in time travel); and are attacked by assorted mercenaries on three-wheel motorcycles.

Amid the action, the relationship between Fontana and Hunter changes from a battle between the sexes to romance. These scenes, which occur on the journey upriver, are patterned after *The African Queen*. *Eliminators* presents an updated version, with Hunter immediately jumping in to fix Fontana's old battered engine and defiantly drinking Fontana's last swig of whiskey. There is even a scene where Fontana pulls the boat through shallow water while Hunter taunts him. Rather than surface with leeches, however, Fontana is captured by an underwater cage set by the Neanderthal tribe. Though the romance is predicated on sexual equality, that liberal morality is offset by the villains being portrayed through homosexual and racial stereotypes. Even the Neanderthals are called "fruity cavemen" when the chief slaps Fontana on the behind.

Mandroid has all the physical and emotive trappings of the Terminator. Whereas the Terminator is a mere machine, however, Mandroid is a human turned into a machine. He seeks revenge as his only reason for living. As the romance develops between Hunter and Fontana, however, Mandroid becomes marginal to the plot. Paired with S.P.O.T., he is a C3PO-surrogate; as such, he becomes a comic figure even before the journey upriver, when he and S.P.O.T. bicker over whether to watch a soccer game or *The Jetsons*. (This reference to television's *The Jetsons* is an allusion to *The Terminator*, in which the protagonist, Sarah Connor, wears a Jetsons T-shirt.) Reduced to the status of a comic character, Mandroid loses his desire for revenge. Shortly before the attack on Reeves's compound, Mandroid requests that Hunter dismantle him, because he realizes that revenge will not make him whole again. Revenge itself, however, is never questioned, only Mandroid's role in it. Shortly after Hunter refuses to dismantle Mandroid, S.P.O.T. must be destroyed when he returns from reconnaissance, having been reprogrammed by Reeves.

The group attacks the compound. With the help of Kuji's impressive kung fu fighting, they are able to kill or scare away Reeves's mercenaries. Mandroid then challenges Reeves, who emerges in full Roman armor. He has transformed himself into a youthful cyborg with twice the power of Mandroid. The two fight, and Mandroid is quickly defeated and killed. Hunter, Fontana, and Kuji race to the time machine but are too late to stop Reeves from entering. Hunter tries to access the computer in the control room but is unable to before Reeves reaches Ancient Rome. Fontana—reflecting the frustration of the computer illiterate in the 1980's—laments the fact that he never learned computer programming as he strokes the keyboard with his fist and then punches it. The shock causes the time machine to continue traveling back in time until it reaches 435,000,000 B.C., where Reeves is stranded, the ruler of nothing. The film ends with Reeves crying out and Hunter, Fontana, and Kuji laughing.

In *Eliminators*, passion triumphs over technology, which is seen as inherently evil. This sentiment is unusual in a genre that glorifies technology and Manichaean battles, typified in the mid-1980's by the ubiquitous "Transformers" and "Gobots," anthropomorphic technologies that carry on the struggle between good and evil in film and television cartoons, comic books, and toys. After all, cyborgs from Steve Austin in *The Six Million Dollar Man* to Luke Skywalker in the *Star Wars* trilogy learn to live with their "value-free" bionics and to triumph over those who put superior bionics to evil use. Not so Mandroid. Yet to make its point, *Eliminators* must portray Mandroid as better off dead and must equate being whole with having all one's limbs. When Hunter sees Mandroid's bare chest, she gives him a look that causes him to put his chest plate back on quickly: Humans and machines must not be conjoined. As with the presentation of sexual quality, the film's critique of technology contains a negative subtext; here the subtext appears to be one that eliminates the disabled.

Eliminators, which failed to be the mainstream hit intended, nevertheless sold fifty thousand video units for approximately $2.5 million. Therein lies its importance. With the home video market firmly established, individual B pictures and exploitation films have been given an extended life. Those who missed *Eliminators* at the theater can now rent it at their local video store, so that what was once disposable becomes a permanent feature of popular culture.

Of the few reviews given the film, all but one deplored *Eliminators* on aesthetic grounds, although cinematographer Mac Ahlberg and special effects makeup artist John Buechler were highly praised. The *San Francisco Chronicle,* taking the popularity of the exploitation film at face value, called *Eliminators* "a very likable B-grade movie" and a "PG *Terminator.*" Implicit in these reviews is the idea that *Eliminators* is simply entertainment, albeit exploitive. Given the popularity and long life of films such as *Eliminators*, it is important to consider the aesthetic pleasures, the issues raised or exploited, and the subtexts of the genre and of individual films.

Chon Noriega

Reviews
Los Angeles Times. January 31, 1986, VI, p. 8.
New Statesman. CXII, August 29, 1986, p. 22.
The New York Times. CXXXV, January 31, 1986, p. C5.
San Francisco Chronicle. February 1, 1986, p. 39.
Variety. CCCXXII, February 5, 1986, p. 32.

FERRIS BUELLER'S DAY OFF

Production: John Hughes and Tom Jacobson; released by Paramount Pictures
Direction: John Hughes
Screenplay: John Hughes
Cinematography: Tak Fujimoto
Editing: Paul Hirsch
Narration: Matthew Broderick
Art direction: John W. Corso
Costume design: Marilyn Vance
Music: Ira Newborn
MPAA rating: PG-13
Running time: 103 minutes

Principal characters:
Ferris Bueller . . . . Matthew Broderick
Cameron Frye . . . . Alan Ruck
Sloane Peterson . . . . Mia Sara
Ed Rooney . . . . Jeffrey Jones
Jeanie Bueller . . . . Jennifer Grey
Katie Bueller . . . . Cindy Pickett
Tom Bueller . . . . Lyman Ward
School secretary . . . . Edie McClurg

Ferris Bueller's Day Off, or "one man's struggle to take it easy," is a likable and entertaining film and was one of the major hits of the summer of 1986, earning more than fifty million dollars between Memorial Day and Labor Day and continuing its run well into the fall. It was targeted toward the teenage market and was perfectly crafted to fit the expectations of that audience by John Hughes, who both directed and wrote the screenplay.

Hughes has a particular genius for writing screenplays that appeal to teenagers. *Sixteen Candles*, which he wrote and directed in 1984, was enormously popular, as was *The Breakfast Club* in 1985, with its ensemble of high school misfits who, forced to spend a Saturday together on detention, discover they have more in common than they would have dreamed possible. Hughes also wrote the screenplay for *Pretty in Pink* (reviewed in this volume), released early in 1986, concerning a potentially comic romance between a solidly middle-class boy and an attractive and perky girl from the wrong side of the tracks.

With *Ferris Bueller's Day Off*, Hughes avoids the pathos of *Pretty in Pink* and works entirely for comedy. As a result, he has produced the perfect "goof-off" picture, which therefore became the perfect summer film. What is interesting about this film is its comic formula, which hearkens back to the earlier days of American screen comedy. In the days of silent comedy, filmmakers would begin by fabricating a situation and then work to see what could be done to make that situation as humorous as possible.

Ferris Bueller's Day Off is not, perhaps, a masterpiece of comic invention in this regard, but it nevertheless succeeds, thanks to the comic talents of Matthew Broderick in the title role, Alan Ruck as his friend Cameron Frye, Jennifer Grey as his spiteful sister Jeanie, and especially Jeffrey Jones as Principal Rooney, who is determined not to let Ferris succeed with his truancy scheme, but who is constantly outsmarted by the boy.

Matthew Broderick is brilliantly charming as Ferris when he takes the audience into his confidence and explains why this day away from the tedium of his Chicago high school is so important to him. He has planned his day off for some time and executes his plan to perfection. He has also worked out a justification for his scheme: "Life moves pretty fast. If you don't stop once in a while and look around, you could miss it." His sister Jeanie is outraged. She knows full well that Ferris is faking his ailments (a stomachache and a fever), and she is resentful: "If I was bleeding out of my eyes, you'd make me go to school," she protests to her parents.

"This is my ninth sick day this semester," Ferris explains to his sympathetic audience. "It's getting tough coming up with new illnesses. . . . So I better make this one count." In order to make the day "count," he has to go in style, so he contacts his friend Cameron, who really is sick. Cameron's father owns a classic car he keeps as a sort of museum piece, a red 1961 Ferrari 250 GTS. "It has a market value of $165,000," Cameron explains. "My father spent three years restoring it. It is his joy; it is his passion; it is his love."

After tricking his parents and the school authorities (except for Principal Rooney, who really is not fooled and perfectly understands Ferris' attitude toward school), Ferris gets together with Cameron and talks his friend into taking his father's red convertible to the Loop for a joyride. Ferris has a real talent for talking people into doing things they would not ordinarily do.

For a perfect "day off," Ferris needs some female companionship as well, so he invents a scheme to get his girlfriend, Sloane Peterson (Mia Sara), out of school for the day, too. Ferris has Cameron, impersonating Sloane's father, call Mr. Rooney to ask that Sloane be excused because her grandmother has died. Rooney is suspicious when Cameron calls, but when Ferris himself calls Rooney on another line, the principal is fooled. Sloane is freed, and the boys pick her up at school (Ferris at the wheel, in disguise).

The three kids drive around downtown Chicago, then leave the valued Ferrari at a parking garage, where, unknown to them, the parking attendants take it out for a joyride of their own. The viewer fears that something is going to happen to the car, but Hughes saves that development for later, while Ferris and his friends enjoy themselves downtown.

Their adventures downtown do not amount to much. They have lunch at a classy restaurant (will they be recognized there?), stop by the art museum, and go to Wrigley Field to watch some baseball. Ferris enters into a German-American parade downtown and sings "Twist and Shout," his idea of a good time. Ferris disappoints the audience, however, by lacking the imagination to make the best of his "day off."

What sustains interest here is that Ferris' nemesis, the dim-witted Principal Rooney, may catch him away from home. Rooney certainly knows that something is going on, and he is determined to investigate the matter. This picture, however, is aimed at teenagers; thus the adults are complete idiots, and all Rooney finds is frustration. Ferris' sister could get revenge on her conniving brother, but she, like the audience and like Cameron, is ultimately taken in by his charm and helps him execute his plan to perfection.

The film needs a conclusion, however, and Cameron provides it by rebelling against his rather stupid, materialistic father, who apparently values his Ferrari more than his son. The father keeps a close watch over the odometer, so, after their mindless "day off," Ferris and Cameron block up the rear wheels and run the engine in reverse, attempting to restore the miles they have put on the automobile. This scheme does not work. While the wheels are spinning, Cameron has an epiphany: "I gotta take a stand," he opines, as resentment toward his father builds. Enraged by the thought of his father, Cameron kicks the car so hard he knocks it off the jack. The car, engine running at full tilt, shoots out of the garage and crashes into a ravine. Now Cameron will really have to take a stand, but as far as the conniving, self-indulgent Ferris is concerned, everything is "cool."

Leaving Cameron alone to face his father at home, Ferris heads for his own house. Mr. Rooney is there waiting for him, and it looks as though Ferris is trapped, but at this point Jeanie saves the day for him. To the end, then, Ferris is free and clear. He lives a charmed life.

Clearly there is not much substance to this picture, populated as it is by impudent kids and moronic adults. Its style, however, is consistent and flawless, and the dialogue has exactly the right tone and is authentically adolescent. *Variety* criticized the film for its "paucity of invention," protesting that "Hughes has gone to this well at least once too often" and describing the characters as "airheads without a cause."

Likewise, Paul Attanasio of *The Washington Post* thought the script was "off-balance" and dismissed the film for its celebration of "mindlessly rich kids." Although Attanasio nicely described Hughes as a "teen anthropologist," his review misses the film's charm and in no way accounts for its considerable popular appeal. His colleague at *The Washington Post*, Rita Kempley, was more on target, calling Ferris "one terrific kid" and the film "one terrific movie," acted "with assurance, directed with precision, and written with universal appeal." She concluded that the film "takes you out of yourself for a while—like a Ferris-wheel ride," enabling the viewer to "appreciate the carnival."

Reviewers whose film consciousness was shaped by the politics of the 1960's are offended by the general silliness of films such as this one, which have dominated the market in the 1980's. Liberals are inclined to accept cinema as a potential instrument of policy; conservatives are more contemptuous of "movies." George Will, one of the most articulate voices of the American Right, praised *Ferris Bueller's Day Off* as the "greatest movie" of the summer of 1986, the "moviest movie, the one most true to the general spirit of movies, the spirit of effortless escapism." Will conceded that *Ferris Bueller* is "not serious," but, then, he added, "few movies are, and fewer should be." His latter point is debatable. By trivializing the cinema, Will attempts to discredit such criticism of the current power structure as the medium may offer. The fact that *Ferris Bueller's Day Off* could be found so amusing by so pedantic and fussy a fellow as George Will, however, speaks volumes for its entertainment value. Will is not entirely humorless, but he takes himself seriously indeed, and he is not often moved to comment about trivial entertainments. His response, therefore, is a tribute to John Hughes's adolescent vision and to this film's universal appeal.

James M. Welsh

Reviews

The Humanist. XLVI, September, 1986, p. 41.
Los Angeles Times. June 11, 1986, VI, p. 1.
The New York Times. CXXXV, June 11, 1986, p. C24.
Newsweek. CVII, June 16, 1986, p. 75.
Seventeen. XLV, August, 1986, p. 187.
Teen. XXX, March, 1986, p. 48.
Time. CXXVII, June 23, 1986, p. 74.
Variety. CCCXXIII, June 4, 1986, p. 16.
The Wall Street Journal. CCVIII, June 17, 1986, p. 26.
The Washington Post. June 12, 1986, p. D4.

FIFTY-TWO PICK-UP

Production: Menahem Golan and Yoram Globus; released by Cannon Films
Direction: John Frankenheimer
Screenplay: Elmore Leonard and John Steppling; based on the novel of the
  same name by Elmore Leonard
Cinematography: Jost Vacano
Editing: Robert F. Shugrue
Production design: Philip Harrison
Art direction: Russell Christian; set decoration, Max Whitehouse
Special effects: Eric Allard
Makeup: Dee Mansano
Costume design: Ray Summers
Sound: Ed Novick
Music direction: Paula Erickson
Music: Gary Chang
MPAA rating: R
Running time: 114 minutes

> *Principal characters:*
> Harry Mitchell .... Roy Scheider
> Barbara Mitchell .... Ann-Margret
> Doreen .... Vanity
> Alan Raimy........................ John Glover
> Leo Franks .... Robert Trebor
> Bobby Shy.................. Clarence Williams III
> Cini.............................. Kelly Preston
> Jim O'Boyle .... Lonny Chapman
> Mark Averson .... Doug McClure

Fifty-two Pick-up is a slick, at times distasteful, extortion thriller which
brings a well-heeled Los Angeles suburbanite into head-on collision with the
criminal underworld. The film lacks the degree of suspense necessary to
make it an outstanding example of its genre, but its brisk pace, technical
polish, and some excellent acting in the secondary roles lift it out of the
ranks of the merely average. Like *Death Wish* (1974) and its sequels, it deals
with a respectable businessman who, being pressed to the limits by corrupt
forces, takes the law into his own hands. *Fifty-two Pick-up*, however, incorporates more subtle forms of interaction between the chief adversaries and,
while it does not pass up opportunities to depict violent confrontations, is
more interested in exploring the role of verbal manipulation as a means of
overcoming the opposition.

Fifty-two Pick-up is adapted from Elmore Leonard's 1974 novel of the same title. Leonard, who cowrote the screenplay for *Fifty-two Pick-up* with playwright John Steppling, has earned recognition as one of America's leading crime-fiction writers after making his initial mark as an author of Westerns. Nicknamed the "Dickens of Detroit" because of his skill in creating colorful, lowlife characters, the Michigan-based author has adapted several other of his novels for the screen, including *The Moonshine War* (1970), *Mr. Majestyk* (1974), and *Stick* (1985). None of these films, however, met with either commercial or critical success. *Hombre*, a 1967 motion picture based on one of Leonard's Westerns, fared much better, but it was scripted by Irving Ravetch. *Fifty-two Pick-up* ranks as an effective screen translation of Leonard's work. Although there are some differences between novel and film in terms of plot, *Fifty-two Pick-up* faithfully reproduces the writer's skillful handling of language, action, and shady characters. As in the book, the film's dialogue is tough, terse, and firmly rooted in the milieus of the central figures.

Harry Mitchell (Roy Scheider) is a middle-aged industrialist who keeps in shape with a morning dip in his pool and pampers himself with a snappy Jaguar XKE. His wife, Barbara (Ann-Margret), is a striking redhead with prospects of a bright future in local politics. The film's opening scenes, in which dialogue, editing, and cinematography combine to create a sense of distance between the couple, suggest that all is not well with the marriage. What has so far been implied is confirmed as Harry is shown arriving at the apartment of his young mistress, Cini (Kelly Preston). Instead of finding his lover, however, he is greeted by a trio of blackmailers who force him to watch his adultery on videotape. Dismayed to learn that Cini works as a nude model in a seedy flesh parlor, Harry realizes that he has been set up. The crooks lay down their terms—$105,000 in exchange for the tape—and leave Harry to contemplate the crisis into which his libido has led him.

Harry confesses his transgressions to his disgusted wife and confides details of the scam to his lawyer-friend Jim O'Boyle (Lonny Chapman). Fearing that the ensuing scandal would jeopardize Barbara's budding political career, Harry rejects O'Boyle's advice to go to the police. The villains, meanwhile, return to their Los Angeles netherworld. The three are classic Leonard ne'er-do-wells—mean, nasty men whose criminal ambitions are doomed to failure by their ineptitude. The ringleader, Alan Raimy (John Glover), is a pornographic theater manager and pervert who fancies himself an amateur filmmaker. Leo Franks (Robert Trebor) runs the nude modeling agency where Cini and her beautiful black friend Doreen (Vanity) ply their trade. A sweaty, blubbery sycophant who guzzles alcohol at moments of stress, Leo is a born loser. The most menacing member of the trio is Bobby Shy (Clarence Williams III), a cocaine user who is not above suffocating his girlfriend almost to the point of death if it will advance his interests.

The blackmailers escalate the pressure on Harry to meet their demands.

They subject him to a Raimy-crafted snuff film in which Cini is brutally murdered, and Raimy steals Harry's gun and other items from under Barbara's nose in order to frame Harry with the murder. Although cornered, Harry is determined not to sell his home or business to raise the blackmail. He embarks on a carefully calculated plan of attack in which the villains' already tenuous cohesion is swiftly dismantled. Far from avoiding his adversaries, he actively seeks them out, playing one off against the other. He even invites Raimy to inspect his books, which provide conclusive evidence of Harry's inability to raise the required money.

With the stakes adjusted downward to fifty-two thousand dollars, Raimy increases his potential share by eliminating Leo and Bobby. In a last-ditch effort to force Harry's compliance, he calmly returns to Harry's home, kidnaps Barbara, and renders her senseless with heroin. These events prepare the way for the final showdown, in which Harry's guile triumphs over Raimy's greed. The film title's double meaning—a reference both to the amount Raimy hopes to collect and to a cheap card trick in which one person makes a fool of another—acquires its full significance in this last scene.

In terms of plot, *Fifty-two Pick-up* contains few surprises. The film is littered with stock genre devices such as the frame-up, the hostage, and the process of divide-and-conquer. The film's chief strength lies in the performances of Glover, Trebor, and Williams as the bumbling crooks. Glover, who won an Emmy nomination for his brief but memorable portrayal of an AIDS victim in the television film *An Early Frost* (1985), gives another memorable performance as the cocky, sadistic Raimy. Like Trebor and Williams, Glover tempers his portrait of corruption with gestures and mannerisms which make him more than merely a cardboard villain. All three actors do full justice to Leonard's clever blueprints for these roles. In contrast, the character of Harry Mitchell seems underdeveloped almost to the point of one-dimensionality. Some of the problem derives from the acting of Roy Scheider, who wears a masklike expression throughout the film and who provides little insight into the inner workings of Harry's mind. It is a remarkably uninteresting performance from an actor who lit up the screen in Bob Fosse's *All That Jazz* (1979) and who was so effective in *The French Connection* (1971) and *Jaws* (1975). The script must also bear part of the blame for the thinness of Harry's character. Unlike Leonard's novel, which is set not in Los Angeles but in Detroit, the film makes little effort to probe Harry's reasons for dealing with the blackmailers on his own terms. The novel is much more explicit about Harry's rise to fortune from a blue-collar background and the way this fuels his determination not to be intimidated.

The female characters in *Fifty-two Pick-up* are uniformly less interesting than their male counterparts, and do little more than represent familiar stereotypes—the wronged wife, the exploited innocent, the ravenous sex kitten. Ann-Margret, whose performances in *Carnal Knowledge* (1971), *The*

Return of the Soldier (1982), and *Twice in a Lifetime* (1985) have proved her to be an actress of considerable ability, is here given little to do. Even though her character is potentially more interesting in the film than in the novel, where she is not an aspiring politician but a housewife, she becomes merely another object for Raimy's delectation. Indeed, it is the representation of women in *Fifty-two Pick-up* which at times make it seem less like a polished thriller and more like a tawdry exploitation film. This duality may reflect the involvement of Cannon Films, a production company owned and run by Menahem Golan and Yoram Globus. At one time associated chiefly with low-budget sex-and-violence films, Cannon Films diversified during the mid-1980's into glossy, expensive productions in a bid for prestige and a share of the mainstream box-office.

Of greater interest than any of *Fifty-two Pick-up*'s plot developments is John Frankenheimer's credit as director. Frankenheimer, who began his directorial career in the demanding conditions of live television drama, rose to prominence in the early 1960's. Two films in particular, the chilling political thrillers *The Manchurian Candidate* (1962) and *Seven Days in May* (1964), led to his being hailed as one of America's most outstanding directors. His youthful promise was compared to that of Orson Welles, and his mastery of suspense was compared to that of Alfred Hitchcock. During the late 1960's and early 1970's, however, his career and reputation spiraled downward, allegedly because of too many box-office flops and an excess of temperament. Since then, only *French Connection II* (1975), with its fine tuning between action and observation of character, marked a clear return to form. Although Frankenheimer has long ceased to be a major presence in American cinema, those familiar with his early achievements may well consider *Fifty-two Pick-up* a sorry vehicle for his talents.

Since it is hard to care about the fate of characters as bland and as inscrutable as Harry and Barbara, *Fifty-two Pick-up* fails to generate much suspense. Robert F. Shugrue's editing, however, sustains interest in the unfolding events by moving the action along briskly. Jost Vacano, whose cinematography greatly augmented the mood of claustrophobia in the submarine settings of *Das Boot* (1981), is responsible for *Fifty-two Pick-up*'s pronounced visual clarity. Vacano's bright, sharp images seem well suited to a plot in which exposure is a recurrent theme.

Leonard's novel inspired an earlier Golan and Globus production, *The Ambassador* (1984), which was filmed in Israel and starred Robert Mitchum and Ellen Burstyn. The screenplay for this earlier film was written by Max Jack. The plot of *The Ambassador*, which involves its protagonist in Arab-Israeli conflict, has little in common with *Fifty-two Pick-up* beyond the use of filmed evidence of adultery to blackmail the main character.

Fiona Valentine

Reviews

American Film. XII, November, 1986, p. 77.
Chicago Tribune. November 11, 1986, V, p. 3.
Films in Review. XXXVIII, February, 1987, p. 106.
Los Angeles Times. November 7, 1986, VI, p. 8.
The New York Times. November 7, 1986, p. C10.
Newsweek. CVIII, November 17, 1986, p. 89.
People Weekly. XXVI, November 24, 1986, p. 10.
Variety. CCCXV, November 12, 1986, p. 14.
Video. XI, June, 1987, p. 81.
The Village Voice. XXXI, November 18, 1986, p. 58.
The Washington Post. November 12, 1986, p. D6.

THE FLY

Production: Stuart Cornfeld; released by Twentieth Century-Fox
Direction: David Cronenberg
Screenplay: Charles Edward Pogue and David Cronenberg; based on a story
  by George Langelaan
Cinematography: Mark Irwin
Editing: Ronald Sanders
Production design: Carol Spier
Art direction: Rolf Harvey; set decoration, Elinor Rose Galbraith and
  James McAteer
Makeup: Chris Walas and Stephen Dupuis (AA)
Costume design: Denise Cronenberg
Music: Howard Shore
MPAA rating: R
Running time: 100 minutes

> *Principal characters:*
> Seth Brundle .... Jeff Goldblum
> Veronica Quaife .... Geena Davis
> Stathis Borans .... John Getz
> Tawny.............................. Joy Boushel
> Dr. Cheevers .... Les Carlson

David Cronenberg's *The Fly* belongs to a particular type of horror film that has developed in recent years, one that achieves its major effect by producing a feeling of revulsion in the viewer. This cinema of revulsion is light-years away from the classic horror films produced by Hollywood in the 1930's, which provoked a more decorous and controlled effect of tension and fright in the audience by silence and the unseen, suggestion and delay. The mass of lower-quality horror films that followed in the 1940's and 1950's tended to undercut their own capacity to frighten with self-deprecating exaggerations of character and action, but these films still did not stress violence, gore, or the repulsive.

The less savory developments in the horror film in recent decades are the product of several causes: the breakdown of film censorship by both the industry and governmental agencies; the prolific presentation of real violence on television during the Vietnam War; the development of special effects and makeup for the cinema that allow realistic and graphic representations of acts of violence, which have virtually become the foci of many films; and the increasing appetite of young audiences for visual feasts of sadism and horror. *The Fly* may well be the most elegant and intelligent horror film of revulsion yet to appear, but there can be no doubt that its main intent is to shock and horrify its audience by showing in great detail the gradual and nauseating physical deterioration of its protagonist as he gradually changes into an oversize insect. In this respect, the film also belongs to another subgroup within the horror genre, the mutation film, which rose to prominence during the 1950's in response to the public's fear of nuclear war and the physical transformation, violation, and disfigurement that such a holocaust would cause. Mutation, however, has always been a feature of the horror film, though in varying degrees, reflecting the basic human fear of becoming a monster, ugly and repulsive like Frankenstein's monster, or some lower form of life, such as an ape, alligator, or snake.

Cronenberg's *The Fly* is also one of a group of horror films that are remakes of earlier classics in the genre and use the original versions as springboards for demonstration of changes in the culture and advances in film technology. Motion pictures such as John Carpenter's 1982 version of *The Thing* (based on the 1951 film directed by Christian Nyby and produced by Howard Hawks) and Paul Schrader's 1982 version of *Cat People* (based on the 1942 film directed by Jacques Tourneur and produced by Val Lewton) have been more effective than remakes of works in other genres because they have been able to extend the mythic appeal of their originals into a contemporary world and to make explicit what before could only be suggested. Certainly Cronenberg's *The Fly* extends the nightmare that was first presented in Kurt Neumann's 1958 film of the same name, increasing its intensity and horror with a far more graphic visual dimension, involving the audience with characters that are more credible and complex, and entrapping viewers in a grotesque situation that resonates more deeply in the unconscious. For these reasons, the present film is also more upsetting to watch and far less enjoyable than the original.

The original film was suggested by George Langelaan's short story "The Fly," which had appeared in the June, 1956, issue of *Playboy* magazine. Twentieth Century-Fox, seeing potential in the project, allowed the production a budget of $400,000, a significant outlay for a horror film, and decided to produce the work in color and CinemaScope. Neumann hired James Clavell to write his first screenplay. Clavell stayed reasonably close to the source and wrote a screenplay that plausibly developed its outrageous premise with seriousness and a heightening suspense. Two very important scenes in the original that did not appear in the remake occur when Helene (Patricia Owens) unveils the large fly head of her husband, Andre (Al "David" Hedison), and when, at the end of the film, the little fly, with Andre's tiny head, screams "Help me! Help me!" as it is about to be devoured by a spider. The film was successful enough for Twentieth Century-Fox to finance two rather dismal sequels, *Return of the Fly* in 1959 and *Curse of the Fly* in 1965.

Cronenberg and Charles Edward Pogue rewrote the original screenplay, making some crucial changes. In the original film, the scientist undergoes a partial physical transformation all at once, and much of the tension in the film derives from his and his wife's frantic search to find the little fly with his head and hand. In the remake, the molecules of man and fly blend, and much of the tension the audience experiences derives from the witnessing of the inevitable physical and mental deterioration of the protagonist as he changes into a slimy and creepy creature. An interesting love relationship, both erotic and tender, is also added to the story and contributes a tragic and upsetting contrast between physical love and physical corruption.

Seth Brundle (Jeff Goldblum), while attending a science exhibition, is attracted to Veronica Quaife (Geena Davis), a reporter for *Particle*, a science magazine. He takes her back to his laboratory, a loft in an old building in a run-down section of town, to see the remarkable project in which he is engaged. Seth is working on teleportation—the transmission of objects through space. His equipment includes two telepods and a computer that controls the disintegration of an object in one telepod and its reintegration in the other. Seth demonstrates his wonderful machinery with Veronica's panty hose and persuades her to write a story for her magazine that will describe his final work on the invention. He still is having problems transporting live creatures, however, as demonstrated in a later scene when a baboon arrives in the second telepod inside out. As Seth perfects his machine, he and Veronica begin a love affair, much to the chagrin of her editor, Stathis Borans (John Getz), who had formerly been her lover. In a sudden fit of jealousy over Stathis, a slightly drunk Seth teleports himself, unaware that a fly is being transmitted with him. At first Seth is rejuvenated, performing acrobatic feats on a gymnastic bar in his loft and sexual feats with Veronica in bed, but soon a strange transformation begins to take place. Seth grows some unpleasant wiry hairs, his skin becomes mottled, and his disposition becomes mercurial. Seth learns from his computer that his genes were merged with those of a fly during transmission. From this point on, the physical and biological changes of "Brundlefly," as Seth refers to himself, are graphically portrayed. Veronica soon discovers that she has been impregnated by Seth and is horrified by the possibility that she is carrying some type of monstrosity. In a particularly unsettling dream, she undergoes an abortion in which a long, slimy maggot baby is removed from her womb (Cronenberg wickedly plays the obstetrician in this scene). Before she can undergo an abortion in reality, she is carried away to the laboratory by Seth, who has acquired the demented notion from his computer that he can clean up his body by merging his molecules with hers. Borans attempts to rescue Veronica but in the process has a hand and ankle dissolved by Seth's corrosive fly-vomit. He is, however, able to rescue Veronica from her telepod before she is transmitted. Seth smashes the door on his telepod but is himself transported. Made even more grotesque by his fusion with parts of the telepod, he persuades Veronica to kill him with Borans' rifle.

Such a description of the plot cannot suggest the visual impact on the viewer of Seth's transformations as he becomes an increasingly grotesque human insect. For this remarkable achievement, the film is much indebted to Chris Walas and Stephen Dupuis who designed the various stages of Brundlefly's appearance and won an Academy Award for creating the film's makeup effects, and to Mark Irwin, the director of photography, who has achieved some impressive lighting and colors for Seth's transformations. This is not a film of razzle-dazzle laboratory effects—at one point Veronica describes the telepods as designer phone booths. It is, however, a film upsettingly obsessed with bodies and flesh, with mutation and mutilation, with physical corruption and degeneration—with a biological horror already explored by Cronenberg in such earlier films as *They Came from Within* (1976), *Rabid* (1977), and *The Brood* (1979).

What makes the viewer even more acutely aware of the biological horror is the vital physical relationship of Seth and Veronica in the first part of the film. Jeff Goldblum and Geena Davis play their parts with a warmth, humor, and natural intimacy that both engages the audience and yields a distinct foreboding about things to come. Physical intimacy turns to physical violence after Seth has taken his ride in the telepods and proceeds to shatter a man's arm when arm wrestling in a seedy bar for the favors of a woman. Biology becomes revolting when Seth demonstrates to Veronica how he eats like a fly, preparing his food for digestion by decomposing it with his vomit. Veronica, however, is meant to be a sharp contrast to the shrinking heroines of the horror films of the past. A modern woman of feeling and strength, she embraces Seth with compassion and love after his human ear falls from his head into his own hand.

It is in the final stages of the lovers' relationship that the audience sees how deeply unsettling is Cronenberg's fantasy about human bodies and human relationships—the audience is made uneasy not merely in Seth's attempt to merge his debased body with Veronica's but also by the fetus he leaves within her. Veronica's nightmare about the maggot in her womb makes the viewer uncertain about her actual pregnancy, about the nature of the fetus that carries Brundlefly's genes. Amid all the horrors that Cronenberg presents regarding physical mutation and mutilation, amid his Grand Guignol display of biological horrors, is his demonic thrust at mankind's deepest fears about procreation—about the monsters produced from man's own body. Cronenberg's cinema of biological revulsion is as much about birth and life as it is about decay and death.

Ira Konigsberg

Reviews

American Film. XXXVII, July, 1986, p. 81.
Cinefantastique. XVII, January, 1987, p. 46.
Films in Review. XXXVII, November, 1986, p. 548.
The Humanist. XLVI, November, 1986, p. 40.
The Nation. CCXLIII, September 20, 1986, p. 257.
The New York Times. CXXXV, August 15, 1986, p. C18.
The New Yorker. LXII, October 6, 1986, p. 126.
Newsweek. CVIII, August 18, 1986, p. 59.
Time. CXXVIII, August 18, 1986, p. 75.
Variety. CCCXXIV, August 13, 1986, p. 11.
The Wall Street Journal. CCVIII, August 7, 1986, p. 16.

F/X

Production: Dodi Fayed and Jack Wiener; released by Orion Pictures
Direction: Robert Mandel
Screenplay: Robert T. Megginson and Gregory Fleeman
Cinematography: Miroslav Ondříček
Editing: Terry Rawlings
Production design: Mel Bourne
Art direction: Speed Hopkins; set decoration, Steven Jordan
Special effects: John Stears
Makeup: Carl Fullerton
Costume design: Julie Weiss
Music: Bill Conti
MPAA rating: R
Running time: 107 minutes

Principal characters:
Rollie Tyler	Bryan Brown
Leo McCarthy	Brian Dennehy
Ellen	Diane Venora
Lipton	Cliff De Young
Mason	Mason Adams
Nicholas DeFranco	Jerry Orbach
Andy	Martha Gehman

This Orion motion picture takes its title from the shorthand term used by the technicians responsible for a given film's "F/X" or special effects. Since the popular success of *Star Wars* (1977) and *Close Encounters of the Third Kind* (1978), model builders, matte artists, and optical houses, which generate light and laser effects, have figured prominently, or even more prominently, than the actors in science-fiction films. Concurrently, the emergence of makeup artists skilled in particularly gory wounds, decapitations, and dismemberments, such as Tom Savini, who did the "splatter" effects for two seminal late 1970's gore films, George Romero's *Dawn of the Dead* (1979) and the *Friday the Thirteenth* series of films (which include five movies, in 1981, 1982, 1984, 1985, and 1986, in addition to the original 1980 horror entry), has made makeup effects artists integral to practically every major horror film in the 1980's. It seems appropriate that a major Hollywood studio would at last release a fairly slick and classy motion picture featuring a makeup and effects technician as the lead character. Yet *F/X* is not a mere biography or a parodic send-up of this relatively new type of creative artist, but more obviously a suspense and adventure film which recalls the Alfred Hitchcock films of the 1950's, in which an ordinary citizen is caught up in a conspiracy, accused of a crime he did not commit, and pursued by both police and the sinister originators of the plot while trying to figure out (and consequently allow the audience to figure out) the details and mechanics of what he has gotten himself into and how to get himself out of it. Here, instead of a Midwestern American type actor such as James Stewart playing the ordinary man caught in a web of paranoia, Australian actor Bryan Brown is cast as the innocent hero. His character, Rollie Tyler, a special-effects and makeup expert, has more than only his wits to rely on: He has a substantial array of special-effects equipment loaded inside his specially designed van.

The film opens with a clever scene in which the viewer believes that he or she is witnessing a gangland slaying in a posh restaurant, a scene which is meant to parody the excesses of violence in Brian DePalma's remake of *Scarface* (1983). Yet one soon realizes that this scene is merely one being shot for a film. When the camera pulls back, it reveals technicians standing around commenting on the engineering of the gunshot effects. Rollie Tyler has been on many such sets, doing the effects for exploitation pictures with titles such as *I Dismember Mama* and *Song of the Succubus*, even getting deported from his native Australia for a film called *Vermin from Venus*.

Tyler, now one of the foremost special-effects creators working in film, is approached by Justice Department agents from the Witness Relocation Program with an offer of thirty thousand dollars to stage what must be made to look like a real assassination of a gangster, a Mafia boss who has agreed to inform on his pals in court and now must be given a new identity. What better way to guarantee the success of this new identity than to kill off the old one?

Tyler is skeptical at first whether the con will be convincing enough to fool the local police and news media, but he eventually decides to take on the job. At the last moment, Agent Lipton (Cliff De Young) begs Tyler to play the gunman who pulls the trigger himself, to guarantee that the effects will come off as planned. Agent Lipton and his superior, Colonel Mason (Mason Adams), assure Tyler that he will be spirited away before the police can catch him and that no one will recognize him as the assassin. Tyler relents, the shooting incident is successful, but Agent Lipton unsuccessfully attempts to kill Tyler in the fleeing getaway car. Moreover, it appears to Tyler that the mob boss has really been murdered, and the police are now in hot pursuit.

Tyler, it seems, is being framed for the murder, which may or may not be real, and he must keep one step ahead of the police and at the same time unravel the plot into which he has stepped. The people at the Witness Relocation Program act as if they have never heard of him, and no one will believe his claim that agents approached him to stage the assassination. The only people willing to listen and to help him are his girlfriend, Ellen (Diane

Venora), an actress, and his colleague, Andy (Martha Gehman). After Ellen is murdered, Andy helps Tyler confound the police and conspirators with an array of cheap but convincing special effects. *F/X* now becomes the fairly simple story of Tyler trying to avoid his various pursuers, although this hour-long chase is never dull. Director Robert Mandel has a flair for witty and clever twists along the way, and the cinematography by Miroslav Ondříček (who shot the 1984 film *Amadeus*) makes the rain-slicked and darkened streets of New York City appear menacing and thrilling.

After the staged assassination of mobster Nicholas DeFranco (Jerry Orbach), a somewhat renegade police detective, Leo McCarthy (Brian Dennehy), begins his own investigation into the scheme because he has a hunch that DeFranco may be alive after all. This subplot is given equal time to that of Tyler's pursuit. The excellent parallel plot structure, like parallel lines that never cross, does not allow McCarthy to link up with Tyler until the very end of the film, when they both have unraveled the scheme and discovered that Agent Lipton and Colonel Mason are corrupt and were paid off by the still-living Mafioso DeFranco to frame Tyler for the murder. Tyler and McCarthy turn the tables on the corrupt government agents, steal the payoff money, and flee the country, leaving the agents and their old occupations behind in New York City.

The ending of *F/X* is very different from Alfred Hitchcock's films of the 1950's, being rather cynical and amoral, a viewpoint which Hitchcock and the filmmaking standards of the 1950's would have never allowed. When Tyler and McCarthy steal the money from the corrupt agents, the filmmakers are indirectly condoning corruption of a sort (though it is disguised as a kind of revenge). Furthermore, *F/X* is wittier in a self-conscious and parodic way than any Hitchcock film of the 1950's was. Director Robert Mandel here generates a crackling and intense suspense. Even though some of the scenes are violent and gory, there is a spirit of fun and imagination which makes the net effect of the film cheerful and, oddly, innocent. As a director, Mandel's touch is quick, sharp, and clean, as is editor Terry Rawlings'.

The most striking aspect and the source of the film's overall success in creating suspense is the extraordinary job that director Mandel achieves with his actors. The casting is consistently perfect, and the actors all turn in performances that are superior. Both Bryan Brown and Brian Dennehy establish a warm and compassionate rapport with the viewer, so that the audience is likely to care and actually to believe that the situation portrayed on the screen could happen in real life. Mandel's accomplished skill with actors should not be surprising after one views his first film, *Independence Day* (1983), a generally overlooked small-town drama in which actress Dianne Wiest turns in a moving portrait of a woman who is a victim of physical abuse from her husband.

Since the 1970's, it has been a common complaint from critics and the public that films which utilize an abundance of special effects tend to dwarf the characterizations and acting in many films; directors are so distracted in constructing convincing special effects that the acting must take a backseat to the light show and blood splattering that goes on. The special effects in *F/X* are employed, not merely for dazzle, but to move the story along. The strength of the film rests ultimately on its strong and convincing characterizations.

Bill-Dale Marcinko

Reviews
American Film. XI, April, 1986, p. 30.
Commonweal. CXIII, June 20, 1986, p. 374.
Films in Review. XXXVII, May, 1986, p. 304.
Los Angeles. XXXI, March, 1986, p. 50.
The Nation. CCXLII, March 29, 1986, p. 468.
The New York Times. CXXXV, February 7, 1986, p. C1.
The New Yorker. LXII, February 24, 1986, p. 93.
People Weekly. XXV, February 24, 1986, p. 10.
Time. CXXVII, February 24, 1986, p. 71.
Variety. CCCXXII, January 29, 1986, p. 15.
The Wall Street Journal. CCVII, January 30, 1986, p. 28.

GINGER AND FRED
(GINGER E FRED)

Origin: Italy
Released: 1985
Released in U.S.: 1986
Production: Alberto Grimaldi for PEA (Rome), Revcom Films in association with Les Films Ariane–FR3 Films (Paris), Stella Films in association with Anthea (Munich), and with the collaboration of RAIUno.; released by Recorded Releasing
Direction: Federico Fellini
Screenplay: Federico Fellini, Tonino Guerra, and Tullio Pinelli; based on a story by Federico Fellini and Tonino Guerra
Cinematography: Tonino Delli Colli and Ennio Guarnieri
Editing: Nino Baragli, Ugo De Rossi, and Ruggero Mastroianni
Art direction: Dante Ferretti; set decoration, Nazzareno Plana
Costume design: Danilo Donati
Music: Nicola Piovani
MPAA rating: PG-13
Running time: 127 minutes

Principal characters:
Amelia Bonetti, "Ginger"..........Giulietta Masina
Pippo Botticella, "Fred".......Marcello Mastroianni
Show host ....Franco Fabrizi
Admiral.................Frederick von Ledenburg
Transvestite ....Augusto Poderosi
Assistant producer ....Martin Maria Blau
Flying priest...............Jacques Henri Lartigue
Toto.............................Toto Mignone
Intellectual........................Ezio Marano
Absentee.....................Antoine Saint Jean
Prisoner ....Frederick von Thun
TV inspector.....................Antonio Ivorio
Journalist........................Barbara Scoppa
Journalist ....Elisabetta Flumeri
Mother of ghost ....Ginestra Spinola
Mafioso.........................Stefanie Marini
Mafioso ....Francesco Casale
Lawyer.....................Gianfranco Alperstre
Mrs. Spretato...................Cosima Chiusoli
Son of ghost ....Sergio Ciulli
Continuity girl................Laurentina Guidotti

Spretato . . . . Luciano Lombardo
Literary critic . . . . Elena Magoia
Editor . . . . Mauro Misul
Assistant director . . . . Nando Pucci Negri
Patient . . . . Elena Cantarone

As with all of Federico Fellini's films, *Ginger and Fred* defies simplistic characterization. The Ginger and Fred of the title are the stage names of two aging vaudevillian dancers, Amelia Bonetti (Giulietta Masina) and Pippo Botticella (Marcello Mastroianni), who were renowned in the 1940's for their imitation of Ginger Rogers and Fred Astaire. After a separation of more than thirty years, the couple have agreed to do a reunion performance in a segment of a popular contemporary television show called "We Are Proud to Present." Fellini employs an episodic treatment of the preparation for and actual mounting of the show as a framework for a biting satire on society's media mania and an eloquent meditation on the position of art and the artist in contemporary times.

The pervasive visual texture of *Ginger and Fred* is established in the opening moments of the film. In the frenetic world of the Rome train station, a female studio emissary who has been sent to meet Ginger raises a sign which proclaims, "We Are Proud to Present." Having disembarked from her train, Ginger spies the sign carrier, and, betraying her own consciousness of image, she quickly checks her face in a mirror. Soon after, Fellini cuts to a huge electric sign in the station which flashes, "You'll Be Better Looking, Stronger and Richer When You Use . . ." Seconds later, a grotesquely huge fake pig decorated with lights swings down on a hoist from the ceiling of the station. A man dressed in a tasteless, glittering red costume wishes everyone a Merry Christmas and urges the consumption of the free sausage and lentils which are part of an advertising promotion for a particular company.

Throughout the film, Fellini's *mise-en-scène* is literally crammed with various signs and images, television images in particular, which are themselves signs of society's obsession with media. As the film progresses, Fellini introduces many of the celebrities who are going to be on the same show as Ginger and Fred. These include an ancient, almost catatonic admiral, a midget musical group, a mother and son who profess to tape-record voices from the beyond, a transvestite whose self-appointed mission is to gratify lonely men in prison, a cow with eighteen teats, and innumerable lookalikes of a wide variety of personalities ranging from Clark Gable and Telly Savalas to Marcel Proust and Franz Kafka. Fellini depicts a truly circuslike world which has become one big show for public consumption.

Although the world that is depicted in the film is something of a chaotic wasteland, the director's own artistic vision is highly integrated, and Fellini's satiric purpose is itself multidimensional. One of the pervasive ironies revealed by the film is that, despite the proliferation of media devices such as cameras, televisions, microphones, and billboards, truly vital human communication has become virtually nonexistent. A vivid exemplification of this point occurs early in the film. After meeting the studio emissary, Ginger is ushered into a van which will take her and other guests on the show to the hotel. As the van starts off, Fellini cuts to a large billboard, "Keep Rome Clean," beneath which is one of several piles of garbage that dot the urban landscape. Later, upon arriving at the hotel, the studio emissary reports to a man at the hotel desk who is so engrossed in a television soccer game that he does not even look at her. Similarly, when Ginger has her first encounter with the assistant director of the show, the latter remains engrossed in his own work while talking to Ginger and does not look at her. Even when he requires her publicity photos from her he does not make eye contact, but only sticks out his hand in her direction.

This scene involving Ginger and the assistant director also pertains to another facet of Fellini's satire. During their pseudoconversation, the assistant director asks Ginger whether she and Fred are married. The fact that Ginger and Fred are not married to each other disappoints the assistant director, who claims that the audience likes a love story and that the dancing couple would draw more audience sympathy if they were married. The assistant director takes for granted the need to pander to an audience. Yet as Fellini makes clear throughout the film, the very audience that is pandered to is in fact enslaved by various vested interests who exploit media addiction for monetary gain. Hence, in Fellini's film, the corollary to an emphasis on the omnipresence of media is an emphasis on advertising and rampant commercialism. The bizarre sausage promotion at the beginning of the film certainly suggests the crass commercialization of Christmas. As the van which is to carry Ginger to the Hotel Manager pulls out of the station, the camera follows the van through streets dotted with vendors and advertising billboards. When the van stops to pick up another celebrity, vendors selling lighters and Kleenex rush up to the windows, and a man dressed in a Santa Claus suit asks the television crew to hire him.

Fellini's understanding of how extensively media is dedicated to selling also manifests itself in the focus in the film on the commercial exploitation of female sexuality. Near the beginning of the film, Fellini offers a fine example of sexual exploitation and media overkill as the studio van goes by two identical billboards, each of which displays a woman with large, bare breasts, holding a plate of sausage. Later, as Ginger watches television in her hotel room, she flips the channel to an advertisement in which an erotically dressed woman leans forward, offering her scantily clad bosom to the viewer and urging the purchase of a particular brand of olive oil.

It is one of the ideological strengths of the film that Fellini highlights this form of media exploitation but also shows that female sexuality is only one of countless aspects of human experience that have become mere grist for the media mill. The dizzying variety of subject matter on the various televisions in the film is itself testimony to the way in which all of human experience has been packaged for consumption. Similarly, the circuslike variety of acts which are to appear on "We Are Proud to Present" suggests the way in which the whole spectrum of human experience has been turned into a show. Even the fact that there is a range of lookalikes from Kojak to Proust suggests that society has become lost in a labyrinth of imitations of imitations, where gradations of relative value have become obliterated, with images taking on a fetishistic value which is being exploited by advertisers.

Since both Mastroianni and Masina have worked in other Fellini films and since Masina is actually married to Fellini, the very presence of these two famous performers in *Ginger and Fred* cannot help but give the film an autobiographical dimension. Yet, Fellini avoids the kind of facile indulgence in nostalgia that such casting might encourage. Nor does the director simply project Fred and Ginger as heroic figures in a fallen world. Indeed, one of the ways that the film evades rigid interpretation is in its richly multivalent characterization of Ginger and Fred. On one level, as performers paid to imitate, Ginger and Fred are themselves emblematic of the social ill that Fellini is investigating. Furthermore, the fact that Ginger and Fred imitated Rogers and Astaire in the 1940's suggests that the contemporary malaise has been an evolving phenomenon which originated in the imitation and indiscriminate consumption of American culture. Yet, on another level, Ginger and Fred are deeply sympathetic, seemingly anachronistic characters who are manipulatively ushered from place to place like pawns in a chess game.

Fred, in particular, is a richly symbolic character. The stage name of Fred not only refers to Fred Astaire but also suggests Federico. The viewer's conviction that Fred is an alter ego for Fellini is confirmed when one recalls that it was again Mastroianni in the role of Guido, Fellini's alter ego in *8½* (1963). It is not surprising that since Fellini himself has grown older, the aging, somewhat pathetic Fred is quite a different character than the younger, precocious Guido. Through the character of Fred, Fellini is clearly contemplating and attempting to come to terms with the specter of aging and bodily decay. Fred is a balding, unkempt character who becomes short of breath after the least exertion. By his own admission he occasionally wets the bed, and his embarrassment at undressing in front of women suggests that he is conscious of his own waning virility. He confides to Ginger that he often encounters objects in such a way that these objects seem to be bidding him a final farewell.

What simultaneously saves Fred from being a totally pathetic creature and instills the character with an added symbolic dimension is that this aging man is also an exuberant life force. He is the author of unabashedly bawdy rhyming aphorisms, and he takes a childlike delight in many of the other acts that are going to be on the show. In the context of the film, the depiction of a character who is at once anachronistic and exuberant is not the contradiction that it might seem. What is sympathetic about Fred is that despite all of his problems and his innate human fallibility, he is intensely alive, a breath of fresh air in the artificial world of media hype. Through the character of Fred, Fellini suggests that it is life and spontaneity themselves which are in danger of becoming anachronistic in a sterile world. At one point in the film, Fred complains to Ginger that they are surrounded by dilettantes, and his complaint underscores the predicament of a true artist such as Fellini who is dedicated to life but who finds himself in a dead world of bad imitations.

Paul Salmon

Reviews
Films in Review. XXXVII, August/September, 1986, p. 425.
Macleans. XCIX, April 14, 1986, p. 65.
National Review. XXXVIII, May 9, 1986, p. 54.
The New Republic. CXCIV, April 14, 1986, p. 24.
New York. XIX, March 31, 1986, p. 82.
The New Yorker. LXII, April 21, 1986, p. 97.
Newsweek. CVII, March 31, 1986, p. 72.
Sight and Sound. LV, Spring, 1986, p. 137.
Time. CXXVII, March 31, 1986, p. 74.
Variety. CCCXXI, January 15, 1986, p. 22.
Washingtonian. XXI, April, 1986, p. 69.
World Press Review. XXXIII, February, 1986, p. 57.

THE GOLDEN CHILD

Production: Edward S. Feldman and Robert D. Wachs; released by Paramount Pictures
Direction: Michael Ritchie
Screenplay: Dennis Feldman
Cinematography: Donald E. Thorin
Editing: Richard A. Harris
Production design: J. Michael Riva
Art direction: Lynda Paradise; set decoration, Marvin March
Special effects: Industrial Light and Magic
Costume design: Wayne Finkelman
Music: Michel Colombier
MPAA rating: PG-13
Running time: 93 minutes

> *Principal characters:*
> Chandler Jarrell . . . . Eddie Murphy
> Sardo Numspa . . . . Charles Dance
> Kee Nang . . . . Charlotte Lewis
> The Golden Child . . . . J. L. Reate
> Old man . . . . Victor Wong

At the beginning of *The Golden Child*, Eddie Murphy's character, Chandler Jarrell, is portrayed as a dedicated, if eccentric, Los Angeles social worker whose mission is to find missing children. Although this is primarily a comedy-adventure film, there is an undercurrent of social criticism. Murphy's fast-talking insouciance would seem at odds with his character's fervent interest in saving children, yet this has become the Murphy *persona* in film after film—the child-man who upsets societal rules but who helps restore order and sound values nevertheless. *The Golden Child* makes this point by having Jarrell appear on a television talk show dominated by a host more interested in himself than in his guest's cause. Rather than obeying the proprieties of the interview program, Jarrell suddenly ignores the announcer and addresses the television audience directly, thrusting into view the photograph of a missing child and obliterating the image of the narcissistic media personality. There is a sweet, caring quality in Murphy's screen characters that is the flip side of his smart-aleck takeoffs on human foibles.

It is Chandler Jarrell's fanatical devotion to helping children that attracts the notice of a group of Tibetans, who have had their "Golden Child" stolen from them by Sardo Numspa, the devil's agent—played very suavely by Charles Dance. Only once in a thousand generations, Jarrell is told by his lovely Tibetan girlfriend Kee Nang (Charlotte Lewis), does such a child come into the world. A child from an earlier generation, who bore the gift of justice, did not survive to manhood. Now a child bearing the gift of compassion may also be lost. In Tibetan lore it has been decreed, Kee Nang says, that a figure such as Jarrell must be the one to rescue the child. The plot of *The Golden Child* is quite silly and unbelievable. Reviewers have complained that its special effects overwhelm the story line. In many of Murphy's recent action pictures, not enough play has been given to his personality; it has not been allowed to develop but instead has been interrupted by car chases and shoot-outs. Slick editing of fast-moving sequences has prevented him from displaying fully his comic genius. Yet, as Susan Stark in *The Detroit News* writes, Murphy's humor saves the film, for "by acting the consummate skeptic, Murphy lightens the burden of skepticism for the audience." He too is doubtful about the presence of a real devil and of the Tibetans' explanation about the cosmic importance of a Golden Child. Whenever Kee Nang is especially somber about her beliefs, Jarrell is always there to puncture her self-importance with an irreverent joke.

What makes *The Golden Child* refreshingly different from other Murphy films is that this hip, know-it-all black man can be surprised and even somewhat disconcerted about things that are not in his ken. That his Tibetan girlfriend, for example, has a judolike prowess in combat amazes him, and it is mildly amusing to see them shatter the film stereotype of the delicate, vulnerable, and exotic maiden in need of the protection of a strong white male. The offbeat casting of an Asian woman with a black man is a welcome change—although reviewers are right to say that the romance between Murphy and Lewis never quite works. *The Golden Child* does not make good on the unusual romantic pairing; in the end, Murphy remains what the reviewer in *New York* magazine calls "the complete urban man who can talk his way into and out of any situation." Had Murphy been allowed to show a little more vulnerability in his love for Lewis, as well as in his quest for the Golden Child, the film might have made an original contribution to screen comedy and to social criticism.

How can the audience believe that these two very different people can come together without conflict? There is some measure of tension between them, since Jarrell has a hard time taking seriously the Golden Child story, but, in the main, the film shifts attention instead to the adventure plot now taking place in Katmandu and to pictorial vignettes of Nepal's unearthly looking, snow-covered mountains. Here Jarrell has his troubles with the cold weather, the food, and the music. He is cheated in the marketplace by a street merchant, whose quickness is even more impressive than Jarrell's. What makes their scene together especially humorous is that the young city slicker is taken by the old, shifty-eyed con man. This is, so to speak, a cross-cultural joke, a comment on the bargaining that seems universal in the commerce between human beings in all cultures.

Dance excels as the sophisticated devil's henchman who is contemptuous of Jarrell's ignorance of the cosmic peril he invites by trying to rescue the Golden Child. It is Numspa's very sense of superiority that is his downfall, for he badly underestimates the seemingly casual naïveté of Jarrell. Numspa can learn nothing because his worldview cannot tolerate the existence of a Chandler Jarrell. Jarrell, on the other hand, may discount the devil at first, but he is capable of adjusting to new realities—including the devil himself, who materializes as a hideous demon with wings and fangs. However fantastic the notion of a kidnapped Golden Child may have seemed at first to Jarrell, it has been his life's goal to recover children who have been lost. He has been the one who must rescue the child because for him all children are golden. This is the intuitive logic of the film—a logic most reviewers missed in their desire for a literal explanation of why Jarrell is chosen to recover the child.

J. L. Reate, a young girl playing the male role of the Golden Child, never speaks a line, yet the child has an almost hypnotic presence, a knowing, compassionate eye in scenes in which he is shown to be entrapped by the devil and apparently cut off from help. There is a sense of mystery in his expression, an ineffable quality that is particularly satisfying in view of the literalness of the special effects. His calm is a welcome contrast to scenes with a dragon lady, "astral rumblings, dragon rapes, kung fu, magic daggers, drooling monsters, dancing Pepsi cans, and dead birds that come to life"—to cite critic Stark's catalog of special effects. Against this barrage of film wonders that are designed to wow the audience with the palpability of the supernatural, the child's serene, inscrutable face is impressive precisely because he evokes what cannot be visualized: a faith in the good and the true, in the compassion the child is meant to embody.

Carl E. Rollyson, Jr.

Reviews
American Film. XII, December, 1986, p. 65.
The Detroit News. December 12, 1986, p. 3C.
Films in Review. XXXVIII, February, 1987, p. 104.
Los Angeles Times. December 12, 1986, VI, p. 1.
New York. XX, January 5, 1987, p. 46.
The New York Times. December 12, 1986, p. C19.
Newsweek. CVIII, December 22, 1986, p. 75.
People Weekly. XXVII, January 12, 1987, p. 10.
Time. CXXVIII, December 22, 1986, p. 70.
Variety. CCCXXV, December 17, 1986, p. 20.
The Wall Street Journal. December 23, 1986, p. 18.
The Washington Post. December 12, 1986, p. C1.

THE GREAT MOUSE DETECTIVE

Production: Burny Mattinson; released by Buena Vista
Direction: John Musker, Dave Michener, Ron Clements, and Burny Mattinson
Screenplay: Ron Clements, Burny Mattinson, Dave Michener, John Musker, Pete Young, Vance Gerry, Steve Hulett, Bruce M. Morris, Matthew O'Callaghan, and Melvin Shaw; based on the novel *Basil of Baker Street,* by Eve Titus
Animation camera: Ed Austin
Editing: Roy M. Brewer, Jr., and James Melton
Art direction: Guy Vasilovich
Supervising animators: Hendel Butoy, Mark Henn, Glenn Keane, and Robert Minkoff
Computer animation: Phil Nibbelink and Ted Gielow
Color styling: Jim Coleman
Special photographic effects: Phillip L. Meador
Music: Henry Mancini
MPAA rating: G
Running time: 72 minutes

> *Voices of principal characters:*
> Basil . . . . Barrie Ingham
> Dr. David Q. Dawson. . . . . Val Bettin
> Olivia Flaversham. . . . . Susanne Pollatschek
> Professor Ratigan. . . . . Vincent Price
> Fidget . . . . Candy Candido
> Flaversham. . . . . Alan Young
> The queen. . . . . Eve Brenner
> Dance-hall singer. . . . . Melissa Manchester

Since the death of Walt Disney in 1966, the animated feature has been in gradual decline, as Walt Disney Productions and their competitors have relied on tired conventions, patched-together situation-comedy stories, and animation either too clichéd or too crude to compare favorably with the classic animated features. The non-Disney films especially have degenerated into sad marketing ploys for toy companies.

It makes little difference whether the filmmakers' goal is a merchandising field day or a cringingly respectful attempt to recapture old glories through slavish imitation and repetition. The biggest failure of all these films has been their inability to create memorable, lovable characters around which to build stories at once thrilling, heart tugging, and funny.

Stories and characters that the audience can care passionately about are rare enough in live-action films these days. Audiences have ceased looking to animated films to find the kind of character that can touch them, make them laugh, and strike some chord deep within them, some universal feeling, or basic human concern. Such an audience-character bond is now more likely to occur in a film such as *E. T.: The Extraterrestrial* (1982). Many have made the observation that the Steven Spielberg/George Lucas/Jim Henson triumvirate has taken over or surpassed what Disney used to do best.

The Black Cauldron (1985) is a good example of Disney's loss of mastery in the field, and it was the studio's first animated feature to fail at the box office on its initial release since *Sleeping Beauty* in 1959. The thirty-million-dollar epic emphasized spectacle over story and died under the weight of its showy, derivative animation and lumbering, familiar plot. The failure of *The Black Cauldron* was a major blow to the studio, but it appears, along with a shake-up in studio management, to have been exactly what was needed.

The Great Mouse Detective is a lean, tightly crafted film. It has the feel of a stripped-down, efficient machine while hardly sacrificing any of the graceful, all-but-extinct quality of animation that is Disney's trademark. Although flawed in minor ways, it is consistently imaginative, interest-holding, and entertaining. It does not insult one's intelligence, yet it has no pretensions beyond telling a clever story and telling it well. As a result, *The Great Mouse Detective* comes closer to capturing the feel of the classic features than any Disney film made since Walt Disney's death.

The film plunges the audience into an involving story and treats them to a carefully structured blend of thrills, suspense, comedy, and pathos. While the animation may not be as polished, fluid, or as warmly dimensional as it once was, the efficient boldness of story construction and the surprising cleverness of execution hearken back to the golden era of *Dumbo* (1941), *Bambi* (1942), and *Cinderella* (1950).

The story begins in London in 1897, in a miniature counterpart to the human world. Flaversham the toy maker is seen demonstrating a mechanical doll to his young daughter, Olivia, when, in a flash, a grotesque bat crashes through the window and abducts Flaversham, leaving behind a distraught Olivia.

After the credits sequence, the film introduces Dr. David Q. Dawson, a portly old mouse who will relate the rest of the story. Dawson discovers Olivia in the street and, learning of her plight, brings her to the home of the world's greatest detective, Basil of Baker Street, who is patterned after Sherlock Holmes (down to the deerstalker cap, pipe, and violin) and who in fact lives beneath the master sleuth's house.

Basil applies his keen powers of deduction and concludes that the villain is his archenemy, Professor Ratigan (the mouse version of Professor Moriarty). The oozingly villainous Ratigan, who claims to be the world's greatest criminal mind and who, although huge and ratlike in every way, tries to pass for a mouse, is indeed holding Flaversham and, aided by his peg-legged bat assistant, Fidget, is forcing him to design a robot version of the queen, which he plans to substitute for Her Highness at the upcoming Diamond Jubilee. Accompanied by his stooges, Ratigan nimbly performs a hilarious song and dance that celebrates his villainous ingenuity and details his subsequent plans to take over "all mousedom." When one of his lackeys slips and calls him a rat, Ratigan has him fed to Felicia, an enormous cat.

Meanwhile, Basil enlists Dawson's aid (thus placing Dawson in the role of Dr. Watson), and, accompanied by Olivia, they follow Fidget's footprints to a human toy shop and look for clues among the eerily oversized dolls and games. A battalion of toy soldiers suddenly springs to life and atacks the trio; in the fracas, Fidget appears and snatches Olivia.

While Basil and Dawson search for Ratigan's hideout, Ratigan uses Olivia to force Flaversham to make the robot immediately. Ratigan is furious to discover that Basil is on the case, but he decides that he will destroy Basil as part of his plan.

Eventually, Basil and Dawson (after investigating a waterfront dive, comically disguised as sailors) spot Fidget and follow him through the sewers to Ratigan's hideout, where they are caught trying to free Olivia. Ratigan puts Basil and Dawson in a giant mousetrap timed to spring to the accompaniment of a record of Ratigan singing "Goodbye So Soon" and then takes off in a dirigible with the decoy queen robot.

When the end seems near, Basil finds a way out and they escape. At the palace, Ratigan has substituted the robot for the queen; the false queen announces that Ratigan is her new royal consort. Basil and Dawson arrive in time to save the queen from being fed to Felicia the cat by Fidget and to sabotage the robot as it speaks to the crowd. Ratigan flees in his dirigible, and Basil and Dawson follow, hanging on party balloons.

The chase ends in a harrowing battle between Ratigan and Basil atop—and inside the gears of—Big Ben. Basil narrowly escapes with his life as Ratigan flies off into the night, only to be battled again in the future.

At the end of the film, Flaversham and Olivia are reunited. Dawson, for his part, looks forward to other adventures with Basil.

The idea of telling a familiar story with animals in human roles is nothing new, but it is the kind of thing Disney does best. In *The Great Mouse Detective*, the animators frequently rise above merely copying old situations or even equaling previous treatments, providing ingenious plot twists, sight gags, characterizations, and visuals.

The film's opening efficiently and effectively introduces the ingenious Flaversham and adorable Olivia, establishing their bond and his cleverness as he demonstrates the dancing doll he has made for her. The tender moment is startlingly shattered when Fidget crashes through the window and Flaversham quickly hides Olivia in a cabinet before he is abducted. (The opening was reportedly redone at the insistence of studio production head Jeffrey Katzenberg, who thought that it lacked action and involvement.) In a few minutes, the audience has been pulled into the story through its interesting setting, appealing characters, and dramatic turn of events.

After Dawson's sympathetic introduction, Basil's introduction is dramatically delayed as Olivia and Dawson wait to meet him, surveying his book- and invention-filled study. His powers of deduction are impressively demonstrated as he quickly determines their problem and Dawson's background from the slightest of clues. His discomfort in dealing with the child is humorous and reveals a character so steeped in reason and knowledge that relating to a simple little girl is difficult.

The animators' design and execution of Basil's superior attitude, racing mind, charm, and style, his posing and impatience, yield animated acting of the highest order. The audience can actually see his mind working—and how it works—through his facial expressions and postures. His precise, flexible design is strongly complemented by the sharp and stylish vocal performance of Barrie Ingham.

The animators clearly enjoyed bringing to life the delightfully diabolical Ratigan. The brilliant vocal characterization by Vincent Price is clearly reflected in the artists' treatment of Ratigan's sublimely theatrical villainy. He is both truly comic and seriously threatening—a perfect foil for Basil. Ratigan is such a strong figure that he nearly overpowers the film; nevertheless, Basil's quieter force, plus the strength of Dawson, Olivia, and the hilariously maniacal Fidget, balances the cast.

Overall, the quality of drawing and design is excellent. The mouse-size interiors of Basil's study, Flaversham's workshop, and Ratigan's hideout are cleverly detailed (Ratigan's lair is a lush, rococo, subterranean palace), and the oversize settings of London's streets and the human toy shop are intriguing in their use of scale and perspective. The climactic battle, which moves from the sheer face of Big Ben to the threatening, intermeshing gears within, is the film's highlight and indeed is one of the finest pieces of animation the studio has produced. The rigid precision of computer animation is effectively exploited in the realistic treatment of the clockworks' turning wheels and flying weights as Basil and Ratigan fight each other. The computerized Automatic Camera Effects System (ACES) enabled the filmmakers to present the scene using a dizzying variety of dramatic camera angles and movements.

All the elements that make up an animated feature are masterfully blended in *The Great Mouse Detective*. Henry Mancini's score effectively underlines the film's moods, and the sprinkling of songs, while not exactly memorable, are pleasant or amusing enough to add greatly to the scene. The story may lack the heart-tugging pathos of *Bambi*, but it is suspenseful and witty, always moving forward but leaving room for well-placed pauses or surprises. The success of this film clearly shows that when visual skills are matched by an entertaining, involving, tightly structured story, contemporary filmmakers can approach the quality of the classic animated features. While *The Great Mouse Detective* may have occasional lapses of originality or polish, its well-rounded characters and confident style suggest that it will become a classic in its own right.

Paul Cremo

Reviews

Chicago Tribune. July 2, 1986, p. CT5.
Los Angeles Times. July 2, 1986, VI, p. 1.
New Statesman. CXII, November 7, 1986, p. 23.
The New York Times. CXXXV, July 27, 1986, II, p. 16.
Time. CXXVIII, July 7, 1986, p. 65.
Variety. CCCXXIII, July 9, 1986, p. 15.
The Washington Post. July 7, 1986, p. B8.

GUNG HO

Production: Ron Howard (executive producer) and Tony Ganz and Deborah Blum; released by Paramount Pictures
Direction: Ron Howard
Screenplay: Lowell Ganz and Babaloo Mandel; based on a story by Edwin Blum, Ganz, and Mandel
Cinematography: Don Peterman
Editing: Daniel Hanley and Michael Hill
Production design: James Schoppe
Art direction: Jack G. Taylor, Jr.; set decoration, John Anderson
Special effects: Stan Parks
Makeup: Ric Sagliani and Janet Flora
Costume design: Betsy Cox
Sound: Richard S. Church
Music: Thomas Newman
MPAA rating: PG-13
Running time: 120 minutes

Principal characters:
Hunt Stevenson . . . . Michael Keaton
Kazihiro . . . . Gedde Watanabe
Buster. . . . . George Wendt
Audrey . . . . Mimi Rogers
Sakamoto . . . . Soh Yamamura
Junior . . . . Jihmi Kennedy
Googie. . . . . Rick Overton
Willie. . . . . John Turturro
Saito . . . . Sab Shimono
Paul . . . . Clint Howard
Heather. . . . . Michelle Johnson

Ron Howard's *Gung Ho* is a topical film which capitalizes on the competition between Japanese and American automobile manufacturers. Inspired by a *60 Minutes* segment about Nissan opening an automobile plant in Smyrna, Tennessee, *Gung Ho* juxtaposes two cultures and explores the differences between their management styles and work ethics. These differences are comically presented as a series of stereotypical dichotomies (team-individual, company-family, craftsmanship-work) that portray the Japanese as more productive but less human workers than their American counterparts. Ultimately, however, *Gung Ho* is not as much about the differences between two static cultures as it is about what those cultures really have in common and how they can profitably work together toward attaining the ideal relationship between management and labor, work and family, and productivity and mental health.

During the opening credits, Howard cuts from one culture to the other and juxtaposes Hunt Stevenson (Michael Keaton) and Kazihiro (Gedde Watanabe): While Hunt, who is typically late and casual, drives a car that is typically American in its messiness, Kazihiro, who is considered an inept manager because of his American (that is, relaxed and sympathetic) concern for his workers, is being humiliated and trained to become a better Japanese (that is, efficient and firm) manager. Hunt, who has unaccountably been assigned to save Hadleyville by inducing Assan (innuendo undoubtedly intended) Motors to locate a plant there, travels to Japan, where his inept but personable Occidental presentation is contrasted with Oriental efficiency and technology.

Inexplicably, the Japanese do decide to build a plant in Hadleyville, and when they arrive, the welcoming ceremony stresses the well-intentioned but gauche American response to an essentially alien culture: Young American boys dress in "typical" Japanese garb—karate outfits—and the traditional red carpet treatment causes the Japanese, as well as their American hosts, to remove their shoes. Clearly, the gap between the two cultures must be breached, and the task can best be accomplished by Hunt, whom Kazihiro remembers from his visit to Japan.

Hunt, the employee liaison for Assan, must introduce company policies to the American workers, who regard him as a peer whose only concern is their best interest, an impression for which Hunt is responsible. As a result, Assan depends on Hunt, who assures his fellow employees that he can "take 'em" by "picking his spot" as he had done in a state championship basketball game. Because they believe in Hunt, the workers reject union advice and accept a less lucrative contract than they had with their previous employer. Hunt is put to the test the first day on the job, when the American workers balk at doing Japanese exercises before work. Though he gets the workers to comply, subsequent differences are not so easily resolved: The Japanese aim for zero defects, while the Americans are willing to let the dealers handle defects; the Japanese want all the workers to learn every job, while the Americans want to specialize; the Japanese want no music, no smoking, and no extensive bathroom breaks, while the Americans want to avoid work.

To Kazihiro's dismay, production lags, primarily because morale is low at the plant, and the incipient conflict surfaces in a bitterly contested softball game between Japanese management and American workers. Because Buster (George Wendt) intentionally injures a Japanese infielder, the Americans win the game, but the antagonism deepens. The resourceful Hunt responds to his threatened firing by striking a deal with Kazihiro about pay raises for increased production, but in the face of peer pressure, he misrepresents the deal to the workers, who do increase production but cannot attain the fifteen-thousand-car goal needed to get the pay raise and job security.

Just as Hunt's position becomes increasingly precarious, Kazihiro's position is also constantly threatened. His work is monitored by Saito (Sab Shimono), the prototypical Japanese manager and the nephew of Assan president Sakamoto (Soh Yamamura). Sakamoto is concerned with production goals not being met, and when Buster leads a walkout, the president decides to close the Hadleyville plant. At the Fourth of July celebration— one of the film's many ironies—the mayor blames Hunt, who confesses that he lied to his fellow employees. A despondent Hunt finds an equally distraught Kazihiro, who has been fired, and the two decide to return to the plant to build cars in a futile attempt to reach the fifteen-thousand-car goal. Eventually, Kazihiro's supervisory staff joins the work effort, and Buster and the other American workers—with their outlawed radios blaring— reenter the plant as well.

At this point, the Japanese and the Americans work together in a blending of cultures: Buster, formerly a sloppy welder who had been demoted to custodial service, supervises the welding in true Japanese style; Japanese supervisors dance as they work; and the products are produced with Japanese speed but with American standards. When Hunt proudly drives one of the cars out of the plant, it quickly falls to pieces. The Americans still are six cars short of their goal when the time expires, and they technically have failed, but an impressed Sakamoto praises the workers as a "good team," a Japanese concept. Kazihiro, who has adopted American values, corrects his superior and calls them "good men," thereby stressing the value of the individuals involved. The triumphal blending of the two cultures is affirmed by Sakamoto's decision not to close the plant and by his demotion of his nephew Saito to the janitorial position that Buster had held.

Actually, the Americanization of the Japanese supervisors should come as no surprise, since Howard begins his film with a shot of a McDonald's in Tokyo and then demonstrates the impact of American popular culture on Kazihiro's family by photographing his children playing with G. I. Joe and Cabbage Patch dolls, watching MTV, and eating Jimmie Dean sausage. When his wife buys their son a bicycle from Sears, the conversion seems complete. In fact, in the domestic squabbling related to American icons, Kazihiro's wife asserts herself in a decidedly un-Japanese manner by telling her husband that he needs to spend more time with his family. A liberated Kazihiro then supports a Japanese supervisor's desire to be with his pregnant wife during labor. The message which emerges from these vignettes is that the Japanese need to relax, to relate to people, to become less strict and rigid.

The American workers, on the other hand, do not seem to need to change quite as much as they need to regain what once was theirs: At one point, Hunt tells the workers that they have got to get the spirit (work ethic, pride, craft) back and that the Japanese now have the spirit. Ironically, when the Americans are most productive, they revert to their radios and do it their way: As Buster says, "We have our own way of making cars." In fact, Buster's case reflects the triumph of the American way. Demoted for sloppy work and beaten by Hunt in a fistfight, Buster leads the walkout, but he somehow gets the spirit back (Howard seems to indicate that it simply was dormant in Buster) and is integrated into the company at the end of the film. On the other hand, Saito, Buster's Japanese counterpart, is excluded from the comic ending and relegated to the broom.

Howard also tips the scales in favor of the Americans by his affectionate treatment of Hunt: He is an irresponsible, egotistic, gauche, frivolous, yet charming individualist who relies on his personality to get through many of life's more delicate situations. Nevertheless, despite his comic gifts, Hunt is not an appealing hero. He calls attention to how he won the basketball championship, promises what he cannot deliver, lies when he is under pressure, tries to evade responsibility (he literally tries to run from the enraged workers but fails when his American car breaks down), steals from the grocery store that his girlfriend, Audrey (Mimi Rogers), manages, and attempts to joke his way out of any serious situation. Two of his remarks to the Japanese ("Dad was over here [Japan] with the army" and "Why didn't you win the Big One?") are played for laughs, but they are neither appropriate nor amusing. Hunt's Willie Loman-like belief in personality is, however, reinforced by Sakamoto's explanation of why he is keeping the plant open (and probably why he located it in Hadleyville): "I like you. You make me laugh."

Howard's *Gung Ho*, like his earlier *Splash* (1984) and *Night Shift* (1982), is amusing, but unlike those films it has content which lends itself to significant social commentary about cultural differences. Unfortunately, *Gung Ho* relies on obvious one-liners, stereotypical caricatures, and a facile resolution. Part of the problem may result from the casting, since Keaton is more of a comic than an actor, and the audience is not encouraged to penetrate beneath the flip façade that he affects. After his confession to the town, Hunt is presumably humiliated and despondent, but Howard next shows him with his head in the mouth of a cannon. Ultimately, the answer to personal failure, as well as to a community's economic plight, is slapstick humor. In *Modern Times* (1936), another film about industry and the work force, Charles Chaplin demonstrates that comedy is not antithetical to seriousness of purpose. While it is entertaining comedy, *Gung Ho* does not live up to its potential.

Thomas L. Erskine

Reviews

Los Angeles Times. March 14, 1986, VI, p. 14.
Macleans. XCIX, March 31, 1986, p. 54.
The New Republic. CXCIV, April 21, 1986, p. 24.
New York. XIX, March 24, 1986, p. 86.
The New York Times. CXXXV, March 14, 1986, p. C8.
Newsweek. CVII, March 17, 1986, p. 81.
Texas Monthly. XIV, May, 1986, p. 169.
Time. CXXVII, March 31, 1986, p. 75.
Variety. CCCXXII, March 12, 1986, p. 14.
The Wall Street Journal. CCVII, March 13, 1986, p. 28.
The Washington Post. March 14, 1986, p. WE27.
The Washington Post. March 22, 1986, p. C7.

HALF MOON STREET

Production: Geoffrey Reeve for RKO Pictures in association with Showtime/The Movie Channel; released by Twentieth Century-Fox
Direction: Bob Swaim
Screenplay: Bob Swaim and Edward Behr; based on the novella "Doctor Slaughter" by Paul Theroux
Cinematography: Peter Hannan
Editing: Richard Marden
Production design: Anthony Curtis
Art direction: Peter Williams; set decoration, Peter Young
Makeup: Linda De Vetta
Costume design: Louise Frogley
Sound: Nicholas Stevenson
Music direction: Richard Harvey
Music: Richard Harvey
MPAA rating: R
Running time: 98 minutes
Running time in U.S.: 90 minutes

Principal characters:
Lauren Slaughter	Sigourney Weaver
Lord Bulbeck	Michael Caine
General Sir George Newhouse	Patrick Kavanaugh
Lady Newhouse	Faith Kent
Lindsay Walker	Ram John Holder
Hugo Van Arkady	Keith Buckley
Mrs. Van Arkady	Annie Hanson

What happens to a sensational French director whose film breaks box-office records, sweeps the French Academy Awards with Best Picture, Best Actor, Best Actress, and then becomes a success in the United States? If he also happens to be American, he goes back to speaking English and makes *Half Moon Street*, a contemporary love story-thriller starring Sigourney Weaver and Michael Caine. For Bob Swaim, whose *La Balance* was indeed the top-grossing French film in 1983, *Half Moon Street* provided a change of language and an escalation of budget as well as production methods. Nevertheless, it is consistent with the themes and taut style of his previous hit. *La Balance* was a fast-paced thriller about the attempts of a policeman (Richard Berry) to pressure a prostitute (Nathalie Baye) and her pimp (Philippe Léotard) into helping him catch a major criminal.

Half Moon Street, adapted from Paul Theroux's "Doctor Slaughter" (which was published as *Half Moon Street* in the United States in 1984), focuses on a fiercely independent American woman living in London. Lauren Slaughter (Sigourney Weaver) is a postdoctoral student in Middle Eastern Studies who is unable financially to make ends meet. She becomes an "escort girl" for a high-class agency, dating and often sleeping with rich clients from a variety of countries. One of her dates is Lord Bulbeck (Michael Caine), a high-ranking politician in charge of peace treaties between Arabs and Israelis. They develop a close relationship—despite the fact that she is a security risk for him.

Lauren's outspokenness and independence are refreshing, but they coexist with the naïveté of a 1980's Jamesian heroine abroad: She falls prey to a scheme that a wealthy Palestinian and an English millionaire have concocted in order to kill Bulbeck—and Lauren, if necessary. She becomes a pawn in the climactic final scene, where she ultimately risks her own life to save Bulbeck. *Half Moon Street* shares with *La Balance* the idea that a prostitute and the man who loves/uses her are never sure if they can trust each other in a world of treachery; nevertheless, in the French film the blackmail is overt, both physically and psychologically, whereas the lovers in *Half Moon Street* are unaware of what is happening around them.

Moreover, Lauren is not so much a prostitute as an intelligent and free-spirited businesswoman. For example, she refuses the advances of the smug Hugo Van Arkady (Keith Buckley)—although he is rich—yet accepts an interlude with a young plumber when she cannot afford to pay him for fixing her shower. (This scene was eventually cut from the American version.) At moments, *Half Moon Street* is reminiscent of Alan J. Pakula's *Klute* (1971), and not only because the protagonist is a feisty woman who thinks that she is in control (even when she is forced to sleep with strangers), but also because an atmosphere of paranoia is induced by tapes, and the audience cannot see who is masterminding events via surveillance.

Like *Klute*, *Half Moon Street* works on four levels: It is simultaneously a thriller, a love story, a feminist exploration, and a portrait of a city. Together with coscriptwriter Edward Behr (European cultural editor of *Newsweek* with a thorough knowledge of London), Swaim made some radical departures from Theroux's book, reducing much of the suspense and adding the romance. Lord Bulbeck, who was a minor—and seventy-five-year-old—character in the novella, became the considerably younger male lead in the film. As incarnated by the ever-seductive Michael Caine, Bulbeck is a perfect complement to Weaver's portrayal of a classy and sardonic call girl with a doctoral degree.

Lauren insists on using her own name in a London that she finds hypocritical, class-oriented, and misogynist. The juxtaposition of this frank heroine with the city she encounters suggests that London has a very different character from the swinging 1960's of Michelangelo Antonioni's *Blow-Up* (1966), for example. It is a violent place, whose social unrest and bleakness are translated into bombings and assassinations. In this sense, *Half Moon Street* is closer to the tone of *Mona Lisa*, the critically acclaimed drama of 1986 (reviewed in this volume) which also depicted a high-class call girl (Cathy Tyson)—and also costarred Michael Caine. While this film, directed by Neil Jordan from a script by David Leland, is arguably the more powerful of the two, its perspective is entirely British; *Half Moon Street*, on the other hand, presents a quintessentially American heroine, whose directness contrasts with Tyson's mysterious *persona*. Indeed, Swaim's film reveals the hybrid quality of his own background as well as the film's genesis. Like Lauren, to some extent, Swaim was an American who did postgraduate work abroad and had to adapt to a foreign culture. He initially came to Paris, armed with a degree in anthropology, to study with Claude Lévi-Strauss. He discovered film, however, remained in France, and entered the film industry there.

His return to the English language (onscreen) came about through two individuals: the American producer Edward Pressman, who had been impressed by *La Balance* and who subsequently took *Half Moon Street* to RKO Pictures (his partner on the film version of *Plenty*, 1985), and Geoffrey Reeve, the British producer of *The Shooting Party* (1985), who originally bought the rights to Theroux's work. With one American and one British producer behind him, the Franco-American Swaim created a film of cultural tensions whose foreign characters are as sharply drawn as its American heroine. Although *Half Moon Street* was not much of a critical or commercial success in the United States—is Lauren too hard a character to like?—it remains an exciting story of political and amorous intrigue.

Annette Insdorf

Reviews
American Film. XI, October, 1986, p. 67.
Chicago Tribune. November 10, 1986, V, p. 5.
Horizon. XXIX, September, 1986, p. 19.
Mademoiselle. XCIII, January, 1987, p. 66.
Ms. XV, December, 1986, p. 20.
New York. XIX, November 24, 1986, p. 81.
The New York Times. November 7, 1986, p. C25.
Variety. CCCXXIV, October 1, 1986, p. 13.
The Wall Street Journal. November 6, 1986, p. 30.
The Washington Post. December 25, 1986, p. C6.

HANNAH AND HER SISTERS

Production: Robert Greenhut; released by Orion Pictures
Direction: Woody Allen
Screenplay: Woody Allen (AA)
Cinematography: Carlo di Palma
Editing: Susan E. Morse
Art direction: Stuart Wurtzel; set decoration, Carol Joffe
Makeup: Fern Buchner
Costume design: Jeffrey Kurland
Music: Richard Rodgers and Lorenz Hart, Johann Sebastian Bach, Giacomo Puccini, Jerome Kern, and others
MPAA rating: PG-13
Running time: 107 minutes

Principal characters:
Mickey	Woody Allen
Elliot	Michael Caine (AA)
Hannah	Mia Farrow
April	Carrie Fisher
Lee	Barbara Hershey
Hannah's father	Lloyd Nolan
Hannah's mother	Maureen O'Sullivan
Dusty	Daniel Stern
Frederick	Max von Sydow
Holly	Dianne Wiest (AA)

Hannah and Her Sisters is the most widely acclaimed motion picture by writer-director Woody Allen since *Annie Hall* (1977) and *Manhattan* (1979), his two hits of the late 1970's which the new film most closely resembles. All three comedies are loosely autobiographical, warmly personal celebrations of the many loves in Allen's life: for his favorite locales in Manhattan, for various kinds of traditional music (classical works, Tin Pan Alley show tunes, and jazz standards), and for the beauties and foibles of his lovers and friends. All three films have their particular strengths and represent different breakthroughs for Allen in content and style, but ultimately *Hannah and Her Sisters* is the most expansive and accomplished of the three. In this regard, several critics have compared the film with more traditional art forms as a way of expressing their esteem for it as a work of high culture. Thus, according to these critics, while *Annie Hall* and *Manhattan* might be considered Woody Allen's novellas or chamber pieces, *Hannah and Her Sisters* is his full-fledged novel or symphony.

Allen achieves this effect of high cultural heft through an ingenious synthesis of his previous methods of structuring a narrative. In most of his earlier films, Allen built the plot around the comic *persona* that he plays as an actor: a wisecracking, neurotic nebbish. Because he was not ultimately satisfied with what he could accomplish with that character and structure, Allen excluded or altered this nebbish character in several later films. The most important of these in relation to *Hannah and Her Sisters* was the first Allen-directed film in which he did not appear: *Interiors* (1978), an Ingmar Bergman-style drama about the emotional problems of three sisters, their parents, and their lovers. Most critics and viewers, however, judged this film to be an oversolemn failure. Allen's brilliant stroke in *Hannah and Her Sisters* is to combine these two types of film, leavening the serious story (again one of three sisters, their parents, and their lovers) with more humor than in *Interiors*, and placing the nebbish character (here Mickey Sachs, a hypochondriac television producer) on the periphery of the main story rather than at the center as in *Annie Hall* and *Manhattan*. One critic has likened Allen's New York City in *Hannah and Her Sisters* to William Shakespeare's forest of Arden in *As You Like It*, and indeed Allen rules as wisely and benignly over his comic world as Shakespeare does over his. As in that Renaissance comedy, writer-director Allen keeps the action moving quickly, deftly shifting from one group of romantically involved characters to another, while also providing the contrasting perspectives of the metaphysical clown Mickey (who corresponds to Shakespeare's Touchstone) and the railing malcontent Frederick (Max von Sydow), a character much like Shakespeare's Jaques.

The film begins with a large Thanksgiving dinner given by Hannah (Mia Farrow) for her family and friends in her spacious Upper West Side apartment. The viewer learns that the serene Hannah, the oldest of three daughters, is the patient provider of advice and financial support for the middle sister, Holly (Dianne Wiest), a frantic and intense woman who is having trouble settling on a career, finding a man, and avoiding cocaine. Also dependent on Hannah are her parents, a brassy and flirtatious alcoholic mother (Maureen O'Sullivan) and a sentimental, insecure father (Lloyd Nolan). This pair of aging actors takes great pride in the way Hannah has managed to succeed both as a stage actress and as a wife and mother. All Hannah's success seems to have become a bit boring, however, to her husband, Elliot (Michael Caine), a circumspect financial consultant, for he has become passionately infatuated with Hannah's youngest sister, Lee (Barbara Hershey). Lee, in turn, is a voluptuous beauty who nevertheless has problems of her own: She is struggling to maintain control over her alcoholism and to escape her burned-out relationship with an older man, Frederick. This bitterly antisocial artist, who has served as an important mentor and lover in Lee's life but has now become too demanding, has shunned the family gathering.

After this Thanksgiving dinner, Allen interweaves three major plot threads. One follows the affair of Elliot and Lee, who first lunge for each other in a comic scene which also shows Frederick angrily ejecting the vulgar rock star Dusty (Daniel Stern), a client of Elliot who was considering buying some of Frederick's paintings. Elliot wins Lee's heart with a tender E. E. Cummings poem, and despite their ambivalence they pursue a passionate affair in hotel rooms, while Hannah remains unsuspecting but disturbed by Elliot's dark moods. When a year goes by, it becomes clear to Lee that Elliot cannot bring himself to leave Hannah, and she becomes interested in yet a third older man—her literature professor at Columbia University.

Meanwhile, another plot thread follows the rueful misadventures of Holly. While pursuing her acting classes and auditions, she starts the Stanislavski Catering Company with her attractive friend April (Carrie Fisher). At their first party, they meet a charming architect, David (Sam Waterston, in an uncredited role), and the unspoken competition between the two women for his attention becomes intense (and in the viewer's eyes, both comic and sad) as he drives them on an architectural tour of the city. At first it seems that David has more interest in April, but Holly's hopes rise when he takes her to the opera. Though he affects a soulful passion for the arts, David turns out to be a cad. He has allowed his wife to put him through architecture school but then says that he plans to divorce her because she is schizophrenic. Further, he coldly drops Holly without a hint of farewell and then takes up with her friend April as his next opera companion.

The third major strand of the plot—a broadly comic one—runs through several traumatic but hilarious crises in the life of Mickey Sachs. The audience learns through one of Mickey's flashbacks that he was Hannah's first husband. That marriage collapsed, however, when he could not handle the knowledge that Hannah was able to have children while medical tests seemed to prove that he was not. In a flashback scene set during their marriage, Mickey and Hannah ask his scriptwriting partner, Norm (Tony Roberts, in an uncredited role), and his wife, Carol (Joanna Gleason), whether Norm would be willing to contribute sperm for Hannah's artificial insemination. Consequently Hannah gives birth to twins—a result which Mickey considers a rueful joke on his inferior creative powers. A later flashback presents a single disastrous date that Mickey has with Holly after he has divorced Hannah. In this nightmare of incompatibility, he is appalled by Holly's blatant cocaine sniffing and by the deafening punk band she takes him to hear, and she condemns him as old-fashioned for disapproving of drugs and boring her with mainstream jazz (here singer Bobby Short performs as himself in a nightclub sequence).

Mickey's main trauma in the present action of the film, however, is far removed from Hannah and Holly. His wildest hypochondriac fears seem to be coming true when a series of solemn doctors and alienating clinical tests appear to be leading him to the conclusion that he has a malignant brain tumor. The news that he does not have a tumor plummets him into an unexpected state of depression, for his imagined brush with mortality makes him all the more desperate to find some meaning in life and some hope of life after death. At the television studio, his earthy, gravel-voiced colleague Gail (Julie Kavner) advises him to take a Caribbean vacation or visit a brothel, but he leaves his job proclaiming, "I'm going to get some answers." Though he is conspicuously Jewish in manner and temperament, Mickey tries to convert to Roman Catholicism (thus shocking his parents), and when that effort fails, he even questions a Hare Krishna devotee about their doctrine of reincarnation.

Woody Allen skillfully builds toward his happy ending by bringing his two most hapless characters—Mickey and Holly—unexpectedly together. Mickey runs into her at a Tower Records store, and Holly, who has spent some months trying her hand as a writer, prevails upon him to read one of her scripts. Mickey is impressed, a romance develops, and in a flashback Mickey relates that he has tried to shoot himself but missed. After this bungled suicide attempt, Mickey wanders into a revival showing of the Marx Brothers film *Duck Soup*. There, he experiences the rejuvenation of laughter and the realization that even if there is no God or afterlife, life itself is still worth living for all that can be experienced.

The concluding scene, set a year after Mickey and Holly's reunion, once again brings *As You Like It* to mind as it choreographs most of the major characters into a reaffirmation of what the film sees as a healthy community's values—in this case, those of marriage, childbearing, and the extended family. Allen's moving camera tracks through the satisfying spectacle of Thanksgiving at Hannah's, which is significantly more harmonious than the two Thanksgivings shown earlier in the film. Elliot has come to realize that he deeply loves Hannah, and Lee has married her Columbia professor. The mother and father (who earlier in the film suffered through a quarrel that Hannah helped them resolve) now gather with others around the piano to enjoy the father's rendition of "Isn't It Romantic?" The camera moves to a close shot of Holly seen in a dark mirror, and it seems for a melancholy moment as if she might still be cut off from the happiness of the family and all of its couples. Mickey enters the frame, the viewer learns that they are married, and in a *deus ex machina* as incredible and satisfying as the appearance of the marriage god Hymen in the final scene of *As You Like It*, Holly tells her husband that she is pregnant. Mickey—who was seen earlier in the film as infertile, divorced, and suicidal—seems to have been brought back to productive life by the powers of laughter and marital love.

Many aspects of *Hannah and Her Sisters* show how masterful Woody Allen has become in blending techniques of cinematic realism and stylization. The inexpensive production was shot entirely on location in New York City, and Allen worked closely with Carlo di Palma, the great Italian cinematographer of *Red Desert* (1964) and *Blow-Up* (1966), to achieve the precise emotional atmosphere he wanted for each scene—from the warmth of Hannah's apartment to the chill of Frederick's Soho loft to the grandeur of some of Manhattan's landmark buildings.

Allen chose his cast carefully, drawing both on his personal feelings for the people and on the associations that each carries into a film. In many ways the film is an affectionate valentine to Mia Farrow—Allen's close companion for a number of years and a star in his last five films. To underscore his feeling that Farrow is the center of a loving world that radiates out from her, Allen used Farrow's apartment as Hannah's apartment, cast Farrow's mother, Maureen O'Sullivan, as Hannah's mother, and included seven of Farrow's eight children as Hannah's children. Allen saw in Barbara Hersey not only the ideal object for a brother-in-law's lust but also an intelligent and feeling woman, and she rises to the opportunity with a fine performance. Michael Caine, with his reserved manner, understated sex appeal, and hint of a larcenous spirit, was the perfect choice for the adulterous Elliot. In the role of the raging painter, Max von Sydow brought to the film a powerful charge of angst and torment from his many films with Ingmar Bergman. Hollywood veteran Lloyd Nolan, who died shortly after the film was completed, provided an immensely poignant stimulus to the audience's memories as the father who enjoys nothing better than sitting at the piano, playing his old sweet songs. Dianne Wiest, Carrie Fisher, Julie Kavner, and Sam Waterston were cast with the same overriding intelligence and directed with the same intimate skill.

Allen's skill at choosing and directing actors is further enhanced by his meticulous attention to both costumes and music. In interviews, Barbara Hershey has marveled at how definite Allen's ideas were about how his actresses should be clothed, and the results add much to their characterizations: plain, toned-down, masculine clothes for Lee (which ironically increase her sexual vibrancy), tailored earth tones for the perfect Hannah, and a busy array of pins, scarves, and offbeat styles for the frantic Holly. Despite the wide variety of musical styles included in the film, no musical director is listed in the credits, but it is likely that Allen took charge of that function himself. His tastes in jazz and classical music have been featured prominently on his sound tracks ever since *Sleeper* (1973), but in *Hannah and Her Sisters* the music is more closely involved with the action than ever before. Certain pop standards—"You Made Me Love You," "Bewitched," and "I've Heard That Song Before"—are repeated throughout the film in connection with all the film's romances: These are the stages, the songs seem to say, that all intense love stories go through. At other times, the music serves as an ironic counterpoint: The deep emotions that the architect David professes to feel during an opera performance do not extend to his human relationships, and the ebullient accompaniment to Mickey's release from his brain tumor scare—Count Basie's "Back to the Apple"—seems incongruous when Mickey abruptly stops short on the sidewalk with his newest anxiety.

Ultimately, however, it is Woody Allen's mastery of narrative and visual form that gives the film a feeling of such simultaneous control and expansiveness. On the one hand, some of his techniques create the impression of a carefully designed analytic novel. His insertion of titles on the dark screen between scenes seems to divide the film into chapters, and by presenting the voice-over ruminations of five major characters (Elliot, Lee, Mickey, Holly, and Hannah), Allen skillfully creates an effect of alternating among limited first-person points of view. On the other hand, he is also capable of shifting from such a limited viewpoint to a more comprehensive view of social situations which are so expansive or volatile that it is hard to conceive of them being contained by the linear, analytic discourse of a novel. To this end, Allen has become a master of the moving camera and the long take, which sometimes allow him to connect the diverse but related activities of a number of characters in motion (as in the Thanksgiving scenes in Hannah's apartment) and at other times enable him to suggest the surging complexity of people's conflicting feelings (as in the powerful scene where Frederick discovers Lee's affair and she declares that she is moving out). Conversely, Allen is also adept at shifting from a comprehensive to a limited point of view. In a scene where the three sisters are about to have lunch together, Allen stops his moving camera for a long shot in which Hannah and Lee pause at the entrance to the restaurant. The camera sees Lee, but its view of Hannah is momentarily cut off by a wall. Nevertheless, the viewer then hears Hannah saying to Lee, "I can't believe Elliot, and I can't think of someone nice for you to go out with." Thus, very subtly, Allen shifts momentarily to Lee's point of view and conveys how a sharp pang of guilt makes her feel isolated from her unsuspecting and generous sister. Further, several memorable vignettes in the film occur when Allen pauses from his camera movement for lingering close shots that adore one of the sisters in a particularly beautiful moment: Lee as seen by Elliot in the opening scene of the film, Hannah by her father's piano after she has brought peace to a parental spat, Holly as seen by Mickey inside the record store as he is about to fall in love with her.

A number of Woody Allen's less admiring critics have often raised the question of whether he is capable of making a film that is not constricted by his own obsessions, with characters that are something more than reflections of his own ego. The answer suggested by *Hannah and Her Sisters* is a triumphant but qualified yes: if he provides his ego with a circumscribed place within the film. By consigning the character of Mickey Sachs to the periphery of the narrative through most of the film, Allen is able to exercise his obsessions with death and meaninglessness without imposing them on the other characters or the film as a whole. This strategy enables him both to develop a contrasting perspective on the other characters and to view them with a more open responsiveness than he has demonstrated in earlier films. The richly comic spectacle that results—the spectacle of a number of intelligent people struggling and growing through a period of their own individual befuddlements—makes *Hannah and Her Sisters* Woody Allen's most dramatically satisfying achievement to date.

Terry L. Andrews

Reviews
America. CLIV, April 19, 1986, p. 325.
Christian Century. CIII, April 2, 1986, p. 330.
Commonweal. CXIII, March 14, 1986, p. 150.
Films in Review. XXXVII, May, 1986, p. 301.
National Review. XXXVIII, March 14, 1986, p. 57.
The New Republic. CXCIV, February 10, 1986, p. 24.
The New Statesman. July 18, 1986, p. 25.
The New Yorker. LXII, February 24, 1986, p. 90.
Newsweek. CVII, February 3, 1986, p. 67.
Time. CXXVII, February 3, 1986, p. 77.
Variety. CCCXXI, January 22, 1986, p. 18.
The Village Voice. February 11, 1986, p. 53.
Vogue. CLXXVI, February, 1986, p. 60.

HEARTBREAK RIDGE

Production: Clint Eastwood for Malpaso Productions; released by Warner Bros.
Direction: Clint Eastwood
Screenplay: James Carabatsos
Cinematography: Jack N. Green
Editing: Joel Cox
Art direction: Edward Carfagno; set decoration, Robert Benton
Music: Lennie Niehaus
MPAA rating: R
Running time: 130 minutes

Principal characters:
Gunnery Sergeant Thomas
  "Gunny" Highway .... Clint Eastwood
Aggie........................... Marsha Mason
Major Malcolm Powers .... Everett McGill
Sergeant Webster.................... Moses Gunn
Mary Jackson..................... Eileen Heckart
Roy Jennings .... Bo Svenson
Lieutenant Ring .... Boyd Gaines
Stitch Jones .... Mario Van Peebles
Choozoo .... Arlen Dean Snyder
Profile............................. Tom Villard

Heartbreak Ridge is not what one might expect the film to be. For all but about twenty of the film's much-too-long 130 minutes, *Heartbreak Ridge* is really a comedy. The combat-action sequences that the film's title (along with the newsreel footage of Korean War battles which runs behind the opening credits) seems to promise arrive only after three-quarters of the film is over, and even the combat sequences are a perfunctory, gag-riddled charade. Producer-director Clint Eastwood and writer James Carabatsos do seem to want to say something thought-provoking about the state of American military readiness, but even the eventual substance of their statement is laughably jingoistic.

Heartbreak Ridge is more the story of its hero, Marine Gunnery Sergeant Thomas "Gunny" Highway (Clint Eastwood), than it is of Korea, the United States Marines, or warfare. *Tightrope* (1984) suggested that Eastwood had some intention of breaking out of the stereotyped *persona* and hackneyed tales which most of his films feature, but *Pale Rider* (1985) told viewers that they should have known better. *Heartbreak Ridge* presents what one might call Dirty Harry in the Marine Corps.

Highway has drunk, brawled, wenched, and cursed his way through twenty-four years in the Marine Corps, from war in Korea, where he won the Congressional Medal of Honor, through duty in the Dominican Republic in the mid-1960's and three tours of duty in Vietnam, back to postings in the United States.

As *Heartbreak Ridge* begins, the black-and-white of the Korean combat scenes gradually fades into the color of the film's narrative proper. The scene is a jail drunk tank late at night or early in the morning, where Highway spins war yarns to an audience of inmates including bikers, college-age kids, and a farmer or two. The transition from the documentary shots of the war where Highway distinguished himself to the ebb to which he has now sunk is nicely effected: Yesteryear's hero is today's military relic, reduced to reliving the highlights and low points of his life.

Highway works a routine job now as a supply sergeant, and, one assumes, he seeks relief from such petty concerns in habitual drunkenness and fighting. The film's initial sequences clearly characterize its hero: His supreme gifts are physical courage, mental toughness, and a talent for obscene verbal jousting. In fact, far too many scenes of *Heartbreak Ridge* depend on nothing more than Highway's skill in topping an adversary by creatively questioning his sexual orientation. In the drunk tank, a sadistic giant of a man grows weary of Highway's war stories, and their verbal exchanges eventually develop into a brief fight which ends when the sergeant deftly subdues his opponent—much to the surprise and admiration of the motley circle of onlookers.

The next day, after Highway has his day in court on charges of public drunkenness and indecent exposure, he returns to his base. Highway is true to the Marine code in his fashion, and he refuses a contraband Cuban cigar with which another sergeant attempts to bribe him. Damage, however, has been done. Highway soon finds that he is to be transferred again, this time back to his old unit, the Second Reconnaissance Division of the Second Marine Batallion.

On the bus which will take him to his new assignment, Sergeant Highway meets Stitch Jones (Mario Van Peebles), a young marine who moonlights as a rock singer, the Earl of Funk. Highway wears his machismo on his sleeve as openly as he sports his numerous campaign ribbons on his chest, and he is quickly offended when Jones takes the seat next to him, still clad in his studded black-leather jacket and dangling a silver cross from his left earlobe. Once again, Highway's perspective marks him as a creature who has materialized from a time warp—he tries to put Jones in his place by calling him a hippy.

The joke is on Jones, however, because he will soon discover that Highway is his new platoon sergeant, and Jones has already incurred the wrath of Gunny Highway by stealing his money and bus ticket while the sergeant was dallying with a waitress at a roadside bus stop.

Like everyone else whom Highway encounters, it seems, Highway's new commanding officer, Major Malcolm Powers (Everett McGill), makes fun of his age and is appalled by his conduct record. Powers issues Highway the challenge of whipping into shape the reconnaissance platoon of his outfit, a group of undisciplined, unmotivated misfits.

At this point in the film, it becomes apparent that *Heartbreak Ridge* possesses two narrative centers of interest. Above all, the film pits Highway against what the Marine Corps has become in 1983—a haven for society's outcasts, a once-proud organization now staffed by junior-officer Annapolis or ROTC graduates (such as Major Powers and Lieutenant Ring, Highway's platoon leader, who is played by Boyd Gaines) who have never seen combat. These young officers become either martinets, such as Powers, or ineffectual dolts, such as Ring.

On the other hand, Highway's coming home to his old unit gives him the opportunity to reconcile with his former wife, Aggie (Marsha Mason), who is now a barmaid in a tavern near the base. Although the ultimate outcome of the Gunny-Aggie intrigue is thoroughly predictable, Highway's awkward attempts to regain Aggie's hand (he secretly reads women's magazines, trying to find a clue as to how to proceed) and Aggie's violent protests against her former husband's hardheadedness provide the film's most satisfying and believable situations and character studies. Highway's first visit to Aggie's home ends in a quarrel which culminates in an amusing role reversal. Highway clumsily and halfheartedly tries to placate Aggie with trendy sociological jargon as she lambastes him with marine obscenities.

Also predictable is Highway's success in winning the favor of his men and turning them into the kind of troops which he knows that they should be. Highway achieves these goals despite a challenge from the platoon bully, the objections of Major Powers to Highway's unorthodox methods (the use of live ammunition during field exercises, for example), and the bumbling incompetence of Lieutenant Ring. Eventually, Highway's men become so proficient that they twice defeat Powers' men in field maneuvers, something which Powers cannot abide. After the second embarrassment, Powers makes the mistake of challenging Highway to a fistfight, with foreseeable results.

It is not difficult to understand why United States Marine Corps officials have not been pleased with the unflattering picture which Eastwood and Carabatsos give of the Corps. The premium which Highway places on improvisation, both in his personal life and in the tactics which he teaches his men, is not exemplary. Such free-lancing manifests itself in Highway's liberal use of foul insults and impatience with rules, authority, and established procedure.

The gung-ho slogans which Highway makes his men repeat over and over do seem archaic in what Major Powers calls the "new marines." The strait-laced major, on the other hand, longs for armed conflict and grieves over the recent war record of the United States as though war were volleyball—no wins, one tie (Korea), and one loss (Vietnam).

Finally, all the apparently senseless training of the marines is to be tested. After one full battle-dress alert proves to be merely that, an alert, a real opportunity to show what they can do, comes to the marines. Powers and Highway lead their men in an invasion of Grenada; the objective is to rescue American civilians trapped on the island.

While the brief combat sequences are realistically staged, the invasion of Grenada, as it is depicted in the film, is a paltry imitation of Guadalcanal and Inchon: The entire operation becomes a black joke. Highway and his men confront and kill several Cuban soldiers as they make their way inward from their beachhead, but the enemy is faceless. Highway now allows himself the pleasure of smoking a Cuban cigar which he took from the pocket of a man whom he shot several times. Only one of his men expresses any remorse when he takes the life of another human being (and even in this instance viewers do not see the face of the dead man).

Eventually, Highway's platoon carries out the rescue of the Americans, who seem to be mostly preppy college students. The marines enthusiastically accept the embraces of their liberated fellow countrymen. The operation, however, is not over yet. Powers orders Highway's men to reconnoiter one of the island's last pockets of enemy resistance, located strategically on a promontory. Cuban tanks are entrenched on the hill, and some heavy fighting ensues; in fact, one of Highway's men is killed, but no one pays much attention.

Farce comes into play even here. When the platoon's radio is put out of action, Lieutenant Ring orders an air strike on the hill by means of a long-distance credit-card telephone call to the Marine Corps base in Camp Lejeune, North Carolina. All ends well, however; Highway's men have given a sterling account of themselves, and even Ring has learned something about leadership.

After the island has been secured for democracy, Powers nevertheless berates Highway and Ring for disobeying orders. Justice, however, is served: The batallion commander arrives, praises Ring and Highway for their initiative, and relieves the foolish Powers of his command.

The fuzzy thinking and questionable taste of Eastwood and Carabatsos will be evident to most viewers. Are the writer and director of *Heartbreak Ridge* really implying that the tactical success of the Grenada mission somehow makes up for the sense of frustration and futility with which wars in Asia have left Americans? Apparently they are: After the mission has been completed, Highway gloats to one of his marine old-timer colleagues that the United States is no longer laboring under a no-win, one-tie, one-loss record. Eastwood and Carabatsos are so intent upon presenting battle as a cartoon short that they do not make the slightest allusion to the political reasons for the invasion of Grenada or its consequences.

Even Highway ultimately seems disaffected with the sorry conclusion of things. At the end of the film, having been reunited with Aggie, he decides at last to retire, muttering that there is no place for him in this day's marines. Amen.

Gordon Walters

Reviews
American Film. XII, December, 1986, p. 65.
Films in Review. XXXVIII, February, 1987, p. 102.
Los Angeles Times. December 5, 1986, VI, p. 1.
The New Republic. CXCVI, January 5, 1987, p. 24.
The New York Times. December 5, 1986, p. C3.
The New Yorker. LXII, December 29, 1986, p. 85.
Newsweek. CVIII, December 15, 1986, p. 83.
Time. CXXVIII, December 8, 1986, p. 103.
Variety. CCCXXV, December 3, 1986, p. 19.
The Washington Post. December 5, 1986, p. C1.

HEARTBURN

Production: Mike Nichols and Robert Greenhut; released by Paramount
Pictures
Direction: Mike Nichols
Screenplay: Nora Ephron; based on her novel of the same name
Cinematography: Nestor Almendros
Editing: Sam O'Steen
Production design: Tony Walton
Art direction: John Kasarda; set decoration, Susan Bode
Costume design: Ann Roth
Sound: James Sabat
Music: Carly Simon
MPAA rating: R
Running time: 108 minutes

Principal characters:
Rachel	Meryl Streep
Mark	Jack Nicholson
Richard	Jeff Daniels
Vera	Maureen Stapleton
Julie	Stockard Channing
Arthur	Richard Masur
Betty	Catherine O'Hara
Harry	Steven Hill
Dmitri	Miloš Forman

Heartburn presents the film fan and film critic with a number of problems. These problems make the film inherently interesting, but whether it is
ultimately deemed successful depends on the viewer's reaction to the way
the problems are resolved. The first problem the film brings forward is that
it is based on Nora Ephron's best-selling novel of the same name. Film adaptations of novels are notoriously problematic—fans of the book inevitably
picture the characters as somehow different from the film. A second problem is that the novel is a roman à clef, a thinly disguised version of the
author's troubled marriage to Watergate journalist Carl Bernstein. The
question of truthfulness, or gossip, is invariably invoked, and much time is
inevitably spent wondering who the supporting characters "really are." Yet a
third problem arises when superstars with well-known personalities—in this
case, Meryl Streep and Jack Nicholson—are asked to portray fictional characters based on real-life models. With all of this going on, it is no wonder
that the important issues the film raises, and the insights it brings to bear,
tend to get lost in the confusion.

Meryl Streep stars as Rachel, Ephron's autobiographical stand-in, who sees Mark (Jack Nicholson) at a friend's wedding and is immediately attracted to him. Through her editor-friend Richard (Jeff Daniels), Rachel learns the particulars about Mark: that he is a Washington columnist and divorced. The viewer soon learns that Rachel, too, is divorced. On their first date, Rachel and Mark reveal strong feelings for each other and some hesitation, but marriage and a move to Washington, D.C., soon follow. In Washington, Rachel befriends Arthur (Richard Masur), Mark's lawyer, and his wife, Julie (Stockard Channing). She also develops an affection for Betty (Catherine O'Hara), a television journalist-cum-gossip monger. Not much more happens by way of plot, as the film tries to detail the little things in the day-to-day life of the for-now happy couple.

To this end, the film is marvelously successful. Plot-oriented American filmgoers may not be used to the sight of a film heroine learning to cook, to care for her home, to rear her children, to relax with friends. Rachel herself is constantly amazed at how happy she is, how content she is to do nothing more than these (seemingly) little things. She must force herself to think about returning to her writing career. Her bliss is short-lived, however, for she soon learns of her husband's affair. This sends her packing, children in tow, to her father's apartment in Manhattan and back to the bosom of her group-therapy sessions (memorably led by Maureen Stapleton as Vera). Mark follows, begging her to come back to him, which she does. Their happiness, however, is only temporary as Rachel, much to her shock, soon realizes.

The film is told basically from Rachel's point of view, and so very little is learned about Mark. All the viewer sees of him is what Rachel sees, and perhaps all that is really known of him is colored by Rachel's (or Ephron's) viewpoint. Thus, one learns of Mark's affair only when Rachel does, and if one may not be quite as shocked as she, one still feels her pain of betrayal. Mark's explanation for his infidelity, if explanation there can be, is absent. Yet Mark is not portrayed as a villain. A particularly delightful scene, for example, shows Mark's genuine joy at learning that Rachel is pregnant. The two of them sing every show tune they can think of with the word "baby" in it, and Mark's humorous rendition of the soliloquy from *Carousel* ("My Boy Bill . . .") is a genuinely touching segment. Yet if Mark's treatment of Rachel seems harsh and his attitude inexplicable, his feelings may not be so different than those of Rachel's father, Harry (Steven Hill): Harry suggests that if Rachel wants revenge, she should leave the children with their father. Harry, and possibly Mark, simply have no idea how Rachel feels, how much her self-worth and identity are tied up with her family, possibly with the idea of family in general. She may have idealized marriage and motherhood, but she also works at them; she could no sooner abandon her family than her self. Perhaps the film is trying to say that, whether culturally or biologically, in this respect women are different from men. Such differences make marriage and family very difficult, and such a realization makes the film very important.

By any objective standards, however, there are a number of weaknesses in *Heartburn*. Early in the film, for example, there is a scene in which Rachel is having second thoughts on her wedding day. As the guests gather and wait, Rachel hides in her room, as one after another of the main characters try to calm her down and reassure her. Director Mike Nichols crosscuts between Rachel and her guests, who assume various poses of boredom and disarray to indicate the passage of time. The problem with this scene is that it is clearly the kind of thing that only happens in the movies (the sequence is not even in Ephron's novel)—in real life people simply do not hide in their rooms on their wedding day while their guests interminably wait. While realism is not necessarily a standard of value to apply to films, this particular scene is so clearly phony, so clearly calculated to draw laughs, that it detracts from the very real doubts of the characters and the insights of the filmmakers. Another sequence of events which similarly smacks of filmdom and not life revolves around the couple's efforts to renovate their high-priced Georgetown townhouse. Contemporary viewers may be uncomfortably reminded of Steven Spielberg's presentation of Richard Benjamin's disastrous *The Money Pit* (1986), while film historians may recall H. C. Potter's far superior *Mr. Blandings Builds His Dream House* (1948). In both cases, however, the scenes in question add nothing to the film's themes.

A somewhat more serious flaw lies precisely in the area of the film's themes. The film suffers from a certain schizophrenia, an inability to decide what it is trying to say, or at least on what, or whom, to place the blame for the failure of Rachel's marriage. Primarily, the film is torn between showing the relationship between Rachel and Mark, revealing Rachel's desires, hopes, and dreams, and delivering a satirical look at upwardly mobile Washington, D.C. Toward this latter end, the film unfavorably compares Washington to Manhattan and concludes that, despite the crime, Manhattan is a more honest, real environment. Rachel's shuttling back and forth between the two cities becomes something of a recurring motif in the film, with the implication, perhaps, that Washington life is simply wrong, that no marriage could survive in that fishbowl atmosphere, in the gossip-ridden parties and get-togethers that distinguish Rachel's marriage. This is where Betty comes in. It is a running gag that every time she appears on-screen, she has more juicy bits of gossip to relate to Rachel and her friends, more stories of who is doing what to whom. One hears more from Betty than from Mark, who is a political columnist—as if the film were trying to say that gossip has replaced political reporting in Washington, which may or may not be true, but which surely cannot be blamed for the breakup of Rachel's marriage.

The blame for the breakup of Rachel's marriage lies in her own fantasies, her own inner voices which seem to be at variance with the contemporary, unromantic, me-oriented, selfish society of the 1980's. This is where the film is at its strongest, where it, in fact, contains its greatest insights, for the viewer learns intimately of Rachel's feelings toward marriage, of her love for Mark, and her overwhelming happiness when the marriage produces children. Her attitude toward being a mother, her romanticization of the role combined with her genuine feelings of fulfillment, prevent her initially from seeing the reality of her situation, which is that Mark's commitment to the marriage is fading. When she finally does make the break permanently, taking her children on the shuttle from Washington, D.C., to Manhattan for the last time, there is a strong feeling of poignancy and pathos. The life of a single mother, even a very talented and successful one, with two children is a difficult life. If the film refuses to blame Mark, or to blame men in general, it also makes no excuses for such insensitive, inexplicable behavior.

In perfectly capturing the milieu of its characters and its evenhanded treatment of all concerned, *Heartburn* is very much in keeping with the best films of its director, Mike Nichols. Nichols has demonstrated his sensitivity to the way men and women interact in all of his films: his stunning debut film, *Who's Afraid of Virginia Woolf?* (1966), followed by *The Graduate* (1967), *Carnal Knowledge* (1971), and the controversial *Silkwood* (1983). It was *Silkwood* that originally brought Meryl Streep, Mike Nichols, and Nora Ephron together. The same careful attention that lent authenticity to *Silkwood*, which depicted rural, working-class life, is present in *Heartburn*, which paints a convincing portrait of successful urbanites who unsuccessfully marry. Yet on this score, there is perhaps a certain hesitation on the filmmakers' part, for in making a film so obviously close to home, they tend to hold back a little, denying the full impact of their insight into the characters' Jewish backgrounds. The ethnicity is there, alluded to and implied, but never really allowed to surface. Nevertheless, this is a minor point compared to the unhesitatingly bold look at the way women and men sometimes simply see things differently, with unhappy but still comic results.

David Desser

Reviews
American Film. X, July, 1986, p. 81.
Commonweal. CXIII, August 15, 1986, p. 436.
Films in Review. XXXVII, October, 1986, p. 481.
Ms. XV, August, 1986, p. 12.
National Review. XXXVIII, August 29, 1986, p. 46.
The New Republic. CXCV, July 28, 1986, p. 26.
The New York Times. CXXXV, July 25, 1986, p. C16.

The New Yorker. LXII, August 11, 1986, p. 77.
Newsweek. CVIII, July 28, 1986, p. 70.
Time. CXXVIII, August 4, 1986, p. 71.
Variety. CCCXXIII, July 16, 1986, p. 14.

HOOSIERS

Production: Carter De Haven and Angelo Pizzo for Hemdale Film and
Orion Pictures; released by Orion Pictures
Direction: David Anspaugh
Screenplay: Angelo Pizzo
Cinematography: Fred Murphy
Editing: C. Timothy O'Meara
Production design: David Nichols
Art direction: David Lubin; set decoration, Janis Lubin and Brendan Smith
Makeup: Ronnie Specter
Costume design: Jane Anderson
Basketball coordinator: Spyridon "Strats" Stratigos
Technical advisers: Tom McConnell and Tom Abernathy
Sound: Bill Phillips
Music: Jerry Goldsmith
MPAA rating: PG
Running time: 114 minutes

Principal characters:

Coach Norman Dale	Gene Hackman
Myra Fleener	Barbara Hershey
Shooter	Dennis Hopper
Cletus	Sheb Wooley
Opal Fleener	Fern Persons
Whit	Brad Boyle
Rade	Steve Hollar
Buddy	Brad Long
Everett	David Neidorf
Merle	Kent Poole
Ollie	Wade Schenck
Strap	Scott Summers
Jimmy	Maris Valainis

Hoosiers opens in a leisurely fashion as Norman Dale (Gene Hackman)
approaches the town of Hickory through a golden-filtered Indiana autumn,
his car edging with telephoto slowness through corn fields and tiny towns.
Once a big-time college coach, he lost that career in a single moment's burst
of anger when he struck one of his own players. Now, some ten years later,
he has a second chance. Yet his penance is to coach a tiny rural high
school's team in a state where the sport of basketball, especially high school
basketball, is a very serious business.

The team he finds in Hickory is an undisciplined group for whom good basketball is a smooth jump shot from fifteen feet. When Dale institutes a regimen of endurance and agility drills and demands that his players learn to pass before they shoot, he discovers that it is easier to control his players' frustrations than the impatience and growing outrage of the local collection of Monday-morning coaches who gather in the town's barbershop to lament each weekend's loss. The one glimmer of hope for the Hickory Huskers is a boy, Jimmy (Maris Valainis), whose jump shot is the best that the basketball fanatics of Hickory have ever seen. Jimmy, however, is off limits. Still in mourning for the previous coach, who had been as close to him as a father, Jimmy is directed to more academic pursuits by a young teacher, Myra Fleener (Barbara Hershey), who sees a future for the boy outside Hickory.

The town's desperation leads to a showdown in a local church hall, where the gathered crowd votes overwhelmingly to fire the coach. The vote is thrown out, however, when Jimmy appears to announce that he is finally willing to play ball—but only if Coach Dale stays. Norman Dale can now lead his team with a new weapon, just in time for the beginning of the state championship tournament. The Huskers grind their way through rough, close battles to their destiny in Indianapolis.

Hickory's march through the state tournament is based on the story of Milan, a tiny, rural, southern Indiana high school, which emerged from a field of 751 teams to win the 1954 championship, playing a school ten times its size in the final game. The last-second jump shot by the team's star shooting guard is enshrined in a gray kinescope which plays daily at the Indiana Basketball Hall of Fame and is remembered fondly by thousands of the state's basketball devotees.

The mysterious Jimmy, who spends hours shooting baskets alone at home and lurks about the gym on game nights, never becomes much of a character in the film. After his dramatic support of the coach at the church meeting, the filmmakers lose interest in his problems off court. The only Husker whose personal life is a factor in the second half of the film is Everett (David Neidorf, the only professional actor among the Husker players), son of the town drunk, Shooter (Dennis Hopper). At first, it is only an embarrassment to the player that Norman Dale wants to make Everett's father assistant coach, to give him a reason to stay sober. Yet Shooter's determination to hold on to this last chance wins for him his son's respect. *Hoosiers* withholds any certainty for Shooter's future, except to suggest that communication between father and son has been restored. That Coach Dale feels an association between Shooter's situation and his own is only implied by the film. The explosive temper that destroyed the coach's college career still threatens his future. *Hoosiers* offers no insight into the root of this problem, content to provide glimpses of Norman Dale's struggle to subdue his rage.

There is no comfortable fit between the tale of damaged characters clinging to a second chance and the incident of Indiana sports history—the miracle of Milan. The first half of the film probes the surfaces of its characters' psychic wounds with a cinematic reticence in keeping with what Myra says about the people of Hickory—that people's private matters stay pretty much their own. In the second half of the film, as the basketball momentum builds, this very unfinished observation of Hoosier characters is overwhelmed by the action. While few viewers outside Indiana are likely to recognize the Milan story, the film's conclusion offers little surprise, since many more have seen *Rocky* (1976) or some other specimen of the triumph-against-the-odds sports film genre. Yet *Hoosiers* has none of the cynical hard-sell of *Rocky* and its clones. Like Frank Capra in the 1930's, Angelo Pizzo and David Anspaugh have given their film a measure of optimism based on compassion and hard work. Yet unlike many Hollywood studio products, *Hoosiers* draws its characters and paints its background with a passion for the particular—the regional peculiarities of rural Indiana and a visual fidelity to the early 1950's. The film was shot on location in Indiana and uses local residents as extras. More unusual than that, however, in an era of teenage stars, this is a film with nonprofessional performers from Indiana playing all but one of the young athletes. That casting decision works. It is difficult to imagine this film featuring Tom Cruise or Michael J. Fox.

Dennis Hopper emerged in 1986 as a serious character actor. *Hoosiers* is the film for which the Academy of Motion Picture Arts and Sciences chose to honor him with an Oscar nomination. While his Shooter cannot dominate the film the way his Frank Booth took charge of *Blue Velvet* (1986; reviewed in this volume), Hopper is convincing as a man whose life has drifted into an alcoholic fog after the brief glory of high school sports stardom.

The director, Anspaugh, and the writer, Pizzo, grew up in Indiana and met as students at Indiana University. These circumstances, rather than an anticipation of financial success, illuminate the conception of *Hoosiers*. Perhaps Anspaugh's television success directing episodes of *Hill Street Blues*, *St. Elsewhere*, and *Miami Vice* encouraged financial backing of a project which could not have seemed a likely box-office champion. It may be that *Breaking Away*, a sleeper hit in 1979 and also a sports film made in Indiana, suggested itself as a promising precedent. Yet *Breaking Away* was southern Indiana springtime, fresh and optimistic, while *Hoosiers* is the cooler rural autumn of 1951. In spite of its triumphant finish, hope for the characters of *Hoosiers* has the desperate flavor of a last chance. Orion Pictures, which distributes the film, recognized possible box-office deficiencies in *Hoosiers* and released the film slowly, first in Indiana and Los Angeles in late 1986. The film was then held back for two months before going into wide release in February, the heart of the basketball season and in time to benefit from its Oscar nominations—Dennis Hopper's for best supporting actor and

Jerry Goldsmith's for best original musical score.

Basketball images of actual games are usually long shots, since a narrow angle of view would require of the cinematographer more ability to antici- pate action than it is practical to expect. Closer shots are limited to pauses in the action or to replay shots. The staged basketball action of *Hoosiers* gave the cinematographer, Fred Murphy, and his director, Anspaugh, an opportunity to present the sport in less traditional terms. Tight close-ups of short duration together with occasional uses of slow motion emphasize the physical effort of the game and its violence. At other times, the Steadicam glides up court with the guards, past the coach and the screaming fans, their cheers muted by a constantly repeating musical beat. Steadicam's eerily smooth, gyroscopic movement, which seems to deny any physical relation- ship to solid ground, encourages a dreamlike attitude at these moments when the viewer almost floats alongside the players.

In the aftermath of Hickory's championship victory, the reactions staged for the camera are familiar: winning players screaming and hugging one another, losing players suddenly subdued or in tears, comforted by friends and coach. The Hickory Huskers are all white boys, surrounded by their white supporters. The stunned and crying losers are mostly black, as are their fans and the coach. *Hoosiers'* audience, which must root for the Husk- ers as inevitably as the Huskers must win, could not escape recognition of this racial split, an uncomfortable but accurate representation of the racial politics of sports in the early 1950's. Interestingly, the coach of the losing team is played, not by an actor but by a former coach, Ray Crowe, who coached Indiana's first all-black high school basketball champions in 1955, after losing to Milan in a semifinal game the year before.

There is no irony in *Hoosiers'* representation of a community for which a high school sports team can be the central emotional focus and chief source of pride and identity. The significance of *Hoosiers* is not in any judgment Pizzo and Anspaugh have to offer of the phenomenon their film describes. Much more important is that a film with such modest ambitions and, at the same time, scrupulous authenticity in the pursuit of an idiosyncratic subject can still emerge from Hollywood.

Ann Harris

Reviews
American Film. XI, October, 1986, p. 67.
Commonweal. CXIV, April 10, 1987, p. 215.
Films in Review. XXXVIII, April, 1987, p. 229.
Los Angeles Times. December 11, 1986, VI, p. 1.
The New York Times. February 27, 1987, p. C10.

Newsweek. CIX, February 9, 1987, p. 73.

Sports Illustrated. LXVI, February 2, 1987, p. 2.

Time. CXXIX, February 9, 1987, p. 74.

Variety. CCCXXIV, October 15, 1986, p. 21.

The Wall Street Journal. April 2, 1987, p. 24.

THE KARATE KID PART II

Production: Jerry Weintraub; released by Columbia Pictures
Direction: John G. Avildsen
Screenplay: Robert Mark Kamen
Cinematography: James Crabe
Editing: David Garfield, Jane Kurson, and John G. Avildsen
Production design: William J. Cassidy
Art direction: William F. Matthews
Costume design: Mary Malin
Martial arts choreography: Pat E. Johnson
Music: Bill Conti
MPAA rating: PG
Running time: 113 minutes

Principal characters:
Daniel . . . . Ralph Macchio
Miyagi . . . . Noriyuki "Pat" Morita
Sato . . . . Danny Kamekona
Kumiko . . . . Tamlyn Tomita
Yukie . . . . Nobu McCarthy
Chozen . . . . Yuji Okumoto
Toshio . . . . Joey Miyashima
Miyagi's father . . . . Charlie Taminoto

The Karate Kid Part II was released in the summer of 1986; it offered changes in neither cast, crew, nor concept from the original. Indeed, it is very nearly seamless in its continuation of a boy's quest for maturity and identity. Along the way, it manages to touch most of the standard film themes of the 1980's: the individual, the teenager, a return to values, and a palpable ambivalence toward popular modern culture. It is not so much an exploitation film as it is a manufactured one, designed to appeal but not to pander. As such, it has more in common with the "made for television" genre than it does with the cinema, but this in itself cannot be read as an indictment.

First and foremost, the film is about the relationship between men-boys and their fathers. About the only role not reprised in this sequel is that of Daniel's mother, who appears offscreen, and then only in the beginning. Her major contributions to the film's plot are that she moves and that she allows Daniel (Ralph Macchio) to live with his *sensei*—his spiritual father, Mr. Miyagi (Pat Morita). It is as if Daniel, having reached a level of maturity and spiritual awakening, no longer needs his mother. The father theme is mirrored by the event which sets the scene for the remainder of the film—Miyagi's father has taken ill, and his son's presence is required. It is revealed that Miyagi has fled his native Okinawa and has lived away from his family and out of touch with his father since his departure. Perhaps in response to being separated from the family, he has had to turn inward, to karate, but this is only implied in the film, peopled as it is with rootless men and boys. It is a measure of his estrangement that his father is unsure that Miyagi's return is not a dream, because it is certainly nothing he would have expected. Following his father's death, Miyagi is comforted by his protégé, Daniel, in a scene that is awkward in its attempt to be accurate.

There are other paternal relationships embodied in the film: a primary one between Sato (Danny Kamekona), the rival and tormentor of Miyagi, and Sato's prize student, Toshio (Joey Miyashima), who is Daniel's nemesis. Sato is also the chief presence in Miyagi's old village, now surrounded by an American air force base. In this latter relationship, he is a cruel and uncaring father, exploiting the peasants in a largely feudal sense. Toshio is as much his student/son as he is his henchman, empowered if not assigned to do his dirty work. That it is impossible to tell how much of his cruelty is innate and how much is institutional is the result of the film's concentration on plot and atmosphere, at the expense of character. This is ironic in that the film's ostensible purpose is to chronicle the development of Daniel's character and, to a lesser extent, that of Miyagi.

Although Sato's power over the village is in some sense paternalistic, it is not benevolent. It is included in the plot because it is the only reference in the film to institutional power. For the characters in the film, there are no governments, no police, no authorities, only their spiritual leaders and themselves. To the extent that this situation is true, it appears odd that the village is situated near a major American base.

There are at least two scenes in which helicopters fly in and out of the base. Likewise, there are two encounters with the American presence on the island; the first occurs when Daniel and Mr. Miyagi (he has no first name) are in a cab trying to get to the village. The only path to the village lies through the base, and the soldiers are less than helpful. In the second incident, Daniel and his romantic interest, Kumiko (Tamlyn Tomita), enter a bar (at Daniel's request and against Kumiko's advice) where a karate contest is in progress. Here the soldiers are boorish and merely set the scene for yet another encounter between Daniel and the taunting, mocking, and hapless Toshio. The presence of the airbase and the authorities must be meant to imply irrelevance if not impotence, a sentiment underscored by Miyagi's comment about his attitude toward his World War II medal; here again, the concept of heroism must arise from within.

If the central theme of the film is the relationships between men and their male children, and that of a man to his government, then a secondary theme lies in the role of tradition and Western tradition in particular. In this sense, Western encompasses the European civilization as well as the more recent Western in cowboy/pioneer sagas. There is much lip service paid to the word "honor": the reason why Miyagi left Japan originally, the reason why Sato has to confront and fight Miyagi, and the reason why Toshio must confront Daniel. The statement "You have offended my honor" is used when pride is punctured, or ego, or self-esteem. There is a definite confusion about honor, unless one defines honor as the precursor to deference— that is, honor is a power relationship. If Sato is an honorable man, why does he do dishonorable things such as allow the villagers to be cheated by dishonest weights? It is much like the classic cowboy confrontation between the man who wants to fight and prove himself and the old hand who recognizes the futility of fighting. Another echo of the gunfight occurs at the end of the film, in the climactic fight scene between Daniel and the now disgraced Toshio. In the midst of a crowd, the two opponents face each other, and the crowd parts, not trying to stop the confrontation, merely hoping that their champion wins this fight to the death.

There is a marked ambivalence displayed toward Western values. The primary villains, Sato and Toshio, are shown in Western dress, formal for the circumstances, with Sato's bull-like neck pressed against a tie in his gray suit, and with Toshio's young-man-from-Beverly-Hills costume replete with tight jeans and gold chains. Even their car is a classic bad-guy vehicle, an old Cadillac. In contrast, native Okinawan traditions are accorded respect, even by the sound track. Indeed, the fight scene that ends the film erupts in the Bone Dance, a traditional ceremony of great importance to the village. Much time and care are lavished on the ceremonies, partly as a means of building suspense (by delaying the plot) and partly as a means of lifting the film past the exploitation level.

Perhaps the most puzzling aspect of the film lies in the way that the young have become so thoroughly Americanized, albeit into the 1950's. One of the more important scenes takes place when Kumiko and Daniel go to a dance, one straight out of *American Bandstand*, complete with costumes and music. It is one way of establishing a rapport, both between the natives and Daniel and between the film and the audience. It is interesting, nevertheless, that one can infer that the Oriental contribution to this civilization is karate and spiritual insight, as well as tradition and depth, while America and by extension the West has contributed rock and roll and the fulfillment of the innate desire to be Elvis Presley.

The weakness of the film is revealed in its endings, relying on storms and artifice to bring issues to a resolution. First, instead of the promised fight between Sato and Miyagi that the film has been hinting at throughout, a typhoon unexpectedly assails the village. It is hard to imagine a village in the midst of an air/naval base that would not have some warning of a major tropical storm. Sato is taken by surprise and caught in a building that collapses about him, pinning him under a massive rafter. His student, the hated Toshio, runs out of the building, looking for shelter. Miyagi frees his erstwhile enemy by breaking the beam with a single blow of his hand, gaining Sato's favor and forgiveness. Toshio is banished. The next scene shows Sato's trucks, which had been introduced previously as they tried to tear up the town, returning to help it rebuild. Daniel, who had become a hero by rescuing the girl who rang the bell that warned the villagers and who was trapped by the sudden onslaught of the winds, makes more points by getting the Bone Dance reinstated in its traditional home, a castle that belongs to Sato. It would seem that this is the ending, but director John G. Avildsen toys with the audience. Toshio leaps in and challenges Daniel to a fight to the death, or he will kill Kumiko. There is finally a fight, and Toshio shows his utter villainy by punching Kumiko. Just as in the first film, the fight is won by Daniel, realizing the purpose and nature of a karate move (there the crane, here the drum). Daniel wins and forces his opponent's head back and prepares to kill him. Despite Toshio's defiance, Daniel relents and settles for honking his foe's nose. It is not clear how humiliating an opponent will have long-term beneficial consequences, except for the director who is free to bring the loser back in a sequel, hungry for revenge. In a film that talks of honor and growth, that has Daniel wondering how he can defuse a situation without fighting, it seems absurd to end with a public humiliation. He does not allow Toshio to save face, or retain any honor, nor does he grow from the experience. The ending works neither as realism nor as allegory and serves primarily to end the film, not to resolve issues.

The film's strength lies in its facile accessibility; its failures can be attributed to its lack of commitment. It is a karate movie without a karate ballet and a teen movie whose hero does not really resolve his problems. Scene by scene, it seems to work, or at least there is something to enjoy, but in sum, the effect is diminished. It lacks the focus of Avildsen's previous films—*Rocky* (1976) and *The Karate Kid* (1985)—and it lacks the intensity of the sound track that made them so compelling. The psychological hook of the outsider training and overcoming odds, thereby becoming accepted, if not respected, is lacking here because Daniel always has been respected by the villagers and by his mentor. The major transformation is wrought upon Sato, and he is a cipher throughout the film, probably more as the result of the direction than to any limitations of Kamekona's acting ability. Both Morita and Kamekona are forced to be stoic and cryptic, speaking in a semblance of English that restricts their ability to project emotions and limits them to a dated and flawed Oriental mysticism. Not only are there few female roles, but also, as in *Rocky* and *The Karate Kid*, the one female role is reserved for the romantic interest of the hero. Women here are seen primarily as upholders of tradition and traditional values, whereas men can set tradition as well as follow it. That it is an unequal world is taken as natural, another manifestation of the film's overwhelming conservatism. There are other, more mundane flaws in this film as well. It is hard to explain the inclusion of a scene from *The Karate Kid* in which Miyagi tells Daniel that there is no defense against the crane in karate, only later to have Daniel try to use it against Toshio and have it deftly and automatically countered, and painfully so, at that. There is no reason to have Daniel's opponent from the first film show up at Sato's karate school in Okinawa and then disappear. That was not a background shot, but a foreshadowing one, yet nothing was done with it, leaving one either to shake one's head in wonderment or to decide to ignore all but the surface of the film.

Richard A. Strelitz

Reviews
Chicago Tribune. June 20, 1986, p. CT7.
Films and Filming. August, 1986, No. 383, p. 38.
Los Angeles Times. June 20, 1986, VI, p. 1.
Macleans. XCIX, July 7, 1986, p. 53.
The New York Times. June 20, 1986, p. C17.
Philadelphia. LXXVII, August, 1986, p. 60.
Variety. CCCXXIII, June 18, 1986, p. 19.
Video. X, January, 1987, p. 75.
The Washington Post. June 20, 1986, p. D6.

LEGAL EAGLES

Production: Ivan Reitman; released by Universal
Direction: Ivan Reitman
Screenplay: Jim Cash and Jack Epps, Jr.
Cinematography: Laszlo Kovacs
Editing: Sheldon Kahn, Pem Herring, and William Gordean
Production design: John De Cuir
Art direction: Ron Hobbs and David Chapman; set decoration, Thomas L.
　Roysden and Alan Hicks
Music: Elmer Bernstein
MPAA rating: PG
Running time: 116 minutes

　　　Principal characters:
　　　Tom Logan .... Robert Redford
　　　Laura Kelly .... Debra Winger
　　　Chelsea Deardon .... Daryl Hannah
　　　Victor Taft .... Terence Stamp
　　　Cavanaugh .... Brian Dennehy

　　In *New York* magazine, David Denby called *Legal Eagles* a "redoing" of
"forties romantic comedy, with some thrills and violence thrown in." Indeed, viewers may be reminded of the Spencer Tracy-Katharine Hepburn
husband-and-wife attorney team in *Adam's Rib* (1949). The very title, *Legal
Eagles*, however, suggests a bolder and less witty humor than is to be found
in the cinema of an earlier age. Ivan Reitman, the highly successful coproducer of *National Lampoon's Animal House* (1978) and the producer
and director of *Meatballs* (1979), *Stripes* (1981), and *Ghostbusters* (1984),
has cast Robert Redford and Debra Winger in roles that befit the 1980's.
　　Tom Logan (Robert Redford), a powerful assistant district attorney, confronts a young and feisty defense attorney, Laura Kelly (Debra Winger).
While she admires his adversarial style, she also challenges his comfortable
niche in the legal system. Will he continue to groom himself as the next district attorney, or will he follow her lead in exposing the corrupt dealings in
the art world that involve the cover-up of a great artist's death? Jeopardizing
a career to pursue one's own convictions seems an especially courageous
thing to do in a time dominated by young, urban, upwardly mobile professionals who are averse to risk taking.
　　Redford looks and acts his part extremely well. His slightly wrinkled features hold together well as if they have been chiseled by experience. He is
attracted to but believably disconcerted by Chelsea Deardon (Daryl Hannah), the performance-artist daughter of the painter who perished in a fire

that supposedly destroyed his work. She suspects that the paintings survived the fire, including one that was given to her by her father on her eighth birthday. When she is accused of stealing the painting and then of murder, she is represented in court by Laura Kelly. Kelly believes Deardon, but no one else does, and Kelly has a hard time convincing Logan to join her in Deardon's defense. Deardon, appropriately enough, plays with fire in the performance piece she seductively puts on for Logan. Although he succumbs (once) to this nubile temptation, his sense of romance (as a divorced man with a young daughter) is awakened by the wide-eyed Kelly. She is straightforward and embarrasses Logan about his attraction to Deardon. He is made to seem foolish because Kelly confronts him directly, making him choose between her adult and demanding sexuality and Deardon's pliant but vacuous eroticism.

As long as one does not inspect the plot too closely (it is full of holes), the chemistry between Winger and Redford carries the film, especially when it is put in the context of the duplicitous art world Kelly and Logan investigate. As light entertainment, the picture pleases, for one wants to know how the great art dealer Victor Taft (Terence Stamp) has been able to defraud Chelsea Deardon of her deceased father's work. Stamp produces the most intriguing character in the film. His Victor Taft is suave and steely-eyed, the consummate professional whose greed has overridden every other emotion. He is a character that the attorneys cannot crack. He is a very dangerous man.

Surprisingly, little is made of Winger's character. As soon as Kelly persuades her male counterpart to take on the case, her personality is subsumed in the plot. There is very little to learn from the couple's contentious scenes—something one could never say of Tracy and Hepburn's more quarrelsome conversations. Reitman has cautioned against this comparison with earlier screen teams of lover lawyers and other professionals—and rightly so, since the very notion of marriage is much more tenuous for the 1980's than it was for mature husband and wife teams such as Garson Kanin and Ruth Gordon, the authors of *Adam's Rib*.

For Reitman, the director of *Legal Eagles*, the film represents a kind of transition to adult themes—an approach to mature subjects—not a retrospective conclusion about them. He views his own audience as growing older and speaks in *The New York Times Magazine* of "targeting an audience over twenty-five." Judging by *Legal Eagles*, that audience—in spite of its prosperity and ambition—is a far less confident generation than Tracy and Hepburn's. Both Logan and Kelly are insomniacs, workaholics, and rather clumsy persons, with none of the comic panache of, say, Cary Grant and Rosalind Russell. Winger and Redford move well in their roles, but their characters are imitators and are not certain of their own authenticity. Logan, for example, is Kelly's model for a lawyer; she is his emulator. Unable to sleep, Logan watches Gene Kelly on television and mimics his dance in *Singin' in the Rain*.

This questioning of authenticity is a theme that is enhanced by the art-world setting of connivers and charlatans and by genuine works of art. Several original works of art by Alexander Calder, Jim Dine, Hans Hofmann, Willem de Kooning, Pablo Picasso, and Louise Nevelson can be seen on-screen. Yet the bogus art looks as good as the genuine articles, and the picture seems to ask: How does one tell the real from the fake? Whom does one trust? In *Art News*, Arnold Glimcher, director of the Pace Gallery in New York City, describes a sculpture he created for the film: "I think it looks quite good, it's just not very original." Some critics have said the same of *Legal Eagles*, but at least the film is honest enough to raise the issue of genuineness. If the film breaks no new ground, it does point to the need for self-evaluation and for moral and aesthetic standards that can create some sense of stability, some alternative to trendiness. To that extent, Reitman has succeeded in his claim that his effort on *Legal Eagles* is "not so much to recreate the movies of the 1940's but to recreate the sensibilities where people stood up for what was right, where people trusted each other, where there was an order to life." If that is an excessively naïve view of what life was like in the 1940's, it is, nevertheless, a fairly accurate reading of the way those 1940's films made people feel. Laura Kelly does make Tom Logan stand up for what is right, and as a couple they do learn to trust each other. Like most comedy thrillers, *Legal Eagles* does solve a mystery and restores some "order to life."

As Vincent Canby points out in his *The New York Times* review, the special effects—two fires and a warehouse explosion—are well done. The film's technique is conventional, with crosscutting sometimes establishing the comic parallels between Logan and Kelly; each is at home alone and completely at a loss. Their work is evidently totally absorbing, and in the crosscutting one can see why their barren personal lives almost guarantee that their professional association will be intense and fulfilling. The cross-cutting, in effect, establishes their need to be together. In this sense, the film's meaning merges with technique and becomes the story of how this couple finds their satisfaction in each other.

Carl E. Rollyson, Jr.

Reviews
Art News. LXXXV, Summer, 1986, p. 188.
Commonweal. CXIII, July 11, 1986, p. 405.
Films in Review. XXXVII, October, 1986, p. 479.
Macleans. XCIX, June 30, 1986, p. 50.

Magill's Cinema Annual 1987

The New Republic. CXCV, August 4, 1986, p. 25.
New York. XIX, June 23, 1986, p. 54.
The New York Times. CXXXV, June 18, 1986, p. C17.
The New Yorker. LXII, June 30, 1986, p. 53.
Newsweek. CVII, June 30, 1986, p. 60.
Time. CXXVII, June 23, 1986, p. 74.
Variety. CCCXXIII, June 18, 1986, p. 18.
Working Woman. XI, August, 1986, p. 113.

LETTER TO BREZHNEV

Origin: Great Britain
Released: 1985
Released in U.S.: 1986
Production: Janet Goddard and Caroline Spack; released by Circle Films
Direction: Chris Bernard
Screenplay: Frank Clarke
Cinematography: Bruce McGowan
Editing: Lesley Walker
Production design: Piers Player
Art direction: Lez Brotherston, Nick Englefield, and Jonathan Swain
Makeup: Viv Howells
Costume design: Mark Reynolds
Sound: Charles Ware
Music direction: Wolfgang Kafer
Music: Alan Gill
Song: Margi Clarke and Alan Gill, "Letter to Brezhnev"
MPAA rating: R
Running time: 94 minutes

Principal characters:

Peter	Peter Firth
Sergei	Alfred Molina
Tracy	Tracy Lea
Elaine	Alexandra Pigg
Teresa	Margi Clarke
Josie	Angela Clarke
Man from Foreign Office	Neil Cunningham
Newspaper reporter	Ken Campbell

Chris Bernard's *Letter to Brezhnev*, along with *My Beautiful Laundrette* (1986; reviewed in this volume) and *Mona Lisa* (1986; reviewed in this volume) marked a new British invasion in cinema. The films recall British cinema of the 1960's, when low-budget films depicting working-class life poured out of England. Working with Frank Clarke's romantic but knowing script, Bernard has taken the spirit and story line of the 1960's films and adapted them to a New Wave sensibility. While *Letter to Brezhnev* is a sympathetic valentine to the working-class people of Liverpool, its slick sound track and carefully edited cuts are very sophisticated. It is a film that is equally heartfelt and street-smart, visually and narratively.

The film opens with two parallel stories. At the port of Liverpool, a burly Russian sailor calls excitedly to his friend Peter, announcing their arrival at their destination. In another part of town, two young women in their twenties, Tracy (Tracy Lea) and Elaine (Alexandra Pigg), spill out of a double-deck bus, pausing to smoke a cigarette before they enter a bar. The two exchange bored conversation. Tracy complains about her boyfriend Mick, and Elaine expresses her unhappiness at being stuck in Liverpool, wistfully speaking of romantic cities like Casablanca. The women, who are dressed almost identically, are bored with frequenting the same working-class Liverpool bars.

Once inside the bar, which is filled with restless, lower-class young people, they are joined by Teresa (Margi Clarke), a chatty, bubbly young woman who has just gotten off from her job at a chicken-processing plant. She animatedly describes her job duties, which consist of pulling out and then restuffing chicken organs into roasters. Elaine and Tracy are revolted by her job, but they silently acknowledge that she is lucky to be working. Like most of the people in the bar, they are unemployed. Once Tracy finds Mick's new girlfriend, she leaves her friends to pick a fight and reclaim her man. Elaine and Teresa become depressed with the bar, which offers refuge in alcohol but no escape. They decide to splurge on a cab and go to a bar across town.

Teresa lets herself be picked up by a Cypriot who has lots of money, and while they dance, she proceeds to pick his pocket. Armed with a bulging wallet, the two women run out of the bar. The Cypriots chase them, but they leave their expensive car momentarily. With a BMW and a stolen wallet, Elaine and Teresa enter a nightclub that is worlds beyond the bars they usually frequent. Teresa heads toward the bathroom, removing her work uniform and emerging as a poor man's version of Marilyn Monroe, complete with dyed blonde hair and ruby lipstick. During her absence, Elaine makes eye contact with Peter (Peter Firth), the young Russian sailor. When Teresa returns, Peter and his friend Sergei (Alfred Molina) join them at their table.

Fun-loving Sergei and Teresa immediately click and head for the dance floor. Elaine and Peter talk of the differences between the Soviet Union and England. Peter romantically characterizes the spirit of Russia, expressing his love for the different regions and people. Yet he also freely admits that if one does not work in Russia, one does not eat. Elaine, keenly aware of her unemployed status, tells him that those are the rules in England as well. Peter does not understand her ironic reference and asks her in a concerned manner if she has not eaten. Elaine explains her remark and asks him to dance. Throughout the film, language barriers and cultural differences are bridged through affection and humor.

As Elaine and Peter dance, the pulsating disco beat becomes a lushly orchestrated waltz in their minds. After an impromptu consultation in the ladies' room, Elaine and Teresa decide to spend their stolen kitty on a hotel room. The two couples walk through the now-quiet streets of Liverpool.

Peter stops to show Elaine the star that guides him to every port, the star that always reminds him of Russia but that will now remind him of Elaine. Elaine's guarded cynicism melts as she falls in love with the romantic sailor. Yet there are constant reminders of what happens to romance in Liverpool, as they pass a bickering couple.

Teresa balks once they reach the hotel, expressing her weariness at having sex be the dominant reason for men's interest in her. Elaine reminds her that she may be on the verge of a real romance with a man who is from another country. Reassured, Teresa goes to Sergei, who carries her to a bedroom.

Teresa and Sergei make love, while Elaine and Peter talk through the night, baring their souls. They wake up early next morning and tour Liverpool, while Teresa and Sergei remain in the bedroom. Elaine's everyday haunts take on a special meaning with Peter. Unlike Peter, who has sailed around the world, Elaine has traveled only on the Liverpool ferry, which shuttles back and forth to the same place day after day. When she rides it with Peter, however, she begins to think that anything can happen. Later that day, Peter gives Elaine his grandfather's watch, offering it as a sign that they will meet again. When Peter returns to the port before his departure, the lovers are parted behind a fence, a metaphorical separation between East and West as well as the disunited hearts of the young lovers. Peter urgently implores Elaine to marry him, to remember always the star. He assures her that they will be together again. As he runs to make roll call, he tosses his hat over the fence, leaving a part of himself with her. Elaine clutches the hat as she walks home.

The romantic possibilities that Peter brought to her life contrast sharply with Elaine's daily routine as an unemployed woman living with an angry, lower-class family. Elaine feels frustrated and trapped by her family and working-class social circle, who have long ago resigned themselves to Liverpool and who have abandoned hope for a better life. Elaine vents her frustration at not being able to be with Peter to Teresa, who halfheartedly suggests that she write to the man in charge.

Elaine takes her suggestion seriously and rushes home to write a friendly, simple letter to Secretary Leonid Brezhnev, asking him to reunite her with Peter. Miraculously, Elaine receives a personal response and a plane ticket to Moscow. The news of her trip puzzles her family and all of Liverpool. Reporters and broadcasters ironically note Elaine's desire to seek refuge behind the Iron Curtain. People react against the Russians on the basis of news stories that they have heard. They tell Elaine that the Russians are cold, calculating, and only interested in denying people their human rights. With the support of her friend Teresa, Elaine gamely challenges these assumptions, knowing full well that her freedom in the West means very little if she has no reason for living.

Before Elaine departs, she has a meeting with a representative from the Foreign Office (Neil Cunningham). Over tea, the official impresses Elaine with his extensive knowledge of the Russian language, the people, and their customs. At first, he approaches Elaine very politely, asking her if she has really considered the ramifications of living in the Soviet Union. Elaine balks when she realizes that she does not know the language, the culture, or, as the official points out, the currency. Her belief that love conquers all remains unshakable until the officer pulls out a photograph of Peter with another woman, whom he identifies as his wife. Stunned, Elaine runs out of the office.

The devastating news forces Elaine to relinquish her hope of ever seeing Peter again, or of escaping from her dismal surroundings. As an unemployed young woman, Elaine knows that her only ticket out of Liverpool will be the one that was given to her by Brezhnev. Teresa points out that the woman in the photograph could be anyone and that she should go to see for herself if Peter is married. Her encouragement boosts Elaine's confidence, and she decides to go.

Teresa drives her to the airport on the day of Elaine's flight. As the blonde, ordinary woman from the chicken factory sees her friend off on an extraordinary adventure, she is filled with a bittersweet sorrow. While she and many others will be stuck with the routine of the grimy port city, Elaine is escaping. Elaine encourages Teresa to follow her own dreams, but Teresa shakes her head sadly. She tells Elaine that she will never leave, she has forgotten how to dream. As the women embrace and say goodbye, Teresa calls out to Elaine, asking her to tell Sergei that she loves him.

Letter to Brezhnev explores the idealism of the spirit in spite of political and personal restrictions. While director Bernard very realistically captures all the limitations that can squelch a young woman's dream, political barriers, working-class problems, and day-to-day ugliness are overpowered by the indestructible belief in a spiritual ideal.

Working with Clarke's touching and humorous screenplay, Bernard has directed a film that is both fantastic and true to life. He has his finger to the pulse of the Liverpudlian, to his singsong dialect, common frustrations, and secret hopes. All the characters have distinctive personality traits so that even minor parts, such as the roles of the taxi driver and the bickering couple, reveal something meaningful about the story being told. By dividing the action into spheres—the world of night versus the reality of day, finite political boundaries versus love that transcends culture—Bernard stacks the odds against his innocent characters and the whimsical story. The film derives its energy from forcing the characters and the audience to make the existential leap of faith and to believe for just a moment in the impossible.

Shot in only three weeks with a seventy-thousand-dollar budget, *Letter to Brezhnev* was the first feature production for most of the cast and crew.

Three members of the Clarke family (screenwriter Frank and actresses Margi and Angela) worked with close friends (director Bernard and actress Alexandra Pigg) on what was a labor of love for all native Liverpudlians involved.

As Teresa and Elaine, Margi Clarke and Alexandra Pigg are a winning pair of heroines. Clarke, who was the model for the character that Julie Walters played in *Educating Rita* (1983), is a gifted comedienne who captures Teresa's rapier tongue with tenderness and wit. Pigg gives Elaine both a sweet romanticism and a dogged determination that are equally credible. Actor Peter Firth, who starred in the film version of *Equus* (1977), is charming as Peter, the Russian sailor who rescues Elaine by giving her hope.

Bruce McGowan's cinematography captures all the film's different moods, from the soft, lush night scenes to the starkness of the Liverpool port where Peter and Elaine say goodbye. The film's use of unusual angles complements Lesley Walker's imaginative, fast-paced editing. For a low-budget film, *Letter to Brezhnev* has a strong and polished visual style. The sound track is used to create different levels of reality: Alan Gill's lyrical string score infuses the scenes between Elaine and Peter with romance, while a score of pop songs by current British bands roots the films in the present-day world of England's restless young people. Just as *Georgy Girl* (1966) was a product of England in the 1960's, so is *Letter to Brezhnev* a very contemporary look at the problems and personalities of Liverpool in the 1980's.

Critics lauded the film for its deceptively simple but imaginative story, its actors and actresses, and its style. *Letter to Brezhnev* explores the universal themes of the triumph of love and hope over despair in a lighthearted way, while it very tenderly portrays the stories of everyday people. The humor and courage that director Bernard reveals in the plucky Liverpudlians is reminiscent of the humanist works of French directors Jean Renoir and Marcel Pagnol. *Letter to Brezhnev* is a lively and innocent film that makes the extraordinary seem within reach of anyone with some measure of hope.

Laura Gwinn

Reviews
Chicago Tribune. July 11, 1986, VI, p. 37.
Films in Review. XXXVII, August, 1986, p. 428.
Los Angeles Times. June 11, 1986, VI, p. 5.
Macleans. XCIX, June 16, 1986, p. 53.
National Review. XXXVIII, July 4, 1986, p. 44.
The New Republic. CXCIV, April 28, 1986, p. 24.
New Statesman. CX, November 8, 1986, p. 31.

The New York Times. May 2, 1986, p. C20.
The Progressive. L, July, 1986, p. 38.
The Washington Post. May 24, 1986, p. C4.

LITTLE SHOP OF HORRORS

Production: David Geffen; released by Warner Bros.
Direction: Frank Oz
Screenplay: Howard Ashman; based on his own musical play of the same
name
Cinematography: Robert Paynter
Editing: John Jympson
Production design: Roy Walker
Art direction: Stephen Spence; set decoration, Tessa Davies
Special effects: Bran Ferren
Audrey II design: Lyle Conway
Costume design: Marit Allen
Choreography: Pat Garrett
Music: Alan Menken and Miles Goodman (original motion-picture score)
Song: Alan Menken, with lyrics by Howard Ashman
MPAA rating: PG-13
Running time: 88 minutes

> *Principal characters:*
> Seymour Krelborn . . . . Rick Moranis
> Audrey . . . . Ellen Greene
> Mushnik . . . . Vincent Gardenia
> Orin Scrivello, D.D.S. . . . . Steve Martin
> Crystal. . . . . Tichina Arnold
> Chiffon. . . . . Tisha Campbell
> Ronette . . . . Michelle Weeks
> Patrick Martin . . . . James Belushi
> Wink Wilkinson . . . . John Candy
> First customer . . . . Christopher Guest
> Arthur Denton . . . . Bill Murray
> Audrey II . . . . voice of Levi Stubbs

Little Shop of Horrors is an entertaining musical adaptation by Muppet-
master Frank Oz of an off-Broadway play that was inspired by a perfectly
ridiculous B-movie science-fiction spoof, produced and directed by Roger
Corman in 1961. The original film, crudely shot in black and white in two
days, tells a ghastly, gothic story about a young man named Seymour Krelborn (Jonathan Haze) who works for Mushnik the florist (Mel Welles) on
Skid Row and who cultivates a mysterious plant that turns out to be a
treacherous man-eating monster from outer space. In the Frank Oz musical
adaptation, which owes more to Howard Ashman's play than to Roger
Corman's original film, Rick Moranis plays the part of Seymour and Vin-

cent Gardenia plays the part of Mushnik.

The general design of the plot is the same in all versions. The plant is a novelty at first and brings fame to Seymour and profit to Mushnik; the problem is that the plant thrives on human flesh. Seymour, who is something of a nitwit, names the plant "Audrey II" in honor of Audrey, the girl of his dreams (Ellen Greene in the remake, Jackie Joseph in the original). She also works for Mushnik and is romantically involved with a sadistic dentist, who is eventually punished for his brutality by being turned into plant food.

Much of Corman's original story is not translated into Howard Ashman's musical play, which became a considerable hit off Broadway and in London, or into the Frank Oz film adaptation. The Corman film follows Seymour home to visit his ailing mother, for example, but this character is dropped in the musical, since the stage play concentrates on the Skid Row setting of the florist shop, economizing on the number of sets but retaining Seymour, Mushnik, Audrey, the dentist (played by Steve Martin in the Frank Oz version in a spectacular cameo), and his masochistic patient (played by Jack Nicholson in the original and by Bill Murray in the musical remake). In all the versions, the plant craves human blood, grows to gigantic proportions, learns to talk, and demands to be fed. In the musical, it sings for its supper.

After working his fingers to the bone to nourish the monster plant with his own blood, Seymour, in a trance in the original, goes out to forage for food for his insatiable plant—a railroad worker who is run over by a train, for example, and a prostitute who is hit over the head by a rock. ("Your place or mine?" she propositions Seymour. "We'll flip a coin," Seymour answers, but he does not have a coin and flips a rock instead—"wet side or dry?"—and the rock conveniently kills her.) The next victim in the original is the dentist; in the musical, he is the first victim, compressing the story. The original, seventy-minute, trashy Corman film, which has become a cult classic, features some memorably idiotic dialogue that is omitted in the adaptation, such as Mushnik's comment to Audrey, "I'll be back in a flash with the cash."

The plot of the Frank Oz adaptation follows the musical fairly closely but changes the conclusion, adding a wicked little twist. The focus here is squarely upon Seymour, his discovery, and his dilemma. The plant he has nourished turns him into a celebrity and brings fame and fortune to Mushnik and his flower shop. Seymour's success gives him the courage to court Audrey, bruised and battered as she is by her sadistic biker-dentist boyfriend.

By the time the dentist gasses himself into oblivion and is fed to the plant, Audrey is receptive to Seymour's proposal of marriage. The musical number that results from this romantic coupling, "Suddenly Seymour," is a wonderful parody of American ambition and materialism, as Seymour and Audrey dream of their very own little house in the suburbs. When their dream is finally realized, as the film permits it to be by adding a happy ending, Oz undercuts their bliss by showing a bed of little Audrey II's growing happily outside the house.

At the same time, however, Oz and Ashman knew that they would have to preserve enough of the original musical to make the film agreeable to those who had seen and enjoyed the play on stage. The stage version added lyrics by Ashman, set to the music of Alan Menken in a 1950's mixture of soul and rock and roll, and provided a dramatic and lyrical chorus of black singers (Crystal, Ronette, and Chiffon, played by Michelle Weeks, Tichina Arnold, and Tisha Campbell in the film). Their songs provided transitions and quickened the pace agreeably. The major changes of the stage version sharpened the focus on the plant, allowing it to sing aggressively for its supper, and expanded the characters of the dentist, Orin Scrivello, D.D.S. (Doctor of de Sade), and of Audrey, who is played as a comic blonde bimbo by Ellen Greene, true to the spirit of the stage musical. Greene is the best Audrey imaginable, overly made-up, but pretty in a hard sort of way, well-shaped, sexy, hopelessly naïve, and altogether likable.

The actors in the musical adaptation play their parts with comic excellence. Gardenia makes an agreeable Mushnik, and Moranis is wonderful as Seymour Krelborn. Director Oz brilliantly animates the plant monster (created and designed by Lyle Conway) into a "mean, green, eating-machine," and Levi Stubbs of the Four Tops provides the plant with the perfect singing voice.

The *Variety* reviewer had reservations about the film's chances for large-scale success—"It's too weird to be involving"—but the weirdness is exactly what made the musical and the film fascinating and enjoyable to watch. In *The New York Times*, Janet Maslin praised the picture for its "good-natured material's durability" and for the way Oz treated that material. Most reviewers were charmed by the soulful "Greek" chorus provided by the three black doo-wop singers. *Variety* was particularly impressed by Roy Walker's Skid Row set (complete with a "working" elevated train), which opens the picture as the camera moves in at street level to establish the scene. Technically, this musical looks more like a film of the 1950's until Bran Ferren's special effects and Conway's mechanical monster remind the viewer that the film has to be a product of the 1980's.

Ellen Greene, a native New Yorker, played Audrey on stage for two years off Broadway and in Los Angeles and London. For the film role she wanted "clothes that suggested cast-offs from Kim Novak and Rita Hayworth." She portrays a bewildered innocent as a tart with a heart of gold. Moranis was producer David Geffen's choice to play Seymour long before his successful supporting roles in *Streets of Fire* (1984) and *Ghostbusters* (1984). Ron Taylor, the black actor who originally created the voice of Audrey II off

Broadway, was replaced by Stubbs, "who was real black, real street," according to Oz, and "who had a touch of malevolence but could be real silly and funny at the same time." The director was awed by this "incredible singer."

The film is remarkably inventive in its handling of the musical spectacle. Conway, who had worked with Oz on television's *The Muppet Show* and the film *The Dark Crystal* (1982), brilliantly designed the man-eating plant—twelve-and-a-half feet tall, ornamented with fifteen thousand handmade leaves, and mechanized with eleven-and-a-half miles of cable, "just slightly more cable than was used to build the Brooklyn Bridge," Conway claims. Oz animates this mechanical carnivore in such a way as to give it a distinct personality. The resonant singing voice of Stubbs provides the perfect final touch, making the plant seem dangerous but also amusingly aggressive and oddly likable. Rita Kempley of *The Washington Post* called it "vege-magic."

Little Shop of Horrors is a wonderfully entertaining adaptation of a stage musical to the screen and deserves to be considered one of the best pictures of 1986, even if it was too strange to warrant attention by the Academy of Motion Picture Arts and Sciences as one of the year's best. It delights both the eye and the ear, besides being satirically pleasing and offering an all-star comic cast. Finally, the film was too macabre, too weird, to qualify as an agreeable family picture; smaller children could easily be confused and frightened by its black humor, which tends to limit its appeal to a cult audience. Regardless, the songs are well executed while the special effects are dazzling and represent a very agreeable transformation of theatrical spectacle and music to the motion-picture screen. *Little Shop of Horrors* was one of the most unjustly undervalued pictures of 1986.

James M. Welsh

Reviews
American Film. XII, November, 1986, p. 77.
Commonweal. CXIV, January 30, 1987, p. 55.
Los Angeles Times. December 19, 1986, VI, p. 1.
The New Republic. CXCVI, January 26, 1987, p. 26.
The New York Times. December 19, 1986, p. C5.
The New Yorker. LXII, January 12, 1987, p. 92.
Newsweek. CIX, January 5, 1987, p. 56.
Time. CXXVIII, December 29, 1986, p. 71.
Variety. CCCXXV, December 10, 1986, p. 14.
The Washington Post. December 19, 1986, p. C1.

LUCAS

Production: David Nicksay for Lawrence Gordon; released by Twentieth Century-Fox
Direction: David Seltzer
Screenplay: David Seltzer
Cinematography: Reynaldo Villalobos
Editing: Priscilla Nedd
Art direction: James Murakami; set decoration, Linda Sutton
Makeup: Jamie Sue Weiss
Costume design: Molly Maginnis
Music: Dave Grusin
MPAA rating: PG-13
Running time: 100 minutes

Principal characters:
Lucas .... Corey Haim
Maggie .... Kerri Green
Cappie............................. Charlie Sheen
Alise..................... Courtney Thorne-Smith
Rina .... Winona Ryder
Bruno........................ Thomas E. Hodges
Ben .... Ciro Poppiti
Coach............................... Guy Boyd
Spike.............................. Jeremy Piven
Tonto .... Kevin Gerard Wixted

Lucas is something of a rarity among the plethora of teen films in the 1980's. Unlike the most exploitative of the genre—for example, *Porky's* (1982) and *Revenge of the Nerds* (1984)—it offers a picture of adolescence as something more than a prolonged sexual grope. Unlike the more polished examples—most notably, John Hughes's slick *Sixteen Candles* (1984), *The Breakfast Club* (1985), and *Pretty in Pink* (1986; reviewed in this volume)—it offers a view into the teenage years that acknowledges the awkwardness and uncertainty of that often painfully embarrassing time.

The film opens with title character Lucas Blye (Corey Haim) observing bugs through a magnifying glass. From his tiny size to his scientific paraphernalia, from his thick glasses to his eternally open mouth, Lucas is iconographically encoded as the timeless nerd. Screenwriter/director David Seltzer undermines this coding, however, by cutting, in this and subsequent scenes, from Lucas to shots of another rare specimen: locust nymphs emerging from their seventeen-year cycle. The similarity between the two names should be noted. There is even an affinity between the two slowly growing creatures, as Lucas is both fascinated by and protective of the emerging bugs. Further underscoring his theme of maturity as a lengthy journey, Seltzer has Lucas haunt the train tracks in both the opening and other sequences. Another coming-of-age film, *Stand by Me* (1986; reviewed in this volume), also centers on the image of boys traversing tracks.

In the midst of his explorations, Lucas spies Maggie (Kerri Green) practicing tennis. They strike up a conversation, which leads to her giving him a ride to the mansion he points out as his home. In the course of this drive, the already-smitten Lucas learns that Maggie is sixteen, new in town, about to enter his school in the fall, and furious at her father, who has abandoned his family for a nineteen-year-old woman. Maggie learns that Lucas is fourteen and accelerated academically. The intimacy between the two proceeds from there, blossoming into a close summer friendship. For Lucas, however, this is hardly enough.

The tenor of Lucas' school days is revealed on the first day, when he is dragged up on stage at a pep rally by football star and resident bully Bruno (Thomas E. Hodges). As the rest of the school laughs and cheers, Maggie and Lucas' other friends watch in horror. Although he clowns onstage once he is released from Bruno's grip, Lucas is pained that Maggie has witnessed his humiliation. In sympathy, she invites him to the movies, where Lucas and his friend Ben (Ciro Poppiti) are again harassed by Bruno. This time, however, football hero Cappie Roew (Charlie Sheen) intervenes, taking the outcasts under his wing for the evening.

An attraction arises between Cappie and Maggie during the car ride home, much to the consternation of Cappie's longtime girlfriend, Alise (Courtney Thorne-Smith). Following a minor mishap in a home economics class, Cappie and Maggie end up in the school basement, where she launders his soiled shirt and their attraction deepens. Despite the jock stereotype, Cappie is humorous and sensitive; he feels indebted to Lucas, who tutored him daily during a long illness. Cappie suggests that Maggie try out for the cheerleading squad, and her subsequent success at this brings the two of them together on the football field each day. When Cappie and Alise eventually break up, Lucas is left without his companion.

In the most daring ploy for Maggie's attention, Lucas determines to beat Cappie at his own game and tries out for the football team. Although the coach (Guy Boyd) is contemptuous, Lucas threatens him with the Sexual Discrimination Act and is thus permitted to practice with the team until the principal protectively forbids him to continue. During the big game, however, the home team is being beaten so badly that Lucas suits up and begs to go into the game. In despair, the coach allows him to do so. Lucas triumphantly catches a long pass, fumbles it, and is buried beneath a pile of players as he tries to tackle the opponent who recovers the ball. The pile disbands to reveal him unconscious and bleeding from the head.

While Lucas is in the hospital, Cappie, Maggie, and Rina (Winona Ryder), a girl who suffers from unrequited love for Lucas even as he does for Maggie, go to his house to find his father. They drive to the mansion where Maggie left Lucas the day they first met, but Rina informs them that Lucas merely works at the mansion and lives in a desolate trailer park with his alcoholic father. This then further accounts for Lucas' defensiveness and loner status.

Lucas recovers and returns to school amid whispers and stares. As he makes his way up the stairs toward his locker, the football players, led by Bruno, lie in wait. Lucas keeps a tentative eye on them as he approaches his locker, while they stand staring at him and a small crowd gathers. Opening his locker, Lucas finds a letter sweater; the crowd, led by Bruno's group, bursts into cheers, and Lucas, sweater on, throws up his arms in victory.

Despite this cozy ending, there is a verisimilitude to many of *Lucas*' scenes which accounts for the film's favorable reception. The dialogue, particularly the awkward pauses between Cappie and Maggie, is closer to the reality any adult viewer remembers than is the studied earnestness of John Hughes's teenage characters in *The Breakfast Club*. Lucas' humiliation at the hands of his tormentors evokes the actual, often sexual cruelty of youth. In the film's most brutal scene, the football bullies hold Lucas down on a massage table in the locker room and rub a deep-heating ointment onto his genitals, then deposit him outside with only a towel to cover himself, whereupon he runs across the field and climbs into a water fountain to soothe his burning flesh. The ingenuity of this torture, and the sexual basis of anti-Lucas sentiment, is in sharp contrast to the well-reviewed *The Karate Kid* (1984). In the latter film, teen violence is carried out neatly through the discipline of karate and completely predicated on a rigid and potentially explosive teenage class antagonism. This same paradigm is visible in *The Flamingo Kid* (1984) and *Pretty in Pink*, to name only two.

It is ironic that, given the prurient appeal upon which the whole concept of the teen film rests so securely, this displacement serves to desexualize both the films and the teenagers with whom they purport to deal. Like *Smooth Talk* (1985), however, *Lucas* attempts to examine—though more gently—adolescent sexual and gender identity. Seltzer's nerd, like all nerds before and after, is primarily intimidating not because of his brains, but because, with his lack of brawn, he reflects a terrifying image of sexual ambiguity at a time when young men are asked to prove, most overtly, a commitment to masculinity and heterosexuality which will propel them, in a few years, down the road to marriage, family, and the American way. In a highly charged scene that reflects these anxieties, the football bullies squeeze oranges between their biceps and each others' foreheads. Prior to Lucas' locker-room torture, he has been taunting Bruno for being semierect in the shower in response to the former's deprecatory comments about Lucas' penis size. Only those free of the fears that Lucas can invoke—the equally marginalized Ben, the handsome Cappie, and the girls—can accept his differences.

Because the film is tightly structured, these themes are easily discernible. There is a visual symmetry here. Throughout the film, for example, the sexually stunted Lucas is shown—in a Hitchcockian trope—to be an inveterate peeper. Not quite ready to act, Lucas looks: first at cheerleaders practicing at school, then at Maggie, and finally at Cappie and Maggie kissing. Cinematographer Reynaldo Villalobos, who has shot such visually stylish films as *Risky Business* (1983) and *Desert Bloom* (1986; reviewed in this volume), often uses a semidocumentary style more reminiscent of independent films such as *Smooth Talk* than of Hollywood teen films. Because the story unfolds primarily from Lucas' perspective, this style is particularly effective in such scenes as the orange-squeezing sequence, which has a grotesque irony not visible in less critical teen films. The film also shows a real sense of technical humor, which gives the slight sound track the best use of diegetic music since *Valley Girl* (1983).

Despite its strong points and its subtleties, however, *Lucas'* ultimate morality provides a problematic twist. While Lucas is a refreshing antihero, and while Seltzer is to be commended for avoiding an embarrassing cliché by having Lucas win the big game, the film's happy ending is only a small step from such a predictable resolution. Peer acceptance is an overwhelming need of the adolescent years, to be sure. In the end, *Lucas* shows that the pleasures of group acceptance are worth a high price, whether it be one's morals or one's health. With history so full of evidence to the contrary, however, perhaps it is time to stop perpetuating this particular message.

Gabrielle J. Forman

Reviews

Chicago Tribune. March 28, 1986, VII, p. 29.
Christian Century. CIII, May 21, 1986, p. 533.
Christian Science Monitor. LXXVIII, April 23, 1986, p. 24.
Films in Review. XXXVII, June/July, 1986, p. 362.
Los Angeles Times. May 1, 1986, VI, p. 1.
Macleans. XCIX, March 31, 1986, p. 54.
The New Republic. CXCIV, April 28, 1986, p. 24.
New York. XIX, April 19, 1986, p. 92.
The New York Times. CXXXV, March 28, 1986, p. C22.
San Francisco Chronicle. March 31, 1986, p. 58.
Variety. CCCXXII, April 2, 1986, p. 16.
Video. X, January, 1987, p. 72.
The Wall Street Journal. CCVIII, March 27, 1986, p. 30.
Washington Post. March 29, 1986, p. C9.

THE MANHATTAN PROJECT
The Deadly Game

Production: Jennifer Ogden and Marshall Brickman for Gladden Entertainment; released by Twentieth Century-Fox
Direction: Marshall Brickman
Screenplay: Marshall Brickman and Thomas Baum
Cinematography: Billy Williams
Editing: Nina Feinberg
Production design: Philip Rosenberg
Art direction: Robert Guerra; set decoration, Philip Smith and Nina Ramsey
Special effects: Bran Ferren
Makeup: Richard Dean
Costume design: Shay Cunliffe
Music: Philippe Sarde
MPAA rating: PG-13
Running time: 117 minutes

Principal characters:
John Mathewson . . . . John Lithgow
Paul Stephens . . . . Christopher Collet
Elizabeth Stephens . . . . Jill Eikenberry
Jenny Anderman . . . . Cynthia Nixon
Lieutenant Colonel Conroy . . . . John Mahoney
Scientist . . . . Adrian Sparks
Scientist . . . . Curt Dempster
Night guard . . . . Sully Boyar

The Manhattan Project: The Deadly Game draws its name from the massive top-secret United States Army program that produced the first three atomic weapons during World War II. Writer-producer-director Marshall Brickman, who cowrote *Annie Hall* (1977) and *Manhattan* (1979) with Woody Allen, had long been fascinated with the history of the Manhattan Project and had hoped to one day make a film about the scientists who worked on the project. Brickman, however, soon realized that the rising cost of filming a period piece prohibited such a film. Instead, he placed the story of the Manhattan Project within the teen-science film genre: *WarGames* (1983), *Real Genius* (1985), *Weird Science* (1985), and *My Science Project* (1985). The reason may have been primarily economic, but Brickman also thought that a male teenager could best portray the last outburst of innocence that surrounded the original Manhattan Project, as well as the seductive lure of the "gadget" on that innocence.

Nuclear scientist John Mathewson (John Lithgow) is contracted by the military to design an excimer laser to refine plutonium to 99.997% purity for nuclear weapons. Mathewson is given a lab in Ithaca, New York, with the false identity of Medatomics, a nuclear medicine research facility. What is not mentioned in the film is that research on the excimer laser is conducted under the auspices of the Strategic Defense Initiative, commonly known as "Star Wars." Thus, *The Manhattan Project*, like *Real Genius*, uses the teen-science film genre to address the moral issues raised by the new Manhattan Project, "Star Wars."

In Ithaca, high school student Paul Stephens (Christopher Collet) pulls a prank that causes a rival student's science drawer to explode during a dull lecture on plutonium and nuclear weapons. After class, Jenny Anderman (Cynthia Nixon) invites Paul to study with her while she babysits her younger brother. Meanwhile, Mathewson is looking for an apartment at the real estate office of Elizabeth Stephens (Jill Eikenberry), Paul's mother. He asks her out on a date, but she refuses just as Paul arrives. When Mathewson learns that Elizabeth is divorced and at the same time sees that Paul has an issue of *Scientific American* devoted to lasers, he sees an opportunity: "I just happen to have access to one of the sexiest lasers in the entire free world." He offers to give Paul a tour in return for a dinner date with Paul and his mother.

The relation between sex and nuclear weapons takes place on two levels. First, the weapons themselves are seen as sexy, so that by extension nuclear war becomes sex. American nuclear war strategists actually refer to all-out nuclear war as a "wargasm." Second, nuclear weapons become a sign of the maker's potency. Mathewson's nuclear laser allows him to use Paul to date his mother. Paul deeply resents being used, and an Oedipal rivalry, or "missile envy," develops between Paul and Mathewson. Paul must somehow outdo Mathewson in order to affirm his sexuality. While Paul's high school prank piques Jennifer's interest in him, it is his decision to build a nuclear weapon that leads her to kiss him. In fact, each time Jennifer kisses Paul it is only after he has mentioned the bomb.

Paul visits the lab, where he sees a robotic arm placing plastic bottles filled with green fluid into cylinders along a plexiglass wall. He quickly realizes that the green fluid contains plutonium. Later, at the promised dinner, Paul breaks into Mathewson's glove compartment and finds access cards for major United States nuclear weapons facilities. He leaves Mathewson and his mother to go to Jenny's house, where he tells her about his discovery. Paul, however, is not as upset at what goes on in the lab as at the fact that Mathewson lied to him and must therefore consider him "some kind of wimp."

Paul convinces Jenny to help him steal some plutonium. Using Mathewson's access card, Paul easily breaks into the lab while Jenny distracts the one guard. Now it is Paul's turn to use the equipment. He uses the robotic arm and its visual system to retrieve a plutonium filled bottle, which he attaches to a remote controlled toy truck. He then uses the laser to cut a hole through the lab wall and places the truck just outside. After a game of cat and mouse between the guard and the truck, Paul is able to escape.

Once outside the compound, Jenny hopes to write an exposé in the vein of Bob Woodward and Carl Bernstein. Paul, on the other hand, wants to build "the first privately built nuclear device in the history of the world." As with Mathewson, bragging about having a nuclear device brings sexual results: Jenny kisses him. Paul's ostensible reason for building the bomb is to take first prize at a science fair.

A long, wordless montage depicts Paul building his bomb. The sequence is reminiscent of the montage used in most teen films to condense the usual group efforts at community service or school projects. In this context, however, the upbeat music evokes Hiroshima and the American cowboy ideals parodied in *Dr. Strangelove* (1964): While the horns play a slow theme evocative of the music in Western films, the strings play a high staccato variation of the same theme that evokes stereotypical Japanese music. The music reveals that Paul becomes a Dr. Strangelove, the same name he uses to describe Mathewson, thereby subverting the visual depiction of teenage innocence and American know-how.

Paul takes his bomb to the forty-fifth Annual Science Fair in Manhattan. Meanwhile, Mathewson has discovered the missing plutonium and quickly realizes that Paul stole it. Jenny and Paul arrive at the fair and go to their hotel room. Once again, Paul mentions the bomb and Jenny begins to kiss him. Before they get too involved, however, Mathewson and Lieutenant Colonel Conroy (John Mahoney) break into the room. The military injects Paul with truth serum, but before he can tell them anything, a group of sympathetic science nerds shut off the electrical power in the hotel and help Paul and Jenny escape, and the two board a bus to Ithaca.

Back in Ithaca, Jenny wants to give the bomb back, but Paul refuses. He wants to get material for Jenny's article, or, in Jenny's parlance, to "do something." Actually, Paul wants a showdown with Mathewson, otherwise he could present the bomb to the national news media, who are already reporting the military's version that Paul is a teenage terrorist.

Paul meets Mathewson at Medatomics, while Jenny makes telephone calls to rally the town behind Paul. Paul realizes that unless he gets public support, the military will kill him in order to keep their secrets. Inside the lab, Paul passes an X-ray detector that reveals that the bomb is unassembled. A soldier tries to shoot Paul, who shields himself behind the plexiglass wall lined with the green bottles. Quietly Paul assembles the bomb and sets the timer for two minutes. All he has to do is turn the key.

Conroy tells Mathewson, whom the boy trusts, to talk to Paul and disarm

Magill's Cinema Annual 1987

him. The implication is that Mathewson must help kill Paul. Mathewson walks over to Paul, who is very frightened. When he tells Paul that his actions accomplish nothing, Paul replies that they do: The proof that his privately made deterrence works is the fact that he is still alive. Unfortunately, Paul realizes that he is not crazy enough to turn the key and therefore gives the bomb to Mathewson and prepares to be killed. Paul's actions acknowledge that deterrence relies not only on a threat to blow up everybody but also on a credible intention actually to do so.

While Paul is not crazy enough to play "nuclear chicken," however, Mathewson is. He threatens to turn the key unless he and Paul are allowed to leave the lab. Outside the lab, sharpshooters are ready to shoot Mathewson, when the bomb begins to count down spontaneously. Soon everyone is united in an effort to disarm the weapon. Paul suggests that they explode the bomb at a nearby quarry, whereupon Mathewson reveals that, because the plutonium is so pure, the bomb's yield is between fifty and seventy kilotons, or about five times larger than the bomb dropped on Hiroshima. After some very tense moments, Mathewson is able to disarm the bomb. The townspeople arrive in time to prevent Mathewson and Paul from being killed. Paul and Jenny embrace as Conroy escapes in his helicopter. Then Paul and his mother embrace, while Mathewson looks on. The Cold War continues, but the Oedipal rivalry is resolved.

To build the Medatomics lab, special effects person Bran Ferren went to the nuclear facilities at Oak Ridge, Los Alamos, and Lawrence Livermore to buy surplus atomic research parts: the same places to which Mathewson had access cards. The purpose behind purchasing the surplus was to make a naturalistic film. The cinematography likewise reflects Brickman's desire for the film to look real. The film was unfogged and unfiltered and used no high-speed film, no preflash, and no postflash. The lasers in the film are actual lasers and, though unable to cut through metal, were powerful enough to burn through a retina. As a precaution, the camera operator was unable to look through the reflex camera when shooting the laser scenes. The robotic arm with its visual system was programmed by Ferren and, after filming, was to be used in a project Ferren had with the navy. Ultimately, the desire to create a nuclear weapons lab that looked real makes *The Manhattan Project* complicitous with its subject; the film itself becomes a link in the military-industrial complex.

The recent teen-science films that deal with nuclear war—*WarGames*, *Real Genius*, and *The Manhattan Project*—express popular anxieties about our lack of control over nuclear weapon technologies and the people who might use them. The teen-science film generally depicts the world in gross stereotypes, while also empowering and sanctifying teenage males. *Real Genius* and *WarGames* follow this pattern, providing neat resolutions to the complex, open-ended, and ambiguous problems that characterize the Cold

War. Unlike the teenage males in these films, Paul deliberately builds a nuclear weapon that could destroy New York and possibly trigger a nuclear war. Paul's reasons for building the bomb are never very clear; and even when they border on social protest, his means hardly justify the end. Because Paul becomes as morally ambiguous and as potentially destructive as the military establishment he opposes, the film's happy ending lacks credibility. Ironically, this may be a good thing, since the problems and anxieties that the film expresses cannot be reduced to a sugarcoated resolution. *The Manhattan Project* conveys in a more troubling and intelligent way the message in *WarGames*: With nuclear weapons "the only winning move is not to play." While Paul and Mathewson agree to stop playing, the viewer nevertheless glimpses how deterrence make society increasingly willing to play.

Chon Noriega

Reviews
Chicago Tribune. June 13, 1986, VII, p. 38A.
The Christian Science Monitor. June 13, 1986, p. 26.
Glamour. LXXXIV, July 1986, p. 111.
Los Angeles Times. June 13, 1986, VI, p. 1.
The New Republic. CVC, July 7, 1986, p. 34.
New York. XIX, June 23, 1986, p. 55.
The New York Times. June 13, 1986, III, p. 8.
The New Yorker. LXII, June 30, 1986, p. 52.
People Weekly. XXV, June 23, 1986, p. 8.
Popular Mechanics. CLXIII, August 1986, p. 20.
Time. CXXVII, June 9, 1986, p. 76.
USA Today. CXV, September 1986, p. 93.
Variety. May 14, 1986, p. 16.
The Wall Street Journal. June 12, 1986, p. 27.
The Washington Post. June 13, 1986, IV, p. 9.

MARLENE

Origin: West Germany
Released: 1983
Released in U.S.: 1986
Production: Zev Braun and Karel Dirka for OKO-Film; released by Alive Films
Direction: Maximilian Schell
Screenplay: Meir Dohnal and Maximilian Schell
Cinematography: Ivan Slapeta, Pavel Hispler, and Henry Hauck
Editing: Heidi Genée and Dagmar Hirtz
Narration: Marlene Dietrich and Maximilian Schell
Makeup: Regine Kusterer
Costume design: Heinz Eickmeier
Sound: Norbert Lill
Music: Nicholas Economou
MPAA rating: no listing
Running time: 94 minutes

Of the great, or the most significantly characteristic, stars of past eras in cinema, some in their old age are prepared to talk about themselves revealingly, some not. Asta Nielsen, for example, among the earliest of the exotic glamour stars, did not want to be seen or photographed in old age but was prepared to comment about herself and her legend. Louise Brooks, with a wonderful openness, not only permitted herself to be filmed in her lonely seclusion in Rochester, New York, but also wrote autobiographically (*Lulu in Hollywood*, 1983). Brooks commented with intelligence and insight on the period of her ascendancy in film, working with G. W. Pabst in the late 1920's, and also on her decline when back in the United States; she also consented to undertake filmed interviews in 1984, which were admirably conducted by Richard Leacock (*Lulu in Berlin*). Greta Garbo (perhaps the greatest of all stars in the high season of female stardom, the 1920's and 1930's), on the other hand, has maintained an absolute silence, withdrawing from the screen forever in 1941 and retiring into a totally private life to enjoy the wealth her fame had brought.

Among these great women, setting a perhaps outrageous pace in their time as models for their sex, was Marlene Dietrich (born 1901 Maria Magdalene von Losch—Losch being her stepfather's name, and Dietrich that of her natural father). She became a hardworking star of stage and screen during the later 1920's in Berlin and Vienna, training initially with Max Reinhardt. She mainly impersonated relatively youthful *femmes du monde*, but she also appeared successfully in plays by George Bernard Shaw. She was well educated, as befitted a daughter of an officer in the Royal Prussian Police, and her cool, disdainful beauty was likened by Victor Barnowsky, the Reinhardt of Vienna, to a portrait by Toulouse-Lautrec.

In private life she became, initially at least, a happily married woman, with a much-beloved daughter, Maria (later Maria Riva, actress). She was literally taken over by the American director Josef von Sternberg and developed into the femme fatale of his special, exotic vision for the early German sound film *The Blue Angel* (1930). He claimed that both her beauty and her personality as an actress had been undervalued and, in her own words, he "made her over." For a period, in the early 1930's, she became, as it were, subservient to his Svengali-like influence. He took her to Hollywood, became her close companion (though both of them were married), fostered her star contracts with Paramount Pictures, and launched her into a public world in a succession of exotic films—*Morocco* (1930), *Dishonored* (1931), *Shanghai Express* (1932), *Blonde Venus* (1932), *The Scarlet Empress* (1934), and *The Devil Is a Woman* (1935)—until Paramount could stand his extravagances no longer. By that time, Dietrich, Paramount's star of stars, had no rival but Metro-Goldwyn-Mayer's Garbo, whose beauty, screen personality, and acting talent were of a different order.

Dietrich's husband and daughter joined her in America, and she became a United States citizen in 1939, refusing all attempts made by the Nazi authorities to induce her to return to Germany. She was strongly anti-Hitler, and her sister was to be among those liberated from Bergen-Belsen concentration camp after the war. Dietrich became increasingly international in outlook and in the choice of her celebrated male escorts—she saw little of her husband by this time. After her career with Sternberg, she appeared in films directed by Ernst Lubitsch, Fritz Lang, Orson Welles, Billy Wilder, Stanley Kramer, and Alfred Hitchcock. Then, gradually abandoning films when in her fifties and sixties, she returned to the stage as a cabaret-singer, dressing and acting the part with a fabulous kind of international success, singing with studied emotional intensity while appearing clothed in elaborate costumes which became part of her self-created image, the image she was to maintain into her seventies. Both as film star and as a live performer, Dietrich has always remained the exacting professional.

How can such a personality, surviving with vigorous intelligence in her eighties, be represented once again through the screen to an international public, the majority of whom had never known her except as a famous name? She absolutely refused (like her predecessor Asta Nielsen, but unlike her contemporary, Bette Davis) to be filmed in her old age in the cold light of the interview camera. Maximilian Schell's courageous, feature-length study of her, therefore, is a case of voice of the present over image of the past.

The troubled evolution of this film "collage" is interesting. It is German in origin because, in the words of its Munich producer, Karel Dirka, Dietrich is the only German female superstar. This feature-documentary was originally to have been a straightforward anthology of extracts from Dietrich's key films with her own commentary on them, plus some form of anchor-narration to hold the film together. This narration was provided by Schell, who is fluent in English and enjoys a sound contemporary reputation as feature director, actor, and writer. Schell was finally invited to direct as well as narrate, though he was at first resistant to this idea because of his lack of experience in the documentary form. Dietrich, however, insisted that he should direct; she knew him, they had appeared together in *Judgment in Nuremberg* (1961), the film that had brought him an Oscar for his role as a defense attorney. After prolonged debate on different approaches to the film, it was agreed and contracted that Dietrich should take part in a re-corded audio interview with Schell of up to forty hours for editing into the film. The first attempt at taping this, in September, 1982, failed—the desired conversation simply dried up. In a second attempt, a video-recorder was put in her apartment, and a discussion of her films between herself and Schell took place. Sometime later, a further interchange between them was improvised in a workshop set constructed in Munich, but another conversa-tional impasse between interviewer and subject resulted. It appears that they never really understood each other in relation to the project.

For the film to reach feature length, some kind of impressionistic continu-ity had to be devised by Schell out of the material at his disposal, visual and aural. It is patent from her somewhat rasping voice that Dietrich was in a contrary mood most of the time. She begins by asserting that *The Blue Angel* was rubbish and that Emil Jannings was nothing but an "old ham." (Jannings did not want to have her in the film in any case.) Lola-Lola, she says, was more "snotty" than erotic. (Perhaps she is right on both counts.) She condemns *Dishonoured* as kitsch and *Rancho Notorious* (1952; directed by the "absolute monster," Lang) as plain bad, but she does think well of *Touch of Evil* (1958), since she holds Welles to have been "a great, great man—a genius." Schell, however, stands his ground firmly enough to in-clude in the film her shout (at the end, no doubt, of some breakdown in the interviews): "Nobody ever walks out on me." He includes a film clip from her London stage show, in which she was swathed in blue and seen singing with a slow kind of professional determination to inspire the maximum emo-tion the songs could carry. Calling the effect a kind of cream of kitsch, he means it as a compliment, but she resents it. He also contrasts her later, live renditions of "See What the Boys in the Back Room Will Have" with the scene as she sang it in *Destry Rides Again* (1939). She does have a prefer-ence among her films, Sternberg's *The Devil Is a Woman*.

These persistent interviews with their visually absent subject create a ghostly atmosphere—the ghost petulant and anxious to preserve her star-dust memories while passing waspish comments on such topics as women's liberation and penis envy. What the film does contain, though, with the star's acerbic asides, are clips representative of more than fifty years of her filmmaking: *Tragedy of Love* (1923), *I Kiss Your Hand, Madame* (1929), *The Blue Angel, Morocco, Dishonored, Blonde Venus, The Scarlet Empress, The Devil Is a Woman, Desire* (1936), *Destry Rides Again, Stage Fright* (1950), *Witness for the Prosecution* (1957), *Touch of Evil, Judgment at Nuremberg,* and *Just a Gigolo* (1978). Schell allows his audience to share actively in his process of filmmaking, the desperate act of editing, trying to make some sense out of it all. The result seems a most regrettable muddle, hardly worthy of Dietrich, the great professional, as Hitchcock called her— "professional actress, professional wardrober, professional lighting technician." If she had collaborated with goodwill and real interest in the making of this film study of her, she could without doubt have given Schell, and the viewer, what Brooks managed so readily and so courageously to give Leacock in his interview film, *Lulu in Berlin.*

Roger Manvell

Reviews
The Christian Science Monitor. LXXVIII, November 14, 1986, p. 27.
Films in Review. XXXVIII, April 27, 1987, p. 232.
Los Angeles Times. December 18, 1986, VI, p. 1.
Macleans. C, January 12, 1987, p. 48.
Ms. XV, December, 1986, p. 20.
The New Republic. CXCV, December 8, 1986, p. 28.
New Statesman. CXI, February 7, 1987, p. 33.
The New York Times. September 21, 1986, I, p. 66.
Newsweek. CVIII, November 24, 1986, p. 88.
Variety. CCCXIV, March 7, 1984, p. 368.

MEN
(MÄNNER)

Origin: West Germany
Released: 1985
Released in U.S.: 1986
Production: Olga Film in association with Zweites Deutsches Fernsehen; released by New Yorker Films
Direction: Doris Dörrie
Screenplay: Doris Dörrie
Cinematography: Helge Weindler
Editing: Raimund Barthelmes and Jeanette Magerl
Art direction: Jörg Neumann, Gabriele Hochheim, and Friedrich Natus
Makeup: Werner A. Püthe
Costume design: Jörg Trees, Claudia Leinert, and Samir Jahach
Sound: Michael Etz and Berthold Posch
Music: Claus Bantzer
Song: Helmut Hartl, Eric Burdon, "When I Was Young"
MPAA rating: no listing
Running time: 99 minutes

> *Principal characters:*
> Julius Armbrust .... Heiner Lauterbach
> Stefan....................... Uwe Ochsenknecht
> Paula Armbrust .... Ulrike Kriener
> Angelika..................... Janna Marangosoff
> Lothar .... Dietmar Bär
> Marita Strass .... Marie-Charlott Scüler
> Frau Lennert .... Edith Volkmann
> Florian.............................. Lois Kelz
> Caro .... Cornelia Schneider
> Juliane Zorn.................... Sabine Wegener
> Woman in bar .... Monika Schwarz
> Jeweler........................... Gerd Huber
> Salesman .... Werner Albert Püthe

Men is a great rarity. A German-language comedy, independently made and firmly seen as an "art-house movie" in terms of commercial exhibition, it achieved popular and financial success. Its success refuted the axiom that there is no significant audience for comedy in West Germany: *Men* finally out-grossed *Rambo: First Blood Part II* (1985), and it is estimated that ten percent of Germans have now seen it. In the United States, the film was a phenomenon on the independent cinema circuit, popular in fifty cities.

Discovering a modern comedy of manners which makes lucid points about the dilemmas facing men in the modern world and which can communicate its charm to an international audience is a very rare experience. Much of the film's charm comes from the certainty of touch of screenwriter/director Doris Dörrie. In several interviews she has mentioned the distinctive "research" methods through which her acute and largely successful screenplay was constructed. In her view, only through the unobtrusive observation and careful recording of men's patterns of conversation when discussing major "male" topics could she create a convincing film. Fully aware of the fact that her very presence would in some way influence these conversations, she began anthropological research, looking for men who embodied certain qualities. In an interview in *Kino* magazine, Dörrie explained that she sought a male equivalent of Marilyn Monroe, someone who is "extremely authentic and at the same time completely fantastic."

So, here they are, two idealized versions of men with very ordinary everyday preoccupations. What they have in common is a woman, Paula (Ulrike Kriener), with whom they are both in love. Paula is the wife of Julius Armbrust (Heiner Lauterbach), a packaging designer living the life of the ideal successful executive. His character is sketched with great economy in the opening scenes. Not averse to indulging in extramarital relations with his secretary, he is nevertheless shocked when Paula reveals that she, too, is having an affair, with Stefan (Uwe Ochsenknecht), a free-lance designer with an alternative life-style. Julius' reaction is extreme. Telling all concerned that he is taking a summer break, he begins to follow secretly every move of Stefan and Paula. In an ugly street scene, Stefan disposes of his live-in girlfriend. Her room in Stefan's house is free, and Julius takes his chance. Posing as an unemployed man called Daniel, Julius moves in with Stefan, who is unaware of Daniel's true identity.

Having created this imbalanced relationship, Dörrie sets to work, applying her field observations to create a wry examination of male interaction. Daniel is greeted by a house meeting, at which he is introduced to the essentials of communal living by Stefan and his flatmate Lothar (Dietmar Bär), who expresses his fears that Stefan is falling under the influence of his new bourgeois girlfriend. When Daniel joins Stefan in his customary jog around town, a key scene follows as both men feel bound to turn the jogging trip into a competition. Daniel is beaten and attacks Stefan; the men roll on the floor in what amounts to a schoolyard fight about who is the toughest.

The wrestling match initiates a new phase in Daniel and Stefan's relationship. Stefan allows Daniel to help him with some of his graphic work, and Daniel encourages Stefan to put his talents to use on a more permanent basis. Daniel now harnesses his aggressive feelings toward Stefan into a campaign to make Stefan more like Julius. He acknowledges to himself that he has come to live in the house to discover the secret of Stefan's attraction for Paula and that the secret is Stefan's life-style, which implicitly rejects Paula's values, her way of life, and her bourgeois husband. As Stefan is slowly fired with more enthusiasm to join the mainstream, Daniel is unearthing some motivation within Stefan that he can recognize. The relationship is further developed in a scene where Daniel, in a moment of frustration caused by Stefan and Paula's affair and Stefan's lack of ambition, sprays paint over Stefan's current work and his studiously underdecorated room. Stefan's response, understandably angry, shows a developing pride in, and reliance on, his work. Daniel offers to redecorate the room. As Stefan develops a greater interest in clothes and a new interest in Porsches, Daniel repaints the room, this time in an austere, unimaginative, but chic industrial white.

As the film proceeds, it offers more and more evidence in support of the view which Daniel has expressed earlier about the fundamental (and frustrating) difference between men and women: "A man is what he does; a woman is what she is." A masterly aspect of the screenplay is to contrast Stefan's introduction to this point of view and his willing acceptance of it to Daniel's sense of loss and anxiety about dropping out of the system by which he defined himself and his status. The audience, witnessing the change, is prepared for the ultimate outcome of the story: Paula will discover that she loves Stefan less as he becomes more like Julius and will then discover who has guided Stefan toward materialism and gain. In fact, this is the only aspect of the story which Dörrie fails to exploit fully. A climax of high farce is reached when Daniel's attempts to avoid meeting Paula are confounded. Paula joins Stefan and Daniel at an impromptu breakfast. Caught unawares, Daniel has to resort to a disguise involving a gorilla mask and boxing gloves. Ironically, through some bantering and animalistic behavior, he succeeds not only in concealing his true identity but also in enamoring Paula of himself by his outlandishness. Finally, Julius believes that he has gained ascendancy in the triangle and returns home smug in his reaffirmed status of husband/lover/provider, and it is here that Dörrie fails to exploit the situation for full effect. A rather too playful final scene reveals true identities only after Paula has already made her decision to abandon the newly besuited and remuneratively employed Stefan for her returned husband. Julius returns to the office only to discover that he is to work with newly hired Stefan, and Paula arrives at the office, dutifully bringing a tie for Julius to wear, just in time to see the two men in her life confronting each other. She learns the truth a little too late.

This glib conclusion is at odds with the tone of ironic knowingness which is so skillfully maintained throughout. *Men* could easily be termed a serious comedy, finding humor in the fragility of human relationships, of life decisions, and of the often-unfounded assumptions that people make about one another. It is all the more pity, then, that the final scene fails to face up to the consequences of the approach to human relationships made in the rest of the film.

Men is Dörrie's first comic feature film, although it has parallels to *In the Belly of the Whale* (1985), which is also concerned with a manipulative triangle (mother, father, and daughter) and which fails to realize its potential in a strangely distorted melodramatic final scene. It is to Dörrie's great credit that she has achieved such a lightness of touch in *Men*. She and her small but skillful and extremely well-directed cast have exploited a significant theme—the disillusionment of a certain generation with the anticapitalist idealism of the 1960's and 1970's—for maximum comic potential. Domestic detail is well observed and used most economically to develop the characters and their respective contexts. Julius, during his feverish surveillance of the lovers, is discovered hiding in his own hedge by his archetypal suburban neighbor, and Stefan, during his materialist "rehabilitation," symbolically rediscovers his favorite toy Porsche. This use of the mundane to create comic points also meshes with the restrained, objective camera style, used throughout to evince a rather unreal and hermetically sealed environment for Dörrie's specimens with the action largely confined to Stefan's huge house.

The end credits of a film may seem an unexpected place to find clues to a director's seemingly effortless mastery of comedic tone, but again, *Men* has a surprise in store. Using an open-fronted elevator which figures in the final scene, both cast and crew suddenly appear, identifying themselves to the camera as the elevator takes them slowly through the shot in a sort of living caption. As the distinction between reality and fiction is playfully blurred, Dörrie herself moves by in the midst of a series of buoyant martial arts poses. *Men* sets out as an attack on the rediscovered materialism of Dörrie's own generation and on its futility and its enshrinement of male egotism. Its failure to follow these arguments through to the bitter end may indicate a simple lack of resolve or perhaps a little hardheaded commercial pragmatism.

Peter Tasker

Reviews
Film Comment. XXII, September, 1986, p. 42.
Films and Filming. November, 1986, p. 40.
Films in Review. XXXVII, November, 1986, p. 551.
Los Angeles Times. August 20, 1986, VI, p. 1.
Ms. XV, October, 1986, p. 14.
The New Republic. CXCV, August 25, 1986, p. 26.

The New York Times. July 30, 1986, p. C13.
The New Yorker. LXII, September 8, 1986, p. 108.
The Wall Street Journal. July 29, 1986, p. 24.
The Washington Post. August 22, 1986, p. D1.
World Press Review. XXXIII, October, 1986, p. 59.

MÉNAGE
(TENUE DE SOIRÉE)

Origin: France
Released: 1986
Released in U.S.: 1986
Production: René Cleitman; released by Cinecom International
Direction: Bertrand Blier
Screenplay: Bertrand Blier
Cinematography: Jean Penzer
Editing: Claudine Merlin
Art direction: Théobald Meurisse
Music: Serge Gainsbourg
MPAA rating: no listing
Running time: 84 minutes

Principal characters:
Bob .... Gérard Depardieu
Antoine .... Michel Blanc
Monique .... Miou-Miou
Art collector .... Bruno Cremer
Depressed man .... Jean-Pierre Marielle
Pedro .... Michel Creton
Depressed woman................. Caroline Sihol
Man in nightclub .... Jean-Yves Berteloot

Bertrand Blier's Oscar-winning *Get Out Your Handkerchiefs* (1978) opens in a restaurant where a bored wife is having lunch with her husband, who, it seems, is incapable of making her happy. Noticing another customer who has been surreptitiously eyeing his wife, the husband goes over and offers her to the stranger for the weekend. The proposal is accepted, and the remainder of the narrative chronicles the working out of the resulting *ménage à trois*.

The first scene of *Ménage* or *Tenue de soirée* is remarkably similar. It is set in a large Parisian café, where another ill-matched couple is having an unpleasant night out on the town. The wife, Monique (Miou-Miou), heaps abuse on her devoted husband, Antoine (Michel Blanc). He can only gaze on her adoringly and reply that he loves her, a response that merely fuels her fury. Poverty has reduced them to a sordid state, and she sees little hope for improvement. Just then an extraordinary person, Bob (Gérard Depardieu), bursts into their life. A professional burglar, he is elegantly attired and flush with francs, which he showers on the astonished couple. Bob is immediately and obsessively attracted, not to the pretty Monique but to her mousy husband, and the rest of the film explores the fate of this bizarre threesome.

Often, as in *My Best Friend's Girl* (1983), Blier's films present offbeat variations on the love-triangle theme. Blier either writes or cowrites his films, which frequently star Depardieu and which are distinguished by sexually explicit dialogue. *Ménage* perhaps outdoes all of his earlier films in this respect; the dialogue is raunchy and laced with argot, causing Vincent Canby to remark that even the English subtitles are too much at times.

Other key elements in these two opening scenes also run through Blier's films. Throughout his career, he has shown a predilection for working against audience expectations, as when Bob zeros in on Antoine instead of Monique. His particular brand of comedy, which turns bourgeois mores inside out, seeks not only to make viewers laugh but also to make them uneasy, even indignant.

According to Molly Haskell, there was ample evidence that these ends were achieved at the Cannes Film Festival, where Michel Blanc won the prize for best actor, sharing it with Bob Hoskins for his role in *Mona Lisa* (1986; reviewed in this volume). Apparently, the audience felt unnerved by the scenes in which Bob seduces Antoine. Depardieu, who has come to dominate this epoch of French cinema as Jean Gabin, Jean-Paul Belmondo, and Alain Delon have in the past, but with far greater range, is completely convincing as Bob, the massiveness of his frame contrasting with Blanc's puniness and lending a certain inevitability to his efforts. The seduction scenes are quite tender, yet far less explicit visually than in the language, which is extremely frank and specific.

Nevertheless, the courtship came under fire from homosexuals at the festival, who, despite Blanc's fine performance, objected to the casting of such a wimpishly unalluring character as the object for Bob's affections, criticizing the relationship as embodying the heterosexual world's misconceptions of seduction among men. Blier originally intended to have the late Patrick Dewaere, a handsome and forceful screen presence, play the role, but it is precisely because Blanc is so nondescript and dour that Bob's determination is so bizarre and Depardieu's part so challenging.

Blier was also accused at the festival of demeaning women, a tendency already pronounced in earlier films such as *Going Places* (1973), which also starred Miou-Miou. Haskell goes so far as to call misogyny the animus of the film. It is certainly true that the character of Monique lends itself to such a charge. In the opening scene, her complaining monologue is cut short when Bob belts her out of her chair and onto the floor. When he tosses a wad of crisp franc notes her way, however, any resentment she might have felt vanishes; indeed, she seems to be impressed only by cash and expensive clothes and views Bob as the means to get them. She clearly finds him quite fabulous, but he has nothing but contempt for women, whom he considers too easily won sexually to present any challenge. He allows himself to be seduced by her, but the intensity of her passion during their lovemaking is counterpointed by his utter indifference. Afraid that Bob might become frustrated and disappear from their lives as abruptly as he entered, Monique even urges her reluctant husband to give in to Bob's advances. The odd person out in the triangle, she gradually loses all spirit and sense of self as the film progresses.

Her interest in Bob is perfectly understandable, for it is at the film's beginning that his power is at its zenith. He erupts into the drab lives of Monique and Antoine like some mythical being. His expensive, high-fashion clothes point up their shabbiness, and he dispenses largesse in the manner of a medieval prince. He is a burglar who, walking down the street, can sniff out the presence of gold bars nearby. No need for messy break-ins: The houses of the wealthy open their doors to him willingly and reveal to him the location of the loot. Like an urban Robin Hood, he steals from the rich and gives to the poor (Monique and Antoine). The rich are so corrupt and jaded that they appear to long secretly for the violations of their mansions and their persons as an all-too fleeting relief from boredom.

If Bob is a fairy godfather, however, he is a malevolent one. Although he describes himself as being in a state of grace, he is a former convict. The couple is forced to throw their lot in with him because a fire of mysterious origins causes their trailer to blow up after he mysteriously appears outside in the middle of the night. After he finally seduces Antoine, Bob tries to turn him over immediately to a particularly decadent art collector, whose specialty seems to be nude male statues. Bob describes the man as his mentor, from whom he accepts a wad of franc notes in return for his gift of Antoine. Unfortunately, he has to give them back when Antoine balks at his end of the deal.

It is at this point that the film, so far full of mirth and wonderments, begins to descend into the prosaic, into a universal meanness of spirit. Bob's character loses its magical quality. Suddenly, there is no more mention of marvelous burglaries like the ones with which he dazzled Monique and Antoine near the film's beginning. The three settle down to a rather ordinary life in a Montmartre flat, but they are ill-suited to domesticity. Life becomes too humdrum and bourgeois. Monique is reduced to the role of housekeeper, and Bob browbeats her harshly for her lack of talents on the domestic front. When finally, by trickery, he turns her over to a pimp, she is eager to escape (she thinks to Spain).

Antoine takes her place as wife and housekeeper, and Bob, apparently bored, begins to abuse him as well, staying out late, not showing up for meals which Antoine has prepared for him. When Antoine protests that he is being neglected, Bob brings home gifts—women's clothes and makeup— that complete the transformation of Antoine from heterosexual to transvestite. Although Antoine objects, he is persuaded to attend a gala dance in drag. He looks quite stunning, but Bob dumps him for a cruising male whore. Monique resurfaces as a prostitute, abused now by her pimp, Pedro (Michel Creton). When Pedro administers a particularly vicious beating to her, Antoine intercedes and kills him.

There follows an unsettling narrative gap of five years, after which the three reassemble for a final appearance as streetwalkers, with Bob also in drag. He has lost all of his charm, and looks absurd in a fur coat. It is here also that Monique's son, abandoned at some earlier stage in her life, is mentioned, awkwardly, for the first time. Blier has admitted to being dissatisfied with this patchy ending, one of several he considered.

If the ending as a whole does not work, the final sequence of the film is extremely effective. Bob and Monique have left the bar where the three had taken temporary refuge from the cold to return to the barren and customerless pavement. Antoine remains, orders another beer, and takes a hand mirror from his purse to check his makeup. As he reapplies his lipstick, the camera moves simultaneously to the right and in for the closeup with which the film ends. It is a new, self-satisfied Antoine that is revealed. He looks terrific, much better than he ever did as a mousy male, and he knows it. He turns toward the camera as it approaches and primps as if the lens were a mirror, smiling with pleasure at his imaginary reflection and, at the same time, with coy coquettishness out at the audience.

This long, unedited take echoes a similar one at the film's beginning, when Bob first enters the café and interrupts Monique's scathing monologue. The camera advances on the arguing couple from Bob's point of view. Although Monique is in the foreground, facing more toward the camera than toward Antoine, she fades completely out of focus, becoming an unrecognizable blur, as the lens focuses on Antoine, bringing his hangdog expression into sharp focus, making clear at the outset precisely where Bob's interest lies.

The lengthy, final shot of Antoine is crucial, because it reveals just how much he has changed since he became, almost in spite of himself, a murderer. This violent act has liberated him at last, freed him from his bondage, first to Monique and then to Bob. These two clearly no longer have any hold over him. On the contrary, the vectors of power have shifted, probably for the last time. Antoine can linger comfortably in the bar, while the others freeze outside, because he is now in the position of control in the triangle. In a film which is as much about power as it is about sex, this is important.

John Martin

Reviews

Chicago Tribune. October 31, 1986, VII, p. 45.
Film Comment. XXII, September, 1986, p. 22.
Los Angeles Times. October 24, 1986, VI, p. 1.
National Review. XXXVIII, November 21, 1986, p. 63.
The New Republic. CXCV, November 3, 1986, p. 26.
New York. XIX, October 13, 1986, p. 93.
The New York Times. October 1, 1986, p. C21.
The New York Times. October 5, 1986, p. B19.
Newsweek. CVIII, October 27, 1986, p. 104.
Time. CXXVIII, November 3, 1986, p. 82.
Vogue. CLXXVI, October, 1986, p. 78.
The Washington Post. November 18, 1986, p. D12.

THE MISSION

Origin: Great Britain
Released: 1986
Released in U.S.: 1986
Production: Fernando Ghia and David Puttnam for Goldcrest and Kingsmere Productions; released by Warner Bros.
Direction: Roland Joffé
Screenplay: Robert Bolt
Cinematography: Chris Menges (AA)
Editing: Jim Clark
Production design: Stuart Craig
Art direction: George Richardson and John King
Special effects: Peter Hutchinson
Makeup: Tommie Manderson
Costume design: Enrico Sabbatini
Sound editing: Chris Ackland
Choral direction: David Bedford
Music: Ennio Morricone; Indian instrumentation, Incantation
MPAA rating: PG
Running time: 130 minutes

> *Principal characters:*
> Rodrigo Mendoza .... Robert De Niro
> Father Gabriel .... Jeremy Irons
> Altamirano .... Ray McAnally
> Felipe .... Aidan Quinn
> Carlotta .... Cherie Lunghi
> Don Cabeza .... Chuck Low
> Hontar .... Ronald Pickup
> Fielding .... Liam Neeson
> Guaraní chief .... Asunción Ontiveros
> Father Sebastian .... Daniel Berrigan

Among a group of films released in the mid-1980's which focused on primitivism (*The Mosquito Coast*, 1986, reviewed in this volume, and *The Emerald Forest*, 1985, were two notable others), *The Mission* was the most indebted to recorded history. Political maneuvering against Jesuit missionaries in South America was conducted jointly by Spain and Portugal following the Treaty of Madrid in 1750. Injustices which occur before and after a visit to the area by a papal representative form the basis of Robert Bolt's original script.

This was not Bolt's first attempt to dramatize conflict and conscience among the church hierarchy and clergy. In 1966, he had transformed his successful theatrical play (staged in 1960) about Sir Thomas More, *A Man For All Seasons*, into an Oscar-winning screenplay. In *The Mission*, his subject is more obscure but no less dramatically challenging. Directing the complex story was Roland Joffé, in his first assignment since his acclaimed study of Southeast Asia, *The Killing Fields* (1984).

The Mission begins as a recollection by Altamirano (Ray McAnally), a distinguished churchman who had been assigned by Pope Benedict XIV to evaluate the situation and ease tensions. His solemn expression indicates that he did not succeed, and the memory is not a happy one. His story develops partially through his own voice-over, starting with a panorama of a spectacularly beautiful rain forest, where much later the boundaries of Paraguay, Argentina, and Brazil would converge. Some time before the Spanish-Portuguese treaty, the Jesuits—then referred to as the "shock troops of the church"—attempt to establish a mission in land populated by Guaraní Indians. The Guaraní are a tribe not easily drawn to civilization or structured religion but are amazingly adept at creating musical instruments. An earlier Jesuit effort fails tragically and symbolically; the Guaraní float a crucified priest downstream to the roaring Iguaçu Falls.

Another attempt is launched up the steep rocks alongside the waterfall by a slender, dedicated Jesuit named Gabriel (Jeremy Irons). In the jungle, he plays softly on a woodwind and is soon joined by Guaraní warriors whose fierce expressions belie their obvious fascination with the priest's melody.

Gabriel succeeds where his predecessors had failed. The natives trust him and they work together to establish the mission of San Carlos. One of the most formidable obstacles to the cooperative venture is a mercenary named Rodrigo Mendoza (Robert De Niro), who periodically invades the area above the falls to steal young Guaraní and sell them to the Spanish territorial governor, Don Cabeza (Chuck Low). Although Portugal continues to employ slaves in the New World, Spain has by this time officially outlawed the practice. Cabeza, however, a bug-eyed swine out of some Orwellian nightmare, views the Guaraní as a subhuman labor force that will help him balance the economic books against his Portuguese counterpart, Hontar (Ronald Pickup). Both men feel threatened by the Jesuits' farming and instrument-producing ventures with the Guaraní.

Mendoza's financially successful life as a slave trader and man of influence takes an unexpected turn one day during a street festival at Asunción. His mistress, Carlotta (Cherie Lunghi), tells him that she is in love with his young brother, the sensitive and literate Felipe (Aidan Quinn). At first, Mendoza seems to accept the disclosure sadly and philosophically. When he confronts the lovers later, however, his jealousy explodes and, after an angry sword fight, he kills Felipe.

Several months later, Father Gabriel visits Mendoza, who is suffering from severe melancholy and guilt and wishes to speak to no one. The priest assures him that there is redemption for everyone, even a mercenary and a murderer. Mendoza is barely touched. Broken in spirit but not ready to give up completely, he follows Gabriel back into the jungle.

During the arduous journey back to the mission at San Carlos, the guilt-wracked Mendoza punishes himself by dragging up armaments and other burdens from his past, attached to his back in a ropelike harness. When another priest in the traveling group begs Gabriel to intervene, the wise clergyman says that only Mendoza himself can know when he has done enough penance. Eventually, a young Guaraní cuts the baggage loose from the weak, mud-caked man. The other natives smile, then burst into spontaneous laughter, and after a moment of self-recognition, Mendoza laughs along with them.

During his early days at San Carlos, the former slave trader discovers a kind of peace. In their simple art and natural beauty, the Guaraní seem quietly driven by a constantly expanding need to create music and musical instruments. They also work the soil with great success, and the priests share the labor and the harvest but take no more than their share. In short, Mendoza learns about a wonderful life of which he was previously unaware. He eventually tells Gabriel that he wants to become a Jesuit.

After the Treaty of Madrid adjusts the territorial boundaries between the Spanish and Portuguese empires, several missions, including San Carlos, are ordered to be evacuated. The Vatican is warned by the Portuguese throne that if the priests do not comply, Jesuits will face expulsion from territories all over the new world.

As Spain's representative, Cabeza finds no difficulty in supporting the shift of land. Neither he nor the Portuguese Hontar sees anything in the jungle missions except land to be exploited for profit. There is no earthly paradise, they say, and they agree that the Jesuits are already much too powerful.

The papal representative Altamirano arrives to give final considerations prior to giving an ultimatum to the Jesuits. During an open hearing, he is informed that missions such as San Carlos provide sanctuary to the Guaraní. Mendoza interjects that this means protection from the Spanish slave-traders. When Cabeza denies that Spain deals in slaves, Mendoza calls him a liar, but he later apologizes when ordered to do so by Gabriel. While admitting nothing, Cabeza cynically notes that slavery fulfills the law of supply and demand. He says also that the mission teaches contempt for property and lawful profit, by allowing the Guaraní to earn from their farming and production of musical instruments.

Altamirano visits some of the missions and is astounded by their beauty and scope. Not only are these cooperatives self-sustaining, but each seems invested with an Edenic purity, while their richness seems to have been spiritually inspired. Ultimately, however, Altamirano's original intention has not altered. He tells Gabriel that, if the Jesuit order is to survive at all in the world, the mission must be sacrificed to the Portuguese. The Guaraní must learn to submit to the will of God, he says. They must put down their tools of production and go back into the bush.

Neither Gabriel nor Mendoza accepts the ruling, but the mission founder knows that he must submit. Mendoza has other ideas. His former militarism returns, and with support from a few other rebellious priests, he sets out to defend the mission against the invading Portuguese. Gabriel does not try to stop him, but neither does he bless Mendoza.

The defenders cause some initial problems, but their primitive weapons are much too feeble for them to contend with the well-trained, well-equipped Europeans. As the life-embracing chants of the Guaraní children fill the background, the soldiers advance and indiscriminately execute everyone in sight—not only Mendoza and his band of resisters, but also Gabriel and many women and children, who are gathered at the end for a benediction service only to be burned out of their shelters and slaughtered in a cloud of gunpowder. Some children who survive crawl into a canoe and move slowly upstream, carrying a battered violin.

Altamirano recalls his initial revulsion when he heard the news of the battle. When Cabeza and Hontar casually state that the world is often harsh, the churchman rejects their rationalization, saying that they, and he, have made the world what it is.

The Mission is an often angry film that manages to retain its panoramic, breathtaking beauty in the midst of harsh, sometimes grotesque scenes. Bolt's script clearly attacks the forces of economic expediency, showing how exploitative land-developers and quick-profit hucksters were already operating in such remote, lush lands nearly 250 years ago. The governing anger becomes evident in his and director Joffé's suggestion that those forces always win, even if temporarily, whether they destroy the natural balance by paving jungle trails with asphalt or by simply mowing down hundreds of pesky natives and priests.

Viewed from the morally ambiguous perspective of the major church figure, Altamirano, the picture is even more distressing. Because Bolt establishes early the cold, contemptuous lack of humanity in both Hontar and Cabeza, the churchman's ultimate decision to order the priests and natives out of the missions is disgraceful. In effect, he allies himself with gangsters in order to preserve official alliances.

The photographic beauty of *The Mission*, controlled so perfectly by the Oscar-winning cinematographer Chris Menges, helps to cover up some unsightly patches in its continuity. The film seems to have been shortened in its early sequences, as if a production decision were made to improve its chances at the box office. For example, the motivation of Mendoza is at first sketchy. The scene in which he kills his brother seems forced or at least clumsy, suggesting that preliminaries and immediate consequences, along with the feelings of the woman they had been fighting over, were not essential. Yet the killing completely changes Mendoza's life, and development of the earlier segments should have been slower. To keep the length of the film manageable, some of the repetitious canoe journeys and rock climbs could have been cut without loss.

Irons' role is pivotal. In his Christ-like face can be traced lines of humility and compassion but also repressed anger at a pontifical edict he finds as hateful as does Mendoza. De Niro is less overwhelming than usual, but he manages well the stark emotional transformations of his character.

With all of its flaws, *The Mission* is a strong film which both celebrates the rich potential of human culture and exposes the destructive underside of "civilization."

Andrew Jefchak

Reviews
America. CLV, November 15, 1986, p. 302.
The Christian Century. CIII, December 24, 1986, p. 1181.
Commonweal. CXIII, November 21, 1986, p. 632.
Films in Review. XXXVIII, January, 1987, p. 47.
Los Angeles Times. November 14, 1986, VI, p. 1.
National Catholic Reporter. XXIII, November 21, 1986, p. 13.
The New Republic. CLXLVIII, December 1, 1986, p. 26.
New Statesman. CXII, October 24, 1986, p. 25.
New York. XIX, November 10, 1986, p. 109.
The New York Times. October 31, 1986, p. D13.
Newsweek. CVIII, November 3, 1986, p. 81.
Time. CXXVIII, November 10, 1986, p. 111.

MONA LISA

Origin: Great Britain
Released: 1986
Released in U.S.: 1986
Production: Stephen Woolley and Patrick Cassavetti; released by Handmade
   Films
Direction: Neil Jordan
Screenplay: Neil Jordan and David Leland
Cinematography: Roger Pratt
Editing: Lesley Walker
Production design: Jamie Leonard
Art direction: Gemma Jackson
Costume design: Louise Frogley
Sound: David John
Music: Michael Kamen
Song: Genesis, "In Too Deep"
MPAA rating: R
Running time: 100 minutes

   Principal characters:
   George .... Bob Hoskins
   Simone............................ Cathy Tyson
   Mortwell......................... Michael Caine
   Anderson......................... Clarke Peters
   Cathy .... Kate Hardie
   Thomas.......................... Robbie Coltrane
   Jeannie .... Zoe Nathenson
   May.............................. Sammi Davies
   Terry.............................. Rod Bedall
   Dudley .... Joe Brown
   Dawn .... Pauline Melville
   Devlin.......................... David Halliwell

   Neil Jordan's *Mona Lisa*, while centering on the criminal underworld,
prostitution, drug addiction, and violence, has a lush and romantic soul.
Like Jordan's *The Company of Wolves* (1984), *Mona Lisa* is a film that explores the psychological resonance of its genre's boundaries and conventions
at the same time as it derives momentum from the audience's familiarity
with these conventions. *The Company of Wolves* is basically a Freudian
reworking of the Little Red Riding Hood fairy tale that was, unfortunately,
marketed and received as a horror film. In *The Company of Wolves*, Jordan
uses a continually receding, internal dream structure to explore the ways in

which fairy tales and folklore are used to condition and fix women's sexuality. While the film is analytical and psychologically dense, Jordan's obvious fascination with the erotic and horrific lure of these tales propels the viewer along. In a similar way, *Mona Lisa* explores the ways in which society attempts and often succeeds in perverting the sexual identities of women and men through the trappings of popular culture, represented here by the structure of the *film noir* gangster picture as well as the mythologizing tone of Nat "King" Cole's popular romantic ballad that serves as the film's theme. As in *The Company of Wolves*, Jordan's affection for these romantic conventions allows *Mona Lisa* simultaneously to capture the viewers' imaginations and cause them to question their preconceptions.

Mona Lisa opens on George (Bob Hoskins), who has just been released from prison seven years after having apparently taken the fall for his former crime boss, Mortwell (Michael Caine, in a thoroughly chilling performance). George goes to Mortwell looking for work and is hired to chauffeur a stylish black call girl named Simone (Cathy Tyson) from one client to another. They despise each other at the outset; Simone is disgusted by George's gaudy appearance and lower-class behavior, and he is enraged by her contempt and condescension. George soon falls under the spell of Simone's alluring mystique, however, and she gradually comes to admire his genuineness and intense loyalty. George and Simone become inextricably bonded when Simone asks George to help her find a fifteen-year-old prostitute, a close friend from whom Simone was separated when she left London to escape the brutal control of their pimp, Anderson (Clarke Peters). George finds that Anderson is pimping for Mortwell, and he eventually locates the girl, who is a drug-addicted pawn in Mortwell's schemes to gain power and control over influential people. The unfolding mystery that has brought George and Simone together becomes the source of their destruction when George learns that Simone and this girl are, in fact, lovers and when Simone is brought into violent and cathartic confrontation with both Mortwell and Anderson. George is left to pick up the pieces of his life alone, although he is reunited with his estranged daughter, whose desire to know her long-imprisoned father is used as poignant counterpoint to the disturbing developments of the film's plot.

What distinguishes *Mona Lisa* from other *film noir* mysteries is that it is extremely aware of its genre's conventions and manages to defy the audience's expectations on almost every significant plot point. The central character of George, though streetwise and capable in the tradition of Humphrey Bogart and James Cagney, is completely lacking in the savvy and worldliness that one normally associates with such heroes. Instead, he is simple and quite ignorant; his brutal side is both a way he has learned to operate effectively in his world and a defense mechanism for his naïveté. George yearns to be a knight in shining armor for the emotionally needy

Simone, but he is never allowed to vanquish her foes as he desires and as the audience expects. Rather, he always seems two steps behind in the mystery that consumes him, and Simone is left to take control of her own situation. George's romantic gullibility and simpleness, qualities which both endear him to the audience and elevate him above the moral corruption of the other characters, are never rewarded by the events of the film's plot. Quite the contrary: George's inability to see beyond his fantasy image of Simone, at least until it is too late, becomes an increasingly painful source of frustration to him and ultimately ruins everything that is special about their relationship.

In this respect, *Mona Lisa* is a tragedy in an almost classical sense: George's most endearing and human quality, his lack of sophistication, is also the source of his failure. The casting of Bob Hoskins and the uniqueness of George's character, the way in which George's singular charm and sweetness is capable of exploding into brutally violent rage, is perhaps the film's greatest asset (and was recognized by the Academy with a nomination for the Best Actor Award). Bob Hoskins' George, like Orson Welles's Charles Foster Kane, Charles Chaplin's Tramp, or Diane Keaton's Annie Hall, is that rarity of rarities: a character virtually unimaginable without the actor who brings it to life. Short and stocky but wired to spring, Hoskins is a beefy, sweaty, and palpably real screen presence; his George is an outsider who is constantly trying to get in. He suffers no embarrassment about his ignorance and lack of propriety, but he does become angry when others recoil from his blunt tactlessness. In an elegant cocktail lounge, he walks up to a waiter and asks for a drink and, when ignored, begins shouting across the crowded room. Though open and nonjudgmental, George can also be harsh and insensitive. When he finds a pornographic videotape featuring Simone, he puts it into a machine and plays it for her and is then stunned by her violent reaction. George lays all of his cards on the table and has no ability to intuit truth and complexities in those who hold back. This quality both makes him an easy target for Mortwell's devious exploitation and prevents him from recognizing the important role that he plays in Simone's life. Hoskins' complete lack of self-consciousness as an actor is essential for this emotionally needy man who, without a trace of self-pity, has no awareness of his impact on the world.

Simone, on the other hand, as played by Cathy Tyson (a twenty-year-old actress making an astonishing film debut), measures everything by the impact she makes on others. After suffering years of degradation and abuse at the hands of her pimp and her clients, she has worked her way up from the streets and back alleys to the high-priced mansions and hotels of London. In order to survive, she has learned to manufacture an exotic and alluring image; in the process, she has closed herself off from her emotions and needs. At one point Simone tells George, upon learning that he is single, that everyone needs someone to go home to; when he points out that she too is alone, she claims that she is different, that she is the person people go home from. George, however, is drawn by the image she projects. Although he drives Simone from client to client and is the primary agent in her obsessive search for the friend she left behind in the dangerous world of the streets, George is blinded by his own romantic image of her. Seeing only the veneer which Simone presents to the world, George is incapable of seeing the pain that drives her on. Consequently, he feels used and betrayed when he discovers that Simone and her friend are lovers. Significantly, George plays Nat "King" Cole's "Mona Lisa" on a tape deck in his car, the lyrics of which include, "Are you warm, are you real, Mona Lisa, or just a cold and lonely, lovely work of art?" This song conveys perfectly George's romantic confusion; to George, Simone is Mona Lisa, while to the audience she is a haunted and cynical victim.

Simone's lesbianism is presented as a logical defense against the exploitation she has experienced at the hands of men. Jordan wisely shies away from overexplaining this sexual preference; since her sexuality is a tool in the heterosexual world, it seems perfectly logical that she would not make herself vulnerable to men in her private life. The depth of Simone's rage against men, however, is not fully realized until the climax, in which she kills Mortwell and Anderson. In a fury spinning wildly out of control, Simone nearly kills George as well; she is simply unable to check her blind, directionless, and necessary outburst. For George, who wants to be uniquely important to Simone, this is unforgivable, and, in rage, he too strikes out at her. This scene seems both shocking and inevitable; it is the sudden distillation of sexual confusion and anger that has been present from the beginning between them. For an audience that has come to sympathize deeply with the pain and humanity of George and Simone, however, this encounter has a startling and bitter finality.

Director Neil Jordan is adept at conveying the seediness of the pornographic underworld without resorting to graphic exposition. The neon lure of this world is there for those who choose not to recognize the hopelessness that lies beneath it. In addition, Jordan is most impressive in the way he stages the film's scenes of violence; they tend to erupt very suddenly in tight, controlled frames that propel the viewer right into the center of their dynamic fury. Although they are handled much less obviously, the thematic concerns of *The Company of Wolves* are present in *Mona Lisa* as well. While Rosaleen (Sarah Patterson), the central figure of *The Company of Wolves*, is trained to fear men and to resist her own sexual urges, Simone, in *Mona Lisa*, has been taken advantage of by men and has separated herself from her sexual identity, which she has learned to market successfully. The heavily stylized atmosphere of *The Company of Wolves* has given way to a more straightforward narrative in *Mona Lisa*, though Jordan still employs some heavily symbolic touches in the latter. At one point, a white horse is seen tethered outside a roadside diner; at another, George and Simone knock over some enormous plastic hearts as they flee from Anderson. This is as it should be, however, for Jordan is exploring the mythologizing conceits of popular romance that have distorted George's view of women. A man who confronts reality with the expectations and formulas of fiction, George finds nothing but disillusionment.

Jeffrey L. Fenner

Reviews
Commonweal. CXIII, July 11, 1986, p. 405.
Films and Filming. Number 382, July, 1986, p. 36.
Films in Review. XXXVII, October, 1986, p. 483.
National Review. XXXVIII, July 18, 1986, p. 56.
The New Republic. CXCIV, June 23, 1986, p. 27.
The New York Times. CXXXV, June 13, 1986, p. C23.
The New Yorker. LXII, June 16, 1986, p. 114.
Newsweek. CVII, June 16, 1986, p. 75.
Time. CXXVIII, July 14, 1986, p. 62.
The Wall Street Journal. CCVIII, June 17, 1986, p. 26.

THE MORNING AFTER

Production: Bruce Gilbert for American Filmworks; released by Twentieth Century-Fox
Direction: Sidney Lumet
Screenplay: James Hicks
Cinematography: Andrzej Bartkowiak
Editing: Joel Goodman
Production design: Albert Brenner
Art direction: Kandy Stern; set decoration, Lee Poll
Costume design: Ann Roth
Music: Paul Chihara
MPAA rating: R
Running time: 103 minutes

> *Principal characters:*
> Alex Sternbergen.....................Jane Fonda
> Turner Kendall ....Jeff Bridges
> Joaquin Manero.......................Raul Julia
> Isabel Harding ....Diane Salinger
> Sergeant Greenbaum ....Richard Foronjy
> Bobby Korshack ....Geoffrey Scott
> Frankie ....James (Gypsy) Haake
> Red ....Kathleen Wilhoite
> Hurley...............................Don Hood

A prolific filmmaker, director Sidney Lumet has surely grown accustomed to the mixed reactions his films so often evoke. *The Morning After*, advertised largely as a mystery, is no exception, having had a lukewarm critical and commercial reception. Yet a dissenting opinion, favorable to the film, has been expressed by feminists concerned about rising alcoholism among women as well as by fans of Jane Fonda. This dissenting opinion rests its praise on Fonda's performance as an aging former starlet, sinking into a confirmed alcoholism yet still capable of great strengths of emotion. Ultimately, the fairest response to *The Morning After* may be a hung jury, since those elements of the script that work toward its success as a character study sometimes work against its success as a mystery, and vice versa. The consequence is that *The Morning After*'s parts are greater than its whole.

The Morning After starts from a powerful premise: Alex Sternbergen (Jane Fonda), a woman not unaccustomed to one-night stands, wakes up one morning in a stranger's bed uncertain whether she is responsible for the knife buried in his very cold chest. She is certain, though, as she watches a television news story on commercial pornography in which the stranger discusses his involvement in response to an interviewer's questions, that she cannot stand the man and would never have gone to bed with him.

Nevertheless, she cannot remember how she got where she is, so she calls Joaquin Manero (Raul Julia), her husband in name only but still her friend. She reaches him over the phone in his jeep; despite the open blue skies behind him as he drives through the hills above Los Angeles, Manero's first appearance has something sinister about it. Yet Alex clearly trusts him. Playing up ambivalent aspects of his character, Julia uses his opening scene to increase audience discomfort and curiosity. This discomfort stems from basic confusion about who these people are, how they are related to each other, and what they are doing. Why, for example, do viewers first meet Manero in the ambiguous context of driving his jeep and only later see him in the more informative surroundings of the successful salon he owns? Why, having left the murder victim's loft, does Alex later return to clean it up? This coy obfuscation is frustrating, but curiosity about the mystery will carry the audience through to the film's end.

Still, some viewers may be disconcerted to find that much of *The Morning After* focuses on a double character study: Ignoring Manero's advice to call the police, Alex Sternbergen instead flees to the airport, where she impulsively confides her dilemma to a scruffy stranger, Turner Kendall (Jeff Bridges), who is working on his car in the airport parking lot. Kendall is a curious character, ambivalent like Manero in that he, too, poses a vague menace while offering much-needed help and understanding. A former police officer, Kendall clearly hides many secrets under his apparently open exterior. Alex both rejects him and relies on his help. She makes fun of his redneck ways—"What are you, the Klan anthropologist?"—but when she examines his unexpectedly large library, she is touched by his owning copies of Nancy Drew novels. Through it all, she drinks, often to the point of oblivion, always leaving herself vulnerable. Is it Manero, Kendall, or yet another party that takes advantage of her vulnerability, and why?

Lumet's films generally take place either in such claustrophobic settings as the jury room of *Twelve Angry Men* (1957) and the snowbound train of *Murder on the Orient Express* (1974) or on the streets of Manhattan, as in *Serpico* (1973) and *Prince of the City* (1981). Although he has relied heavily on a variety of stage plays and novels—*A View from the Bridge* (1962), *Long Day's Journey into Night* (1962), *Fail Safe* (1964)—Lumet's films also often deal with cops and robbers fighting over control of their city. With the exception of his 1966 film version of Mary McCarthy's novel *The Group* (1963), Lumet's work also has focused primarily on male protagonists. Although in many ways *The Morning After* resembles Lumet's earlier work, it also represents a departure for him in two major respects: It was filmed on location not in New York City but in Los Angeles; and it features a female protagonist. Lumet examines her flaws as well as her strengths, and Alex

Sternbergen gradually emerges as an ordinary but complicated woman. This impression no doubt derives in part from the superrealistic believability of her surroundings—an endless sidewalk abutting a warehouse wall harshly reflecting the relentless sun; glitzy hair salons and concrete airports; her tacky house in sunny suburbia—surroundings into which she blends so well. Credit for the strong impression many of these images make must go to cinematographer Andrzej Bartkowiak, but it should also be acknowledged that Lumet uses many of his settings to establish character, usually to emphasize the discrepancy between their surface appearances and their true selves. Kendall, for example, lives in an old garage, but, being handy with tools, he has converted its interior into a comfortable place with a kitchen especially well equipped for his gourmet cooking. Alex, in contrast, despite her middle-class home, lives less well; her house is messy and her refrigerator is bare of almost everything except cheap wine and mayonnaise, which she stocks in absurd abundance. When Manero picks up Isabel Harding (Diane Salinger), the establishment heiress he plans to marry, he finds her at the family dining table, a very formal affair in a mahogany-paneled room that emphasizes the stuffiness of the Harding family. Manero himself is associated after his first appearance with his high-tech, elaborately lighted salon, a world of mirrors and false appearances.

Why, though, when Alex Sternbergen wakes up next to a dead man, does she first call her husband for advice and then ignore it? Only once she has met Kendall can her bits and pieces of conversation with him provide the background so painfully absent from the film's opening (just as his background also comes to viewers only in bits and pieces at various points in the story). What one learns is that, although her career as an actress got off to a good start, her drinking problem even then interfered with her success. Most important of all, though, is the fact that she once drunkenly assaulted her husband with a knife and thus already has a police record. Guilty or innocent, she does not want to go back to jail, and, given her record, she assumes that the police will give her no benefit of the doubt. Kendall agrees with her that circumstantial evidence does imply her guilt, but he seems to believe her innocent, anyway.

It is Kendall, too, who provides the first conclusive proof of her innocence. Having invited him to eat dinner with her, Alex drinks until, in the midst of another phone call with Manero, she passes out. On his way out, Kendall inadvertently opens the wrong door, thereby proving to himself and the audience that her shower stall is empty. The next morning, though, when Alex awakens she is again startled to discover the same dead body, now mysteriously transported to her shower stall. Kendall and Alex now know that she is innocent of murder, but how can they prove it to the police?

The police, in the meantime, are closing in on Alex. As a former policeman, Kendall has been carrying on his own investigations. Alex continues to turn to Manero for help, and the climactic scene for the mystery takes place in his private apartment. There, viewers learn that all the earlier casual, joking references to race and class were clues to what turns out to be the mystery's fairly predictable origins and solution.

In fact, James Hicks's script seems to be the real culprit in *The Morning After*. Yet it provides Jane Fonda with one of her best roles in a while. Some credit for her success must go to Jeff Bridges, whose offbeat, laid-back character provides not only a foil for Alex's brittle nervousness but also a stabilizing counterbalance to Fonda's tendency to overplay her roles. Again, part of *The Morning After*'s success and failure lies in the script's odd combination of comic elements with the dramatic interaction between Kendall and Alex.

There is, for example, something curious about the way they meet. Alex flees to the airport, leaving her car illegally parked. After putting on a convincing performance as a mother trying to return to her daughter's sickbed only to find that Thanksgiving traffic has made it impossible for her to get a seat on any flight out of Los Angeles, Alex returns to her car to find that it has attracted the attention of various passersby, a traffic cop, and a cabbie. Having infuriated the cabbie, she deserts her car and finds sanctuary in Kendall's car, unbeknown to him. At first grateful to Kendall, she quickly grows dismayed to find that he and his car have become a fixture in her life. To Kendall, the old Chevy is a real prize, but to Alex it is merely a dump. A sticky passenger door becomes a leitmotif, as Alex learns how to deal with it, while Kendall gets stuck behind it at crucial moments.

As the focal character of the film, Alex poses several enigmas that weaken the film in various ways. If Alex is the alcoholic she seems to be, how is it that she has retained her beauty and her fit appearance? Her husband contributes to her financial support out of gratitude to her for having originally funded his first salon, but what ties does she have with the gay friend who provides her with clothes, or the bartender who provides her with cash on Thanksgiving Day? If she can pull herself together with such a degree of self-confidence as she does in the end, when she stops drinking cold turkey, how is it that she has been so dependent in the past and how is it that she has been able to tolerate her previous existence? These questions pose a greater mystery than the murder itself, but *The Morning After*'s ambiguous ending provides no real answers.

Harriet Margolis

Reviews
American Film. XII, December, 1986, p. 65.

Commonweal. CXIV, January 30, 1987, p. 55.
Films in Review. XXXVIII, April, 1987, p. 231.
Los Angeles Times. December 25, 1986, V, p. 1.
The New Republic. CXCVI, January 5, 1987, p. 24.
The New York Times. February 8, 1987, II, p. 21.
The New Yorker. LXXII, December 29, 1986, p. 84.
Time. CXXVIII, December 29, 1986, p. 71.
Variety. CCCXXV, December 24, 1986, p. 12.
The Washington Post. December 25, 1986, p. C1.

THE MOSQUITO COAST

Production: Jerome Hellman; released by Warner Bros.
Direction: Peter Weir
Screenplay: Paul Schrader; based on the novel of the same name by Paul Theroux
Cinematography: John Seale
Editing: Thom Noble
Production design: John Stoddart
Art direction: John Wingrove; set decoration, John Anderson
Makeup: Judy Lovell, Michelle Myers, and Rosalina Silva
Costume design: Gary Jones
Music: Maurice Jarre
MPAA rating: PG
Running time: 119 minutes

Principal characters:
Allie Fox ....Harrison Ford
Mother...........................Helen Mirren
Charlie ....River Phoenix
Mr. Haddy ....Conrad Roberts
The Reverend Spellgood............André Gregory
Emily Spellgood.................Martha Plimpton
Tiny Polski ....Dick O'Neill
Jerry ....Jadrien Steele
April ....Hilary Gordon
Clover ....Rebecca Gordon
Ma Kennywick................Butterfly McQueen

The conflict between civilization and more primitive or traditional cultures has been the theme of a number of prominent films in recent years, including *The Mission* in 1986 (reviewed in this volume), *Out of Africa* and *The Emerald Forest* in 1985, and *Greystoke: The Legend of Tarzan, Lord of the Apes* and *The Gods Must Be Crazy* in 1984. In whatever time or place these films are set, they all reflect the misgivings that artists and audiences have toward the state of civilization in the mid-1980's—toward a way of life that has provided unprecedented profits and luxury for many, while also ignoring important spiritual values, wantonly exploiting people and natural resources, and threatening the very survival of the planet with pollution and nuclear weapons. In this social and cinematic context, both audiences and critics eagerly anticipated *The Mosquito Coast*, a film project which gathered an impressive array of talent in adapting Paul Theroux's best-selling novel of the same name. First published in 1982, this psychological adventure novel traces the tragicomic odyssey of Allie Fox, a maverick American inventor who drags his family into the Honduran jungle and ultimately fails in his obsessive attempts to create a new and purified civilization. The much-anticipated film adaptation, however, met with only limited box-office and critical success, and this initial disappointment caused the film to be ultimately underrated. Though by no means a great film, *The Mosquito Coast* does mark an interesting point in the evolution of several cinematic careers, and it merits further consideration as a serious exploration of the theme of civilization versus nature.

The enterprise of filming *The Mosquito Coast* attracted a number of people who seemed ideally suited to the project. Independent producer Jerome Hellman, whose other prestigious, socially minded projects have included *Midnight Cowboy* (1969) and *Coming Home* (1978), bought the rights to the book when it was first published and was determined to bring a faithful adaptation to the screen. To develop the script, Hellman hired Paul Schrader, an eminent screenwriter and director whose treatment of monomaniacal protagonists in such films as *Taxi Driver* (1976), *Hardcore* (1978), and *Raging Bull* (1980) made him an ideal choice to reimagine the character of Allie Fox in cinematic terms. Similarly, Hellman seemed to exercise unerring judgment in engaging Peter Weir to direct, for a major theme running through virtually all the Australian director's films, from *Picnic at Hanging Rock* (1975) through *The Last Wave* (1977), *The Plumber* (1980), and *The Year of Living Dangerously* (1982), is the confrontation of civilized protagonists with ominous forces that seem beyond the limits of the kinds of rational understanding favored by Western culture. While Weir waited for the business arrangements to be completed that would allow him to begin shooting *The Mosquito Coast*, he directed the enormously successful *Witness* (1985), yet another film about the conflict of modern civilization with a more traditional way of life. The American Academy of Motion Picture Arts and Sciences honored *Witness* with one Oscar (Thom Noble for Editing) and with a number of nominations (for Best Picture, Weir for Best Direction, Harrison Ford for Best Actor, Maurice Jarre for Best Original Score, and John Seale for Best Cinematography) that helped to unify these artists into a team which continued to work together on *The Mosquito Coast*.

The deficiencies in these filmmakers' work on *The Mosquito Coast* are fairly inconspicuous in the early comic scenes, set in rural Massachusetts, where Allie (Harrison Ford) is employed by Tiny Polski (Dick O'Neill), an asparagus farmer who becomes exasperated by the irregular behavior of his hired handyman. While entertaining in a broadly humorous way, these early scenes are also important in that they establish both Allie's domineering, ranting, technically ingenious character and the double perspective with which his thirteen-year-old son Charlie (River Phoenix) views him. On the one hand, Charlie, who is the first-person narrator in the novel and a voice-over narrator in the film, worships his father and enjoys being swept along in his manic attitudes and projects, but on the other, especially since Charlie is emerging into manhood, he begins to view his father from a more detached and critical perspective—to be puzzled by his contradictions, embarrassed by his social eccentricities, and frightened by his fallibilities as he thrusts himself and his family into situations he may not be able to control. Weir finds effective visual terms to accentuate Charlie's double perspective by alternating between two cinematic styles. When Charlie is feeling compelled by his father's overbearing personality, as in an early scene in a hardware store, Weir uses tighty framed close-ups and a swiftly moving camera to express the hectic, breathless pace of Allie's life and Charlie's confinement within it. On the other hand, Weir pulls back to long- or extreme-long-shot range when Charlie reflects in voice-over or when the director wants to express Charlie's comic perspective on his father, as in a scene where Allie goes raging through a junkyard looking for a used part.

Even in these early scenes, however, some of the weaknesses of the film begin to emerge. These flaws range from technical mistakes (one scene begins in the house of migrant farm workers, but when Charlie and his brother move into another room, they are inexplicably back in their family's home) to a timid and overschematic handling of the materials of the book. In Theroux's novel, Charlie experiences his father's contradictions and his own fear of them in deep and complex ways. For example, Allie is both fascinated and repelled by the black migrant workers, whom he calls "savages," and in one of the most haunting passages in the early chapters, Charlie dreams (or does he actually walk out of his house and hallucinate?) that he sees his father dead after a late-night crucifixion by torch-bearing natives, and that he, Charlie, leads his mother and three siblings away from burning fields and a blood-red sky. Schrader and Weir eliminate this powerful and prophetic vision and create instead a bedtime conversation involving Charlie, his younger brother Jerry (Jadrien Steele), and his mother (Helen Mirren). This rather conventional scene seems to fix the characters' roles and the family dynamics as they will appear throughout the film. Jerry voices his fears of (and later his hostility toward) his father. Charlie, as he hears his own feelings being expressed but in a child's way, either remains silent or defends his father. Mother tries to cover her own fears as well, as she sympathizes with Jerry but remains primarily loyal to her husband. As the film progresses, it is marred not only by the repetitiveness and predictability of these responses, but also by the miscasting and limitations of the role of Mother. Helen Mirren brings such associations of intelligence and strength from her previous screen work—including fine performances in the British Broadcasting Company's *Shakespeare Plays* and in such films as *The Long Good Friday* (1980), *Cal* (1984), *2010* (1984), and *White Nights*

(1985)—that she seems out of place in her one-note role of a sympathetic but usually submissive earth mother.

Despite these flaws, the middle section of the film—the boat trip to the tropics and the rejuvenation of a dilapidated river village called Jerónimo into a thriving utopian community—largely succeeds in diverting the viewer through its comic touch and energetic performances by several fine character actors. Onboard the *Unicorn*, a run-down cargo ship, the atheistic Allie matches wits with the Reverend Spellgood (André Gregory), an evangelical missionary who alternates between preaching at drive-in parking lots in Baltimore and at the Honduran river village of Guampú. As the aggressively pious and self-important Spellgood, Gregory gives an entertaining performance that is quite different from his sophisticated role as himself in *My Dinner with André* (1981). Martha Plimpton, who was seen previously in *The River Rat* (1984) and *The Goonies* (1985), also presents her liveliest performance to date as Emily Spellgood, the reverend's sexually assertive teenage daughter who tries to convince Charlie to become her boyfriend. Though their parts skirt uncomfortably close to the racist stereotypes of earlier Hollywood films, a number of black performers contribute vivid characterizations as Jerónimo villagers, including Butterfly McQueen as Ma Kennywick—a virtual reprise of her role as Prissy, the skittish and fearful maid to Scarlett O'Hara in *Gone with the Wind* (1939). Also memorable in a larger supporting role is Conrad Roberts as Mr. Haddy, the warm-hearted Creole boatman who ferries the Fox family to their new jungle home and who reappears to supply and aid them at key points later in the film.

The garrulous, grandiose character of Allie Fox clearly marks an ambitious step for Harrison Ford, who had established a laconic, understated *persona* as the tough-guy hero in three *Star Wars* films (*Star Wars*, 1977, *The Empire Strikes Back,* 1980, and *Return of the Jedi,* 1983), two Indiana Jones films (*Raiders of the Lost Ark,* 1981, and *Indiana Jones and the Temple of Doom,* 1984), *Blade Runner* (1982), and *Witness*. In the first half of *The Mosquito Coast*, Ford is more than adequate as an obsessive perfectionist who drives himself and all those around him with unceasing manic energy and constant jeremiads aimed at the corruption, waste, and approaching nuclear doom of American society. Under Weir's direction, Ford achieves some wonderfully comic moments, as when he calls a town meeting, ostensibly to offer the natives a choice of what improvements they will tackle first ("I'm here to work for you"), and interprets one man's nervous cough to mean "planting." Later, he continues his nonstop diatribe against American civilization, even to natives who understand very little of what he is saying and even while using a chainsaw that drowns out his every word. The film attains an exhilarating sense of wonder as Allie's hard work and paternalistic rule mold the village into the practical utopia he had envisioned, with its roomy platform house for his family; its systems of fans, pulleys, and revolving buckets; and even its old rusty bicycle that he has transformed into a washing machine so that his young twins, April and Clover (Hilary and Rebecca Gordon), can have fun as they agitate the family's laundry.

From this ebullient high point in the family's adventure, however, both the film as a whole and Ford's performance in particular begin to deteriorate— for reasons that are traceable to the novel as well as to the film. One point is that the narrow political vision of Theroux and Weir begins to become more apparent. A bounteous Thanksgiving scene reveals how Allie has provided an ideal life for his wife and four children worthy of the Swiss Family Robinson, but what of the natives he has so aggressively colonized? He has provided them with new clothes and a party before his own Thanksgiving dinner, but how do they feel about their new life of constant toil? Have their living quarters been improved so as to compare with Allie's luxurious platform house? The audience perceives the natives' point of view only in brief reaction shots and never sees where they live; Weir (like Theroux) fails to give Allie's ideal of a benign colonialism the serious scrutiny it deserves.

Instead, it is Allie's political and technological overreaching that rapidly causes his downfall. Having achieved the ideal, so satisfying to contemporary audiences, of a perfect society set apart from corrupt civilization, both Theroux and Weir hasten to show that it is impossible, which is, paradoxically, also a notion comforting to apathetic audiences who are not interested in being challenged to change their present luxurious and wasteful life-styles. The overarching irony of both the novel and film is that Allie cannot escape the destructiveness of civilization: He carries too much of it within him, and there is too much of it around him, even in the jungle. When the Reverend Spellgood pays Jerónimo a visit, Allie does not strike the conciliatory note that might have allowed him to live in harmony with his neighbors, but harshly drives Spellgood away. Further, in order to achieve his long-held ideal of producing ice in the jungle, he builds an enormous ice-making plant (appropriately named "Fatboy," carrying connotations of decadence to which Allie is oblivious) and forces his sons and some of the natives to help him drag a block to the "pure" primitive natives deep in the jungle. When the expedition reaches a suspicious village and discovers that the ice has completely melted, Charlie is ironically forced into the role of a hollow salesman, assuring the natives that "Ice can be used for a number of things," while Allie spots three sordid-looking white men, whom he assumes are prisoners. When these three later make their way to Jeronimo, however, they turn out to be threatening outlaws; Allie tries to freeze them to death inside Fatboy, but they try to shoot their way out and set off a conflagration that destroys the village, scorches the countryside, and poisons the river.

By this point, it seems clear that Allie is such a self-absorbed character that he will not learn his lesson and that more setbacks like the destruction of Jeronimo are inevitable. Allie Fox, however, does not have the larger-than-life stature of a King Lear or a Captain Ahab, or even of a Captain Bligh, that might have given the story tragic dimensions. In the book, Theroux circumvents this problem to some extent by creating some suspense around the Oedipal issue of whether or when Charlie is going to rebel against his father's despotism. What appears in the film as a mere play lagoon for the children is, in the book, a serious political alternative called the Acre, where Charlie likes to imagine that the children could survive without his father's slave driving, and where he does in fact bring his whole family to save them when Jerónimo explodes. In the film, however, though River Phoenix emotes the adulation and the worry in Charlie's character well enough, he is no smoldering rebel along the lines of Clark Gable's Fletcher Christian, and Harrison Ford is too matter-of-fact an actor to heighten Allie's self-absorption to the point of grandly tragic monomania.

Thus, much of the second half of the film seems predictable and dramatically flat. After the destruction of Jerónimo, the family travels by boat down to the seacoast, where Allie is determined to create another thriving village, this time without chemicals. Foolishly, he rejects Mr. Haddy's generous offer to take them to his coastal village, where they could avoid the coming tropical storms. Allie's antisocial paranoia now begins to loosen his grip on reality, and he claims that civilization has been destroyed in a nuclear war and that he and his family are lucky to be among the few survivors. When the storms Mr. Haddy predicted do come and tear the family from their tenuous outpost, the Foxes travel back upstream. They happen upon Spellgood's missionary village, but Allie's antisocial nature, now more virulent than ever, once again leads to disaster. While Charlie finally summons the nerve to try to pull his family away from his father and seeks help from Emily Spellgood, Allie sets the church on fire and is shot by the vengeful Reverend Spellgood. The Fox family closes ranks once again and floats downstream, though they continue to assure Allie, who is delirious and dying, that they are headed upstream. As they reach the ocean after Allie's death, Weir opts for an uplifting and affirmative ending: The camera pulls back and up to an extreme long shot showing the boat arriving at a picturesque seacoast, and Charlie declares in a voice-over, "Once I had believed in Father, and the world seemed small and old. Now he was gone, and I wasn't afraid to love him anymore, and the world seemed limitless."

Like Charlie, who never becomes an entirely decisive liberator of his family, *The Mosquito Coast* ultimately lacks the nerve to delve into more frightening emotional and political depths and become the dramatic, disturbing work that it might have been. To view a film that treats the conflict between nature and civilization with more energy and emotional resonance, one might well go back to the original *King Kong* (1933); or, for a film on this theme with more political awareness, one would do well to reexamine Weir's own *The Last Wave* or Werner Herzog's masterpiece *Aguirre, the Wrath of God* (1972). One can be certain of one thing, however: As the threat posed by civilization to the natural environment becomes more dire in coming decades, artists will continue to address themselves to this crucial issue.

Terry L. Andrews

Reviews
Commonweal. CXIII, December 26, 1986, p. 689.
Films in Review. XXXVIII, February, 1987, p. 103.
Los Angeles Times. November 26, 1986, VI, p. 1.
The Nation. CCXLIII, December 13, 1986, p. 683.
The New Republic. CXCV, December 22, 1986, p. 26.
New Statesman. CCXIII, February 13, 1987, p. 24.
The New York Times. December 7, 1986, II, p. 23.
Newsweek. CVIII, December 1, 1986, p. 88.
Time. CXXVIII, December 1, 1986, p. 74.
Variety. CCCXXV, November 19, 1986, p. 16.
The Washington Post. December 19, 1986, p. C1.

MOTHER TERESA

Production: Ann Petrie and Jeanette Petrie; released by Petrie Productions
Direction: Ann Petrie and Jeanette Petrie
Screenplay: no listing
Cinematography: Edward Lachman and Sandi Sissel
Editing: Tom Haneke
Narration: Richard Attenborough
Art direction: no listing
Sound recording: Barbara Becker
Sound editing: Donald Klocek
Music: Suzanne Ciani
MPAA rating: no rating
Running time: 81 minutes

For anyone who has traveled extensively in India, travel by train often provides an opportunity for contemplation, even illumination, as one feels both separation and union with the complex world of beauty and misery outside the moving windows. On a train winding through the quiet, beautiful mountains of northeast India in 1946, a thirty-six-year-old Catholic nun experienced a call to serve "the poorest of the poor." Born in Skopje, in what is now Yugoslavia, of Albanian descent, she had chosen the veil at eighteen and had been living in India since 1929 as a teaching nun. The call she heeded on the train led to a life trajectory which, beginning with her single-handed labors among the dying, the leprous, the utterly lost on the streets of Calcutta, raised her to great, though unsought fame as Mother Teresa, and brought about the creation of the Missionaries of Charity. The order is dedicated to labor for the poorest of the poor, and operates nearly three hundred centers scattered throughout the world. In Calcutta alone, at the time of the filming, forty-two thousand of the diseased and the moribund had been raised from the streets, through the efforts of the Missionaries of Charity, and nursed back to life or toward a tended death in bed.

This is without doubt the work of a saint or, in terms of formal canonization, a saint-to-be; and this documentary is essentially a work of hagiography, an approach which raises the difficult problem of presenting absolute good, as seen and felt by the artist, in a manner which transcends sentimentality and simplistic piety. Both pitfalls are avoided in *Mother Teresa*, although it is also, as befits hagiography, not a work which raises questions or doubts or any trace of negative judgment. Some might argue, for example, that support for this kind of work may serve as a salve for the conscience of people opposed to greater help for the poor through wide-ranging social change, an issue with which Mother Teresa does not seem to be concerned.

Mother Teresa was directed and produced by two sisters, Ann and Jeanette Petrie, whose brother is a Sacred Heart priest and has worked with the Missionaries of Charity for many years. The film is a labor of love which took five years to complete and involved extensive and sometimes dangerous travel. Except for the expressionistic opening and close of the film, it is a documentary that does not call attention to technique. The Petries present the life and work of Mother Teresa in a rather simple style, through a mixture of interviews, stills, old black-and-white film used for atmosphere and historical background, as well as closely observed color sequences of Mother Teresa's active, eloquent, and joyful presence in the world.

Preceding the title of the film is a montage sequence of black-and-white film clips and still photographs, presented in spasmodically slow motion and camera movement, which is set to slow elegiac music. The sequence is a flow of human suffering—images from World War II, from the concentration camps, faces of East Asians and blacks in pain, the diseased near-dead of the Calcutta streets—moving finally to a nun in a white sari, arching in from the right-hand side of the screen, who appears like a ministering angel to stretch out a hand and fold and unfold a blanket (shown in forward and reverse motion) across the face of a muffled, perhaps dying figure. The sequence, and a voice-over narration by Richard Attenborough, introduces the background of human suffering in relation to which Mother Teresa's life has unfolded and asserts the film's central credo, that the light of spiritual force can outshine even the darkest experiences of humanity. The title, *Mother Teresa*, appears briefly, followed by an extreme close-up of an eye in a black-and-white photograph. As the camera slowly pulls back, the viewer sees the face of a young, attractive woman with dark hair. It is Mother Teresa when she was still Agnes Gonxha Bojaxhiu and one hears her strong, heavily accented voice speaking Indian-lilted English in her vigorous seventies. She talks of God speaking "in the silence of the heart," a striking initial statement. Silence is an impressive aesthetic tool in the Petries' film while their most successful use of sound consists of the cadences of Mother Teresa's own husky, unwavering voice.

The viewer then sees the streets of Calcutta, in sudden brilliant color, and the nuns of the Missionaries of Charity moving, in the plain white saris with blue borders which are their habits, among the colors and miseries of those streets, examining the fingerless hands of lepers or carrying those who have fallen in the street to the order's Home for the Dying. In the quietly elegant cinematography of Ed Lachman and Sandi Sissel, the visual contrast established here—between the white of the calmly moving nuns and the colors of turmoil and suffering around them—threads a steady leitmotif throughout the many locations of the film, which include Guatemala, Lebanon, Italy, and the United States as well as India. Mother Teresa appears at the hospice, touching and tending the dying, then at the order's Home for Children, where she soothes and caresses the orphans, while her voice is heard explaining that her order fights abortion through adoption, and one sees footage of Westerners playing with children they have chosen to adopt. One sees her discussing the requirements for induction into her order, total love and total labor, and then the camera moves to various areas of the world, where she goes to establish a center, minister directly to the poor, receive the Nobel Peace Prize or an honorary doctorate from Harvard University.

Wherever she appears, the tones of absolute certainty in her voice and the craggy face capable of sudden smiling radiance or calm, unyielding stubbornness exercise their power and succeed in securing her goal, which is always direct assistance to those most desperately in physical need. With unswervable faith, she sees such success as the will and love of Christ working through her as a mere channel. "There are no shadows about her," says Mother Teresa's niece, in one of the many cameo interviews with those who have known or served with her, which often culminate in a memorable phrase about Mother Teresa or her work.

The spoken word is very important to this film, not so much in Richard Attenborough's occasional voice-over narration as in the statements of nuns (and a few priests) about their own emotions in relation to the work or the centrality of faith to Mother Teresa's mission. Most important, it is the words of Mother Teresa herself, on camera in public or in voice-over to an interviewer, which condition the viewer's perception of her work and linger in the mind. Her comments steadily restrain one from concentrating entirely on the social aspect of her activities and insistently refer to her own sense of her vocation, the manifestation in action of Christ as love.

Then there is the role of silence in the film. The first words one hears from Mother Teresa refer to "the silence of the heart," and silence figures at least as eloquently as words: the silent passage of the nuns on their errands of mercy, the movements of their hands as they minister and soothe, Mother Teresa's characteristic gesture of greeting or comfort, cupping a face at the cheeks or at the temples with both her open palms. Silence speaks most eloquently perhaps in the amazing sequence of the Beirut children which seems to center and sum up so much of the film. On a day of cease-fire during the Israeli siege of Beirut, Mother Teresa and her nuns rescue, rapidly and efficiently, numerous seriously handicapped, spastic children who have been trapped in Moslem Beirut, their hospital deprived of essential services by the bombardment. In a silence broken only by brief snatches of talk and the occasional outcries of the children, the nuns, including Mother Teresa herself, clean, tend, and comfort the children. In one, very long camera take, one sees a severely contorted and anguished child being stroked, with steady circling motions, in absolute silence by an Indian nun until the anguished body calms and the eyes lost inward in pain open and look up, with awed awareness of his benefactress. And Mother Teresa herself moves among the children, showing as always closely individualized concern without a shred of abstract heartiness.

The film ends with a visual culmination of the leitmotif of the white-and-blue saris as Mother Teresa returns to the Mother House in Calcutta. Here, where the nuns live in extreme simplicity, there are no contrasting colors. The excitement of the nuns at her arrival conveys a kind of sparkling joy, reciprocated by her pleasure in them and her laying-on of hands as nun after nun kneels before her to be blessed by the firm touch of Mother Teresa's palms. In the film's final shot, the camera, from a height, catches a large group of nuns crowding, in orderly but excited motion, toward Mother Teresa. From this perspective, the blue borders of the saris disappear and they show entirely white. The screen lightens and becomes whiter and whiter, and the nuns of the Mother House in Calcutta with their zeal to greet Mother Teresa turn from a flock into a unified white radiance, on which *Mother Teresa* closes.

Mira Reym Binford

Reviews
The Christian Century. CIV, March 18, 1987, p. 260.
Commonweal. CXIV, February 13, 1987, p. 82.
Los Angeles Times. November 19, 1986, VI, p. 7.
National Catholic Reporter. XXIII, February 6, 1987, p. 14.
The New York Times. November 28, 1986, p. C14.
Variety. CCCXXV, November 6, 1986, p. 28.
The Wall Street Journal. January 12, 1987, p. 20.
The Washington Post. November 22, 1986, p. G8.

MY AMERICAN COUSIN

Origin: Canada
Released: 1985
Released in U.S.: 1986
Production: Peter O'Brian; released by International Spectrafilm
Direction: Sandy Wilson
Screenplay: Sandy Wilson
Cinematography: Richard Leiterman
Editing: Haida Paul
Art direction: Paul Schmidt; set decoration, Joey Morgan
Makeup: Jayne Dancose
Costume design: Philip Clarkson and Sheila Bingham
Sound: Bruce Nyznik
Music: no listing
MPAA rating: PG
Running time: 92 minutes

Principal characters:
Sandy Wilcox	Margaret Langrick
Butch Walker	John Wildman
Major Wilcox	Richard Donat
Kitty Wilcox	Jane Mortifee
Lenny McPhee	T. J. Scott
Shirley Darling	Camille Henderson
Thelma	Darsi Bailey
Lizzie	Alison Hale
Sue	Samantha Jocelyn

My American Cousin is the first Canadian, English-language, fictional feature film directed by a woman in ten years—since Joyce Wieland's *The Far Shore* (1976). It was made on a low budget—of $1.2 million—and in British Columbia, a province well removed from the mainstream of Ontario and Quebec. Yet it garnered six Genies (Canadian Academy Awards) in March, 1986, including Best Film, Best Director, Best Screenplay, Best Editing, Best Actress, and Best Actor. In the process, *My American Cousin* upset the aspirations of those connected with *Joshua Then and Now* (1985)—the most expensive Canadian film ever made, with a budget of more than eleven million dollars—and ushered in the freshest new wave of quality native productions seen in more than a decade, including *Loyalties* (1986), *The Decline of the American Empire* (1986; reviewed in this volume), *Anne Trister* (1986), and *Dancing in the Dark* (1986).

Sandy Wilson, the writer-director, has made a number of short films since

1974, and she conceived the idea for *My American Cousin* in 1982, after receiving a scriptwriting grant for another project. She was listening to a Johnny Horton hit song, "The Battle of New Orleans," on a Vancouver radio station, and the music reminded her of the summer of 1959, when her own American cousin visited the family ranch in Penticton, British Columbia. The resulting film is to a large extent autobiographical and was shot on the ranch, with the interiors filmed inside the house where she grew up. Apart from the two leads and three other actors, all the cast members were from Wilson's hometown, including her mother, sister, brother, and their children.

Like many contemporary Hollywood releases, *My American Cousin* focuses on the problems of adolescence, specifically male-female relationships, but, uncharacteristically (and like *Smooth Talk*, 1985), the film has a female protagonist and perspective, and, even more unusual, this protagonist is preteen—she is twelve years old—and the film deals with the period prior to full sexual awakening. These unusual elements, however, which may work against the film's commercial potential, are balanced by its placement in the late 1950's, which, together with the early 1960's, has emerged as a popular period for film treatment, as shown by the success of *Peggy Sue Got Married* and *Stand by Me* (both 1986 releases that are reviewed in this volume).

My American Cousin opens with an extreme long shot of the night that zooms in slowly to a house by a lake as the strains of "Some Enchanted Evening" can be heard, presumably coming from a radio. After the credits end, the film abruptly cuts to the interior of the house to introduce Sandy (Margaret Langrick), simultaneously writing in large letters in her diary and reciting, "Nothing ever happens." Parental authority is introduced through Sandy's mother, Kitty (Jane Mortifee), who berates her daughter, whom she calls Sandra, for staying awake too long. Then Sandy's voice-over recounts, "I first saw my American cousin in the golden summer of 1959." He arrives unannounced and introduces himself to his Aunt Kitty and Uncle John (Richard Donat) as Butch Walker (John Wildman). He claims that he has come to Canada for a holiday. The theme music, signifying enchantment for Sandy, is carried over by a nondiegetic piano sound track, as the scene ends with Butch noticing Sandy and one of her younger sisters peering at him from their bedroom doorways.

The next day is ushered in with the camera looking directly at the front of a bright red Cadillac framed in front of pine trees and set against a picturesque backdrop of mountains separating a bright blue lake and sky. The camera tracks right to show Sandy setting up to take a snapshot of her cousin and one of her sisters next to his car with her Brownie camera. Butch is wearing a white T-shirt and blue jeans while Sandy is dressed in red shorts and a white blouse with a floral pattern. Her other brothers and sisters arrive to spoil the intimacy of the occasion, her parents then arrive to complete the family group, and Butch obligingly immortalizes them on film.

Butch then leaves with his uncle, the "Major"—he always wears khaki—to go cherry picking, while Sandy and her sisters join their mother in the kitchen. After one of many arguments with her mother, Sandy goes for a drive with her father, who has returned from picking cherries, to her grandmother's place. Along the way, he tries to tell her the "facts of life," warning against "uncontrollable urges" exhibited by males.

Later that day, Butch meets Shirley Darling (Camille Henderson), the blonde girlfriend of a fellow cherry picker, Lenny McPhee (T. J. Scott), the strains of "Theme from a Summer Place" playing in the background. Sandy, clearly jealous of Butch turning his attention away from her when he learns of her tender age and vowing suicide, can be seen in the background walking into the lake while the camera is focused on her cousin talking to Shirley.

The next day, Sandy longs to go for a ride in Butch's car and gets her wish. They drive into town, and he reluctantly agrees to take her and three of her friends, Thelma (Darsi Bailey), Lizzie (Alison Hale), and Sue (Samantha Jocelyn)—all of whom are, to him, "ugly"—to the next town and back. All three friends wear glasses, and the four ride in the backseat of the convertible, putting on bright headscarves for protection against the wind. From their screams and laughter it is clear that they are thrilled by the experience, and they sing along to "Sea Cruise" on the car radio. The speed with which Butch is driving eventually sickens them, however, especially when he becomes involved in a race with Lenny. Nevertheless, they recover when Butch spectacularly avoids a police chase. Then they all go swimming. Butch plays with the girls being awestruck by his all-American coolness; he threatens to swim nude—leading Sandy to worry that he will get an "uncontrollable urge"—and invites Lizzie into the front seat on the drive back if she will remove her glasses. He offers Camels all around from a pack he keeps in his shirt sleeve, and then kisses Lizzie near the concession stand on Penticton beach.

Meanwhile, the Major has called Butch's parents and discovered that the teenager has run away with his mother's car. On their return, Butch and Sandy learn that they only have a few more hours together as Butch's parents will be arriving the next day. So Butch and Sandy steal away after she finds the car keys to the Cadillac that her father has confiscated. They go to the Dominion Day teen dance in Penticton, which gives Butch the opportunity to be alone with Shirley. The scene crosscuts from the young lovers, to Lenny gathering a crowd to look for them, to Sandy at the dance with her friends, to her father looking for her, all the while pop hits by groups such as The Everly Brothers and Buddy Holly and The Crickets, performed by a local band, are playing in the background. Eventually Lenny and Butch fight, and the Major separates them and sends his nephew home; Butch finds Sandy in the backseat of his Cadillac as he leaves. After they run out of gas, her romantic fantasy shattered, Sandy finally, and ironically, gets to kiss her cousin.

Sandy's desire to get away from Paradise Ranch is so great that she decides to escape with Butch the next day, packing a suitcase and placing it in the Cadillac. Meanwhile, Butch's parents have arrived. They are stereotyped as American by their coarseness and materialism—Butch's father, Al (Terence Moore), views the ranch as a potential money-making resort. Butch's parents unwittingly foil Sandy's plan, however, for when she goes to the ranch gate—which has functioned as a motif representing the possibility of her escape—and the red Cadillac arrives, it is driven by Uncle Al, thus leaving Sandy stranded. The film ends with a reprise from Sandy in voice-over telling the viewer of Lenny and Shirley's marriage, of how, thereafter, she always thought of Butch whenever she opened the gate, and that her mother was right in saying that "boys are like buses. You miss one; another will be along shortly."

My American Cousin succeeds in a number of ways. The autobiographical portrait of Sandy Wilson at twelve is beautifully realized by Margaret Langrick, and the interrelationships with her girlfriends and younger sisters are equally well conveyed. A feeling for the late 1950's is also evoked through these performances and through Butch's action and dialogue. Further, the music and the costumes accurately represent teenage tastes of the times, but these elements also work on deeper levels. The songs carry a strong emotional charge, and often they correspond to some aspect of the scene—"Sea Cruise" for the joyride, "Summertime Blues" to convey Sandy's boredom, and "Some Enchanted Evening," which returns one final time when Sandy loses her Prince Charming. Also, the color of the clothing implies an additional layer of meaning. Butch's white and blue outfit seen against the red Cadillac conjures an image of the American flag (which was also the color scheme of the Canadian flag, the Union Jack, in 1959). The girls are also seen in combinations of these colors, and here, red predominates—the swimsuits of Sandy and her friends are all variations on this primary color, and Sandy wears red lipstick during her sojourns with Butch. Perhaps the director intended an allusion here to the Canadian flag with the red maple leaf design which was introduced in the early 1960's, so that together with the more traditional, emotional association of the color with awakening sexual passion, it invokes an awakening national independence as well. Certainly, a central theme in *My American Cousin* is the inferiority that Canadians feel toward their American neighbors, who exhibit a more developed sense of themselves, and Wilson may be using color to convey this idea.

Richard Leiterman's cinematography is one of the most remarkable of the film's achievements, presenting a somewhat garish, picture-postcard view of the place and period while also displaying the world in pop art poster color as though it were seen through a young person's eyes. Both views succeed in yielding a decidedly nostalgic perspective.

The way in which Wilson's film does not come together successfully is in its mixture of acting styles. Although there is verisimilitude in the performances of all the girls, the adults are caricatured to varying degrees. In part, this might be deliberate, to continue Sandy's point of view, but it also seems that some of the adult performers are not relaxed, which lends an overall unevenness to the acting in the film. The same criticism could possibly be leveled at the narrative style of *My American Cousin*, where at times the camera is set back, filming action in long shot and extreme long shot while voices can be heard as though the characters were in close-up. This method, however, allows the viewer to take in the great natural beauty of the British Columbian landscape, which provides a different perspective from that of Sandy—who refuses to recognize her surroundings—and it is surely a directorial strategy to present an objective viewpoint in order to balance the subjective one. It is indeed no accident that at the end of the film, the adult Sandy declares that, after her father sold Paradise Ranch, she missed it more than she ever thought possible. While Wilson's writing and direction reveal an all-too-familiar modest and self-effacing young Canadian, mildly rebelling against authority and longing to be somewhere else, Leiterman's cinematography lovingly presents one of the real glories of Canada on the screen—its natural beauty. Finally, while many Canadian films can be praised for their verisimilitude, their accurate sense of time and place, and some for their style, *My American Cousin* is above all simply enjoyable.

Peter Rist

Reviews
The Canadian Forum. LXV, March, 1986, p. 40.
Cinema Canada. June, 1986, p. 30.
Macleans. XCVIII, November 4, 1985, p. 77.
Ms. XIV, December, 1985, p. 26.
The New York Times. CXXXV, August 15, 1986, p. C13.
Newsweek. CVIII, August 25, 1986, p. 63.
Seventeen. XLV, June, 1986, p. 67.
Time. CXXVIII, September 1, 1986, p. 76.
Variety. CCCXXII, April 16, 1986, p. 7.
The Wall Street Journal. CCVIII, August 21, 1986, p. 21.

MY BEAUTIFUL LAUNDRETTE

Origin: Great Britain
Released: 1985
Released in U.S.: 1986
Production: Sarah Radclyffe and Tim Bevan for Film Four International; released by Orion Classics
Direction: Stephen Frears
Screenplay: Hanif Kureishi
Cinematography: Oliver Stapleton
Editing: Mick Audsley
Art direction: Hugo Luczyc Whyhowski
Music: Ludus Tonalis
MPAA rating: R
Running time: 93 minutes

> *Principal characters:*
> Johnny . . . . Daniel Day-Lewis
> Omar . . . . Gordon Warnecke
> Nasser. . . . . Saeed Jaffrey
> Papa. . . . . Roshan Seth
> Rachel. . . . . Shirley Anne Field
> Tania . . . . Rita Wolf
> Salim. . . . . Derrick Branche
> Cherry. . . . . Souad Faress
> Bilquis . . . . Charu Bala Choksi
> Genghis . . . . Richard Graham

Two brief scenes at the start of *My Beautiful Laundrette* serve as an overture for the film's themes, atmosphere, and technique. In the first, a pile of furniture tumbles into a tenement hallway as a group of black men break in to evict two whites sleeping in a room upstairs. One of the squatters, a punk sporting a bleached blond brush cut, called Johnny (Daniel Day-Lewis), rouses his groggy friend, detains a gigantic intruder with a gesture of compliance, and scrambles out the window into the gray dawn of a London slum. Johnny then disappears from the film for more than twenty minutes. The next scene opens on the terrace of an equally dreary flat situated beneath a railroad line. Omar (Gordon Warnecke), a young Pakistani, begins the day by wringing out his father's dirty pajamas. Inside, the bedridden old man starts to pour himself a glass of vodka but then impatiently presses the bottle to his lips. Calling his son over, he chides Omar for his lugubrious bearing and wryly informs him that he is arranging a summer job for him with his wealthy brother Nasser. In the fall, his father maintains, Omar must carry on the family's intellectual heritage by enrolling at university.

That Omar and his schoolfriend Johnny will advance no further than their South London neighborhood seems a certainty arising not merely from economic oppression but also from the peculiar claustrophobia of the film's milieu. Gritty, overcast, and neon-lit, the city itself seems a perpetual interior, filtered through dirty windows or framed by storefronts and scrap heaps. Both young men wish to rise above these circumstances and seize the opportunity when Uncle Nasser (Saeed Jaffrey) promotes Omar from a car washer in his garage to manager of a decaying laundrette. Omar promptly steals a delivery from the family's cocaine connection in order to turn the dingy premises into an art deco suds palace, cunningly named Powders. Still, through it all, he remains, as his father bitterly puts it, "in the business of cleaning underpants." Nor can Johnny put his life as a street fighter behind him: He must not only play the role of bouncer at the laundrette but must also serve as Nasser's "unscrewer," forcibly evicting impoverished tenants from the slumlord's properties. Though Omar may turn a profit laundering clothes (and money) and Johnny may enjoy economic privileges denied his resentful skinhead friends, one cannot ignore the prevailing irony that neither escapes the activity in which he was first presented. *My Beautiful Laundrette* is, however, far more than a sociological treatise on life in the British underclass or an indictment of Thatcherite capitalism. Omar and Johnny are not merely business partners but lovers as well, whose improbable but wholly convincing passion survives the hostility of their separate communities. Above all, they are counterparts in cultural alienation, dual registers for the racial tensions that are at the heart of director Stephen Frear's remarkable film.

Two generations after their importation into England as menial labor, however, the Pakistani, once a romantic symbol of Britannia's might, have become entrepreneurs in a time of economic depression and inverted the colonialist formula. Uncle Nasser, a plump man of promiscuous affections and manifold appetites, has learned to "squeeze the tits of the system," supplementing his various enterprises by trading with English businessmen in drugs and pornographic tapes. When Johnny questions his eviction of a penniless black poet, Nasser summarizes the new ethic: "I'm a professional businessman, not a professional Pakistani."

A London-born Pakistani himself, screenwriter Hanif Kureishi bears witness to the loss of tradition and collapse of ideals among his fellow émigrés. The remnants of Pakistani culture that emerge are either preposterous or destructive. At home, Nasser luxuriates on silk cushions while his three daughters rub his temples and feet, but when his wife, Bilquis (Charu Bala Choksi), discovers that he keeps a mistress, Rachel (Shirley Anne Field), she concocts a potion from leaves and dead mice that causes Rachel to break out into a violent rash. Salim's wife, Cherry (Souad Faress), marvels that Omar can call a little island off the coast of Europe his home, but he, like most of his generation, has never visited the subcontinent where, Cherry proudly reports, his aristocratic relatives meet Saturday nights for bridge, bourbon, and VCR. Doe-eyed and smiling, Omar is as impervious to his aunt's deluded nationalism as he is to his father's alcoholic socialism. Once a brilliant journalist in Bombay, Papa (Roshan Seth) had been the eloquent voice of an exiled people until Omar's friends, Johnny included, began to march in neo-Fascist demonstrations against the Pakistani. Political despair and cultural dislocation led him to berate his wife, eventually driving her to suicide. Sharp-tongued and sodden, he remains an unregenerate idealist who looks to his son to atone for his own failures.

Omar is a dreamer of a different kind, having been convinced by his uncle that London abounds with money for the taking. Though he resents Johnny for breaking his father's heart, he rarely allows this to interfere with their passion or their enterprise. As a lover, he is passive yet tender; as a businessman, he is as naïve as he is amoral and self-serving. In confiscating and then selling a drug shipment that Salim sends him to collect, it never occurs to Omar that his uncle might hold him responsible. He demonstrates a similar penchant for blind risk-taking by lording it over the white toughs in the neighborhood. The boys who once beat him up in grammar school now loiter menacingly outside the laundrette. As they watch Johnny paint the exterior one day, Omar ostentatiously pays his lover for the work and receives in return a voluptuous lick on the ear.

Here, as elsewhere, Johnny's response indicates an understanding of this reversal of fortunes that is far subtler than Omar's. The lick is more than a bit of daredevil eroticism—it is a gesture that transforms the master-slave relationship into a parody of itself. Johnny is willing to serve as Omar's employee and Nasser's strongarm not merely for love but also out of guilt for his past association with the reactionary National Front. Unlike Omar, who holds expediency above racial loyalty, he still values his white friends, understands their anger, and realizes how pathetic and childlike they are under their loudmouth jeering. He seems on the verge of balancing their friendship with his love for Omar, until Salim runs down a white youth with his Mercedes, maiming him. Caught between clashing cultures, Johnny emerges as the film's surprising moral center. Though he despises Salim as a racist, he finds that he cannot remain a passive spectator when revenge-seeking whites smash the Pakistani's car and nearly beat him to death. As he tries to stop his friend Genghis (Richard Graham), the gang batters him with clubs, fists, and hobnail boots. In the film's closing scene, Omar tenderly washes his cuts, and the two splash each other with water at the laundrette, but Johnny knows that the price of this love has been estrangement from his own race through the defense of a man he hates.

If Johnny may be said to evolve, it is clear that the individuals and circumstances that surround him cannot. This sense of moral stasis is entirely a matter of design: Frears frequently urges his cast toward caricature, and his style is both antipsychological and antidramatic. The film's texture is a series of quick, startling images. Rather than building a conventionally unified narrative, Frears compresses scenes that often appear truncated and disconnected, as if the tissue of causal logic had been clipped away. Seemingly unrelated incidents are intercut, events turn unexpectedly, and characters sometimes veer into strange behavioral orbits. Papa rises from his sickbed and wanders into the laundrette at three in the morning, Nasser's rebellious daughter Tania (Rita Wolf) flashes her breasts for Omar at a family party, and Salim suddenly throws Omar to the floor and grinds his foot into his face after a drug pickup. Motivation in such instances is never explicit, and one occasionally has the disarming sense that some essential information has been left out.

The film's jagged consistency may be a result, in part, of its curious origins. Commissioned for British television's Channel 4 and shot in 16 millimeter, *My Beautiful Laundrette* was originally planned as a three-to-four-hour, sprawling family saga. In condensing this material into ninety-three minutes, Kureishi seems to have retained the story's entire skeletal structure but abbreviated its episodes. Far from distorting the script's intentions, the film's directorial technique is perfectly suited to its overriding tone. Frears's dislocations and staccato shifts maintain an ironic pitch by keeping the viewer at an emotional and psychological distance from characters who inhabit a palpable but slightly skewed world. Some of his most striking effects involve visual juxtapositions. Moments before the gala opening of "the Ritz among laundrettes," Johnny (always the sexual aggressor) and Omar make love in a darkened office in the foreground, while behind them, seen through a half-shuttered window, Nasser and Rachel waltz around gleaming washers and dryers to the music of Johann Strauss.

Though Omar and Johnny's love is clandestine and tainted by racial resentment, it is easily the most vital relationship in the film. Heterosexual relations are inevitably subordinate to the cash nexus, and women, be they mothers, daughters, or mistresses, exist only to serve the needs of men. Teenage Tania reviles her father's English mistress, Rachel, as a parasite. When the two meet at the laundrette's unveiling she cannot answer Rachel's challenge, "Whom do you live off of?" After failing to seduce both Omar and Johnny, Tania prepares to leave home, and in the film's penultimate scene the audience catches a glimpse of her standing on the train platform near Omar's apartment. The shot occurs within a stunning montage in which Nasser visits Papa to lament his estrangement from Rachel while Johnny is silently bludgeoned by his friends outside the laundrette. As Nasser spots his daughter, a train roars by—when it has passed, she is gone. Is one to understand that she has boarded, though the train never stops? Or has Tania, like Omar's mother, jumped on the tracks? It is a cultivated ambiguity typical of a film that eschews all resolutions. Tania's freedom, along with the survival of Omar and Johnny's love, remains, at best, a potential in a world where the only certainties are economic strife and racial distrust.

Philip Sicker

Reviews
Commonweal. CXIII, May 9, 1986, p. 278.
Films in Review. XXXVII, June, 1986, p. 362.
The Nation. CCXLII, April 19, 1986, p. 560.
The New Republic. CXCIV, April 7, 1986, p. 24.
New Statesman. CX, November 15, 1985 p. 33.
The New Yorker. LXII, March 10, 1986, p. 117.
Newsweek. CVII, February 24, 1986, p. 82.
Sight and Sound. LV, Winter, 1985, p. 67.
Time. CXXVII, March 17, 1986, p. 78.
Variety. CCCXX, August 21, 1986, p. 16.

MY SWEET LITTLE VILLAGE
(VESNICKO MA STREDISKOVA)

Origin: Czechoslovakia
Released: 1986
Released in U.S.: 1986
Production: Barrandov Film Studio; released by Circle Releasing Company
Direction: Jiří Menzel
Screenplay: Zdenek Sverak
Cinematography: Jaromir Sofr
Editing: Jiří Brozek
Art direction: Zbynek Hloch
Music: Jiří Šust
MPAA rating: PG
Running time: 100 minutes

Principal characters:
Otik	Janos Ban
Pavek	Marian Labuda
Skruzny	Rudolf Hrušínský
Mrs. Pavek	Milena Dvorska
Rumlena	Ladislav Zupanic
Turek	Petr Cepek
Mrs. Turek	Libuse Safrankova
Kaspar	Jan Hartl
Odvarka	Evzen Jegorov
Kunc	Oldrich Vlach

One of the foremost of the young Czech directors who came to prominence during the brief burst of creative and artistic energy known as the Prague Spring was Jiří Menzel, whose *Closely Watched Trains* (1966) won an Oscar as Best Foreign Language Film in 1967. The Prague Spring ended with the Soviet invasion in August, 1968, and Menzel was among those directors banned from the Czech film industry for the ideological content of their films. In Menzel's case, the ban was ended when he agreed to recant his earlier position, but his subsequent films have received little attention in the West.

With *My Sweet Little Village*, however, Menzel has again received the acclaim and interest that attended *Closely Watched Trains*, and the film was nominated for an Academy Award (losing to *The Assault*, 1986; reviewed in this volume, from the Netherlands). A warmly comic look at life in a small Czech village where many of the residents work for a collective farm, it tells a story as universal as the laughter it evokes; indeed, there are sentiments at work here that Frank Capra would recognize and applaud.

The story centers on two men, Pavek (Marian Labuda), a portly truck driver, and his slow-witted assistant, Otik (Janos Ban). Otik is that immediately recognizable figure, the village idiot, watched over by his neighbors and for five years instructed, chided, and tolerated by the older Pavek. After a series of mistakes on Otik's part, however, Pavek insists that he be assigned another assistant as soon as the year's harvest is over. For Otik, the news is devastating, and when the director of the company that manages the farm offers to transfer him to Prague and buy his house as a weekend vacation home, he agrees. As the fabric of village life unfolds, the film draws in subplots involving the poetic, absentminded village doctor; Pavek's son and his crush on his sister's lovely teacher; a wandering artist who catches the teacher's eye; and the love affair of one of the young company officials with another truck driver's wife. Each story is interwoven with the connecting thread of Otik's possible move to Prague and an existence stripped of the support system that makes him an integral part of village life.

The story is resolved with a heartwarming happy ending when Pavek arrives in Prague on Otik's first day of work at his new job. As Otik follows his coworkers across a bridge, trying unsuccessfully to fall into step with them as he once did with Pavek, he hears Pavek's familiar whistle. Otik returns with him to their village, and the pair resume their old routine, walking in unison down the road together, the harmony of village life restored.

The film's central theme is the interconnectedness of life in the village and the manner in which the overriding sense of community provides each character with the security of an extended family. There are few secrets in Menzel's small town, and no one—from the doctor to the charwoman—hesitates to comment on a neighbor's private life. The only inhabitants who remain largely outside the ebb and flow of village life are the "Prague weekenders"—a chic, well-to-do couple with a weekend home in the village whom the villagers themselves regard with benign indifference. The full-time inhabitants watch over one another with affection, humor, and a familial nosiness that will strike a chord with anyone familiar with life in a small town. Interestingly, this is a theme which has also found voice recently in Peter Weir's *Witness* (1985), which treats the same subject with less humor but with an equal regard for the basic human values which flourish in a close-knit community.

Menzel's view of his community is an undeniably rosy one—Peter Bogdanovich's *The Last Picture Show* (1971) presents the dark flip side of small-town life—and his village is a bucolic blend of old-fashioned values and modern socialism at work. Much of the life and work of the village is tied to the cooperative farm, providing the villagers with a common goal, while the faceless Prague crowds and the sheer size of the city are seen as a threatening contrast to the harmony of the smaller community. The local company head describes the morals of the village as "unspoilt" as he chastises the young official (who is, significantly, from Prague) for his adulterous affair, and many of the inhabitants seem almost to lead charmed lives: the doctor who survives car wreck after car wreck, the farm worker who is run over by a thresher and emerges unscathed. *My Sweet Little Village* is clearly intended to be both a very human comedy and a modern-day fable, and it is perhaps not stretching a point too far to see the village as Menzel's representation of Czechoslovakia and the depersonalized, monolithic portrayal of Prague as a stand-in for the Soviet influence that so harmed Menzel's career. (It should be noted that the United States, too, comes in for its share of satirizing as the villagers watch, in horrified fascination, an American film on television that seems to be one long car chase and gun battle.)

Yet if the film's portrait of the village is painted in glowing colors, it is a knowing and many-faceted depiction as well, touched by moments of sorrow, pettiness, and disappointment. Turek (Petr Cepek), the disagreeable driver whose wife eventually leaves him for her lover, is the closest thing the village has to a local villain, an angry, jealous man who spikes Otik's beer at the town fair and beats his wife when he discovers her infidelity. Yet the doctor, who serves as the town's whimsical sage and poet, refuses to report Turek's drunkenness on the job to the safety inspector, knowing that the driver will soon lose his wife and could not stand to lose his job as well. The film also features a startling, if halfhearted, suicide attempt by Pavek's son when his crush on his sister's teacher goes unrequited—proof that young love is painful even in Menzel's idyllic village. Additionally, there are several instances of villagers taking advantage of Otik: the above-mentioned spiking of his drink, jokes played on him by his coworkers, and the stratagems of the two lovers, who trick him into going to the cinema so that they can use his house for their trysts.

My Sweet Little Village demonstrates Menzel's sure grasp of one of the fundamental rules of comedy: The truest and best moments of humor are those which grow naturally out of the story's characters. The film's physical comedy—the doctor's car wrecks, Otik's mishaps at work—arises directly from the particular character traits of the individuals involved, giving its humor an engagingly human flavor that is lost in comedies where a series of slapstick gags are imposed on the characters. Menzel's affection for his characters, evident throughout the film, is strongest in his depiction of Otik and Pavek. Like a Czech Stan Laurel and Oliver Hardy, after whom they have clearly been patterned, the two form a wonderfully incongruous duo: Otik, tall, gangly, and slow-witted, and Pavek, short and fat, a gruff father figure, who gives a masterful rendition of that venerable comic reaction, the "slow burn." The sight of Otik alone in his modern high-rise apartment in Prague is one of the film's most touching moments, and the joyous little skip the two add to their morning walk to work after their reunion captures the unexpressed delight they feel at returning to their old routine.

The rest of the villagers form the film's supporting cast, and they are a memorable collection of personalities: the charwoman who freely offers advice during council meetings and tartly tells the traveling artist to stand up when he speaks to her; the doctor careening blithely down the country roads, too busy rhapsodizing over the beauty of his home to pay attention to his driving; the bespectacled worker run over by the thresher, posing happily by the plaster statue taken from his impression in the dirt; the self-satisfied man who has ignored warnings throughout the film about putting used matches back in the box suddenly finding his pants on fire. Together these characters and their neighbors round out the film's portrayal of village life.

My Sweet Little Village is a charming, wistful look at a way of life that contrasts sharply with the world most city-dwellers know. In his characters and the overlapping patterns that shape their daily existence, Jiří Menzel has created a community in the truest sense of the word: people bound together by ties of affection and familiarity which go beyond geographic boundary lines. The result is a thoughtful, unhurried approach to life that recognizes the inextricable ties between the good of the many and the good of the few.

Janet E. Lorenz

Reviews
Chicago Tribune. January 9, 1987, VII, p. 39.
Commonweal. CXIV, February 13, 1987, p. 82.
Films in Review. XXXVIII, April, 1987, p. 230.
Hollywood Reporter. July 22, 1986, p. 3.
Los Angeles Times. January 16, 1987, VI, p. 8.
The New York Times. January 9, 1987, p. C6.

THE NAME OF THE ROSE

Origin: West Germany, France, and Italy
Released: 1986
Released in U.S.: 1986
Production: Bernd Eichinger; released by Twentieth Century-Fox
Direction: Jean-Jacques Annaud
Screenplay: Andrew Birkin, Gerard Brach, Howard Franklin, and Alain Godard; based on the novel of the same name by Umberto Eco
Cinematography: Tonino Delli Colli
Editing: Jane Seitz
Production design: Dante Ferretti
Art direction: Giorgio Giovannini and Rainer Schaper; set decoration, Francesca Lo Schiavo
Special effects: Adriano Pischiutta
Makeup: Hasso von Hugo
Costume design: Gabriella Pescucci
Supervising historical adviser: Jacques Le Goff
Music: James Horner
MPAA rating: R
Running time: 130 minutes

> *Principal characters:*
> William of Baskerville . . . . Sean Connery
> Bernardo Gui . . . . F. Murray Abraham
> Adso of Melk . . . . Christian Slater
> Severinus . . . . Elya Baskin
> Jorge de Burgos . . . . Feodor Chaliapin, Jr.
> Ubertino de Casale . . . . William Hickey
> Abbot . . . . Michael Lonsdale
> Salvatore . . . . Ron Perlman
> Malachia. . . . . Volker Prechtel
> Remigio de Varagine . . . . Helmut Qualtinger
> Girl. . . . . Valentina Vargas
> Berengar. Michael Habeck

The Name of the Rose, the first work of fiction by a noted professor of semiotics, Umberto Eco, seems a most unlikely novel to have become a runaway best-seller, with some four million copies sold internationally since its original publication in Italian in 1980. Some five hundred pages long, Eco's imaginative tour de force drew on his medieval learning, his fascination with language and Christian dialectic at a period poised on the threshold of Renaissance rationalism. It is also, however, a murder-mystery story set in a fourteenth century monastery in northern Italy riven by dogmatic casuistry. The tension of the book lies mostly in the threats to the monastic community generated by the semirepressed sexual needs of certain of its inmates and by the investigative agents of the all-powerful Inquisition, for the secret recesses of the monastery's renowned library appear to have become the source for a variety of heretical interests. A visiting English Franciscan monk, William of Baskerville, a former Inquisitor, is prevailed upon by the abbot to investigate the mystery of why a succession of murders is taking place at the monastery at the time of his arrival.

When Eco's novel was published in French translation in 1982, it caught the eye of maverick director Jean-Jacques Annaud and his producer-agent, Gerard Lebovici. They acquired the film rights. In March, 1984, Lebovici was shot in Paris, but Annaud, already heavily committed to the production, was able to obtain the financial backing of the young German producer Bernd Eichinger, the project by then climbing to a commitment of some twenty million dollars. Eichinger, both as producer and distributor, was used to the unusual; he had been, for example, producer of Hans-Jürgen Syberberg's *Hitler, a Film from Germany* (1977) and the distributor of Edgar Reitz's *Heimat* (1984) and Annaud's own *Quest for Fire* (1982), a study of an advanced human tribe that lived in prehistoric times and its discovery of the secret of making fire. Annaud, a student of medieval history, put the script of *The Name of the Rose* through some fifteen revisions, working with two French writers, Alain Godard (who had collaborated with Annaud before) and Gerard Brach (the notable scriptwriter who had worked for Roman Polanski); Andrew Birkin, a British writer previously affiliated with David Puttnam; and an American writer, Howard Franklin. Eco's prolix but fascinating study had to be rendered by these writers into a gothic-style horror film, a mystery story tracing who did the murders and why.

The year is 1327, and the monastery, a massive Benedictine edifice, is isolated in the mountains of northern Italy, border territory between northern Europe, center of medievalism, and central Italy, birthplace of Renaissance art and thinking. William of Baskerville (Sean Connery), a medieval Sherlock Holmes, is accompanied by his novice, sixteen-year-old Adso of Melk (Christian Slater), in both novel and film narrator of the story as recollected in his old age; they arrive at the monastery for a high-level conference to determine church policy. The abbot (Michael Lonsdale), however, has a more immediate concern—the investigation of the recent, violent death of a brilliant young illuminator, which has filled the neurotic monks with fear. He begs William, now celebrated (or notorious) for his quick and penetrating mind, to investigate the death, which is almost immediately followed by a second, the victim in this instance a translator from the Greek. William, grave, learned, skeptical, but in his amused, restrained way worldly-wise, interrogates Severinus (Elya Baskin), herbalist and anatomist, Malachia (Volker Prechtel), supervisor of the scriptorium, and the aged Jorge de Burgos (Feodor Chaliapin, Jr.), forbidder of laughter, as it is a sign of possession by the Devil. Meanwhile, at night, the handsome, innocent Adso, wandering alone, is seduced by a village girl (Valentina Vargas), who climbs often to the monastery to offer the more lascivious of the brethren sex in return for scraps of food.

By the time of the arrival of William's former antagonist, senior inquisitor Bernardo Gui (F. Murray Abraham), William has become convinced that the clue to the murders—which increase to three when the homosexually avid assistant librarian, Berengar (Michael Habeck), is found drowned—lies in the secret, upper library housed in the monastery's massive tower, entrance to which has been forbidden William by the abbot. At night, William and Adso manage to acquire access to the tower; there they find an astonishing labyrinth of stairways and rooms where a great collection of ancient works, many thought irretrievably lost, are hidden away. Bernardo, intent on rooting out the least suspicion of heresy, begins his own investigations and catches a piteous hunchback monk, Salvatore (Ron Perlman), with the peasant girl; he regards both as possessed by the Devil. Along with Remigio de Varagine (Helmut Qualtinger), the cellarer, who admits to possession in order to escape confession under torture, they are condemned to be burned at the stake. William finally solves the mystery of the murders in the library before it is consumed by fire, just as the pyres are being lit outside to consume the bodies of the condemned. The monastery and its precious manuscripts are destroyed, including Aristotle's lost study of comedy, root of the trouble in the library. The climax, simplified and romantically melodramatized for the film, involves the death of Gui, chased away by the angry villagers when the monastery is burning, and the escape of the girl from the fire.

The film is subtitled a "palimpsest" of Eco's novel; a palimpsest is a manuscript page the initial text of which has been erased and the page then reused—the word therefore implying a "reprocessing" of the novel in a new and filmlike form. What inevitably happens is that William's seven-day investigation of the murders becomes the hard spine of the action, while the architectural beauty of the monastery, contrasted with the obsessive, often insane preoccupations of its inhabitants, provides the rich flesh of the film. All the key interiors were finally shot, after a search involving some three hundred European abbeys, in Kloster Eberbach, a twelfth century Cistercian edifice near Frankfurt, which has remained virtually unchanged for eight hundred years. The massive exterior was a film set built under the supervision of production designer Dante Ferretti on a hilltop near Rome. This set, said to be the largest exterior set constructed in Europe since those built for Joseph L. Mankiewicz's *Cleopatra* (1963), was destroyed by fire for the film's climax. Tonino Delli Colli (Italian director of cinematography for the period films of Pier Paolo Pasolini) was inspired by Annaud to study the mood lighting of more northerly painters, such as Jan Steen and Rembrandt, and also to capture some of the Romantic melodrama of Gustave Doré's nineteenth century engravings and the painterly qualities in the work of Michelangelo da Caravaggio and the French seventeenth century painter Georges de La Tour. The use of wide-aperture lenses allowed Delli Colli to capture the magnificent interiors of the monastery while faithfully evoking the limited lighting of medieval dwellings.

The manuscripts and other major properties and furniture were produced by craftsmen in Italy under the guidance of medieval historian Jacques Le Goff; close-up shots of the illuminated manuscripts in Latin, Greek, and Arabic are a notable decorative feature of the film. Even more striking are the close-ups of the carefully made-up grotesque features of the monks whom William has individually to confront; they have the visages of medieval gargoyles. In marked contrast is Sean Connery's handsome, thoughtful face, silver-bearded, eminently sane and ironic, the rational man quietly contending with manifestations of the irrational. Connery plays William in an entirely modern style, his vocal inflections clear and insistent against the repressed hysteria of the opposing monks. F. Murray Abraham, however, is less effective as the dread inquisitor, lacking the depth and menace demanded by such a role.

The film, with all of its scholarly and artistic accoutrements, remains a superior and original work in gothic horror, occasionally cheapened by overdwelling on the flaying of beasts and the bloody dismemberment of corpses. It is a film both involving and haunting in its extraordinary beauty and saved from its occasional excesses by the sardonic humor of Sean Connery's restrained and masterly performance.

Roger Manvell

Reviews
Christian Science Monitor. LXXVIII, September 26, 1986, p. 25.
Commonweal. CXIII, October 24, 1986, p. 553.
Films in Review. XXXVII, December, 1986, p. 620.
Los Angeles Times. September 24, 1986, VI, p. 1.
The New Republic. CXCV, October 6, 1986, p. 24.
The New York Times. CXXXVI, September 24, 1986, p. C21.
Newsweek. CVIII, September 29, 1986, p. 62.
Time. CXXVIII, October 13, 1986, p. 107.
The Wall Street Journal. CCVIII, September 25, 1986, p. 28.
The Washington Post. September 27, 1986, p. C5.

'NIGHT, MOTHER

Production: Alan Greisman and Aaron Spelling for Universal
Direction: Tom Moore
Screenplay: Marsha Norman; based on her play of the same name
Cinematography: Stephen Katz
Editing: Suzanne Pettit
Art direction: Jackson De Govia
Music: David Shire
MPAA rating: PG-13
Running time: 96 minutes

Principal characters:
Jessie Cates.........................Sissy Spacek
Thelma (Mama) Cates ....Anne Bancroft

This remarkable film details the final hour and a half of the life of Jessie Cates (Sissy Spacek), from the moment she tells her mother that she is going to commit suicide until the moment she carries out her promise. It is a film that shows a human being at a moment of decision: to end a life without freedom, without purpose, without hope. Equally important, it is a film in which a mother becomes conscious for the first time of the reality, the individuality of her offspring. Devastating in its carefully orchestrated and inexorable journey from decision to fulfillment, the film is an adaptation of the 1983 Pulitzer Prize-winning Broadway play of the same title by Marsha Norman, who also wrote the screenplay for the film. Sissy Spacek, a four-time Academy Award nominee and an Oscar winner in 1980 for her portrayal of Loretta Lynn in *Coal Miner's Daughter*, personally requested the role of Jessie on film; with the addition of Anne Bancroft, one of the world's most respected and versatile actresses, in the role of Mama, the film version becomes a cinematic record of the ideal stage performance, with the added advantage of the camera's eye.

Given the tendency of contemporary stage plays to deal with small casts and single interior sets, it is often difficult to transform the dramatic core of the work for the screen without damaging the intimate and enclosed ambience of the original. With *'night, Mother*, the problem is exacerbated by the central character's social isolation; to give the camera free play in Jessie's world would be to relieve the very tensions that precipitate the dramatic conflict. Thus, Tom Moore and Marsha Norman's decision to keep the entire action inside the "pressure cooker" of the Cates house (with the exception of one or two scenes on the lawn, seen through the doorway) allows the story to unfold naturally; the film takes place in real time, with virtually no camera movement other than follow shots, and the cuts are seamless. What has been lost in cinematic flexibility and variety is made up for with intimate closeups and selective editing, giving visual attention to detail in a way not available to the stage experience while maintaining the "present tense" of the stage's ability to parallel stage time with real (audience) time.

On the surface, the subject of *'night, Mother* is suicide: Jessie Cates, divorced and abandoned by her husband and delinquent teenage son, has moved in with her mother, Thelma (whom she calls "Mama"), some years before the evening of the film's opening. This evening, however, is different from all the others on which Jessie has taken care of her loquacious and shallow-minded mother; calmly, Jessie informs Mama that she plans to commit suicide that very evening. The film is taken up with Mama's desperate attempts to talk Jessie out of shooting herself with her father's pistol, a carefully planned act of choice. Using every device she can think of, Mama cajoles, threatens, pleads, reminisces, and offers compromise and change to Jessie. Jessie's resolve, however, reflected in the meticulous preparations she has been making over the past months and in the check-off list of things to do before dying, will not be swayed. When the time comes, Jessie whispers, " 'night, Mother," and locks herself in her room. As Mama pounds on the door, crying and pleading, a single shot is heard. The stage direction in the play reads, "And we hear a shot, and it sounds like an answer, it sounds like No."

In the course of the play it becomes clear that Jessie has had her choices taken away from her since childhood, partly by domineering parents, partly through a willingness to subsume her own personality under the demands of others, partly from ignorance about herself. For example, Jessie is enraged to learn that she has been having epileptic seizures since childhood, but her parents never told her about them. "That was mine to know, Mama, not yours," Jessie says. As the evening progresses, the camera follows Jessie from room to room as she makes final arrangements, filling candy dishes, packing clothes, and instructing her mother on the everyday chores of staying alive; the viewer learns about her husband Cecil, who deserted her, her son Ricky, who stole from her, her brother Dawson, who judged and censored her, her sister-in-law Loretta, who will have to care for Mama after Jessie's death, and especially her mother, who has taken her for granted, using her like a servant, never seeing her as anything more than a possession. "You're my child," says Mama, and Jessie answers, "I'm what became of your child." In the final anguished scene, Mama admits, "Jessie, child . . . forgive me. I thought you were mine."

It is this deeper theme, then, that makes *'night, Mother* universal in its impact: Humanity shares with Jessie a sense of anguish, forlornness, and despair over being alive without meaning. Jessie's tragedy is not that she does not see enough but that she sees too much, she sees into the meaninglessness of existence behind the disguise of everyday activity. She views her suicide as an act of will, something that will work, something that will irrevocably testify to her ability to choose: "No, Mama. *This* is how I have my say. This is how I say what I thought about it *all* and I say no. To Dawson and Loretta and the Red Chinese and epilepsy and Ricky and Cecil and you. And me. And hope. I say no!"

Director Tom Moore also directed the play on Broadway in 1983, when it was honored with the Pulitzer Prize. Working on his first film, and coming from a stage-directing background, Moore filmed the scenes in sequence, thus affording the two actresses the opportunity to sustain a high emotional level from day to day without the disjunctions of out-of-sequence shooting. Anne Bancroft's Mama, possibly the finest screen role in her career, is both entertaining and unfeeling, fast-talking and superficial, the portrait of a woman awakening to her own insensitivity. In the last shot of the film, she clutches her saucepan to her breast like a child as she waits for the outside world to intrude on this last, and only, moment of intimacy between herself and her daughter. Sissy Spacek's portrayal of Jessie brings the determination of the quiet character to life, so that she finally convinces Mama and the audience that her decision is in fact her own, and the right one.

The film received excellent reviews but was withdrawn from general distribution when the producers were reluctant to spend the advertising dollars necessary for it to find its audience. It remains as a masterpiece of characterization for both Bancroft and Spacek, and it is possibly the most successful of many recent attempts to transfer the small-cast, single-set play onto the large screen.

Thomas J. Taylor

Reviews
Commonweal. CXIII, September 12, 1986, p. 471.
Films in Review. XXXVII, November, 1986, p. 548.
Glamour. XVII, December, 1986, p. 30.
Los Angeles Times. September 12, 1986, VI, p. 1.
Ms. XV, October, 1986, p. 20.
The New Republic. CXCV, October 13, 1986, p. 26.
New York. XIX, September 22, 1986, p. 157.
The New York Times. CXXXV, September 12, 1986, p. C7.
Newsweek. CVIII, September 22, 1986, p. 81.
Time. CXXVIII, October 6, 1986, p. 94.
USA Today. CXV, November, 1986, p. 94.
Variety. CCCXXIV, September 10, 1986, p. 18.
The Wall Street Journal. CCVIII, September 11, 1986, p. 28.

OTELLO

Origin: Italy and the Netherlands
Released: 1986
Released in U.S.: 1986
Production: Menahem Golan and Yoram Globus; released by Cannon Group
Direction: Franco Zeffirelli
Screenplay: Adapted from the libretto by Arrigo Boito; based on the play *Othello* by William Shakespeare
Cinematography: Ennio Guarnieri
Editing: Peter Taylor and Franca Silvi
Production design: Franco Zeffirelli
Art direction: Gianni Quaranta; set decoration, Bruno Carlino and Stefano Paltrinieri
Music direction: Lorin Maazel
Music: Giuseppe Verdi
MPAA rating: PG
Running time: 122 minutes

> *Principal characters:*
> Otello .... Plácido Domingo
> Desdemona...................... Katia Ricciarelli
> Iago .... Justino Diaz
> Emilia........................... Petra Malakova
> Cassio .... Urbano Barberini
> Lodovico .... Massimo Foschi
> Montano.......................... Edwin Francis
> Roderigo.......................... Sergio Nicolai
> Brabanzio .... Remo Remotti
> Doge .... Antonio Pierfederici

Franco Zeffirelli, who has a reputation for creating elaborate, richly detailed (some will say overproduced) work for both the operatic stage and the cinema, has designed and directed a sumptuous version of *Otello*. From the drenching rain of the opening scene to the final overhead shot of the dead Otello (Plácido Domingo) and Desdemona (Katia Ricciarelli), there are many beautiful and striking images. One such image is that of Iago (Justino Diaz) singing his "Credo" in a dazzlingly lit chapel, starkly empty except for an eerie Gothic crucifix, which hangs high in its center. Far above the crucifix is a skylight through which shafts of light play tricks on the eye, lending the room an infinite variety of perspectives.

The fact that Zeffirelli designs his own productions speaks of the high priority he gives to design. Indeed, he began his career as a stage designer, working in opera with Luchino Visconti, and many of Zeffirelli's choices as a director result, partly at least, from his instincts as a designer. There are magnificent rugs, tapestries, art objects, opulent period furniture, and doors wrought in intricately patterned openwork. During the Otello-Desdemona love duet, flashbacks to Desdemona's house when she was being wooed by Otello and to the palatial court where the Doge (Antonio Pierfederici) endorsed Otello's marital claim to Desdemona are included not only for the cinematic purpose of opening up the stagebound action but also, perhaps, to provide Zeffirelli the opportunity to display two additional lavish rooms. The flashback to the court is, in fact, potentially confusing. It does not take place in Giuseppe Verdi's opera, and the viewer who does not know William Shakespeare's play on which the opera is based is not likely to understand shots of Brabanzio (Remo Remotti), Desdemona's father, looking forlorn over the Doge's verdict.

The story, which involves principally Otello, Iago, and Desdemona, was immortalized by William Shakespeare in his early seventeenth century dramatization of a mid-sixteenth century Italian novella by "Il Cinzio" (Giambattista Giraldi) and has, since that time, inspired adaptations in the forms of opera and ballet. Gioacchino Rossini's 1819 operatic version was eclipsed by Verdi's masterwork, which was performed for the first time in Milan in 1887. The tragic tale of the Venetian Moor, who is convinced of his wife's infidelity by the lies and machinations of a military subordinate, is one of powerful emotions gone out of control.

The story's potential to move the viewer, in both Shakespeare's play and Verdi's opera, depends to a great extent on the portrayal of Otello. The character must have great range: He must possess heroic stature yet be convincingly unsophisticated in the ways of the Venetian society for which he leads an army; he must be mighty enough to keep brawling soldiers in check and to subdue an enemy in combat yet extraordinarily tender in his love for his fair Venetian wife, Desdemona. When Laurence Olivier decided to play Othello for the National Theatre's 1963-1964 season, despite his reputation as one of the great voices of the classical theater, he did vocal exercises over a period of months and sought help from a coach to achieve the rich bass sound he considered essential for the role. It is true that an actor essaying the role in the play has Shakespeare's magnificent verse to assist him while in the opera there is Verdi's glorious music. Yet the task is formidable. Zeffirelli's choice of a performer to portray Otello was a crucial one. Even those who tend to disagree with several of Zeffirelli's other directorial choices will find it difficult to fault his selection of Plácido Domingo.

What makes Domingo's feat so remarkable is that he is not only the foremost singer of *Otello* (with the possible exception of Canadian tenor Jon Vickers) since the 1960's but also one of the best actors to play the role.

Under the scrutiny of Ennio Guarnieri's frequently close-up camera, Domingo's portrayal of pain, jealousy, and rage is consistently convincing. One typically powerful sequence begins when, shortly after Iago has convinced him that Desdemona is disloyal, Otello sees her enter the room and has a renewed faith in her innocence, only to have that faith crushed when she begins to plead on behalf of Cassio (Urbano Barberini), the very man whom he suspects as Desdemona's paramour, for reinstatement as Otello's lieutenant. Later, as Desdemona is singing to envoys from Venice of her grief at Otello's inexplicable abuse, Otello separates himself from the throng and wanders around like a trapped animal; as he hears her heartrending plea, one can see his grief, his regret, his love for her. Then he sees Cassio kneel to help her and his rage is instantly sparked. Olivier himself has stated that he envies the exceptional accomplishment of Domingo's performance, which succeeds in moving audiences, making them care about the man Otello.

Zeffirelli, like certain of his compatriots—including Federico Fellini and Luchino Visconti—has demonstrated skill at casting for the cinema. Zeffirelli's well-publicized search for two teenagers to play the leads in his film *Romeo and Juliet* (1968) resulted in one of the most well-received cinematic adaptations of a Shakespearean drama. His selection of principal performers for *Otello* was perhaps more difficult because of the need to find outstanding singing actors who would look right for the camera, but he succeeded, for the cast makes a potentially melodramatic and difficult tale credible and often deeply moving. Katia Ricciarelli makes a beautiful Desdemona, joyous and glowing in her love during the early scenes, and, later, touchingly vulnerable. Justino Diaz as Iago is quite impressive in his display of authority and vitality as well as the intensity of evil with which he pursues his hell-bent course. Also noteworthy is the performance of Urbano Barberini as Cassio, although he must be judged only for his acting and lip-synching, since the role is sung by tenor Ezio Di Cesare. Cassio's fairness and youthful visage are the perfect foil for the dark, hulking, middle-aged Otello. One can understand how Otello might begin to question his ability to hold onto his fair Venetian wife as he observes her in friendly discourse with Cassio. They appear comfortable within the same cultural sphere, while Otello is clearly the outsider. He becomes a ready target for Iago's malignant plot.

Still, there have been and there will be objections to certain directorial choices. It would be impossible to satisfy the contradictory demands of the musical purists, the opera fans, the devotees of Shakespeare's play, and, finally, those who would advocate indifference to the concerns of all the above groups for cinematic purposes. For example, the film begins with Verdi's famous opening chord, but it is partially obliterated by the sounds of a realistic storm and the crashing of waves. This opening is typical of Zeffirelli's bold style, which some critics regard as heavy-handed.

In the past, Zeffirelli has often been criticized for his sentimentality. In Zeffirelli's remake of *The Champ* (1979), for example, Ricky Schroder probably sets a record for sustained, profuse weeping on-screen. The fact that he plays a young boy who has just lost his father, to whom he was deeply attached, makes the display of emotion understandable. In *Otello*, however, to see Cassio, who is not a boy but a soldier in Otello's command, weeping profusely over the deaths of his general and the general's wife, is a bit disconcerting. In the same scene, Zeffirelli cuts to repeated shots of Lodovico (Massimo Foschi), the leader of the delegation from Venice, looking pityingly toward Otello and the dead Desdemona and then slowly away, overcome with what is meant to be unspeakable grief. The powerful performances of Domingo and Ricciarelli do not need the assistance of these devices, especially the false echo of Lodovico's grief.

Another directorial choice likely to arouse discussion is a scene in which Iago is attempting to stir Otello's jealous rage. In this scene, the viewer sees only the obscene picture Iago puts into Otello's mind, which is that of a naked and reclining Cassio lusting for Desdemona. The viewer who is unfamiliar with the story might be confused and think that Cassio indeed desires the general's wife, but in neither Shakespeare's play nor Verdi's opera does Cassio harbor such feelings. Further, Shakespearean purists are likely to object to the scene in which Otello kills Iago with a spear, an event that happens in neither the play nor the opera. In both, Iago is captured but lives on.

Nevertheless, when one considers the fundamental difficulty of translating the melodramatic and overblown medium of grand opera to the realistic medium of film, Zeffirelli's remarkable achievement is clear. When Otello makes his triumphant way onto the island of Cyprus carried on the shoulders of his adoring soldiers, accompanied by Verdi's rousing music and the praise of the chorus, Zeffirelli achieves an integration of visual and aural elements that sweeps away all tendencies to analyze and question—there is only deeply felt emotion. With *Otello* added to *The Taming of the Shrew* (1967), *Romeo and Juliet*, and *La Traviata* (1982), Zeffirelli has consolidated his reputation as one of the preeminent adapters of Shakespearean and operatic masterpieces to the medium of cinema.

Cono Robert Marcazzo

Reviews
Christian Century. CIII, October 22, 1986, p. 920.
Films and Filming. Number 384, September, 1986, p. 39.
Films in Review. XXXVII, November, 1986, p. 554.
Los Angeles Times. September 19, 1986, VI, p. 1.

The New Republic. CXCV, October 6, 1986, p. 24.
The New York Times. CXXXVI, September 12, 1986, p. C4.
Opera News. LI, December 6, 1986, p. 62.
Philadelphia Magazine. LXXVII, November, 1986, p. 71.
Time. CXXVIII, October 6, 1986, p. 94.
World Press Review. XXXIII, May, 1986, p. 57.

PARTING GLANCES

Production: Yoram Mandel and Arthur Silverman for Rondo Productions; released by Cinecom
Direction: Bill Sherwood
Screenplay: Bill Sherwood
Cinematography: Jacek Laskus
Editing: Bill Sherwood
Production design: John Loggia
Art direction: Daniel Haughey and Mark Sweeney; set decoration, Anne Mitchell
Makeup: Franco
Costume design: Sylvia Heisel
Sound: Scott Breindel
Music: Frédéric François Chopin, Johannes Brahms, Johann Strauss, Wolfgang Amadeus Mozart, and Bronski Beat
MPAA rating: R
Running time: 90 minutes

Principal characters:
Michael......................Richard Ganoung
Robert ....John Bolger
Nick ....Steve Buscemi
Joan............................Kathy Kinney
Peter ....Adam Nathan
Betty ....Yolande Bavan
Cecil..............................Patrick Tull
Douglas ....Richard Wall
Sarah..........................Kristin Moneagle
Klaus..........................Theodore Ganger
Liselotte ....Nada

Parting Glances was perhaps the most unexpected film success of 1986. The debut feature of previously unknown director/writer/editor Bill Sherwood, the ultralow-budget film refracted a typically sentimental story through an uncompromising gay sensibility. It was also the first American theatrical release to integrate a potentially off-putting Acquired Immune Deficiency Syndrome (AIDS) theme into its narrative and, on top of that, to take a jaundiced, sharply satirical view of the killer virus in the process.

The project, clearly, was fraught with commercial pitfalls. By relying, however, on a well-modulated combination of sharp dialogue, quirky humor, and naturalistic performances and cinematography, Sherwood and his un-

familiar cast created a warm and believable character-oriented piece resonant with complex emotions and a precisely observed social context. Even
on the occasions when it flirts with mawkishness or cliché, *Parting Glances*
never seems exploitative or contrived.

Robert (John Bolger), an athletic and handsome fellow who works for an
international hunger relief organization, has been living in a Manhattan apartment with the more intelligent and sensitive Michael (Richard
Ganoung), an editor. It is the day before Robert is to be transferred to a
post in Africa, and though they make love and josh around, Michael is
noticeably more upset about the move than Robert.

Michael buys a Mozart album at a record store where a handsome young
clerk, Peter (Adam Nathan), wangles an invitation from him to Robert's
surprise going-away party that night. The album is a gift for Nick (Steve
Buscemi), a pop songwriter and Michael's former lover. Nick is dying of
AIDS, and Michael visits and cooks for him regularly, gently forcing a
macrobiotic diet down the nihilistic, sarcastically witty Nick's throat.

That evening, Michael and Robert attend a goodbye dinner at the home
of Robert's boss, Cecil (Patrick Tull), a pretentious, middle-aged closet
homosexual, and his Caribbean wife, Betty (Yolande Bavan). After the
meal, Betty gets Michael alone and expresses her sympathy over his
impending abandonment, convinced the whole while that Cecil does not
know that the young men are gay. In another room, out of earshot of his
blissfully unaware wife, Cecil recounts some of his own homosexual escapades to an amused Robert.

In the cab on the way home, Robert confesses to Michael that he
requested the African transfer, partly because their relationship was becoming predictable. He also indicates a repressed jealousy over Michael's concern for Nick. Michael is hurt, but that does not stop him from making love
with Robert when they arrive home.

The men get dressed and visit Joan (Kathy Kinney), a struggling artist
friend. Her loft is the site of the surprise party and is filled with Robert's
gay acquaintances, old college friends, and some colorful weirdos, among
them Klaus (Theodore Ganger) and his tattoo-torsoed wife, Lisolette
(Nada), German performance artists. Peter is there, constantly making suggestive advances toward Michael. All Michael is interested in, however, is
sharing his conflicting feelings with the sympathetic, understanding Joan.
He confesses to her that he has always loved Nick more than Robert, although he has never told Nick that.

Nick comes to the party, sneering that he dragged himself out of bed only
to say goodbye to Robert. He fails to cross paths with Robert but has
bizarre encounters with everyone else, such as Klaus (who wants Nick to appear in a performance piece made up entirely of terminally ill participants)
and Peter (who expresses an amoral worldview that is part abject material-

ism and part sensual abandon and concludes with the dream of becoming a doctor—Nick accuses the young man of being a Republican).

Nick leaves, and the party ends soon after that. Extremely drunk, Michael, Peter, and a friend head for a gay disco, where a shirtless Robert calls the sleeping Nick to say goodbye. Half awake, Nick has a vision of a friend (Daniel Haughey) who died from AIDS complications, wearing a suit of armor. The shade tells Nick to hang onto life as long as he can, because Heaven is a real bore.

After taking a cab home at dawn, Michael runs into the park with the apartment keys. Robert pursues him; if he does not leave soon, he will miss his plane. They have a fight, primarily over Nick. Robert finally admits that he thinks that Michael should spend more time with Nick before Nick dies and that he is leaving to get out of the way.

Michael sees Robert to the airport. In the waiting room, Robert is surprised to encounter Cecil, who has abandoned his wife in favor of checking out the young men of Sri Lanka. Michael stops off at Nick's apartment on the way home to tell Nick how much he loves him. Back at his own apartment, Michael receives a phone call from Nick, who has gone out to Long Island. Nick sounds suicidal.

Michael frantically calls for an air taxi. As he is about to leave, Robert enters the apartment, saying he has changed his mind and will not go to Africa. Michael tells Robert about Nick's dilemma, kisses him, and rushes out the door.

Michael flies to Long Island. He finds Nick standing on the beach, feeling fine; Nick just wanted to see how serious Michael was about still being in love with him. Nick asks Michael to go on a trip with him, then spins Michael—his eyes closed and one arm outstretched—around like a human compass magnet, to determine where they will go.

Parting Glances is fundamentally an old-fashioned romantic triangle story with a have-your-cake-and-eat-it-too ending tacked on. It is a conclusion which perhaps is possible only in a gay love story (a happy ending to any heterosexual threesome would inevitably leave dangling questions about parental claims to any resulting offspring). It is also a cunning statement on the differences between physical and emotional love. It is quite apparent to everyone why Michael finds the dashing, athletic Robert attractive; it is equally apparent that Nick has the much more interesting, intelligent, and seductive personality, not to mention the vulnerability his disease engenders. Since Michael is not, therefore, going to have sex with Nick again, he has to learn to separate his lust from his affection, something more people (whether homosexual or heterosexual) than would care to admit do every day.

This is probably a bit unfair to Robert, reducing him as it does to little more than sex object. It also negates his initial reason for wanting to leave

Michael, however: that the relationship was becoming predictable. There is nothing predictable about never being sure of your lover's true feelings. That, it seems, combined with a desire to settle down (Robert certainly has the potential to be a part of Michael's life long after Nick is gone) and a sense of gay solidarity over the AIDS crisis, is what brings Robert back from the airport.

The film's key moment is the scene in which the drunk, jealous, and somewhat confused Robert calls Nick from the disco. He wants to confess that he understands the situation thoroughly and that he would perhaps emulate Michael's behavior if he were in his shoes (too drunk and, maybe, inarticulate to say that, Robert simply tells Nick that he will write). He tells Michael as much the next morning, and when he returns from the airport to see Michael rushing out to save Nick, Robert's concern is instantly focused on Nick's predicament.

This uplifting suppression of personal sexual politics in favor of a united front against the disease (and the panic it has created in society at large) is *Parting Glances'* true claim to greatness. There are numerous reasons for enjoying the film as sheer entertainment, however, chief among them Buscemi's bravura performance as Nick, who is so quick and caustic and full of nervous energy that he makes all the other characters appear to be the ones on death's doorstep. Then there is Sherwood and cinematographer Jacek Laskus' uninflected, highly accurate portrayal of the SoHo art scene milieu, which they subtly play for both laughs and riveting social commentary.

Finally, there is Sherwood's astounding ear for specific/universal dialogue and his dead-on ability with actors. Aside from Nick, practically every character in the film is a gay stereotype, yet Sherwood invests them all with such well-observed habits, fantasies, and compassion—in short, so much convincing humanity—that there is never a question of offensiveness. *Parting Glances* deftly appropriates some of the cinema's most manipulative (and beloved) conventions to fashion a story that is timely, emotionally honest, and wickedly entertaining.

Robert Strauss

Reviews

Chicago Tribune. March 14, 1986, VII, p. 30.
Los Angeles Times. March 6, 1986, VI, p. 11.
Macleans. XCIX, April 21, 1986, p. 75.
The Nation. CCXLII, March 8, 1986, p. 283.
The New York Times. February 19, 1986, p. C21.
Newsweek. CVII, June 9, 1986, p. 80.

Variety. CCCXXII, January 29, 1986, p. 19.
The Village Voice. February 25, 1986, p. 58.
The Washington Post. March 15, 1986, p. B7.
Washingtonian. XXI, April, 1986, p. 70.

PEGGY SUE GOT MARRIED

Production: Paul R. Gurian for Rastar; released by Tri-Star Pictures
Direction: Francis Coppola
Screenplay: Jerry Leichtling and Arlene Sarner
Cinematography: Jordan Cronenweth
Editing: Barry Malkin
Production design: Dean Tavoularis
Art direction: Alex Tavoularis
Special effects: Larry Cavanaugh
Makeup: E. Thomas Case
Costume design: Theadora Van Runkle
Choreography: Toni Basil
Sound: Richard Bryce Goodman
Music: John Barry
MPAA rating: PG-13
Running time: 101 minutes

Principal characters:
Peggy Sue Bodell	Kathleen Turner
Charlie Bodell	Nicolas Cage
Richard Norvik	Barry Miller
Carol Heath	Catherine Hicks
Maddy Nagle	Joan Allen
Michael Fitzsimmons	Kevin J. O'Connor
Evelyn Kelcher	Barbara Harris
Jack Kelcher	Don Murray
Elizabeth Alvorg	Maureen O'Sullivan
Barney Alvorg	Leon Ames
Delores Dodge	Lisa Jane Persky
Rosalie Testa	Lucinda Jenney
Beth Bodell	Helen Hunt

Long a staple of popular fiction and of film, time travel blends quite readily with nostalgia and the classic, seductive notion of "If I knew then what I know now, would things have turned out any differently?" These are the key ingredients of *Peggy Sue Got Married*, the latter—and primary—element receiving the generally serious approach it deserves, though leavened with considerable warmth and some humor. The film also served as a rather odd "comeback" project for director Francis Coppola, whose work usually occupies a far larger and more technically ambitious canvas.

Peggy Sue Bodell (Kathleen Turner), now in her early forties, has reared a family, built her own business, and been deserted by her philandering husband, Charlie (Nicolas Cage), the high school sweetheart she married at age eighteen. The cumulative unhappiness and disappointments of her life are closing in at the worst possible moment—as she prepares to attend the twenty-five-year reunion of her high school class. Despite the uncomfortable possibility of seeing Charlie there, she decides to attend the reunion, nervously wearing her silver prom dress of all those years ago.

Her appearance, particularly in that dress, seems almost to defy the years, even as she is surrounded at the reunion by photographic enlargements from the yearbook, memories, comparisons and contrasts of the people she knew then with their adult counterparts. Richard Norvik (Barry Miller) has made the most startling transformation: Disdained back then as the class bookworm—by everyone except Peggy Sue—he has become a self-assured, computer industry multimillionaire. Peggy Sue and Richard are designated the queen and king of this gala affair.

Called on for a speech, Peggy Sue stammers out a few words before fainting dead away (the viewer ultimately learns that her spell was a potentially serious cardiac incident), thus leading into the film's elegant time transitions. She wakes up in the same high school gym—in 1960—apparently having passed out while giving blood in a school blood drive. It is Peggy Sue's adult consciousness, however, that now resides in her teenage self. Naturally, her shock, disorientation, and disbelief are extreme, and, even as she goes through the motions of trying to cope with this bizarre situation, her first theory is that she has died. Her strange behavior, adult perspective, and 1980's attitudes are typically misunderstood—if they register at all—by the people of her 1960's past.

As events progress, she willingly gives in to this new reality. It is a chance to relive at least some of the spirit and dizzying emotions of youth; a chance to reconsider family relations one has taken for granted and to cherish relatives now gone; a chance at the satisfaction of applied hindsight; and, dangerously but irresistibly, a chance to take other forks in life's road, averting pivotal mistakes one has made. This time, Peggy Sue can and does have that fling with the class rebel, Kerouac idolizer Michael Fitzsimmons (Kevin J. O'Connor), which she had always regretted resisting. More critically, she can alter her entire destiny by discouraging the determined romantic overtures of Charlie. Inevitably, however, things are not that simple.

High-toned fantasy that asks to be taken seriously is very hard to accomplish in film. One thinks of models such as William Dieterle's *Portrait of Jennie* (1948) or Frank Capra's *It's a Wonderful Life* (1946, which, thematically, is somewhat comparable to *Peggy Sue Got Married*). While clearly not of this stature, *Peggy Sue Got Married* aspires to their company. Although Jerry Leichtling and Arlene Sarner's script (whose existence actually predates that of the adventure-comedy *Back to the Future*, a 1985 hit also about time travel) has a wonderfully appealing concept and many clever details, it is, for the most part, skin-deep and insufficiently developed. This is immediately apparent in the presentation of the central choice facing Peggy Sue, that of marrying Charlie, which could conceivably have been a real dilemma, but is a bogus issue in the film, as she would never "undo" her two children, the only bright spots in her life.

Even as the viewer enjoys the deft, direct hits on the most obvious targets—satirical period contrasts, deserved putdowns undelivered the first time around, the dismissal of high school algebra—there is also a persistent feeling of missed opportunities. The central fantasy situation is not mysterious or spooky, as one might expect, but, rather, handled in a light comedic vein. Though the story is slight, many implications are raised along the way, only to remain unexplored. Further, Peggy Sue's predicament is nothing if not emotional, yet the abundant emotion rarely cuts very deep. Nevertheless, the film's core scenes are genuinely powerful: Peggy Sue having another opportunity to visit her beloved grandparents (Maureen O'Sullivan and Leon Ames), with its bittersweet *Our Town*-like echoes, and a wrenching confrontation with Charlie, in which Peggy Sue cannot begin to explain her knowledge that his quest for a musical career will come to naught, that bitterness and betrayal will ultimately doom their relationship as well.

There is some real poignancy in the push-pull, from original attraction to knowing repulsion to attraction reluctantly rekindled, that Peggy Sue feels for Charlie; the depth and sincerity of his need for her is never in doubt. Still, this is very much an actor's picture, and here the casting, acting, and direction of Nicolas Cage poses considerable problems. With his voice ("reedy and strangulated," in one critic's apt description), his weird admixture of hangdog look, hoodish cool, and generally goofy manner (not without a certain charm), his Charlie is a striking creation, but one that does not well serve the film. Rarely does he seem to be even remotely on the same wavelength as Peggy Sue, which makes it difficult to imagine what she sees in him.

Peggy Sue Got Married is a triumph for Kathleen Turner, who does not look like a teenager (beyond the suggestion of hairstyle and dress) and so must rely on her abilities as an actress. She pulls off the part through gesture, attitude, and vocal inflection, managing the difficult feat of being seventeen and forty-three at the same time. Peggy Sue starts out as a wounded individual who must regain her zest for life and is then taken on a rollercoaster ride of quickly shifting reactions and often delicate, ambiguous emotions that set the film's tone. Turner handles this challenge with aplomb. Her work is so good, so heartfelt and sympathetic that it carries the film.

The uniformly good supporting cast tends to be hampered by their characters, who are either stereotypical (such as Michael, the would-be Beat poet) or one-dimensional and unchanging (Peggy Sue's girlfriends). Kevin J. O'Connor, as Michael, more than gets by on intensity. Veterans Ames and

O'Sullivan make the most of their brief screen time through their great experience and appeal. Barry Miller lifts Richard Norvik out of the familiar nerd classification with a wariness that shows every slight he has endured. His friendship with Peggy Sue is touching, and their sharing of her time-travel secret and the satirical look ahead that she gives him provide some of the film's most satisfying moments.

Like Turner, director Coppola was not originally attached to the project. (Debra Winger was to play Peggy Sue, with Penny Marshall directing.) Here, he eschews the technical flash and experimentation of his more recent—and commercially unsuccessful—films *One from the Heart* (1982), *Rumble Fish* (1983), and *The Cotton Club* (1984), in favor of letting his story unfold in a natural, relaxed manner. While the results are consistently smooth and entertaining, there is also a restraint bordering on detachment. Almost an anonymous hired hand this time, and one determined to play it safe, Coppola fails to energize or challenge the material, to make it his own, or to delve beyond the surfaces of feelings and situations.

The film's evocation of 1960 offers little more than the window dressing. A more notable contribution is the dependably excellent camera work of Jordan Cronenweth. From the smoky, blue-fringed lighting at the reunion dance to the burnished wood tones of Peggy Sue's childhood home (giving one the sense of literally stepping back in time with her), the cinematography establishes the right mood. John Barry's heavy-handed score is far less of an asset.

Peggy Sue Got Married is one of those motion pictures whose deficiencies do not seem to hurt it nearly so much as would ordinarily be the case. There are lines of dialogue that drop with a thud yet nevertheless seem in keeping with things these people might have said. Even a rather ridiculous scene set at the lodge of Peggy Sue's grandfather manages to be charming and amusing, and Nicolas Cage's quirky overacting and poor makeup job are tolerable.

A mixed blessing is the thinly scripted hospital scene, where Peggy Sue is recovering from her attack, that concludes the film (added to replace a more downbeat ending that had been shot originally). Wisely, there is neither denial nor absolute confirmation of what Peggy Sue has experienced. Further, there is no pat reconciliation between her and Charlie, only the clear hope that one may be possible. Some sort of change—over and above Charlie's deep concern for her—has occurred. The approach is not really a matter of whether history can be changed but that, given a person's character and emotional makeup, try as he or she might, he will probably end up making the same choices. Such questions and issues, touched upon with a mature and melancholy contemplation, separate *Peggy Sue Got Married* from a purely entertaining, youth-oriented confection such as *Back to the Future*.

As far as audiences are concerned, the film simply has a high "likability factor" that insulates it from its failings. Critical reaction was divided about evenly, between those critics who overpraised the film straight onto their "Ten Best" lists and those who found it inadequate in most departments, often expressing their views in very unkind terms. Coppola, because of his stature in American filmmaking, straddling the worlds of both commercial and artistically ambitious cinema, seems to be a lightning rod for such criticism. In the case of *Peggy Sue Got Married*, it is the favorable audience response that will be heard.

Jordan Fox

Reviews
Commonweal. CXIII, October 10, 1986, p. 534.
Films in Review. XXXVIII, January, 1987, p. 41.
Los Angeles Times. October 8, 1986, VI, p. 1.
Ms. XV, November, 1986, p. 17.
The New Republic. CXCV, November 10, 1986, p. 27.
The New York Times. CXXXVI, October 19, 1986, II, p. 21.
The New Yorker. LXII, October 20, 1986, p. 113.
Newsweek. CVIII, October 6, 1986, p. 73.
Time. CXXVIII, October 13, 1986, p. 104.
Variety. CLXXVI, November, 1986, p. 90.

PLATOON

Production: Arnold Kopelson (AA) for Hemdale Film; released by Orion Pictures
Direction: Oliver Stone (AA)
Screenplay: Oliver Stone
Cinematography: Robert Richardson
Editing: Claire Simpson (AA)
Production design: Bruno Rubeo
Art direction: Rodel Cruz and Doris Sherman Williams; set decoration, Roy Lachica
Special effects: Yves de Bono
Makeup: Gordon J. Smith
Costume design: Kathryn Morrison
Sound: Simon Kaye (AA)
Music direction: Budd Carr
Music: Georges Delerue
MPAA rating: R
Running time: 120 minutes

Principal characters:
Sergeant Barnes . . . . Tom Berenger
Sergeant Elias . . . . Willem Dafoe
Chris Taylor . . . . Charlie Sheen
Sergeant O'Neill . . . . John C. McGinley
King . . . . Keith David
Big Harold . . . . Forest Whitaker
Bunny . . . . Kevin Dillon
Rhah . . . . Francesco Quinn
Lieutenant Wolfe . . . . Mark Moses
Gardner . . . . Bob Orwig
Sal . . . . Richard Edson
Junior . . . . Reggie Johnson
Lerner . . . . Johnny Depp
Tex. . . . . David Neidorf
Manny . . . . Corkey Ford

Like Francis Coppola's *Apocalypse Now* (1979), which appropriated the characters and plot of Joseph Conrad's *Heart of Darkness*, Oliver Stone's Academy Award-winning *Platoon*, based on his own experiences in Vietnam, insistently relies on symbolism to convey its meaning. Unlike *Apocalypse Now*'s episodes of escalating psychological and moral insanity, however, *Platoon*'s action unrelentingly assaults the viewer. So much happens to its characters that the plot almost seems contrived (like the telescoped true events in Stone's *Salvador*, 1986; reviewed in this volume); the action even threatens to overshadow the psychological and moral progress of Stone's hero, Chris Taylor (Charlie Sheen).

The film opens in Vietnam, September, 1967. As Taylor and other rookies deplane and march off through the noise and dust, they pass by files of body bags awaiting evacuation. (At once, the requiemlike strains of Samuel Barber's "Adagio for Strings" begin, a piece that Stone introduces too soon and repeats too often.) Soon Taylor and his platoon are making their way through the comparative quiet of the dense, humid—and, at times, radiantly beautiful—jungle. Sergeant Elias (Willem Dafoe), who is first seen with his arms draped Crucifixion-style over the ends of the machine gun he carries across his shoulders, amiably attends Taylor when he collapses from exhaustion. Later, as he digs his nightly foxhole, Taylor complains in the first of his many voice-over letters to his Grandmother—the only family member, he believes, who listens to him—that no one in this Hell teaches the new recruits anything, and that he now regrets his decision to drop out of college and volunteer to fight with the anonymous poor and uneducated—the "grunts."

The first of the four skirmishes/battles that shape the narrative occurs on a night patrol/ambush. Before departing, Elias tries, unsuccessfully, to convince Staff Sergeant Barnes (Tom Berenger) to keep back the rookies. Another, Sergeant O'Neill (John C. McGinley), mocks Elias' concern: "This guy is in three years and he thinks he's Jesus. . . ." Just before daylight, the enemy walks into the unsuccessful ambush and rookie Gardner (Bob Orwig) is killed. Taylor, though he is convinced that he is dying, receives only a slight wound, which earns for him three days of light duty back at base camp and an introduction by King (Keith David), a wise, black "short-timer," to the underground recreation bunker of the "hopheads." King announces, "Your highness has arrived," and Rhah (Francesco Quinn), surprised to find the clean-cut youth there, asks, "What are you doing in the underworld, Taylor?" "This ain't Taylor," proclaims King, "Taylor's been shot. This is Chris. He's been resurrected!" Chris does not resist the drug-induced, almost erotic comradeship—later, they are seen dancing together—that unites these men: Elias, his high cheekbones and sensuous lips enlarged by a wide-angle close-up, blows marijuana smoke down a gun barrel into Chris's mouth. The "underworld" is immediately contrasted to the aboveground tent-barracks, where Barnes, O'Neill, Bunny (Kevin Dillon), and others smoke cigarettes, drink beer, play cards, pray, and joke about getting a woman.

The second skirmish takes place New Year's Day, 1968. When underground tunnels are discovered, Elias enthusiastically sloshes through them until he ferrets out and kills an enemy soldier. Meanwhile, Manny (Corkey

Ford) goes astray, and, just as orders are received to move to a nearby village where Vietcong have been sighted, another grunt is blown apart by a booby trap. A moment later, Chris happens upon Barnes alone, sitting and staring. It appears that this battle-hardened, even callous man—his face stitched together as testimony to his experience—is vulnerable after all. What is Barnes feeling—fear, pity, despair, or frustrated hatred?

En route to the village, the missing Manny is found tied to a pole, his throat cut. As the camera pans the horrified faces of his men, Barnes cries out in anger. Reacting not only to his recent view of the solitary Barnes, but also, like the others, to the two gruesome deaths, Chris, in voice-over, asserts that they all looked to Barnes to set things right: "That day we loved him." Immediately, Barnes shoots an unidentified Vietnamese running in the distance.

The subsequent scenes in the village constitute the film's foremost achievement. Viewers not only experience what being an infantryman in Vietnam felt like but also understand how one could commit (or accede to) acts of which one did not believe oneself capable. The GI's drive or drag screaming villagers and animals from their huts and underground shelters in a cacophony of gunfire, explosions, and screeching human and animal sounds. The viewer too is infected with a hysteria-born paranoia: who amongst the villagers are Vietcong soldiers or sympathizers, who simply innocent farmers? As a hysterical Chris flushes out of a hole a frightened old woman and her idiot son, a black soldier behind him shouts, "Be cool, be cool, they're scared!" Chris screams back, "Oh, they're scared, huh? What about me?" Annoyed by the idiot's smile, Chris fires at the uncomprehending man's feet to make him "dance." When Chris begins to calm down— regrettably, Sheen's passion is not credible and he is unable to negotiate the scene's seesawing emotions—baby-faced Bunny pushes him aside and crushes the idiot's skull with his rifle butt, observing with amused surprise how easy the head comes apart and how curious brains look. Dillon's performance is unnervingly perfect; this is the film's truest and most chilling moment. Meanwhile, the overwrought Barnes, who already has shot a woman point-blank in the face because she would not stop screaming, threatens to shoot her child unless its father reveals the Vietcong. Elias arrives and struggles with Barnes over the child. Finally parted, Barnes swears revenge, while Elias berates the ineffectual Lieutenant Wolfe (Mark Moses) for not having prevented the murders. The officer pretends ignorance, however, and orders the village reduced to ashes. Chris looks admiringly at Elias, and on the way out of the village, he stops several of his fellow soldiers from raping a young woman.

Back in the company area, Elias informs the harried but concerned company commander that he intends to press charges against Barnes and Wolfe. Soon, there is civil war in the platoon. Half the men side with Barnes, whose ruthless, animal instinct for survival, they believe, will bring them through; the other half side with the "water-walker" Elias and believe that things have gone too far. Chris, no longer certain of what is right or wrong, is among the latter.

In the third battle, Elias volunteers to cut off retreating enemy ambushers. Running and screaming with exhilaration, he kills one after another. Chris sets out to find him, but Barnes orders him back to the evacuation area, assuring him that he will find Elias. He does. As Elias emerges from the undergrowth, he sees Barnes and smiles. He then realizes, though, that Barnes's raised rifle is aimed at him, and, as viewers are hit point-blank by giant close-ups of their eyes, Barnes fires three bullets into Elias.

Returning, Barnes informs Chris that he found Elias dead and that the whole area is swarming with Vietcong. A few minutes later, however, as the platoon is being helicoptered out, the men see Elias below, somehow still alive, and being chased by the Vietcong. The onboard machine guns rake the pursuers, but it is futile; Elias, his arms raised to the heavens, falls in slow motion, a solemnizing device that, along with the reverential adagio, adds to Elias' mythic dimension. Chris stares at Barnes with hatred.

Back in "the underworld," and unaware that Barnes is listening, Chris tries to convince six comrades that Barnes murdered Elias and should be fragged. Rhah points out that Barnes, already having been wounded seven times, obviously is not meant to die, that only Barnes can kill Barnes. Barnes makes his presence known, mocking their affection for Elias and their cowardice. Almost as if he desires it, he challenges them to kill him, and, when they do not, he spits out his utter contempt for them. Screaming an obscenity and cheered on by others, Chris charges Barnes, but Barnes soon has his knife at Chris's throat. Only when someone whispers to Barnes that he will get ten years for killing an enlisted man does he draw back, but not before he knicks Chris under the eye. Then, bitterly declaring, "Death, what do you all know about death?" he laughs and walks out.

The next night, a major battle is fought and the Americans are soon overrun, causing the captain to call in an air strike on his own position. The first explosions stop Barnes, who is in the act of killing Chris.

Daybreak finds Chris alive but wounded. As he opens his eyes, he observes a deer grazing, oblivious to the human carnage. Struggling to his feet, he wanders about the landscape of wounded and dead, coming upon Barnes, badly wounded. Barnes commands Chris to get him a medic, but the intent in Chris's eyes and his raised rifle cause Barnes (possibly like Conrad's Kurtz, who was sickened by his own evil) to order, "Do it!" With three quick shots, Chris does.

For the wounded Chris, the war is over. As his helicopter rises into the sun and with the adagio helping to seal the scene, he salutes those he leaves behind. For a few moments, his body shakes with sobbing. Then, before his tearful face, caked with mud and blood, is washed out by the sunlight, the dispassionate conclusions he later draws from his experience are heard in voice-over: The enemy has really been themselves; the two sides of his character, represented by "fathers" Barnes and Elias who fought for his soul, will always be at war. Even so, he concludes, his duty—and the duty of the other survivors—is to teach what they learned. The words, unfortunately, reduce the complexity of what the audience has experienced. Nevertheless, in spite of Stone's penchant for overwriting and Sheen's limitations as an actor, Stone's "lesson," his film, is a harrowingly immediate and haunting accomplishment.

Hubert Cohen

Reviews
The Boston Phoenix. January 13, 1987, III, p. 4.
Nation. CCXLIV, January 17, 1987, p. 54.
The New Republic. CXCVI, January 9, 1987, p. 24.
The New Yorker. LXII, January 12, 1987, p. 94.
Newsweek. CIX, January 5, 1987, p. 57.
Rolling Stone. January 29, 1987, p. 23.
Time. CXXIX, January 26, 1987, p. 54.

PRETTY IN PINK

Production: John Hughes and Michael Chinich (executive producers) and
Lauren Shuler; released by Paramount Pictures
Direction: Howard Deutch
Screenplay: John Hughes
Cinematography: Tak Fujimoto
Editing: Richard Marks
Art direction: John W. Corso; set decoration, Jennifer Polito and Bruce
Weintraub
Special effects: John Frazier
Makeup: Tommy Cole
Costume design: Marilyn Vance
Music: Michael Gore
MPAA rating: PG-13
Running time: 96 minutes

> *Principal characters:*
> Andie Walsh . . . . Molly Ringwald
> Jack Walsh . . . . Harry Dean Stanton
> Duckie Dale . . . . Jon Cryer
> Blane . . . . Andrew McCarthy
> Iona . . . . Annie Potts
> Steff McKee . . . . James Spader
> Simon . . . . Dweezil Zappa

Although *Pretty in Pink* is directed by Howard Deutch, the film clearly
belongs to John Hughes, who wrote the screenplay and served as an executive producer. Hughes, who had earlier collaboration with Molly Ringwald
in the popular *Sixteen Candles* (1984) and in *The Breakfast Club* (1985) as
both those films' screenwriter-director, here continues his exploration of the
teenage world. Ringwald, for whom the film was written, plays Andie, a
poor girl whose obsession with the prom and with Blane (Andrew McCarthy), a rich boy, is the focus of the film. Although Blane is attracted to
Andie, his snobbish friend Steff (James Spader) and a bevy of blonde
WASP coeds exert enough peer pressure to threaten the budding relationship. Also compounding Andie's problem are the attentions of Duckie (Jon
Cryer), a fellow outsider with the proverbial heart of gold.

The opening sequence takes place on Andie's side of town, a lower-
middle-class neighborhood. After dressing in one of her modest yet stylishly
thrown together outfits—clothes are the principal determinant of class in
the film—Andie urges her father (Harry Dean Stanton) to get up and find a
job. Her despondent, lethargic father, who still broods over his wife's run-

ning away, asks Andie about the prom, which is, despite her resourcefulness and common sense, her obsession.

At school, the gap between Andie and her fellow have-nots and Blane and the haves is reinforced in their clothes (the haves are dressed in expensive, tailored, preppy wardrobes) and by their turf. In fact, the film further suggests that this contemporary Romeo and Juliet have no place where they both can feel comfortable together. Andie is embarrassed about Blane seeing her house. When Blane takes Andie to Life, a have-not teenage nightclub, he is an obvious target, and Duckie actually tries to precipitate a fight with him. Yet Blane and Andie are no more at home in one of his hangouts or at Steff's house, where the haves are partying and trashing his parents' home. One of the blondes actually insults Andie with an obscene remark and taunts her about her appearance. Still, Andie reassures Blane, "I'd be happy with you in a Turkish prison."

From her first appearance, when she, ironically, mothers her father and gives him adult reminders about responsibility, Andie seems more mature than her peers. Undaunted by the blonde's vicious comments and by Steff's crude sexual advances, Andie perseveres, mostly on her own, and seems not to suffer from the insecurity of Blane or the immaturity of Duckie. In the relationship with Blane, she is in charge, from the moment the two exchange computer small talk to their meetings at the record store where Andie works. Even when Blane succumbs to peer pressure and avoids seeing Andie because he is simply too weak to tell her he has changed his mind, she confronts him and astutely assesses his motives: She knows that he is afraid. At the end of the film Blane concurs: "I believed in you—I didn't believe in me."

This is not to say that Andie does not develop or experience any emotional turmoil, for she does. Blane's rejection is a traumatic event, but it only serves to strengthen her character. When she plans on going to the prom with Blane, she enters an exclusive clothing store to look at evening gowns, but the saleswoman's condescending manner and the presence of the blondes make her realize that she does not belong in that world. She recovers from that setback, however, when she symbolically creates a pink gown from the tacky monstrosity that her father buys for her and from the old dress that her older friend Iona (Annie Potts) gives to her. Since Iona serves at times as a kind of surrogate mother, Andie's dress comes from her parents, but is her own creation, just as she shapes herself rather than being shaped by others. As she tells her father when he asks why she is going to the prom unescorted, "I'll let them know they didn't break me."

Iona, who is in her late thirties, serves not only as a surrogate mother but also, since Andie has no girlfriends her own age, as a confidante. The friendship makes Andie seem mature and Iona immature, since she follows, like a fourteen-year-old, one fashion after another and affects, at times, vulgar and obscene language. The world seems to have passed Iona by, and she is left reminiscing about her youth, which is represented by the pink prom dress that her mother had given her. Iona is, in dramatic terms, a foil to Andie: Despite the age discrepancy, they share the same tastes in clothes and in popular culture, and they both have fallen in love with preppies. While Andie can love Blane and simultaneously retain her standards and values, however, Iona buys into the life-style that her boyfriend represents.

At the end of the film, Andie emerges as her own person with her values intact, but she has also changed, even if in subtle ways. For example, while she wisely advises her father to accept her mother's absence and to make a new life for himself, she is still child enough to keep her mother's photograph near her bed, thereby suggesting that she remains emotionally dependent on the missing mother and still suffers from the same futile hopes that her father does. Then, when she creates her dress, surely a task a mother would participate in with her daughter, she puts her mother's photograph away, indicating that she has taken her own advice and is her own woman.

Pretty in Pink not only depicts Andie's maturation but also the conflict between two social classes in an America where money talks. Duckie states, "There are people who have money and people who don't." Sociopolitical theory is hardly Hughes's focus, but it is a subsidiary concern, for the only classroom scene depicted in the film shows a discussion of Franklin Delano Roosevelt's New Deal. Blane acknowledges ruefully that in America corporate families have replaced royal ones and that he is himself the crown prince of his father's company.

The have-nots, rather than attempt to compete with the haves, retreat to an unorthodox form of dress to defy the establishment and convince the haves (and perhaps themselves) that they reject their values. Duckie, Andie's unsuccessful suitor, is the articulate spokesman for his group, but his frenzied posturings and his intellectual put-downs do not reflect a viable alternative to Steff and the blondes. Though he is sensitive and caring, he is also narrow-minded because he regards Blane not as an individual but as a member of a group, and he even attempts to start a fight with him. Duckie retreats from reality into a fantasy world involving Andie, and it is not until the end of the film that he understands that Blane is not "one of them." At that point Duckie shakes Blane's hand and then advises Andie to go to him. Blane and Andie are reunited in the parking lot, and the unselfish Duckie is rewarded for his gesture by a blonde falling for him.

Duckie's integration, or inclusion, into the opposing camp is played primarily for laughs rather than for its message and is one of the more unconvincing moments in an otherwise fairly realistic film. While it is difficult to understand why Blane would be friends with a person such as Steff, Blane's yielding to peer pressure is perfectly understandable. Less convincing is Blane's reformation, but then Blane's character is not entirely consistent. Part of the problem may lie in Hughes's exaggeration of the split between the two groups: The wealthy students are so obnoxious and vicious, and the poor students so defensive and defiant, that a reconciliation between them may be impossible. After all, while the film ends with Blane and Andie embracing in the parking lot, there still does not appear to be a place in the real world where they can feel comfortable together.

Thomas L. Erskine

Reviews
Films in Review. XXXVII, May, 1986, p. 300.
High Fidelity. XXXVI, June, 1986, p. 63.
Los Angeles. XXXI, March, 1986, p. 44.
New York. XIX, March 10, 1986, p. 93.
The New York Times. CXXXV, February 28, 1986, p. C8.
The New Yorker. LXII, April 7, 1986, p. 91.
Newsweek. CVII, March 17, 1986, p. 81.
Teen. XXX, February, 1986, p. 44.
Time. CXXVII, March 3, 1986, p. 83.
Variety. CCCXXII, February 12, 1986, p. 24.
Washingtonian. XXI, April, 1986, p. 70.
The Washington Post. February 28, 1986, p. D1, WE11.

A ROOM WITH A VIEW

Origin: Great Britain
Released: 1986
Released in U.S.: 1986
Production: Ismail Merchant for Goldcrest Films; released by Cinecom
International
Direction: James Ivory
Screenplay: Ruth Prawer Jhabvala (AA); based on the novel of the same
name by E. M. Forster
Cinematography: Tony Pierce-Roberts
Editing: Humphrey Dixon
Art direction: Gianni Quaranta and Brian Ackland-Snow (AA)
Costume design: Jenny Beavan and John Bright (AA)
Music: Richard Robbins
MPAA rating: no listing
Running time: 110 minutes

Principal characters:
Charlotte Bartlett . . . . Maggie Smith
Lucy Honeychurch . . . . Helena Bonham Carter
Mr. Emerson . . . . Denholm Elliott
George Emerson . . . . Julian Sands
Cecil Vyse . . . . Daniel Day-Lewis
The Reverend Beebe . . . . Simon Callow
Miss Lavish . . . . Judi Dench
Mrs. Honeychurch . . . . Rosemary Leach
Freddy Honeychurch . . . . Rupert Graves
Mr. Eager . . . . Patrick Godfrey
Catherine Alan. . . . . Joan Henley
Mrs. Vyse . . . . Maria Britneva
Cockney signora . . . . Amanda Walker
Sir Harry Otway . . . . Peter Cellier

A Room with a View follows *A Passage to India* (1985) as the second of
E. M. Forster's novels to be adapted for the screen in as many years. The
book draws on Forster's keen observations of the behavior of Englishmen
abroad—knowledge gathered during his own travels on the Continent as a
young man and put to good use in his deliciously ironic portrait of his fellow
countrymen setting out warily in pursuit of local color with their guidebooks
clutched firmly in their hands.

Happily, the novel's translation to the screen has been overseen by the
skilled team of director James Ivory, producer Ismail Merchant, and writer

Ruth Prawer Jhabvala, a trio whose combined talents seem uniquely suited to the task. Since the 1960's, the three have collaborated on a number of exquisitely crafted films (*Shakespeare Wallah*, 1965; *The Europeans*, 1979; *Heat and Dust*, 1982; *The Bostonians*, 1984) which deal with the subtle shadings of cultural and ideological conflicts—the heart and soul of Forster's story and a theme easily mangled by less experienced hands. *A Room with a View* has enjoyed a degree of popularity unequaled by any of the trio's earlier films, and its enthusiastic reception was highlighted by its eight Academy Award nominations. In addition to its three Oscars for Screenplay Adaptation, Art Direction, and Costume Design, the film was nominated for Best Picture, Best Director, Best Cinematography, and Best Supporting Actor (Denholm Elliott) and Actress (Maggie Smith).

Ultimately, *A Room with a View* is a love story, but one in which the obstacles standing in the way of the heroine's happiness are largely those she places there herself. The film opens in Florence as Lucy Honeychurch (Helena Bonham Carter) and her spinsterish cousin and chaperon, Charlotte Bartlett (Maggie Smith), arrive at a pensione and are disappointed to discover that their rooms do not have the promised view of the city. At dinner that evening, an eccentric Englishman, Mr. Emerson (Denholm Elliott), and his son, George (Julian Sands), offer to trade rooms with the two women—a proposition which horrifies Charlotte until she is persuaded to accept by the Reverend Beebe (Simon Callow).

Charlotte strikes up a friendship with another of the pensione's guests, Miss Lavish (Judi Dench), a novelist who sets off in search of the local sights with Charlotte in tow, leaving Lucy to explore Florence on her own. Lucy's wanderings bring her to the site of a violent street fight, where she faints and is assisted by George Emerson. The experience is cataclysmic for both of them, and, during a picnic the following day, George impulsively kisses Lucy in a field of tall grass. Charlotte witnesses the embrace and promptly nips the romance in the bud.

Safely back in England with her mother (Rosemary Leach) and her lively younger brother, Freddy (Rupert Graves), Lucy becomes engaged to the stuffy Cecil Vyse (Daniel-Day Lewis), a man as prim and pompous as George Emerson was open and spontaneous. Unbeknown to Lucy, however, Cecil has made the acquaintance of Mr. Emerson and George and, knowing nothing of his fiancée's encounter with them in Italy, has arranged for them to rent a local house. George and Freddy quickly become friends, and Lucy finds herself once again thrown into George's company.

It is soon clear that George's feelings remain unchanged—a situation made more difficult for Lucy by the arrival of Charlotte and the revelation that her cousin has described the kiss in the field to Miss Lavish, who has included the incident in her latest novel. When George confronts Lucy with his feelings (this time in Charlotte's presence), telling her that Cecil neither loves nor understands her, she orders him away. That night, however, she breaks off her engagement with Cecil and decides that she must leave England before word of the rift becomes widely known.

The Emersons, too, are planning to leave now that George's hopes regarding Lucy are gone. Charlotte realizes, however, that her earlier meddling has been a mistake, and she arranges for Lucy to meet with Mr. Emerson, who is distraught over his son's unhappiness. The older man's simplicity and honesty force Lucy to face the truth, and she at last admits to her love for George, the depth of her feelings written clearly on her radiant face. The film ends with George and Lucy—now husband and wife—back at the pensione in Florence, embracing at the window of their room with a view.

The premise for *A Room with a View* is set forth early in the film by the Reverend Beebe, who, as he listens to Lucy's passionate interpretation of a piece by Ludwig van Beethoven on the piano, comments, "If Miss Honeychurch ever takes to live as she plays, it will be very exciting . . . both for us and for her." The question of whether Lucy will indeed ever live as she plays—that is, trust to her emotions and instincts—becomes the film's central dramatic conflict, with George Emerson representing the possibilities of that choice and Cecil Vyse the barrenness of a life without passion or depth of feeling. Lucy is at her most engaging in the presence of George Emerson, drawn to him by inclination yet driven toward Cecil by social convention and her own sense of panic. There is a sulky, impatient side to her personality that is partly residual adolescent discontentment and partly the frustrated yearnings of a young woman whose potential is as yet unrealized. As the film progresses, she becomes more and more deceitful (a fact amusingly emphasized by descriptive title cards introducing various segments of the story) the further she moves from accepting George and, hence, herself.

In sharp contrast to Lucy's confusion and avoidance of the truth are the Emersons themselves, a father and son wholly unconcerned with social façades and interested solely in finding truth in their lives. For George, who has shaped the food on his plate into a giant question mark when Lucy first meets him, life is meaningless until his encounter with her. Mr. Emerson has taught his son to trust to the power of love, and this George does, without regard for Lucy's disavowal of her own feelings or her engagement to Cecil. The uncomplicated nature of his love for Lucy both baffles and frustrates her, admitting as it does none of the barriers she has erected between them. Like his son, Mr. Emerson is open and straightforward by nature, goodhearted, wise, and incapable of deception. It is his honesty that finally breaches Lucy's defenses and shows her a picture of herself that shatters her view of her own actions. Upon hearing Lucy's unhappy argument that she cannot possibly tell her family that she has always secretly loved George because they trust her, Mr. Emerson responds, "Why should they when you've deceived everyone?" It is a statement which shakes her perceptions to their core and frees her at last to follow her heart.

Cecil Vyse, too, is uncomplicated, but in quite another fashion. He is the epitome of bourgeois convention, regarding Lucy as an ornament with which to decorate his life, and his air of fussy self-satisfaction annoys her even before George's reappearance. Yet Cecil is a figure of amusement, not a villain, and his thoughtful, stricken reaction to Lucy's decision not to marry him brings out a finer side to his nature than he has hitherto seemed to possess. Day-Lewis' performance is one of the film's best, and a comparison of his work here with his portrayal of a homosexual street punk in another of the year's most intriguing films, *My Beautiful Laundrette* (1985; reviewed in this volume), shows him to be a young actor of exceptional versatility.

The central cast of characters is rounded out by Charlotte Bartlett, or "poor Charlotte," as Mrs. Honeychurch often calls her. Unmarried and spinsterish in her manner, Charlotte represents the repression of all the joys that life with George holds for Lucy, and Smith's performance captures each nuance of Charlotte's flustered, slightly martyred air. Yet Charlotte is also well meaning and capable, finally, of helping the young couple, an action that earns for her a friendly letter from Lucy when she and George arrive in Florence near the story's conclusion. The resulting scene is one of the film's most poignant, as Charlotte reads the letter alone in bed and muses on their happiness with an expression of wistful longing.

Lucy Honeychurch's story is that of a young woman's gradual awakening to the joys of a life lived in harmony with one's own nature, and it is Italy which first stirs that knowledge in her. There is a voluptuous beauty to the country as it is depicted in the film, and a sense of passions given free rein, which affect the sensibilities of the British guests at the pensione in very individual ways. For Charlotte, the atmosphere of the country is unsettling and vaguely dangerous—an invitation to relax the standards of behavior that govern one's life at home. Lucy, however, hears an answering chord in her own character and has her life changed by her stay.

Ivory's films excel at conveying atmosphere and mood, and *A Room with a View* is beautifully photographed with an eye to details which serve to evoke a stunning portrait of a very particular place and time. The film's lush depiction of Florence and the surrounding countryside helps to create a palpable sense of the culture shock experienced by the story's characters—a crucial step in understanding the forces at work in Lucy's life. The depiction of England is no less lovely, but the element of passion is lacking, and the languorous beauty and spontaneous violence which first draw George and Lucy together would seem out of place in its gardens and country lanes. It is these details which give the film its depth and subtlety, presented as they are as part of the story's fabric and never spelled out or overemphasized.

A Room with a View is a film of wit and intelligence, and it is one which refuses to underestimate the intelligence of its audience as well. From the ironic humor of its title cards to its carefully shaded performances, the film allows the comedy innate in human foibles to unfold in an unforced, unhurried manner. Humor which grows naturally from character and character interaction is a refreshing alternative to the broadside style of many current comedies, and *A Room with a View* emerges as one of the year's unexpected cinematic delights: a splendid, sophisticated film and a remarkable achievement among literary adaptations.

Janet E. Lorenz

Reviews
Christian Century. CIII, May 21, 1986, p. 533.
Commonweal. CXIII, April 11, 1986, p. 213.
Hollywood Reporter. January 29, 1986, p. 3.
Los Angeles Times. March 21, 1986, VI, p. 1.
Macleans. XCIX, March 31, 1986, p. 56.
National Review. XXXVIII, April 25, 1986, p. 60.
The New Republic. CXCIV, March 24, 1986, p. 24.
New Statesman. CXI, April 11, 1986, p. 26.
New York. March 17, 1986, p. 79.
The New Yorker. LXII, March 24, 1986, p. 112.
Newsweek. CVII, March 10, 1986, p. 74.
Time. CXXVII, March 10, 1986, p. 80.
Variety. January 30, 1986, p. 3.
Village Voice. March 11, 1986, p. 53.
Vogue. CLXXVI, March, 1986, p. 70.

'ROUND MIDNIGHT

Origin: France and the United States
Released: 1986
Production: Irwin Winkler; released by Warner Bros.
Direction: Bertrand Tavernier
Screenplay: David Rayfiel and Bertrand Tavernier
Cinematography: Bruno De Keyzer
Editing: Armand Psenny
Production design: Alexander Trauner
Art direction: Pierre Duquesne
Costume design: Jacqueline Moreau
Music: Herbie Hancock (AA)
MPAA rating: R
Running time: 130 minutes

> *Principal characters:*
> Dale Turner .... Dexter Gordon
> Francis Borier .... François Cluzet
> Berangère .... Gabrielle Haker
> Buttercup .... Sandra Reaves-Phillips
> Darcey Leigh .... Lonette McKee
> Sylvie .... Christine Pascal
> Eddie Wayne .... Herbie Hancock
> Ace .... Bobby Hutcherson
> Madame Queen .... Liliane Rovère
> Goodley......................... Martin Scorsese
> Ben............................... John Berry
> Redon .... Philippe Noiret

Although it served as subject matter for experiments in film sound as early as the mid-1920's, jazz has been a disappointment in motion pictures. Modest success was achieved when popular artists such as Louis Armstrong and Benny Goodman appeared in shorts or were spotted by production numbers interpolated into features that otherwise concentrated on comic or suspenseful stories. Also worthy of note is the occasional improvised or jazz-inflected sound track. Stan Getz supplied backgrounds to *Mickey One* (1965). Miles Davis recorded the music for *Frantic* (1958). Benny Carter has composed a variety of film scores, including *Edge of Doom* (1950) and *Buck and the Preacher* (1972). Duke Ellington's music for *Anatomy of a Murder* (1959) both supports the melodrama of Otto Preminger's film and stands comfortably on its own merits.

Turgid drama often triumphed when music was the center of attention, as in *Young Man With a Horn* (1950) or *Syncopation* (1942). Somehow, the actual life experiences of jazz musicians have never been considered sufficiently engaging or perhaps palatable enough to warrant the financial gambles of feature film, an attitude reinforced by the fact that most great figures in jazz history have been black.

It is, then, the more remarkable that '*Round Midnight* maintained both musical and social integrities throughout production, based as it is on anecdotal histories of the great black jazz performers to whom it is dedicated, Bud Powell and Lester Young. Although he died in 1959, well after the swing idiom had run its popular course, Lester Young contributed a tenor saxophone style still reflected among musicians performing in the 1980's. Immensely successful in the 1930's and 1940's, his languorous, harmonically innovative approach set Young apart from the driving, arpeggio-styled mainstream of saxophone soloists. At the height of his powers, Young was inducted into the army, a nightmarish experience that climaxed with a year's confinement in detention barracks and a dishonorable discharge. After that experience, Young's playing, like his personality, underwent drastic change. The flowing lines of his earlier solos turned fragmented, phrases now wisps of melancholy ellipsis and innuendo. Demoralized, his health deteriorating, Young abused his body with drugs; he was periodically hospitalized both for health reasons and for depression. After a series of appearances in Paris, Young spent his last days in New York City.

Bud Powell, a highly influential bop pianist with virtuoso skill and imagination, belonged to jazz's next generation. Powell, too, suffered emotional difficulties during most of his professional life. He was institutionalized in a Long Island hospital in 1945 at the age of twenty-one. In the late 1940's, he was severely beaten on the head by Philadelphia police. After suffering further setbacks in the early 1950's, Powell finally moved to Paris, where success was interspersed with the ravages of alcoholism and mental illness. He died from their consequences in 1966. A song he played regularly since his youth was called " 'Round Midnight."

Against this background may be set the traditionally zealous French enthusiasm for American popular culture, including jazz music. Critical writing and audience fervor helped to make Paris a center for black American musicians, largely free from the racism of their own country. The adulation which the expatriate musicians enjoyed there was generally short-lived but intense.

'*Round Midnight*'s director, Bertrand Tavernier, comes from a generation slightly younger than that of France's first New Wave filmmakers such as Jean-Luc Godard and François Truffaut, but he repeated a similar youthful pattern. Tavernier abandoned the study of law to write interviews and film reviews for journals such as *Cahiers du cinéma* and *Positif*. Having served as an assistant under director Jean-Pierre Melville on *Léon Morin Prêtre*

(1961), Tavernier made his film debut two years later with an episode in *Les Baisers*. Tavernier's premier feature, *The Clockmaker* (1974), won France's most esteemed award, Le Prix Delluc. Here as in some of his later works, the director's enthusiasm for American film ambience and visual style is much in evidence. Tavernier's other side, a brooding pessimism about modern life, appears in *The Judge and the Assassin* (1976) and the remarkable *Death Watch* (1980). In *Death Watch*, the director's first English-language venture, a woman's fatal illness is avidly followed on national television through the agency of a cameraman in whose eyes an electronic camera has been implanted.

In 1985, working with an American filmmaker, Robert Parrish, Tavernier made a short film about Southern musicians, *Mississippi Blues*, reflecting his interest in jazz and its roots. He collaborated with the writer David Rayfiel on *'Round Midnight*'s screenplay, "inspired by incidents in the lives of Francis Paudras and Bud Powell."

'Round Midnight is set in 1959 in Paris, marking the arrival of a famous black American tenor saxophone player, Dale Turner (Dexter Gordon). Turner is a confirmed alcoholic whose erratic behavior is constrained by a collection of sympathetic black American expatriates. They lock the musician in his room, escort him to the Blue Note, the club which has engaged him, and attend him minute-to-minute. For his part, Turner plays to a rapt audience, cadges what money he can from fans and unwary patrons, and tries constantly to escape from his keepers, heading for a little bar across the street or yet farther afield.

Each night that Turner performs, an impoverished young French graphic artist named Francis Borier (François Cluzet playing the Francis Paudras of the screenwriters' reference, the man who befriended Bud Powell) stands or crouches outside a transom at the Blue Note to hear him play. Borier's enthusiasm for the music approaches idolatry; he says that his first exposure to Dale Turner changed his entire life. Separated from his wife, Borier lives and works in a tiny, crowded flat with his daughter Berangère (Gabrielle Haker), whom he abandons nightly to pursue his musical obsession. Turner and Borier finally meet.

The American initially sees the Frenchman as another potential source for drinking money, but their relationship gradually changes. When Turner escapes from his keepers, Borier tracks him down, sometimes finding him in police custody, sometimes hospitalized, once under psychiatric observation. Borier takes Turner home, absorbs him into his cluttered life, and undertakes a program of reform. In a painful sequence, the Frenchman borrows money from his wife to find larger quarters, including a piano so that Turner can return to composition. He introduces the musician to his friendly, unmusical parents, who live in the suburbs.

Rehabilitated, Turner records fresh compositions and finally decides to return to New York, accompanied by his new friend. Anxious about life's new perils for Turner in this seedy, cynical, drug-infested world, Borier stays as long as he can, but he must finally return to Paris. Later he receives a telegram announcing Turner's death.

If 'Round Midnight has its deficiencies, it is nevertheless exceptional for the authenticity of its dialogue and the quality of its music. Both are largely attributable to the American musician who plays Dale Turner, Dexter Gordon. In many respects he is ideally suited to the part. Gordon was perhaps the first tenor saxophonist to assimilate effectively the harmonies of bebop, performing in a style whose roots reflect the relaxed, vibrato-flattened phrasing of Lester Young. After a California prison term for narcotics, Gordon returned in 1960 as an actor and performer in playright Jack Gelber's work about drugs, The Connection. Two years later, Gordon emigrated to Europe, recording with Bud Powell, among others.

Himself physically unwell, Gordon has accommodated the idiosyncrasies of his personal manner to those remembered from Lester Young with uncanny effect. There is Young's private language (everyone is "lady") and the elfin yet insistent hand and finger gestures that are ever ready to substitute for speech, to move in lieu of music. This is a man who exists for two reasons: to play jazz and to narcotize himself against the cruelties of life. At one point, Turner recalls a conversation with another musician named Hershal. (Hershal Evans was Lester Young's saxophone campanion in the Count Basie band.) When Hershal said, "You won't play no different in Paris," Turner replied, "No cold eyes in Paris."

Performing with such jazz artists as Wayne Shorter, Tony Williams, and Herbie Hancock (who won an Academy Award for the musical score), Gordon evokes the deceptively simple phrases of Lester Young's last years while retaining a personal skill and manner. Except for cutaways to blissful French nightclub audiences, the music is presented with understanding and integrity. Its musicians are seen listening to one another as they play.

One of 'Round Midnight's most charming sequences defines a loving relationship between Dale Turner as the Lester Young figure and a beautiful singer named Darcey Leigh (Lonette McKee), a surrogate for Billie Holiday, including the gardenia in her hair. Their oblique expressions of affection particularly mark screenwriter Rayfiel's skills. Subsequent to the film, McKee impersonated Billie Holiday in a New York stage drama written as a cabaret act, Lady Day at Emerson's Bar and Grill.

Jazz fans came from all across France to make up the film's Blue Note audience. A viewer's response to 'Round Midnight may depend substantially on sympathy toward Dale Turner and his world. If one is moved by the music and the history of its artists, then Francis Borier's monomania is at least comprehensible. The film's explicit romanticism about suffering artists is grounded in genuine sentiment, however hackneyed the expression.

(Vibraphonist Ace, played by Bobby Hutcherson, says of Turner, "When you have to explore every night, even the most beautiful things you feel can be the most painful.") In the film, Francis Borier's memories of Dale Turner are preserved in black-and-white home movies. For audiences too young to have seen and heard Lester Young, the Dexter Gordon performance may serve a like purpose. For others, what might be considered winsome and warm becomes sentimental.

John L. Fell

Reviews
Essence. XVII, November, 1986, p. 36.
Film Quarterly. XL, Spring, 1987, p. 2.
Films in Review. XXXVIII, January, 1987, p. 43.
Los Angeles Times. October 16, 1986, VI, p. 1.
The New Republic. CXCV, November 3, 1986, p. 26.
The New York Times. September 30, 1986, p. C11.
The New York Times. October 17, 1986, p. B2.
Newsweek. CVIII, October 20, 1986, p. 79.
Time. CXXVIII, October 6, 1986, p. 94.
The Wall Street Journal. October 9, 1986, p. 32.
Whole Earth Review. Winter, 1986, p. 87.

RUNNING SCARED

Production: David Foster and Lawrence Turman; released by Metro-Goldwyn-Mayer
Direction: Peter Hyams
Screenplay: Gary DeVore and Jimmy Huston; based on a story by DeVore
Cinematography: Peter Hyams
Editing: James Mitchell
Art direction: Albert Brenner; set decoration, George P. Gaines
Stunt coordination: Carey Loftin and Bill Couch, Sr.
Music: Rod Temperton
MPAA rating: R
Running time: 108 minutes

> *Principal characters:*
> Ray Hughes .... Gregory Hines
> Danny Costanzo..................... Billy Crystal
> Frank .... Steven Bauer
> Anna Costanzo .... Darlanne Fluegel
> Tony .... Jonathan Gries
> Captain Logan .... Dan Hedaya
> Snake........................... Joe Pantoliano
> Julio Gonzales .... Jimmy Smits
> Maryann .... Tracy Reed
> Vinnie............................ John DiSanti
> Ace............................... Larry Hankin

Peter Hyams' *Running Scared* is the kind of comedy/thriller which has become so familiar in films and television in the 1980's. Hyams has been active in the crime-thriller genre, directing (and often writing) such good films as *The Star Chamber* (1983), *Outland* (1981), and *The Hunter* (1980). *Running Scared*'s comic dimension is something which Hyams, who in addition to directing the film also served as its cinematographer, has not attempted before in a thriller, and the results of his experiment are reasonably positive.

Since *Running Scared* stars Billy Crystal and the versatile Gregory Hines, the viewer is prepared for comedy. In fact, the film consists of a long, episodic series of sketches, gag setups which feature energetic dialogue interspersed with scenes of police procedural business, shoot-outs, and car chases. While the production design and photography of *Running Scared* provide the viewer with pungent realism, and while one does laugh at the lively patter of Crystal and Hines, the film suffers somewhat from a lack of credibility, of both plot and characterization.

Danny Costanzo (Billy Crystal) and Ray Hughes (Gregory Hines) are undercover detective partners assigned to the narcotics detail of the Chicago Police Department. While their profession is clearly dangerous, Danny and Ray do not seem to take anything very seriously. Indeed, Danny's former wife, Anna (Darlanne Fluegel), divorced him because she found him to be immature. Wisecracking may in fact be one way in which police officers deal with the stress of their jobs, but it is difficult to believe that two men could carry on a running comedy routine while engaged in life-threatening gunplay and wild vehicle chases. It appears that the writers of *Running Scared* (Gary DeVore and Jimmy Huston) expect their viewers to suspend disbelief and accept Danny and Ray as characters similar to those which appear in television's *Hill Street Blues* or in *Beverly Hills Cop* (1984) and the action films of Burt Reynolds or Clint Eastwood.

Danny and Ray are hot on the trail of ambitious drug dealer Julio Gonzales (Jimmy Smits), who has set his sights on becoming Chicago's underworld czar. In the opening sequence of *Running Scared*, the two scruffy cops catch sight of one of Gonzales' thugs, Snake (Joe Pantoliano), as he appears in one of the city's uglier ghettos. A considerable amount of time is spent convincing Snake to reveal Gonzales' whereabouts, and after much illegal persuasion, Snake agrees to wear a radio transmitter to a rendezvous with his boss.

It is at moments such as this that *Running Scared*'s rather unnerving lack of continuity and smooth narrative transitions surfaces. In short order, Danny and Ray arrive at the scene of a policeman's apparent suicide (the viewer—and the detectives—later learn that the officer did not jump but was thrown from atop a building); then, Danny remembers that he must attend his Aunt Rose's funeral; soon after attending the funeral, the partners are accosted by a pair of muggers, and after a confrontation during which all four men draw guns, Danny and Ray apprehend the would-be robbers.

In all fairness, one must note that not all such interludes are completely irrelevant to the plot's development. Gonzales had murdered the policeman; and Danny eventually discovers that, much to his understandable delight, the late Aunt Rose has left him forty thousand dollars.

The planned ambush of Gonzales develops into an embarrassing double cross. Danny and Ray do survive and arrest Gonzales, but their free-lancing has ruined the undercover work of the two Federal agents who had to rescue them. As a result, the detectives' superior, Captain Logan (Dan Hedaya), suspends Danny and Ray, and another tangent is pursued, which is designed to showcase the fun-loving side of the two detectives.

Their brash confidence shaken, Danny and Ray take a vacation in Key West, Florida, where, amid verbal jokes and sight gags (Danny and Ray sport T-shirts with women's breasts silk-screened on their fronts and pose for pictures next to swordfish that disgorge beer cans when they are hung upside down), the primary subject of their conversations is what Danny should do with his inheritance and the thankless nature of police work. Ultimately, the two decide to buy a bar in Florida.

Cutting quickly back to Chicago, Danny and Ray roller-skate into Logan's office and announce that they are quitting the force. Logan, however, knows his men too well: He only has to tell them that Gonzales is back on the streets, and Danny and Ray are once again in business. As a form of harassment, however, Logan saddles Danny and Ray with the training of their replacements, Tony (Jonathan Gries) and Frank (Steven Bauer), the same two young undercover agents who had saved Danny and Ray from Gonzales. Tony and Frank remind the older detectives of themselves when they were eager and overconfident—before they lost their edge and started "running scared" from police work.

The chase after Gonzales is on again, and it becomes a game of wits. The police close in on an alleged three-million-dollar shipment of cocaine at O'Hare Airport only to discover bags of manure. Danny and Ray spot a priest and a nun who appear to be likely drug couriers; it develops that the religious are in fact just that, religious. All is not lost, however, for the nun and the priest have, in fact, unwittingly carried dope into the country.

After a frantic car chase that features spectacular photography and stunt driving as Danny and Ray pursue Gonzales on Chicago's elevated railway tracks, Gonzales takes Anna as a hostage and, thus, sets up the film's mind-boggling finale.

Danny agrees to exchange Gonzales' cocaine for Anna, and a meeting is set to take place in the gigantic State Building in downtown Chicago. It appears that Gonzales has the upper hand: Danny and Ray (with help from Tony and Frank, who arrive close behind) go in against an entire corps of armed goons disguised as state policemen. As the viewer knows full well, Danny and Ray will manage an absolutely outrageous rescue of Anna and kill every villain in sight. They are also able to teach Tony and Frank some lessons on bold police work, saving Tony's and Frank's lives in the process. How tens of men armed with automatic weapons could carry on a fifteen-minute gun battle in a massive edifice in the heart of a major city without attracting any attention at all remains a mystery to the film's end.

As befits a fairy tale, however, all ends happily: Anna's heart gets the best of her head, and she sees that Danny is still the man for her after all. Danny, Ray, Tony, and Frank have gained respect for one another as well.

Running Scared is decent entertainment if one accepts the film as just that—entertainment. The dialogue is often irresistibly funny, and viewers will find that they are caught up in most of the action sequences almost in spite of themselves.

The visual appeal of the film owes much to Hyams and production designer Brenner's depiction of the sleaziness of Chicago's mean streets, on the one hand, and the majestic glitter of the heart of the city, on the other. The sun never shines in Chicago, it seems, and even in the scenes shot in interiors, a pervasive haze suggests the moral confusion of the characters. Indeed, if the worldview which *Running Scared* presents is to be taken seriously at all, the perspective is not a pretty one. Danny and Ray and their police colleagues seem to be less concerned with duty and the system of justice than with looking out for themselves and one another and satisfying their own pragmatic code of honor—which clashes with legal procedures most of the time. The heroes' indifference to the bigger picture is understandable, given the existence of a thankless public, lawyers who are interested only in scoring points for their clients, and police salaries which in no way compensate for the risks that peace officers take daily.

Gordon Walters

Reviews
Chicago Tribune. June 27, 1986, p. CT7.
Ebony. XLI, October, 1986, p. 100.
Films in Review. XXXVII, October, 1986, p. 480.
Los Angeles Times. June 27, 1986, VI, p. 1.
The New York Times. June 27, 1986, p. C10.
Newsweek. CVII, June 30, 1986, p. 60.
People Weekly. XXV, June 30, 1986, p. 10.
Time. CXXVII, June 30, 1986, p. 87.
Variety. CCCXXIII, June 25, 1986, p. 32.
The Wall Street Journal. June 26, 1986, p. 29.

RUTHLESS PEOPLE

Production: Michael Peyser for Touchstone Films; released by Buena Vista
Direction: Jim Abrahams, David Zucker, and Jerry Zucker
Screenplay: Dale Launer
Cinematography: Jan De Bont
Editing: Gib Jaffe and Arthur Schmidt
Art direction: Donald Woodruff; set decoration, Anne McCulley
Costume design: Rosanna Norton
Music: Michel Colombier
MPAA rating: R
Running time: 93 minutes

Principal characters:
Barbara Stone .... Bette Midler
Sam Stone .... Danny DeVito
Ken Kessler .... Judge Reinhold
Sandy Kessler .... Helen Slater
Carol .... Anita Morris
Earl .... Bill Pullman
Police commissioner............... William Shilling

For a variety of economic and practical reasons, American films have come to look increasingly like American television. *Ruthless People* is a mutt of a film: part cinema, part television, and even part stand-up comedy.

Television does not demand the viewer's attention; in fact it courts the viewer's disconnection. Every ten or eleven minutes, the audience's focus will be shifted to stories about soap and beer. The fabric of a work is lost in a mix and jumble of disconnected images and sound. The resulting new video narrative, which programs like *Hill Street Blues* and *St. Elsewhere* fostered, is built with short episodes of character interaction. Each episode is a joke or mininarrative unto itself.

Ruthless People is a film with three directors: Jim Abrahams, David Zucker, and Jerry Zucker. This kind of group filmmaking worked well for their collections of visual puns and jokes, *Airplane!* (1980; reviewed in this volume) and *Top Secret* (1984), in which they parodied the cinematic clichés of 1970's disaster epics and World War II spy-adventure films. In such works, the joke is more important than character development or storytelling; one joke can follow another without much concern for style, consistency, or design. When, however, such a formula is applied to the complex plot of a film such as *Ruthless People*, it leads to an awkward, uneven work.

Sam Stone (Danny DeVito) is the Spandex miniskirt king. The viewer meets him in the opening scene of the film dining with Carol (Anita Morris), his mistress. He reveals to her his plan to kill his wife, Barbara (Bette Midler). True to his word, and the film's title, he excuses himself and heads home for the afternoon's work.

The Stone home is one of the few elements of the film which is treated with the care and craft considered cinematic. The camera, hiding in a corner of the living room, looks across a sparsely furnished space dotted not with furniture but with post-modernist *objets d'art* of plastic and enamel. It is all slick and spotless and superficial, just like the Stones' marriage. Every glimpse of Sam and Barbara's life together is as lifeless as this museum of New Wave design, a motif echoed throughout the film. The truly ruthless people are found in lifeless homes and offices. The not-so-truly ruthless but simply hapless middle-class folks are found in cluttered, comfortable, lived-in settings. It is a romantic notion as old as Western storytelling: The bad people are rich and showy, the good people are poor and modest.

Barbara is not home. She has been kidnapped by some simple, middle-class folks who have been wronged by ruthless Sam Stone. Sandy Kessler (Helen Slater) is the true designer of the Spandex miniskirt. Sam Stone stole her designs and made his fortune without even a nod to Sandy. She and her husband, Ken (Judge Reinhold), are holding Barbara until Sam agrees to pay $500,000 in ransom. Sam, however, is delighted to think that Barbara's murder will be taken care of for him as long as he does not act to free her.

Sam's wife is a demanding, stormy woman. When the viewer first sees her emerging from a large gunnysack which Ken and Sandy clumsily carry from their car and bounce down the cellar steps, she is understandably loud, abusive, and unpleasant. It is clear from the start that Ken and Sandy have more than they can handle. They wait impatiently for Sam to call and agree to pay the ransom. The joke of this film is set: The kidnappers cannot wait to be rid of their victim. The victim makes a miserable guest. The husband will not pay the ransom. Not only will the kidnappers have to make more modest demands, but they might also end up paying the victim's husband to take her off their hands.

This is a familiar story. O. Henry told it in "The Ransom of Red Chief." Here screenwriter Dale Launer embellishes it with layer upon layer of blackmail and mistaken identity. Sam's mistress, Carol, has a second lover, Earl (Bill Pullman), and the two of them are as ruthless as Sam. They videotape what they think is Sam murdering Barbara in a parked car on a hillside. What they really have filmed, however, is the police commissioner (William Shilling) and his mistress involved in the throes of passion. Carol and Earl threaten to blackmail Sam with the tape, but Sam knows that he is the most innocent of all these ruthless characters. Carol, convinced that Sam is lying about not having killed Barbara, calls the police and offers the videotape which she thinks shows the crime in progress. Carol is baffled when the commissioner frantically reacts on the assumption that he is the one being blackmailed.

Meanwhile, back at the Stone house, the police find evidence that makes them suspect that Sam may have killed his wife and only invented the kidnapping story. To avoid being thrown in jail on suspicion of murder, he contacts the kidnappers and, to their surprise, makes a generous offer to buy back Barbara.

Throughout this mayhem, there are some isolated moments—little films within the film—which are distinguished more by the actor's performance than the directors' vision. These moments, however, clever as they are, interrupt rather than advance the film. Barbara spends her time in the basement watching exercise programs on television. Her workouts are little islands of slapstick in the turbulent plot, inventive and funny. There is also a running gag about the Stones' dog, Muffie. Sam is determined to do away with the dog while his wife is gone. He buys a large and reputedly vicious dog to do the job. Muffie and her intended assailant, however, grow increasingly close and in the end turn on Sam. Ken, too, is allowed moments which have little to do with the plot. He works in a stereo equipment store, and the audience realizes how gentle he is when, determined to behave ruthlessly, he begins to pitch a huge stereo system to a teenage boy by equating a large woofer with masculinity. When the boy's pregnant girlfriend enters, however, Ken returns to trying to sell the best bargain equipment. These scenes have a realistic, almost theatrical look, unlike the garish, close-up style of the rest of the film.

Barbara's exercise program pays off for her. Because she loses so much weight, she must ask Sandy for better-fitting clothes. Sandy is anxious to oblige, and the film's one and only tender moment unfolds. Sandy offers Barbara some of the dressy fashions she has designed, and Barbara thinks that they are wonderful. The two women become instant friends, and Barbara is freed from the cellar. Ken, at first dubious, finally agrees to elevate Barbara from victim to accomplice. Knowing that they can manipulate the situation to their advantage, the three of them taunt and tease Sam and finally force him to agree to pay the ransom.

All the complexities of the plot come together in a long and ponderous scene when Sam and Earl meet with Ken and fight over the money. The obligatory chase scene, with cops chasing two sets of robbers, ends with Ken's car careening off the end of a pier into the water. The money and the kidnapper seem lost. Barbara appears for a final bit of nasty revenge. After convincing Sam that all is forgiven, she turns their affectionate clutch into a nasty punch. For his part, Sam has achieved what he set out to do: He is rid of his wife. This conclusion is a mere afterthought: The story was complete long before the chase began.

There is, however, a final, unexpected twist: an epilogue in which Ken surfaces on a distant beach, carrying a briefcase filled with the ransom money. He is joined by Sandy, and they are joined by Barbara; arm in arm they walk off into the sunset. As mean and nasty and black as this film struggles to be, it is finally sweet and good-natured: Justice comes to those most wronged.

As feature films become more costly to produce, it seems inevitable that the lucrative television aftermarket will have even greater impact on the form and content of American cinema. European films, which are not tied so intimately to the television industry, are the last hope of the film purist. Films such as *Ruthless People* will satisfy those who go to the theater expecting nothing more than an extended situation comedy without commercials.

Peter Moller

Reviews
Film Comment. XXII, July, 1986, p. 26.
Los Angeles Times. June 27, 1986, VI, p. 1.
Macleans. XCIX, July 7, 1986, p. 53.
The New York Times. CXXXV, July 6, 1986, II, p. 18.
The New Yorker. LXII, July 14, 1986, p. 66.
Newsweek. CVII, June 30, 1986, p. 59.
Time. CXXVII, June 30, 1986, p. 87.
Variety. CCCXXIII, June 25, 1986, p. 32.
The Wall Street Journal. CCVIII, June 26, 1986, p. 29.
The Washington Post. June 27, 1986, p. D1.

THE SACRIFICE
(OFFRET)

Origin: Sweden and France
Released: 1986
Released in U.S.: 1986
Production: Katinka Farago for Swedish Film Institute and Argos Films in association with Film Four International, Josephson and Nykvist, Sveriges Television/SVT2, and Sandrew Film and Teater; released by Sandrew Film and Teater
Direction: Andrei Tarkovsky
Screenplay: Andrei Tarkovsky
Cinematography: Sven Nykvist
Editing: Andrei Tarkovsky and Michal Leszczylowski
Art direction: Anna Asp
Special effects: Svenska Stuntgruppen, Lars Hoglund, and Lars Palmqvist
Costume design: Inger Pehrsson
Sound: Owe Svensson, Bosse Persson, Lars Ulander, Christin Loman, and Wikee Peterson-Berger
Music: Johann Sebastian Bach, *The Saint Matthew Passion* and Swedish and Japanese folk music
MPAA rating: PG
Running time: 149 minutes

Principal characters:
Alexander .... Erland Josephson
Adelaide .... Susan Fleetwood
Julia .... Valérie Mairesse
Otto .... Allan Edwall
Maria .... Gudrún Gísladóttir
Victor .... Sven Wollter
Little Man .... Tommy Kjellqvist

Andrei Tarkovsky, who died in exile in Paris in December, 1986, was probably the greatest Soviet filmmaker since Sergei Eisenstein. Unlike Eisenstein, however, Tarkovsky found his inspiration not in the spirit of the Russian Revolution but in the spirituality of the Russian literary masters of the nineteenth century. His heroes were closer to Leo Tolstoy's Ivan Ilyich than to Eisenstein's Ivan the Terrible, and the questions his films posed were not about the nature of political power but about the possibilities of personal salvation.

His last film, *The Sacrifice*, shows Tarkovsky at his most poetic and his most prophetic. The poetry in the film resides in his absolute control of composition and narrative rhythm, perhaps best exemplified by the two astonishing single takes that constitute the opening and penultimate scenes; in his idiosyncratic imagery (here the crashing to the floor of a jug of milk suggests a whole world about to become unstable); and in his ability to establish an uneasy, menacing atmosphere that is palpable without being overtly portentous. In his roll as prophet, Tarkovsky once again warns mankind that it is on a wrong road, a dangerous road, on which there is an imbalance between man's material and spiritual development and where scientific breakthroughs are being put in the service of evil. *The Sacrifice* is an apocalyptic film that implicitly asks what the artist can do in a nuclear age. The urgency of its message has only been amplified by the contaminated clouds of Chernobyl.

At his birthday party, a former actor, now a lecturer and writer, Alexander (Erland Josephson), awakens from a rest to find his family and guests seated anxiously around the television, listening to a newscast which seems to speak of a major nuclear crisis. The unthinkable, for which the postwar generation has been waiting in trepidation, has finally happened, and Tarkovsky for a moment observes the impact of catastrophe on character. It drives Alexander's wife, Adelaide (Susan Fleetwood), into hysterics and toward a confession that the man she loves and wishes she had married is not Alexander but the doctor, Victor (Sven Wollter). The bland Victor's reaction to this disaster is to offer either soothing or fatal palliatives—a sedative to Adelaide's daughter, Julia (Valérie Mairesse) and a gun obligingly at the service of anyone who wishes to use it. Another guest, the postman Otto (Allan Edwall), consoles himself with drink, but it is Alexander's response which is to form the core of the film's drama.

Alone in his room, Alexander offers up a prayer to God: Reverse the events of this day, and he will give up all that he most values. Later that night, Otto visits him and says that the spell can be broken if Alexander sleeps with the maid, Maria (Gudrún Gísladóttir), who has strange powers. He does so. The next day everything seems to have returned to normal, and Alexander must honor his promises of the previous night—his vow of silence, his renunciation of home, wife, and son. Having tricked the others into going for a stroll, Alexander begins to make preparations for setting fire to his house.

The professor is the kind of hero who has always interested Tarkovsky: a man under moral or ethical pressure, at a crisis in his life that will either make or break him. He is also an artist, and as with the eponymous heroes of *Andrei Rublev* (1966) and *Stalker* (1979), there is an element of self-portraiture in Tarkovsky's depiction of Alexander. In his book, *Sculpting in Time: Reflections on the Cinema* (1987), Tarkovsky writes about the necessity of man's willingness for sacrifice, without which he ceases to be a spiritual being. As a dissident artist expelled from his native country,

Tarkovsky would certainly know about the sacrifices imposed on the artist who feels compelled to speak the truth as he sees it. Yet, as in *Stalker*, Tarkovsky does not romanticize or sentimentalize. He perceives the danger of this fearful frankness moving into, or being mistaken for, an arrogant self-righteousness, and he does not disguise the suffering of other people, notably the artist's family, who become implicated in the consequences of his uncompromising nature. For it is not only Alexander who suffers from his sacrifice.

It is probably significant that Alexander's greatest roles as an actor were as Richard III and Fyodor Dostoevski's Prince Myshkin—extremes of destructive selfishness and divine selflessness, respectively. It is a detail which neatly expresses the duality and ambiguity of Alexander's character and actions. It is revealed that he gave up acting because, rather like the actress in Ingmar Bergman's *Persona* (1966), he suddenly became embarrassed by his presence on the stage. The suggestion is that he was afraid that he might either reveal or surrender his ego and that his identity might dissolve altogether—something to bear in mind when one assesses his act of sacrifice. Does it enhance the sacrifice's nobility or make it even more ambiguous? Alexander has the complexity of a true tragic hero. In the astonishing, single-shot penultimate sequence in which his house explodes, his family, guests, and the ambulancemen gather in horror, and he rushes round in crazy circles, he resembles nothing so much as a modern King Lear—a man who has surrendered everything in a fallen world, a man who might be on the brink of discovering the true value of life as opposed to its materialist and symbolic appurtenances, but who is in danger of being misunderstood and perceived by society as an obsessive madman.

Many critics have commented on the similarity of the film's world to that of Ingmar Bergman. The similarity is reinforced by the film's setting on the Swedish island of Gotland, which Bergman first used in *Through a Glass Darkly* (1961), by Tarkovsky's use of the skills of Bergman's regular cameraman, Sven Nykvist, and by the film's casting of some of the actors and the art director from *Fanny and Alexander* (1982). Perhaps the strongest connection, though, is the intensity of the film's religious imagery, which, away from the constraints of the Soviet Union, Tarkovsky employs with great force. For example, the credits appear over a close camera examination of a detail from Leonardo da Vinci's painting *The Adoration of the Three Kings*. At one point, Alexander and Otto discuss the painting, Otto finding it frightening, Alexander being awed by it. Tarkovsky composes a marvelous shot of their faces reflected on the painting's protective glass covering, an image that suddenly unites in a single frame, and with great majesty and mystery, the human, the artistic, and the religious.

There are three details in the painting that will be mystically transformed in the texture of the film's narrative. The Virgin Mary will be metamorphosed in Tarkovsky's tale into the maid Maria, a guardian angel whose benevolent love will literally sweep Alexander off his feet. The tree in the painting will anticipate the appearance of a tree which Alexander is planting in the opening scene with the help of his temporarily mute son (Tommy Kjellqvist). In the final scene, his speech now restored, the son will return to this tree and tend to it: the tree of life, perhaps, or knowledge, which will blossom if nurtured properly by a younger generation now finding its own voice. Finally, as in the painting, Alexander will receive three gifts on his birthday, all of which will prove significant: a book of religious paintings, which will foreshadow Alexander's recourse to prayer as a means of surviving the crisis; a model of his beloved house, the destruction of which will become the principal symbol of his sacrifice; and a map of seventeenth century Europe, which illustrates how man has always attempted to make charts of his world but which also highlights how that world has constantly been changed by conquest and catastrophe.

The Sacrifice is a haunting film, and it would be quite tempting to interpret it as a dream or a nightmare, with Tarkovsky offering several different tantalizing possibilities about where the dream starts. Is it when Alexander collides with his son, which seems to disorient him and trigger a frightening vision of debris and panic? Or when he rests prior to going down and hearing the newscast? Or is it even a dream of his young son as he sleeps upstairs while the crisis explodes? Nykvist's marvelously shaded photography gives a complex and varied visual texture to the film's shifts of mood and tone, and the characters are also more multilayered than they initially appear: The maid may be a Madonna, and the postman is also a philosopher and occultist. Some critics have suggested that Tarkovsky rather indulges himself here, particularly in two anecdotes, one in which Otto tells a story about a photograph on which a dead son appears ghostlike with his mother, and the other in which Alexander tells Maria a parable about an attempt of his to improve his mother's unruly garden, which has actually ruined it. Yet both stories point to a moral that is thematically crucial to the film: that there are more things in heaven and earth than are dreamt of in man's philosophy, and that man's arrogant attempt to impose his own will on Nature is dangerously destructive.

The Sacrifice is a long film, but its impeccable compositions and concentration of action over a twenty-four-hour period compel one's attention. If Eisenstein brandished his camera like a fist, Tarkovsky uses it with painterly precision. On one level, *The Sacrifice* resembles a Chekhovian country-house drama, in which a group of comfortable, self-important, dissatisfied people regretfully and terrifyingly begin to crack open the shell of their empty lives. The difference is that the cloud that hovers over them in the twentieth century is not simply personal regret but global annihilation. The intrigue of the plot in *The Sacrifice* makes it perhaps the most accessible of all Tarkovsky's films, but not to the point of sacrificing that characteristic air of ambiguity and apprehension as humanity makes its way along a path that is winding and increasingly treacherous.

Last year it was Akira Kurosawa's *Ran* (1985) which offered a glimpse of the apocalyptic, and Kurosawa's final image of humanity in that film—that of a blind man staggering towards an abyss—was a terrifying warning. *The Sacrifice* is also a warning, but its tone is more temperate and its conclusion more hopeful. There is still time, disaster can be averted, and humanity can still aspire to a burgeoning spirituality and selflessness. In *The Sacrifice*, Tarkovsky seems to have been reflecting on his own imminent death as well as the possibility of the world's, and it is a measure of his courage and confidence that he felt that he could dedicate the film to his son in a spirit of hope for the future. Tarkovsky once said that the artist exists because the world is not perfect. Perhaps so, but artistry on the level of *The Sacrifice* makes the world seem a little less imperfect.

Neil Sinyard

Reviews
The Christian Science Monitor. October 31, 1986, p. 25.
Los Angeles. XXXII, February, 1987, p. 213.
Los Angeles Times. December 22, 1986, VI, p. 1.
New Statesman. CXIII, January 23, 1987, p. 23.
New York. XIX, November 3, 1986, p. 83.
The New York Times. September 26, 1986, p. C12.
Newsweek. CVIII, November 24, 1986, p. 90.
Philadelphia. LXXVIII, February, 1987, p. 49.
Time. CXXVIII, November 24, 1986, p. 97.

SALVADOR

Production: Gerald Green and Oliver Stone; released by Hemdale Film
  Corporation
Direction: Oliver Stone
Screenplay: Oliver Stone and Richard Boyle
Cinematography: Robert Richardson
Editing: Claire Simpson
Production design: Bruno Rubeo
Art direction: Melo Hinojosa; set decoration, Milo Needles
Special effects: Yves De Bono
Music: Georges Delerue
MPAA rating: R
Running time: 123 minutes

> *Principal characters:*
> Richard Boyle...................James Woods
> Dr. Rock.........................James Belushi
> Ambassador Thomas Kelly.........Michael Murphy
> John Cassady ....John Savage
> María............................Elepedia Carrillo
> Major Max ....Tony Plana
> Jack Morgan ....Colby Chester
> Colonel Hyde.....................Will MacMillian
> Archbishop Romero ....José Carlos Ruíz

In a famous scene from the film *Becket* (1964), the late Richard Burton,
in the role of Henry II, asks the ostensibly rhetorical question: "Will no one
rid me of this troublesome priest?" Three of his vassals take the hint and
run out to assassinate the Archbishop of Canterbury, whose martyrdom had
but little impact on the political affairs of England—whatever it may have
done to the state of Henry's soul. In *Salvador*, Major Max (a thinly disguised version of Major Roberto D'Aubuisson, leader of the Salvadoran
right wing, played with convincing menace here by Tony Plana) circles a
sumptuously appointed table at which are seated various members of the
Salvadoran bourgeoisie and its military henchmen. Major Max curses the
clergy, the foreign press, and the current American ambassador and concludes with a question rather less ambiguous in intent than that of Henry II:
"Who will be the one among you to rid me of this Romero?" In the film,
the subsequent assassination of Archbishop Romero (José Carlos Ruíz) is
framed by the attempt of protagonist Richard Boyle (James Woods) to reform his life in order to marry his Salvadoran girlfriend, María (Elepedia
Carrillo), and deliver her from the country. What was historically one of the

most dramatic events in the Salvadoran struggle to date is thus turned into a mere backdrop for the story of the film's decadent but irresistible hero. The same pattern is repeated often, as the major historical events of El Salvador, from early 1980 through the first two months of 1981 (to which the film is on the whole reasonably faithful, although the time scale is considerably compressed), are focused on their interaction with Boyle's career. This is the source both of the film's narrative coherence and of its weakness as an analytic account of Salvadoran politics and history. Another way of making the same point is to say that the ideological limits of *Salvador* are largely visible in the decision to make it the story of the journalist hero rather than that of the Salvadoran people.

In contrast to Stone's popular triumph with *Platoon* (1986; reviewed in this volume)—which won Academy Awards for Best Picture and Best Direction—*Salvador*, by any standard a superior film, received only one nomination (James Woods for Best Actor), making the ideological limits of his project even clearer. The brutal naturalism of combat in *Platoon* focuses exclusively on the sufferings and tragedy of "our boys," while the Vietnamese soldiers appear only as ghosts in the night, menacing wraiths scarcely distinguishable from the animals who inhabit the jungle. The indigenous peasants, when they are not simply pitiful, are sneaking, sly, and untrustworthy. The notable scene in which a village is put to the torch leaves open the question whether the villagers were Vietcong sympathizers. Nowhere in the film are the heroism and fortitude of the Vietnamese people portrayed.

That *Salvador* is a film for the *norteamericanos* is made perfectly clear in the guerrillas' short-lived triumph at the battle of Santa Ana during the January, 1981, Farabundo Martí National Liberation Front (FMLN) offensive. Faced with the arrival of tanks and air support (made possible by the American ambassador's decision to release embargoed American military aid in the form of fuel), the guerrillas decide to execute the few remaining members of the National Guard before retreating. Boyle, who has appeared somewhat miraculously on the scene in time to witness the guerrillas' stirring cavalry charge which forces the garrison to surrender, characteristically jumps into the middle of the action, shouting: "You're becoming just like them, you're becoming just like them." For the audience who recoiled in horror earlier when a helpless young campesino was executed by this same National Guard, Boyle's words can only ring true—and thus stand in irrevocable judgment on the acts of violence the guerrillas commit in the name of political expedience or necessity. It is quite difficult even to hear the reply of the young fighter who momentarily halts Boyle with the barrel of his rifle to say: "It's war, gringo." That voice, which speaks the historical truth about El Salvador, in 1986 more than ever, is all but muted by the drama of Boyle's personal tragedy, the real subject of this film. (To some degree, this was inevitable, since the real Richard Boyle who lived out these incidents collaborated with director Oliver Stone on the screenplay. Nevertheless, the biographical accuracy of Boyle's story does not entail its broader historical truth. Individual perceptions of historical processes are no less ideological for their being the testimony of an eyewitness.)

Salvador continues a tradition of semifictionalized filmmaking about contemporary or recent political struggles witnessed by Western journalists, from Volker Schöndorff's *Circle of Deceit* (1982), which chronicles the Lebanese civil war of the late 1970's, to *The Year of Living Dangerously* (1982), the Peter Weir film about the fall of Sukarno in 1965, to Roger Spottiswoode's film about the Sandinista revolution in Nicaragua, *Under Fire* (1983), to Roland Joffe's *The Killing Fields* (1984), which is based on *The New York Times* reporter Sydney Schanberg's account of 1970's war-torn Cambodia. In each of these films, the historical sequence is an occasion for psychological exploration or romantic plotting, so that however much one is reminded of the actualities of political power and the brutality of repressive state apparatuses, in the end the life of the hero is the viewer's principal concern. In all the climactic scenes, violence against the hero himself becomes the focus of the narrative, his survival and escape the viewer's only concern. These films ostensibly represent the trajectory of actual historical events in the so-called Third World, but what they more powerfully project is the ideological image of the Western witness to the inhumanity and brutality that are assumed to be endemic to non-Western societies.

All this said, one must concede that *Salvador* remains a powerful film and is, given the standard views of Latin America presented in the mainstream media since the early 1980's, a welcome counterweight to the conventional images of the struggles of Central American peoples against American-sponsored repression by their own governments. When Boyle returns to the city after photographing a guerrilla training camp in the mountains, he visits the American embassy in an attempt to trade his photos (which reveal nothing in particular) for a voter registration card that will guarantee the relative safety of María from the death squads. Neither the embassy aide Jack Morgan (Colby Chester) nor the military attaché Colonel Hyde (Will MacMillian) can accept Boyle's claims that the guerrillas have nothing but captured or stolen weapons, mostly relics of past wars. They press him to reveal what they "already know": that the guerrillas are being supplied by Nicaragua and Cuba with modern hardware, thus confirming the official view of the war as an extension of Communist aggression in the region. Boyle, who is more concerned about his girlfriend's safety than about the grand political strategy that is at stake in the war, finally realizes that he is getting nowhere and delivers what is surely the film's most direct political judgment, linking Central America to Vietnam and denouncing the United States for its stupid blindness to the facts of social and political life in both: that the poverty, suffering, and degradation of the indigenous populations of these nations are the true source of rebellion and that America's support of murderous re-gimes will in the long run simply drive more and more people to support the guerrillas. Boyle's parting shot to the American colonel recalls his similar outburst against the guerrillas' execution of the National Guardsmen and summarizes the film's general view regarding American policy in El Sal-vador: "You should fit right in here, Colonel; you talk just like a gangster."

One of the oddly winning aspects of *Salvador* is its blending of buffoonery with seriousness, low comedy with high drama. The focal point of most of the film's humor is Dr. Rock (James Belushi), an aging disc jockey whose marriage has recently broken up and who comes along to El Salvador for the ride with his sometime buddy Boyle. Jolted momentarily into sobriety when his own life appears at risk, Rock nevertheless bounces from one drunken or drug-induced stupor to another, until he latches onto a more or less permanent situation with a former prostitute whom he first meets when she is pursuing her trade. Initially desiring only to return to San Francisco, he appears ready, by the film's end, to remain in El Salvador indefinitely. This is a recurrent motif in the film; Boyle himself leaves less from fear for his own safety than from the conviction that only by taking María and her children to California will they be safe from the death squads who murdered her brother.

This romance of the region "south of the border" may provide a key to what is surely the film's most puzzling feature: its stubborn optimism, despite all the evidence it offers that the historical situation in El Salvador offers no foreseeable hope for its people or any relief from their suffering. Boyle and María escape, if only in the end to have her caught by United States immigration and deported. The viewer learns, in a series of printed conclusions after the final shot, that she is rumored to be living in a refugee camp in Guatemala. Boyle himself keeps hope alive by searching for her, and he manages to publish combat footage which his friend John Cassady (John Savage) shot just before his death. The war itself has escalated since 1981, with American military assistance enabling the Salvadoran army to carry out virtual genocide against its own people in the countryside, but the spirit of *Salvador* runs directly counter to the historical pessimism which many of its sequences and events would seem to warrant.

What sticks in one's mind even more vividly than the images of carnage and the memories of brutality are the scenes of life in the guerrillas' moun-tain camp, where soldiers are trained and a close-knit community functions under the most primitive conditions. When pressed by Boyle to consider that the Pentagon will almost certainly not allow the guerrilla offensive to succeed, FMLN commander Martí (Miguel Ehrenberg) triumphantly re-plies: "The will of the people and the march of history cannot be stopped, not even by the *norteamericanos*"—which sounds laughably naïve, particu-larly in the light of what has happened during the intervening five years.

This faith in the inevitable triumph of popular will and the irresistible force of the revolutionary process throughout Central America and the Caribbean is, to be sure, no less ideological than the residual "gringoism" noted earlier. For an American audience largely anesthetized to the revolutionary politics of the Third World, it may be a means of opening up a small corner of the truth about wars of national liberation. The more Americans who realize that the indigenous populations of the underdeveloped world will fight to the death for the basic economic and political rights generally taken for granted by citizens of the free world, the sooner will the revolutionary optimism expressed by Captain Martí no longer be a strictly utopian vision.

Michael Sprinker

Reviews
California Magazine. XI, June, 1986, p. 47.
Los Angeles Times. April 12, 1986, V, p. 1.
The New York Times. CXXXV, March 5, 1986, p. C22.
The New Yorker. LXII, July 28, 1986, p. 77.
Newsweek. CVII, March 17, 1986, p. 80.
Variety. CCCXXII, March 5, 1986, p. 14.
Video. X, October, 1986, p. 85.
The Wall Street Journal. CCVII, March 20, 1986, p. 28.
Washingtonian. XXI, May, 1986, p. 101.

SHERMAN'S MARCH
An Improbable Quest for Love

Production: Ross McElwee; released by First Run Features
Direction: Ross McElwee
Screenplay: Ross McElwee
Cinematography: Ross McElwee; New York statue camerawork by Michel
    Negroponte
Editing: Ross McElwee
Narration: Ross McElwee
Reading of historical narration: Richard Leacock
Art direction: no listing
Sound: Ross McElwee
Music: no listing
MPAA rating: no listing
Running time: 155 minutes

> *Principal characters:*
> Ross McElwee .... Himself
> Mary .... Herself
> Pat .... Herself
> Charleen .... Herself
> Dee Dee .... Herself
> Karen .... Herself

Some of the earliest films ever made were documentaries. The program of shorts at the Grand Café in Paris on December 28, 1895—probably the first time films were projected to a paying public—included brief, nonfiction film clips of workers leaving a factory, waves crashing on a shore, and scenes of Lyons traffic. Indeed, the invention of cinema was inspired in part by the desire to capture reality for present and future generations. Once the medium discovered the possibilities in a fictional narrative, however, the fictional film became the dominant form and remains so to this day. Nevertheless, the documentary has continued to flourish and has had its own illustrious history, though one of which the film-going public is largely unaware. Against this backdrop it was both surprising and gratifying to have so many commercially and critically successful documentaries emerge during the mid-1980's. *Marlene* (1983), *Twenty-eight Up* (1984), *The Times of Harvey Milk* (1984), *Stop Making Sense* (1984), *Shoah* (1985), and others all found a reasonably widespread audience—minuscule perhaps in relation to a major studio hit, but significant enough on the art-house circuit. Certainly one of the most aesthetically challenging nonfiction films of the 1980's, *Sherman's March: An Improbable Quest for Love* is an unusual work which begins as a documentary about the lingering effects of the Civil War on the American South and ends as filmmaker Ross McElwee's search for romance. McElwee sees himself as a modern-day embodiment of General William Tecumseh Sherman, but his exploits are sexual, not military, and, unlike Sherman's battlefield triumphs, McElwee's attempted conquests end in comic failure.

McElwee was schooled in the documentary tradition known as cinema verité. While it has historical antecedents as diverse as Louis and Auguste Lumière, Robert Flaherty, Jean Renoir, Italian neorealism, and the French New Wave, cinema verité had its immediate roots in both France and the United States during the late 1950's and early 1960's. Aided by compact sixteen-millimeter cameras and portable sound recorders, cinema verité filmmakers attempted to capture reality directly on film without directorial manipulation or control. Technical quality was sacrificed in order to achieve spontaneity and immediacy. In the United States, one of the movement's earliest practitioners was Richard Leacock, who later founded the film department at the Massachusetts Institute of Technology. McElwee both studied and lectured at M.I.T. and names Leacock as one of his more important influences. Despite McElwee's background, however, *Sherman's March* is not really cinema verité. Certainly McElwee's film, shot over the course of seven months in 1981 with a sixteen-millimeter camera and a handheld Nagra tape recorder, owes much to the cinema verité tradition. McElwee rejects, however, cinema verité's pretense to objectivity. He continually inserts his presence into the film, relishing rather than avoiding the power of the filmmaker to shape the events being filmed. In *Sherman's March*, McElwee shows what happens when the filmmaker steps out from behind the shield of the camera and becomes a part of the film itself.

Sherman's March began in 1981 as an idea to make a film about Sherman's march to the sea during the American Civil War. McElwee had planned not a somber educational work but a conversational one in which the filmmaker was to retrace Sherman's route and interview Southern people along the way. Just as filmmaking was to begin, however, McElwee's girlfriend left him. Dejected and confused, he decided to begin his odyssey anyway, unsure of what he would find. The opening of *Sherman's March* presents what presumably would have been the beginning of the original project. A red line on a map of the United States slowly traces Sherman's path as a solemn narrator (Richard Leacock) gives the essential historical background. As the map gives way to black-and-white photographs of the destruction caused by Sherman, the film's sound track reveals a brief conversation between McElwee and Leacock, who wants to try another take of his narration. The unexpected intrusion of this small, self-referential moment sets the tone for the film, which gradually evolves into an investigation of both filmmaker and filmmaking.

McElwee returns to his native South to attend a family gathering. While canoeing with his sister, he hits upon the *modus operandi* of the film. She suggests that he regard his camera as a conversation piece and use it to be more outgoing with women. The idea strikes a responsive chord, and from that point onward the camera almost never leaves McElwee's shoulder. Whereas the first few scenes had established the camera as an objective recorder of events, the film becomes told primarily from McElwee's point of view, the pattern broken only for those moments in the film when he turns the camera on himself. The point-of-view technique is so total that the audience (as they might in a traditional cinema verité film) almost accepts it as natural. McElwee continually disrupts the point-of-view approach, however, by reminding the audience of his directorial presence, and, more often than not, it is these dislocations that are the sources of the film's comedy.

The first woman he films is Mary, a childhood friend of McElwee and a recent divorcée. When McElwee surprises her at a fashion show, she runs up and hugs him, virtually kissing the camera in the process. Shortly thereafter, she leaves town, again embracing both camera and filmmaker. These rather direct acknowledgments of the camera establish the connection between McElwee's aesthetic compulsion to film and his sexual desire to meet women. The emotions are revealed as one and the same, and the rhythm and structure of the film become dependent on the status of McElwee's love life.

As the work progresses, McElwee's interest in filming women gradually becomes an obsession. During the sequences with Pat, an aspiring actress, McElwee confesses that he cannot seem to stop filming her. When she goes to Hollywood to audition for a part in a film, McElwee complains that he will not have anything to film after she leaves. The two first meet, appropriately enough, when Pat asks McElwee to film her performing her anticellulite exercises, a routine which consists primarily of Pat swinging somewhat suggestively to and fro. McElwee's microphone mysteriously (almost discreetly) turns off, and the viewer is left to watch the event silently. The moment draws the audience's attention to its own voyeurism and links McElwee's desire to film to the viewer's desire to see.

Without a subject for his camera, McElwee's film comes to a screeching halt. His life and film in limbo, he turns the camera on himself and delivers a dryly funny monologue from a hotel bed about his despair. These deadpan monologues are the most obvious way in which McElwee intrudes himself into the filmmaking process, as McElwee talks directly to the camera as if it were another person. The camera does in fact become a third party in the relationships between McElwee and the women he films, forming a perverse *ménage à trois*.

Ultimately, McElwee's obsession to film becomes overpowering. He goes to see Charleen, a former teacher and an exuberant matchmaker. As she introduces him to Dee Dee, Charleen begs him to put down the camera; this is not art, she says, this is life. McElwee can only reply that he must film. Later in the film, after two more failed attempts at love, McElwee decides to look up Karen, an old girlfriend. It is during these scenes that the film becomes most uncomfortable for the viewer. McElwee is clearly still obsessed with Karen, and he begs her to love him. Karen implores him to put down the camera while they discuss the relationship, but he cannot. The comic bantering with Charleen about his obsession to film turns serious. McElwee realizes that it is time to end his journey.

McElwee comes to the end of Sherman's march and the end of his film simultaneously. He has no money, no girlfriend, no reason to film anymore. He goes to New York and visits the statue of Sherman. In a voice-over, he tells of Sherman's death. Finally, McElwee seems to be cured of his dual obsession for women and film. (Appropriately, the New York footage is not even shot by McElwee but by his occasional collaborator Michel Negroponte.) When McElwee returns to Boston, however, resolving to enjoy a period of solitude, the camera is back on his shoulder. Later, during a music appreciation class, McElwee pans to the left and slowly zooms in on his teacher, whom he realizes is a rather attractive woman. The camera almost appears to have a life of its own, as it inexorably seeks out another woman. McElwee's obsessions have the final word.

David Rivel

Reviews

Chicago Tribune. September 12, 1986, VII, p. 48.
Film Quarterly. XL, Spring, 1987, p. 41.
Los Angeles Times. January 15, 1987, VI, p. 3.
The New Republic. CXCV, October 13, 1986, p. 26.
New York. September 8, 1986, p. 71.
The New York Times. September 5, 1986, p. C12.
Newsweek. CVIII, September 22, 1986, p. 84.
Variety. CCCXXIII, July 2, 1986, p. 13.
Vogue. CLXXVI, December, 1986, p. 70.
The Wall Street Journal. September 9, 1986, p. 26.
The Washington Post. December 25, 1986, p. C8.

SHE'S GOTTA HAVE IT

Production: Shelton J. Lee for Forty Acres and a Mule Filmworks; released by Island Pictures
Direction: Spike Lee
Screenplay: Spike Lee
Cinematography: Ernest Dickerson
Editing: Spike Lee
Production design: Wynn Thomas
Art direction: Ron Paley; set decoration, Clarence Jones
Costume design: John Michael Reefer
Sound: Barry Alexander Brown
Music: Bill Lee
MPAA rating: R
Running time: 84 minutes

Principal characters:

Nola Darling	Tracy Camila Johns
Jamie Overstreet	Tommy Redmond Hicks
Greer Childs	John Canada Terrell
Mars Blackmon	Spike Lee
Opal Gilstrap	Raye Dowell
Clorinda Bradford	Joie Lee
Dr. Jamison	Epatha Merkinson
Sonny Darling	Bill Lee
Ava	Cheryl Burr
Noble	Aaron Dugger
Keva	Stephanie Covington
Shawn	Renata Cobbs

Appropriate to its free-spirited nature, Spike Lee's film *She's Gotta Have It* emerged spontaneously from a false start. Lee, who had received two grants to make his first film since he was graduated from New York University film school, was stymied when it came to completing the initial funding for the project (a film about a bike messenger from Brooklyn and his family). One of the donors was willing to transfer its grant to a new project, while the other withdrew, leaving Lee with the staff and equipment to make a film but little money.

So, in a true improvisational spirit, Lee wrote a new script which required a minimum of characters, locations, and properties. (He also made good use of relatives; besides Spike, three Lee family members are credited in *She's Gotta Have It.*) He and his crew completed their work in a week and a half, spending their nights after shooting writing letters and phoning for contributions. Their efforts are reflected in a film which depends for its success almost entirely on a strong, witty story and clear, concise characterizations. In its reliance on these elements, often neglected in the realm of multimillion-dollar budgets, Lee's film reaffirms the creative potential of small, independent feature filmmaking.

The story of *She's Gotta Have It* is the story of Nola Darling (Tracy Camila Johns), a black, Brooklyn-based graphic artist who happens to be the female fixation for at least three men. The film unfolds to reveal certain aspects of Nola's personality, both in her own words and those of her three suitors, a sex therapist, her father, her former roommate, and a lesbian acquaintance. The resulting portrait, which Nola herself characterizes as highly subjective and therefore inauthentic, describes the life and style of an attractive, charismatic, and thoroughly modern woman.

After a series of still photographs woven among the opening credits which establish the character of Brooklyn's Bedford-Stuyvesant neighborhood, the setting for the film, the viewer is introduced to Nola unraveling herself from her sheets, sitting up in bed to face the camera and a new day. Her speech provides the prologue for *She's Gotta Have It*; she wants to exonerate herself of the charges made against her by numerous people who believed it their duty to consign her to inappropriate pigeonholes. She challenges the labels and asserts her independence.

After this scene, the viewer hears from the crowd of observers who claim to know Nola. First to speak is Jamie Overstreet (Tommy Redmond Hicks), a sympathetic and faintly intellectual man who confronts the camera from a bench in a children's playground. Jamie is convinced that for every person in the world there is one other who truly is meant for him or her, a mate in heart, body, and soul. He believes that Nola fills this role for him. (Jamie's role in the film is that of both suitor and narrator/mediator; he is often shown on this playground bench, revealing salient aspects of Nola's character and detailing her progress through the fields of romance.) Jamie introduced himself to Nola after following her on the street, a chance encounter which to him seemed predestined.

After a sensual and illuminating description of an episode in Jamie and Nola's love life, alluding to the sexual potency which lures men to her, the film introduces Clorinda Bradford (Joie Lee). At one time, Clorinda shared Nola's apartment; she explains that the constantly changing parade of men she encountered mornings in the bathroom ultimately caused an unbridgeable rift between the roommates, and that since the apartment was in fact Nola's she had to accept the flux or move out. On her own, Clorinda is self-sufficient and content, though she does admit to missing her roommate; Nola's presence is nothing if not enlivening.

Another witness to the life of Nola, and the second of her lovers, is Mars

Blackmon (played by director Spike Lee). A series of close-ups summarize Mars's character—the arrow design shaved out of his close-cropped hair, his designer glasses, his bike cap, his untied basketball shoes, and his belt buckle and neck-chain emblazoned "Mars." In distinct contrast to Jamie, Mars is the jovial product of a concrete environment. His speech is rife with street vernacular, and, though small in stature, Mars is expansive in gesture and spirit. He is also direct: When he first sees Nola's spacious apartment, he proposes moving in with her.

Nola's physical presence draws forth two more commentators—Opal Gilstrap (Raye Dowell) and Greer Childs (John Canada Terrell). It is Nola's apparent enjoyment of sex which attracts Opal, along with Opal's conviction that one should be open to experiences on both sides of the gender line. Greer, on the other hand, has no interest in such explorations. Strikingly handsome, he considers Nola an accessory, an attractive complement to his own fashionable self. As Nola intimates, Greer would marry himself if he could.

Until that concept is a reality, Greer must content himself with the imperfect nature of women such as Nola. In one of the film's most amusing scenes, Nola, after hearing that Greer is to be on the cover of *Gentleman's Quarterly*, induces him to make love to her, eyeing him as she slowly removes her leotard. Greer responds with similar but more excruciating slowness; before joining Nola on the bed (and responding to the African drumbeat on the sound track), he meticulously folds and arranges his T-shirt and shorts. Their lovemaking, shot from above, resembles a photo flip-book whose pages have been randomly sequenced.

For a sense of Nola's history, the film next introduces Nola's father, Sonny Darling (Bill Lee, who also provided the jazzy score for the film). Sitting at a piano, he turns to face the camera and explain that Nola received all the parental indulgences of an only child and that she was never able to concentrate for long on any one thing—dance and music lessons to schoolwork (and, beyond the range of his commentary, men). He reiterates that she disliked being classified, especially as "normal," and confesses, when asked if he recalls anything unusual about Nola's childhood, that she crawled backward until she walked.

So, with some background information and various interpretations of her present state, Nola's story proceeds. Jamie, the romantic, provides her with an elaborately staged dance performance for her birthday. This sequence effects a humorous reversal of *The Wizard of Oz*—Jamie instructs Nola to close her eyes, click her heels, and repeat, "There's no place like home." Instead of transporting Dorothy and Toto back to monotone Kansas, however, the ritual places Nola and Jamie in a park, seated before a monument festooned with balloons and birthday banners, a scene shot in color, in contrast to the rest of the film's black-and-white. Back in bed (and in monotone) after the spectacle, practical Nola offers to pay for half of her present. Jamie demurs.

Mars, who called to convey birthday greetings, is convinced that Jamie and Greer are both unfit for her and that she should recognize his as true love. Yet Mars's success with Nola is based on his ability to amuse her; when he inquires about his lovemaking as compared to Jamie's and Greer's, Nola's cold response suffices to restore his role as bed jester. While they frolic, the phone rings; Mars, who refuses to remove his high-top sneakers in bed, answers by kicking the phone off its bedside table. On the other end of the line, Jamie is thoroughly disconcerted. For all Nola's protestations of love for him, her actions with Greer and Mars contradict her words.

At Greer's instigation (he claims that her sexual activity is abnormal), Nola visits a sex therapist. Dr. Jamison (Epatha Merkinson) expresses her professional opinion that, although excessive sex can be viewed as an addiction, Nola is a perfectly healthy woman. In Nola's words, it was Greer who had the problem, and he would be the first to go in any progress toward monogamy.

Before any such trimming occurs, however, Nola brings all three of her lovers together in an attempt to create harmony among them. This ill-fated effort provides the film with its most evocative and humorous scene. During the course of a Thanksgiving dinner which she has prepared, the three men jockey for position, each attempting to gain favor with Nola while putting down the others as unworthy. When Mars and Greer exchange barbs, nearly progressing to physical violence, Nola pleads with them to behave; Jamie tries to make a good impression by remaining aloof and controlled. After this exasperating experience, the four attempt to come to terms over a game of Scrabble—another fiasco, as Greer considers himself the elite arbiter of words and discounts Mars's efforts to place street vernacular on triple-word spaces. The exhausting evening is brought to a close in a bed-centered tableau shot from above—Jamie and Nola entwined on the mattress, Mars seated at their feet and leaning toward Nola, and Greer set off by himself in a chair at the head of the bed.

The remainder of the film devolves from this scene. Nola determines that the juggling has become too complex for her; the first to go is Greer. He accepts her rejection, though he suggests that it reflects poor judgment on her part. Ridding herself of Mars is not as easy for Nola. He is more understanding and compassionate than Greer, though he still claims that he has to end the relationship, not she. They part on good terms, with Mars jokingly imploring her to return.

Left with Jamie, Nola attempts to work out a relationship. The two stay together for a time, but Nola comes to the realization that she cannot be faithful to one man. The penultimate scene encapsulates the nature of Nola's relations with men; meeting Jamie on his playground bench, she tells him that she wants to be with him, that she has forsworn the others, but she needs some time to herself. Jamie protests, but she hugs him, whispers "I love you" in his ear, and walks away. The camera stays on her, backing up as she approaches and holding her in a constant medium shot. As she moves away from him, Jamie shrinks in size, though his image remains perched on her left shoulder. He calls her back, and the shrinking is reversed as the camera advances again to bring Jamie back to scale and reunite the two; Nola did not need much time to be alone, for her self-determination prevails.

The film closes in a visual reversal of its opening. Nola asserts that each person claiming to know her may indeed understand a part of her, but only she can define the whole. She proclaims her inability to be a one-man woman, and the camera follows as she returns to bed and wraps herself in the sheets, resuming the position from which she emerged at the beginning to relate her story. The camera tracks out but holds in a shot slightly tighter than the opening; the audience, too, has moved a little closer to her in the course of the film.

Yet Nola's character is not completely revealed. Given the form of the film, an unfiltered portrayal of Nola Darling is impossible. *She's Gotta Have It* exists as a multilevel narrative, contained within the space of one woman's day. The only opportunity the audience has to view Nola in her everyday pursuits is a brief scene following her father's revelations about her childhood; Nola is alone in her apartment, working at her drafting table and on a wall-covering collage of her paintings and clipped newspaper headlines.

Given Nola's description of herself as independent, it is revealing that the film portrays her always as subject to the descriptions of others; it is precisely this subjectivity that *She's Gotta Have It* questions and ultimately finds wanting. The male-centered nature of the commentary thwarts the viewer's desire to delve more deeply into Nola's personality. In this, the film is as much about men's attitudes toward women as it is about Nola. At one point, Nola opines that most men know nothing about her or women in general. She also introduces her rogues' gallery of dogs—come-on artists with little or no sensitivity in their approach. Clorinda offers the only female companionship evidenced in the film (Opal's interests are too similar to those of the predatory males).

Nola's mural, her personal work, is of interest on several levels. First, it confronts the issues of blackness and racism. With one exception, the cast of *She's Gotta Have It* is composed entirely of blacks, an anomaly in contemporary films. Lee has made a film about very specific human issues, some linked to being black, others more universal. Nola's mural depicts a world torn by violence; the painting appears to be her *Guernica*, a passionate response to the racist attitudes which killed such leaders as Martin Luther King, Jr.

The painting offers Nola an opportunity to express feelings that she cannot share with her men and does not share with Clorinda (with whom she rarely communicates). When Nola calls Jamie late one night and tells him to come over immediately, Jamie arrives to find nothing wrong; she just wanted to be with him. Angered by what he regards as callous manipulation, Jamie throws her on the bed and abuses her, verbally and physically. Rather than film her screams, the camera cuts to an anguished, open-mouthed face in the painting.

The idea for *She's Gotta Have It* was, as mentioned earlier, directly linked to funding, or the lack thereof. Lee made good use of economic necessity in another way. To sell the film to audiences, rather than simply assemble a standard trailer of film clips, he made the sales pitch himself: Standing by a curbside table covered with merchandise, Lee pleaded with viewers to see his film so that he would be able to stop selling socks on the street.

George Slade

Reviews
Black Enterprise. XVII, December, 1986, p. 56.
Film Comment. XXII, September/October, 1986, p. 46.
Films in Review. XXXVII, November, 1986, p. 549.
Jet. LXXI, November 10, 1986, p. 54.
Ms. XV, October, 1986, p. 14.
The New Republic. CXCV, September 15, 1986, p. 30.
New Statesman. CXII, October 24, 1986, p. 27.
New York. XIX, August 18, 1986, p. 59.
The New York Times. CXXXVI, November 14, 1986, p. C10.
The New Yorker. LXII, October 6, 1986, p. 128.
Newsweek. CVIII, September 8, 1986, p. 65.
Time. CXXVIII, October 6, 1986, p. 94.
Variety. CCCXXII, April 2, 1986, p. 20.
The Wall Street Journal. CCVIII, November 12, 1986, p. 32.

SID AND NANCY

Origin: Great Britain
Released: 1986
Released in U.S.: 1986
Production: Eric Fellner; released by Samuel Goldwyn Company
Direction: Alex Cox
Screenplay: Alex Cox and Abbe Wool
Cinematography: Roger Deakins
Editing: David Martin
Production design: Andrew McAlpine
Art direction: J. Rae Fox and Lynda Burbank
Makeup: Peter Frampton
Costume design: Cathy Cook and Theda De Ramus
Sound: Peter Glossop
Music: Joe Strummer, The Pogues, and Pray for Rain
MPAA rating: R
Running time: 111 minutes

Principal characters:
Sid Vicious	Gary Oldman
Nancy Spungen	Chloe Webb
Malcolm McLaren	David Hayman
Johnny Rotten	Andrew Schofield
Phoebe	Debby Bishop
Steve	Tony London
Paul	Perry Benson
Linda	Anne Lambton
Wally	Graham Fletcher Cook
Brenda	Kathy Burke
Bowery Snax	Xander Berkeley
Methadone caseworker	Sy Richardson

Alex Cox made a minor art-house splash in 1984 when his first film, *Repo Man*, sneaked into theaters and captured the imagination of a small but blossoming independent market. Though it had an undeniably wacky freshness, *Repo Man*, even then, seemed too easily cynical, too fashionably apathetic, and too calculatedly geared toward a ready-made cult audience (and without the stylistic consistency and imagination of, for example, Jim Jarmusch's 1984 film, *Stranger than Paradise*) to really mark Cox as an important new film talent. It therefore comes as some surprise that *Sid and Nancy*, Cox's second film, is a major achievement: a film that mixes brutal realism with the blackest of comedy to provide a deeply resonant account of the late 1970's punk movement as embodied in the violent and stormy ro-mance of Sex Pistol Sid Vicious and his heroin-addicted, groupie girlfriend, Nancy Spungen. With the same obvious affection that he displayed in *Repo Man* toward society's outsiders, Cox here takes a strong and complex moral position with regard to his characters and risks alienating both those main-stream members of the audience who disdain the crassness and aggressive-ness of the punk movement as well as those fringe members of the audience who view punkers as heroic exemplars of progressive antisocial behavior. Sid and Nancy are, at the same time, victims of their sociopolitical environment and knowing architects of their own destruction. Their love is inseparable from their addiction; it simultaneously binds them together and tears them apart. No starry-eyed hero-worshiper, Cox sees their lives as a tragic waste, though he views them with sympathy.

Sid and Nancy opens at the end of their story, with a strung out Sid (Gary Oldman) being questioned by the police as the dead body of Nancy (Chloe Webb) is hauled out of their Chelsea Hotel room in a body bag. Although a frequently awkward and misused device, the flashback structure serves *Sid and Nancy* well, for it gives an immediate indication that Nancy's death has deeply affected Sid. It lends weight to the importance of their union and provides the audience with a needed indication that their relationship will deepen from its offhand, childish, casually brutal origins. The film then moves back to the day Sid joined The Sex Pistols as their supremely untalented bass player. He meets Nancy at the home of a mutual friend and dominatrix, Linda (Anne Lambton), and Nancy latches onto him immedi-ately. In a strange and unpleasant way, they complete each other. Sid, though obnoxious and destructive, is a bit of a naïve innocent, and Nancy, relentlessly and gratingly selfish, has a certain worldliness. Nancy introduces Sid to drugs, the ultimate vehicle for his self-destructive impulses, and Sid offers Nancy the fame and notoriety she so desperately craves.

Their fierce devotion to each other begins to drive everyone else away; the other Sex Pistols want to get rid of Sid, but their manager, Malcolm McLaren (played as an unfeeling vulture by David Hayman), considers Sid an important component of the band, for he "embodies the dementia of a nihilistic generation." This is not without truth in Cox's unglued London of the period, a London in which girls casually smash cars with hockey sticks on their way home from school. The tensions in the band come to a head during their disastrous American tour, and the band breaks up. Sid and Nancy move to New York's Chelsea Hotel and, with Nancy acting as Sid's manager, they try to launch Sid on a solo career. They are, however, so strung out by this point that they cannot make anything work. Through the last third of the film, they do little more than shoot heroin and lie in bed, staring blankly into the harsh light of a flickering television screen. Nancy cannot even remember when they last had sex. Hallucinatory fantasies (such as the image of them kissing in an alley as garbage cascades down on them) are the only moments of beauty left in their lives; no real joy ever intrudes on their blank existence. Nancy convinces Sid to enter into a suicide pact (so they can go out in a "blaze of glory"), but Sid is unwilling to go through with it and accidentally stabs Nancy to death in the drug-crazed argument that ensues. (Sid eventually died of a drug overdose, but this is not depicted in the film.)

Sid and Nancy could have easily slid into the same unbearable state of morbidity and boredom that takes over its main characters were it not for Alex Cox's streak of black humor and his subtly inventive command of style. Hardly a scene goes by that does not have both a pitifully tragic and darkly comic dimension; these seemingly opposite frames of reference feed off each other with dizzying skill. In a hilariously grotesque parody of domestic life, Sid and Nancy fight about housework while Sid plays with his Action Man doll and Nancy reminisces about her "Special Hair Barbie" (and laments that she will never look like Barbie because "Barbie doesn't have bruises"). As out-of-control and childish. as both Sid and Nancy's behavior becomes in this scene, Nancy still manages to cross some barely detectable threshold of Sid's endurance, and he punches her in the face. They are like little children playing; their fun can change to despair in the flash of a careless instant and, just as quickly, turn to fun again.

As random and improvisational as the film may feel at times, one is repeatedly struck by the carefully thought-out stylistic choices that Cox makes. Unlike film-school wizards such as Joel and Ethan Coen (whose goal in both *Blood Simple*, 1985, and *Raising Arizona*, 1987, seems to be, first and foremost, to show what they can do), Cox takes the chance that the audience might not recognize the skill of his work (a sure sign that he is capable of much more than simply technical excellence). His depiction of the first night Sid and Nancy spend together (which is also the first time Sid shoots up) begins with a shot of their friend, Wally (Graham Fletcher Cook), watching Sid's heaving back in the foreground. What one initially thinks is the movement of Sid and Nancy making love turns out to be the gyrations of Sid vomiting into a toilet bowl. Then, and only then, when the loosening effects of the drugs allow Sid to display tenderness, do they make love. All of this takes place in the presence of the bored Wally, who is as interested in the toy cars with which he plays as he is in the strange ritual going on before him. When Sid and Nancy are through making love, Nancy automatically gathers her clothes to leave, and Sid asks her to stay; they are inseparable from this point onward, forever joined as a couple by this artless moment of acceptance. Even from the beginning, however, their love and drug use are indistinguishable.

Drugs are Sid and Nancy's primary means of shared expression; by the end, when lovemaking, music, and their sense of adventure have all failed them, drugs become their only real bond. The critics who labeled *Sid and Nancy* an antidrug tract seem to have missed the point; drugs destroy them, but they also provide relief. Cox, along with cinematographer Roger Deakins, sought to evoke Sid and Nancy's drug-induced hallucinations in all their trashy beauty and surrealistic pleasurableness. These sequences are not earmarked as such, but they do give the audience an indication of how Sid and Nancy pull away from the rest of the world. This is first evident when, after a Sex Pistols concert on the *Queen Elizabeth* erupts in violence between the punks and the police, Sid and Nancy are seen walking through the riot, oblivious to the action around them and even amused by it, draped over each other in a romantically blissful, unconcerned haze. What begins as a liberating retreat from harsh reality, however, turns into the harshest of realities; Sid and Nancy become vomiting, paranoid zombies frantically jabbing dirty needles into bruised and bloody flesh, waiting in vain for a calm that never comes. Cox treats drug abuse for the depraved condition that it is, but he does not pass easy moral judgment; in the punk ethos of masochism elevated to a form of social action, what alternative do Sid and Nancy have? Toward the end of the film, there is a powerful scene in which a methadone clinic caseworker (Sy Richardson) chastises the pair for being strung out on drugs when they could be promoting "healthy anarchy." Sid and Nancy are too stuporous to care what the caseworker is saying. Throughout the film, one is continually aware of Cox's dedicated political sensibility flirting with and superseding his adulation of mere subversiveness.

Sid and Nancy would not be nearly as powerful without the startling performances of Gary Oldman and Chloe Webb, yet it is very difficult to appreciate fully the measure of their achievement. Since they are both making their film debuts here, it is tempting to underestimate them and to assume that Cox selected them because they were so like these characters. Oldman, however, has already proved this incorrect with his strikingly different portrayal of playwright Joe Orton in Stephen Frears's 1987 film, *Prick Up Your Ears*, and one suspects that Webb has similar tricks up her sleeve. It is with some astonishment, therefore, that one views the absolutely compelling metamorphoses of Oldman and Webb into Vicious and Spungen. Oldman displays a glazed-over, slack-jawed thickheadedness and clumsy, rubbery body movements that can snap to alertness with quick and shocking aggression. By the end, his romantic and moral confusion in the face of his overwhelming ignorance has grown quite moving. Webb (who was named Best Actress of 1986 by the National Society of Film Critics) uses a screechy, whiny voice for the greedy, self-absorbed Nancy. She is like an overgrown child always trying to get what she wants, as if her parents were too afraid of her ever to tell her no. Together, Oldman and Webb connect on an unfathomable level; always finding the edge of wit in Sid and

Nancy's overweening stupidity, as well as the cutting cruelty in their most childish arguments, they are bonded in destructiveness. Their descent into the hellish world of drug abuse is genuinely hair-raising. Many admirers of The Sex Pistols and the punk movement have criticized *Sid and Nancy* for not lending more credence and attention to The Sex Pistols' cultural impact and the social forces that gave rise to the punk movement in general. Cox, however, has wisely avoided this: Films emphasizing movements and themes more than the complexities of human interaction inevitably grow polemically simpleminded. Besides, Cox has found a richer truth in Sid and Nancy's relationship—a truth which can, in turn, be applied to the failure of punk to make more than a glancing cultural impact. Opting for an insular and destructive retreat from the mainstream instead of a collective and purposeful challenge to it guaranteed Sid and Nancy only agonizing self-defeat. The embodiment of a nihilistic generation, indeed.

Jeffrey L. Fenner

Reviews
Film Quarterly. XL, Spring, 1987, p. 33.
Films in Review. XXXVIII, February, 1987, p. 105.
Los Angeles Times. October 16, 1986, VI, p. 1.
Ms. XV, October, 1986, p. 21.
The Nation. CCXLIII, November 1, 1986, p. 463.
The New Republic. CXCV, October 27, 1986, p. 24.
New York. October 20, 1986, p. 92.
The New York Times. October 3, 1986, p. C5.
Newsweek. CVIII, October 27, 1986, p. 103.
Time. CXXVIII, November 3, 1986, p. 82.
Vanity Fair. October, 1986, p. 131.
The Washington Post. November 8, 1986, p. D9.

SOMETHING WILD

Production: Jonathan Demme and Kenneth Utt; released by Orion Pictures
Direction: Jonathan Demme
Screenplay: E. Max Frye
Cinematography: Tak Fujimoto
Editing: Craig McKay
Production design: Norma Moriceau
Art direction: Steve Lineweaver; set decoration, Billy Reynolds
Costume design: Eugenie Bafaloukas
Music: John Cale and Laurie Anderson
MPAA rating: R
Running time: 116 minutes

> *Principal characters:*
> Charles Driggs......................Jeff Daniels
> Audrey Hankel ....Melanie Griffith
> Ray Sinclair.........................Ray Liotta
> Irene ....Margaret Colin
> Country squire.....................Tracey Walter
> Peaches.............................Dana Preu
> Larry Dillman ....Jack Gilpin
> Peggy Dillman........................Su Tissue
> Tracy..............................Kristin Olsen
> Motorcycle cop ....John Sayles
> Used car guy........................John Waters
> The Willies ....The Feelies
> Waitress....................."Sister Carol" East

The conflict between safety and adventure, between the call of society and the call of the wild, has always been a popular film theme. In countless *films noir*, Hitchcock thrillers, and screwball comedies, characters have stumbled into adventures that alter their normal lives, bringing them equal doses of danger and romance. It is only fitting, then, to find a number of films in the 1980's which test the mettle of "yuppies," young professionals known for leading conservative lives and preferring to work within the system rather than rebel against it. John Landis' *Into the Night* (1985) starred Jeff Goldblum as a bored electronics specialist who finds himself chased by gangsters and the Central Intelligence Agency (CIA) after rescuing a woman (Michelle Pfeiffer) in a parking lot. In Martin Scorsese's *After Hours* (1985), Griffin Dunne played a word processor who meets an intriguing woman (Rosanna Arquette) in a diner one night and soon finds himself in a madcap adventure in which he almost loses his life. Blake Edwards'

Blind Date (1987) starred Bruce Willis as a business executive whose career is wrecked by his date with a beautiful alcoholic (Kim Basinger). In all of these films, the yuppie protagonist has his mundane life-style disrupted after a fateful meeting with a beautiful, mysterious woman. Jonathan Demme's *Something Wild* treats a similar story line in a refreshing manner. The film starts like a screwball comedy but ends like a *film noir*, with a harrowing, violent climax. Demme takes what initially seems a lightweight situation and invests it with real emotion, creating what is easily the most involving film in the mini-genre which can be called "yuppie *noir*."

It is fitting that the film blends two genres, for its theme is split identity. Both the main characters are transformed during the course of their journey, and their identities are presented as masquerades. The film suggests that style and appearance are skin deep, that something wild lies under our social mask. Yet these ideas are not presented in a dry manner. The lively sound track blends reggae, soul, and New Wave music, and the film careens along like a fast-paced road picture, taking its characters from New York through New Jersey, Pennsylvania, and Virginia in a wild weekend adventure.

The film opens with a song, "Loco de amor" (performed and written by David Byrne), and a surprising view of Manhattan. The city is seen as an island in a series of shots taken from a speeding motorboat traveling around the East River and Hudson River. Byrne's song, and the rest of the music throughout the film, will be used in association with Audrey's free-spirited way of life and in contrast to Charlie's white, middle-class trappings.

The audience first meets Audrey (Melanie Griffith) and Charlie (Jeff Daniels) at a diner in Lower Manhattan. Charlie Driggs, dressed in a business suit, taps away at a calculator while finishing his lunch. He is being watched by Audrey Hankel, who has a Louise Brooks hairdo and is dressed East Village style, ornamented with large, colorful, African-style jewelry. Charlie, impatient to get back to work, looks around, pockets his check, and walks out of the diner. He is confronted in the street by Audrey, who introduces herself as Lulu. Embarrassed, and thinking that she is a waitress, Charlie fumbles for money. With an electronic paging device on his belt and an umbrella in his hand (despite the fact that it is a warm, sunny afternoon), he looks ridiculously encumbered. Because of the check incident, however, Lulu sees something else and tells Charlie that he is a closet rebel.

She offers him a ride back to work in her car, and the adventure begins as she heads through the Holland Tunnel, away from New York City. At this point, the film seems like a madcap comedy bearing a strong resemblance to *After Hours*. Scorsese's hero, played by Griffin Dunne, was a lightweight comic buffoon, however, reacting in disbelief to increasingly absurd situations, and the audience never felt much genuine concern for him. Demme, who has shown an ability to treat eccentric situations with real warmth in movies such as *Handle With Care* (1977) and *Melvin and Howard* (1980), has real affection for the characters in *Something Wild*. He frequently cuts to close-up reaction shots of Daniels and Griffith, and their reactions show a wide range of feelings. Demme is more concerned with the characters than the situation.

Charlie's first reaction is mild shock and intrigue. Lulu tosses Charlie's electronic pager out the window and tells him that he deserves a break. She stops at a liquor store where she robs the cash register while Charlie is outside telephoning his office. Though Charlie seems genuinely flustered, it is clear that Lulu is too playful and high-spirited to be truly dangerous. Charlie's first real display of anxiety is when Lulu pulls off the road and stops at a motel. Realizing that Lulu wants to have sex, Charlie is both excited and uncomfortable. He has clearly never done anything like this. In the room, he quickly undresses, leaving on his underpants, socks, and T-shirt as he hops under the covers. Lulu takes a pair of handcuffs out of a bag, and, after cuffing Charlie to the bed, they make love. Later, Lulu tells Charlie that she is taking him to her hometown in Pennsylvania.

As they continue their journey, Charlie finally relaxes. After eating at a roadside place, Mom and Dad's Restaurant, Lulu playfully leaves the restaurant to get her car, knowing that Charlie does not have enough money to pay the check. Seeing Lulu outside, Charlie runs out of the restaurant and dives into the car.

He is now simply enjoying the adventure and is even falling for Lulu. As they drive on, Charlie lies down on the front seat, his head in Lulu's lap, his feet sticking out of the car, with "Wild Thing" playing on the sound track. After they stop at a motel for the night, Charlie, still a little apprehensive, fakes a telephone call to his wife. In fact, he has been separated for nearly a year. Charlie and Lulu spend the night together. The next morning, as Charlie and Lulu leave the motel, a policeman is ticketing Lulu's car. They walk by it and to a used car lot, where Lulu buys a car and pays with cash, presumably from the liquor store robbery. She lies to Charlie, telling him that she got the money from a divorce, one of many white lies told by Audrey and Charlie to each other.

When they stop at a clothing store in Lulu's hometown, Charlie buys a blue, trendy-looking jacket at Lulu's urging, and she buys a feminine, old-fashioned summer dress. They seem like different people from their earlier images; Charlie looks more stylish, hardly like an executive, and Lulu looks like a pleasant small-town girl. Before they enter Lulu's mother's house, Lulu tells Charlie to call her "Audrey," her real name. Charlie and Audrey pose as a happily married couple for Audrey's mother, Peaches, a wonderfully gracious, absent-minded woman played by Dana Preu. Later in the evening, Audrey transforms herself once again, taking off her Louise Brooks wig and appearing in short, blonde hair.

Finally, the audience learns the reason for Audrey's adventure as she drives Charlie to her high school reunion. Charlie plays along with her plan and poses as her husband. He nearly loses his composure when he runs into a worker from his office, Larry Dillman (Jack Gilpin). Audrey walks up to Charlie while he is talking to Larry and introduces herself as Charlie's lover, calling him the probable father of her child. Charlie panics, with visions of his career going down the drain, but Dillman looks at Charlie with admiration. Later in the evening, feeling that the masquerade has gone too far, Charlie pleads with Audrey, "Let me go back to my safe, boring life." He decides to stay, however, a choice he will soon regret.

Ray, Audrey's real husband, appears. Played in an intense, electric manner by Ray Liotta, Ray brings a note of true danger to the adventure. He has just been released from prison, and it is clear from the look in his eyes that he is obsessed with Audrey. Audrey wants to avoid Ray and abruptly leaves with Charlie.

Ray follows Charlie and Audrey into the parking lot and invites himself and a friend, Irene (Margaret Colin), to go out for a drink with Audrey and Charlie. Audrey is reluctant, but Charlie good-naturedly agrees to the idea. The foursome stops at a convenience store. When Audrey and Irene go in to buy cigarettes, Ray and Charlie talk about Audrey. Charlie tells Ray that he has been married to Audrey for more than a year. Ray then startles Charlie by asking him, in vulgar language, what Audrey is like in bed.

Ray becomes more dangerous as the night progresses. He has an argument with Audrey, who tells him that she does not love him anymore. Ray abandons Irene, drives away with Audrey and Charlie, and stops at another convenience store, which he holds up at gunpoint. He beats Charlie, who tries to stop him, and forces Audrey and Charlie to come with him to a motel room, where Ray announces that it is time to play "true confessions."

First, Ray tells Audrey that he knows that she is not married to Charlie because he would have been notified about a divorce while he was in prison. Ray, in fact, is still married to Audrey. Ray then announces, for Audrey's sake, that he knows that Charlie is not still married, that he has been separated for months—something Ray found out from Larry at the reunion. Audrey is visibly upset by this revelation. Ray tells Charlie to leave the motel, and Audrey does not protest.

Charlie, however, realizing that he is in love with Audrey, follows Ray and Audrey as they drive together into Virginia. He pursues them throughout the day and stops at a diner where they are eating. Noticing police cars in the parking lot, he goes into the diner and sits down in the same booth as Ray and Audrey. Knowing that he can turn Ray over to the police if he wants, Charlie demands the car keys and leaves with Audrey.

The two of them drive away. Audrey stops the car and confronts him about the fact that he lied to her. After some tense, heated moments, Charlie and Audrey are able to look at each other for who they really are, and they decide to stay together. They get back into the car to drive home to New York, to Charlie's peaceful, suburban home in Stony Brook. As Charlie recuperates in the house, Audrey asks, "What are you going to do now that you've seen how the other half lives?" "What other half?" he asks. She responds, "The other half of you."

In the meantime, Ray has managed to track Charlie down, and he bursts into the house in Stony Brook. Ray beats up Charlie, handcuffs him to a pipe, and attacks Audrey. Charlie breaks free and rescues Audrey. This life-and-death struggle, which concludes with Ray impaling himself on a kitchen knife when he lunges at Charlie, is truly harrowing, a physically brutal struggle in which the audience cares deeply about all the characters. Even though Ray is clearly the bad guy, one sympathizes with him. He is psychopathic, but there is strong feeling in his desperation for Audrey. The police arrive, and they take Audrey away for questioning as Charlie looks on from the back of an ambulance.

In the story's epilogue, set a few days later, the audience sees Charlie at his office, his arm in a sling. He has quit his job and is packing to leave. The camera cuts to him searching the streets for Audrey. He goes back to the diner where he first saw her, but she is not there. He eats and leaves money for the check on the table. A waitress ("Sister Carol" East) follows him outside and begins yelling at him for not paying. Audrey then appears. She has the money in her hand.

Charlie, dressed in casual, trendy clothing, is a free man, with no clear future. Audrey, in a 1940's-style black-and-white dress and a tilted hat, has adopted yet another look. They drive off together in Audrey's car, on to their next adventure, and the camera pans back to the diner, where the waitress is standing outside, singing a reggae version of "Wild Thing" as the credits roll.

A plot description cannot capture the flavor of the film, and *Something Wild* has a rich sense of atmosphere. Tak Fujimoto's crisp, sunny color photography captures with postcard clarity a rural American landscape, complete with roadside diners, motels, gas stations, stores, restaurants, and country highways. Demme also has a great sense for background characters: The taciturn restaurant owner (Kenneth Utt) who picks up the phone and says, "Mom and Dad's Restaurant. Dad speaking," the breathless teenage girl, Tracy (Kristin Olsen), who falls prey to Ray's manipulative charm, the sleazy used-car salesman, played by film director John Waters, are all charming and memorable cameos. The film's landscape is also populated with musicians. Charlie and Audrey pick up some hitchhiking kids and a guitar player, and they all sing "Wild Thing," the film's anthem. The New Wave group The Feelies performs as The Willies at the high school reunion. When Charlie walks out of a gas station, a group of black kids is seen rapping and break dancing in the background. Demme, who directed the acclaimed Talking Heads concert film *Stop Making Sense* (1984), fills the film with music.

It is not the background atmosphere alone, though, which makes the film so emotionally involving. Jeff Daniels and Melanie Griffith create three-dimensional characters, making them ring true through small, quirky bits of behavior. Charlie could easily be a caricature, a repressed businessman displaying disbelief through the entire ordeal. Daniels, however, plays Charlie as a high-strung, energetic, adaptable man whose youth is reignited during the adventure. Early in the film he enthusiastically tells Audrey, "You're right, I am a rebel, but I funnel it into the system. Deep down, I've got what it takes." Daniels shows the audience both sides of Charlie at the same time: the nervous, materialistic citizen who wants a quaint suburban life and the brash, boyish Charlie who wants to feel alive. Among the small details of Daniels' performance that flesh out his character are the way he constantly turns his head to look behind him, as though he is a bad boy and thinks that someone is following him; the way he dances at the high school reunion, gradually loosening up and adding bold hand and body gestures; the way he calls all waitresses and gas station attendants by their first name, reading their name tags, because "it makes it more personal."

Griffith also brings depth to her character, making the audience believe that she can be both Lulu and Audrey. Even when she dons dominatrix gear and handcuffs Charlie during their first motel stop, there is a sweetness in her manner. Griffith makes it clear that her character is only playing, acting the role of Lulu for the sake of adventure. She is comfortable as an East Village vamp and as a small-town girl who wants to get married. Griffith and Daniels let the audience see that their characters do not take their masks too seriously; deep down, they have both "got what it takes." Films have always favored characters like these, and, ultimately, despite all the elements of the counterculture which flavor the picture, *Something Wild* is a well-made, old-fashioned film, as American as George Bailey (Jimmy Stewart) wanting to get out and see the world in *It's a Wonderful Life* (1946).

David Schwartz

Reviews
The Christian Century. CIII, December 24, 1986, p. 1181.
Films in Review. XXXVIII, February, 1987, p. 104.
Los Angeles Times. November 6, 1986, VI, p. 1.
The New Republic. CXCV, November 24, 1986, p. 31.
The New York Times. November 7, 1986, p. C8.
The New Yorker. LXII, November 17, 1986, p. 139.

Newsweek. CVIII, November 10, 1986, p. 86.
Time. CXXVIII, November 10, 1986, p. 111.
Variety. CCCXXV, October 29, 1986, p. 11.
The Washington Post. November 7, 1986, p. C1.

STAND BY ME

Production: Bruce A. Evans, Raynold Gideon, and Andrew Scheinman; released by Columbia Pictures
Direction: Rob Reiner
Screenplay: Raynold Gideon and Bruce A. Evans; based on the novella "The Body" by Stephen King
Cinematography: Thomas Del Ruth
Editing: Robert Leighton
Art direction: Dennis Washington
Music: Jack Nitzsche
MPAA rating: R
Running time: 87 minutes

Principal characters:

Gordon "Gordie" Lachance	Wil Wheaton
Chris Chambers	River Phoenix
Teddy Duchamp	Corey Feldman
Vern Tessio	Jerry O'Connell
Denny Lachance	John Cusack
Ace Merrill	Kiefer Sutherland
Gordon Lachance (as an adult)	Richard Dreyfuss

The film industry discovered long ago that the largest segment of American filmgoers consists of young people, age twelve to twenty-four. For years Hollywood provided for this audience films about the romance and adventure of their elders; inevitably, however, the fare became more youth oriented. These viewers began to watch themselves on the screen—their own romance and adventure. The quality of such films has varied widely, from the exploitation of puberty to the serious treatment of young people's concerns. Occasionally films of considerable merit are made in this genre. One such film is *Stand by Me*, directed by Rob Reiner.

Reiner is proving himself to be an accomplished and sensitive director. He is alert to the nuances of realistic dialogue, to the little details that so concisely characterize people. In his films there runs a thread of genuine humor, from the wacky satire of *This Is Spinal Tap* (1984) to the girl-loathes-but-finally-loves-guy syndrome of *The Sure Thing* (1985). Always there is a ring of truth to the fun, the creation of an appeal for the viewer which is rooted in an honest and sympathetic understanding of human nature. In *Stand by Me* this understanding pervades the film, rendering both its hilarity and its pathos effective, neither undermining the other.

Stand by Me, based on the novella "The Body" (1982) by Stephen King, treats the archetypal theme of the rite of passage, in this case involving the lives of four adolescents who move toward manhood through a series of adventures sparked by the accidental death of a young boy. Uncharacteristically, the boys' fathers do not play the initiatory role but remain largely absent from the scene and, if anything, play a negative role in the story. Around this age-old theme, the film develops the attendant themes of friendship and loyalty so important to the adolescent.

Stand by Me is a memory film narrated in the first person by one of the characters, a mature author, Gordon Lachance (Richard Dreyfuss), whose brief appearances at the start and close of the film frame the story. The narration also provides a double point of view which adds depth to the story but at the same time inevitably raises some questions about the authenticity of certain details: Are twelve-year-old males capable of either a continuous barrage of dirty language or a remarkable depth of insight, both of which are indigenous to the story? Is adolescence the only time one experiences uncorrupted friendship?

The narrator, prompted by the newspaper account of the death of a friend, looks back to the summer of 1960 when he and three of his pals encountered for the first time a dead body. The narrator, Gordie Lachance (Wil Wheaton), and his pals, Chris Chambers (River Phoenix) and Teddy Duchamp (Corey Feldman), are engaged in a card game in their treehouse when the youngest of the crew, Vern Tessio (Jerry O'Connell), bursts in to tell them that he has overheard a conversation between his older brother and a friend. The two older boys have accidentally discovered the corpse of a young lad who has been missing for several days. The older boys must keep their find a secret, so the question arises in the minds of the younger boys: Is it possible to use this information to "discover" the body themselves and thereby benefit by gaining the attention of the whole community? They plan their alibis, gather their gear, and set off along the railroad track to find the body.

During the two-day journey, the boys have a number of adventures by means of which their personalities are made ever more clear: their adolescent braggadocio, their deepest fears, their backgrounds, and the ecstasy and terror residing within them. For the most part, Reiner is able to communicate all of this within a believable child's point of view. For example, early in the film, the boys discover that, despite all of their planning, they have neglected to bring one essential item—food. Vern, the slowest and least mature of the four, offers his solace—he has brought a comb. So when the great moment arrives and they are confronted by the media, they will be prepared to look their best.

As the journey progresses, each boy is put to the test; each responds with a mixture of childish fear or grief within his burgeoning manhood. Each is developed as a distinct character. Teddy, the wildest, most unpredictable of the four, has suffered cruel abuse at the hands of a lout of a father, now incarcerated in an asylum. With almost irrational fervor, Teddy reveres his father as a hero who stormed the beach at Normandy, and he attempts to prove his own bravery by taking chances, often at the risk of his own life. His bravado is ultimately shown up in a confrontation with a nasty junkman who taunts him by calling his father a "loony." Insanely angry and frustrated, Teddy ultimately breaks down in anguish at the unfairness of a world which can only mock heroism and which shows no pity for the outcast.

Night comes, and as the boys sit around the campfire, alternately demonstrating their cool and cringing at the increasingly terrifying howl of the nearby coyotes, the mixture of child and man is shown again. Even Chris, the most mature of the four, finally breaks down, sharing his sorrow and frustration with Gordie, for he must bear the stigma of being one of those no-good Chambers kids, with a no-good father, a no-good older brother, and the reputation of being a thief. He explains to Gordie that, despite his attempt to atone for his petty theft, the adult world ultimately double-crossed him. In an especially tender scene, Chris's façade of manly demeanor breaks, and the child who lives deep within him reveals himself.

Gordie, too, bears his cross. Already an embryonic writer, Gordie is the most sensitive of the boys, but this sensitivity has its price. As the quartet moves ever closer to the corpse, the reason for Gordie's fascination with the prospect grows increasingly evident to him, for he is no stranger to death. His older brother, Dennis (John Cusack), athletic hero and pride of their parents, had been accidentally killed a short time before, and ever since, Gordie has suffered not only the loss of his closest friend but also lives with a father who, out of his own grief, continually rejects him. Gordie realizes that he must confront this corpse in order to exorcise the trauma, allowing him to live normally again.

Throughout the film there exists a further impediment to the boys' fulfillment of their desires—their older brothers. The critical conflict occurs when the gang of older boys, led by Ace Merrill (Kiefer Sutherland), challenges them to the right of discovery. How the four manage this crisis will determine in their own eyes whether they have successfully passed into manhood. Everything that follows this crisis winds down to the film's bittersweet ending.

The techniques of the film consistently present the adolescent rite in the context of both the social setting of the era and the eternal movement of nature and time. Director of photography Thomas Del Ruth consistently enhances the film's themes. The focus is principally upon the boys themselves. Sometimes they are seen in a long shot, walking along the railroad track, across a trestle, or, in a final silhouette, across the wide fields. There, the great expanse of nature forms the backdrop—they are simply little children in the big world. More often a low angle is combined with the close-up, each boy's face revealed in telling detail, and the viewer experiences the boy's emotion. Striking shots punctuate the film: an enormous full moon hanging in the sky, the great globe of the rising run, the watery waves of heat rising from the rails at midday, the firelight reflected in the faces of the boys huddled about the campfire. Unusual camera technique is rare: in the flashbacks occurring in Gordie's mind, where either a sepia tone or coated lens is used, or on the one occasion when Gordie tells a story, where the entire sequence is overexposed, which gives it the quality of fantastic exaggeration.

Reiner effectively places his story in the period by continuously undergirding the action with the music of the time. The boys march through the countryside to the beat of "The Ballad of Paladin," radios blare, the older boys career through the film in their autos to such standards as "Lollipop," "Every Day," or "Let the Good Times Roll." Juxtaposed against these sounds of the pop culture are those more elementary and timeless: a loon, crickets, the coyotes, and the haunting music by Jack Nitzsche that often underscores the young boys' sadness.

The screenplay by Raynold Gideon and Bruce A. Evans is a comparatively faithful adaptation of the King novella. The characterization of the adolescents captures both an underlying sameness—the unmistakable presence of the child within the developing youngster—and each distinctive personality. Occasionally, a slight shift of emphasis has been made. In the film, it is Chris, rather than Gordie, who pulls daredevil Teddy off the rails when Teddy attempts to prove his bravery by dodging an oncoming locomotive. The cruelty and potential violence of the older boys are present in the film but are toned down from the novella. Indeed, the entire ending of the film is softened considerably. The filmmakers opted for a conclusion mellower than King's. The film was shot on location in Oregon; likewise, the setting of the film was moved from Maine to Oregon without disturbing the ambience of the story.

With Gordie as narrator-participant, a significant part of the film concerns the development of the sensitive and perceptive writer. Reiner has chosen to retain one of King's exempla to illustrate Gordie's embryonic literary attempts. It is a particularly hilarious tale involving a pie-eating contest and a local rube, the butt of community humor. The story contains many of the common ingredients of the adolescent tale: ribald humor, grossness, exaggeration, and the theme of revenge. When Gordie relates the story to his friends, the difference between the imaginative young writer and his buddies is made clear. They are both pleased with the story and disappointed in its ending, which to them is totally inconclusive. They want a formula ending; Gordie gives them the "unsatisfying" ending, so much more like life as it is. It is ironic that *Stand by Me* is rated R, undoubtedly for the film's strong language. It is, therefore, supposedly "off limits" to those who presumably make this language their daily fare. The voice-over narration, which occurs throughout the film, occasionally intrudes to too great an extent, interfering with the viewer's ability to "see" the film for himself.

Stand by Me is a serious contribution to the body of films about adolescence. Rob Reiner's film is a touching and humorous revelation of what it is like to be a young boy, where, beneath the façade of bluster, there exists the authenticity of tender friendship and loyalty.

Norman Carson

Reviews
Christian Century. CIII, October 22, 1986, p. 920.
Films in Review. XXXVII, November, 1986, p. 550.
Los Angeles Times. August 8, 1986, VI, p. 1.
The New York Times. CXXXV, August 8, 1986, p. C14.
The New Yorker. LXII, September 8, 1986, p. 110.
Newsweek. CVIII, August 25, 1986, p. 63.
Time. CXXVIII, August 25, 1986, p. 62.
Variety. CCCXXIV, July 30, 1986, p. 16.
The Wall Street Journal. CCVIII, August 7, 1986, p. 16.
The Washington Post. August 22, 1986, p. D1.

STAR TREK IV
The Voyage Home

Production: Harve Bennett with Industrial Light and Magic for Paramount
  Pictures Corporation
Direction: Leonard Nimoy
Screenplay: Harve Bennett, Peter Krikes, Steve Meerson, and Nicholas
  Meyer; based on a story by Leonard Nimoy and Bennett, which was
  inspired by the television series *Star Trek* created by Gene Roddenberry
Cinematography: Don Peterman
Editing: Peter E. Berger
Production design: Jack T. Collis
Art direction: Joe Aubel and Pete Smith; set decoration, James Bayliss,
  Richard Berger, and Dan Gluck
Special effects: Michael Lanteri
Special visual effects supervisor: Kenneth Ralston
Makeup: Jeff Dawn, Wes Dawn, and James L. McCoy
Costume design: Robert Fletcher
Sound: Gene S. Cantamessa
Music: Leonard Rosenman
MPAA rating: PG
Running time: 118 minutes

> *Principal characters:*
> Admiral James T. Kirk . . . . William Shatner
> Captain Spock . . . . Leonard Nimoy
> Dr. Leonard "Bones" McCoy . . . . DeForest Kelley
> Chief Engineer Montgomery
>   "Scotty" Scott . . . . James Doohan
> Commander Hikaru Sulu . . . . George Takei
> Commander Pavel Chekov . . . . Walter Koenig
> Commander Nyota Uhura . . . . Nichelle Nichols
> Dr. Gillian Talyor . . . . Catherine Hicks

Star Trek IV: The Voyage Home was released on the twentieth anniversary
of the debut of the television series. Ironically, critics found it the most successful of the four "Star Trek" films, not because it paved new ground in
plot or in special effects but because *Star Trek IV* best recaptured the sense
of a noble mission and developed the wit and banter of cast interaction
present in many of the early television episodes.

These factors are not mere additives. The "Star Trek" universe is informed by its own history. Kirk (William Shatner), Spock (Leonard Nimoy),
and McCoy (DeForest Kelley) have aged noticeably, but so have their characters. The stuff of their memories has been played out on television screens

and in theaters for more than two decades. As the insufferably logical Spock (a half-breed, product of an Earth woman and a Vulcan man) rediscovers his human (emotional) side in *Star Trek IV*, he is once again the focus of good-natured kidding from Kirk and McCoy. It all rings true.

The appearance of other characters from the television series adds to the inner verisimilitude of *Star Trek IV*. There are cameo appearances by Spock's father, Ambassador Sarek (Mark Lenard), Sarek's wife, Amanda (Jane Wyatt), Chief Nurse Christine Chapel (Majel Barrett), and even Chief Petty Officer Janice Rand (Grace Lee Whitney). For the film viewer aware of the "Star Trek" history, there is a kind of knowing delight when the familiar characters rub up against the real world of 1986. Despite its somber opening scenes, the core of *Star Trek IV* is a lighthearted culture critique with an ultimate "save the whales" ecological message.

That, however, comes later. As the film begins, it is dark indeed for Admiral Kirk and his crew. The Klingon ambassador (John Schuck) is addressing the United Federation of Planets, meeting at the Federation's headquarters in San Francisco. The ambassador charges the crew of the starship *Enterprise* with destruction of Klingon life and property during a battle in space for the secret of the so-called Genesis device, which had been created by Kirk's son. Planets can be created and destroyed using a Genesis torpedo; in the ensuing struggle with the Klingons (sworn enemies of the Federation), Kirk and his crew witness the destruction of the *Enterprise* yet manage to escape to Vulcan, Spock's home planet, in a captured Klingon Bird of Prey spaceship. Now the Klingon ambassador demands that Kirk be extradited as a terrorist. Though the ambassador's demands are ignored, the Federation president notes that Kirk has been charged with the violation of Federation regulations: the theft and willful destruction of the *Enterprise* in the crew's desperate effort to save the life of Captain Spock, and the disregarding of direct Starfleet commands. This scene is an effective and fast-paced summary of what has gone before; it is not forced but follows naturally from events.

On Vulcan, the Genesis-regenerated body of the once-dead Spock has been reunited, through alien metaphysics, with its living essence. After months of retraining, Spock, not yet himself, is ready to make the voyage to Earth, as are the rest of the *Enterprise* crew. His mother, Amanda, is concerned that the human side is still submerged in her son; Spock is merely being logical when he offers to return to Federation headquarters to testify on behalf of Admiral Kirk. The idea of friendship is still foreign to him.

There is no Federation greeting party as the Bird of Prey nears Earth. Instead, Uhura (Nichelle Nichols) can pick up only a static-filled warning from Starfleet Command in San Francisco that all spacecraft stay away. Earth is now ringed by clouds; the life-giving sun is blocked while powerful storms rage below. The source of the destruction is a mysterious cylindrical alien probe now circling high above the planet. Uhura intercepts the probe's message, which resembles the song of the humpback whale. The probe, as Spock observes, has little concern for the human race; it is seeking out whales, long since extinct in the twenty-third century. The next step, to Kirk at least, is obvious: The crew must rely on Spock's calculations, swing the Klingon craft in a slingshot effect around the Sun, and return to the twentieth century to retrieve creatures who can respond to the probe. Kirk is able to communicate his mission to Starfleet Command, and with "Scotty" (James Doohan) nursing the engines, the Bird of Prey makes the time jump.

There is now an abrupt change in the tone of the film. Desperate circumstances are no less desperate, yet the dramatic intensity gives way to a flirtation with rather broad humor as two cultures clash. The Klingon vessel lands in Golden Gate Park in San Francisco. A cloaking device renders the craft invisible, but Scotty despairs that power will last only twenty-four hours. Worse, the engine's crystals need an influx of high-energy photons for the return time trip. Chekov (Walter Koenig) and Uhura are assigned to scout out an atomic power plant from which to collect the photons; Sulu (George Takei), Scott, and McCoy are charged with constructing a tank for the whales on board the Bird of Prey; and Kirk and Spock are to retrieve the whales, two humpbacks located at the nearby Cetacean Institute.

While Chekov stands on a street corner asking passersby in his Russian accent where the nuclear vessels might be located, and Scotty encounters an old-fashioned computer that is not voice-activated (even speaking into the "mouse" does not arouse the machine), the focus of the film is on Spock and Kirk, and Institute guide Dr. Gillian Taylor (Catherine Hicks). Taylor is enamored of her two humpbacks, which must be released into the open sea for lack of Institute funding. She is intrigued by the two strangers yet orders them away after Spock jumps underwater to "mind-meld" with the whales. (Not only do the creatures give permission for the abduction, but also Spock learns that one whale is pregnant and can help repopulate the oceans of the twenty-third century.)

Later, as Taylor is driving her pickup truck, she again notices the odd pair, eventually accepting a dinner invitation from Kirk. The Admiral reveals his preposterous mission and Taylor half believes him.

Chekov, the navigator, meanwhile, has fallen into trouble. Though Uhura is safely "beamed" (transported) back to the Klingon ship, Chekov is discovered by those guarding the atomic reactor (coincidentally on board the twentieth century USS *Enterprise*) and, injured while trying to escape, is now in the hospital, dying. At that moment Dr. Taylor arrives in Golden Gate Park, feeling betrayed because her precious whales have been removed overnight without her knowledge. She had dropped Kirk at the park after dinner, and she is back for help. She witnesses a helicopter commandeered by Sulu as it lowers a large plexiglass sheet into what appears to be thin air. Taylor is beamed inside the Klingon craft and realizes that all Kirk has said was true.

Kirk, McCoy, and Taylor don medical garb to spirit Chekov from the hospital. Wryly noting the primitive medical techniques, McCoy in moments is able to restore the navigator to health. Safely aboard the Bird of Prey, the crew tracks the whales to the open ocean and beams them aboard as they are about to be harpooned. Spock is forced to use his human, intuitive side in guessing at the time-warp calculations; as usual, he is correct. The vessel reappears in the twenty-third century in the midst of a furious storm and smashes into the sea. Kirk manages to release the whales from the tank, and the creatures sing to the alien probe. Moments later, as the probe heads back to the stars, the storm subsides and all is calm.

Yet now Kirk and his crew must face Federation charges, all but one of which are dismissed in view of Kirk's world-saving efforts. For disobeying Starfleet orders in the Genesis affair, Kirk is reduced to the rank of Captain and given the greatest honor he could wish: the command of the new starship *Enterprise*. Dr. Taylor, refusing to be left behind, tells Kirk that this world of the future needs a marine biologist who is a whale specialist. Taylor is pert and intelligent and hints that she will someday see Kirk again. Ambassador Sarek, welcoming back his son Spock, is to take a message to Amanda. Spock explains to his bewildered father that now he does indeed feel with his emotions.

The film ends on a note of nostalgia. Captain Kirk and his crew power up the new *Enterprise*, which disappears in warp drive, the bold mission to explore the universe somehow beginning again. If the acting in *Star Trek IV* is patterned and familiar, if Nimoy the director is straightforward in his presentation, the old friends do not disappoint.

Dan Barnett

Reviews
Chicago Tribune. November 26, 1986, V, p. 3.
Cinefantastique. March, 1987, p. 24.
Films in Review. XXXVIII, February, 1987, p. 102.
Los Angeles Times. November 26, 1986, VI, p. 1.
Macleans. XCIX, December 8, 1986, p. 74.
The Magazine of Fantasy and Science Fiction. May, 1987, p. 109.
The New York Times. November 26, 1986, p. C14.
Newsweek. CVIII, December 1, 1986, p. 89.
Time. CXXVIII, December 8, 1986, p. 99.
Variety. CCCXXV, November 19, 1986, p. 16.
The Wall Street Journal. November 28, 1986, p. 8.
The Washington Post. November 26, 1986, p. D1.

SUMMER
(LE RAYON VERT)

Origin: France
Released: 1986
Released in U.S.: 1986
Production: Margaret Menegoz for Les Films du Losange; released by
   Orion Classics
Direction: Eric Rohmer
Screenplay: Eric Rohmer
Cinematography: Sophie Maintigneux
Editing: Maria-Luisa Garcia
Art direction: no listing
Sound: Claudine Nougaret
Music: Jean-Louis Valero
MPAA rating: R
Running time: 90 minutes

Principal characters:
Delphine.........................Marie Rivière
Manuella..........................Lisa Heredia
Béatrice ....Béatrice Romand
Françoise ....Rosette
Edouard ....Eric Hamm
Young girl in Cherbourg............Vanessa Leleu
Irène............................Irène Skobline
Lena ....Carita
Joël ....Joël Comarlot
Pierrot ....Marc Vivas
Jacques ....Vincent Gauthier

Summer is the fifth in director Eric Rohmer's series "Comedies and Prov-
erbs," which includes *The Aviator's Wife* (1981), *Le Beau Mariage* (1982),
Pauline at the Beach (1982), and *Full Moon in Paris* (1984). This series of
films, like its predecessor "Six Moral Tales," is concerned with its characters' romantic choices and the way they rationalize them. Rohmer has
changed neither his basic style nor his interests since *My Night at Maud's*
(1969) made him an overnight sensation. Yet *Summer*, with its largely improvised dialogue and its episodic structure, carries Rohmer's realist aesthetic a bit further. Like most of his films, it contains no stars, though some
of its actors have appeared in previous Rohmer films. Marie Rivière, for
example, appeared in *The Aviator's Wife*, and Béatrice Romand, who plays

one of her friends, was the charming young girl in *Claire's Knee* (1970) as well as the heroine of *Le Beau Mariage*.

The film's American title is unfortunate, for the French title, *Le Rayon vert*, is the same as the title of an 1882 Jules Verne novel that figures prominently in the film. A literal translation would be "The Green Ray." Verne's novel concerns a girl who decides that she must see the green ray, a rare meteorological phenomenon, before deciding whom to marry. Sometimes, when the sun sets, there is a brief moment, usually after the sun sinks into the horizon, when all the red-orange light has been absorbed and the blue-violet shades have been scattered into the atmosphere so that only the green remains visible. Verne's novel romanticizes this phenomenon, describing its color as the most ethereal shade of green: the precise color of hope. Additionally, according to a legend mentioned in the novel, whoever sees the green ray, which melts away lies and illusions, will make no mistake in love. Rohmer's film is not a version of the novel, but there are many loose parallels between the two. Both have heroines prone to superstition and fantasy, and both culminate in a sighting of the green ray, though Verne's heroine, Helena Campbell, is so busy staring into the eyes of her lover, Olivier Sinclair, that she herself misses the sight.

Each of the film's various episodes is preceded by its respective date. On July 2, two weeks before her scheduled vacation trip to Greece, Delphine (Marie Rivière), a young Parisian secretary, receives a call from her traveling companion, who has canceled the vacation plans with Delphine in order to travel with her boyfriend. Desolate, Delphine begins searching unsuccessfully for new vacation plans. Some relatives who are about to go camping in Ireland invite her along, but, craving sun, she finds the idea of the rainy climate too depressing. She calls her former boyfriend, Jean-Pierre, to borrow his summer place, but he is planning on using it and offers instead his Alpine apartment, which she rejects. Still flailing around, she dines with some friends, Manuella (Lisa Heredia), Béatrice (Béatrice Romand), and Françoise (Rosette), who try to talk her out of her depression and into vacationing alone, or at least actively searching for a new man. Delphine lies to put them off and tells them that she has a new man already. She explains her personal superstitions to them: the fact that she constantly finds meaningful cards in the street, and that ever since a medium friend declared green to be her color this year she finds little green things too. Driven to tears by the conversation, she sulks on a nearby step. Her friend Françoise tries to console her and convinces Delphine to join her and her fiancé and family in Cherbourg. There, near the water, Françoise tries to get Delphine to pick up Edouard (Eric Hamm), but Delphine, finding him suspicious, backs off. That evening, eating with the family couples and their children, Delphine refuses the main course, a large, beautiful platter of pork chops, explaining that she is a strict vegetarian. She then argues with the family members who try to reason her out of her refusal. Though her position, she states, is instinctual, she does run through a list of her reasons. Vegetables are more removed from humans, cheaper to raise, tastier than meat. Being lighter, they aerate her.

Delphine tries to be pleasant and enjoy herself by playing with the children or taking solitary country walks, but she does not quite fit into this family scene, and when Françoise and her boyfriend leave for Paris, she goes with them. Once back, she takes up Jean-Pierre's offer and leaves for his Alpine apartment. Arriving on a morning bus, she takes a solitary walk while waiting for the friend with the keys but then panics and leaves that very evening without even staying overnight. The next Friday, after walking by the Seine, she encounters an old friend, Irène (Irène Skobline), at an outdoor café. Irène offers Delphine her brother-in-law's apartment at Biarritz. There, after swimming and wandering around the shore, Delphine overhears a group of plain, middle-aged women enthusiastically discussing Jules Verne's novel *Le Rayon vert*. An elderly man joins the women and offers a detailed scientific explanation of the ray. The sun then sets, but no green ray appears.

The next day on the beach, Delphine meets Lena (Carita), an adventurous, uninhibited Swede. Lena is everything Delphine is not. She adores traveling alone, eyes and chases men, rejects a regular boyfriend or fiancé, and goes joyfully topless on the beach. Out drinking one evening with Delphine, Lena explains her ideas about how to relate to men and provides a virtuoso display of her tactics. Explaining that life is like a card game and that one must dissemble and not reveal one's hand, Lena chooses to play with people rather than reveal herself. Delphine is unconvinced, claiming that her hand is empty. Lena then attracts two nearby men, Joël (Joël Comarlot) and Pierrot (Marc Vivas), to their table and proceeds to tease Joël by changing her language from minute to minute and claiming to be first Spanish, then German, and finally English. Delphine gradually withdraws from this scene and, finally, unable to bear it any more, she runs away, pursued briefly by Pierrot, who has taken a liking to her.

On August 4, at the Biarritz train station, she sits reading Fyodor Dostoevski's *The Idiot* while waiting for the train back to Paris. Jacques (Vincent Gauthier), a young cabinetmaker, sits across from her and they begin to flirt. Delphine, however, has changed. She looks back at him invitingly, and, shortly after he joins her on her bench, she asks to accompany him to Saint-Jean-de-Luz. There she strolls with him, speaking frankly of her loneliness, her dissatisfaction with one-night stands, and her general suspicion of men. Jacques invites her to go away with him to a place near Bayonne, but she is indecisive. After they pass a souvenir shop called Le Rayon vert, she asks him to watch the sunset with her. As the sun sinks, she bursts again into tears, but while he strokes her face she suddenly cries

"Yes!" as she sees the fabled green ray.

There is no fancy camera work; the film is even simpler, closer to television than Rohmer's previous films. Because of its improvisational character, it has an almost documentary look. Most of the time the various characters are framed in medium shots while they talk. Occasionally the camera will slide over to one of the companions, zoom in a bit closer, or employ a straightforward shot-countershot. Sometimes a random shot intrudes—for example, the momentary glimpse of the Oriental tourists at the next table while Delphine talks to Irène at the sidewalk cafe. The film's genius is demonstrated by the fact that in spite of its loose, almost aimless structure, a tension builds up toward its end so that the final sequence, in which Delphine sees the green ray and accepts Jacques, is extremely moving and satisfying.

The film's ending stirs the audience partly because Delphine gradually acquires their sympathy throughout the film. She is restless, passive, and empty, yet devoid of vanity and narcissism. The people she flees do seem insensitive, shallow, even predatory. Most important, she is ever hopeful. She has an affinity, even a hunger, for nature. Her friends tease her, telling her that she is a plant, or like the solitary mountain goat represented by Capricorn, her zodiac sign. Because of her sensitivity to chance and fable, her gentle nature, her love of natural beauty, however, she seems to deserve the magic spectacle. The viewer's curiosity about the ray develops along with Delphine's. One feels vicarious joy for her at the end, but there is also the more immediate, childlike pleasure of seeing it oneself.

Rohmer's new brand of realism, however, is not as naïve as it might seem. The old man at Biarritz who explains the ray states clearly that one is not really seeing the sun, which has already disappeared as one watches its colors set. Rohmer's sunset is a reflection, and perception of it is filtered through a legend, a novel, and the film itself. His vision is an openly Platonic one: At the heart of the world is a fierce mathematical beauty which reveals itself in flashes to those who, dissatisfied with the formlessness of everyday experience, seek it.

Joan Esposito

Reviews

The Christian Science Monitor. August 29, 1986, p. 23.
Los Angeles Times. October 19, 1986, p. C22.
Mademoiselle. XCII, November, 1986, p. 98.
The New Republic. CXCV, September 1, 1986, p. 25.
New Statesman. CXIII, March 13, 1987, p. 21.
New York. XIX, September 8, 1986, p. 70.

The New York Times. August 29, 1986, p. C5.
Newsweek. CVIII, September 22, 1986, p. 84.
Variety. CCCXXVII, April 22, 1986, p. 23.
Vogue. CLXXVI, September, 1986, p. 108.
The Washington Post. October 20, 1986, p. C9.

THAT'S LIFE!

Production: Tony Adams; released by Columbia Pictures
Direction: Blake Edwards
Screenplay: Milton Wexler and Blake Edwards
Cinematography: Anthony Richmond
Editing: Lee Rhoads
Art direction: Tony Marando
Music: Henry Mancini
MPAA rating: PG-13
Running time: 102 minutes

Principal characters:
Harvey Fairchild . . . . Jack Lemmon
Gillian Fairchild . . . . Julie Andrews
Holly Parrish. . . . . Sally Kellerman
Father Baragone. . . . . Robert Loggia
Megan Fairchild Bartle . . . . Jennifer Edwards
Steve Larwin . . . . Robert Knepper
Larry Bartlet . . . . Matt Lattanzi
Josh Fairchild. Chris Lemmon
Janice Kern. . . . . Cynthia Sikes
Fanny Ward . . . . Dana Sparks
Kate Fairchild . . . . Emma Walton
Madame Carrie . . . . Felicia Farr

It would be a gross understatement to call *That's Life!* a personal film. The project is loaded with references to director Blake Edwards, his wife, Julie Andrews, and actor Jack Lemmon. Andrews plays Gillian Fairchild, a renowned singer and entertainer. Lemmon, in an oblique reference to Edwards himself, plays her husband, a successful architect. Edwards' daughter from a previous marriage, Jennifer, appears as one of the Fairchilds' children. The other offspring are played by Lemmon's son, Chris, and Andrews' daughter from an earlier marriage, Emma Walton. Lemmon's wife, Felicia Farr, appears as Madame Carrie. The primary setting of the film, a sprawling Malibu estate, is Edwards and Andrews' actual home. Neighbors Dana Sparks and Sally Kellerman—the latter is the wife of the film's executive producer, Jonathan Krane—also have roles in the film. The screenplay was written by Edwards and his psychiatrist, Milton Wexler, with most of the dialogue improvised by the actors themselves and many of the film's scenes drawn from actual incidents.

The autobiographical aspects of Edwards' film go even deeper. Lemmon is a stand-in for Edwards; in fact, Edwards even considered playing the role of Harvey Fairchild himself. Like Edwards, Harvey is an artist. The job of the architect is analogous to that of the film director: planning a production, then overseeing its construction by others. Harvey's disillusionment with his commercial success and his yearning for an artistic triumph can be read as Edwards' own dissatisfaction with his career to date. Just as Harvey must cater to the whims of ignorant and tasteless clients, so has Edwards fought with studio executives over the final editing of his films. His legendary battles with the studios on *Darling Lili* (1970), *Wild Rovers* (1971), and *The Carey Treatment* (1972), all of which was later lampooned in his vicious satire *S.O.B.* (1981), nearly ruined him, and he was only able to revive his ailing career by filming seemingly endless sequels to *The Pink Panther* (1964). While Edwards' "commercial" projects, primarily the Pink Panther films, have much to recommend them, his artistic frustrations can be understood. As Edwards has said in an interview, "It bothers me that I haven't got to do the ultimate thing I want to do, and there isn't a piece of work of which I can say, 'That's the definitive one.' "

That's Life! is similar in many ways to other Edwards films. Throughout his career Edwards has been particularly concerned with the idea of chaos. From the comic chaos of the Pink Panther films to the dramatic chaos of *Days of Wine and Roses* (1962), Edwards depicts the fragility of the human condition. His characters often find themselves in a world falling apart, and the challenge of his characters is to survive, either by existentially accepting disorder, like Inspector Clouseau, or by conquering it through a commitment to meaningful human relationships.

That's Life! takes place during the course of a weekend at the Fairchild household. Harvey is facing the stress of his sixtieth birthday; Gillian is stoically awaiting the news of a test for throat cancer. (In real life it was Edwards, not Andrews, who had a biopsy.) Each is a typical Edwards character in that they face the possible disintegration of their worlds, but since *That's Life!* concerns Edwards' own world, the film is the depiction of his life in the terms of his artistic vision. *That's Life!* is therefore the ultimate meeting of art and reality.

Though Edwards is probably better known to the public as a director of comedies, he has actually functioned equally well with dramatic material. Moreover, his comic approach is informed by drama. The source of his comedy is invariably pain or humiliation, and even his funniest films contain dark overtones. In *That's Life!* comedy and drama are brought together in bittersweet combination through the use of the two central characters. Harvey is primarily a comic character. His anxieties about aging are treated with humor, and each of the film's long comedy sequences is dominated by his presence. Gillian, on the other hand, is the dramatic character. Her fears are treated solemnly, and the audience is asked to empathize with her predicament. It is this juxtaposition of comedy and drama, embodied in the lead couple, that lends *That's Life!* its unique qualities.

The film opens quietly. As the credits appear, the sounds of a procedure inside an operating room are heard. A patient's throat sample is removed to a laboratory, where over the next two days it will be analyzed. The clinical, claustrophobic close-ups of Gillian's tissue sample, which recur throughout the film, provide striking counterpoint to the comic treatment of Harvey's medical problems, both real and imagined. After Gillian returns home from the hospital, the audience is introduced to Harvey, returning home from work. As he crosses his estate in long-shot, the lawn sprinklers slowly and inexorably begin to erupt. Harvey attempts to evade the streams of water, eventually jumping across some bushes to the safety of his driveway. This short scene perfectly illustrates Edwards' view of the world. An orderly and safe world is illusory. Even a seemingly benign lawn can conceal hidden danger. The comic episode with Harvey is ended by a cut to Gillian resting silently on her bed. She hears Harvey playing the piano and goes downstairs. In a long comic monologue, photographed by Edwards in a single unbroken take, Harvey describes his day's problems. These early scenes clearly identify Harvey with comedy and Gillian with drama. The alternation of scenes containing each character takes the audience from comedy to drama and back and establishes the overall structural pattern of the film.

Later that evening Harvey and Gillian go out for dinner. At the restaurant Edwards frames the two of them together. (Like nearly all Edwards' films, *That's Life!* is filmed in a wide-screen format.) Harvey continues his comic monologue; Gillian silently holds her throat. The audience is torn in two directions at once. Lemmon's performance is a tour de force, and his dialogue is genuinely funny; Andrews' understated stoicism is no less appealing. Edwards does not allow the audience to side with one character or the other. Harvey talks of his dissatisfactions. Success breeds failure, he says, reasoning that commercial success means designing private homes for wealthy clients and making artistic compromises in the process. He longs to create an aesthetic masterpiece. That Edwards has been relatively more successful in realizing his dreams than his alter ego, Harvey, is evidenced by the fact that Edwards is making *That's Life!* while Harvey is designing fast-food restaurants emblazoned with the slogan "We Be Food."

That evening Harvey and Gillian watch son Josh (Chris Lemmon) in his weekly television show. Edwards frames the television within the wide-screen space of his film and asks the audience to examine the television image. Later in the scene Harvey walks to the bathroom mirror and gazes at his own weathered image. The juxtaposition of the youthful Josh on television with his older father in the mirror reminds the audience that the film is not only about Blake Edwards but also about Jack Lemmon. Lemmon, after all, has been identified with some of the best screen comedy, from his debut in *It Should Happen to You* (1954) through the blockbuster successes of *Some Like It Hot* (1959) and *The Apartment* (1960). His aging is an integral part of the film.

The next morning Harvey goes for a physical checkup while the Fairchild children begin arriving for Harvey's sixtieth birthday celebration. In the doctor's office Harvey is photographed from a slightly high camera angle, and the crosscutting between him and his doctor emphasizes his weakened position. Meanwhile, Gillian meets daughter Kate (Emma Walton) at the airport. When they return home, daughter Megan (Jennifer Edwards) also arrives. The young Fairchilds are undergoing personal crises of their own (the working title of the film, in fact, was "Crisis"), but Edwards wisely chooses not to focus too closely on the children's problems, so that the focus on the central couple is not diluted.

The culmination of the film's middle sequences comes at an outdoor dinner at the Fairchild home which brings together most of the film's main characters. Edwards sets up and photographs the scene magnificently, bringing out each of the subplots contained around the dinner table. The important juxtaposition, once again, is poignant one-shots (shots of only one character in the scene) of the quietly suffering Gillian to Harvey and his humorous asides about the other guests. The scene ends with a long-shot of the group, beautifully framed between a pair of glowing candles. The solidarity of a loving family unit is the haven from the swirling and unpredictable chaos of the world. Edwards, however, breaks the balanced and pleasing composition with a slow zoom toward Gillian. The internal conflicts of the family have not yet been resolved at this point in the film, and the composition cannot be maintained.

The next day, Sunday, Harvey stops on his way to church to consult with Madame Carrie, the local clairvoyant. The fortune-telling session gradually turns romantic, and at church Harvey discovers an uncomfortable feeling in his crotch. The long comic sequence of Harvey dealing with his case of crab lice is typical Edwards. The bit is carried far beyond the point of hilarity to outright absurdity, culminating in Harvey's frantic visit to a hospital emergency room. Edwards daringly juxtaposes Harvey's comic suffering with the real suffering of the emergency room. Screams are heard, patients are wheeled by, a bloodied man staggers in. The giddy contrast is alarming and sums up the comic-dramatic dichotomy of the film.

That's Life! concludes with Harvey's sixtieth birthday party Sunday evening. (It is worth noting that at the time of filming Lemmon was sixty and Edwards was sixty-four.) As the sequence unfolds, the family's personal crises first escalate, then gradually diminish. Kate and her boyfriend settle their differences; Larry (Matt Lattanzi) and Megan also become reconciled. Even oversexed Holly (Sally Kellerman) finds her match in Father Baragone (Robert Loggia). The crises of the central couple, however, continue to linger. In perhaps the film's most moving episode, Gillian finally explodes with pent-up emotion and chastises Harvey for his immature behavior. The message of her short speech—that the solution to his fears about dying is to join her in a loving relationship—is Edwards talking. As the stunned Harvey is brought his birthday cake, Edwards cuts to his point of view. The wide-screen frame harmoniously filled with family and friends is Harvey's alternative to his suffering. Only after Gillian learns that her tumor is benign, however, is a final reconciliation possible. Gillian explains to Harvey what has happened, and then she dances lovingly with him in close-up.

The final shot of the film frames the outdoor party between two lanterns. The composition—toward which the entire film has been evolving—recalls the family dinner earlier, but now there is nothing to disrupt the formal balance and purity of the frame. The wide-screen space of the film, which is potentially chaotic (the lawn sprinkler sequence) or disjointed (the comic suffering of Harvey framed with the real suffering of Gillian or of the hospital patients), has become intimate and friendly.

David Rivel

Reviews
Films in Review. XXXVII, December, 1986, p. 619.
Glamour. LXXXIV, October, 1986, p. 226.
Los Angeles Times. September , 1986, VI, p. 1.
Macleans. XCIX, October 6, 1986, p. 79.
The New Republic. CXCV, October 20, 1986, p. 25.
The New York Times. CXXXVI, September 26, 1986, p. C1.
Newsweek. CVIII, October 6, 1986, p. 72.
Time. CXXVIII, September 29, 1986, p. 72.
Variety. CCCXXIV, September 3, 1986, p. 14.
The Wall Street Journal. CCVIII, October 9, 1986, p. 32.

THREE MEN AND A CRADLE
(TROIS HOMMES ET UN COUFFIN)

Origin: France
Released: 1985
Released in U.S.: 1986
Production: Jean-François Lepetit for Flach Film, Soprosfilms, and TF1 Productions; released by Samuel Goldwyn Company
Direction: Coline Serreau
Screenplay: Coline Serreau
Cinematography: Jean-Yves Escoffier and Jean-Jacques Bouhon
Editing: Catherine Renault
Art direction: Yvan Maussion
Music: no listing
MPAA rating: PG-13
Running time: 100 minutes

Principal characters:
Michel .... Michel Boujenah
Pierre............................ Roland Giraud
Jacques .... André Dussollier
Sylvia .... Philippine Leroy Beaulieu
Baby Marie (as an infant) ...... Gwendoline Mourlet
Marie (as a toddler) .... Jennifer Moret

Coline Serreau's *Three Men and a Cradle* is essentially a one-joke farce. While the film's comic premises are amusing enough, Serreau is able to sustain the audience's interest in the narrative primarily because of careful pacing, the acting skills of Michel Boujenah (who, in appearance and manner, reminds one of Harpo Marx) and Roland Giraud, and the visual style brought to the production by cinematographers Jean-Yves Escoffier and Jean-Jacques Bouhon and production designer Yvan Maussion.

Although Serreau seems to want to make some at least semiserious statements about gender roles, the heart of her story is the chaos which is brought into the lives of three bachelors by an infant girl who is almost literally thrown into their midst.

Michel (Michel Boujenah), Pierre (Roland Giraud), and Jacques (André Dussollier) are successful, devil-may-care young men who share elegant living quarters in a chic section of Paris. Michel is a cartoonist whose work is much in demand, Pierre has a flourishing career in advertising, and Jacques is a dashing commercial pilot who flies to all corners of the world. The professional, social, and sexual whirl of the men's lives is disrupted when a baby is left on their doorstep. Baby Marie (Gwendoline Mourlet) is the fruit of the passion of Jacques (who has trouble remembering the names of the women with whom he shares one-night stands) and Sylvia (Philippine Leroy Beaulieu), a model who has gone to work in the United States for six months. When Sylvia leaves Marie at the apartment, Jacques has left for Asia; hence, the burden of caring for the baby falls for several months on Michel and Pierre. At first, the two clumsy bachelors seem ready to throttle the child, but eventually, in spite of themselves, they become doting parents.

The plot begins to thicken before Jacques leaves for Japan and Thailand. At a party on the eve of his departure, a pilot friend of his asks a favor of Jacques: He is expecting a package and he would like to have it delivered to the apartment of Jacques and his roommates. The friend's request appears to be innocent enough, but Jacques forgets to tell Michel and Pierre about the arrival of the package until just before he leaves Paris. When Marie turns up, Jacques's roommates think that Jacques has played a nasty trick on them—that the baby is the package.

In reality, the package which Jacques's pal was expecting contains heroin, and this bundle shows up shortly after Marie's appearance. Soon, a couple of young men arrive at the apartment and ask for the package. Michel and Pierre are relieved at this point, for they think that the men have come to take the baby off their hands. The drug couriers are suitably confused, but Michel and Pierre persuade them to take both Marie and the much smaller package (of whose contents Michel and Pierre are completely ignorant). When Pierre realizes that the two men had not come for Marie, however, he pursues them, and, after an argument, he retrieves the baby—and the heroin.

Unfortunately, a policeman has witnessed the confrontation between Pierre and the thugs. The officer accompanies Pierre back to his apartment, and he is still present when Jacques telephones from Thailand. The policeman overhears enough of a double-meaning conversation to cause him to suspect that Michel and Pierre are party to drug-smuggling. On the one hand, then, the crooks are determined to retrieve their booty—they break into the apartment and leave it a shambles. In addition, the police become more and more convinced that Jacques, Pierre, and Michel are trafficking in drugs, and they give the apartment a thorough going-over themselves.

Pierre and Michel are now under constant surveillance. Michel ultimately arranges to pass the contraband to a gang member during a meeting in the Parc Monceau; he is able to get rid of the infamous package, despite the fact that the police are watching, by concealing it in a dirty diaper.

At long last, Jacques, the third member of the formerly happy trio of friends, arrives home, completely unaware of the mess which has materialized. Not only was he not expecting the arrival of Marie, he also had no idea that his friend's package contained what it did. Pierre and Michel are understandably annoyed with what they have had to endure, and Serreau and her cinematographers provide several humorous takes of the two men pouting amid their once-sumptuous furnishings.

After considerable bickering with his roommates, Jacques takes Marie to the home of his mother in Nice, hoping that she will take the baby off his hands. Jacques's mother, however, is a liberated woman: She and a friend have planned an extended vacation, and it is clear that she, despite her attraction to her only grandchild, has no intention of giving up her freedom to come and go and do as she pleases. The joke is again on Jacques—his own mother, upon whose maternal instincts he has counted so heavily, turns out to be as hedonistic as he.

Jacques and Marie are forced to return to Paris, and since Sylvia refuses to come back to France, Jacques attempts to hire a nanny. The now experienced Pierre, however, is convinced that he is more qualified to care for Marie than any hired hand, and he goads the nurse into beating an angry and hasty retreat.

As time has passed, Pierre, Michel, and, finally, even Jacques have become quite attached to Marie. The three vie for the opportunity to feed her, bathe her, tuck her in for the night—without revealing to the others the extent of their devotion. Jacques is the last to succumb to the baby's charms— he even interrupts making love to one of his girlfriends late one night when the baby begins to cry. Jacques's carnality having given way to his paternal instincts, his miffed girlfriend leaves in a snit. Later, a grand dinner party in the apartment is reduced to a shambles because all three of the men in turn neglect their dinner guests in order to cater to the child's needs. Pierre even insults his young, free-spirited friends when they express a dislike of infants.

The wretched end to the dinner party is the last straw for Michel, Pierre, and Jacques, and they quarrel in frustration over the extent to which their lives have been altered by Marie's presence.

One morning, however, Sylvia turns up unexpectedly at the apartment. She confesses that she now misses the baby and has come to take her back. At first, Pierre, Michel, and Jacques are relieved: They are looking forward to sleeping late when they please and pursuing their sexual conquests uninhibited by responsibility to Marie. Each man in turn, however, soon realizes how empty his life is now without the baby.

Jacques joyfully flies off to Caracas only to brood alone in his hotel room; Michel cannot even concentrate on his girlfriends; Pierre is seen lying face down on his bed, clutching Marie's rubber giraffe. In one of the film's most successful scenes, Jacques, having sullenly returned to Paris, gets quite drunk and pads his abdomen in a parody of pregnancy. He delivers a comic speech of self-pity, bemoaning the futility of his life—indeed, protesting the lot of men everywhere, men who build machines and architectural wonders but cannot truly create as women can. Men, snivels Jacques, can never bring anything from within themselves.

All is not lost, however. Sylvia overestimated her own motherly stamina, and, looking very much the worse for wear, she brings Marie back to her father surrogates. Sylvia complains that she cannot handle the stress of caring for a baby and that her career is suffering, and she asks Pierre, Michel, and Jacques if they would be so kind as to keep Marie for a few days. Sylvia is, of course, only going through what the men had coped with for months, and they gleefully gloat over their hard-earned expertise in child care.

The film's last scenes are of Sylvia curled up in Marie's cradle, in a fetal position, with her thumb in her mouth. Suddenly, Marie, who has survived the trauma of the past few months quite well, comes toddling into the room.

Three Men and a Cradle is not a profound film, and it is most successful when it focuses on the flustered pseudofathers and their eventual coming to terms with caring for Marie. When Serreau tries to give some sort of serious dimension to the situation—as with Jacques's drunken philosophizing—no real depth materializes. The film is nevertheless something of a satire on the egocentric life of "swinging singles": Pierre, Michel, and Jacques, who use and discard women casually, are completely undone by a baby girl.

One of the real charms of *Three Men and a Cradle* is the cinematography of Escoffier and Bouhon and the atmospheric decor wrought by Maussion. The bachelor apartment, where most of the film's action takes place, is a treat to behold in itself, but one notes the irony of its furnishings: Shots of Michel, who has spent the night comforting the colicky Marie, sitting stuporously beneath a painting of a peaceful landscape symbolize his humorous predicament, and the plethora of female faces and figure studies which hang on the walls of the apartment indicate that for the inhabitants women are only decoration, things to be enjoyed in a passive, unthinking fashion.

The camera of Escoffier and Bouhon frequently tracks forward and backward through the apartment, especially from room to room and down the corridors, and nicely translates the confusion and frenzy of Pierre and Michel early in the film.

The gags which are the very substance of the comedy of *Three Men and a Cradle* are those which feature the ghastly things that a baby can do—to furniture, clothing, comfortable routines. It is Serreau's skill in pacing her film that gets the most from these situations and maintains one's interest.

Gordon Walters

Reviews
Chicago Tribune. May 2, 1986, p. CT7.
Films in Review. XXXVII, August, 1986, p. 423.
Los Angeles Times. May 9, 1986, VI, p. 1.

Macleans. XCIX, May 5, 1986, p. 52.
The New York Times. April 25, 1986, p. C8.
Newsweek. CVII, May 26, 1986, p. 72.
The Wall Street Journal. CCVIII, April 29, 1986, p. 28.
The Washington Post. May 10, 1986, p. C1.
Washingtonian. XXI, April, 1986, p. 73.

TOP GUN

Production: Don Simpson and Jerry Bruckheimer; released by Paramount Pictures
Direction: Tony Scott
Screenplay: Jim Cash and Jack Epps, Jr.
Cinematography: Jeffrey Kimball
Editing: Billy Weber and Christopher Lebenzon
Art direction: John F. De Cuir, Jr.; set decoration, Robert R. Benton
Special photographic effects: Gary Gutierrez
Music: Harold Faltermeyer
Song: Giorgio Moroder and Tom Whitlock, "Take My Breath Away" (AA)
MPAA rating: PG
Running time: 112 minutes

Principal characters:
Lieutenant Pete "Maverick" Mitchell . . . . Tom Cruise
Charlotte "Charlie" Blackwood . . . . Kelly McGillis
Lieutenant Nick "Goose"
    Bradshaw. . . . . Anthony Edwards
Commander Mike Metcalf. . . . . Tom Skerritt
Tom "Iceman" Kazansky. . . . . Val Kilmer
Dick "Jester" Wetherly . . . . Michael Ironside
Bill "Cougar" Cortell . . . . John Stockwell
Ron "Slider" Kerner . . . . Rick Rossovich
Carole Bradshaw . . . . Meg Ryan

Of the films of 1986, the most heartless, the most programmatically manipulative, and also the slickest and most technically polished may well have been *Top Gun.* The truly offensive thing about this film is not that its screenplay and direction are so abysmal, nor is it the fact that such a shallow film was one of the top-grossing attractions of 1986. No, what makes *Top Gun* a worthy target for critical darts is precisely its high finish and technical sophistication, the always artful, occasionally brilliant employment of action footage, the advantage it takes of all the lessons taught by *Miami Vice* and MTV in how the camera and the sound track can become the real heroes of the action, and the use to which it puts the by-now nearly iconic innocence of Tom Cruise. Like most really evil artworks, *Top Gun* is ideologically successful precisely to the degree that it is aesthetically effective.

Consider, for example, the film's opening scene, which follows hard upon an explanation of the title (Top Gun is the nickname for the navy's combat-fighting school, begun during the Vietnam War to rehone American pilots' dog-fighting skills) and the opening credits. The heavy beat of New Wave rock commences with the credits and moves up a notch in intensity as the screen is filled with images of dawn on the deck of an aircraft carrier from which fighter planes are being launched into action. The sequence is presented mostly in slow motion, and it is eerily reminiscent of a science-fiction fantasy, the strange creatures who guide the planes into position and supervise their launch into space resembling automatons more than men. Coproducer Jerry Bruckheimer has been entirely candid about the associations these scenes are meant to evoke in the audience: "I knew it could be like 'Star Wars' on earth." The remainder of the film features innumerable similar set pieces—in the air, on the ground (with the Tom Cruise character zooming along the highway on a motorcycle), and back again on the deck of the aircraft carrier. Indeed, the navy was so delighted with the film and with the quality of its production that it has used several cuts in its recruiting ads. This alone should make producers Bruckheimer and Don Simpson nervous, if not ashamed.

Both ideologically and in terms of the nuts and bolts of the narrative itself, *Top Gun* picks up where *An Officer and a Gentleman* (1982) left off. The earlier film (another Simpson production) took hero Zack Mayo (Richard Gere) up to the moment of graduation from the Naval Aviation Officers Candidate School, next stop flight training. The story resumes with Cruise in the lead role of Lieutenant Pete "Maverick" Mitchell, now the most gifted fighter pilot in the navy, driven by the legacy of his fighter-pilot father to fly higher, faster, and more daringly than anyone else. Also, as in the earlier film, the hero's career is nearly terminated when his closest friend dies, but, predictably, Maverick ultimately recovers and graduates with his class. The only twist here is that the film does not end with Maverick's surviving this test of his moral and psychological fiber; *Top Gun*, which after all is about combat, not simply building character, ends with a real dog fight between outnumbered Americans and better-equipped but morally inferior Russians. The latter are, predictably, faceless, their visors blackened so that the viewer never gets to look into their eyes.

What emerges as the dominant motif in this sequence, in the failure of Maverick's chief rival, Tom "Iceman" Kazansky (Val Kilmer), to defend himself successfully against the Russian fighters, is the ultimate superiority of unorthodox daring and innovation, of personal initiative, one might say, over mere technical brilliance. Iceman has won the trophy as the best of the best at Top Gun. When the game is for real, however, it is Maverick's skill and guts (boosted by a shot of inspiration from the memory of his dead friend whose dog tags he clutches while intoning "Talk to me, Goose") that prove decisive in routing the hapless Russians, who are no match for the guile and heart of clean-cut (and superbly schooled) American youth. This outcome has, to be sure, a long heritage in Westerns and war pictures, down to Luke Skywalker's infamous reliance on the mystic aid of "the force" in *Star Wars* (1977). Here, however, the need for personal initiative and ingenuity is part and parcel of the film's curious attempt to say two entirely contradictory things: On the one hand, it promotes the romance of high-technology combat, featuring at every opportunity shots of very slick, very sophisticated machines (and the people who operate them); on the other, it lionizes the boyish naïveté and unbridled high spirits of Maverick. By pitting Iceman's cold perfection against Maverick's rule breaking and giving the nod finally to the latter, the film valorizes on the level of the plot the obverse of what it practices and extols in its images: the irresistible lure of high technology. It is yet another mark of the film's achievement as well as its ideological power that the viewer scarcely notices the contradiction during the course of watching it. Even the most hard-hearted and analytic of filmgoers could not resist rooting for Maverick in that climactic dog fight.

The same tension underlies the character of Charlotte "Charlie" Blackwood (Kelly McGillis), an ambitious astrophysicist and civilian instructor at Top Gun who falls in love with Maverick. One of the recurrent figures in the film's dialogue represents erotic encounters in the jargon of air combat. When Maverick first makes a pass at Charlie in a local singles bar (dubbed by Maverick and Goose a "target-rich environment"), she asks him whether he has ever tried the same technique of picking up women before. He replies: "Yeah once, but I crashed and burned." The film consistently and intentionally images human relationships in the language of war and combat, and this central fact produces the character of Charlie. Her identity constantly, from the first time she appears in the singles bar, shifts between highly skilled and essentially affectless technician and sexual object. When she invites Maverick to her house for dinner, she admits that she cannot decide whether her genuine desire to hear the story of his encounter with a Russian Mig or her sexual attraction to him has been the primary motivation. Is she Charlie, or is she Charlotte? If this were her film, that contradiction might have been fruitful, but *Top Gun* is not about women. It is about men (more precisely, boys) and war. Charlotte's position in the film's structure is quickly resolved: The next scene shows her humiliating Maverick in front of the other pilots, followed by her chasing him in her Porsche as he speeds off angrily on his motorcycle, ending with her confession of love and their slow-motion sex bathed in the now-standard love-scene cast of the blue lens filter. Next morning, Charlie/Charlotte awakes to discover a paper airplane Maverick has left on the pillow, just in case the viewer (or she) were in any doubt about where Maverick's heart really lies.

The two previous Simpson-Bruckheimer blockbusters, *Flashdance* (1983) and *Beverly Hills Cop* (1984), both generated hit sound tracks, and *Top Gun* has followed in that tradition. What has made this film so popular is not merely its clever use of contemporary music to punctuate and supplement the otherwise slender plot. Rather, like the contradiction between plot and image that pits the creative instincts of individuals such as Maverick against the merciless power of hardware, weaponry, and technical efficiency, it is the music's persistent evocation of nostalgia on the ground in opposition to the affectless New Wave beats backing up action in the air. The entire film is structured around this split in the lives of the pilots between what they are out of uniform and what they become once they don flight suits, and it is keyed by the division of labor in the musical score. High technology wins out—how could it be otherwise?—when the pilots are cruising along at Mach II on the lookout for bogeys, but back on terra firma, they are free to indulge their memories, lusts, and frivolous wishes and to sing (generally off key) "You've Lost That Lovin' Feelin'" and "Great Balls of Fire."

In 1980, Bertrand Gross wrote a semipopular book on the reconfiguration of American politics and ideology at the dawn of the age of Ronald Reagan. The title, *Friendly Fascism*, might be appropriated to describe films such as the Steven Spielberg-George Lucas-Harrison Ford vehicles and a rash of other less successful rock-'em, sock-'em action films that, with varying degrees of virulence, pit clean-cut, right-thinking white folks against the dark-skinned, morally corrupt races of the world. With *Top Gun*, "friendly fascism" has acquired a new wrinkle: It combines the daring of the hero with the romance of space-age technology. Actually, this was pioneered by *Star Wars*, with its combination of futuristic machines and weaponry and the mystical power of "the force." Now, something like the real thing has indeed descended: F-14's do indeed exist, and as the bombing of Libya in the spring of 1986 illustrated, they can get the job done. *Top Gun* must have already been in the can and ready for release when President Reagan ordered American planes to scour the North African desert in search of menacing Arabs, so it cannot be that Simpson and Bruckheimer conceived this project to capitalize on the wave of chauvinism those events instigated. As they say in the business, however, bombing Tripoli did not exactly hurt them at the box office. One can only speculate what Hollywood producers think that they are doing when they make a film that exploits all the cheap, tawdry emotional strings that American patriotism still touches. What can be said with confidence is that the glamorizing of modern warfare, which is the most powerful message communicated by *Top Gun*, not only occults the brutal realities of combat, but it also mystifies the structures of power that rule over military life. The navy founded Top Gun to give American pilots a competitive edge; the war then being waged in Indochina was unaffected by this initiative. Real wars, unlike the imaginary ones fought on the silver screen, are won and lost not by individuals but by the social structures that produce them.

Michael Sprinker

Reviews

Commonweal. CXIII, June 20, 1986, p. 375.
Cosmopolitan. CCI, July, 1986, p. 22.
Films and Filming. Number 384, September, 1986, p. 43.
The New Republic. CXCIV, June 9, 1986, p. 24.
The New York Times. CXXXV, June 8, 1986, II, p. 23.
The New Yorker. LXII, June 16, 1986, p. 118.
Newsweek. CVII, May 19, 1986, p. 72.
Time. CXXVII, May 19, 1986, p. 105.
Variety. CCCXXIII, May 14, 1986, p. 14.
The Wall Street Journal. CCVIII, May 22, 1986, p. 29.

TOUGH GUYS

Production: Joe Wizan for Touchstone Pictures in association with Silver
   Screen Partners II and Bryna Productions; released by Buena Vista
Direction: Jeff Kanew
Screenplay: James Orr and Jim Cruickshank
Cinematography: King Baggot
Editing: Kaja Fehr
Production design: Todd Hallowell
Art direction: Michael C. Corenblith; set decoration, Jeff Haley
Special effects: Chuck Gaspar, Joe D. Day, and Stan Parks
Makeup: Robert J. Schiffer and Michael F. Blake
Costume design: Erica Phillips
Sound: C. Darin Knight
Music direction: Ken Kushnick and David Passic
Music: James Newton Howard
Song: Burt Bacharach (music), Carole Bayer Sager (lyrics), and Kenny
   Rogers (performer), "They Don't Make Them Like They Used To"
MPAA rating: PG
Running time: 103 minutes

Principal characters:
Harry Doyle	Burt Lancaster
Archie Long	Kirk Douglas
Deke Yablonski	Charles Durning
Belle	Alexis Smith
Richie Evans	Dana Carvey
Skye Foster	Darlanne Fluegel
Leon B. Little	Eli Wallach
Vince	Monty Ash
Philly	Billy Barty
Schultz	Simmy Bow
Gladys Ripps	Darlene Conley
Jimmy Ellis	Nathan Davis
Man in gay bar	Matthew Faison
Gang leader	Corkey Ford
Federale captain	Rich Garcia
Richie's boss	Graham Jarvis

A fine sense of nostalgic melancholy and good-natured camaraderie min-
gles uncomfortably with contrived supporting characterizations and unbelievable situations in *Tough Guys*. Despite its drawbacks, however, the
film succeeds as light entertainment, almost entirely as a result of the cha-

risma of its leads, real-life buddies and frequent coworkers Burt Lancaster and Kirk Douglas. In their seventh screen outing together—the others were *I Walk Alone* (1947), *Gunfight at the OK Corral* (1957), *The Devil's Disciple* (1959), *The List of Adrian Messenger* (1963), *Seven Days in May* (1964), and the television film *Victory at Entebbe* (1976)—Douglas and Lancaster not only have a wonderful time trying to steal scenes from each other, but also, in their characters' bewildered disdain for the uncouth, dehumanizing modern world, enjoy poking a little sly fun at the sorry state of filmmaking in the 1980's.

The film opens with a slow pan across a collection of 1950's memorabilia, pausing on a framed newspaper clipping about the 1956 attempted robbery of the Gold Coast Flyer. The headline reads, "Train Bandits Get Thirty Years." Harry Doyle (Burt Lancaster) removes the keepsake from the wall of his prison cell while, a few feet away, his partner-in-crime and cellmate Archie Long (Kirk Douglas) presses dumbbells and mutters—as he has every day for the past thirty years—that they could have gotten away with it.

Looking dapper, Doyle and Long walk out of prison to begin their parole. The first thing that they see on the outside is a newspaper in a vending machine, which informs them that the Gold Coast Flyer will make its final run in a week. Long is miffed that the article does not mention their hijacking, which was the last train robbery attempt in United States history.

Richie Evans (Dana Carvey), a criminology buff-turned-parole officer and an admirer of Doyle and Long, meets the "Tough Guys" and offers to drive them to his office. While Richie goes to get his car, Doyle and Long are suddenly attacked by a myopic, screaming man with a shotgun, Leon B. Little (Eli Wallach). They escape, driving off in Richie's car at breakneck speed.

At Los Angeles Police Department headquarters, Sergeant Deke Yablonski (Charles Durning) learns of Doyle's and Long's paroles. Frustrated over having been retired from detective work to the payroll department, Yablonski—who captured the Tough Guys in 1956—tries to convince his skeptical, younger bosses that the convicts will return to crime with only a little encouragement.

While cashing their release checks, Doyle and Long easily foil a bank robbery, commenting afterward that crooks are not as tough as they used to be. Later, in Richie's office—which is a shrine to the Gold Coast Flyer heist— Long is given a job lead while Doyle is told that, although he wants to work, he is to move into a retirement home. The old pals are also informed that, since they are both convicted felons, the terms of their parole dictate that they cannot associate with each other for the next three years. Outside the office, they each complain about the other's habits, insist they will be happy to be rid of each other, and part tough.

After a few humorous encounters with a changed modern world, Long and Doyle meet again and vow not to let any stupid regulation keep them apart. They are cornered by the persistent, inexplicable Little, whom they lead into an open manhole. Moments later, they are accosted by six young street punks, whom the Tough Guys easily dispatch with a few well-placed groin kicks. At the retirement home, Doyle leads the elderly inmates in a protest against the inferior food and runs into an old flame, Belle (Alexis Smith), who has become a health-food enthusiast and an aerobics instructor.

Long quits his job at a frozen-yogurt stand after throwing a bowl of the gooey stuff at an obnoxious child. He visits his old gymnasium, now a co-educational fitness spa run by sexy young Skye Foster (Darlanne Fluegel). Attracted by his outstanding physique, Skye soon has Long wearing New Wave fashions, slam-dancing in rock clubs, and making love to her five or six times a day.

Doyle rekindles his romance with Belle, to the chagrin of the already outraged retirement-home staff. Richie has to reprimand Doyle for his behavior, hurting the old man's pride in the process. Long, meanwhile, repeatedly objects to the menial jobs that Richie finds for him. The situation is aggravated by Yablonski, who has taken it upon himself to needle the Tough Guys personally, hoping to provoke them into criminal acts.

Finally, his self-worth decimated and physically worn out by Foster, Long leaves the young woman, finds the morose Doyle drowning his sorrows in a bar, and proposes getting the old gang back together for a bank robbery. This proves easier said than done: Their old criminal cronies are all either deaf, invalids, or incontinent. Long and Doyle therefore hijack an armored car, only to discover that it is empty.

The Tough Guys show Richie the stolen vehicle, and Richie believes that he has failed as a parole officer. Long suggests that he join the gang for their last big caper: the successful hijacking of the Gold Coast Flyer. Both Richie and Doyle reject the proposal, and Long drives away angry, determined to pull the job on his own. That night, Doyle has a nightmare about Long being killed while robbing the train.

The next day, armed with a submachine gun, Long hijacks the train. He is hardly surprised to find a grinning Doyle waiting there to help him, but they are both caught off guard by Little, who finally explains that he was hired by a rival mobster thirty years ago to assassinate the Tough Guys, and—being a dedicated professional—he intends to fulfill the contract no matter how long it takes him.

When Yablonski arrives at the train yard with a SWAT division, the Tough Guys and Little agree to fight the police together, then settle their differences later. A shootout appears imminent, but the train unexpectedly lurches forward; Richie, disguised as a SWAT officer, has sneaked into the engineer's cab and started the locomotive.

The Gold Coast Flyer barrels south toward the Mexican border, Yablonski tailing it in a police helicopter. The Tough Guys kick Little out into a shallow river, then disconnect a passenger car while Richie is in it, so that he will not be implicated in their crime.

The train jumps the tracks, which end fifty yards before the border. The locomotive screams past a squad of border guards and through the fence, finally coming to rest a hundred feet inside Mexico. Even Yablonski cheers the Tough Guys' success, and orders his chopper to return home. Dusty but chipper, Doyle and Long crawl out of the cab. They are met by jeepfuls of Mexican police, whose commander informs them that they are under arrest. Outnumbered again, the Tough Guys resort to the same groin-kicking tactic that they used earlier on the Los Angeles street gang.

Despite the script and director Jeff Kanew's insistence on emphasizing either laughs or macho posturing in virtually every scene, Lancaster injects a high level of sensitivity and poignance into his portrayal of a man doubly at odds with society, outside both the law and his time. His quiet realization that he is not as tough as he was in his prime, his elegant courting of his lost love, Belle (by far the film's most mature, intelligent passage), and his final decision to place loyalty to Long above more comfortable—and craven— good sense all add up to the kind of class act whose passing the film constantly laments, but otherwise rarely evokes.

Douglas' more physical, volatile Archie Long provides almost all the film's forward momentum. He is the instigator, the hothead, and the man who tackles the new world head-on. It is a demanding, bravura performance, incredibly vital for an actor who was sixty-nine at the time. Although it required less introspection than did Lancaster's role (one cannot fault this film for casting; Lancaster has always been more adept at subtler emotions than the more intense Douglas), Douglas manages at least one remarkably tender moment. When, exhausted and hating himself, he says final goodbyes to his young mistress, both the reluctant realization of his own limitations and the warmth of his feelings for her are achingly palpable. Nowhere else in the film, before or after, does Long display such vulnerability.

The supporting characters are a mixed bag ranging from mediocre to embarrassingly poor. This is more because of the way the script was written than because of the generally capable cast's performance. Smith comes off best as Belle; the actress' polished professionalism is the perfect reflection of the character's civilized survivor's instinct. In descending order from there, Carvey is suitably earnest as the naïve, hero-worshipping Richie; Fluegel manages to transcend the air-headed nymphomaniac role by keeping control over a wide range of conflicting emotions (while wearing an electric blue wig, no less) in the powerful farewell scene with Long; Durning tries but fails to add some complexity to his mean-spirited, two-dimensional antagonist; and Wallach, saddled with the film's most ridiculous character, seems to have wandered in from a bad Borscht Belt routine. He is all flailing arms, overemphasized squints, and shrill screechings of humorless lines. Director Kanew, a former film editor, brings to *Tough Guys* the kind of detached commercial sheen that might be expected from someone who started cutting trailers for United Artists. The director of such teen farces as *Revenge of the Nerds* (1984) and *Gotcha!* (1985), Kanew certainly was not prepared to explore the darker questions about growing old in America that *Tough Guys* implicitly poses. Kanew's best creative decision was probably to keep the movie percolating at a quick, surface-entertainment tempo and to leave the addition of any depth into the proceedings solely up to Lancaster and Douglas.

Like Kanew, screenwriters James Orr and Jim Cruickshank come from a teen-comedy background. They scripted *Tough Guys* specifically for Douglas and Lancaster, and although Doyle and Long are well-drawn, with obvious affection for the two actors' screen *personae*, in many instances the authors seem to be attempting something along the lines of *Animal Retirement Home*. (Does Douglas really need to throw food at a kid, or Lancaster at a dining room attendant? Must Doyle get in Dutch for having a woman in his room?) To their credit, Orr and Cruickshank do manage to produce a decent percentage—by current commercial comedy standards, anyway—of funny gags, and they keep the hoary 1950's versus 1980's jokes to a tolerable minimum. Still, even as featherlight a concoction as *Cocoon* (1985) provided more insight into and gleaned sharper humor from the plight of the aged.

Despite its failings, however, *Tough Guys* is a likable celebration of old-fashioned star power and a cakewalk triumph for its two great leads.

Robert Strauss

Reviews
Chicago Tribune. October 3, 1986, VII, p. 40.
Commonweal. CXIII, October 24, 1986, p. 553.
Films in Review. XXXVII, December, 1986, p. 618.
Glamour. LXXXIV, December, 1986, p. 182.
Los Angeles Times. October 2, 1986, VI, p. 1.
The New York Times. October 3, 1986, p. C4.
Newsweek. CVIII, October 20, 1986, p. 79.
Time. CXXVIII, October 13, 1986, p. 107.
Variety. CCCXXIV, October 1, 1986, p. 13.
The Washington Post. October 8, 1986, p. D15.

TRUE STORIES

Production: Gary Kurfirst; released by Warner Bros.
Direction: David Byrne
Screenplay: Stephen Tobolowsky, Beth Henley, and David Byrne
Cinematography: Edward Lachman
Editing: Caroline Biggerstaff
Art direction: Barbara Ling
Costume design: Elizabeth Mcbride
Music: David Byrne and the Talking Heads
MPAA rating: PG
Running time: 111 minutes

Principal characters:
Louis Fyne......................John Goodman
Narrator ....David Byrne
Lying woman....................Jo Harvey Allen
Kay Culver......................Annie McEnroe
Earl Culver ....Spalding Gray
Ramon.......................Humberto Larriva
Mr. Tucker.................Roebuck Pops Staples
Miss Rollings, the lazy woman........Swoosie Kurtz
Cute woman ....Alix Elias
Preacher ....John Ingle
Computer guy ....Matthew Posey

David Byrne's first film, the musical *True Stories*, carries with it the flavor of his rock group, the Talking Heads. Byrne's background defies categorization, as does the film, but terms such as parody and synthesis appear frequently in discussions of his work. A clear understanding of the film may be aided by familiarity with the music of the Talking Heads and with Byrne's collaboration with Jonathan Demme on the concert film *Stop Making Sense* (1984), but Byrne's deadpan delivery does not immediately suggest a particular attitude toward his film's subject, the imaginary American everytown of Virgil, Texas. Like film director and theoretician Lev Kuleshov's blank face, in which viewers may read a variety of emotions, *True Stories* coolly presents a set of locations and characters only slightly exaggerated, leaving audiences to interpret Byrne's depiction as condescending or affectionate, biting or bland.

An examination of David Byrne's place in the American musical and artistic milieu helps to account for the synthetic and elusive quality of his work. Ranging through interests as varied as dinosaurs, pure science, visual art, music, and screenplay writing, Byrne draws the label of Renaissance man of the 1980's from popular magazines. His work resides within the cultural context of a postmodern avant-garde, a category which includes composer Philip Glass, playwright and conceptual artist JoAnne Akalaitis, choreographer Twyla Tharp, playwright Robert Wilson, filmmaker Jonathan Demme, performer Laurie Anderson, and writer Beth Henley. While varied in their styles and approaches, all these artists present a bafflingly stark façade upon which audiences may project a rich variety of interpretations.

Although *True Stories* is a musical of sorts, comparisons with more traditional representatives of this genre prove relatively fruitless. Critics have noted its stronger ties with what one might call American grotesque, a genre created in such films as Susan Seidelman's *Desperately Seeking Susan* (1985), Jonathan Demme's *Something Wild* (1986; reviewed in this volume), David Lynch's *Blue Velvet* (1986; reviewed in this volume), Beth Henley's *Crimes of the Heart* (1986; reviewed in this volume), and Joel and Ethan Coen's *Raising Arizona* (1987). Life in the middle America of these trendy films emerges a bit askew; beneath the veneer of ordinariness lurk eccentricity, perversity, and alienation, and while depiction of this kind of disparity may not be new, the quirky, almost lighthearted black humor derived from these subjects is distinctive.

David Byrne's cool chronicle of the human, technological, and architectural oddities of Virgil, Texas, may appear condescending in the light of his avant-garde origins. His is one of several 1986 films from downtown New York, including Jim Jarmusch's *Down by Law* (reviewed in this volume), JoAnne Akalaitis' *Dead End Kids*, and Laurie Anderson's *Home of the Brave*, but *True Stories* received the most popular acclaim. While some critics found in the film sneering contempt for his subject, others found fault with Byrne's apparent refusal to judge, viewing his introductory remark that it is "OK" to like things now as a validation of Reaganesque optimism.

If any evidence supports the notion of *True Stories* as good-natured fun, the music does, in the degree to which it operates integrally with characters and themes. At times, nondiegetic steel-string harmonies accentuate a feeling of being on the road, through the heartland of America. Music glides as effortlessly into the film as does narrator Byrne's red Chrysler Le Baron convertible, and music is the bond linking director and subject. Byrne likes his offbeat characters, whom he describes as "completely normal," even in the midst of their 150th "Celebration of Special-ness." He also puts a gentle spin on the music such characters would like, including gospel, zydeco, country, and Mexican, all of which weave their way through the film, sometimes unobtrusively and at other times compellingly.

True Stories has nothing so strong as a plot or so deep as characterization, and yet it holds together, gracefully avoiding the segmented feel of vignettes or the shallowness of caricature. Facing the camera unsmilingly, cowboy-suited Byrne introduces locales and concepts, but the characters present themselves through self-description, conversation, and incidents, only rarely interacting with one another. The touring narrator enters into casual conversations with Louis Fyne (John Goodman), whose search for a wife is the closest thing to an emotional center of the film.

All the individuals are peculiar yet believable. Indeed, some, including Louis' character, come from tabloid accounts of real people. The film was constructed from newspaper stories and photographs, with the unifying theme of tension between isolation and a yearning for connectedness. This loving satire captures the "specialness" and peculiarity of individuals, but it is the kind of satire that recognizes common humanity. On its way to this conclusion, the film makes a virtue of spareness and understatement.

Ed Lachman's cinematography crystallizes the barren beauty of the Texas landscape, opening with a shot of a perfectly straight white road shooting off into an empty, flat, green horizon. A girl in a white dress meanders down the road, humming the same repetitive Meredith Monk refrain that is playing in the background, music as cheerily flowing and oceanic as the mindless movements of the girl's clasped hands. In a similar way, the narrator undulates through the town of Virgil, beginning by giving a visual and verbal digest of prehistoric oceans, dinosaurs, and Indian, Spanish, and white settlers—a capsule tour that winds up neatly inside Varicorp, a "multi-purpose shaped" box of a building housing a microcomputer-chip industry. The opening Tennysonian preoccupation with time gives way to other themes, including architecture, entertainment, alienation, and love.

The opening scene inside Varicorp begins with a tracking shot down the assembly line, with each character giving his or her views on love. One woman (Alix Elias), obsessed with cuteness, remarks that love is like a puppy. Another woman, a compulsive liar played by Jo Harvey Allen, claims that Burt Reynolds, smitten with her, was ready to give her all of his money. Ramon (Humberto Larriva) explains how he picks up transmissions from people's noses, and, in playful flirtation, he grabs the woman next to him and tells her he feels hot vibrations coming from her. John Goodman's bearlike Louis Fyne recounts his unsuccessful attempts to find a wife, a description interspersed with shots of Louis putting a "Wife Wanted" sign in the yard, Louis attempting yoga positions with a latter-day flower child, Louis having dinner with a woman and her huge brood of squalling children.

Although most of the characters in *True Stories* are not united intimately by plot connections, the relative lack of complex interaction does not suggest an overall sense of dislocation or total alienation. Even such characters as Kay and Earl Culver (Annie McEnroe and Spalding Gray), community leaders who communicate only secondhand through their children, are more whimsical than disturbing. Swoosie Kurtz, as Miss Rollings, the lazy woman who is so wealthy she never leaves her bed, lives alone except for her contact with television and servants. In answer to her isolation and to Louis' climactic plea for love in the song "People Like Us," their marriage unites soul mates and community.

Much of the cohesion, depth, and warmth of the film derives from the musical score, with its varied rhythms, textures, verses, and cultural sources. The audience receives a sense of a society united by music through key scenes, including a lip-synch and dancing talent show done to the Talking Heads song "Wild Wild Life," during which young and old, fat and skinny, black and white, conventional and bizarre, beautiful and homely all take their brief turn in the spotlight as an indulgent audience enjoys the spectacle. In the most outrageous and unexplained sequence, shopping mall patrons murmur appreciatively as fashion show participants parade costumes made of imitation astroturf, brick material, and wedding cakes. Byrne's affinity for video collage appears as the preacher (John Ingle) and a gospel chorus deliver a rousing conspiracy song, "Puzzlin' Evidence," with shots of politicians and products filling a large screen behind them. In a television piece viewed by the lazy woman, Byrne and the Talking Heads appear singing in a montage of products until they finally become products themselves, dipped in chocolate and wrapped in foil. All of these scenes have the edge of satire, but the gleeful energy of Byrne's musical score obviates cynical or sinister connotations.

True Stories excels both visually and musically, seamlessly intertwining the absurd and the romantic, creating beauty by juxtaposing spare images of empty horizons and prefabricated buildings with intricate rhythms, rich melodies, lyrics sometimes melancholy, at other times absurd. If the film suffers structurally, it does so in its flatness, its reflection of the landscape and the two-dimensional characters inhabiting this world. Like the Crayola colors of Lachman's gorgeous photography, *True Stories* has a certain opacity; it resists high emotion or dramatic conflict, hence rolling along with a homogeneity of pace and tone that some viewers may find as featureless as the plains of Texas. This effect does not violate Byrne's minimalist intention or quotidian subject, for he states that he deliberately picked topics so trivial that no one had bothered to form strong opinions about them. For appreciators of David Byrne, *True Stories* subtly manages, where more grandiose efforts have failed, to make art from the true stories of people such as Louis, who answer the telephone, who just want someone to love, whose oddities and foibles sing in harmony with dinosaurs and shopping malls, with the ebb and flow of time.

Rebecca Bell-Metereau

Reviews
The Christian Science Monitor. LXXVIII, October 9, 1986, p. 25.
Films in Review. XXXVIII, January, 1987, p. 44.
Los Angeles Times. October 23, 1986, VI, p. 1.
Macleans. XCIX, October 27, 1986, p. 70.
The New Republic. CXCV, November 10, 1986, p. 26.
The New York Times. October 4, 1986, II, p. 7.
The New Yorker. LXII, October 20, 1986, p. 112.
Newsweek. CVIII, October 27, 1986, p. 103.
Rolling Stone. November 6, 1986, p. 21.
Time. CXXVIII, October 27, 1986, p. 80.
Variety. CCCXXIV, October 8, 1986, p. 21.
The Wall Street Journal. October 9, 1986, p. 30.

TURTLE DIARY

Origin: Great Britain
Released: 1986
Released in U.S.: 1986
Production: Richard Johnson; a CBS Theatrical Films presentation of a United British Artists/Britannic production; released by Samuel Goldwyn Company
Direction: John Irvin
Screenplay: Harold Pinter; based on a novel of the same name by Russell Hoban
Cinematography: Peter Hannan
Editing: Peter Tanner
Art direction: Leo Austin
Music: Geoffrey Burgon
MPAA rating: PG
Running time: 97 minutes

> *Principal characters:*
> Neaera Duncan .... Glenda Jackson
> William Snow .... Ben Kingsley
> Mr. Johnson .... Richard Johnson
> George Fairbairn................ Michael Gambon
> Mrs. Inchcliff .... Rosemary Leach
> Miss Neap........................ Eleanor Bron
> Mr. Sandor .... Jeroen Krabbe
> Harriet.......................... Harriet Walter
> Bookshop customer................. Harold Pinter

Turtle Diary is a wonderful, offbeat film: subtle, unpredictable, and resolutely outside the cinematic mainstream. Based on a novel by Russell Hoban, the film's screenplay is the work of Harold Pinter, and its odd, quiet moments and flashes of dry wit mark it as a script of rare intelligence and insight. With fine, sensitive performances by Glenda Jackson and Ben Kingsley in the leading roles, the film offers a portrait of ordinary lives altered by a single, eccentric act, and its sophisticated approach to its subject is refreshing in an era of underlined points and overstated themes.

At the heart of *Turtle Diary*'s story are loneliness and isolation, qualities which permeate the lives of the film's major and minor characters. The isolation here is not desperate or dramatic (with one exception), but rather the result of lives that have been allowed to fall into tightly circumscribed patterns. Breaking those patterns is the story's central concern, and the changes which result are rarely those which one might expect. This is not a story of heroic deeds or superhuman acts; it is a gentle tale of lives which touch each other with unusual and unlooked-for repercussions. The film opens with images of giant sea turtles swimming in their tank in the London Zoo. Watching them with a shared sense of melancholy are William Snow (Ben Kingsley) and Neaera Duncan (Glenda Jackson), both of whom feel that the turtles would be happier in the sea. William and Neaera have not yet met, although their interest in the turtles brings them increasingly into each other's orbit. William is divorced and works in a bookstore, while Neaera writes and illustrates children's books. As their paths cross repeatedly, each notices the other and senses an answering concern for the fate of the turtles, and when Neaera learns that William has spoken to the zookeeper, George Fairbairn (Michael Gambon), about the possibility of freeing the animals, she contacts him and asks to be included in the plan. William finds a sympathetic ally in Fairbairn as well, who promises to assist him in the theft the next time the tanks are cleaned.

Terrified but exhilarated at the prospect of taking action to return the turtles to the sea, William begins his preparations, building crates and renting a van to haul the huge animals. On the day of the tank cleaning, he leaves the crates with the keeper, returning later with Neaera to collect their unusual cargo. They drive to the coast, stopping periodically to douse the turtles with water, and finally arrive at their destination, where they carry the turtles down to the sea and set them free. The following morning they return to London, where William continues his affair with Harriet (Harriet Walter) and Neaera embarks on a romance with the zookeeper. Liberated by the experience, William at last stands up to one of his fellow rooming-house boarders, the belligerent, slovenly Mr. Sandor (Jeroen Krabbe), and both men are injured slightly in the ensuing fight. A third boarder, the lonely, withdrawn Miss Neap (Eleanor Bron), shocks the others by committing suicide, an incident which makes painfully clear the isolation in which so many of the characters are living. Not long after his adventure, William drops by the zoo with a bottle of champagne and finds Neaera with George Fairbairn. The three drink a toast and promise to do it all again in another twenty years, and William and Neaera part company to resume their separate lives.

The symbolic act which is at the center of John Irvin's film has a quirky authenticity. The image of the turtles swimming for thirty years in aimless circles powerfully conveys the sense of entrapment which William and Neaera feel before their decision to free the helpless creatures. Liberated by that decision, William begins his affair with Harriet, and his uncharacteristic confrontation with Mr. Sandor comes soon after his sense of triumph at putting the turtles back into the ocean. For Neaera, who has reached a standstill in her work, the experience is also critical, leading her to her affair with the amiable zookeeper—a surprising turn of events and one of the film's most engaging developments. In freeing the turtles, Neaera and William free themselves, breaking the pattern of lives that have become as constricting as the glass tanks in which the animals swim.

In the tragic Miss Neap, one sees a life that never manages to break free of its isolation, ending in despair with a suicide that shocks her fellow boarders because they have been so unaware of her deep unhappiness. Reading her suicide note, they realize that they have never known her first name, although they have lived under the same roof and shared the same kitchen and bath; as one of them comments, "We never asked." Miss Neap passes through the film as a sad, awkward reminder of the lengths to which people are driven by loneliness; Bron, who is best known for her work in comedies, gives a touching performance in the role.

Indeed, *Turtle Diary* is rich in strong performances. Jackson's Neaera is wistful and unhappy as the film opens, conveying the impression that she is puzzled by her own vague sense of depression. Neaera is not a woman given to emotional extremes, and Jackson is as subdued in her portrayal of the shift her character's mood later undergoes as she is in her earlier scenes. This is quiet, understated work and a pleasure to watch. Kingsley, too, is superb, capturing William's unassuming manner and nervous excitement—or perhaps disbelief—at the venture he is undertaking. William's pride and self-respect are reawakened by his actions and Kingsley's bright eyes and small smile convey the great importance the undertaking has for him. Together, Jackson and Kingsley bring to life the unlikely friendship that springs up between these two lonely individuals.

One of the most intriguing aspects of *Turtle Diary* is the way in which it manages to avoid predictable plot developments. Early in the story, it seems certain that this will be a tale of two people who fall in love as they help the turtles, and the discreet emotional distance the pair maintains even after their long drive to the seaside is quite surprising. The same is true for Neaera's blossoming relationship with George the zookeeper, a twist that is at once unexpected and delightfully appropriate. The direction these characters' lives take is as unpredictable as real life often is, and the film steadfastly avoids the clichés that would have turned the freeing of the turtles into simply the prelude to a love story. Even the plotting of the story seems at odds with traditional drama, in which the sight of the turtles finally swimming free in the ocean would normally serve as the film's climax. Here, however, the viewer follows the characters back into their everyday lives, observing the changes their actions bring about. It is a dramatic choice that is both strikingly original and far more compelling than traditional plotting would be.

To anyone familiar with Pinter's plays (*The Birthday Party, Old Times, Betrayal*), the clipped, enigmatic dialogue and glancing wit of *Turtle Diary* is unmistakable. Pinter excels at subtle chartings of emotional terrain; the intelligence, complexity, and understated humor of the film are Pinter trademarks as well. (His other film scripts include *The Servant*, 1963, *The Go-Between*, 1970, and the screen adaptation of *Betrayal*, 1983.) Pinter himself makes a cameo appearance in an amusing scene in the bookshop.

Unlike most of Pinter's work, however, *Turtle Diary* is refreshingly optimistic. The isolation that characterizes so many lives is indeed felt throughout the film, but the rewards of shattering the patterns that create that isolation are at the heart of this remarkable film's illuminating message.

Janet E. Lorenz

Reviews
America. CLIV, May 10, 1986, p. 385.
Chatelaine. LIX, May, 1986, p. 10.
Films in Review. XXXVII, March, 1986, p. 176.
Los Angeles Times. February 14, 1986, VI, p. 1.
Macleans. XCIX, April 7, 1986, p. 62.
The New Republic. CXCIV, March 10, 1986, p. 26.
The New York Times. March 7, 1986, p. C8.
The New Yorker. LXII, March 24, 1986, p. 115.
The Washington Post. February 28, 1986, p. D2.
Whole Earth Review. Spring, 1986, p. 32.

TWIST AND SHOUT

Origin: Denmark
Released: 1985
Released in U.S.: 1986
Production: Per Holst Film Produktion and Palle Fogtdal in collaboration with the Danish Film Institute, the Children's Film Council, and the Coproductions Fund of Danmarks Radio
Direction: Bille August
Screenplay: Bille August and Bjarne Reuter
Cinematography: Jan Weincke
Editing: Janus Billeskov
Art direction: Soren Krag Sorensen
Music: Bo Holten
MPAA rating: no listing
Running time: 100 minutes

Principal characters:
Bjorn .... Adam Tonsberg
Erik .... Lars Simonsen
Anna.......................... Camilla Soeberg
Kirsten .... Ulrikke Juul Bondo
Henning .... Thomas Nielson
Bjorn's mother .... Lone Lindoff
Bjorn's father .... Arne Hansen
Erik's mother .... Aase Hansen
Erik's father .... Bent Mejding

Twist and Shout is a wonderful little film about coming of age in Denmark during the mid-1960's. Unlike many coming-of-age films, this one manages not only to maintain a sense of balance but also to view the process with something approaching a consistent point of view, thereby providing a film with a notably hard-edged finish as well as an understanding glimpse of adolescence.

The film begins at the Blue Moon dance hall where Bjorn (Adam Tonsberg) is dancing with Kirsten (Ulrikke Juul Bondo) to the Beatles' music played by a local rock group. Bjorn has eyes for Anna (Camilla Soeberg), whom he sees watching the dancing from the sidelines. Bjorn's friend Erik (Lars Simonsen), who likes Kirsten, must leave the dance early in order to take care of his invalid mother (Aase Hansen) while his father (Bent Mejding) attends his weekly Friday night meeting. Erik's home life explains his rather standoffish behavior at the dance as he apparently has had to assume responsibilities well beyond his years. In sharp contrast is Bjorn's family, who are seen sometime later at a lunch where his mother announces, much to the consternation of her husband, that they are going to move to a larger flat. Theirs is a large, extended family who enjoy spending time outdoors and gently kidding Bjorn's father about his new promotion and imminent move.

The second scene at the Blue Moon features Bjorn's small rock group, performing a spirited if slightly off-key rendition of "Twist and Shout," much to the delight of Anna, who is in the audience. Against the growing attraction between Anna and Bjorn is set Erik's continual mooning after Kirsten, whom he worships from afar. In a brief but telling scene during which Erik tries to entertain Kirsten at home without introducing her to his ailing mother, it becomes evident that Erik's desires will remain unfulfilled. The encounter between Kirsten and Erik's mother obviously upsets and embarrasses the girl and reveals her lack of compassion and understanding.

The scenes with Bjorn's family again provide a contrast: Moving day is one of energy and joy; a clothes-buying shopping expedition reflects the warmth and closeness between Bjorn and his mother. The tension between Bjorn and Kirsten is revealed at her birthday party where Kirsten is angered at the attention Bjorn is paying to Anna and gives her first and only real outburst of passion. In contrast to the controlled and warm Anna, Kirsten is alternately shrill and cool. Although Bjorn apparently continues to see Kirsten, he has become increasingly involved with Anna, and after she returns from a short trip they make love, an event which leads to Anna's pregnancy and eventually finishes the relationship between Bjorn and Kirsten.

The pregnant Anna goes to an abortionist, and Bjorn, who accompanies her home, witnesses the expulsion of the fetus, a scene horrifying in its realism. The experience drives a permanent wedge between the two lovers, and Anna stops taking Bjorn's phone calls. In a chilling scene between Anna and her mother concerning the abortion, Anna's mother shows a callous lack of interest in her daughter's well-being. Bjorn resumes his relationship with Kirsten, and goes off to the country with Kirsten, her sister, and her brother-in-law. The trip produces the engagement which it was apparently designed to encourage, and Kirsten's family gives a party to announce their betrothal.

The party itself reveals the difference in class between the families of the bride-to-be and her groom. Both Bjorn's father and mother are clearly uncomfortable at the affair. Erik suddenly shows up needing his friend's help, and Bjorn confesses that he cannot marry Kirsten because he does not love her. He apologizes to the families and leaves with Erik. In the meantime, Erik has an unpleasant confrontation with his father. Angry with his son for encouraging his mother, the father becomes enraged when he discovers that Erik has continued to borrow books from the library for his mother. It becomes quite clear from these outbursts that Erik's father is not really interested in having his wife well again. Erik's shock of recognition comes when he discovers that his father's Friday night "meetings" are with a prostitute, and the confrontation between father and son reveals the boy's maturity and understanding. This confrontation provides Erik with the courage to take his mother to her family in the country, the scene which ends the film and brings it full circle.

There are some nice touches in *Twist and Shout* which help to elevate it above the clichéd coming-of-age film. The music is downplayed, providing only a background to the nightclub scenes, thereby avoiding the throbbing and intrusive sound track which so often mars films about adolescence. Sex, although a constant preoccupation of the principal characters, is treated with a refreshing maturity. It is interesting that the scenes of recognition for the two boys come through the abortion and the visit to the prostitute. Sexuality for both young men loses something of its fascination and becomes associated with the idea of betrayal.

Twist and Shout is also a film about two young men who rebel against the mores and attitudes of their parents' generation. Most films about youth contain such fantasies, and such films as *Zéro de conduite* (1933), *If . . .* (1968), and *Zabriski Point* (1969) come to mind, but in *Twist and Shout* the rebellion seems more thoughtful and positive, less violent and self-destructive. Perhaps the point is that in modern society, where many traditional rigidities have been abandoned, wrenching breaks from the past are often unnecessary. In the end, both Erik and Bjorn seem more sensitive, more genuinely mature, so that the film ends on a positive note and does not simply glorify an endless adolescence of sniggering sex and mindless immaturity.

Twist and Shout received limited distribution in the United States, which is unfortunate, since the film is both sensitively made and insightful and could provide an example to American filmmakers of how to treat the subject of adolescence with something other than exploitative crassness. The performances of the young actors are uniformly good, especially Adam Tonsberg as Bjorn and Camilla Soeberg, in her first film role, as Anna. Even the parents, while primarily seen from the youthful viewpoint of the main characters, exhibit a refreshing depth, especially in their concern for and bewilderment over their children. *Twist and Shout* is a wonderful small film which deserves a much wider audience and broader discussion.

Charles L. P. Silet

Reviews
Chicago Tribune. September 19, 1986, VII, p. 42.
Los Angeles Times. August 22, 1986, VI, p. 12.
The New York Times. September 26, 1986, p. C1.
People Weekly. XXVI, November 10, 1986, p. 10.

UFORIA

Production: Gordon Wolf; released by Universal
Direction: John Binder
Screenplay: John Binder
Cinematography: David Myers
Editing: Dennis M. Hill
Art direction: William Malley; set decoration, Carl Biddiscombe
Music: Richard Baskin
MPAA rating: PG
Running time: 100 minutes

Principal characters:
Arlene	Cindy Williams
Sheldon	Fred Ward
Brother Bud	Harry Dean Stanton
Naomi	Beverly Hope Atkinson
George Martin	Harry Carey, Jr.
Celia Martin	Peggy McKay
Delores	Diane Diefendorf
Emile	Robert Gray
Toby	Darrell Larson
Brother Roy	Alan Beckwith

"Why is it every woman I meet is too young, too old, drunk, crazy, or out of my reach?" wonders Sheldon (Fred Ward), a handsome drifter who likes to think that he bears a strong resemblance to country singer Waylon Jennings. He does, but when the audience first sees Sheldon, he is down on his luck, as usual. With one hand on the steering wheel, a beer in the other, and a foot on the dashboard, he is cruising through the Mojave Desert as Jennings wails "I've Always Been Crazy" on the car radio.

He stops at a gas station to refuel and distracts the attendant long enough to steal the quarters from the condom dispenser in the men's room. Sheldon's next stop is a supermarket in a dusty California desert town. He shoplifts his way toward the cash register, where Arlene (Cindy Williams) is waiting for him with a knowing look. Pretty and sweet-tempered, and clearly finding him attractive, she lets Sheldon take a six-pack of beer without paying for it.

Sheldon then visits an old friend, Brother Bud (Harry Dean Stanton), a traveling evangelist and faith healer whose trailer is plastered with slogans— "Blessed are those who give." That night, Sheldon hobbles up to the stage at Brother Bud's crusade and emotionally tells the crowd that he lost his wife and child in an accident which permanently injured his leg. After Bud cures him and Sheldon takes a seat, he looks around and notices Arlene, who gives him another knowing look.

The next day, Sheldon goes to the supermarket to ask Arlene for a date. He takes her to a bar, though she is a born-again Christian and has sworn not to drink. Soon he is teaching her how to drink tequila, and she is telling him about her own peculiar brand of religion. Arlene believes that Jesus came to Earth in a flying saucer and that Adam and Eve were the astronauts. Sheldon simply laughs, as he does again that night after they make love, and Arlene moans that she loves Jesus and feels guilty for breaking all of her promises of good behavior.

Arlene is clearly lonely, while Sheldon honestly admits that sleeping with her is simply better than sleeping in his car. When Arlene sees a tourist couple, George and Celia Martin (Harry Carey, Jr., and Peggy McKay), on television recounting their sighting of a UFO (unidentified flying object) in the desert, she becomes convinced that a UFO will soon land in the vicinity. Furthermore, Arlene believes that the spaceship will be a modern-day Noah's Ark and that she has been chosen to be Noah.

At first Sheldon dismisses Arlene as crazy and repeatedly threatens to leave her. Arlene's sweetness and naïveté affect him, however, and he gets a job hauling stolen cars across the state border so that Bud can auction them off in the name of Jesus. Soon Arlene's obsession becomes evangelistic. She converts Toby (Darrell Larson), a hippie who lives with his wife and baby, Krishna Jesus, in a pyramid-shaped house. The tourist couple and others soon follow, and Arlene, determined to spread her message, goes to a convention which is televised on a program called *Cults and Crazies*. When Bud sees her on television, he realizes that Arlene's message offers an opportunity for a new kind of crusade. "You get enough people believing they're going up in a spaceship, they'll leave a lot behind," Bud points out to Sheldon, who eagerly supports using Arlene to make some quick money. Sheldon dons a singing-cowboy outfit like that of his idol Waylon Jennings and makes use of his considerable charm, while Arlene serves as a prophet in a flowing white robe. When Bud makes the pitch for donations, however, Arlene becomes enraged. Bud and Arlene have a falling out, and in a fit of anger, Arlene calls the police to report Bud's stolen car activities.

By this point, Sheldon has begun to believe in Arlene, or, rather, through her he has developed a need to believe in something, and Arlene's unshakable faith has converted him to her cause. He delivers a truckload of stolen cars at the claimed UFO landing site just as a squadron of police cars arrives to arrest Bud. In the midst of the chaos, Arlene and Sheldon slip away into the desert. A police helicopter spots them, but as the officers move in, a flying saucer appears on the horizon. It glides across the sky and hovers above Arlene and Sheldon, who are transported in a beam of light into the spaceship.

UFOria was not a box-office success when it was released. Though it was actually filmed in 1980, Universal shelved the film until 1985, when it opened briefly in Los Angeles. It was not given a general release until 1986, but the low-budget film had a skimpy advertising campaign and correspondingly short runs in most cities.

The lack of star names in the cast did not help to attract audiences, though Cindy Williams was recognizable from her years on television's *Laverne and Shirley*. Audiences seemed to enjoy the film, and it was favorably reviewed by most critics. It also made a few of the more eclectic ten-best lists in the country.

Though writer and director John Binder concocted an engaging, idiosyncratic story line, the film was often compared with both *Repo Man* (1984) and *Stranger than Paradise* (1984), two UFO-related films that had recently preceded it, and with *Close Encounters of the Third Kind* (1977), which had a similar ending. The tone of *UFOria*, however, is completely different from that of any of these films. While *Repo Man* was a black comedy with a cynical edge, and *Stranger than Paradise* was an extremely stylized New Wave urban nightmare with comic overtones, *UFOria* is a straightforward, old-fashioned romance with an ultracontemporary twist and a slyly satirical bent.

Binder, a former partner in the documentary film company that made *Woodstock* (1970) and *Marjoe* (1972), made his directing debut with *UFOria*. He was previously a screenwriter who cowrote *Honeysuckle Rose* (1980) and wrote the original draft for *North Dallas Forty* (1979). Binder keeps the emphasis of his film on the characters, the film's biggest strength. Even the supporting characters are finely detailed and well drawn, and Binder displays an affection for the wide-eyed believers and smooth cynics who make them their prey. These are archetypal figures from the American landscape, at once familiar and nostalgic. What these characters have in common is a dream of another, better reality, a dream confined only by their lack of assets and imagination.

In Binder's view, the smaller the life, the bigger the dream, and he creates an Arlene lost in her visions of a heaven in outer space and the cynical Bud, for whom money will change everything. Sheldon is by far the most interesting character, however, caught, as he is, between his materialistic ambitions and the knowledge that happiness comes from other, less tangible sources.

Binder and his associates paid careful attention to the telling details that bring both characters and story to life. For example, the supermarket where Arlene works has theme days, and the audience sees her variously wearing a sombrero or a Hawaiian lei as she adds up the cost of the groceries. Much of the film's humor comes from these clever visual asides.

Outstanding performances by Williams, Ward, and Stanton make the audience respond to their rather pathetic characters with warmth and empathy. They also lend a dignity to the film that the shoddy production values deny. The cinematography by David Myers is never more than adequate, and the dim lighting detracts from many of the scenes. Yet the natural scenery of the locations is an asset that Myers exploited to good advantage, and production designer William Malley did brilliant work with a limited budget. An unusually fine score of country-western classics, chosen by Richard Baskin, keeps the film lively.

UFOria has all the ingredients for a simple, charming, and extremely warmhearted satire. What it lacks is a defined style, and enough substance to make it more than a sketch of some appealing misfits. Indeed, Binder's greatest failing is in neglecting to develop his intriguing themes. Connecting religion with the popular fascination with UFO's is an audacious concept with a potential Binder barely taps. He is content to let his themes serve solely as plot points, putting far more energy into the delightful dialogue and thoroughly developed characters that make this film enjoyable despite its flaws.

Marylynn Uricchio

Reviews
Christian Century. CIII, May 21, 1986, p. 533.
Los Angeles Times. July 2, 1985, VI, p. 5.
The New York Times. CXXXV, January 3, 1986, p. C9.
Seventeen. XLV, January, 1986, p. 57.
Variety. CCCXV, July 18, 1984, p. 17.
Washingtonian. XXI, April, 1986, p. 73.

WHERE THE RIVER RUNS BLACK

Production: Joe Roth and Harry Ulfland; released by Metro-Goldwyn-Mayer
Direction: Christopher Cain
Screenplay: Peter Silverman and Neal Jimenez; based on the book *Lázaro*, by David Kendall
Cinematography: Juan Ruiz-Anchia
Editing: Richard Chew
Production design: Marcos Flaksman
Art direction: Paulo Flaksman; set decoration, Alexandre Meyer
Special effects: Edu Paungarten
Makeup: Antonio Pacheco
Costume design: Tetê Amarante
Sound: Romeu Quinto
Music: James Horner
MPAA rating: PG
Running time: 96 minutes

> *Principal characters:*
> Father O'Reilly . . . . Charles Durning
> Lázaro . . . . Alessandro Rabelo
> Segundo . . . . Ajay Naidu
> Eagle Woman . . . . Divana Brandão
> Father Mahoney . . . . Peter Horton
> Orlando Santos . . . . Castulo Guerra
> Mother Marta . . . . Conchata Ferrell

The cinematic terrain of *Where the River Runs Black* could be described as *The Emerald Forest* (1985) meets *The Wild Child* (1970), for it is not only a stunning epic shot in Brazil but is also a poignant tale about an abandoned boy whom society attempts to civilize. Although the two previous features by director Christopher Cain—*The Stone Boy* (1984) and *That Was Then . . . This Is Now* (1985)—displayed his sensitivity to actors as well as his visual craftsmanship, *Where the River Runs Black* transcends them by offering a richness of theme or vision equal to its striking production values. In David Kendall's novel *Lázaro* (1986)—from which Neal Jimenez and Peter Silverman wrote the script—Cain found a story that blends primeval myth with a critique of political manipulation.

The Metro-Goldwyn-Mayer release begins with the focus on Father O'Reilly (Charles Durning), whose confession to another priest engenders a flashback to events of ten years before, in which the missionary travels to the jungle to visit Father Mahoney (Peter Horton), a young, idealistic, long-haired priest who wants to build a school and hospital complex. When O'Reilly does not give him his approval, Mahoney paddles down the river, where he sees a beautiful, naked Indian woman (Divana Brandão) bathing among dolphins. In a sequence particularly remarkable because it has (and needs) no dialogue, they are drawn to each other in an erotic embrace; he paddles away and is killed by a water serpent. In the next scene, a baby wears the cross Mahoney gave the woman.

The boy, Lázaro (Alessandro Rabelo), grows up with the dolphins in a harmonious existence. Some greedy white men seeking gold, however, come from the city, murder his mother, and assume that they have killed the child. Lázaro survives and is later abducted by other men from the city, but O'Reilly finds him and places him in an orphanage. Here, Lázaro is socialized: He learns English and makes friends with the young troublemaker Segundo (Ajay Naidu). The man who killed his mother, Orlando Santos (Castulo Guerra), is now a leading politician running for governor; when he visits the orphanage, Lázaro recognizes him and vows revenge. He and Segundo escape, try to kill Santos, and end up in an enormous gold-mining area owned by the corrupt politician. After being sighted by Santos, they escape back to where the river runs black.

In Lázaro's former home, Santos tries to drown both boys, but Father O'Reilly's boat approaches. He sees not only the politician's attempted murder of the boys but also a dolphin attacking Santos. Consequently, when Santos asks for help, the missionary does nothing, and the villain dies. This, the audience now realizes, is the root of Father O'Reilly's guilt. At the end, he is absolved, and Lázaro remains with the dolphins.

Like John Boorman's *The Emerald Forest* and Roland Joffé's *The Mission* (1986; reviewed in this volume), *Where the River Runs Black* seems to validate Indian experience above and beyond Christianity, as Lázaro is allows to remain joyfully in his habitat. More than François Truffaut's *The Wild Child*—which questioned but appeared ultimately to endorse the removal of the child from the forest for the sake of his integration into human society—*Where the River Runs Black* criticizes white, Anglo-Saxon assumptions. Indeed, it brings to life an Indian legend that is still vital in the rain forests of the Amazon—of a wayward priest who traveled to a place where the river runs black and was seduced by a dolphin who became a beautiful woman. Their son was once taken to another world but could not learn its ways; it is said that he still lives at the water's edge, protected by the mysterious white dolphins of the Rio Negro.

The power of *Where the River Runs Black* can be attributed not only to the story but also to at least three elements that Cain "orchestrated": the casting and direction of the actors, the lush cinematography by Juan Ruiz-Anchia in a breathtaking if treacherous area, and the haunting sound track by James Horner. The director rightfully insisted on casting a native Brazilian in the lead, because he realized that an American actor in the role would look exactly that—an American actor playing a Brazilian boy. The film's authenticity is heightened by the Brazilian actors, as well as by the specificity of the steamy jungle and bustling city.

With its emphasis on percussion and flutes, the music evokes Latin American rhythms and melodies. It is a testament not only to the talent of the composer (whose other credits include *Aliens*, 1986, reviewed in this volume; *Cocoon*, 1985; *The Dresser*, 1983; and *48 HRS.*, 1982) but also to the fact that Cain's university degree was in music. Part of the score's power results from a historical breakthrough: *Where the River Runs Black* is the first film to be recorded entirely in digital sound. Digital recording and mixing afford greater depth and scope which—especially in the case of this film—complement the masterful *mise-en-scène*.

The clarity of the images and sounds gives a paradoxical sharpness to the scenes that pertain to myth or fantasy. As in Jean Cocteau's *Beauty and the Beast* (1946), the visual crispness imparts a sense of reality to events that would seem unlikely in a literary or theatrical presentation.

The only thing that could be faulted about *Where the River Runs Black* is the way it was released in New York during the late summer of 1986. With a minimal publicity campaign—using an image so dark that most people did not know what the story was about—the studio did not handle the picture with the care it deserved. Capitalizing neither on favorable reviews nor on the magical aspects of the on-location shooting in Brazil, MGM gave the film a puny run in one Upper West Side theater. It is likely that a specialized distributor would have allowed the film's critical success and word-of-mouth to build, not unlike the way Cinecom International handled *A Room with a View* (1986; reviewed in this volume) at approximately the same time.

By the end of 1986, *Where the River Runs Black* was almost completely forgotten, as well as eclipsed by the larger-scale fresco of *The Mission*. Nevertheless, it remains a haunting achievement—as poetic as it is political and as universal in its humanist vision as it is specific to its lush locale.

Annette Insdorf

Reviews
Los Angeles Times. September 19, 1986, VI, p. 8.
The New York Times. September 19, 1986, p. C6.
People Weekly. XXVI, October 6, 1986, p. 16.
Variety. CCCXXIV, September 10, 1986, p. 18.
The Wall Street Journal. September 25, 1986, p. 28.

WISE GUYS

Production: Aaron Russo; released by Metro-Goldwyn-Mayer/United Artists
Direction: Brian De Palma
Screenplay: George Gallo
Cinematography: Fred Schuler
Editing: Jerry Greenberg
Production design: Edward Pisoni
Art direction: Paul Bryan Eads; set decoration, Leslie Bloom
Costume design: Richard Bruno
Sound: Les Lazarowitz
Music: Ira Newborn
MPAA rating: R
Running time: 92 minutes

> *Principal characters:*
> Harry Valentini .... Danny DeVito
> Moe Dickstein .... Joe Piscopo
> Bobby Dilea .... Harvey Keitel
> Marco .... Ray Sharkey
> Anthony Castelo .... Dan Hedaya
> Frank "the Fixer" Acavano ..... Captain Lou Albano
> Lil Dickstein .... Julie Bovasso
> Wanda Valentini .... Patti LuPone
> Aunt Sadie .... Antonia Rey
> Grandma Valentini .... Mimi Cecchini
> Harry Jr. .... Matthew Kaye

Brian De Palma is one of the more controversial film directors of the 1970's and 1980's. During this period he has produced a string of films which have aroused considerable indignation, even scorn, albeit there have been critics who have defended him. Films such as *Obsession* (1976), *Carrie* (1976), *Dressed to Kill* (1980), and *Body Double* (1984) reveal De Palma's fascination with illicit sex and violence and his insistence on a surrealistic approach to filmmaking. An admirer of Alfred Hitchcock, De Palma emphasizes the viewer's role as voyeur. Some critics have tended to favor this approach because of their delight with his technique; others have deplored his inattention to such matters as plot structure and his tendency to emphasize set pieces within the film, scenes in which visual stylization becomes the principal concern. There have been critics who see in De Palma's films a Brechtean approach, an attempt to keep viewers at a distance while at the same time they watch what is going on through the peephole, as it were. De

Palma's view of the world has been variously described as absurdist, cruel, and bleak; in his films there is neither justice nor redemption. For many, De Palma is a filmmaker for whom technology and form outweigh all other considerations.

Wise Guys is a departure from De Palma's recent obsessions, his first comedy since *Hi, Mom!* (1969). Here one finds pure farce, even though there is a feeble attempt to say something significant beneath the constant barrage of gags and abusive language.

Under the opening credits Harry Valentini (Danny DeVito) and his next-door neighbor, Moe Dickstein (Joe Piscopo), appear as they prepare to meet the challenges of the new day. The two longtime friends are hoods, but with a difference. In the employ of Tony Costelo (Dan Hedaya), a "Guinea gangster" operating in Newark, New Jersey, their job is to suffer insults from the other gang members, to pick up Tony's groceries and his laundry, and, for excitement, to test a new bulletproof jacket and start his limousine in the morning just in case it has been booby-trapped.

Harry is the innovator, the man with the ideas; his projects inevitably turn sour. Yet Moe argues that they should stick with the business; he remains a hood despite his mother's pleas because organized crime is the fourth largest growth industry in the state. Nevertheless, Harry is beginning to desire respectability and a "normal" life.

The plot thickens when Frank "the Fixer" (Captain Lou Albano) interrupts Moe's birthday party and whisks them away to the racetrack, where they have been instructed to place a ten-thousand-dollar bet for Tony on the second horse in the second race. Harry, his mind always churning, sees a golden opportunity to make a killing. An inveterate gambler, he decides to place the entire amount on another horse—a sure winner—and pocket the prize money. True to form, Moe resists, and Harry asks him why he always wants to hold them back. This is their big opportunity, he insists, to break away from the mob and fulfill their lifelong dream of opening an Italian-Jewish restaurant/delicatessen.

Their horse loses, Tony's horse wins, the pair fail to escape and are tortured. Finally, at Tony's command, each is persuaded privately to murder the other. Why, Tony wonders, are these wise guys loyal to each other and not to me? This will be the supreme test, and, as the pair miserably returns to their sodden row houses in Newark, much of the humor comes from the fact that neither knows what the other has been ordered to do. Despite Tony's orders, neither can steel himself to kill. They confess to their mistreatment of each other and agree to forgive. Meanwhile, their pal, Marco, the bartender (Ray Sharkey), decides to reveal Tony's scheme. He sneaks them into Saint Lucy's Cathedral where they can talk in peace. Unfortunately, the trio is spotted entering the church, and Marco is shot before the altar by the gang, firing, with silencers, from the balcony.

The ever-resourceful Harry has been working on a new idea: They will hurry to Atlantic City, to the home of his Uncle Mike, the retired hood who originally established them in business. Harry and Moe steal the Fixer's gleaming white Cadillac and lark their way to Atlantic City. The trip provides an opportunity to repaint the car and then trash it along the way. They arrive in Atlantic City only to discover that Uncle Mike's wife is less than enthusiastic about their appearance and, worse, that Uncle Mike now resides in an urn on the bedroom mantlepiece. All seems to be lost, when Grandma (Mimi Cecchini) comes to the rescue with the $250,000 necessary to make restitution. Matters take an even better turn when Harry and Moe discover that the casino-hotel at which they are staying is owned by Bobby Dilea (Harvey Keitel), another former Newark citizen who has made it big in the hotel business. DiLea warns them that they are in deep trouble with the Fixer, and he is suspicious when they tell him that Tony will accept the payment of the $250,000.

The Fixer arrives, discovers his trashed Cadillac sitting in front of the hotel, and subsequently discovers that Harry and Moe have run up an astronomical bill on his credit card. At this point, Moe reveals that he is the hit man hired to kill Harry, and Harry confesses to the same. Harry talks Moe out of killing him by showing him the $250,000. Arrangements have been made to spirit them away in a hired limousine, but Harry simply cannot resist gambling one more time before they leave. For him, their failure to take advantage of the situation will prevent them from fulfilling their destiny. The climax is quickly reached when Harry attempts to wrestle Moe's gun away from him at the gaming table and is accidentally killed.

The film ends on a happy note, however, when it becomes evident that all is not what it seems. Retribution is gained, the Grand Design is attained, and the Italian-Jewish restaurant/delicatessan opens in a blaze of glory.

There are moments to savor in *Wise Guys*, but they are characteristically set pieces (comic rather than horrific) which somehow do not add up to a consistently satisfying film, partly because they have been borrowed from other films. They include the early put-down sequence when Harry and Moe come to work, particularly when Harry, in a suspense-filled scene, has to open the boss's automobile door and start the engine. Despite a touch of the De Palma macabre, a hilarious scene is that in which Marco is gunned down, for, just before the fatal shots, he has told Harry and Moe to do exactly as he does. The sight gag of a triple "death scene" as Marco slumps to the floor comes off well. Harry's discovery of Uncle Mike's status and what that means to the two star-crossed hoods is genuinely humorous. In the end, however, the viewer is left with the impression that he has been manipulated from one high spot to another with very little to sustain him in between. The plot is thin and all too reminiscent of *The Sting* (1976), a considerably more satisfying film.

The two stars of *Wise Guys* have made a name for themselves in fast-paced, raucous comedy, both in television and in motion pictures. Piscopo achieved his fame on *Saturday Night Live*, where he specialized in caricatures. Here, however, he plays the straight man to DeVito's wild antics. DeVito, who made his name in the television series *Taxi*, has had considerably more success in film than has Piscopo. After early success in such films as *Romancing the Stone* (1983) and *Jewel of the Nile* (1985), DeVito has become one of the hottest current comedians, starring in *Ruthless People* (1986; reviewed in this volume) and *Tin Men* (1987). The sight of DeVito, barely five feet tall, confronting the much taller world of the criminal is amusing in itself. DeVito's natural genre is abusive comedy, often played at the level of a continuous scream; in *Wise Guys* such shenanigans simply become too much for the thin plot.

While there may be relief from the De Palma trademarks of horror, violent sensuality, surrealism, and sensationalism in *Wise Guys* (some reviewers expressed a desire to have those staples back), the insistence on technique over content remains, and that is patently not enough here to ensure a great film.

Norman Carson

Reviews
Los Angeles Times. April 18, 1986, VI, p. 6.
The New Republic. CXCIV, May 19, 1986, p. 26.
New York. XIX, May 5, 1986, p. 79.
The New York Times. April 18, 1986, p. C8.
The New Yorker. LXII, May 19, 1986, p. 101.
Newsweek. CVII, May 19, 1986, p. 73.
People Weekly. XXV, May 5, 1986, p. 10.
Playboy. XXXIII, July, 1986, p. 20.
Texas Monthly. XIV, June, 1986, p. 152.
Variety. CCCXXII, April 23, 1986, p. 17.
Vogue. CLXXVI, March, 1986, p. 74.
The Washington Post. May 10, 1986, p. C4.

A YEAR OF THE QUIET SUN
(ROK SPOKOJNEGO SLONCA)

Origin: Poland, West Germany, and the United States
Released: 1984
Released in U.S.: 1985; 1986 (general release)
Production: Michal Szczerbic and Michael Boehme for Film Polski, Tele-culture, Inc., and Regina Ziegler Filmproduktion; released by Sandstar Releasing Company
Direction: Krzysztof Zanussi
Screenplay: Krzysztof Zanussi
Cinematography: Slawomir Idziak
Editing: Marek Denys
Art direction: Janusz Sosnowski
Sound: Wieslawa Dembinska
Music: Wojciech Kilar
MPAA rating: no listing
Running time: 106 minutes

Principal characters:
Norman	Scott Wilson
Emilia	Maja Komorowska
Emilia's mother	Hanna Skarzanka
Stella	Ewa Dalkowska
Hermann	Vadim Glowna
David	Daniel Webb
Szary	Zbigniew Zapasiewicz
Adzio	Jerzy Stuhr

Krzysztof Zanussi's *A Year of the Quiet Sun* may at first seem deceptively easy to interpret. The film, which is a Polish-West German-American co-production, bears all the markings of a conventional wartime romance, but it soon reveals itself to be a complex and highly compassionate examination of flawed human behavior. In keeping with Zanussi's recurring concerns, it is also a source of understated but insightful political commentary. *A Year of the Quiet Sun* centers on the uneasy romantic liaison between Norman (Scott Wilson), a traumatized American former POW serving in the occupation forces in postwar Poland, and Emilia (Maja Komorowska), a Polish war widow with many unhappy memories of her own. Norman and Emilia are both faced with the task of reconstructing their lives in the aftermath of the war and finding worthwhile reasons to persist in that struggle.

The story unfolds in a Polish town which had once been considered part of German territory. The landscape is ravaged, a pointed metaphor for the emotional state of its inhabitants. Even after the war is over, the towns-people are subject to random thievery and petty political manipulations at the hands of marauding Germans and various members of the occupying forces. Emilia, who lives with her invalid mother (Hanna Skarzanka) in the shell of a bombed-out building, subsists by turning her apartment into a makeshift bakery. She and her neighbors wander through the town like ghosts, stunned into a kind of emotional nonbeing, overwhelmed by the not-too-distant horrors of war.

Norman and Emilia drift toward each other as similarly wounded individuals in the midst of this war-torn environment. Their relationship develops in a fitful but inexorable fashion despite the barriers of language and their shared fear of human contact.

A Year of the Quiet Sun marks a bit of a departure for Zanussi. The film is pointedly sentimental in tone rather than self-consciously intellectual, more concerned with the heartfelt examination of human behavior than with sustained, impassioned political point making. It also displays a daring willingness to rely on images, rather than dialogue, to elicit a visceral response from the audience. Norman and Emilia share no common language; thus they must rely on their war-ravaged faces to communicate everything that is felt between them. Zanussi has the courage and audacity to let this happen rather than resorting to the use of dialogue at every possible turn. He has previously been renowned for his highly cerebral examinations of individual lives crushed in the midst of repressive political conditions, as in *Family Life* (1971), *Camouflage* (1977), and *The Constant Factor* (1980). As a tale of war-blighted romance, *A Year of the Quiet Sun* is less concerned with rarefied intellectual observations and didactic political point making than with the sympathetic examination of nonspectacular, battered lives. Nevertheless, the film is invested with its share of complex intellectual ideas and scathing political subtexts. For all its seeming romanticism, *A Year of the Quiet Sun* might just as easily be interpreted as a tale of emotional collapse in the midst of oppressive political circumstances. Emilia must strive to reject the learned helplessness which has been ingrained in her by years of exposure to the horrors of war as well as an inept and corrupt political system. Her surroundings have taught her that happiness is impossible or, at least, is more than she has a right to deserve. Her task is to reject these notions, reorder her ways of thinking, and accept the chance for freedom and happiness that Norman comes to signify.

Like Agnieszka Holland's *Angry Harvest* (1985), which concerns the ill-fated love between an escaped Viennese Jewess and a German Catholic who willingly harbors her, *A Year of the Quiet Sun* depicts a relationship between two ordinary people, not the glamorous figures of conventional wartime romances. Norman and Emilia are not heroic; they are not moral archetypes. Their behavior is all the more fascinating because it is flawed, conditioned by human weakness and the failure of emotional connections.

Zanussi was trained as a physicist before embarking upon a career as a filmmaker. He has always been fascinated by the disparity between logical scientific relationships and the flawed functioning of human beings and political systems. Several of his films bear titles drawn from the world of scientific phenomena; the title of *A Year of the Quiet Sun* is itself an obscure reference to sunspots. Springing from a nation in which freedom of thought and action are routinely stifled for arbitrary and capricious reasons, Zanussi has repeatedly depicted the struggle of isolated individuals to overcome a repressive political milieu and regain their force of will. Indeed, his films collectively support Sigmund Freud's assertion that "people must sometimes be forced to be free."

In his films, Zanussi implies that the human urge toward freedom is a conditioned response which may be perverted or unlearned, rather than an innate instinct which persists in spite of all obstacles and demoralizing conditions. Thus, Emilia becomes an emblem for all people—Poles in particular—who are forced to subsist on as little as possible in the way of personal freedom and emotional gratification.

Emilia's uneasy resignation to her way of life is challenged and disrupted by Norman, who, once smitten by her, will not be easily swayed. Norman himself must overcome the recurring memory of his torture at the hands of the Nazis and resume some semblance of an emotional life. Until he encounters Emilia and experiences a rekindling of his emotional responses, Norman is unwilling to readjust to life in postwar America—a way of life which seems foreign and ephemeral.

Their first meeting is not an auspicious one. Emilia, an erstwhile artist, one day takes refuge in an abandoned car and is working there when Norman, not seeing her, comes by to relieve himself. The courtship begins fitfully, benighted by language difficulties, Norman's general uneasiness, and Emilia's deeply ingrained distrust of outsiders. Norman's first visit to Emilia's home consists of several misfired attempts at communication: Norman can only stammer and fret as Emilia and her mother make hilarious asides to each other. Nevertheless, an affinity is struck between Norman and Emilia, and once established, it gathers inexorable force, transcending mere limitations of language.

Norman struggles to express his nascent attraction to Emilia by way of a series of local interpreters—an army officer, a nun—none of whom is especially interested in providing a faithful translation. The moments of humor which mark these occasions serve to offset the very real pain that pervades both of their lives. Norman cannot imagine life without Emilia; he proposes marriage and offers Emilia a life of peace and freedom in America. She cannot imagine why she deserves such happiness or summon the will to accept it once it is offered. Emilia's sickly mother invites death upon herself in order to facilitate her daughter's happiness, and she leaves her with enough money to make the passage to America. Emilia responds by giving the money to her neighbor Stella (Ewa Dalkowska), a prostitute who has survived the horrors of the concentration camps as well as the rigors of postwar Polish life by offering herself to the local soldiers. Emilia's failure to embrace her own happiness is a source of dismay to Norman as well as the audience, but it is signified as the inevitable consequence of a life of repressed yearnings and thwarted expectations.

Zanussi renders the film as a whole in a kind of twilight, reflecting the nascent and still-submerged emotional responses of the characters, punctuated only occasionally by the pale glimmer of an electric light. The interior lighting is harsh, not at all favorable to the characters' war-ravaged faces, but it allows their luminous resiliency to shine through. Zanussi makes extensive use of the hand-held camera, so that the awkward, fitful exchanges between Norman and Emilia are matched by the tremulous movements of the camera itself.

Zanussi also injects elements of fantasy which illumine the main characters' greatest horrors as well as their deeply felt wishes. Norman is tormented by recurrent flashbacks of life in the German POW camp. Emilia, by contrast, generates her own fanciful vision of life with Norman in the mythical "wide-open spaces" of America: She imagines them doing a freewheeling jitterbug in the midst of Utah's primordial Monument Valley, a place she has only seen in films. These compensatory flights of imagination become necessary for the survival of trapped characters such as Emilia who are forced to adjust to life under highly oppressive conditions. Emilia and Norman are eventually separated: Years later, when Norman reiterates his offer of love and marriage in America, and sends her still more money for the passage, Emilia seems prepared to accept and act upon his overtures, but she collapses before she can respond. Her imaginary vision of what life might be like in America is ultimately all that is left to her.

Emilia's failure to act is signified as the inevitable consequence of the life she has endured in Poland—a life fixed by arbitrary, external constraints, in which genuine freedom and emotional satisfaction seem quite impossible, something for which no one has the right to hope. Zanussi implies that Emilia's paralysis of will may be characteristic of the Polish nation as a whole—a nation in which the deformation of individual impulses and emotions is seen as necessary for the continued functioning of the state. Emilia's lack of resolve may seem maddeningly incomprehensible from an American point of view, since Americans are imbued with vastly different notions of individual free will and self-determination, as well as freedom of thought and action. The Polish view of such matters, however—as exemplified by the films of Zanussi—is decidedly different: The will of the individual is always circumscribed by the demands of the state and a corrupt political system; genuine emotional satisfaction is transient if not impossible, and the realm of the imagination is very often the only available refuge.

After the release of *A Year of the Quiet Sun*, Zanussi drew fire from Polish critics for his resolutely dim view of the national state of affairs. The film enjoyed a generally favorable critical response outside Poland, winning the Golden Lion for Best Film at the 1984 Venice Film Festival and serving as a popular selection at the New York and San Francisco Film Festivals in 1985. It was eventually put forth as the official Polish contender for the Academy Award for Best Foreign-Language Film in 1985, but the Polish government abruptly withdrew the film from Academy Award considera-tion—an action which perhaps only served to underscore Zanussi's original assertion that repression does exist along cultural lines and that its force is arbitrary and capricious.

A Year of the Quiet Sun is borne aloft by the luminous performances of Wilson, Komorowska, and Skarzanka in the leading roles, as well as the fine portrayals of the minor characters. The film is also sparked by Zanussi's willingness to rely on imagery, rather than dialogue, to convey complex emotional states and ideas. The political points exist, and are eloquently stated, but are never put forth at the expense of characterization. The film partly concerns the failure of language and didactic political point making in the face of overwhelming human needs and desires: The greatest virtue of *A Year of the Quiet Sun* is perhaps that it tells more by saying less.

Karl Michalak

Reviews
Film Comment. XXI, December, 1985, p. 66.
Los Angeles Times. March 20, 1986, VI, p. 1.
New Statesman. CXI, February 21, 1986, p. 29.
The New York Times. CXXXV, October 9, 1985, p. C21.
Newsweek. CVI, October 28, 1985, p. 92.
Variety. CCXX, October 23, 1985, p. 20.

MORE FILMS OF 1986

Abbreviations: *Pro.* = Production *Dir.* = Direction *Scr.* = Screenplay *Cine.* = Cinematography *Ed.* = Editing *Mu.* = Music *P.d.* = Production design *A.d.* = Art direction *S.d.* = Set decoration *R.t.* = Running time *MPAA* = MPAA rating

ABSOLUTE BEGINNERS (Great Britain, 1986)
Pro. Stephen Woolley and Chris Brown; Orion Pictures *Dir.* Julien Temple *Scr.* Richard Burridge, Christopher Wicking, Don MacPherson *Cine.* Oliver Stapleton *Ed.* Michael Bradsell, Gerry Hambling, Richard Bedford, Russell Lloyd *Mu.* David Bowie, Ray Davies, Gil Evans, Paul Weller, Patsy Kensit, Sade, Tenpole Tudor, Jerry Dammers, Nick Lowe, Ekow Abban, Working Week *P.d.* John Beard *A.d.* Ken Wheatley, Stuart Rose *R.t.* 107 min. *MPAA* PG-13 *Cast:* Eddie O'Connell, Patsy Kensit, David Bowie, James Fox, Ray Davies, Eve Ferret, Steven Berkoff, Sade, Anita Morris, Lionel Blair, Tony Hippolyte.

Teen love is achieved, lost, and regained in this inventive musical that re-creates the period just before the youth-culture explosion of the early 1960's.

THE ADVENTURES OF MARK TWAIN
Pro. Will Vinton; Atlantic Releasing Corporation *Dir.* Will Vinton *Scr.* Susan Shadburne *Ed.* Kelley Baker, Michael Gall, Will Vinton *Mu.* Bill Scream *S.d.* Joan C. Gratz, Don Merkt *R.t.* 90 min. *MPAA* G. *Voices:* James Whitmore, Chris Ritchie, Gary Krug, Michele Mariana, John Morrison, Carol Edelman, Dallas McKennon, Herb Smith, Marley Stone.

Realized in a stop-motion animation process called Claymation, this film draws on Mark Twain's fiction and incidents from his life to create a fantasy-adventure story.

THE ADVENTURES OF THE AMERICAN RABBIT
Pro. Masaharu Etoh, Masahisa Saeki, and John G. Marshall; Atlantic Releasing Clubhouse Pictures *Dir.* Fred Wolf and Nobutaka Nishizawa *Scr.* Norm Lenzer *Mu.* Mark Volman, Howard Kaylan, John Hoier *R.t.* 85 min. *MPAA* G. *Voices:* Bob Arbogast, Pat Freley, Barry Gordon, Bob Holt, Lew Horn, Norm Lenzer, Ken Mars, John Mayer, Maitzi Morgan, Lorenzo Music, Lauri O'Brien, Hal Smith, Russi Taylor, Fred Wolf.

This animated film tells of a mild-mannered rabbit who is chosen to battle evil in the world.

AGENT ON ICE
Pro. Louis Pastore; Shapiro Entertainment *Dir.* Clark Worswick *Scr.* Clark Worswick, Louis Pastore *Cine.* Eric Kollmar *Ed.* Bill Freda *Mu.* Ian Carpenter *R.t.* 97 min. *MPAA* R. *Cast:* Tom Ormeny, Clifford David, Louis Pastore, Matt Craven, Debra Mooney, Donna Forbes, Jennifer Leak.

A former CIA agent uncovers a deal between his previous employers and the Mafia, thus becoming a target for both groups.

THE ALCHEMIST (Great Britain, 1983)
Pro. Lawrence Appelbaum; Empire Pictures *Dir.* James Amante *Scr.* Alan J. Adler *Cine.* Andrew W. Friend *Ed.* Ted Nicolaou *Mu.* Richard H. Band *Pd.* Dale A. Pelton *A.d.* Pam Warner *R.t.* 84 min. *MPAA* R. *Cast:* Robert Ginty, Lucinda

Dooling, John Sanderford, Viola Kate Stimpson, Robert Glaudini. This supernatural horror film depicts the accidental murder of Anna by her husband during a struggle with the alchemist who is trying to seduce her.

AMERICA

Pro. Paul A. Leeman; ASA Communications *Dir.* Robert Downey *Scr.* Robert Downey, Sidney Davis *Cine.* Richard Price *Ed.* C. Vaughn Hazell *Mu.* Leon Pendarvis *A.d.* C. J. Strawn *R.t.* 83 min. *MPAA* R. *Cast:* Zack Norman, Tammy Grimes, Michael J. Pollard, Richard Belzer, Monroe Arnold, Liz Torres, Pablo Ferro, David Kerman, Howard Thomashefsky, Michael Bahr, Laura Ashton.

Terrence Hackley (Zack Norman) decides to wear the plaid skirt his wife (Tammy Grimes) has discovered in his suitcase, explaining its presence by pretending that it is a kilt. His reportage while wearing the skirt makes the television news program for which he works into a hit.

AMERICAN ANTHEM

Pro. Robert Schaffel, Doug Chapin; Columbia Pictures *Dir.* Albert Magnoli *Scr.* Evan Archerd, Jeff Benjamin *Cine.* Donald E. Thorin *Ed.* James Oliver *Mu.* Alan Silvestri *P.d.* Ward Preston *S.d.* Chris Westlund, JoAnn Chorney *R.t.* 100 min. *MPAA* PG-13. *Cast:* Mitch Gaylord, Janet Jones, John Aprea, Michelle Phillips, R. J. Williams, Michael Pataki, Patrice Donnelly, Stacey Maloney, Maria Anz, Andrew M. White.

Two gymnasts become romantically involved.

AMERICAN JUSTICE

Pro. Jack Lucarelli, Jameson Parker; Movie Store *Dir.* Gary Grillo *Scr.* Dennis A. Pratt *Cine.* Steve Yaconelli *Ed.* Steven Mirkovich *Mu.* Paul Chihara *A.d.* Bruce Crone *R.t.* 92 min. *MPAA* R. *Cast:* Jack Lucarelli, Gerald McRaney, Wilford Brimley, Jameson Parker, Jeannie Wilson, Dennis A. Pratt, Danelle Hand, Sherry Adamo, Rick Hurst, Sharon Hughes, Warner Glenn, David Steen, Rosanna De Soto, Roman Cisneros.

A former Los Angeles policeman visits the ranch of his friend and witnesses the murder of a Mexican girl who tries to run away as she is being smuggled across the border to be part of a prostitution ring.

ANGRY HARVEST (*Bittere Ernte.* Germany, 1985)

Pro. Peter Hahne *Dir.* Agnieszka Holland *Scr.* Agnieszka Holland, Paul Hengge *Cine.* Josef Ort-Snep *Ed.* Barbara Kunze *Mu.* Jorg Strassburger *A.d.* Werner Schwenke *R.t.* 102 min. *Cast:* Armin Mueller-Stahl, Elisabeth Trissenaar, Kathe Jaenicke, Hans Beerhenke, Isa Haller, Margit Carstensen, Wojtech Pszoniak, Gerd Baltus.

Nominated for an Academy Award as Best Foreign Film, this powerful film, set during World War II in eastern Poland, focuses on the relationship between a Polish farmer and a beautiful Jewish woman who jumps from a transport going to a death camp.

THE ANNIHILATORS

Pro. Allan G. Pedersen, Tom Chapman; New World Pictures *Dir.* Charles E. Sellier, Jr. *Scr.* Brian Russell *Cine.* Henning Schellerup *Ed.* Dan Gross *Mu.* Bob Summers *A.d.* Simon Gittins *S.d.* Annette Serena *R.t.* 84 min. *MPAA* R. *Cast:* Christopher Stone, Andy Wood, Lawrence Hilton-Jacobs, Gerrit Graham, Dennis Redfield, Paul Koslo, Cavanaugh Yelling, Bruce Evers, Tom Harper, Lonnie Smith,

Josh Patton, Jim Antonio, Bruce Taylor.

In this action film, a group of Vietnam veterans turned vigilantes attempts to clean up a gang-brutalized neighborhood.

APRIL FOOL'S DAY

Pro. Frank Mancuso, Jr.; Paramount Pictures *Dir.* Fred Walton *Scr.* Danilo Bach *Cine.* Charles Minsky *Ed.* Bruce Green *Mu.* Charles Bernstein *A.d.* Stewart Campbell *S.d.* Dell Johnston *R.t.* 90 min. *MPAA* R. *Cast:* Jay Baker, Deborah Foreman, Deborah Goodrich, Ken Olandt, Griffin O'Neal, Clayton Rohner, Amy Steel, Thomas F. Wilson

One by one, the members of a group visiting their friend at her isolated mansion begin to disappear.

ARMED AND DANGEROUS

Pro. Brian Grazer, James Keach; Columbia Pictures *Dir.* Mark L. Lester *Scr.* Harold Ramis, Peter Torokvei *Cine.* Fred Schuler *Ed.* Michael Hill, Daniel Hanley, George Pedugo *Mu.* Bill Meyers *P.d.* David L. Snyder *S.d.* Tom Pedigo *R.t.* 88 min. *MPAA* PG-13. *Cast:* John Candy, Eugene Levy, Robert Loggia, Kenneth McMillan, Meg Ryan, Brion James, Jonathan Banks, Don Stroud, Steve Railsback.

Two bumblers become security guards for a company run by the Mafia.

ARMED RESPONSE

Pro. Paul Hertzberg; Cintel Films *Dir.* Fred Olen Ray *Scr.* T. L. Lankford *Cine.* Paul Elliott *Ed.* Miriam L. Preissel *Mu.* Tom Chase, Steve Rucker *A.d.* Maxine Shepard *R.t.* 85 min. *MPAA* R. *Cast:* David Carradine, Lee Van Cleef, Mako, Lois Hamilton, Ross Hagen, Brent Huff, Laurene Landon, Dick Miller, Michael Berryman, David Goss.

Jim Roth and his father set out to rescue Jim's wife and daughter, who have been kidnapped by a gangster trying to retrieve a stolen jade antique that Jim's brother, a private investigator double-crossed by his partner and then killed, was hired to find.

ARTHUR'S HALLOWED GROUND (Great Britain, 1984)

Pro. Chris Griffin; Cinecom International Films *Dir.* Freddie Young *Scr.* Peter Gibbs *Cine.* Chick Anstiss *Ed.* Chris Risdale *R.t.* 84 min. *Cast:* Jimmy Jewel, Jean Boht, David Swift, Michael Elphick, Derek Benfield, Vas Blackwood, John Flanagan.

An elderly gentleman, who has lovingly tended a cricket field in London for nearly fifty years, must defend the turf against those who would tamper with it.

AVENGING FORCE

Pro. Menahem Golan, Yoram Globus; Cannon Films *Dir.* Sam Firstenberg *Scr.* James Booth *Cine.* Gideon Porath *Ed.* Michael J. Duthie *Mu.* George S. Clinton *P.d.* Marcia Hinds *A.d.* Bo Johnson *S.d.* Michele Starbuck *R.t.* 103 min. *MPAA* R. *Cast:* Michael Dudikoff, Steve James, James Booth, John P. Ryan, Bill Wallace, Karl Johnson, Mark Alaimo, Allison Gereighty, Loren Farmer, Richard Boyle.

A former secret-service agent aids his black friend, who has become the target of a racist terrorist organization because of his bid for a Senate seat.

BAD GUYS

Pro. John D. Backe, Myron A. Hyman; Interpictures Releasing *Dir.* Joel Silberg *Scr.* Brady W. Setwater, Joe Gillis *Cine.* Hanania Baer *Ed.* Peter Parasheles, Christopher Holmes *Mu.* William Goldstein *A.d.* Ivo Cristante *R.t.* 86 min. *MPAA* PG. *Cast:* Adam Baldwin, Mike Jolly, Michelle Nicastro, Ruth Buzzi, James Booth,

Gene LeBell, Norman Burton, Alexia Smirnoff, Jay York, Dutch Mann, Sergeant Slaughter, Allan Rich, Toru Tanaka, Jay Strongbow, Jack Armstrong, Buddha Kahn, Curt Henning, Billy Varga, Pepper Martin.

Two police officers suspended from the force become professional wrestlers.

BAND OF THE HAND

Pro. Michael Rauch; Tri-Star Pictures *Dir.* Paul Michael Glaser *Scr.* Leo Garen, Jack Baran *Cine.* Reynaldo Villalobos *Ed.* Jack Hofstra *Mu.* Michael Rubini *P.d.* Gregory Bolton *A.d.* Mark Harrington *S.d.* Don K. Ivey *R.t.* 109 min. *MPAA* R. *Cast:* Stephen Lang, Michael Carmine, Lauren Holly, John Cameron Mitchell, Daniele Quinn, Leon Robinson, Al Shannon, Danton Stone, Paul Calderon, Larry Fishburne, James Remar.

Five juvenile criminals are sent to the Everglades for a survival course; when they return, they begin cleaning up their inner-city neighborhood.

BEDROOM EYES (Canada, 1986)

Pro. Robert Lantos, Stephen J. Roth; Cinecom International *Dir.* William Fruet *Scr.* Michael Alan Eddy *Cine.* Miklos Lente *Ed.* Tony Lower *R.t.* 90 min. *MPAA* R. *Cast:* Kenneth Gilman, Dayle Haddon, Barbara Law, Christine Cattell.

A young voyeur who has sought psychiatric help witnessess the murder of the woman on whom he has been spying.

BELIZAIRE THE CAJUN

Pro. Allan L. Durand, Glen Pitre *Dir.* Glen Pitre *Scr.* Glen Pitre *Cine.* Richard Bowen *Ed.* Paul Trejo *Mu.* Michael Doucet *P.d.* Randall LaBry *A.d.* Deborah Schildt *R.t.* 101 min. *Cast:* Armand Assante, Gail Youngs, Michael Schoeffling, Stephen McHattie, Will Patton, Nancy Barrett, Loulan Pitre, Andre Delaunay, Jim Levert, Ernie Vincent, Paul Landry, Allan L. Durand, Robert Duvall.

This splendidly detailed period drama, set in Louisiana in the 1850's, depicts an animosity between the locals and the incoming French Cajuns that eventually escalates into violence.

BIG TROUBLE

Pro. Michael Lobell; Columbia Pictures *Dir.* John Cassavetes *Scr.* Warren Bogle *Cine.* Bill Butler *Ed.* Donn Cambern, Ralph Winters *Mu.* Bill Conti *Pd.* Gene Callahan *A.d.* Lee Poll *R.t.* 93 min. *MPAA* R. *Cast:* Peter Falk, Alan Arkin, Beverly D'Angelo, Charles Durning, Paul Dooley, Robert Stack, Valerie Curtin, Richard Libertini, Jerry Pavlon, Steve Altermen, Paul La Greca, John Finnegan, Karl Lukas.

Leonard Hoffman (Alan Arkin) needs money to send his triplets to Yale. When he meets Blanche Rickey (Beverly D'Angelo), whose husband, Steve (Peter Falk), has heart trouble, he sells her an insurance policy that pays double if Steve is killed falling off a train, and they then conspire to bring this about.

BIG TROUBLE IN LITTLE CHINA

Pro. Larry J. Franco; Twentieth Century-Fox *Dir.* John Carpenter *Scr.* Gary Goldman, David Z. Weinstein; adapted by W. O. Richter *Cine.* Dean Cundey *Ed.* Mark Warner, Steve Mirkovich, Edward A. Warschilka *Mu.* John Carpenter, Alan Howarth *P.d.* John J. Lloyd *A.d.* Les Gobruegge *S.d.* George R. Nelson *R.t.* 100 min. *MPAA* PG-13. *Cast:* Kurt Russell, Kim Cattrall, Dennis Dun, James Hong, Victor Wong, Kate Burton, Donald Li, Carter Wong, Peter Kwong, James Pax, Suzee Pai, Chao Li Chi, Jeff Imada, Rummel Mor.

An evil, ancient Chinese magician searches for a green-eyed Chinese woman with whom to mate.

BLACK JOY

Pro. Elliott Kastner, Martin Campbell *Dir.* Anthony Simmons *Scr.* Anthony Simmons, Jamal Ali *Cine.* Philip M. Eheux *Ed.* Thom Noble *Mu.* Lou Reizner *R.t.* 97 min. *MPAA* R. *Cast:* Norman Beaton, Trevor Thomas, Dawn Hope, Floella Benjamin, Oscar James, Paul Medford.

This is a spirited fable about a country boy from Guyana who learns the ways of the big city.

BLACK MOON RISING

Pro. Joel B. Michaels, Douglas Curtis; New World Pictures *Dir.* Harley Cokliss *Scr.* John Carpenter, Desmond Nakano, William Gray *Cine.* Misha Suslov *Ed.* Todd Ramsay *Mu.* Lalo Schifrin *Pd.* Bryan Ryman *R.t.* 100 min. *MPAA* R. *Cast:* Tommy Lee Jones, Linda Hamilton, Robert Vaughn, Richard Jaeckel, Lee Ving, Bubba Smith, Dan Shor, William Sanderson, Keenan Wynn, Nick Cassavetes, Don Opper, William Marquez.

Freelance thief Quint (Tommy Lee Jones) must retrieve evidence that he has stolen from a fancy new car, the Black Moon, which itself is then stolen; the film takes off from there.

BLUE CITY

Pro. William Hayward, Walter Hill; Paramount Pictures *Dir.* Michelle Manning *Scr.* Lukas Heller, Walter Hill *Cine.* Steven Poster *Ed.* Ross Albert *Mu.* Ry Cooder *A.d.* Richard Lawrence *R.t.* 83 min. *MPAA* R. *Cast:* Judd Nelson, Ally Sheedy, David Caruso, Paul Winfield, Scott Wilson, Anita Morris, Luis Contreras.

A young man returns to his hometown to find that his father, the crooked mayor, has been murdered.

BORN AMERICAN (Finland and USA, 1986)

Pro. Cinema Group in association with Larmark; Concorde Cinema Group *Dir.* Renny Harlin *Scr.* Markus Selin, Renny Harlin *Cine.* Henrik Paerchs *Ed.* Paul Martin Smith *Mu.* Richard Mitchell *R.t.* 95 min. *Cast:* Mike Norris, Steve Durham, David Coburn, Thalmus Rasulala, Albert Salmi, Piita Vuosalmi.

Three young Americans find out about Soviet prisons from the inside, after crossing the border into the Soviet Union from Norway on a dare.

THE BOY IN BLUE (Canada, 1986)

Pro. John Kemeny; Twentieth Century-Fox *Dir.* Charles Jarrott *Scr.* Douglas Bowie *Cine.* Pierre Mignot *Ed.* Rit Wallis *Mu.* Roger Webb *P.d.* William Beeton *R.t.* 93 min. *MPAA* R. *Cast:* Nicolas Cage, Cynthia Dale, Christopher Plummer, David Naughton, Sean Sullivan, Melody Anderson, James B. Douglas, Walter Massey, Austin Willis, Philip Craig, Robert McCormick.

The story of Ned Hanlon, a world-class rower from backwoods Ontario, who was at his peak in the 1870's, is depicted in this film biography.

THE BOY WHO COULD FLY

Pro. Gary Adelson; Twentieth Century-Fox *Dir.* Nick Castle *Scr.* Nick Castle *Cine.* Steven Poster, Adam Holender *Ed.* Patrick Kennedy *Mu.* Bruce Broughton *P.d.* Jim Bissell *A.d.* Graeme Murray *R.t.* 114 min. *MPAA* PG. *Cast:* Lucy Deakins, Jay Underwood, Bonnie Bedelia, Fred Savage, Colleen Dewhurst, Fred Gwynne, Mindy Cohn, Janet MacLachlan, Jennifer Michas, Michelle Bardeaux,

Louise Fletcher.

A teenage girl befriends an autistic teenage boy who can fly and who has not spoken since his parents were killed when he was very young.

THE BOYS NEXT DOOR

Pro. Keith Rubenstein, Sandy Howard; New World Pictures *Dir.* Penelope Spheeris *Scr.* Glen Morgan, James Wong *Cine.* Arthur Albert *Ed.* Andy Horvitch *Mu.* George S. Clinton, Geo *R.t.* 91 min. *MPAA* R. *Cast:* Maxwell Caulfield, Charlie Sheen, Patti D'Arbanville, Christopher McDonald, Hank Garrett, Paul C. Dancer, Richard Pachorek, Lesa Lee, Kenneth Cortland, Moon Zappa, Dawn Schneider.

Two alienated teenagers visit Los Angeles on their graduation night and go on a murderous spree.

BULLIES (Canada, 1986)

Pro. Peter Simpson; Universal *Dir.* Paul Lynch *Scr.* John Sheppard, Brian McCann *Cine.* Rene Verzier *Ed.* Nick Rotundo *Mu.* Paul Zaza *A.d.* Jack McAdam *R.t.* 90 min. *MPAA* R. *Cast:* Janet Laine-Green, Stephen Hunter, Jonathan Crombie, Dehl Berti, Olivia D'Abo.

A small town is terrorized by a family.

CACTUS (Australia, 1986)

Pro. Jane Ballantyne, Paul Cox; Spectrafilm *Dir.* Paul Cox *Scr.* Paul Cox, Norman Kaye, Bob Ellis *Cine.* Yuri Sokol *Ed.* Tim Lewis *P.d.* Asher Bilu *R.t.* 95 min. *Cast:* Isabelle Huppert, Robert Menzies, Norman Kaye, Monica Maughan, Banduk Marika, Sheila Florance, Peter Aanensen.

A Frenchwoman visiting Australia is in a car accident that causes the loss of sight in one eye and endangers the other. She learns courage and gains a new outlook on life from a man who has been blind from birth. He in turn learns to let himself open up emotionally to people.

LA CAGE AUX FOLLES III: THE WEDDING (*Il Eizietto III.* France, Italy, 1985)

Pro. Marcello Danon; Tri-Star Pictures *Dir.* Georges Lautner *Scr.* Michel Audiard, Jacques Audiard, Marcello Danon, Georges Lautner, Gerard Lamballe *Cine.* Luciano Tovoli *Ed.* Michelle David, Elisabeth Guido, Lidia Pascolini *Mu.* Ennio Morricone *A.d.* Mario Garbuglia *R.t.* 90 min. *MPAA* PG-13. *Cast:* Michel Serrault, Ugo Tognazzi, Michel Galabru, Benny Luke, Stephane Audran, Antonella Interlenghi, Saverio Vallone, Gianluca Favilla, Umberto Ramo.

In the latest *La Cage aux folles* installment, the gay nightclub owner Albin will receive an enormous inheritance if he marries and fathers a child.

CAMORRA (Italy, 1986)

Pro. Menahem Golan, Yoram Globus; Italian International Film *Dir.* Lina Wertmuller *Scr.* Linda Wertmuller, Elvio Porta *Cine.* Giuseppe Lanci *Ed.* Luigi Zita *Mu.* Tony Esposito *A.d.* Enrico Job *R.t.* 115 min. *MPAA* R. *Cast:* Angela Molina, Francisco Rabal, Harvey Keitel, Daniel Ezralow, Vittorio Squillante, Paolo Bonacelli, Tommaso Bianco.

Director Lina Wertmuller focuses on the deadly Neapolitan crime organization, the Camorra, in this Italian film.

CARAVAGGIO (Great Britain, 1986)

Pro. Sarah Radclyffe *Dir.* Derek Jarman *Scr.* Derek Jarman *Cine.* Gabriel

Beristain *Ed.* George Akers *Mu.* Simon Fisher Turner *P.d.* Christopher Hobbs *R.t.* 89 min. *Cast:* Nigel Terry, Sean Bean, Garry Cooper, Spencer Leigh, Tilda Swinton, Michael Gough, Nigel Davenport, Robbie Coltrane, Jonathan Hyde, Dexter Fletcher, Noam Almaz, Jack Birkett.

This film biography depicts the life of the Italian Renaissance painter Michelangelo da Caravaggio.

CARE BEARS MOVIE II: A NEW GENERATION (Canada, 1986)
Pro. Michael Hirsh, Patrick Loubert, Clive A. Smith; Columbia Pictures *Dir.* Dale Schott *Scr.* Peter Sauder *Ed.* Evan Landis *Mu.* Patricia Cullen *R.t.* 77 min. *MPAA* G. *Voices:* Maxine Miller, Pam Hyatt, Hadley Kay, Cree Summer Francks, Alyson Court, Michael Fantini.

In this animated feature, the Care Bears set out to teach the virtues of caring and sharing to some self-centered children at a summer camp.

THE CHECK IS IN THE MAIL
Pro. Robert Kaufman, Robert Krause; Ascot Entertainment Group *Dir.* Joan Darling *Scr.* Robert Kaufman *Cine.* Jan Kiesser *Mu.* David Frank *R.t.* 91 min. *MPAA* R. *Cast:* Brian Dennehy, Anne Archer, Hallie Todd, Chris Hebert, Michael Bowen, Nita Talbot, Dick Shawn.

This lighthearted comedy features Brian Dennehy as a California pharmacist who is in debt to everyone from the utility companies to a Mafia gambling ring—he resolves to fight back by living outside the system.

CHOKE CANYON
Pro. Ovidio G. Assonitis; United Film Distribution Company *Dir.* Chuck Bail *Scr.* Sheila Goldberg, Ovidio G. Assonitis, Alfonso Brescia *Cine.* Dante Spinotti *Ed.* Robert Silvi *Mu.* Sylvester Levay *P.d.* Frank Vanorio *R.t.* 94 min. *MPAA* PG. *Cast:* Stephen Collins, Nicholas Pryor, Janet Julian, Lance Henriksen, Bo Svenson, Victoria Racimo.

A scientist, who is working on converting sound waves into energy, fights a company that wants to dump radioactive waste into a canyon.

CHOPPING MALL
Pro. Julie Corman; Concorde Pictures *Dir.* Jim Wynorski *Scr.* Jim Wynorski, Steve Mitchell *Cine.* Tom Richmond *Ed.* Leslie Rosenthal *Mu.* Chuck Cirino *A.d.* Carol Clements *R.t.* 76 min. *MPAA* R. *Cast:* Kelly Maroney, Tony O'Dell, John Terlesky, Russell Todd, Paul Bartel, Mary Woronov, Dick Miller, Karrie Emerson, Barbara Compton, Suzee Slater, Nick Segal.

Eight teenagers are trapped in a shopping mall overnight and face three murderous guard robots.

THE CLAN OF THE CAVE BEAR
Pro. Gerald I. Isenberg; Warner Bros. *Dir.* Michael Chapman *Scr.* John Sayles *Cine.* Jan De Bont *Ed.* Wendy Greene Bricmont *Mu.* Alan Silvestri *Pd.* Anthony Masters *A.d.* Guy Comtois, Richard Wilcox *S.d.* Kimberly Richardson *R.t.* 98 min. *MPAA* R. *Cast:* Daryl Hannah, Pamela Reed, James Remar, Thomas G. Waites, John Doolittle, Curtis Armstrong, Martin Doyle, Adel C. Hammoud, Tony Montanaro, Mike Museat.

Daryl Hannah stars in this scenic adaptation of Jean M. Auel's best-selling novel, playing a Cro-Magnon foundling who is reared by Neanderthals and inculcated with their sexist, oppressive ways.

CLASS OF NUKE 'EM HIGH

Pro. Troma Inc. *Dir.* Richard W. Haines, Samuel Weil *Scr.* Richard W. Haines, Mark Rudnitsky, Lloyd Kaufman, Stuart Strutin *Cine.* Michael Mayers *Ed.* Richard W. Haines *Mu.* various composers *A.d.* Richard W. Haines *R.t.* 92 min. *MPAA* R. *Cast:* Janelle Brady, Gilbert Brenton, Robert Prichard, R. L. Ryan, James Nugent Vernon, Brad Dunker, Gary Schneider, Theo Cohan.

This satiric comic-horror film focuses on Tromaville, New Jersey—"The Toxic Waste Capital of the World"—and its unfortunate inhabitants.

CLOCKWISE (Great Britain, 1986)

Pro. Michael Codron; Universal *Dir.* Christopher Morahan *Scr.* Michael Frayn *Cine.* John Coquillon *Ed.* Peter Boyle *Mu.* George Fenton *P.d.* Roger Murray-Leach *A.d.* Diana Charnley *R.t.* 97 min. *MPAA* PG. *Cast:* John Cleese, Alison Steadman, Penelope Wilton, Stephen Moore, Joan Hickson, Sharon Maiden.

An obsessively prompt headmaster, invited to speak at a headmasters' conference, misses his train; thus begins a series of misadventures.

CLUB PARADISE

Pro. Michael Shamberg; Warner Bros. *Dir.* Harold Ramis *Scr.* Harold Ramis, Brian Doyle-Murray *Cine.* Peter Hannan *Ed.* Marion Rothman *Mu.* David Mansfield, Van Dyke Parks *P.d.* John Graysmark *A.d.* Tony Reading *S.d.* Peter Young *R.t.* 104 min. *MPAA* PG-13 *Cast:* Robin Williams, Peter O'Toole, Rick Moranis, Jimmy Cliff, Twiggy, Adolph Caesar, Eugene Levy, Joanna Cassidy, Andrea Martin, Brian Doyle-Murray, Steve Kampmann, Joe Flaherty, Mary Gross.

A man invests in a ramshackle tropical resort that is visited by a variety of eccentrics.

COCAINE WARS

Pro. Roger Corman, Alex Sessa; Concorde Pictures *Dir.* Hector Olivera *Scr.* Steven M. Krauzer *Cine.* Victor Kaulen *Ed.* Edward Lowe *Mu.* George Brock *R.t.* 83 min. *MPAA* R. *Cast:* John Schneider, Kathryn Witt, Federico Luppi, Royal Dano, Rodolfo Ranni, Miguel Angel Sola.

A drug enforcement agency officer goes to a South American country to destroy a cocaine ring that is headed by an evil army officer.

COMBAT SHOCK

Pro. Buddy Giovinazzo; Troma Inc. *Dir.* Buddy Giovinazzo *Scr.* Buddy Giovinazzo *Cine.* Stella Varveris *Ed.* Buddy Giovinazzo *Mu.* Ricky Giovinazzo *R.t.* 88 min. *MPAA* R. *Cast:* Ricky Giovinazzo, Veronica Stork, Mitch Maglio, Aspah Livni, Nick Nasta, Mike Tierno.

Combat Shock is a stark tale of a shellshocked Vietnam veteran who is at the end of his rope.

THE COSMIC EYE

Pro. Faith Hubley; released by Upfront *Dir.* Faith Hubley *Scr.* Faith Hubley *Mu.* Benny Carter, Elizabeth Swados, Dizzy Gillespie, Conrad Cummings, William Russo *Animation:* Fred Burns, William Littlejohn, Emily Hubley *R.t.* 72 min. *Voices:* Dizzy Gillespie, Linda Atkinson, Sam Hubley, Maureen Stapleton.

Director Faith Hubley's first animated feature is nothing less than an inventory of myths about mankind's origins, a review of the current state of planet Earth, plus some hope-filled speculations about the future.

CRAWLSPACE
Pro. Roberto Bessi; Empire Pictures *Dir.* David Schmoeller *Scr.* David Schmoeller *Cine.* Sergio Salvati *Ed.* Bert Glastein *Mu.* Pino Donaggio *P.d.* Giovanni Natalucci *A.d.* Gianni Cozzo *R.t.* 77 min. *MPAA* R. *Cast:* Klaus Kinski, Talia Balsam, Barbara Whinnery, Sally Brown, Carol Francis, Tane, Jack Heller, Kenneth Robert Shippy.

A psychotic doctor rents rooms in his apartment house to pretty young women, spies on them, and then kills them.

THE CRAZY FAMILY (*Gyakufunsha Kazoku.* Japan, 1984)
Pro. Kazuhiko Hasegawa, Toyoji Yamane, Shiro Sasaki; New Yorker Films *Dir.* Sogo Ishii *Scr.* Yoshinori Kobayashi, Fumio Kohnami, Sogo Ishii *Cine.* Masaki Tamura *Ed.* Junnichi Kikuchi *Mu.* 1984 *A.d.* Terumi Hosoishi *R.t.* 106 min. *Cast:* Katsuya Kobayashi, Mitsuko Baisho, Yoshiki Arizono, Yuki Kudo, Hitoshi Ueki.

This Japanese satire on suburbia depicts the lunacy of the Kobayashi household.

CRITTERS
Pro. Rupert Harvey; New Line Cinema *Dir.* Stephen Herek *Scr.* Stephen Herek, Domonic Muir *Cine.* Tim Suhrstedt *Ed.* Larry Bock *Mu.* David Newman *P.d.* Gregg Fonseca *A.d.* Phillip Foreman *S.d.* Anne Huntley *R.t.* 86 min. *MPAA* PG-13. *Cast:* Dee Wallace Stone, M. Emmet Walsh, Billy Green Bush, Scott Grimes, Nadine Van Der Velde, Terrence Mann, Don Opper, Billy Zane, Ethan Phillips, Jeremy Lawrence, Lin Shaye, Michael Lee Gogin, Art Frankel.

A small farm community in Kansas is invaded by otherworldly creatures called Krites, which cause havoc and destruction until extraterrestrial bounty hunters manage to catch up with them.

CUT AND RUN (Italy, 1986)
Pro. Alessandro Fracassi; New World Pictures *Dir.* Ruggero Deodato *Scr.* Cesare Frugoni, Dardano Sacchetti *Cine.* Alberto Spagnoli *Ed.* Mario Morra *Mu.* Claudio Simonetti *A.d.* Claudio Cinini *R.t.* 87 min. *MPAA* R. *Cast:* Lisa Blount, Leonard Mann, Willie Aames, Richard Lynch, Richard Bright, Karen Black, Valentina Forte, Michael Berryman, John Steiner, Gabriele Tinti.

This action drama focuses on the exploits of an American television reporter and her cameraman in the jungles of Latin America.

DANCING IN THE DARK (Canada, 1986)
Pro. Anthony Kramreither; Norstar *Dir.* Leon Marr *Scr.* Leon Marr *Cine.* Vic Sarin *Ed.* Tom Berner *A.d.* Lillian Sarafinchan *R.t.* 98 min. *MPAA* PG-13. *Cast:* Martha Henry, Neil Munro, Rosemary Dunsmore, Richard Monette, Elena Kudaba, Brenda Bazinet.

After twenty years of marriage, meticulous housewife Edna kills her husband when she finds out about his infidelity.

DANGEROUSLY CLOSE
Pro. Harold Sobel; Cannon Films *Dir.* Albert Pyun *Scr.* Scott Fields, John Stockwell, Marty Ross *Cine.* Walt Lloyd *Ed.* Dennis O'Connor *Mu.* Michael McCarty *Pd.* Marcia Hinds *A.d.* Bo Johnson *S.d.* Piers Plowden *R.t.* 95 min. *MPAA* R. *Cast:* John Stockwell, J. Eddie Peck, Carey Lowell, Bradford Bancroft, Don Michael Paul, Thom Mathews, Jerry Dinome.

High school students form a vigilante group employing terrorist tactics in order to clean up their school.

DARK OF THE NIGHT (New Zealand, 1985)
Pro. Robin Laing, Gaylene Preston; Castle Hill Productions *Dir.* Gaylene Preston *Scr.* Gaylene Preston, Geoff Murphy, Graham Tetley *Cine.* Thomas Burstyn *Ed.* Simon Reece *Mu.* Jonathan Crayford *R.t.* 88 min. *Cast:* Heather Bolton, David Letch, Margaret Umbers, Suzanne Lee, Gary Stalker, Danny Mulheron, Perry Piercy, Philip Gordon.

A young woman buys a haunted car.

DEAD-END DRIVE-IN (Australia, 1986)
Pro. Andrew Williams; World Pictures *Dir.* Brian Trenchard-Smith *Scr.* Peter Smalley *Cine.* Paul Murphy *Ed.* Lee Smith *Mu.* Frank Strangio *P.d.* Larry Eastwood *R.t.* 90 min. *MPAA* R. *Cast:* Ned Manning, Natalie McCurry, Peter Whitford, Wilbur Wilde, Brett Climo, Ollie Hall, Sandy Lillingstone, Lyn Collingwood, Nikki McWaters, Melissa Davis, Dave Gibson.

In this futuristic film, the Australian government has turned drive-ins into youth prison camps.

DEADLY FRIEND
Pro. Robert M. Sherman; Warner Bros. *Dir.* Wes Craven *Scr.* Bruce Joel Rubin *Cine.* Philip Lathrop *Ed.* Michael Eliot *Mu.* Charles Bernstein *Pd.* Daniel Lomino *S.d.* Edward J. McDonald *R.t.* 99 min. *MPAA* R. *Cast:* Matthew Laborteaux, Kristy Swanson, Michael Sharrett, Anne Twomey, Anne Ramsey, Richard Marcus.

A boy steals the body of his friend and implants the artificially intelligent brain of his robot into her; she reanimates and seeks revenge on her father, whose push resulted in her death.

DEATH OF A SOLDIER (Australia, 1986)
Pro. David Hannay, William Nagle; Scotti Brothers *Dir.* Phillipe Mora *Scr.* William Nagle *Cine.* Louis Irving *Ed.* John Scott *Mu.* Alan Zavod *A.d.* Geoff Richardson *R.t.* 93 min. *MPAA* R. *Cast:* James Coburn, Reb Brown, Bill Hunter, Maurie Fields, Belinda Davey, Max Fairchild, Jon Sidney.

An American soldier undergoes a military trial for the murder of three women in Australia.

DEATH OF AN ANGEL
Pro. Peter Burrell; Twentieth Century-Fox *Dir.* Petru Popescu *Scr.* Petru Popescu *Cine.* Fred Murphy *Ed.* Christopher Lebenzon *Mu.* Peter Myers *R.t.* 95 min. *MPAA* PG. *Cast:* Bonnie Bedelia, Nick Mancuso, Pamela Ludwig, Alex Color, Abel Franco, Irma Garcia, Michael Shannon, Carlos Marentes, Leonard Lewis, Jon Hart Olson.

After her husband's death, a woman is ordained as an Episcopalian priest and undergoes a pilgrimage of faith when searching for her daughter, who has gone for healing to a Mexican religious zealot.

DEMONS (*I Demoni*. Italy, 1986)
Pro. Dario Argento; Ascot Entertainment Group *Dir.* Lamberto Bava *Scr.* Dario Argento, Lamberto Bava, Franco Ferrini, Dardano Sacchetti *Cine.* Gianlorenzo Battaglia *Mu.* C. Simonetti *R.t.* 90 min. *MPAA* R. *Cast:* Urbano Barberini, Natasha Hovey, Karl Zinny, Paola Cozzo, Fiuore Argento.

A young girl and her friend are trapped in a film theater and threatened by demons, who have already transformed most of the audience into demons.

DESERT HEARTS
Pro. Donna Deitch; Samuel Goldwyn Co. *Dir.* Donna Deitch *Scr.* Natalie Cooper *Cine.* Robert Elswit *Ed.* Robert Estrin *R.t.* 97 min. *MPAA* R. *Cast:* Helen Shaver, Patricia Charbonneau, Audra Lindley, Andra Akers, Gwen Welles, Dean Butler, James Staley, Katie La Bourdette, Alex McArthur, Anthony Ponzini, Denise Crosby, Tyler Tyhurst.

Based on Jane Role's novel *Desert of the Heart*, this film explores the lesbian awakening of a newly divorced woman and the turmoil and ecstasy which it produces in her.

DREAM LOVER
Pro. Alan J. Pakula, Jon Boorstin; MGM/UA Entertainment *Dir.* Alan J. Pakula *Scr.* Jon Boorstin *Cine.* Sven Nykvist *Ed.* Trudy Ship *Mu.* Michael Small *Pd.* George Jenkins *A.d.* John J. Moore *R.t.* 104 min. *MPAA* R. *Cast:* Kristy McNichol, Ben Masters, Paul Shenar, Justin Deas, John McMartin, Gayle Hunnicutt, Joseph Culp, Matthew Penn, Paul West, Matthew Long.

Ben Masters plays a dream researcher who is hired by a young New York woman (Kristy McNichol) to treat her sleeplessness.

DUET FOR ONE
Pro. Menahem Golan, Yoram Globus; Cannon Films *Dir.* Andrei Konchalovsky *Scr.* Tom Kempinski, Jeremy Lipp, Andrei Konchalovsky *Cine.* Alex Thomson *Ed.* Henry Richardson *Mu.* Michael Linn *Pd.* John Graysmark *A.d.* Reg Bream, Steve Cooper *S.d.* Peter Young *R.t.* 107 min. *MPAA* R. *Cast:* Julie Andrews, Alan Bates, Max Von Sydow, Rupert Everett, Margaret Courtenay.

A famed violinist discovers that she has multiple sclerosis.

EAT AND RUN
Pro. Jack Briggs; New World Pictures *Dir.* Christopher Hart *Scr.* Stan Hart, Christopher Hart *Cine.* Dyanna Taylor *Ed.* Pamela S. Arnold *Mu.* Donald Pippin *A.d.* Mark Selemon *R.t.* 90 min. *MPAA* R. *Cast:* Ron Silver, Sharon Schlarth, R. L. Ryan, John F. Fleming, Derek Murcott, Robert Silver, Mimi Cecchini, Tony Moundroukas, Frank Nastasi, Peter Waldren, Gabriel Barre, Ruth Jaroslow, George Peter Ryan, Lou Criscuolo, Tom Mardirosian, Louis Turenne.

When an extraterrestrial lands in New Jersey and begins eating Italians, detective Mickey McSorely (Ron Silver) attempts to solve the case.

EDITH'S DIARY (West Germany, 1983)
Pro. Hans W. Geissendörfer Film Produktion; Greentree Productions *Dir.* Hans W. Geissendörfer *Scr.* Hans W. Geissendörfer *Cine.* Michael Ballhaus *Ed.* Helga Borsche *Mu.* Jürgen Knieper *A.d.* Toni Lundi *R.t.* 108 min. *MPAA* R. *Cast:* Angela Winkler, Vadim Glowna, Leopold von Verschuer, Hans Madin, Irm Herrmann, Sona MacDonald, Wolfgang Condrus, Friedrich G. Beckhaus, Werner Eichhorn.

A magazine editor escapes her boredom and her family problems by creating a fantasy world in her diary.

EIGHT MILLION WAYS TO DIE
Pro. Steve Roth; Tri-Star Pictures *Dir.* Hal Ashby *Scr.* Oliver Stone, David Lee Henry *Cine.* Stephen H. Burum *Ed.* Robert Lawrence, Stuart Pappe *Mu.* James

Newton Howard *P.d.* Michael Haller *R.t.* 115 min. *MPAA* R. *Cast:* Jeff Bridges, Rosanna Arquette, Alexandra Paul, Randy Brooks, Andy Garcia.

An alcoholic sheriff sets out to dismantle a cocaine-dealing ring and becomes involved in buying a prostitute's freedom from her pimp.

ENDGAME (Italy, 1983)

Pro. American National Enterprises *Dir.* Steven Benson *Scr.* Alex Carver *Cine.* Federico Slorisco *Ed.* Tony Larson *Mu.* Carlo Maria Cordio *A.d.* Robert Connors *R.t.* 99 min. *Cast:* Al Cliver, Laura Gemser, George Eastman, Jack Davis, Al Yamanouchi, Gabriele Tinti, Mario Pedone, Gordon Mitchell, Christopher Walsh.

This action film is about life after World War III.

EVERY TIME WE SAY GOODBYE

Pro. Jacob Kotzky, Sharon Harel; Tri-Star Pictures *Dir.* Moshe Mizrahi *Scr.* Moshe Mizrahi, Rachel Fabien, Leah Appet *Cine.* Giuseppe Lanci *Ed.* Mark Burns *Mu.* Philippe Sarde *A.d.* Mickey Zahar *R.t.* 97 min. *MPAA* PG-13. *Cast:* Tom Hanks, Christina Marsillach, Benedict Taylor, Anat Atzmon, Gila Almagor, Moni Moshanov, Avner Hizkiyahu, Caroline Goodall, Esther Parnass, Daphne Armony, Orit Weisman.

This heartwarming, often humorous film is a tale of star-crossed lovers set in Jerusalem, 1942. Tom Hanks plays an American pilot who falls in love with a girl from a Sephardic Jewish family.

EXTREMITIES

Pro. Burt Sugarman; Atlantic Releasing Corporation *Dir.* Robert M. Young *Scr.* William Mastrosimone *Cine.* Curtis Clark *Ed.* Arthur Coburn *Mu.* J. A. C. Redford *P.d.* Chester Kaczenski *R.t.* 90 min. *MPAA* R. *Cast:* Farrah Fawcett, James Russo, Diana Scarwid, Alfre Woodard, Sandy Martin, Eddie Velez, Tom Everett, Donna Lynn Leavy, Enid Kent.

When the man who raped her and stole her wallet invades her home and begins brutalizing and humiliating her, Marjorie is able suddenly to gain the advantage, and she hysterically begins to punish him by subjecting him to the same sort of fear that she has undergone.

EYE OF THE TIGER

Pro. Tony Scotti; Scotti Bros. *Dir.* Richard Sarafian *Scr.* Michael Montgomery *Cine.* Peter Lyons Collister *Ed.* Greg Prange *A.d.* Wayne Springfield *S.d.* Kurt Gauger *R.t.* 90 min. *MPAA* R. *Cast:* Gary Busey, Yaphet Kotto, Seymour Cassel, Bert Remsen, William Smith, Kimberlin Ann Brown, Denise Galik, Judith Barsi, Eric Bolles, Joe Brooks.

A man who has spent time in prison on a false murder charge returns to his small town and seeks revenge on a group of evil motorcyclists who killed his wife after he prevented them from raping a nurse.

FAREWELL ILLUSION (*Adjø, Solidaritet.* Norway, 1985)

Pro. Mefistofilm; International Home Cinema *Dir.* Svend Wam, Petter Vennerod *Scr.* Svend Wam, Petter Vennerod *Cine.* Philip Ogaard *Ed.* Inge-Lise Langfeldt *Mu.* Svein Gunderson *R.t.* 100 min. *Cast:* Svein Sturla Hungnes, Knut Husebo, Jorunn Kjellsby, Wenche Foss, Thomas Foss, Thomas Robsahm, Bjorn Skagestad, Per Frisch, Ellen Horn, Per Sunderland.

The lives of the Norwegian middle class are circumscribed by the rigidity of the economic structure.

FAST TALKING (Australia, 1984)
Pro. Ross Matthews; Cinecom International *Dir.* Ken Cameron *Scr.* Ken Cameron *Cine.* David Gribble *Ed.* David Huggett *Mu.* Sharon Calcraft *P.d.* Neil Angwin *R.t.* 93 min. *Cast:* Rod Zuanic, Toni Allaylis, Chris Truswell, Gail Sweeny, Steve Bisley, Peter Hehir, Tracy Mann, Denis Moore.

With an abusive father, a drug-selling brother, and a runaway mother, Steve Carson seems to have little chance of escaping his life of petty crime, despite the encouragement of his friend Redback, a former convict.

FEMMES DE PERSONNE (France, 1984)
Pro. T. Films, F.R.3; European Classics *Dir.* Christopher Frank *Scr.* Christopher Frank *Cine.* Jean Tournier *Ed.* Nathalie Lafaurie *Mu.* Georges Delerue *P.d.* Philippe Lievre *R.t.* 106 min. *Cast:* Marthe Keller, Jean-Louis Trintignant, Caroline Cellier, Fanny Cottencon, Philippe Léotard, Patrick Chesnais, Elisabeth Etienne, Pierre Arditi, Marcel Bozonnet, Yvette Delauné, Karol Zuber.

This film depicts the lives of four independent and successful women who nevertheless are lonely and desperately searching for love.

A FINE MESS
Pro. Tony Adams; Columbia Pictures *Dir.* Blake Edwards *Scr.* Blake Edwards *Cine.* Harry Stradling *Ed.* John F. Burnett *Mu.* Henry Mancini *P.d.* Rodger Maus *R.t.* 88 min. *MPAA* PG. *Cast:* Ted Danson, Howie Mandel, Richard Mulligan, Stuart Margolin, Maria Conchita Alonso, Jennifer Edwards, Paul Sorvino.

Spence overhears the conversation of two gangsters as they drug a racehorse, and soon he and his friend are being chased all over Los Angeles by the crooks.

FIRE WITH FIRE
Pro. Gary Nardino; Paramount Pictures *Dir.* Duncan Gibbins *Scr.* Bill Phillips, Warren Skaaren, Paul Boorstin, Sharon Boorstin *Cine.* Hiro Narita *Ed.* Peter Berger *Mu.* Howard Shore *Pd.* Norman Newberry *A.d.* Michael Bolton *S.d.* Rondi Johnson *R.t.* 104 min. *MPAA* PG-13. *Cast:* Craig Sheffer, Virginia Madsen, Jon Polito, Jeffrey Jay Cohen, Kate Reid, Jean Smart, Tim Russ.

A juvenile prison inmate and a student at a Catholic boarding school fall in love and attempt to escape their situations.

FIREWALKER
Pro. Menahem Golan, Yoram Globus; Cannon Group *Dir.* J. Lee Thompson *Scr.* Robert Gosnell *Cine.* Alex Phillips *Ed.* Richard Marx *Mu.* Gary Chang *S.d.* Kleomenes Stamatiades *R.t.* 104 min. *MPAA* PG. *Cast:* Chuck Norris, Louis Gossett, Jr., Melody Anderson, Will Sampson, Sonny Landham, John Rhys-Davies, Ian Abercrombie.

Two men, one a martial-arts expert, are asked to accompany a woman on a search for the treasure of an Aztec temple.

FLIGHT OF THE NAVIGATOR
Pro. Robby Wald, Dimitri Villard; Buena Vista *Dir.* Randal Kleiser *Scr.* Michael Burton, Matt MacManus *Cine.* James Glennon *Ed.* Jeff Gourson *Mu.* Alan Silvestri *P.d.* William J. Creber *A.d.* Michael Novotny *S.d.* Scott Jacobson *R.t.* 88 min. *MPAA* PG. *Cast:* Joey Cramer, Veronica Cartwright, Cliff De Young, Sarah Jessica Parker, Matt Adler, Howard Hesseman, Paul Mall, Robert Small, Albie Whitaker, Jonathan Sanger, Iris Acker, Richard Liberty.

Young David Freeman is picked up by an extraterrestrial spaceship and serves as its navigator until he is returned to Earth. Although eight years have passed, it has been only a moment for David, and he does not remember the experience until NASA scientists take an interest in him and the spaceship returns for his help.

FOREIGN BODY (Great Britain, 1986)
Pro. Colin M. Brewer; Orion Pictures *Dir.* Ronald Neame *Scr.* Celine La Freniere *Cine.* Ronnie Taylor *Ed.* Andrew Nelson *Mu.* Ken Howard *P.d.* Roy Stannard *R.t.* 100 min. *MPAA* PG-13. *Cast:* Victor Banerjee, Warren Mitchell, Geraldine McEwan, Denis Quilley, Amanda Donohoe, Eve Ferret, Anna Massey, Stratford Johns, Trevor Howard, Jane Laurie, Rashid Karapiet.

Ram Das travels to London from Calcutta on false seaman's papers, and once there, he begins to practice as a doctor, treating eventually the prime minister himself.

FOXTRAP (Italy and USA)
Pro. Fred Williamson; Snizzlefritz Distribution *Dir.* Fred Williamson *Scr.* Aubrey K. Rattan *Cine.* John Stephens, Steve Shaw *Ed.* Giorgio Venturoli *Mu.* Patrizio Fariselli *R.t.* 88 min. *MPAA* R. *Cast:* Fred Williamson, Chris Connelly, Arlene Golonka, Donna Owen, Beatrice Palme, Cleo Sebastian, Lela Rochon.

A bodyguard takes the assignment of finding a missing woman and discovers that his employer is involved in drugs and prostitution.

FREE RIDE
Pro. Tom Boutross, Bassem Abdallah; Galaxy International *Dir.* Tom Trbovich *Scr.* Ronald Z. Wang, Lee Fulkerson, Robert Bell *Cine.* Paul Lohman *Ed.* Ron Honthaner *A.d.* Daniel Webster *S.d.* Joe Mirvis *MPAA* R. *Cast:* Gary Hershberger, Reed Rudy, Dawn Schneider, Peter DeLuise, Brian MacGregor, Warren Berlinger, Mamie Van Doren.

A teenager and his new girlfriend try to outsmart the mob when the boy accidentally finds a large amount of money.

FRENCH LESSON (Great Britain, 1986)
Pro. Iain Smith; Warner Bros. *Dir.* Brian Gilbert *Scr.* Posy Simmonds *Cine.* Clive Tickner *Ed.* Jim Clark *Mu.* Enya Ni Bhraonain *A.d.* Anton Furst *R.t.* 90 min. *MPAA* PG. *Cast:* Jane Snowden, Alexandre Sterling, Diana Blackburn, Oystein Wiik, Jacqueline Doyen, Raoul Delfosse.

An English teenager sent to learn French in Paris learns much more.

FRIDAY THE THIRTEENTH, PART VI: JASON LIVES
Pro. Don Behrns; Paramount Pictures *Dir.* Tom McLoughlin *Scr.* Tom McLoughlin *Cine.* Jon R. Kranhouse *Ed.* Bruce Green *Mu.* Harry Manfredini *P.d.* Joseph T. Garrity *A.d.* Pat Tagliaferro *S.d.* Jerie Kelter *R.t.* 87 min. *MPAA* R. *Cast:* Thom Mathews, Jennifer Cooke, David Kagen, Kerry Noonan, Renee Jones, Tom Fridley, C. J. Graham, Darcy DeMoss, Vincent Guastaferro, Tony Goldwyn, Nancy McLoughlin, Ron Palillo.

Lightning strikes the dead body of Jason, the psychopathic killer, and reanimates him, and he begins another series of gruesome murders.

FROM BEYOND
Pro. Brian Yuzna; Empire Pictures *Dir.* Stuart Gordon *Scr.* Dennis Paoli; based on a story by H.P. Lovecraft *Cine.* Mac Ahlberg *Ed.* Lee Percy *Mu.* Richard Band *Pd.* Giovanni Natalucci *S.d.* Robert Burns *R.t.* 85 min. *MPAA* R. *Cast:* Jeffrey Combs, Barbara Crampton, Ted Sorel, Ken Foree, Carolyn Purdy-Gordon, Bunny

Summers, Bruce McGuire.

A scientist is killed by a creature from the fourth dimension that has passed through his invention; his assistant and a psychiatrist investigate.

GETTING EVEN

Pro. J. Michael Liddle; American Distribution Group *Dir.* Dwight H. Little *Scr.* M. Phil Senini, Eddie Desmond *Cine.* Peter Lyons Collister *Ed.* Charles Bornstein *Mu.* Christopher Young *Pd.* Richard James *S.d.* Derek Hill *R.t.* 90 min. *MPAA* R. *Cast:* Edward Albert, Audrey Landers, Joe Don Baker, Rod Pilloud, Billy Streater.

The head of a chemical company must work quickly when the city of Dallas becomes a hostage to a man who has stolen a canister of poison gas.

THE GIG

Pro. Norman I. Cohen; Castle Hill *Dir.* Frank D. Gilroy *Scr.* Frank D. Gilroy *Cine.* Jeri Sopanen *Ed.* Rick Shane *R.t.* 95 min. *MPAA* PG-13. *Cast:* Wayne Rogers, Cleavon Little, Joe Silver, Andrew Duncan, Jerry Matz, Daniel Nalbach, Warren Vache, Jay Thomas.

A group of middle-aged men who informally play Dixieland jazz together get a gig at a resort—their first paying job in the music business.

THE GIRL IN THE PICTURE (Scotland, 1986)

Pro. Paddy Higson; Samuel Goldwyn Company *Dir.* Cary Parker *Scr.* Cary Parker *Cine.* Dick Pope *Ed.* Bert Eeles *P.d.* Gemma Jackson *R.t.* 90 min. *MPAA* PG-13. *Cast:* John Gordon-Sinclair, Irina Brook, David McKay, Gregor Fisher, Caroline Guthrie, Paul Young, Rikki Fulton, Simone Lahbib, Helen Pike, Joyce Deans.

A young Glasgow photographer realizes that he really does love his girlfriend after she has moved out, and he clumsily effects a reconciliation.

GIRLS SCHOOL SCREAMERS

Pro. John P. Finegan, Pierce J. Keating, James W. Finegan; Troma *Dir.* John P. Finegan *Scr.* John P. Finegan, Katie Keating, Pierce J. Keating *Cine.* Albert R. Jordan *Ed.* Thomas R. Rondinella *Mu.* John Hodian *R.t.* 82 min. *MPAA* R. *Cast:* Mollie O'Mara, Sharon Christopher, Mari Butler, Beth O'Malley, Karen Krevitz, Marcia Hinton, Monica Antonucci, Peter C. Cosimano, Vera Gallagher, Charles Braun, Tony Manzo, John Turner.

A group of Catholic school teenagers go to a haunted mansion to take inventory of art works.

GOBOTS: BATTLE OF THE ROCK LORDS

Pro. Kay Wright; Clubhouse Pictures *Dir.* Ray Patterson *Scr.* Jeff Segal *Ed.* Larry C. Cowan *R.t.* 75 min. *MPAA* G. *Voices:* Margot Kidder, Roddy McDowall, Michael Nouri, Telly Savalas.

In this animated film, the Gobots battle the evil Rock Lords and renegade Gobots in order to aid the oppressed Rock People.

THE GOODBYE PEOPLE

Pro. David V. Picker; Castle Hill Productions *Dir.* Herb Gardner *Scr.* Herb Gardner *Cine.* John Lindley *Ed.* Rich Shaine *P.d.* Tony Walton *R.t.* 105 min. *MPAA* PG. *Cast:* Judd Hirsch, Martin Balsam, Pamela Reed, Ron Silver, Michael Tucker, Gene Saks, Sammy Smith.

Three people drawn together during a Coney Island sunrise find in one another the strength to pursue their almost forgotten dreams.

GOSPEL ACCORDING TO VIC (Great Britain, 1986)
Pro. Michael Relph; Skouras *Dir.* Charles Gormley *Scr.* Charles Gormley *Cine.* Michael Coulter *Ed.* John Gow *Mu.* B. A. Robertson *P.d.* Rita McGurn *R.t.* 94 min. *MPAA* PG-13. *Cast:* Tom Conti, Helen Mirren, Brian Petlier, David Hayman. A teacher at a small Catholic school seems to be the focus of several miracles.

A GREAT WALL (China and USA, 1986)
Pro. Shirley Sun; Orion Classics *Dir.* Peter Wang *Scr.* Peter Wang, Shirley Sun *Cine.* Peter Stein, Robert Primes *Ed.* Graham Weinbren *Mu.* David Liang, Ge Ganru *R.t.* 97 min. *MPAA* PG. *Cast:* Peter Wang, Sharon Iwai, Kelvin Han Yee, Li Quinqin, Hu Xiaoguang, Shen Guanglan, Wang Xiao, Xiu Jian, Ran Zhijuan, Han Tan.

In this lighthearted comedy, a Chinese computer executive in San Francisco quits his job and returns to China with his American-born wife and son.

HAMBURGER
Pro. Edward S. Feldman, Charles Meeker; FM Entertainment *Dir.* Mike Marvin *Scr.* Donald Ross *Cine.* Karen Grossman *Ed.* Steve Schoenberg, Ann E. Mills *Mu.* Peter Bernstein *P.d.* George Costello *A.d.* Maria Rebman Caso *R.t.* 90 min. *MPAA* R. *Cast:* Leigh McCloskey, Dick Butkus, Randi Brooks, Chuck McCann, Jack Blessing, Charles Tyner, Debra Blee, Sandy Hackett, John Young, Chip McAllister, Barbara Whinnery, Maria Richwine, Karen Mayo-Chandler.

In order to get an inheritance, a college dropout must earn a college degree, so he enrolls at Busterburger University where he learns how to make hamburgers.

HARD CHOICES
Pro. Robert Mickelson; Lorimar *Dir.* Rick King *Scr.* Rick King *Cine.* Tom Hurwitz *Ed.* Don Loewenthal *Mu.* Jay Chattaway *R.t.* 90 min. *Cast:* Margaret Klenck, Gary McCleery, John Seitz, John Sayles, John Snyder, Martin Donovan, Larry Golden, Judson Camp, Wiley Reynolds III, Liane Curtis, J. T. Walsh, Spalding Gray, John Connolly, Ruth Miller, Tom McCleister.

A social worker assists in the escape from prison of one of her young clients.

HARD TRAVELING
Pro. Helen Garvy; New World Pictures *Dir.* Dan Bessie *Scr.* Dan Bessie *Cine.* David Myers *Ed.* Susan Heck *Mu.* Ernie Sheldon *R.t.* 95 min. *MPAA* PG. *Cast:* J. E. Freeman, Ellen Geer, Barry Corbin, James Gammon, Jim Haynie, W. Scott.

A drifter marries and is briefly happy, but, thrown out of work, he kills a businessman during a robbery and is tried for murder.

HARDBODIES II
Pro. Jeff Begun, Ken Solomon, Dimitri Logothetis; Cinetel Films *Dir.* Mark Griffiths *Scr.* Mark Griffiths, Curtis Scott Wilmot *Cine.* Tom Richmond *Ed.* Amy Blumenthal *Mu.* Jay Levy, Eddie Arkin *A.d.* Theodosis Davlos *R.t.* 88 min. *MPAA* R. *Cast:* Brad Zutaut, Sam Temeles, Curtis Scott Wilmot, Brenda Bakke, Fabiana Udenio, Louise Baker, James Karen, Alba Francesca, Sorells Pickard, Roberta Collins, Julie Rhodes, Alexi Mytones, George Tzifos, Ula Gavala, George Kotandis.

Three Americans go to Greece to work on a film and end up taking part in a variety of romantic and sexual encounters.

HAUNTED HONEYMOON
Pro. Susan Ruskin; Orion Pictures *Dir.* Gene Wilder *Scr.* Gene Wilder, Terence

Marsh *Cine.* Fred Schuler *Ed.* Christopher Greenbury *Mu.* John Morris *P.d.* Terence Marsh *A.d.* Alan Tomkins *S.d.* Michael Seirton *R.t.* 82 min. *MPAA* PG. *Cast:* Gene Wilder, Gilda Radner, Dom DeLuise, Jonathan Pryce, Paul L. Smith, Peter Vaughan, Bryan Pringle, Roger Ashton-Griffiths, Jim Carter, Eve Ferret, Julann Griffin, Jo Ross, Ann Way.

A man takes his fiancée to his ancestral home, there to be married, and a variety of mysterious and frightening things begin to happen.

HEAD OFFICE

Pro. Debra Hill; Tri-Star Pictures *Dir.* Ken Finkleman *Scr.* Ken Finkleman *Cine.* Gerald Hirschfeld *Ed.* Danford B. Greene, Bob Lederman *Mu.* James Newton Howard *Pd.* Elayne Barbara Ceder *A.d.* Gavin Mitchell *R.t.* 90 min. *MPAA* PG-13. *Cast:* Eddie Albert, Merritt Butrick, George Coe, Danny DeVito, Lori-Nan Engler, Ron Frazier, Ron James, John Kapelos, Don King, Richard Masur, Rick Moranis, Don Novello, Brian Doyle Murray, Michael O'Donoghue, Judge Reinhold, Jane Seymour, Wallace Shawn.

This film follows the employees of a large corporation, focusing on a young man who witnesses the incompetence and frantic opportunism of his colleagues.

HEATHCLIFF: THE MOVIE

Pro. Jean Chalopin; Atlantic Releasing Corporation *Dir.* Bruno Bianchi *Scr.* Alan Swayze *R.t.* 76 min. *MPAA* G. *Voice:* Mel Blanc.

In this animated film, Heathcliff the cat tells his nephews of his past exploits.

HIGHLANDER

Pro. Peter S. Davis, William Panzer; Twentieth Century-Fox *Dir.* Russell Mulcahy *Scr.* Gregory Widen, Peter Bellwood, Larry Ferguson *Cine.* Gerry Fisher *Ed.* Peter Honess *Mu.* Michael Kamen *P.d.* Allan Cameron *A.d.* Tim Hutchinson, Martin Atkinson *R.t.* 111 min. *MPAA* R. *Cast:* Christopher Lambert, Roxanne Hart, Clancy Brown, Sean Connery, Beatie Edney, Alan North, Sheila Gish, Jon Polito.

An immortal being battles other immortals over the course of five hundred years until he is the last one remaining.

THE HITCHER

Pro. Davie Bombyk, Kip Ohman; Tri-Star Pictures *Dir.* Robert Harmon *Scr.* Eric Red *Cine.* John Seale *Ed.* Frank J. Urioste *Mu.* Mark Isham *P.d.* Dennis Gassner *R.t.* 97 min. *MPAA* R. *Cast:* Rutger Hauer, C. Thomas Howell, Jennifer Jason Leigh, Jeffrey DeMunn.

Not until it is too late does a driver realize that the hitchhiker he has picked up is a psychopathic killer.

HOLLYWOOD IN TROUBLE

Pro. Joseph Mehri; J. M. Pro Film *Dir.* Joseph Mehri *Scr.* Joseph Mehri *Cine.* Bob Voze *Ed.* Reinhard Schreiner *Mu.* Richard Kosinski *R.t.* 93 min. *MPAA* PG-13. *Cast:* Vic Vallaro, Jerry Tiffe, Joan Le Vine, Jerry Cleary, R. W. Munchkin.

A man finances and directs a spoof of bad films with the money he has made in the pizza business.

HOLLYWOOD VICE SQUAD

Pro. Arnold Orgolini and Sandy Howard; Concorde/Cinema Group *Dir.* Penelope Spheeris *Scr.* James J. Docherty *Cine.* Joao Fernandes *Ed.* John Bowey *Mu.* Keith Levine, Michael Convertino *P.d.* Michael Corenblith *S.d.* Donna Stamps

R.t. 200 min. *MPAA* R. *Cast:* Ronny Cox, Frank Gorshin, Leon Isaac Kennedy, Trish Van DeVere, Carrie Fisher, Ben Frank, Evan Kim, Robin Wright, H. B. Haggerty, Joey Travolta, Cec Verrell, Julius W. Harris, Robert Miano, Marvin Kaplan.

A mother asks the captain of the police force to arrest the pimp for whom her runaway daughter works.

HOME OF THE BRAVE

Pro. Paula Mazur; Cinecom International Films *Dir.* Laurie Anderson *Scr.* Laurie Anderson *Cine.* John Lindley *Ed.* Lisa Day *Mu.* Laurie Anderson, Roma Baran *P.d.* David Gropman *A.d.* Perry Hoberman *R.t.* 90 min. *Cast:* Laurie Anderson, Joy Askew, Adrian Belew, Richard Landry, Dollette McDonald, Janice Pendarvis, Sang Won Park, David Van Tiegham, Jane Ira Bloom, Bill Obrecht, William S. Burroughs.

Performance artist Laurie Anderson and her band perform eighteen compositions in this film.

HOUSE

Pro. Sean S. Cunningham; New World Pictures *Dir.* Steve Miner *Scr.* Ethan Wiley *Cine.* Mac Ahlberg *Ed.* Michael N. Knue *Mu.* Harry Manfredini *Pd.* Gregg Fonseca *A.d.* John Reinhart *S.d.* Anne Huntley *R.t.* 92 min. *MPAA* R. *Cast:* William Katt, George Wendt, Richard Moll, Kay Lenz, Mary Stavin, Michael Ensign, Susan French, Eric Silver, Mark Silver.

A Vietnam veteran turned horror-story writer moves into his deceased aunt's spooky house and is visited by monsters.

HOWARD THE DUCK

Pro. Gloria Katz; Universal *Dir.* Willard Huyck *Scr.* Willard Huyck, Gloria Katz *Cine.* Richard H. Kline *Ed.* Michael Chandler, Sidney Wolinsky *Mu.* John Barry *P.d.* Peter Jamison *A.d.* Blake Russell, Mark Billerman *S.d.* Philip Abramson *R.t.* 111 min. *MPAA* PG. *Cast:* Lea Thompson, Jeffrey Jones, Tim Robbins, Ed Gale, Chip Zien, Tim Rose, Steve Sleap, Peter Baird, Mary Wells, Lisa Sturz, Jordan Prentice, Paul Guilfoyle, Tommy Swedlow, Liz Sagal.

Howard the Duck, who lives on a planet populated by ducks, is transported to Cleveland by a misdirected laser experiment that also unleashes the evil forces of the Dark Overlords of the Universe, from whom Howard must save a punk-rock singer who has befriended him.

THE IMAGEMAKER

Pro. Marilyn Weiner, Hal Weiner; Castle Hill Productions *Dir.* Hal Weiner *Scr.* Dick Goldberg, Hal Weiner *Cine.* Jacques Haitkin *Ed.* Terry Halle *Mu.* Fred Karns *P.d.* Edward Pisoni *A.d.* Russell Metheny *R.t.* 93 min. *Cast:* Michael Nouri, Anne Twomey, Jerry Orbach, Jessica Harper, Farley Granger, Richard Bauer, Roger Frazier, Maury Povich, Diana McLellan.

A political media consultant gets entangled in a complicated scheme to raise money for a film about the manipulation of the media.

IN THE SHADOW OF KILIMANJARO

Pro. Gautam Das, Jeffrey M. Sneller; Scotti Bros. Pictures *Dir.* Raju Patel *Scr.* Jeffrey M. Sneller, T. Michael Harry *Cine.* Jesus Elizondo *Ed.* Paul Rubell *Mu.* Arlon Ober *A.d.* Ron Foreman *R.t.* 97 min. *MPAA* R. *Cast:* John Rhys-Davies, Timothy Bottoms, Irene Miracle, Michele Carey, Leonard Trolley, Patty Foley, Cal-

vin Jung, Don Blakely, Jim Boeke, Patrick Gorman, Mark Walters, Carl Vundla.
Villagers in Kenya are threatened by baboons that begin to kill and eat them when their regular food supply dwindles as a result of a drought.

INVADERS FROM MARS

Pro. Menahem Golan, Yoram Globus; Cannon Films *Dir.* Tobe Hooper *Scr.* Dan O'Bannon, Don Jakoby *Cine.* Daniel Pearl *Ed.* Alin Jakubowicz *Mu.* Christopher Young *A.d.* Craig Stearns *R.t.* 100 min. *MPAA* PG. *Cast:* Karen Black, Hunter Carson, Timothy Bottoms, Laraine Newman, James Karen, Louise Fletcher, Bud Cort, Jimmy Hunt.

A little boy sees a spaceship land in his backyard, and soon his parents and others begin to act strangely. He persuades the school nurse to believe his story, and together they manage to get the marines to intervene.

IRON EAGLE

Pro. Ron Samuels, Joe Wizan; Tri-Star Pictures *Dir.* Sidney J. Furie *Scr.* Kevin Elders, Sidney J. Furie *Cine.* Adam Greenberg *Ed.* George Grenville *Mu.* Basil Poledouris *A.d.* Robb Wilson King *R.t.* 119 min. *MPAA* PG-13. *Cast:* Louis Gossett, Jr., Jason Gedrick, David Suchet, Tim Thomerson, Larry B. Scott, Caroline Lagerfelt, Jerry Levine, Robbie Rist, Michael Bowen.

A teenage boy enlists the help of a veteran combat pilot to fly an unauthorized mission to a fictional Arab country where his father is being held captive.

JAKE SPEED

Pro. Andrew Lane, Wayne Crawford, William Fay; New World Pictures *Dir.* Andrew Lane *Scr.* Wayne Crawford, Andrew Lane *Cine.* Brian Loftus *Ed.* Fred Stafford *Mu.* Mark Snow *A.d.* Norman Baron *R.t.* 100 min. *MPAA* PG. *Cast:* Wayne Crawford, Dennis Christopher, Karen Kopins, John Hurt, Leon Ames, Donna Pescow, Roy London, Barry Primus, Monte Markham, Alan Shearman, Rebecca Ashley.

Jake Speed, a pulp novel hero, sets out to save a young American woman who has been kidnapped in Paris by a gang of white slavers.

JO JO DANCER, YOUR LIFE IS CALLING

Pro. Richard Pryor; Columbia Pictures *Dir.* Richard Pryor *Scr.* Rocco Urbisci, Paul Mooney, Richard Pryor *Cine.* John Alonzo *Ed.* Donn Cambern *Mu.* Herbie Hancock *P.d.* John De Cuir *S.d.* Cloudia *R.t.* 97 min. *MPAA* R. *Cast:* Richard Pryor, Debbie Allen, Art Evans, Fay Hauser, Barbara Williams, Carmen McRae, Paula Kelly, Diahnne Abbott, Scoey Mitchell, Billy Eckstine, E'lon Cox.

While he is being treated in the hospital for burns suffered from setting himself afire, Jo Jo Dancer reviews his life, from his troubled childhood to his rise to comedic stardom.

JUMPIN' JACK FLASH

Pro. Lawrence Gordon, Joel Silver; Twentieth Century-Fox *Dir.* Penny Marshall *Scr.* David H. Franzoni, J. W. Melville, Patricia Irving, Christopher Thompson *Cine.* Matthew F. Leonetti *Ed.* Mark Goldblatt *Mu.* Thomas Newman *P.d.* Robert Boyle *A.d.* Frank Richwood *S.d.* Donald Remacle *R.t.* 98 min. *MPAA* R. *Cast:* Whoopi Goldberg, Stephen Collins, John Wood, Carol Kane, Annie Potts, Peter Michael Goetz, Roscoe Lee Browne, Sara Botsford, Jeroen Krabbe, Vyto Ruginis, Jonathan Pryce, Jim Belushi.

A computer programmer working in the foreign exchange department of a banking firm somehow receives a message from a British spy imprisoned in an Eastern Bloc country. In an effort to help, she becomes involved in an espionage plot.

JUST BETWEEN FRIENDS

Pro. Edward Teets and Allan Burns; Orion Pictures *Dir.* Allan Burns *Scr.* Allan Burns *Cine.* Jordan Cronenweth *Ed.* Anne Goursaud *Mu.* Patrick Williams *P.d.* Sydney Z. Litwack *S.d.* Bruce Weintraub, Chris Butler *R.t.* 120 min. *MPAA* PG-13. *Cast:* Mary Tyler Moore, Ted Danson, Christine Lahti, Sam Waterston, Salome Jens, Susan Rinell, Timothy Gibbs, Diane Stilwell, James MacKnell.

Chip Davis involves himself in an adulterous affair with Sandy Dunlap, whose friendship with Holly Davis, Chip's wife, must survive Chip's death and Sandy's pregnancy with his child.

KILLER PARTY

Pro. Michael Lepiner; United Artists/Metro-Goldwyn Mayer *Dir.* William Fruet *Scr.* Barney Cohen *Cine.* John Lindley *Ed.* Eric Albertson *Mu.* John Beal *A.d.* Reuben Freed *S.d.* Enrico Campana *R.t.* 91 min. *MPAA* R. *Cast:* Martin Hewitt, Ralph Seymour, Elaine Wilkes, Paul Bartel, Sherry Willis-Bursh, Alicia Fleer, Woody Brown, Joanna Johnson, Terri Hawkes.

Three friends go through a harrowing sorority initiation.

KING KONG LIVES

Pro. Martha Schumacher; De Laurentiis Entertainment Group *Dir.* John Guillermin *Scr.* Ronald Shusett, Steven Pressfield *Cine.* Alec Mills *Ed.* Malcolm Cooke *Mu.* John Scott *P.d.* Peter Murton *A.d.* Fred Carter, Tony Reading, John Wood *S.d.* Hugh Scaife, Tantar LeViseur *R.t.* 105 min. *MPAA* PG-13. *Cast:* Peter Elliot, George Yiasomi, Brian Kerwin, Linda Hamilton, John Ashton, Peter Michael Goetz, Frank Maraden.

King Kong and Lady Kong escape to the wilderness and have a baby.

KNIGHTS OF THE CITY

Pro. Leon Isaac Kennedy, John C. Strong III; New World Pictures *Dir.* Dominic Orlando *Scr.* Leon Isaac Kennedy *Cine.* Rolf Kesterman *Ed.* John O'Connor, Nicholas Smith *Mu.* Misha Segal *R.t.* 88 min. *MPAA* R. *Cast:* Leon Isaac Kennedy, John Mengati, Nicholas Campbell, Jeff Moldovan, Stoney Jackson, Janine Turner, Michael Ansara.

Three gang members get a chance to exit their street life when they win a musical contest.

LABYRINTH

Pro. Eric Rattrag; Tri-Star Pictures *Dir.* Jim Henson *Scr.* Terry Jones *Cine.* Alex Thomson *Ed.* John Grover *Mu.* Trevor Jones *P.d.* Elliot Scott *A.d.* Roger Cain, Peter Howitt, Michael White, Terry Ackland-Snow *R.t.* 101 min. *MPAA* PG. *Cast:* David Bowie, Jennifer Connelly, Toby Froud, Shelly Thompson, Christopher Malcolm, Natalie Finland. *Voices:* Brian Henson, Rob Mills, David Shaughnessy, Timothy Bateson.

Fifteen-year-old Sarah must venture to the home of the Goblin King to rescue her baby brother.

THE LADIES CLUB

Pro. Nick J. Mileti, Paul Mason; New Line Cinema *Dir.* A. K. Allen *Scr.* Paul Mason, Fran Lewis Ebeling; based on the novel *Sisterhood* by Betty Black *Cine.* Adam Greenberg *Ed.* Marion Segal, Randall Torno *Mu.* Lalo Schifrin *A.d.* Stephen

Myles Berger *R.t.* 90 min. *MPAA* R. *Cast:* Karen Austin, Diana Scarwid, Christine Belford, Bruce Davison, Shera Danese, Beverly Todd, Marilyn Kagan, Kit McDonough, Arliss Howard, Randee Heller, Paul Carafotes, Nicholas Worth, Scott Lincoln.

This formulaic vigilante film depicts a band of rapists' victims who seek revenge.

LADY JANE

Pro. Peter Snell; Paramount Pictures *Dir.* Trevor Nunn *Scr.* David Edgar *Cine.* Douglas Slocombe *Ed.* Anne V. Coates *Mu.* Stephen Oliver *Pd.* Allan Cameron *A.d.* Fred Carter, Martyn Hebert *S.d.* Harry Cordwell *R.t.* 142 min. *MPAA* PG-13. *Cast:* Helena Bonham Carter, Cary Elwes, John Wood, Michael Hordern, Jill Bennett, Jane Lapotaire, Sara Kestelman, Patrick Stewart, Warren Saire, Joss Ackland, Ian Hogg, Lee Montague, Richard Vernon, David Waller, Richard Johnson, Pip Torrens, Matthew Guiness, Guy Henry, Andrew Bicknell.

Lady Jane Grey ruled for only nine days before Mary I took the throne.

LAST RESORT

Pro. Julie Corman; Concorde Cinema Group *Dir.* Zane Buzby *Scr.* Steve Zacharias, Jeff Buhai *Cine.* Stephen Katz, Alex Nepomniaschy *Ed.* Gregory Scherick *Mu.* Steve Nelson, Thom Sharp *P.d.* Curtis A. Schnell *A.d.* Colin Irwin *S.d.* Douglas Mowat *R.t.* 86 min. *MPAA* R. *Cast:* Charles Grodin, Robin Pearson Rose, John Ashton, Ellen Blake, Megan Mullally, Christopher Ames, Scott Nemes.

A Chicago family visits a Caribbean resort that turns out to be a sexually liberated spot on an island about to undergo a revolution.

LEGEND

Pro. Arnon Milchan; Universal *Dir.* Ridley Scott *Scr.* William Hjortsberg *Cine.* Alex Thomson *Ed.* Terry Rawlings *Mu.* Tangerine Dream *P.d.* Assheton Gordon *R.t.* 89 min. *MPAA* PG. *Cast:* Tom Cruise, Mia Sara, Tim Curry, David Bennent, Alice Playten, Billy Barty, Cork Hubbert, Peter O'Farrell, Kiran Shah, Annabelle Lanyon, Robert Picardo.

Two young innocents must face the Prince of Darkness and regain the stolen horn of one of the last two unicorns.

LIES (1984)

Pro. Ken Wheat, Jim Wheat, Shelby Herman; Sandstar *Dir.* Ken Wheat, Jim Wheat *Scr.* Ken Wheat, Jim Wheat *Cine.* Robert Ebinger *Ed.* Michael Ornstein *Mu.* Marc Donahue *A.d.* Christopher Henley *R.t.* 90 min. *MPAA* R. *Cast:* Ann Dusenberry, Gail Strickland, Bruce Davison, Clu Galagher, Terence Knox, Bert Remsen.

A young actress is drawn into a complicated plot concerning a woman who may or may not be dead.

THE LIGHTSHIP

Pro. Moritz Borman, Bill Benenson; Castle Hill *Dir.* Jerzy Skolimowski *Scr.* William Mai, David Taylor *Cine.* Charly Steinberger *Ed.* Barry Vince *P.d.* Holger Gross *R.t.* 90 min. *MPAA* PG-13. *Cast:* Robert Duvall, Klaus Maria Brandauer, Tom Bower, Robert Costanzo, Badja Djola, William Forsythe, Arliss Howard, Michael Lyndon, Tim Phillips.

The leader of a band of robbers and the captain of a ship the robbers have taken over hold a philosophical discussion.

LINK
Pro. Richard Franklin; Cannon *Dir.* Richard Franklin *Scr.* Everett DeRoche *Cine.* Mike Malloy *Ed.* Andrew London *Mu.* Jerry Goldsmith *P.d.* Norman Garwood *A.d.* Keith Pain *R.t.* 103 min. *MPAA* R. *Cast:* Terence Stamp, Elisabeth Shue, Steven Pinner, Richard Garnett, David O'Hara, Kevin Lloyd, Joe Belcher, Locke.

A researcher working with chimpanzees disappears, and his assistant discovers that an evil monkey is responsible for not only the disappearance but also several murders.

THE LONGSHOT
Pro. Lang Elliott; Orion Pictures *Dir.* Paul Bartel *Scr.* Tim Conway *Cine.* Robby Muller *Ed.* Alan Toomayan *Mu.* Charles Fox *A.d.* Joseph M. Altadoona *S.d.* Bob Schulenberg *R.t.* 89 min. *MPAA* PG-13. *Cast:* Tim Conway, Jack Weston, Harvey Korman, Ted Wass, Anne Meara, Jorge Cervera, Stella Stevens, George DiCenzo, Joseph Ruskin, Jonathan Winters.

Some pathetic racetrack aficionados unwittingly enter a race-fixing scheme.

LOOP HOLE (Great Britain, 1983)
Pro. David Korda, Julian Holloway; Almi Pictures *Dir.* John Quested *Scr.* Jonathan Hales *Cine.* Michael Reed *Ed.* Ralph Sheldon *Mu.* Lalo Schifrin *R.t.* 96 min. *Cast:* Albert Finney, Martin Sheen, Susannah York, Colin Blakely, Jonathan Pryce, Robert Morley.

A burglar asks an unemployed architect to help in the robbery of a highly secure bank.

LOOSE SCREWS
Pro. Maurice Smith; Concorde *Dir.* Rafal Zielinski *Scr.* Michael Cory *Cine.* Robin Miller *Ed.* Stephan Fanfara *Mu.* Fred Mollin *A.d.* Judith Lee *R.t.* 75 min. *MPAA* R. *Cast:* Bryan Genesse, Karen Wood, Alan Deveau, Jason Warren.

A group of teenagers are sent to a special school because of their misbehavior, and they vow to have as many sexual escapades as possible.

LOW BLOW
Pro. Leo Fong; Crown International Pictures *Dir.* Frank Harris *Scr.* Leo Fong *Cine.* Frank Harris *Ed.* Frank Harris *Mu.* Steve Amundsen *A.d.* Diane Stevenett *R.t.* 85 min. *MPAA* R. *Cast:* Leo Fong, Akosua Busia, Cameron Mitchell, Troy Donohue, Diane Stevenett, Stack Pierce, Patti Bowling.

A private investigator is hired to rescue a woman from a religious cult.

MALCOLM (Australia, 1986)
Pro. Nadia Tass, David Parker; Vestron Pictures *Dir.* Nadia Tass *Scr.* David Parker *Cine.* David Parker *Ed.* Ken Sallows *Mu.* The Penguin Cafe Orchestra *A.d.* Rob Perkins *R.t.* 90 min. *MPAA* PG-13. *Cast:* Colin Friels, John Hargreaves, Lindy Davies, Chris Haywood, Charles Tingwell, Beverly Phillips, Judith Stratford, Heather Mitchell, Katerina Tassopoulos.

A mechanically gifted young man is taken advantage of by his two boarders, who involve him in a robbery.

A MAN AND A WOMAN: TWENTY YEARS LATER (*Un Homme et une femme: Vingt ans déjà.* France, 1986)
Pro. Claude Lelouch; Warner Bros. *Dir.* Claude Lelouch *Scr.* Claude Lelouch, Pierre Uytterhoeven, Monique Lange, Jerome Tonerre *Cine.* Jean-Yves Le Mever *Ed.* Hugues Darmois *Mu.* Francis Lai *A.d.* Jacques Bufnoir *R.t.* 120 min. *MPAA*

PG. *Cast:* Anouk Aimée, Jean-Louis Trintignant, Richard Berry, Evelyne Bouix, Marie-Sophie Pochat, Patrick Polver D'Arvor, Philippe Leroy-Beaulieu, Charles Gerard, Antoine Sire, Andre Engel, Thierry Sabine, Robert Hossein, Tanya Lopert, Nicole Garcia.

Anne is a film producer who decides that her past love affair with a race-car driver would make a good film, and when she contacts him to ask permission to pursue the idea, their affair blossoms again.

MANHUNTER
Pro. Richard Roth; De Laurentiis Entertainment Group *Dir.* Michael Mann *Scr.* Michael Mann *Cine.* Dante Spinotti *Ed.* Dov Hoenig *Mu.* The Reds and Michael Rubini *P.d.* Mel Bourne *A.d.* Jack Blackman *R.t.* 118 min. *MPAA* R. *Cast:* William L. Petersen, Kim Greist, Joan Allen, Brian Cox, Dennis Farina, Stephen Lang, Tom Noonan.

A former FBI agent, who has the ability to anticipate the twisted logic of killers, is asked to return to the field to find a serial killer.

MAXIMUM OVERDRIVE
Pro. Martha Schumacher; De Laurentiis Entertainment Group *Dir.* Stephen King *Scr.* Stephen King *Cine.* Armando Nannuzzi *Ed.* Evan Lottman *Mu.* AC/DC *P.d.* Giorgio Postiglione *A.d.* Rod Schumacher *R.t.* 97 min. *MPAA* R. *Cast:* Emilio Estevez, Pat Hingle, Laura Harrington, Yeardley Smith, John Short, Ellen McElduff, J. C. Quinn, Christopher Murney, Holter Graham.

When the Earth passes through the tail of a rogue comet, mechanical devices begin to malfunction and start to threaten humans.

THE MEN'S CLUB
Pro. Howard Gottfried; Atlantic Releasing Corporation *Dir.* Peter Medak *Scr.* Leonard Michaels *Cine.* John Fleckenstein *Ed.* Cynthia Scheider, David Dresher, Bill Butler *Mu.* Lee Holdridge *P.d.* Ken Davis *A.d.* Laurence Bennett *S.d.* Thomas Lee Roysden *R.t.* 100 min. *MPAA* R. *Cast:* Roy Scheider, Frank Langella, Harvey Keitel, Treat Williams, Richard Jordan, David Dukes, Craig Wasson, Stockard Channing, Ann Wedgeworth, Jennifer Jason Leigh, Cindy Pickett, Ann Dusenberry, Penny Baker, Gina Gallegos, Claudia Cron, Rebecca Bush, Gwen Welles.

A group of men, most of them professionals, get together to talk about their relationships with women, and they end the night with a visit to a bordello.

MISS MARY (Argentina, 1986)
Pro. Lila Stantic; New World Pictures *Dir.* María Luisa Bemberg *Scr.* Jorge Goldenberg, María Luisa Bemberg *Cine.* Miguel Rodríguez *Ed.* Cesar D'Angiolillo *Mu.* Luis María Serra *R.t.* 100 min. *MPAA* R. *Cast:* Julie Christie, Nacha Guevara, Luisina Brando, Tato Pavlovsky, Gerardo Romano.

An English nanny observes an Argentinian family's sexual repression and politics.

MR. LOVE (Great Britain, 1986)
Pro. Susan Richards, Robin Douet; Warner Bros. *Dir.* Roy Battersby *Scr.* Kenneth Eastaugh *Cine.* Clive Tickner *Ed.* Alan J. Cumner-Price *Mu.* Willy Russell *R.t.* 92 min. *MPAA* PG-13. *Cast:* Barry Jackson, Maurice Denham, Margaret Tyzack, Christina Collier, Linda Marlowe, Helen Cotterill, Julia Deakin, Donal McCann, Marcia Warren, Tony Melody.

In this light comedy, a gardner's affection for women endears him to them.

MODERN GIRLS

Pro. Gary Goetzman; Atlantic Releasing Corporation *Dir.* Jerry Kramer *Scr.* Laurie Craig *Cine.* Karen Grossman *Ed.* Mitchell Sinoway *Mu.* Jay Levy, Ed Arkin *P.d.* Laurence Bennett *A.d.* Joel Lang *S.d.* Jill Ungar *R.t.* 82 min. *MPAA* PG-13. *Cast:* Daphne Zuniga, Virginia Madsen, Cynthia Gibb, Clayton Rohner, Chris Nash, Steve Shellen, Rick Overton, Quin Kessler, Pamela Springsteen.

This film depicts the nightclub-hopping adventures of three young women on a single evening.

THE MONEY PIT

Pro. Frank Marshall, Kathleen Kennedy, Art Levinson; Universal *Dir.* Richard Benjamin *Scr.* David Giler *Cine.* Gordon Willis *Ed.* Jacqueline Cambas *Mu.* Michel Colombier *P.d.* Patrizia Von Brandenstein *A.d.* Steve Graham *S.d.* George DeTitta, Sr. *R.t.* 91 min. *MPAA* PG. *Cast:* Tom Hanks, Shelley Long, Alexander Godunov, Maureen Stapleton, Joe Mantegna, Philip Bosco, Josh Mostel, Yakov Smirnoff, Carmine Caridi.

A couple who have bought a house for a remarkably low price find that it is in almost total disrepair.

MOUNTAINTOP MOTEL MASSACRE

Pro. Jim McCullough, Sr., Jim McCullough, Jr.; New World Pictures *Dir.* Jim McCullough, Sr. *Scr.* Jim McCullough, Jr. *Cine.* Joe Wilcots *Ed.* Mindy Daucus *Mu.* Ron Dilulio *R.t.* 95 min. *MPAA* R. *Cast:* Bill Thurman, Anna Chappell, Will Mitchel, Virginia Loridans, Major Brock, James Bradford, Amy Hill, Marian Jones, Greg Brazzel, Jill King, Rhonda Atwood.

A woman kills her daughter when she finds her worshipping Satan in the basement of their motel; then she goes completely berserk and tries to murder all the motel guests as well.

MURPHY'S LAW

Pro. Pancho Kohner; Cannon Group *Dir.* J. Lee Thompson *Scr.* Gail Morgan Hickman *Cine.* Alex Phillips *Ed.* Peter Lee Thompson, Charles Simmons *Mu.* Marc Donahue, Valentine McCallum *P.d.* William Cruise *S.d.* W. Brooke Wheeler *R.t.* 97 min. *MPAA* R. *Cast:* Charles Bronson, Kathleen Wilhoite, Carrie Snodgress, Robert F. Lyons, Richard Romanus, Angel Tompkins, Bill Henderson, James Luisi, Clifford A. Pellow, Janet MacLachman.

A woman escaped from a lunatic asylum frames the policeman who put her there for the murder of his former wife.

MY CHAUFFEUR

Pro. Marilyn J. Tenser; Crown International Pictures *Dir.* David Beaird *Scr.* David Beaird *Cine.* Harry Mathias *Ed.* Richard E. Westover *Mu.* Paul Hertzog *A.d.* C. J. Strawn *R.t.* 97 min. *MPAA* R. *Cast:* Deborah Foreman, Sam Jones, Sean McClory, Howard Hesseman, E. G. Marshall, Penn Jillette, Teller, John O'Leary, Julius Harris, Laurie Main, Stanley Brock, Jack Stryker, Vance Colvig.

A young woman is hired as a chauffeur into an all-male company, and she and the owner's son fall in love.

MY LITTLE PONY

Pro. Joe Bacal, Tom Griffin, Michael Joens; De Laurentiis Entertainment *Dir.* Michael Joens *Scr.* George Arthur Bloom *Mu.* Rob Walsh *R.t.* 89 min. *MPAA* G. *Voices:* Danny DeVito, Madeline Kahn, Cloris Leachman, Rhea Perlman, Tony

Randall, Tammy Amerson, Jon Bauman, Alice Playten.

In this animated film, ponies are threatened by a wicked witch and her daughters.

THE MYSTERY OF ALEXINA (*Mystère Alexina*. France, 1985)
Pro. René Féret; European Classics *Dir.* René Féret *Scr.* Jean Gruault, René Féret *Cine.* Bernard Zittermann *Ed.* Adriane Boeglin *Mu.* Anne-Marie Deschamps *R.t.* 86 min. *Cast:* Vuillemin, Valérie Stroh, Véronique Silver, Bernard Freyd, Marianne Basler, Pierre Vial, Philippe Clevenot, Isabelle Gruault, Lucienne Hamon, Michel Amphoux, Claude Bouchery, Olivier Sabran, Anne Cornaly.

A person who has been brought up as a woman discovers that she is really a man.

THE NAKED CAGE
Pro. Chris D. Nebe; Cannon Group *Dir.* Paul Nicholas *Scr.* Paul Nicholas *Cine.* Hal Trussell *Ed.* Anthony DiMarco *A.d.* Alex Hajdu *R.t.* 97 min. *MPAA* R. *Cast:* Shari Shattuck, Angel Tompkins, Lucinda Crosby, Christina Whitaker, Faith Minton, Stacey Shaffer, Nick Benedict, Lisa London, John Terlesky, Aude Charles, Angela Gibbs, Leslie Huntly, Carole Ita White, Seth Kaufman, Larry Gelman.

An innocent farm girl type working in a bank is framed on a bank-robbery charge and sent to prison, which proves to be a real eye-opener for her.

NATIVE SON
Pro. Diane Silver; Cinecom Pictures *Dir.* Jerrold Freedman *Scr.* Richard Wesley *Cine.* Thomas Burstyn *Ed.* Aaron Stell *Mu.* James Mtume *P.d.* Stephen Marsh *R.t.* 112 min. *MPAA* PG. *Cast:* Victor Love, Matt Dillon, Elizabeth McGovern, Geraldine Page, Oprah Winfrey, Akosua Busia, Carroll Baker, John McMartin.

A young black man accidentally kills his rich employer's daughter in this film based on the novel by Richard Wright.

NEVER TOO YOUNG TO DIE
Pro. Steven Paul; Paul Entertainment *Dir.* Gil Bettman *Scr.* Lorenzo Semple, Steven Paul, Anton Fritz, Gil Bettman *Cine.* David Worth *Ed.* Bill Anderson, Paul Seydor, Ned Humphreys *Mu.* Chip Taylor, Ralph Lane, Michael Kingsley, Iren Koster *P.d.* Dale Allan Pelton *A.d.* Dean Tschetter, Michelle Starbuck *S.d.* Deborah K. Evans, Carol Westcott *R.t.* 92 min. *MPAA* R. *Cast:* John Stamos, Vanity, Gene Simmons, George Lazenby, Peter Kwong, Ed Brock, John Anderson, Robert Englund.

An evil hermaphrodite sets out to poison the Los Angeles water supply.

NEXT SUMMER (*L'Été prochain*. France, 1986)
Pro. Alain Sarde; European Classics *Dir.* Nadine Trintignant *Scr.* Nadine Trintignant *Cine.* William Lubtchansky *Ed.* Marie-Josephe Yoyotte *Mu.* Phillipe Sarde *R.t.* 100 min. *Cast:* Fanny Ardant, Jean-Louis Trintignant, Claudia Cardinale, Philippe Noiret, Marie Trintignant, Jerome Ange.

Three generations of women experience love, betrayal, and self-discovery.

NIGHT OF THE CREEPS
Pro. Charles Gordon; Tri-Star Pictures *Dir.* Fred Dekker *Scr.* Fred Dekker *Cine.* Robert C. New *Ed.* Michael N. Knue *Mu.* Barry DeVorzon *P.d.* George Costello *A.d.* Maria Caso *R.t.* 88 min. *MPAA* R. *Cast:* Jason Lively, Jill Whitlow, Tom Atkins, Steve Marshall, Allan J. Kayser.

Two college freshmen who want to pledge a fraternity are ordered to place a dead body in a conspicuous place.

NINE AND A HALF WEEKS

Pro. Anthony Rufus Isaacs, Zalman King; Metro-Goldwyn-Mayer/United Artists *Dir.* Adrian Lyne *Scr.* Patricia Knop, Zalman King, Sarah Kernochan; based on a novel by Elizabeth McNeill *Cine.* Peter Biziou *Ed.* Tom Rolf, Caroline Biggerstaff *Mu.* Jack Nitzsche *Pd.* Ken Davis *A.d.* Linda Conaway-Parsloe *S.d.* Christian Kelly *R.t.* 113 min. *MPAA* R. *Cast:* Mickey Rourke, Kim Basinger, Margaret Whitton, David Margulies, Christine Baranski, Karen Young, William De Acutis, Dwight Weist, Roderick Cook.

A stockbroker and an art gallery manager are irresistibly drawn into a bizarre sexual affair.

NINETY DAYS (Canada, 1985)

Pro. David Wilson, Giles Walker; Cinecom International *Dir.* Giles Walker *Scr.* David Wilson, Giles Walker *Cine.* Andrew Kitzanuk *Ed.* David Wilson *Mu.* Richard Gresko *R.t.* 99 min. *Cast:* Stefan Wodoslawsky, Christine Pak, Sam Grana, Fernanda Tavares, Daisy De Bellefeuille.

Two men experience romantic difficulties: One has been left by both his wife and his mistress, the other is thinking of marrying a Korean mail-order bride.

NINJA TURF

Pro. Phillip Rhee; Ascot Entertainment Group *Dir.* Richard Park *Scr.* Simon Blake Hong *Cine.* David D. Kim, Mazimo Munzi *Ed.* Alex Chang *Mu.* Charles Pavlosky, Gary Falcone, Chris Stone *P.d.* David Moon Park *R.t.* 86 min. *MPAA* R. *Cast:* Jun Chong, Phillip Rhee, James Lew, Rosanna King, Bill Wallace, Dorin Mukama, Arlene Montano.

A kung-fu pro, who wishes to return to his homeland, gets mixed up in gang warfare.

NO MERCY

Pro. D. Constantine Conte; Tri-Star Pictures *Dir.* Richard Pearce *Scr.* James Carabatsos *Cine.* Michel Brault *Ed.* Jerry Greenberg, Bill Yahraus *Mu.* Alan Silvestri *P.d.* Patrizia Von Brandenstein *A.d.* Doug Draner *R.t.* 105 min. *MPAA* R. *Cast:* Richard Gere, Kim Basinger, Jeroen Krabbe, George Dzundza, Gary Basaraba.

A policeman follows the woman who is his only lead in the murder of his partner to the bayous of Louisiana.

NO RETREAT, NO SURRENDER

Pro. Ng See Yuen; New World Pictures *Dir.* Corey Yuen *Scr.* Keith W. Strandberg *Cine.* John Huneck, David Golia *Ed.* Alan Poon, Mark Pierce, James Melkonian, Dane Davis *Mu.* Paul Gilreath *R.t.* 83 min. *MPAA* PG-13 *Cast:* Kurt McKinney, Jean-Claude Van Damme, J. W. Fails, Kathie Sileno, Kim Tai Chong.

A boy harassed by bullies takes karate lessons and is soon able to take on the Russian karate champion.

NOBODY'S FOOL

Pro. James C. Katz, Jon S. Denny; Island Pictures *Dir.* Evelyn Purcell *Scr.* Beth Henley *Cine.* Mikhail Suslov *Ed.* Dennis Virkler *Mu.* James Newton Howard *P.d.* Jackson De Govia *A.d.* John R. Jensen *S.d.* Laurie Scott *R.t.* 107 min. *MPAA* PG-13. *Cast:* Rosanna Arquette, Eric Roberts, Mare Winningham, Jim Youngs, Louise Fletcher, Gwen Welles, Stephen Tobolowsky, Charlie Barnett.

A romance with a lighting technician from a visiting theatrical troupe brings a woman out of her depression and gives her a sense of self-worth.

NOMADS
Pro. George Pappas, Cassian Elwes; Atlantic Releasing Corporation *Dir.* John McTiernan *Scr.* John McTiernan *Cine.* Stephen Ramsey *Ed.* Michael Bateman *Mu.* Bill Conti *R.t.* 95 min. *MPAA* R. *Cast:* Pierce Brosnan, Lesley-Anne Down, Anna-Maria Montecelli, Adam Ant, Hector Mercado, Josie Cotton, Mary Woronov, Frank Doubleday, Frances Bay, Tim Wallace.

A doctor treating a dying French anthropologist absorbs and then relives the memories of his battle with hostile wandering spirits.

NOT QUITE PARADISE
Pro. Lewis Gilbert; New World Pictures *Dir.* Lewis Gilbert *Scr.* Paul Kember *Cine.* Tony Imi *Ed.* Alan Strachan *Mu.* Rondo Veneziano *P.d.* John Stoll *R.t.* 106 min. *MPAA* R. *Cast:* Sam Robards, Joanna Pacula, Ewan Stewart, Selina Cadell, Todd Graff, Kevin McNally, Bernard Strother.

A group of volunteers visiting Israel work on a kibbutz and confront problems in communal living, some hostility from their hosts, and the complications of friendship and love across cultural lines.

NOTHING IN COMMON
Pro. Alexandra Rose; Tri-Star Pictures *Dir.* Garry Marshall *Scr.* Rick Podell, Michael Preminger *Cine.* John Alonzo *Ed.* Glenn Farr *Mu.* Patrick Leonard *P.d.* Charles Rosen *S.d.* Jane Bogart *R.t.* 118 min. *MPAA* PG. *Cast:* Tom Hanks, Jackie Gleason, Eva Marie Saint, Hector Elizondo, Barry Corbin, Bess Armstrong, Sela Ward, John Kapelos, Carol Messing.

A womanizing, quick-witted, successful advertising executive must suddenly cope with the dissolution of his parents' marriage. In the process, he learns just how much he and his father, who cannot stand each other, are alike.

THE NUTCRACKER: THE MOTION PICTURE
Pro. Willard Carroll, Donald Kushner, Peter Locke, Thomas L. Wilhite; Atlantic Releasing Corporation *Dir.* Carroll Ballard *Scr.* E. T. A. Hoffmann; conceived by Kent Stowell, Maurice Sendak *Cine.* Stephen H. Burum *Ed.* John Nutt, Michael Silvers *Mu.* Pyotr Ilich Tchaikovsky *P.d.* Maurice Sendak *A.d.* Peter Horne *R.t.* 84 min. *MPAA* G. *Cast:* Hugh Bigney, Vanessa Sharp, Patricia Barker, Wade Walthall, Pacific Northwest Ballet Company.

This lovely film is a re-creation of the classic ballet and is about a young girl, who, in a dream, confronts her fears and hopes and meets her nutcracker prince.

OFF BEAT
Pro. Joe Roth, Harry Ufland; Touchstone Films *Dir.* Michael Dinner *Scr.* Mark Medoff *Cine.* Carlo di Palma *Ed.* Dede Allen, Angelo Corrao *Mu.* James Horner *P.d.* Woods MacKintosh *R.t.* 92 min. *MPAA* PG. *Cast:* Judge Reinhold, Meg Tilly, Cleavant Derricks, Joe Mantegna, Jacques d'Amboise, Amy Wright, John Turturro, James Tolkan, Julie Bovasso, Anthony Zerbe, Fred Gwynne, Harvey Keitel, Victor Argo.

A librarian subs for his police officer friend at the annual police-benefit dance auditions and falls for a policewoman in the show.

ON THE EDGE
Pro. Jeffrey Hayes, Rob Nilsson; Skouras Pictures *Dir.* Rob Nilsson *Scr.* Rob Nilsson *Cine.* Stefan Czapsky *Ed.* Richard Harkness, Bert Lovitt *R.t.* 86 min. *MPAA* PG-13. *Cast:* Bruce Dern, John Marley, Bill Bailey, Jim Haynie.

A runner, banned from racing and the Olympics for accepting financial assistance, returns home twenty years later to prepare for and run in a grueling mountainous course, learning in the process about individual achievement and the importance of group solidarity.

ON VALENTINES DAY

Pro. Lillian V. Foote, Calvin Skaggs; Cinecom International Films *Dir.* Ken Harrison *Scr.* Horton Foote; based on his play *Valentine's Day* *Cine.* George Tirl *Ed.* Nancy Baker *Mu.* Jonathan Sheffer *A.d.* Howard Cummings *S.d.* Donasu Schiller *R.t.* 105 min. *MPAA* PG. *Cast:* Hallie Foote, William Converse-Roberts, Michael Higgins, Steven Hill, Rochelle Oliver, Richard Jenkins, Carol Goodheart, Jeanne McCarthy, Horton Foote, Jr., Matthew Broderick, Irma Hall, Oskar Kelly, Bill McGhee, Tim Green, Peyton Park, Ed Holmes, Artist Thornton, Jack Gould.

Elizabeth and Horace, who eloped on Valentine's Day, 1917, reach a reconciliation with her parents and deal kindly with their eccentric neighbors in this portrait of everyday life in a small Texas town.

ONE CRAZY SUMMER

Pro. Michael Jaffe; Warner Bros. *Dir.* Savage Steve Holland *Scr.* Savage Steve Holland *Cine.* Isidore Mankofsky *Ed.* Alan Balsam *Mu.* Cory Lerios *P.d.* Herman Zimmerman *S.d.* Gary Moreno *R.t.* 93 min. *MPAA* PG. *Cast:* John Cusack, Demi Moore, Joel Murray, Curtis Armstrong, Bobcat Goldthwait, Tom Villard, Matt Mulhern, Mark Metcalf, William Hickey, Joe Flaherty, Kristen Goelz.

An aspiring young cartoonist helps a girl save her home from greedy developers, and they end up falling in love.

ONE MORE SATURDAY

Pro. Tora Laiter, Robert Kosberg, Jonathan Bernstein; Columbia Pictures *Dir.* Dennis Klein *Scr.* Al Franken, Tom Davis *Cine.* James Glennon *Ed.* Gregory Prange *Mu.* David McHugh *S.d.* Karen O'Hara *R.t.* 95 min. *MPAA* R. *Cast:* Tom Davis, Al Franken, Moira Harris, Frank Howard, Bess Meyer, Dave Reynolds, Chelcie Ross, Eric Saiet, Jessica Schwartz.

This film depicts the tedious Saturday night in a small Minnesota town.

OUT OF BOUNDS

Pro. Charles Fries, Mike Rosenfeld; Columbia Pictures *Dir.* Richard Tuggle *Scr.* Tony Kayden *Cine.* Bruce Surtees *Ed.* Kent Beyda *Mu.* Stewart Copeland *P.d.* Norman Newberry *S.d.* Cloudia *R.t.* 93 min. *MPAA* R. *Cast:* Anthony Michael Hall, Jenny Wright, Jeff Kober, Glynn Turman, Raymond J. Barry, Pepe Serna, Michelle Little, Jerry Levine, Ji-Tu Cumbuka, Kevin McCorkle, Linda Shayne, Maggie Gwinn, Ted Gehring, Allan Graf, Meatloaf.

A youth, traveling from Iowa to Los Angeles to visit relatives, accidentally picks up a bag at the airport that is filled with heroin, and he is subsequently pursued by the bag's owners and the police.

PARTISANS OF VILNA

Pro. Aviva Kempner; European Classics *Dir.* Josh Waletzky *Cine.* Danny Shnever *Ed.* Josh Waletzky *R.t.* 130 min.

This documentary tells the story of Jewish Resistance fighters in a town in Lithuania during World War II.

THE PATRIOT

Pro. Michael Bennett; Crown International Pictures *Dir.* Frank Harris *Scr.* Andy

Ruben, Katt Shea Ruben *Cine.* Frank Harris *Ed.* Richard E. Westover *Mu.* Jay Ferguson *A.d.* Brad Einhorn *S.d.* Tori Nourafshan *R.t.* 88 min. *MPAA* R. *Cast:* Gregg Henry, Simone Griffeth, Michael J. Pollard, Jeff Conaway, Stack Pierce, Leslie Nielsen, Glenn Withrow.

A former navy commando is asked to prevent a nuclear holocaust by finding and dismantling a bomb.

PIRATES (France)

Pro. Tarak Ben Ammar; Cannon Films *Dir.* Roman Polanski *Scr.* Gerard Brach, Roman Polanski *Cine.* Witold Sobocinski *Ed.* Herve de Luze, William Reynolds *Mu.* Philippe Sarde *A.d.* Pierre Guffroy *R.t.* 124 min. *MPAA* PG-13. *Cast:* Walter Matthau, Damien Thomas, Richard Pearson, Cris Campion, Charlotte Lewis, Olu Jacobs.

After spending four years on a desert island, a pirate is rescued by a Spanish galleon and promptly incites a mutiny, steals cargo, and kidnaps a woman.

PLACE OF WEEPING: A FILM ABOUT SOUTH AFRICA (South Africa, 1986)

Pro. Anant Singh; New World Pictures *Dir.* Darrell Roodt *Scr.* Darrell Roodt *Cine.* Paul Witte *Ed.* David Heitner *A.d.* Dave Barkharm *R.t.* 88 min. *MPAA* PG. *Cast:* James Whylie, Geina Mhlophe, Charles Comyn, Norman Coombes, Michelle du Toit, Ramolao Makhene, Patrick Shai.

When a black man is killed by a white farmer for stealing a chicken, the victim's sister wants to bring the farmer to justice. As this is not possible under the South African system, justice is accomplished by means of individual revenge.

PLAYING FOR KEEPS

Pro. Allan Brewer, Bob Weinstein, Harvey Weinstein; Universal *Dir.* Bob Weinstein, Harvey Weinstein *Scr.* Bob Weinstein, Harvey Weinstein, Jeremy Leven *Cine.* Eric Van Haren Noman *Ed.* Gary Karr, Sharon Ross *Mu.* George Acogny, Daniel Bechet *P.d.* Walderman Kalinowski *R.t.* 95 min. *MPAA* PG-13. *Cast:* Daniel Jordano, Matthew Penn, Leon W. Grant, Mary B. Ward, Marisa Tomei, Harold Gould, Jimmy Baio, Kim Hauser, Robert Milli, John Randolf Jones.

Three teenagers want to convert a dilapidated hotel into a nightclub-arcade for teenagers, but first they must battle with a corrupt council member who wants to use the site as a toxic waste dump.

POLICE (France, 1985)

Pro. Emmanuel Schlumberger; New Yorker Films *Dir.* Maurice Pialat *Scr.* Catherine Breillat, Sylvie Danton, Jacques Fieschi, Maurice Pialat *Cine.* Luciano Tovoli *Ed.* Yann Dedet, Helen Viard, Nathalie Letrosne *Mu.* Henryk Mikolaj Gorecki *R.t.* 113 min. *Cast:* Gérard Depardieu, Sophie Marceau, Richard Anconina, Pascale Rocard, Sandrine Bonnaire.

A policeman investigating a drug-smuggling ring run by Tunisian gangsters falls in love with one of their members.

POLICE ACADEMY III: BACK IN TRAINING

Pro. Paul Maslansky; Warner Bros. *Dir.* Jerry Paris *Scr.* Gene Quintano *Cine.* Robert Saad *Ed.* Bud Molin *Mu.* Robert Folk *P.d.* Trevor Williams *A.d.* Rhiley Fuller *S.d.* Sean Kirby *R.t.* 90 min. *MPAA* PG. *Cast:* Steve Guttenberg, Bubba Smith, David Graf, Michael Ramsey, Leslie Easterbrook, Art Metrano, Tim Kazurinsky, Bobcat Goldthwait, George Gaynes.

Competition arises between two police academies, as one must be shut down because of budgetary cuts.

POLTERGEIST II

Pro. Mark Victor, Michael Grais; Metro-Goldwyn-Mayer/ United Artists *Dir.* Brian Gibson *Scr.* Mark Victor, Michael Grais *Cine.* Andrew Laszlo *Ed.* Thom Noble *Mu.* Jerry Goldsmith *P.d.* Ted Haworth *S.d.* Roy Barnes, Greg Papalia *R.t.* 90 min. *MPAA* PG-13. *Cast:* Jobeth Williams, Craig T. Nelson, Heather O'Rourke, Oliver Robins, Zelda Rubinstein, Will Sampson, Julian Beck, Geraldine Fitzgerald, John P. Whitecloud, Noble Craig, Susan Peretz, Helen Boll, Kathy Jean Peters, Jaclyn Bernstein.

In this sequel to *Poltergeist,* the Freeling family is again plagued by menacing forces of supernatural evil.

P.O.W. THE ESCAPE

Pro. Menahem Golan, Yoram Globus; Cannon Group *Dir.* Gideon Amir *Scr.* Jeremy Lipp, James Bruner, Malcolm Barbour, John Langley *Cine.* Yechiel Ne'eman *Ed.* Marcus Manton *Mu.* David Storrs *P.d.* Marcia Hinds *R.t.* 90 min. *MPAA* R. *Cast:* David Carradine, Charles R. Floyd, Mako, Steve James, Phil Brock, Daniel Demorest, Tony Pierce, Steve Freedman, James Acheson, Rudy Daniels.

Colonel James Cooper is captured by the Vietnamese not long before the fall of Saigon. He strikes a deal with his captor, Captain Vinh: Vinh will help him and the other prisoners escape if Cooper will help him get to the United States.

POWER

Pro. Reene Schisgal, Mark Tarlov; Twentiety Century-Fox *Dir.* Sidney Lumet *Scr.* David Himmelstein *Cine.* Andrzej Bartkowiak *Ed.* Andrew Mondshein *Mu.* Cy Coleman *Pd.* Peter Larkin *A.d.* William Barclay *R.t.* 111 min. *MPAA* R. *Cast:* Richard Gere, Julie Christie, Gene Hackman, Kate Capshaw, Denzel Washington, E. G. Marshall, Beatrice Straight, Fritz Weaver, Michael Learned, J. T. Walsh, E. Katherine Kerr, Polly Rowles, Matt Salinger, Tom Mardirosian, Omar Torres.

The career of Pete St. John (Richard Gere), an enormously successful media consultant for political candidates, provides a vehicle for director Lumet's reflections on issues of money and morality in today's political campaigns.

PSYCHO III

Pro. Hilton A. Green; Universal *Dir.* Anthony Perkins *Scr.* Charles Edward Pogue *Cine.* Bruce Surtees *Ed.* David Blewitt *Mu.* Carter Burwell *P.d.* Henry Bumstead *S.d.* Mickey S. Michaels *R.t.* 93 min. *MPAA* R. *Cast:* Anthony Perkins, Diana Scarwid, Jeff Fahey, Roberta Maxwell, Hugh Gillin, Lee Garlington, Robert Alan Browne, Gary Bayer, Patience Cleveland, Juliette Cummins, Steve Guevara, Kay Heberle.

In *Psycho III,* Norman Bates again struggles with the conflict between his psychotic attachment to his mother and his affection for a woman who has come to stay at the motel after having accidentally caused the death of a nun while attempting suicide.

QUICKSILVER

Pro. Michael Rachmil, Daniel Melnick; Columbia Pictures *Dir.* Tom Donnelly *Scr.* Tom Donnelly *Cine.* Thomas Del Ruth *Ed.* Tom Rolf *Mu.* Tony Banks *P.d.* Charles Rosen *A.d.* James Shanahan *S.d.* Marvin March *R.t.* 101 min. *MPAA*

PG. *Cast:* Kevin Bacon, Jami Gertz, Paul Rodriguez, Rudy Ramos, Andrew Smith, Gerald S. O'Loughlin, Larry Fishburne, Louie Anderson, Whitney Kershaw, Charles McCaughan.

A brilliant stockbroker who seems to have lost his touch gives up his three-piece suit and becomes a bicycle messenger on the streets of San Francisco.

QUIET COOL
Pro. Robert Shaye, Gerald T. Olson; New Line Cinema *Dir.* Clay Borris *Scr.* Clay Borris, Susan Vercellino *Cine.* Jacques Haitkin *Ed.* Bob Brady *Mu.* Jay Ferguson *R.t.* 80 min. *MPAA* R. *Cast:* James Remar, Adam Coleman Howard, Daphne Ashbrook, Jared Martin, Nick Cassavetes, Fran Ryan.

A policeman joins with the son of a murdered couple to bring the killers to justice.

QUILOMBO (Brazil, 1984)
Pro. Augusto Arraes; New Yorker Films *Dir.* Carlos Diegues *Scr.* Carlos Diegues *Cine.* Lauro Escorel Filho *Ed.* Mair Tavares *Mu.* Gilberto Gil, Walid Salomao *S.d.* Luiz Carlos Ripper *R.t.* 114 min. *Cast:* Antonio Pompêo, Zezé Motta, Toni Tornado, Vera Fischer, Antonio Pitanga, Mauríco do Valle, Daniel Filho João Nogueira, Jorge Coutinho, Grande Otelo, Jofre Soares.

Quilombo tells the story of the Portuguese destruction of a free society that arose in seventeenth century Brazil in a mountainous region known as Quilombo dos Palmares, which served as a haven for escaped slaves, Indians, Jews, and poor whites.

RAD
Pro. Robert L. Levy; Tri-Star Pictures *Dir.* Hal Needham *Scr.* Sam Bernard, Geoffrey Edwards *Cine.* Richard Leiterman *Ed.* Carl Kress *Mu.* James Di Pasquale *A.d.* Shirley Inget *S.d.* Cindy Gordon, Clay Weiler, Grant S. Goodman *R.t.* 93 min. *MPAA* PG. *Cast:* Bill Allen, Lori Loughlin, Talia Shire, Ray Walston, Alfie Wise, Jack Weston, Bart Conner, Marta Kober, Jamie Clarke, Laura Jacoby.

A young boy enters a professional motorcross race that turns out to be rigged.

RADIOACTIVE DREAMS
Pro. Thomas Karnowski, Moctesuma Esparza; De Laurentiis Entertainment Group *Dir.* Albert Pyun *Scr.* Albert Pyun *Cine.* Charles Minsky *Ed.* Dennis O'Connor *Mu.* Pete Robinson *P.d.* Chester Kaczenski *A.d.* Chester Kaczenski *R.t.* 98 min. *MPAA* R. *Cast:* John Stockwell, Michael Dudikoff, Lisa Blount, George Kennedy, Don Murray, Michelle Little, Norbert Weisser, Paul Keller Galan, Demian Slade, Chris Andew.

Two men gain possession of the keys that will launch the only MX missile left after a holocaust, and they are pursued by various factions that want to control the world.

RAINY DAY FRIENDS
Pro. Tomi Barrett, Walter Boxer *Dir.* Gary Kent *Scr.* Gary Kent *Cine.* Ronald Garcia *Ed.* Peter Appleton *Mu.* Jimmie Haskell *R.t.* 105 min. *MPAA* R. *Cast:* Esai Morales, Chuck Bail, Janice Rule, Carrie Snodgrass, Lelia Goldoni, John Phillip Law, Tomi Barrett, Anne Betancourt.

A streetwise Mexican-American boy, dying of cancer, finds hope within himself and through his relationships with his doctor and with another cancer patient.

RATBOY
Pro. Fritz Manes; Warner Bros. *Dir.* Sondra Locke *Scr.* Rob Thompson *Cine.*

Bruce Surtees *Ed.* Joel Cox *Mu.* Lennie Niehaus *P.d.* Edward Carfagno *S.d.* Cloudia *R.t.* 104 min. *MPAA* PG-13. *Cast:* Sondra Locke, Robert Townsend, Christopher Hewett, Larry Hankin, Sydney Lassick, Gerrit Graham, Louie Anderson, S. L. Baird, Gordon Anderson, Billie Bird.

An opportunist discovers Ratboy, who is half human and half rat, and proceeds to cash in, via Hollywood, on this freak of nature.

RATE IT X

Pro. Lucy Winer, Paula de Koenigsberg, Lynn Campbell, Claudette Charbonnenu; Interama *Dir.* Lucy Winer, Paula de Koenigsberg *Cine.* Paula de Koenigsberg *Ed.* Lucy Winer *Mu.* Elizabeth Swados *R.t.* 95 min. *Cast:* Lucy Winer.

Rate It X is an excellent documentary that examines the underlying sexism behind such diverse activities as the advertising for an automatic teller machine and the baking of cakes in the shape of a woman's nude body.

RAW DEAL

Pro. Martha Schumacher; De Laurentiis Entertainment Group *Dir.* John Irvin *Scr.* Gary M. Devore, Norman Wexler *Cine.* Alex Thomson *Ed.* Anne V. Coates *Mu.* Cinemascore *P.d.* Giorgio Postiglione *A.d.* Maher Ahmad *S.d.* Hilton Rosemarin *R.t.* 97 min. *MPAA* R. *Cast:* Arnold Schwarzenegger, Kathryn Harrold, Sam Wanamaker, Paul Shenar, Robert Davi, Ed Lauter, Darren McGavin, Joe Regalbuto, Mordecai Lawner, Steven Hill, Blanche Baker.

A former FBI agent, who is now a sheriff in North Carolina, accepts an assignment to infiltrate a Chicago mob family and learn the identity of the family's government informant.

REBEL (Australia, 1985)

Pro. Phillip Emanuel; Vestron Pictures *Dir.* Michael Jenkins *Scr.* Michael Jenkins, Bob Herbert *Cine.* Peter James *Ed.* Michael Honey *Mu.* Chris Neal *P.d.* Brian Thomason *R.t.* 93 min. *MPAA* R. *Cast:* Matt Dillon, Debbie Byrne, Bryan Brown, Bill Hunter, Ray Barrett, Julie Nihill, John O'May, Kim Deacon, Isabelle Anderson, Sheree Da Costa, Joy Smithers.

A young soldier in World War II Australia, who has deserted from the army, falls in love with a nightclub singer. She hides him and then helps to smuggle him out of the war zone.

RECRUITS

Pro. Maurice Smith; Concorde Pictures *Dir.* Rafal Zielinski *Scr.* Charles Wiener, B. K. Roderick *Cine.* Peter Czerski *Ed.* Stephan Fanfara *Mu.* Steve Parsons *A.d.* Craig Richards *S.d.* Nick White *R.t.* 82 min. *MPAA* R. *Cast:* Steve Osmond, Doug Annear, Alan Deveau, John Canada Terrell, Lolita David, Tracey Tanner, Annie McAuley, Tony Travis, Mike McDonald.

A group of misfits are invited to join the police department in a plot to discredit the mayor, and they cause havoc during training.

REFORM SCHOOL GIRLS

Pro. Jack Cummins; New World Pictures *Dir.* Tom DeSimone *Scr.* Tom DeSimone *Cine.* Howard Wexler *Ed.* Michael Spence *Mu.* Tedra Gabriel *P.d.* Becky Block *S.d.* Tom Talbert *R.t.* 94 min. *MPAA* R. *Cast:* Linda Carol, Wendy O. Williams, Pat Ast, Sybil Danning, Charlotte McGinnis, Sherri Stoner, Denise Gordy, Laurie Schwartz, Tiffany Helm, Darcy DeMoss.

The new girl at the reform school refuses the advances of the corrupt, sadistic in-

mate who has battered into submission all the others at the school.
RESTLESS NATIVES (Great Britain, 1985)
Pro. Rick Stevenson; Orion Classics *Dir.* Michael Hoffman *Scr.* Ninian Dunnett
Cine. Oliver Stapleton *Ed.* Sean Barton *Mu.* Big Country, Stuart Adamson *R.t.* 90
min. *MPAA* PG. *Cast:* Vincent Friell, Joe Mullaney, Teri Lally, Ned Beatty, Rob-
ert Urquhart, Bernard Hill, Ann Scott-Jones.

Two young men become celebrities and even tourist attractions when they begin
holding up sightseeing buses with toy guns filled with sneezing powder.
SAVING GRACE
Pro. Herbert F. Solow; Columbia Pictures *Dir.* Robert M. Young *Scr.* Robert M.
Young, Richard Kramer, David S. Ward, Tom Conti *Cine.* Reynaldo Villalobos
Ed. Peter Zinner *Mu.* William Goldstein *A.d.* Giovanni Natalucci *R.t.* 112 min.
MPAA PG. *Cast:* Tom Conti, Giancarlo Giannini, Fernando Rey, Erland
Josephson, Patricia Mauceri, Donald Hewlett, Edward Olmos, Angelo Evans.

Pope Leo XIV mistakenly locks himself out of the Vatican garden while dressed in
civilian clothes and decides to visit, incognito, a small village, where he tries to re-
pair the aqueduct, bringing comfort to the villagers.
SAY YES
Pro. Rosemary Le Roy Layng, Larry Yust; CineTel Films *Dir.* Larry Yust *Scr.*
Larry Yust *Cine.* Isidore Mankofsky *Ed.* Margaret Morrison *S.d.* John Retsek
R.t. 88 min. *MPAA* PG-13. *Cast:* Lissa Layng, Art Hindle, Logan Ramsey, Jonathan Winters, Maryedith Burrell, Jacque Lynn Colton, Jensen Collier, Devon Er-
icson, Art La Fleur, Laurie Prange, Anne Ramsey, Paula Trueman.

A grandfather bequeaths $250 million to his playboy grandson if he marries before
his thirty-fifth birthday. When he is jilted at the altar, a frantic search for another
mate ensues.
SCORPION
Pro. William Riead; Crown International Pictures *Dir.* William Riead *Scr.* William
Riead *Cine.* Bill Philbin *Ed.* Gigi Coello *Mu.* Sean Murray *A.d.* Heather
Cameron *R.t.* 98 min. *MPAA* R. *Cast:* Tonny Tulleners, Don Murray, Robert Lo-
gan, Allen Williams, Kathryn Daley, Ross Elliott, John Anderson, Bart Braverman,
Thom McFadden, Bill Hayes, Adam Pearson.

A defense intelligence agent is assigned to protect an informant, and when the
informant and another agent are assassinated, he tracks down the murderers.
SEPARATE VACATIONS
Pro. Robert Lantos, Stephen J. Roth; RSL Entertainment *Dir.* Michael Anderson
Scr. Robert Kaufman *Cine.* François Protat *Ed.* Ron Wisman *P.d.* Csaba Kertesz
S.d. Murray Sumner *R.t.* 82 min. *MPAA* R. *Cast:* David Naughton, Jennifer
Dale, Mark Keyloun, Laurie Holden, Blanca Guerra, Suzie Almgren, Lally Cadeau,
Jackie Mahon, Lee-Max Walton, Jay Woodcroft, Tony Rosato, Colleen Embree.

A husband and wife take separate vacations in order to get away from each other
and the kids for awhile. Both are tempted by romantic affairs, but they remain
faithful.
SEVEN MINUTES IN HEAVEN
Pro. Fred Roos; Warner Bros. *Dir.* Linda Feferman *Scr.* Jane Bernstein, Linda
Feferman *Cine.* Steven Fierberg *Ed.* Marc Laub *Pd.* Vaughan Edwards *A.d.*
Thomas A. Walsh *S.d.* Deborah Schutt *R.t.* 90 min. *MPAA* PG-13. *Cast:* Jennifer

Connelly, Maddie Corman, Buron Thames, Alan Boyce, Polly Draper, Marshall Bell, Michael Zaslow, Denny Dillon, Margo Skinner, Matthew Lewis, Tim Waldrip, Billy Wirth, Paul Martel, Terry Kinney.

Three teenage friends attempt their first sexual and romantic explorations.

SHANGHAI SURPRISE

Pro. John Kohn; Metro-Goldwyn-Mayer *Dir.* Jim Goddard *Scr.* John Kohn, Robert Bentley *Cine.* Ernie Vincze *Ed.* Ralph Sheldon *Mu.* George Harrison, Michael Kamen *P.d.* Peter Mullins *A.d.* John Siddall, David Minty *R.t.* 93 min. *MPAA* PG-13. *Cast:* Sean Penn, Madonna, Paul Freeman, Richard Griffiths, Philip Sayer, Clyde Kusatsu, Kay Tong Lim, Sonserai Lee, Victor Wong.

A female missionary in China enlists the aid of an adventurer in helping her find some missing opium.

SHARMA AND BEYOND (Great Britain, 1986)

Pro. Chris Griffin; Cinecom International Films *Dir.* Brian Gilbert *Scr.* Brian Gilbert *Cine.* Ernest Vincze *Ed.* Max Lemon *Mu.* Rachel Portman *A.d.* Maurice Cain *R.t.* 83 min. *Cast:* Suzanne Burden, Robert Urquhart, Michael Maloney, Antonia Pemberton, Benjamin Whitrow, Tom Wilkinson.

Stephen, an English teacher, courts Natasha, daughter of the science-fiction novelist whom he idolizes; she cannot decide whether Stephen is pursuing her in order to get close to her father.

SHORT CIRCUIT

Pro. David Foster, Lawrence Turman; Tri-Star Pictures *Dir.* John Badham *Scr.* S. S. Wilson, Brent Maddock *Cine.* Nick McLean *Ed.* Frank Morriss *Mu.* David Shire *A.d.* Dianne Wager *R.t.* 99 min. *MPAA* PG. *Cast:* Ally Sheedy, Steve Guttenberg, Fisher Stevens, Austin Pendleton, G. W. Bailey, Brian McNamara, Marvin McIntyre, John Garber, Penny Stanton, Vernon Weddle, Barbara Tarbuck, Tom Lawrence, Fred Slyter, Billy Ray Sharkey. *Voice:* Tim Blaney.

A robot, which has been designed as a military weapon, begins to malfunction after being hit by lightning, and it leaves the military complex. The robot meets a young woman and begins to take on human characteristics after reading her books and watching television.

SIGNAL SEVEN

Pro. Don Taylor, Ben Myron *Dir.* Rob Nilsson *Scr.* Rob Nilsson *Cine.* Geoff Schaaf, Tomas Tucker *Ed.* Richard Harkness *Mu.* Andy Narell *R.t.* 92 min. *Cast:* Bill Ackridge, Dan Leegant, John Tidwell, Herb Mills, Don Bajema, Phil Polakoff, Don Defina, Frank Triest, Jack Tucker, David Schickele, Paul Prince.

This excellent small film follows the events of two taxi drivers on one rainy San Francisco night as they take fares, deal with the murder of a fellow driver, audition for a play, and move toward self-awareness.

SINCERELY CHARLOTTE (*Signe Charlotte*. France, 1984)

Pro. Les Films de la Tour, FR3; New Line Cinema *Dir.* Caroline Huppert *Scr.* Caroline Huppert, Luc Beraud, Joelle Goron *Cine.* Bruno de Keyzer *Ed.* Anne Boissel *R.t.* 92 min. *Cast:* Isabelle Huppert, Niels Arestrup, Christine Pascal, Nicolas Wostrikoff, Jean-Michel Ribes, Philippe Delevingne, Laurence Mercier.

A woman, Charlotte, asks a former lover, Mathieu, to help her when she is being chased by the police as a suspect in the murder of her last boyfriend. Mathieu falls back in love with Charlotte and leaves his fiancée.

SIXTEEN DAYS OF GLORY

Pro. Bud Greenspan; Paramount Pictures *Dir.* Bud Greenspan *Scr.* Bud Greenspan *Cine.* Robert E. Collins, Gil Hubbs, Michael D. Margulies, Robert Primes *Ed.* Andrew Squicciarini *Mu.* Lee Holdridge *R.t.* 145 min. *MPAA* G. *Cast:* David Perry, Joan Benoit, Rowdy Gaines, Michael Gross, Juergen Hingsen, John Moffett, Dave Moorcroft, Edwin Moses, Mary Lou Retton, Ecaterina Szabo, Daley Thompson, Yasuhiro Yamashita, Grete Waitz.

This film is a documentary about the 1984 Olympic Games held in Los Angeles.

SKY BANDITS (*Gunbus.* Great Britain, 1986)

Pro. Richard Herland; Galaxy International Releasing *Dir.* Zoran Perisic *Scr.* Thom Keyes *Cine.* David Watkin *Ed.* Peter Tanner *Mu.* Alfie Kabiljo *P.d.* Tony Woollard *A.d.* Malcolm Stone, John Siddall, Jose Maria Taprador *S.d.* Hugh Scaife *R.t.* 93 min. *MPAA* PG. *Cast:* Scott McGinnis, Jeff Osterhage, Ronald Lacey, Miles Anderson, Valerie Steffen.

Two young bank robbers are sent to France to fight in a flying corps whose mission is to destroy a German zeppelin.

SOLARBABIES

Pro. Irene Walzer, Jack Frost Sanders; Metro-Goldwyn-Mayer/United Artists *Dir.* Alan Johnson *Scr.* Walon Green, Douglas Anthony Metrov *Cine.* Peter Mac-Donald *Ed.* Conrad Buff *Mu.* Maurice Jarre *P.d.* Anthony Pratt *A.d.* Don Dossett *S.d.* Graham Sumner *R.t.* 94 min. *MPAA* PG-13. *Cast:* Richard Jordan, Jami Gertz, Jason Patric, Lukas Haas, James Le Gros, Claude Brooks, Peter DeLuise, Peter Kowanko, Adrian Pasdar, Sarah Douglas, Charles Durning.

A group of orphaned children living in a futuristic, drought-ridden world find a round ball, which turns out to be a kindly extraterrestrial. When the orb is stolen, the children plot to get it back.

SOUL MAN

Pro. Steve Tisch; New World Pictures *Dir.* Steve Miner *Scr.* Carol Black *Cine.* Jeffrey Jur *Ed.* David Finfer *Mu.* Tom Scott *P.d.* Gregg Fonseca *A.d.* Don Diers *S.d.* Dorree Cooper *R.t.* 101 min. *MPAA* PG-13. *Cast:* C. Thomas Howell, Arye Gross, Rae Dawn Chong, James Earl Jones, Melora Hardin, Leslie Nielsen, James B. Sikking.

A white boy takes an overdose of tanning pills to seem eligible for a Harvard Law School scholarship for blacks. He obtains it and learns about racism.

SPACECAMP

Pro. Patrick Bailey, Walter Coblenz; Twentieth Century-Fox *Dir.* Harry Winer *Scr.* W. W. Wicket, Casey T. Mitchell *Cine.* William Fraker *Ed.* John W. Wheeler, Timothy Board *Mu.* John Williams *P.d.* Richard MacDonald *A.d.* Richard J. Lawrence, Leon Harris *S.d.* Richard C. Goddard *R.t.* 107 min. *MPAA* PG. *Cast:* Kate Capshaw, Lea Thompson, Kelly Preston, Larry B. Scott, Leaf Phoenix, Tate Donovan, Tom Skerritt, Barry Primus, Terry O'Quinn, Mitchell Anderson.

A group of teenagers at a summer space camp and their teacher-astronaut are accidentally launched into space by a literal-minded robot.

SPECIAL EFFECTS

Pro. Paul Kurta; New Line Cinema *Dir.* Larry Cohen *Scr.* Larry Cohen *Cine.* Paul Glickman *Ed.* Arnold Lebowitz *Mu.* Michael Minard *R.t.* 95 min. *MPAA* R. *Cast:* Zoe Tamarlis, Eric Bogosian, Brad Rijn, Kevin O'Connor, Bill Olland, Richard Greene.

On camera, a film director strangles an aspiring actress; he subsequently attempts to make her husband the culprit.

SPRING SYMPHONY (*Frühlingssinfonie*. Germany, 1983)
Pro. Allianz Filmproduktion and Peter Schamoni Film; Greentree Productions *Dir.* Peter Schamoni *Scr.* Peter Schamoni *Cine.* Gerard Vandenberg *Ed.* Elfie Tillack *Mu.* Robert Schumann *A.d.* Alfred Hirschmeier *R.t.* 106 min. *MPAA* PG-13. *Cast:* Nastassja Kinski, Herbert Grönemeyer, Rolf Hoppe, Anja-Christine Preussler, Edda Seippel, Andre Heller, Gideon Kremer, Bernard Wicki, Sonja Tuchmann, Margit Geissler, Uwe Müller.

Spring Symphony tells the story of the love and marriage of composer Robert Schumann and pianist Clara Wieck.

STEAMING
Pro. Paul Mills *Dir.* Joseph Losey *Scr.* Patricia Losey; based on a play by Nell Dunn *Cine.* Christopher Challis *Ed.* Reginald Beck *Mu.* Richard Harvey *R.t.* 95 min. *MPAA* R. *Cast:* Vanessa Redgrave, Sarah Miles, Diana Dors, Patti Love, Brenda Bruce, Felicity Dean, Sally Sagoe.

Several English women of diverse social backgrounds fight to prevent the closing of the public bathhouse where they meet every week to bare their souls as well as their bodies.

STREETS OF GOLD
Pro. Joe Roth, Harry Ufland; Twentieth Century-Fox *Dir.* Joe Roth *Scr.* Heywood Gould, Richard Price, Tom Cole *Cine.* Arthur Albert *Ed.* Richard Chew *Mu.* Jack Nitzsche *P.d.* Marcos Flaksman *A.d.* Bill Pollock *S.d.* Victor Kempster *R.t.* 95 min. *MPAA* R. *Cast:* Klaus Maria Brandauer, Adrian Pasdar, Wesley Snipes, Angela Molina.

A Russian boxer, who was denied permission to compete because he is Jewish, emigrates to the United States and trains two street kids, who later fight the Russian team.

STRIPPER
Pro. Jerome Gary, Geof Bartz, Melvyn J. Estrin; Twentieth Century-Fox *Dir.* Jerome Gary *Cine.* Edward Lachman *Ed.* Geof Bartz, Bob Eisenhardt, Lawrence Silk *R.t.* 90 min. *MPAA* R. *Cast:* Janette Boyd, Sara Costa, Kimberly Holcomb, Loree Menton, Lisa Suarez, Ellen Claire McSweeney.

This documentary chronicles the lives of five women who have come to Las Vegas to compete at a strippers' convention.

SWEET LIBERTY
Pro. Martin Bregman; Universal *Dir.* Alan Alda *Scr.* Alan Alda *Cine.* Frank Tidy *Ed.* Michael Economou *Mu.* Bruce Broughton *P.d.* Ben Edwards *A.d.* Christopher Nowak *S.d.* John Alan Hicks *R.t.* 107 min. *MPAA* PG. *Cast:* Alan Alda, Michael Caine, Michelle Pfeiffer, Bob Hoskins, Lise Hilboldt, Lillian Gish, Saul Rubinek, Lois Chiles.

A history professor tries to prevent a film-production crew from completely distorting his book on the American Revolution.

TAI-PAN
Pro. Raffaella De Laurentiis; De Laurentiis Entertainment Group *Dir.* Daryl Duke *Scr.* John Briley, Stanley Mann; based on the novel by James Clavell *Cine.*

Jack Cardiff *Ed.* Antony Gibbs *Mu.* Maurice Jarre *P.d.* Tony Masters *A.d.* Benjamin Fernandez, Pierluigi Basile *S.d.* Giorgio Desideri *R.t.* 127 min. *MPAA* R. *Cast:* Bryan Brown, Joan Chen, John Stanton, Tom Guinee, Bill Leadbitter, Russell Wong, Katy Behan.

The Tai-Pan is thrown out of Canton by the Chinese emperor for trading opium, and he goes to Hong Kong, where his enemies threaten his preeminence.

TEA IN THE HAREM (*Le Thé au harem d'Archi Ahmed.* France, 1985) *Pro.* K.G. Production; Cinecom International *Dir.* Mehdi Charef *Scr.* Mehdi Charef *Cine.* Dominique Chapius *Ed.* Kenout Peltier *Mu.* Karim Kacel *R.t.* 100 min. *Cast:* Kader Boukanef, Remi Martin, Laure Duthilleul, Saida Bekkouche, Nicole Hiss, Brahim Ghenaiem, Nathalie Jadot, Frederic Ayivi, Pascal Dewaeme, Sandrine Dumas, Bourlem Guerdjou, Jean-Pierre Sobeaux.

This film depicts the friendship of two tough but goodhearted youths whose pastime is petty crime.

TERRORVISION
Pro. Albert Band; Empire Pictures *Dir.* Ted Nicolaou *Scr.* Ted Nicolaou *Cine.* Romano Albani *Ed.* Tom Meshelski *Mu.* Richard Band, The Fibonaccis *A.d.* Giovanni Natalucci *R.t.* 83 min. *MPAA* R. *Cast:* Diane Franklin, Gerrit Graham, Mary Woronov, Chad Allen, Jonathan Gries, Jennifer Richards, Alejandro Rey, Bert Remsen, Randi Brooks, Ian Patrick Williams, Sonny Carl Davis.

A monstrous alien, transported to Earth accidentally, lurks in the television sets of a zany family, emerging periodically to try to reduce family members to jelly.

THE TEXAS CHAINSAW MASSACRE, PART II
Pro. Menahem Golan, Yoram Globus; Cannon Group *Dir.* Tobe Hooper *Scr.* L. M. Kit Carson *Cine.* Richard Kooris *Ed.* Alain Jakubowicz *Mu.* Tobe Hooper, Jerry Lambert *P.d.* Cary White *A.d.* Daniel Miller *S.d.* Pat Welsome *R.t.* 95 min. *Cast:* Dennis Hopper, Caroline Williams, Bill Johnson, Jim Siedow, Bill Moseley, Lou Perry, Barry Kinyon, Chris Douridas.

In this sequel to *The Texas Chainsaw Massacre*, a family of butchers who make chili out of human flesh are pursued by Lieutenant Enright, whose family was killed by them.

THRASHIN'
Pro. Alan Sacks *Dir.* David Winters *Scr.* Paul Brown, Alan Sacks *Cine.* Chuck Colwell *Ed.* Lorenzo De Stefano, Nicholas Smith *Mu.* Barry Goldberg *A.d.* Katheryn Hardwick *R.t.* 92 min. *MPAA* PG-13. *Cast:* Josh Brolin, Robert Rusler, Chuck McCann, Pamela Gridley, Brooke McCarter, Jr., Josh Richman, Brett Marx, David Wagner.

An aspiring skateboard champion encounters trouble when he falls for the sister of his principal competitor.

THREE AMIGOS
Pro. Lorne Michaels, George Folsey, Jr.; Orion Pictures *Dir.* John Landis *Scr.* Steve Martin, Lorne Michaels, Randy Newman *Cine.* Ronald W. Browne *Ed.* Malcolm Campbell *Mu.* Elmer Bernstein *P.d.* Richard Sawyer *S.d.* Richard Goddard *R.t.* 105 min. *MPAA* PG. *Cast:* Chevy Chase, Steve Martin, Martin Short, Patrice Martinez, Alfonso Arau, Tony Plana, Joe Mantegna.

The Three Amigos, singing film stars, answer a poor Mexican woman's call for help, but they think that they are being invited to put on a show.

3:15

Pro. Dennis Brody, Robert Kenner; Dakota Entertainment *Dir.* Larry Gross *Scr.* Sam Bernard, Michael Jacobs *Cine.* Misha Suslov *Ed.* Steven Kemper *Mu.* Gary Chang *P.d.* Paul Ahrens *S.d.* Anne Huntley *R.t.* 85 min. *MPAA* R. *Cast:* Adam Baldwin, Deborah Foreman, Rene Auberjonois, Ed Lauter, Scott McGinnis, Danny De La Paz, John Scott Clough, Mario Van Peebles.

A boy must fight the head of the gang he used to belong to when he refuses to participate in drug-dealing activity at his high school.

THUNDER ALLEY

Pro. William R. Ewing *Dir.* J. S. Cardone *Scr.* J. S. Cardone *Cine.* Karen Grossman *Ed.* Daniel Wetherbee *Mu.* Robert Folk, Ken Topolsky *A.d.* Joseph T. Garrity *R.t.* 92 min. *MPAA* R. *Cast:* Roger Wilson, Jill Schoelen, Scott McGinnis, Cynthia Eilbacher, Clancy Brown, Leif Garrett, Phil Brock, Brian Cole, Randy Polk.

The rocky road to stardom is followed by a band of young rock musicians led by a wholesome, insecure farm boy.

TORMENT

Pro. Samson Aslanian, John Hopkins; New World Pictures *Dir.* Samson Aslanian, John Hopkins *Scr.* Samson Aslanian, John Hopkins *Cine.* Stephen Carpenter *Ed.* John Penney, Earl Ghaffari, Bret Shelton *Mu.* Christopher Young *A.d.* Chris Hopkins *R.t.* 85 min. *MPAA* R. *Cast:* Taylor Gilbert, William Witt, Eve Brenner, Warren Lincoln, Najean Cherry, Stan Weston, Doug Leach.

A psychopathic killer terrorizes the mother and girlfriend of the detective who is stalking him.

TOUCH AND GO

Pro. Stephen Friedman; Tri-Star Pictures *Dir.* Robert Mandel *Scr.* Alan Ormsby, Bob Sand, Harry Colomby *Cine.* Richard H. Kline *Ed.* Walt Mulconery *Mu.* Sylvester Levay *P.d.* Charles Rosen *S.d.* James Payne, Jean Alan *R.t.* 88 min. *MPAA* PG-13. *Cast:* Michael Keaton, Maria Conchita Alonso, Ajay Naidu, Maria Tucci, Max Wright, Lara Jill Miller, D.V. de Vincentis.

A hockey star falls in love with the mother of the boy who tried to hold him up.

THE TOXIC AVENGER

Pro. Lloyd Kaufman, Michael Herz; Troma *Dir.* Michael Herz, Samuel Weil *Scr.* Joe Ritter *Cine.* James London, Lloyd Kaufman *Ed.* Richard Haines *R.t.* 85 min. *MPAA* R. *Cast:* Andree Maranda, Mitchell Cohen, Jennifer Baptist, Cindy Manion, Robert Pritchard, Gary Schneider, Pat Ryan, Jr., Mark Torgl.

After jumping into a vat of toxic waste, a nerd is transformed into a monstrous hulk, and he sets out to fight evil and corruption.

TRACKS IN THE SNOW (*Pervola, Sporen in de Sneeuw.* The Netherlands, 1986) *Pro.* Jan Musch, Orlow Seunke, Tijs Tinbergen *Dir.* Orlow Seunke *Scr.* Orlow Seunke, Dirk Ayelt Kooiman, Maarten Koopman, Gerard Thoolen *Cine.* Theo Birkens *Ed.* Orlow Seunke, Dorith Vinken *Mu.* Maarten Koopman *R.t.* 95 min. *Cast:* Gerard Thoolen, Bram van der Vlugt, Melle van Essen, Jan Willem Hees, Thom Hoffman, Jaap Hoogstra.

Two estranged brothers are brought together in a dangerous journey into northern wastelands to fulfill their father's wish to be buried in a remote village.

THE TRANSFORMERS: THE MOVIE
Pro. Joe Bacal, Tom Griffin; De Laurentiis Entertainment Group *Dir.* Nelson Shin *Scr.* Ron Friedman *Ed.* David Hankins *Mu.* Vince DiCola *R.t.* 86 min. *MPAA* PG. *Voices:* Orson Welles, Robert Stack, Leonard Nimoy, Eric Idle, Judd Nelson, Lionel Stander, John Moschitta, Roger C. Carmel, Scatman Crothers, Casey Kasem, Don Messick, Frank Welker, Neil Ross, Michael Bell, Corey Burton.

This animated film features the transformers—robots that are able to change into high-tech objects in a flash. The story revolves around their attempts to reclaim their home planet from their enemies.

TRICK OR TREAT
Pro. Michael S. Murphey, Joel Soisson; De Laurentiis Entertainment Group *Dir.* Charles Martin Smith *Scr.* Michael S. Murphey, Joel Soisson, Rhet Topham *Cine.* Robert Elswit *Ed.* Jane Schwartz Jaffe *Mu.* Christopher Young, Fastaway *P.d.* Curt Schnell *A.d.* Colin D. Irwin *S.d.* Doug Mowat *R.t.* 97 min. *MPAA* R. *Cast:* Marc Price, Tony Fields, Lisa Orgolini, Doug Savant, Elaine Joyce, Glen Morgan, Gene Simmons, Ozzy Osborne.

A teenager plays backward the last record of his favorite heavy-metal musician, and the musician's ghost returns to seek revenge on his critics and on the boy's enemies.

TROLL
Pro. Albert Band; Empire Pictures *Dir.* John Buechler *Scr.* Ed Naha *Cine.* Romano Albani *Ed.* Lee Percy *Mu.* Richard Band *A.d.* Gayle Simon *R.t.* 86 min. *MPAA* PG-13. *Cast:* Noah Hathaway, Michael Moriarty, Shelley Hack, Jenny Beck, Sonny Bono, Phil Fondacarro, Brad Hall, Anne Lockhart, Julia Louis-Dreyfuss, Gary Sandy, June Lockhart.

A troll casts a spell over a little girl and attempts to use her to establish a troll kingdom in a San Francisco apartment house.

UNDER THE CHERRY MOON
Pro. Bob Cavallo, Joe Ruffalo, Steve Fargnoli; Warner Bros. *Dir.* Prince *Scr.* Becky Johnston *Cine.* Michael Ballhaus *Ed.* Eva Gardos, Rebecca Ross *Mu.* Prince and the Revolution *P.d.* Richard Sylbert *A.d.* Damien Lafranchi *S.d.* Ian Whittaker *R.t.* 98 min. *MPAA* PG-13. *Cast:* Prince, Jerome Benton, Kristin Scott-Thomas, Francesca Annis, Alexandra Stewart, Steven Berkoff.

A piano player at a Nice resort falls in love with a rich girl whose father is against the romance.

UNFINISHED BUSINESS
Pro. Steven Okazaki *Dir.* Steven Okazaki *Scr.* Steven Okazaki, Jane Kaihatsu, Kei Yokomizo, Laura Ide *Cine.* Steven Okazaki *Ed.* Steven Okazaki *R.t.* 60 min.

This documentary depicts the internment of Japanese-Americans during World War II and the later challenges to the legality of the internment.

THE UNHEARD MUSIC
Pro. Christopher Blakely; Skouras Pictures *Dir.* W. T. Morgan *Scr.* W. T. Morgan *Cine.* Karem John Monsour *Ed.* Charlie Mullin, Kent Beyda, Curtiss Clayton, W. T. Morgan *Mu.* X *P.d.* Alizabeth Foley *R.t.* 86 min. *MPAA* R. *Cast:* John Doe, Exene Cervenka, Billy Zoom, D. J. Bonebrake, Ray Manzarek, Rodney Bingenheimer, Brendan Mullen, Frank Gargani, Alizabeth Foley, Denis Zoom, Dinky Bonebrake, Bob Biggs, Al Bergamo, Tom Hadges, Joe Smith, Jello Biafra,

Robert Hilburn.

This rock documentary traces the origins of the punk band X in the clubs of Los Angeles in the late 1970's.

VAGABOND (*Sans toit ni loi*. France, 1985)

Pro. Cine-Tamaris, Films Az, French Ministry of Culture; International Film Exchange in association with Grange Communications *Dir.* Agnès Varda *Scr.* Agnès Varda *Cine.* Patrick Blossier *Ed.* Agnès Varda, Patricia Mazuy *Mu.* Joanna Bruzdowicz *R.t.* 105 min. *Cast:* Sandrine Bonnaire, Macha Meril, Stephane Freiss, Laurence Cortadellas, Marthe Jarnias, Yolande Moreau, Joel Fosse, Patrick Lepcynski, Yahaoui Assouna, Christian Chessa.

This bleak but compelling film tells the story of a young, alienated woman who wanders through the south of France in the wintertime and eventually dies from the cold.

VAMP

Pro. Donald P. Borchers; New World Pictures *Dir.* Richard Wenk *Scr.* Richard Wenk *Cine.* Elliot Davis *Ed.* Marc Grossman *Mu.* Jonathan Elias *P.d.* Alan Roderick-Jones *R.t.* 94 min. *MPAA* R. *Cast:* Chris Makepeace, Sandy Baron, Robert Rusler, Dedee Pfeiffer, Gedde Watanabe, Grace Jones, Billy Drago, Brad Logan, Lisa Lyon.

Two fraternity pledges agree to find a stripper for the initiation party being held that night and wind up in a nightclub run by vampires.

VASECTOMY: A DELICATE MATTER

Pro. Robert Burge, Lou Wills; Seymour Borde and Associates *Dir.* Robert Burge *Scr.* Robert Hilliard, Robert Burge *Cine.* Gary Thieltges *Ed.* Beth Conwell *Mu.* Fred Karlin *A.d.* Terry Welden, Bruce Cameron *R.t.* 90 min. *MPAA* PG-13. *Cast:* Paul Sorvino, Abe Vigoda, Cassandra Edwards, Lorne Greene, Gary Raff, Ina Balin, Frank Aletter, Catherine Battistone, Suzanne Charney, John Moskoff, Janet Wood, June Wilkinson, William Marshall.

A woman orders her husband to get a vasectomy because she does not want to have a ninth child.

VENDETTA

Pro. Jeff Begun, Ken Solomon, Ken Dalton; Concorde Pictures *Dir.* Bruce Logan *Scr.* Emil Farkas, Simon Maskell, Laura Carestani, John Adams *Cine.* Robert New *Ed.* Glenn Morgan *Mu.* David Newman *A.d.* Chris Clarens *S.d.* Timothy Ford *R.t.* 88 min. *MPAA* R. *Cast:* Karen Chase, Lisa Clarson, Lisa Hullana, Linda Lightfoot, Sandy Martin, Michelle Newkirk, Marianne Taylor, Marshall Teague.

A stunt woman proficient in the martial arts intentionally gets herself incarcerated in order to avenge her sister's murder.

VIOLETS ARE BLUE

Pro. Marykay Powell; Columbia Pictures *Dir.* Jack Fisk *Scr.* Naomi Foner *Cine.* Ralf Bode *Ed.* Edward Warschilka *Mu.* Patrick Williams *P.d.* Peter Jamison *A.d.* Bo Welch *S.d.* Jane Bogart *R.t.* 90 min. *MPAA* PG-13. *Cast:* Sissy Spacek, Kevin Kline, Bonnie Bedelia, John Kellogg, Jim Standiford, Augusta Dabney, Kate McGregor-Stewart, Adrian Sparks.

A photojournalist returns to her hometown on vacation and sees her high school boyfriend, who is now married and the editor of the town's newspaper. The two find that they are still attracted to each other.

THE WALL (*Le Mur.* France, 1983)
Pro. Marin Karmitz; Kino International Corporation *Dir.* Yilmaz Guney *Scr.*
Marie-Helene Quinton, Yilmaz Guney *Cine.* Izzet Akay *Ed.* Sabine Mamou *Mu.*
Ozan Garip Sahin, Setrak Bakirel *R.t.* 117 min. *Cast:* Tuncel Kuritz, Ayse Emel
Mesci, Malik Berrichi, Nicolas Hossein, Isabelle Tissaandier, Ahmet Ziyrek, Ali
Berktay, Selahattin Kuzuoglu, Jean-Pierre Colin, Jacques Dimanche, Ali Dede
Altuntas.
In this film, life in a Turkish prison is depicted, focusing especially on the abused
and neglected children.

WATER
Pro. Ian La Frenais; Atlantic Releasing Corporation *Dir.* Dick Clement *Scr.* Dick
Clement, Ian La Frenais, Bill Persky; based on a story by Bill Persky *Mu.* Mike
Moran *R.t.* 89 min. *MPAA* PG-13. *Cast:* Michael Caine, Valerie Perrine, Brenda
Vaccaro, Billy Connolly, Leonard Rossiter, Dennis Dugan, Fulton Mackay, Chris
Tummings.
When high-quality mineral water is discovered on a remote British colony in the
Caribbean, everyone from Margaret Thatcher to a bat-loving environmentalist con-
verges in attempts to exploit or protect the island.

WEEKEND WARRIORS
Pro. Hannah Hempstead; Movie Store *Dir.* Bert Convy *Scr.* Bruce Belland, Roy
Rogosin *Cine.* Charles Minsky *Ed.* Raja Gosnell *Mu.* Perry Botkin *P.d.* Chester
Kaczenski *R.t.* 85 min. *MPAA* R. *Cast:* Chris Lemmon, Vic Tayback, Lloyd
Bridges, Graham Jarvis, Daniel Greene, Marty Cohen, Brian Bradley, Matt McCoy.
A group of young men who have joined the National Guard to avoid active service
try to impress visiting military leaders.

WHAT HAPPENED TO KEROUAC?
Pro. Richard Lerner; New Yorker Films *Dir.* Richard Lerner, Lewis MacAdams
Cine. Richard Lerner, Nathaniel Dorsky *Ed.* Nathaniel Dorsky, Robert Estrin *R.t.*
96 min. *Cast:* Steve Allen, William S. Burroughs, Carolyn Cassady, Neil Cassady,
Ann Charters, Gregory Corso, Robert Creeley, Diane DiPrima, Lawrence
Ferlinghetti, Allen Ginsberg, John Clellon Holmes, Herbert Huncke, Joyce John-
son, Jack Kerouac, Jan Kerouac, Edie Kerouac Parker.
This documentary on Beat writer Jack Kerouac features interviews with those who
knew him, news and talk-show clips, and home-movie segments.

WHATEVER IT TAKES
Pro. Bob Demchuk, Walter J. Scherr; Aquarius Films *Dir.* Bob Demchuk *Scr.*
Chris Weatherhead, Bob Demchuk *Cine.* John Drake *Ed.* Bob Demchuk *Mu.*
Garry Sherman *P.d.* Maher Ahmad *R.t.* 93 min. *Cast:* Tom Mason, Martin Bal-
sam, Chris Weatherhead, James Rebhorn, Maura Shea, Bill Bogert, Rosetta
Lenoire, Joey Ginza, Fred Morsell, Edward Binns, Thomas Barbour.
A Vietnam veteran supports himself and his father's diner by driving a cab in New
York City while struggling with his daily life, relationships, and aspiration to be a
cartoonist.

WHERE ARE THE CHILDREN?
Pro. Zev Braun; Columbia Pictures *Dir.* Bruce Malmuth *Scr.* Jack Sholder *Cine.*
Larry Pizer *Ed.* Roy Watts *Mu.* Sylvester Levay *P.d.* Robb Wilson King *S.d.* Jane
Cavedon *R.t.* 92 min. *MPAA* R. *Cast:* Jill Clayburgh, Max Gail, Harley Cross,

Elisabeth Harnois, Elizabeth Wilson, Barnard Hughes, Frederic Forrest, James Purcell, Clifton James.

Jill Clayburgh plays a mother with a sordid past whose two children are kidnapped.

THE WHOOPEE BOYS

Pro. Adam Fields, Peter MacGregor-Scott; Paramount Pictures *Dir.* John Byrum *Scr.* Steve Zacharias, Jeff Buhai, David Obst *Cine.* Ralf Bode *Ed.* Eric Jenkins *Mu.* Jack Nitzsche *P.d.* Charles Rosen *S.d.* Don Ivey *R.t.* 88 min. *MPAA* R. *Cast:* Michael O'Keefe, Paul Rodriguez, Denholm Elliott, Carole Shelley, Andy Bumatai, Eddie Deezen, Marsha Warfield, Elizabeth Arlen, Karen A. Smythe, Joe Spinell, Robert Gwaltney, Lucinda Jenney, Dan O'Herlihy, Stephen Davies, Taylor Negron, Greg Germann.

Two poorly mannered street hustlers help out an heiress who runs a school for the underprivileged.

WILDCATS

Pro. Anthea Sylbert; Warner Bros. *Dir.* Michael Ritchie *Scr.* Ezra Sacks *Cine.* Donald E. Thorin *Ed.* Richard A. Harris *Mu.* Hawk Wolinski, James Newton Howard *P.d.* Boris Leven *A.d.* Steve Berger *S.d.* Phil Abrahamson *R.t.* 107 min. *MPAA* R. *Cast:* Goldie Hawn, Swoosie Kurtz, Robyn Lively, Brandy Gold, James Keach, Jan Hooks, Bruce McGill, Nipsy Russell, Mykel T. Williamson, Tab Thacker, Wesley Snipes, Nick Corri, Woody Harrelson, M. Emmet Walsh.

A woman becomes the high school football coach of a group of tough kids.

WIRED TO KILL

Pro. Jim Buchfuerer; American Distribution Group *Dir.* Franky Schaeffer *Scr.* Franky Schaeffer *Cine.* Tom Fraser *Ed.* Daniel Agulian, Franky Schaeffer *Mu.* Russell Ferrante, The Yellow Jackets *A.d.* Diana Williams, Gay Redinger *S.d.* Ainslee Colt De Wolf *R.t.* 94 min. *MPAA* R. *Cast:* Emily Longstreth, Devin Hoelscher, Merritt Butrick, Frank Collison, Garth Gardner, Tom Lister, Jr., Kim Milford, Michael Wollet, Kristina David, Don Blakely, Dorothy Patterson.

The survivors of a virus that has killed millions of people are threatened by marauding criminals, and one boy plans revenge using inventive technology.

WISDOM

Pro. Bernard Williams; Twentieth-Century Fox *Dir.* Emilio Estevez *Scr.* Emilio Estevez *Cine.* Adam Greenberg *Ed.* Michael Kahn *Mu.* Danny Elfman *P.d.* Dennis Gassner *A.d.* Dins Danielson *S.d.* Richard Hoover *R.t.* 109 min. *MPAA* R. *Cast:* Demi Moore, Emilio Estevez, Tom Skerritt, Veronica Cartwright, William Allen Young.

A young man goes on a cross-country spree robbing banks of their mortgage records.

THE WRAITH

Pro. John Kemeny; New Century Productions *Dir.* Mike Marvin *Scr.* Mike Marvin *Cine.* Reed Smoot *Ed.* Scott Conrad, Gary Rocklin *Mu.* Michael Hoenig, J. Peter Robinson *A.d.* Dean Tschetter *S.d.* Michele Starbuck *R.t.* 92 min. *MPAA* PG-13. *Cast:* Charlie Sheen, Nick Cassavetes, Randy Quaid, Sherilyn Fenn, Griffin O'Neal, David Sherrill, Jamie Bozian, Clint Howard, Matthew Barry, Chris Nash.

A stranger comes to town and challenges the members of a tough, murderous gang to car races.

YOUNGBLOOD

Pro. Peter Bart, Patrick Wells; Metro-Goldwyn-Mayer/United Artists *Dir.* Peter Markle *Scr.* Peter Markle; based on a story by Peter Markle and John Whitmore *Cine.* Mark Irwin *Ed.* Stephen E. Rivkin, Jack Hofstra *Mu.* William Orbit, Touchsong *A.d.* Alicia Keywan *S.d.* Angelo Stea *R.t.* 109 min. *MPAA* R. *Cast:* Rob Lowe, Cynthia Gibb, Patrick Swayze, Ed Lauter, Jim Youngs, Eric Nesterenko, George Finn, Fionnula Flanagan.

Leaving the family farm to follow his dream of playing hockey, Dean Youngblood (Rob Lowe) encounters sexual temptation from his landlady and vicious persecution from his teammates.

RETROSPECTIVE FILMS

AIRPLANE!

Released: 1980
Production: Howard W. Koch and Jon Davidson for Paramount Pictures
Direction: Jim Abrahams, David Zucker, and Jerry Zucker
Screenplay: Jim Abrahams, David Zucker, and Jerry Zucker
Cinematography: Joseph Biroc
Editing: Patricia Kennedy
Art direction: Ward Preston; set decoration, Anne D. McCulley
Special effects: Bruce Logan
Makeup: Edwin Butterworth
Costume design: Rosanna Norton
Choreography: Tom Mahoney
Sound: Jim Troutman
Music: Elmer Bernstein
MPAA rating: PG
Running time: 88 minutes

Principal characters:
Roger Murdock	Kareem Abdul-Jabaar
McCroskey	Lloyd Bridges
Captain Oveur	Peter Graves
Elaine	Julie Hagerty
Ted Striker	Robert Hays
Dr. Rumock	Leslie Nielsen
Randy	Lorna Patterson
Kramer	Robert Stack
Johnny	Stephen Stucker

Airplane! is a very silly motion picture that succeeds in illustrating how silly most motion pictures are. As soon as the illusions and clichés of the cinema are exposed, it is very hard to take anything seriously. For example, most films depend on casting stars or celebrities in order to attract a large audience. In *Airplane!*, Kareem Abdul-Jabaar plays Roger Murdock, a commercial pilot, but a boy on board responds to Abdul-Jabaar as basketball player not pilot and criticizes him for not being more aggressive on defense. Clearly trying to stay in character, Abdul-Jabaar squirms under the boy's attack and finally drops his pose as pilot to answer his young critic.

Another favorite ploy of motion pictures is to cast the same actor repeatedly in the same kind of role. Robert Stack, for example, often plays the hero in charge. In *Airplane!*, he plays Kramer, an experienced airline pilot attempting to guide a passenger jet safely to the ground after both the captain and copilot have succumbed to food poisoning. He has to deal with his former fighter pilot subordinate, Ted Striker (Robert Hays), who has never recovered from having sent a fellow pilot on a mission that resulted in his death. Striker has never flown a commercial airliner; he has been afraid of flying since coming home from the war. Stupidly leaving his microphone on, Kramer says that Striker will never be able to land the plane. Filled with his own importance, Kramer ignores the reality of Striker's plight—then makes Striker's dilemma worse by fatuously reminding him that he is in charge of the plane, that he is the "head honcho, the big cheese," and so on. In a similar role, Lloyd Bridges plays McCrosky, the confident air-traffic controller who is addicted to cigarettes and airplane glue. Peter Graves plays Captain Oveur, the stalwart, masculine pilot who propositions a young boy. Both actors parody with straight faces the stereotypes they have patented in previous films.

Airplane! does not have a plot so much as a clichéd cinema situation. Elaine (Julie Hagerty) has left Striker because he has not been able to hold a job or to make any reasonable adjustment to society after his war experiences. At the airport, she tells him that she is leaving him, but he refuses to accept her decision, and he follows her onto a plane bound for Chicago. Soon the plane's crew and many of its passengers become desperately ill from the airplane food. Will Striker be able to overcome his anxieties and land the plane? This is the one piece of suspense on which the film hangs. The tension and humor are aided by flashbacks to Striker's wartime experiences, to his Peace Corps years, and to his relationship with Elaine.

The suffering war-veteran story is perhaps the biggest cliché of all in *Airplane!*, and it is treated with appropriate comic contempt. Every time Striker launches into the long-winded explanation of his past, a fellow passenger commits suicide rather than suffer the boredom of his familiar tale. There are very amusing moments in the flashback sequences. When Striker sees Elaine in a bar, they dance a version of *Saturday Night Fever* (1977) with Elaine doing some extraordinary heavy lifting and swinging of Striker.

Leslie Nielsen's deadpan delivery of Dr. Rumock's lines is flawless. When passengers begin to panic, Dr. Rumock is steady. He is also stupid, the most literal-minded character in a film based on literal-minded humor. Several times, characters address Dr. Rumock with the expression, "surely"—to which he replies, "Don't call me Shirley." The plane almost does not get off the ground because of the names of its crew: Captain Oveur, Roger Murdock, and the navigator, Victor. Confusion abounds with lines such as "What's the vector, Victor?" No one on the crew is clear whether announcements refer to Roger and Oveur or roger and over—the terms used on the plane's intercom.

Some of the humor is dated. There are several airport scenes in which characters are accosted by cultists handing out flowers and asking for donations. Yet much of the film survives because its satirical targets are the perennial clichés of filmmaking. If Ted and Elaine must fall in love in an exotic location, their big love scene also must take place on a beach and be shot in the manner of the torrid embrace of Burt Lancaster and Deborah Kerr in *From Here to Eternity* (1953).

Airplane! suggests that life in America sometimes resembles a second-rate film. Stewardesses aboard airplanes, for example, are there not simply to serve passengers but also to play the role of accommodating hostesses and nurses. The chances that these stewardesses actually feel the warmth that they are taught to emote is highly unlikely. In one of the best scenes in *Airplane!*, Randy, the guitar-playing stewardess, sings a song to amuse and comfort a young girl who is stretched out on a hospital bed receiving some kind of intravenous medication. As Randy gets carried away with her song, she swings the guitar against the tube and knocks it out of the girl's arm. The girl immediately goes into convulsions while Randy and everyone else smile and hum along with the song completely oblivious to the suffering in front of them.

Airplane! creates as much of its humor through visual gags as through verbal jokes. When a passenger requests a "smoking seat" from the attendant at the airline counter, he is handed an envelope that is literally smoking. When it is suggested that the press take some pictures during a briefing about the effort to avoid an air crash, the reporters take the pictures off the airport walls.

At every turn, *Airplane!* pokes fun at the way contemporary life has become routinized. The film opens with two bored voices identifying over the public address system the airport zones that can be used for pickup and parking. The same announcements are repeated several times before dissonance is introduced into the system. The two public address voices begin to argue over which zones are for pickup and parking, and soon their voices degenerate into a bitterly personal quarrel. It is almost as if the uniformity of airports and everything else is lampooned simply for the sake of relieving the stultifying norms of everyday life. Eccentricity in the film has a value in and of itself because so much of the "reality" it attacks is banal.

It would be wrong to suggest some weighty purpose in *Airplane!*. It is a good example of what Stanley Kauffman in *The New Republic* calls "the madhouse film": It "does *anything* for a laugh." For example, Captain Oveur gets a call from the Mayo Clinic and then is interrupted by the operator who says he has an urgent call from Mr. Hamm. Oveur says, "OK, give me Hamm and hold the Mayo." There are many, many jokes of this kind throughout the film. Some reviewers have complained of the repetitiveness of this humor, but that is surely the point of a film that begins with a jet airplane roving back and forth in the clouds, with only its tail fins showing while the ominous theme from *Jaws* (1975) is played.

Carl E. Rollyson, Jr.

Reviews

The Christian Century. XCVII, September 24, 1980, p. 892.
Commonweal. CVII, Septemer 26, 1980, p. 529.
Macleans. XCIII, August 11, 1980, p. 55.
The Nation. CCXXXI, July 19, 1980, p. 93.
The New Republic. CLXXXIII, August 2, 1980, p. 26.
New Statesman. C, August 8, 1980, p. 24.
The New York Times. July 13, 1980, II, p. 15.
The New Yorker. LVI, September 1, 1980, p. 76.
Newsweek. XCVI, July 21, 1980, p. 71.
Rolling Stone. October 1, 1980, p. 31.
Time. CXVI, July 14, 1980, p. 71.
Variety. July 2, 1980, p. 18.

THE CARDINAL

Released: 1963
Production: Otto Preminger; released by Columbia Pictures
Direction: Otto Preminger
Screenplay: Robert Dozier; based on the novel *The Cardinal* by Henry Morton Robinson
Cinematography: Leon Shamroy
Editing: Louis R. Loeffler
Production design: Lyle Wheeler
Art direction: Otto Niedermoser; set decoration, Gene Callahan
Makeup: Dick Smith
Costume design: Donald Brooks
Sound: Harold Lewis, Red Law, Walter Goss, and Morris Feingold
Music: Jerome Moross
MPAA rating: no listing
Running time: 175 minutes

Principal characters:

Stephen Fermoyle	Tom Tryon
Annemarie	Romy Schneider
Mona	Carol Lynley
Lalage Menton	Jill Haworth
Cardinal Quarenghi	Raf Vallone
Cardinal Innitzer	Josef Meinrad
Cardinal Glennon	John Huston
Father Ned Halley	Burgess Meredith
Father Gillis	Ossie Davis
Benny Rampell	John Saxon
Celia	Dorothy Gish
Cardinal Giacobbi	Tullio Carminati
Florrie	Maggie McNamara
Frank	Bill Hayes
Monsignor Monaghan	Cecil Kellaway
Din	Cameron Prud'homme
Kurt Von Hartman	Peter Weck

Director Otto Preminger (1906-1986) was an artist who blended innate cinematic mastery with an unusually well-developed sense of a higher purpose. His expansive dramas of the late 1950's and early 1960's treat a variety of socially significant subjects—the law in *Anatomy of a Murder* (1959), the birth of Israel in *Exodus* (1960), the process of American democracy in *Advise and Consent* (1962), Catholicism in *The Cardinal*, war in *In Harm's*

Way (1965)—and in all these films, Preminger exhibits some degree of the melodramatic finesse that had characterized the celebrated *Laura* (1944) and the other mysteries that dominated the first phase of his career. Just as in those films, however, Preminger always chose a subtle, thoughtful aesthetic approach over an emotionally obvious one. The viewer is not guided into a certain line of thinking by Preminger's style—which is generally distinguished by long-take master shots that do not favor or disfavor characters in ways that make them heroes or villains. However charged a given stretch of material may be, there is always the sense that Preminger's images and manner of storytelling will be most rewarding if one does not try to sift out an attitude from the immediate moment but instead tries to grasp some sense of the interconnectedness of everything, both in the curve of larger events and in the barest stylistic emphasis of individual nuances.

Notwithstanding the artful objectivity for which admiring critics have praised him, Preminger always does have an attitude toward his subjects, and this attitude may be all the more passionate for so thoroughly transcending an explicit position. No film shows this better than *The Cardinal*, a majestic work of the most committed humanism imaginable. Sometimes a bit unwieldy in its attempt to unite highly diverse historical events in one man's personal experience, it nevertheless displays unwavering skill and beauty in articulating the deeper meaning of its protagonist's passage through life. Though visually opulent and filled with dramatic incidents, the film is at heart a character study, and more especially, a study of inner spiritual evolution. Commandingly, Preminger unites that evolution with each event so that a thorough relationship between the character and the actual world finally emerges. Not necessarily the most dazzling or perfect Preminger film, *The Cardinal* is, ultimately, his greatest work because of the maturity and power with which it imposes his admirable vision of life.

Beginning in Rome during World War II, the narrative traces through flashbacks events in the life of Stephen Fermoyle (Tom Tryon), an American priest who has risen in the Church through the years and is now preparing for the ceremony in which he will become a cardinal. The first flashback finds Stephen returning from the seminary in Rome to his home in Boston during the years just before World War I. A parish priest in the service of Monsignor Monaghan (Cecil Kellaway), Stephen has ambitions for higher things—it is revealed that he has excelled in his academic work and is writing a book on the Reformation. Nevertheless, unexpected problems within his own family—which includes a simple, hard-working father, Din (Cameron Prud'homme); a dignified, loving mother, Celia (Dorothy Gish); a sweet-natured, piano-playing brother, Frank (Bill Hayes); a severe, unhappy older sister, Florrie (Maggie McNamara); and a sweet, intense younger sister, Mona (Carol Lynley), who has a special love and high regard for Stephen—immediately claim his attention. Mona falls in love with

Benny Rampell (John Saxon), a Jew, and Stephen feels that he must convert the young man to Catholicism in order that Mona may marry him. Benny, though initially willing, has too much of a mind of his own to embrace all the dogma of the Church, and even after Mona sleeps with him to hold him, Stephen tries to discourage her from continuing the relationship. Benny is drafted into war service, and Stephen believes that will resolve the problem.

Meanwhile, his principal American superior, Cardinal Glennon (John Huston), takes a liking to him but believes that he needs to learn humility. Glennon sends Stephen to a remote village, L'Enclume, to assist Father Ned Halley (Burgess Meredith), a seemingly ineffectual priest who is in truth a saintly, totally giving man completely unembittered by the fact that he is becoming increasingly disabled by multiple sclerosis. Stephen deepens through knowing him, but not enough to help Mona when Frank discovers that she has become a promiscuous, hard-drinking nightclub dancer (for she is now too bitter toward him). Returning to L'Enclume, where the dying Father Halley is attended to by a pious young woman, Lalage (Jill Haworth), Stephen finds that Glennon thinks so much of Halley that he travels to the village to be with him and give him last rites.

Afterward, Stephen makes one more attempt, with Frank and a returned Benny, to help Mona, who is now pregnant and ill. Unfortunately, though, his strict adherence to Catholic law forces him into a position where he must allow her to die rather than let her baby be killed so that she might live. The event haunts him. Traveling to Rome as Glennon's secretary, Stephen learns that Glennon has obtained a prestigious post for him in the Vatican, but he confesses to Glennon that because of Mona's death he no longer feels serene as a priest, and that in fact he never felt fully comfortable in the role, which his family had chosen for him. Glennon obtains for him a special dispensation so he may take a leave of absence and teach.

In Vienna, a lovely and captivating young woman named Annemarie (Romy Schneider) falls in love with Stephen and hopes to entice him to leave the priesthood for good; but though he is tempted by her, he comes to realize that he does want to continue in the priesthood. Though still feeling guilty over Mona's death, he returns to Rome with a new sense of purpose. There he is encouraged and supported by his old teacher, Cardinal Quarenghi (Raf Vallone), but regarded skeptically by the conservative Cardinal Giaccobbi (Tullio Carminati). Thanks to Quarenghi's influence, Stephen is permitted to travel to Georgia to aid a black priest, Father Gillis (Ossie Davis), whose church has been burned by Ku Klux Klansmen. He stops in Boston long enough to meet Mona's daughter (the spitting image of her mother, she is also played by Carol Lynley), a bittersweet reminder of the past; later, he is whipped by Klansmen while in Georgia, but his mission there is a success and when he returns to Rome he is made a bishop.

The narrative climaxes when Germany takes over Austria and Stephen returns to Vienna as the Pope's emissary to deal with Cardinal Innitzer (Josef Meinrad), a man duped by Adolf Hitler (though later regretful of it). During this journey, Stephen meets Annemarie once again; she is now a bitter, seemingly remote woman married to Kurt Von Hartman (Peter Weck), an idealist who in the end commits suicide rather than capitulate to the Nazis. Annemarie, who had kept Kurt in Vienna and even flirted with Nazi loyalty, is arrested by the Nazis, and despite Stephen's impassioned appeal to her to help herself and accept his help, she seems resigned to a grim fate. Finally, as the war continues and the human values that are at stake have come into sharp focus, the narrative returns (for the second time—the death of Mona had prompted the first) to the present and Stephen's serene, hopeful perspective on what he hopes to bring to the world as a cardinal.

Because it incorporates important events in twentieth century history (the rise of Nazism, the subduing of racism in the American South), *The Cardinal* invites speculation that it is meant to be taken as a portrait of the Catholic Church in the modern world. Inevitably, this raises the question of whether it is a straightforward affirmation of the Church's value, as it would certainly be in some hands, or an attack on the Church's complacency, impotence, and lack of humanism, as it would just as surely be in other hands. True to form, Preminger is aloof from either sentiment. Stephen, though his sometimes ambivalent devotion to Catholic principles is strong enough to make him responsible for the death of his own beloved sister, is never a wholly unsympathetic or insensitive man; vitally, it is emphasized that he suffers almost disproportionately for this youthful act, which his role as priest absolutely dictated without regard for his personal anguish. Also, Preminger shows a priest truly devoted to the deepest spiritual principles in the humble Father Halley and two powerful and pragmatic, but compassionate and benevolent, church leaders in Quarenghi and Glennon. At the same time, the Church sometimes seems indifferent to suffering (Cardinal Giaccobbi's cool, aloof attitude toward the Georgian situation and Father Gillis in particular), self-preserving in the face of greater collective needs (Cardinal Innitzer's tragic willingness to cooperate with the Nazis although the Austrian people need a moral example from him), and generally more interested in its own dogma and traditions than the world's needs as they emerge within a historical flow. Intriguingly, the opulence of Church ceremony and dress in Rome is emphasized in Leon Shamroy's vivid Technicolor lighting and Lyle Wheeler's authentic appearing production design; perceived abstractly, this opulence seems almost lurid, and forcefully reminds the viewer, in master colorist Preminger's careful presentation, of the seedy nightclubs and theaters that served as setting for Mona's degradation. On balance, the film unquestionably does nothing to suppress the sense that much of what the Church brings to the world and to individual needs is cold and empty. Many of the film's admirers are convinced that Preminger's characteristic ambiguity and objectivity only make his skepticism of Catholicism's continuing value more forceful.

That view is naïve, and it overlooks the all-encompassing nature of Preminger's interests. For the film is not a catalog of positives and negatives about a religious institution in which the latter outweigh the former. It is about the value that spiritual life can have for an individual and how that value can nourish such an individual's larger purpose within the world. Preminger may not manipulate but he does, over the course of three hours, solicit a reflective empathy in the viewer. In this eye-filling but remote spectacle, the beautifully photographed settings are underlined by Jerome Moross' discreetly used but sweeping score. Characters weave in and out of the narrative in order to propel and broaden it rather than to claim fixed sympathy. (It may be especially noted how Annemarie's function as romantic interest essentially remains while being totally transformed in its dramatic purpose upon her reappearance.) Social and historical issues are asserted strongly only to be reabsorbed into the fabric of the whole, all of which make the film seem absolutely typical of Preminger. It is a mosaic of interlocked thought and drama. Yet within the mosaic is the private interior struggle and gradual enlightenment of Stephen, and it is from these that the true drama and positive value of the film's events is yielded.

With unmistakable stylistic clarity, illumination, and force, Preminger asserts that there is a divine process that permits man to reunite with God. In this process, a true spiritual path may be followed (though not in the way an individual intends—Stephen is spiritualized not by the Church but through his personal experiences), while the most challenging problem can also offer the seeds of a solution to inner struggle. So, the Church, seemingly so heartless in its dictates and so demanding of Stephen's emotions, becomes— in its *negative* aspects—the ironic central force that pushes him into finally becoming, on his own, a commendable human being with a sense of worth. For in compelling Stephen to be his sister's unwilling murderer—and in so doing to throw him into doubt, anguish, and despair—the Church passively and indifferently forces him to cast off his youthful arrogance, complacency, and fundamental misdirectedness. His resolution of his problems, which entails a second, more complicated abuse of a woman's love for him (this time Annemarie—but whether sister or lover, the extent to which this celibate man's life is profoundly affected by women is surely at the heart of what is insightful about Preminger's handling of the story), necessitates that Stephen deepen both within himself and in his response to life. In a wonderfully realized scene in the first Vienna episode, he realizes that he will return to the priesthood when he sees himself in a mirror, well-dressed and dapper after a ball, and looks both melancholy and newly resolved in the same moment.

Stephen grows beyond the Church while remaining within it, and this places him in a special position at film's end. As a powerful Church leader, he can make the Church serve the world in a humanistic way at a crucial time. In the context of eternity, he has become a man of value and purpose, helping the world to sustain hope of ultimate peace and enlightenment.

Preminger shows this process with dramatic vividness simply by bending his stylistic principles in a way that calls attention to and unites two scenes that are far apart in the running time of the film. The first is the scene of Mona coming to Confession to tell Stephen that she has slept with Benny. The film's first large, Panavision-filling closeups, of Stephen and Mona, each in isolation, give an intimate look at each of them as an individual apart from the larger context. (In theory, Preminger never treats a sequence this way, though stylistic theory about directors always breaks down when individual films are analyzed.) Honest, intense, and in touch with her inner conflicts, Mona becomes more sympathetic by the moment, while Stephen, by contrast, seems more and more heartless—here he is severe, judgmental, totally unable to be of any real help to the sister he loves, because he is so inflexible. The interaction sets in motion the chain of events that will lead to Mona's death, so Stephen is seen to be responsible in a larger perspective.

The second comparable sequence, however, shows Stephen in a different light. This is the last flashback scene when Stephen visits Annemarie in prison. Again, isolated large closeups set this scene apart, and further, Annemarie is behind bars, so that her declarations (she feels guilty over Kurt's death because she had always remained in love with Stephen and had not supported her husband when he needed her, and now she is more or less grateful to be punished) come across exactly as if she, like Mona earlier, were in Confession. Yet Stephen's closeups do not show an aloof, rigid man, unable to show love. On the contrary, he has learned about life, about the subtlety and beauty of feeling, and about himself as a flawed human being. In neither word nor look does he try to take himself out of the personal relationship (as he had done with the sister who also needed personal recognition). His warm responses to Annemarie acknowledge his part in her life and show total compassion for her. His face shows both his former worldly affection for her and his present spiritual love, and he tries to dissuade her from guilt—a guilt comparable in every sense to the guilt he lived with for so long—by concluding with passionate conviction that her life has value and that she is an individual with a God-given soul of her own (like him, as well as Mona, the film implies). Annemarie is too bitterly lost in herself and will not transcend her sad sense of herself, but at least she knows that Stephen hears her—he has at last truly responded to another. As Annemarie's final closeup dissolves to Stephen's present-tense one and the camera tracks backward to a wider view of the Roman cathedral in which he now stands in the midst of a group, the viewer is now convinced that this Stephen could have helped Mona, has found peace within himself, and has been spiritually empowered to bring into the world the love he once suppressed. Such is the complexity of life's interconnections that the first, relatively youthful encounter with Annemarie was a key event in helping him to find that greater love and a sense of true communion with others.

Such a lucid presentation of the journey to understanding of one's purpose attests both a highly intelligent and highly idealistic nature. Preminger, sometimes cavalierly described as cold and cynical, certainly deserves the description. In passing, it should be noted that he is an astute producer, also. The much-maligned Tryon—so simple, straightforward, and real—is an inspired casting choice as Stephen. How critics could describe as bland an actor who so sensitively evokes the gradual emergence of inner spiritual strength is beyond comprehension. Yet, many critics of the day did not connect with Tryon's performance, perhaps never understanding that Preminger loves actors (Dana Andrews in his early films, such as *Laura*, is the best example) who can hold back and seem masklike for much of a film, the better to underscore the truth that a human being is complex and difficult to know. In any event, Tryon is not at all inexpressive in difficult scenes of Stephen's deepest anguish and suggests from the beginning a quietly churning inner conflict, as well as convincingly evoking the character's ultimate serenity. The performances of the large cast are characteristically fine—notably Meinrad's even but agitated-under-the-surface Innitzer, Romy Schneider's seductive and mercurial and finally rueful Annemarie, and John Huston's flamboyant but knowing Glennon (a fine professional acting debut for this veteran director)—but Tryon's is especially impressive.

On the whole, Robert Dozier's adaptation of an elaborate novel is taut enough, especially as Preminger does not try to conceal the episodic quality of the narrative, electing—at some expense of conventional tension—an even visual tone in order to highlight the stylistic power of the sustained closeups in the two key scenes involving Mona and Annemarie. Inevitably, concentrations of melodrama and violence can make an episode such as the Georgia-set one seem very contrived within the context of the larger story. Each episode has its place, however, and the important quality of the film is that it does reveal their interconnectedness. The subtle relationship of all events and people that thread through an individual life is a difficult, almost intangible concept that Preminger makes register persuasively, and it gives *The Cardinal* a rare spiritual dimension. A prestigious film in its time, with half a dozen Oscar nominations including one for Preminger's direction, *The Cardinal* deserves to be rescued from its later neglect and experienced by new audiences, less as a film about religion than for what it is, a work that is itself, in the deepest sense, religious.

Blake Lucas

Reviews

Catholic World. CXCVIII, March, 1964, p. 365.
Film Quarterly. XVII, Spring, 1964, p. 61.
Films and Filming. X, November, 1963, p. 11.
Films in Review. XV, January, 1964, p. 46.
The New York Times. December 15, 1963, II, p. 3.
The New Yorker. XXXIX, December 14, 1963, p. 198.
Saturday Review. XLVI, December 7, 1963, p. 32.
Sight and Sound. XXXIII, Winter, 1963, p. 39.
Time. LXXXII, December 13, 1963, p. 97.
Variety. October 16, 1963, p. 6.

THE HEARTBREAK KID

Released: 1972
Production: Edgar J. Sherick for Palomar International Pictures; released by Twentieth Century-Fox
Direction: Elaine May
Screenplay: Neil Simon; based on the story "A Change of Plans" by Bruce Jay Friedman
Cinematography: Owen Roizman
Editing: John Carter
Production design: Michael Hausman
Art direction: Richard Sylbert; set decoration, William O'Connell
Sound: Chris Newman
Costume design: Anthea Sylbert
Music: Garry Sherman
Songs: Cy Coleman and Sheldon Harnick, and Burt Bacharach and Hal David
MPAA rating: PG
Running time: 104 minutes

Principal characters:
Lenny Cantrow . . . . Charles Grodin
Lila . . . . Jeannie Berlin
Kelly Corcoran . . . . Cybill Shepherd
Mr. Corcoran. . . . . Eddie Albert
Mrs. Corcoran . . . . Audra Lindley
Ralph . . . . Mitchell Jason
Kelly's boyfriend . . . . Tim Browne

The Heartbreak Kid is a deceptively simple-looking film. Based on the story "A Change of Plans" by Bruce Jay Friedman, with screenplay by Neil Simon, it gives one every reason to expect to be able to write it off as that dependable entity—"a Neil Simon comedy." Everyone knows the recipe: Mix a lot of screwball zaniness and bickering between the male and female leads with a dash of schmaltz and a pervasive leavening of romance, and top it all off with a whirlwind happy ending to make a sure-fire hit. Yet perhaps the reason that *The Heartbreak Kid* was only a moderate, and not a huge, success at the box office was that, notwithstanding the Simonized story, director Elaine May did not quite adhere to the recipe. The romantic screwiness is frequently more ominous than zany. The farcical high jinks between the leads is at times more frightening than amusing. There is not a drop of sentiment or sentimentality anywhere in sight, and the ending is more disturbing than happy. In Elaine May's and Charles Grodin's transformation of Simon's materials, something almost terrifying is added to the comedy until it comes out as dark, as black, as haunting as Christopher Marlowe's *Tamburlaine* (c. 1587) or *The Jew of Malta* (c. 1589).

The plot is vintage Simon material, even if one feels sure that Neil Simon could not have anticipated how blackly May would treat it. Lenny Cantrow (Charles Grodin) is a good, dutiful Jewish boy on his Miami beach honeymoon with his good, dutiful, Long Island Jewish wife, Lila (played by Jeannie Berlin, Elaine May's daughter). They are the perfectly matched couple: singing Burt Bacharach duets together, eating breakfast in the International House of Pancakes, and sitting in lounge chairs around the hotel pool with hundreds of other newlyweds and newly retireds. The only hitch is that on the first afternoon of the honeymoon, Lenny impulsively decides that he is in love with preppie, blonde, WASPish Kelly Corcoran (Cybill Shepherd) and would rather be married to her than to his wife.

Lenny crazily courts Kelly while he honeymoons Lila. There have been many other films about a man who attempts to keep two women in his life unaware of each other, but *The Heartbreak Kid* takes the situation to the comic *reductio ad absurdum*. While Lenny's behavior is clearly grounds for divorce, it is even more grounds for some of the wildest farce on film. As Lenny juggles his two loves, May and her deadpan star work the material for all it is worth in a hilarious series of near misses.

The situation get even wilder in the second half of the film. Lenny obtains a divorce from Lila and goes on to pursue Kelly back to her home in a posh suburb outside Minneapolis, to attempt to persuade her to marry him. He must outmaneuver her schoolmates, her father, and her mother. He, the nice Jewish boy from Brooklyn, must out-WASP the WASP's back in Lake Minnetonka. Lenny is imaginatively released from all the social systems and values within which his whole life has previously been organized and understood. He becomes a connoisseur of social tones and inflections. In order to impress Kelly's parents and friends, he becomes a comic deconstructionist in a tradition that existed long before the French invented the word, twisting, adapting, manipulating the codes of social life, and hilariously building himself anew around a new set of values and morals.

From *Such Good Friends* (1971) to *Ishtar* (1987), May's films have been studies of the consequences of alienation, but, just as here, they have always understood marginality to be not a lamentable but an empowering condition. Alienation confers freedom. Marginality is the source of creativity on the margins of social situations, May demonstrates, and never have those things been more exuberantly demonstrated than as this good Jewish boy tries to woo the shiksa from Lake Minnetonka. To see through the reigning systems of value, to see their artificiality, is to be free to play with them. Feelings of sadness, nostalgia, or nihilism are the furthest things from May's (or Lenny's) mind. To be displaced from the center of a system onto its margins is potentially to gain imaginative leverage within it, to acquire a capacity for movement among alternative systems of value that is denied both a more dismissive and a more embedded position. One may be irrevocably alienated from the sources of power, but the attainment of a critical distance from a system is potentially the first step toward exercising creativity on its margins.

The practical ramification of this fact is that as he pursues Kelly, initially in hot Miami Beach and subsequently back in frozen Minnesota—visiting her, pestering her parents, eating meals with her family, courting their approval—Lenny is freed to become an uproarious, comic improviser of his own identity. Like a farcical version of Iago, he exuberantly makes himself up as he goes along.

Elaine May began her adult professional career as a stand-up comedienne (working with Mike Nichols, who also subsequently went on to filmmaking), and her characters are never very far from being buoyant, exuberant stand-up comedians to the world. As he improvises his cover stories first to Lila (as he secretly dates Kelly on their honeymoon), and subsequently to Kelly's family and friends (as he travels to her home and steals her away from her college boyfriends), Lenny displays a performative gaiety, gusto, and comic inventiveness that affiliates him with his namesake Lenny Bruce.

One of the things that distinguish *The Heartbreak Kid* from a Howard Hawks or Jerry Lewis film or from a generically similar story such as Billy Wilder's *The Seven Year Itch* (1955), and which hints at some of the darkness of its vision, is that Lenny is not really a victim or a dupe. He is empowered imaginatively, socially, and verbally to the point of brilliance. As a schemer and tale-teller, he may be a comic bungler at times, but he is ultimately stunningly superior to and in control of his destiny. As a liar, a cheat, and a scoundrel, Lenny is of almost legendary panache, daring, and energy, with much more in common with some of the great imaginative schemers of literature than with the mild-mannered bumblers and Milquetoasts played by Cary Grant or Tom Ewell.

Lenny Cantrow, the stylistic parodist, dramatic improviser, and self-made man *par excellence*, summarizes in his character the strange, eccentric connections between Emersonian self-reliance, the all-American traditions of the tall-tale teller and the confidence man, the self-help philosophies of Dale Carnegie and Horatio Alger, the pragmatism of William James, and the aesthetic eclecticism of George Santayana and Wallace Stevens. At best, he represents the possibility of the self making itself up as it goes along and endlessly revising its own identity to suit ever-changing audiences and conditions of performance.

Yet he represents a more nightmarish state of affairs as well. As an endless improviser of his own identity, Lenny represents a state of energy in motion, a condition of destinationless desire that may, the film suggests, be hazardous to one's own and others' health. In becoming a consummate parodist and appropriator of styles and roles, in performing as a stand-up comedian to the world, Lenny treats all life as if it were only a series of free-floating fictions. It is as if there were no reality except whatever one makes up on the spur of the moment. He treats himself as if he had no self, except whatever identity he puts on at that instant.

This conception of the postmodern personality is May's most daring and radical achievement in this film and others (as well as being the link between her work and that of her close friend John Cassavetes). She imagines characters so energetic, so continuously engaged in reformulating and reconstituting themselves in alternately dazzling or daft displays of improvisational inventiveness that they raise questions about whether there is anyone in control of or responsible for their various tones, styles, and spiels. The performer becomes such a quick-change artist, such a masterful parodist of postures and styles that one wonders if there is anyone underneath the masks and costumes.

The issue in both May's and Cassavetes' work is pointedly one of the authenticity of this process of endless appropriation of others' styles and forms of expression. Lenny's self is nothing in itself. If John Keats praised artistic chameleonism in his reflections about negative capability, May worries about the social and ethical consequences of stylistic eclecticism and appropriation as they play out their destiny in American art and culture. The self ceases to mark a real center of action and belief and becomes instead a silence in which inherited styles and tones resonate. It is a vacuum whose emptiness is filled with cultural styles and fantasies which no one in particular authors or controls. Lenny's so-called self is only a kind of black hole in which alternative fantasies about power, romance, blondes, WASP's, money, and social success replace one another endlessly. In allowing the self to become the site for a "free play" of cultural styles and fictions, May suggests that perhaps people play themselves out of meaningful and responsible personal existence. In short, *The Heartbreak Kid* asks whether one may defy the stylistic gravity of the predicaments in which one finds oneself without becoming morally, ontologically, and humanly weightless.

May's figures raise questions about the extent to which people are able to express themselves in socially responsible and responsive identities while still remaining true to the free movements of imagination and desire. *The Heartbreak Kid* is a celebration of the joys of self-revision and reformulation, but it also raises disturbing questions about the hospitality of society to the expression of such free plays of feeling.

Lenny improvises so daringly and changeably, and works up so many conflicting comic bits and alternative versions of himself in the course of *The Heartbreak Kid* that it is difficult to see how there can be any actual role available in society for an imagination so energetic. Think of Lenny Bruce actually attempting to live the nuttiness and the mercurial free associations of his stage routines in his real life, in his offstage relationships (but then again, maybe that is just what Lenny Bruce tragically tried to do). The more brilliant the performer, the more alienated he is from what the world considers to be an acceptable, responsible form of expression.

In his acting, Charles Grodin (an extraordinary comic actor and a graduate of the Actors Studio, who, along with Peter Falk, is one of very few practitioners of the Method to apply it to the practice of comedy) wonderfully captures this condition of slightly dazed expressive disenfranchisement. He lets the viewer know through the comic vacancy of his stare, the flatness and nasality of his tones, and the strange prolongation of his pauses as he does multiple takes and inserts beats (strange ellipses in the text which the customary briskness of the delivery of a Neil Simon joke-fest would never have allowed to emerge, but which May must have encouraged Grodin to employ) that even in his most brilliant performances, Lenny is forever a misfit, a little out of step and out of place. He is imaginatively always somewhere else, somewhere beside himself and off-center from everyone around him, slightly out of synch with the rhythms of other characters, ahead of or behind the pacings of ordinary life.

That appreciation of the inevitable homelessness of the creative spirit is ultimately what makes Grodin's inspired performance almost heartbreaking at times, and it is what makes *The Heartbreak Kid*, unlike Neil Simon's work, the darkest of black comedies. The final scene of the film summarizes the virtually tragic overtones of Lenny's predicament in that it reminds one of the utter inhospitality of the rules and systems of society to all the free movements of consciousness that Lenny so joyously represents. After Lenny's successful second marriage to Kelly, at his second wedding reception, May excruciatingly lingers on his figure as he performs for the dozens of guests, each of whom wants to pin him down on what career or role he will pursue in the future. Society, as May depicts it, inexorably attempts to structure and systematize desire. It labors, with every fiber of its being, repressively to assign a destination to development.

Lenny is about to begin his second honeymoon, with a second bride, at exactly the point at which the film began with the first one. One feels the loneliness and doom of his situation. He is caught in a double irony. Insofar as he is finally placed, and is realizing his dreams of an ideal marriage and upper-class social position, Lenny is being destroyed, since whatever else he represents, he represents an imagination on the margins, a freedom from definition that is anathema to all conventional social structures and moral systems. Yet, insofar as he is unplaceable socially and economically, what has been the point of his feverish pursuit of Kelly? How can this joyous improviser settle down? How can there be any fixed social form for such a shape changer? How can one lock up such mercurial inventiveness in the prison of home and family?

The film ends with the scene of the wedding reception and with those questions hanging in the air. Should one be surprised to learn that May shot another ending that was never used? It follows the wedding reception and shows Lenny and Kelly on the first day of their honeymoon. They have just gone out on a boat when Lenny sees another woman and falls in love with her at first sight, and the chase begins again. The scene was cut from the final print—and wisely—not because it was inconsistent with the film as it now stands, but because it was unnecessary.

Lenny's bereftness at the wedding reception already tells one all one needs to know. It demonstrates that Lenny can never settle down anywhere without giving up everything that the whole film has shown to be interesting about him. He is a principle of imagination that can never have a home. He is a figure of desire that can never have a destination. He is desire itself, and as inevitably homeless as Iago or Tamburlaine. That is what it means to say that he is much closer to being tragic than comic. He speaks to all of us insofar as he raises fundamental questions about the inevitable frustration of our expression of ourselves in the forms and structures of society. The blackness of May's comedy, like Marlowe's before her, is that it tells us we must learn to live with that state of affairs.

Raymond Carney

Reviews
The Christian Century. XC, March 7, 1973, p. 298.
Commentary. LV, May, 1973, p. 81.
Commonweal. XCVII, February 23, 1973, p. 470.
Films in Review. XXIV, February, 1973, p. 117.
Los Angeles Times. December 20, 1972, III, p. 1.
The New Republic. CLXVIII, January 6, 1973, p. 33.
The New York Times. December 18, 1972, II, p. 56.
The New Yorker. XLVIII, December 16, 1972, p. 126.
Sight and Sound. XLII, no. 3, p. 176.
Time. CI, January 1, 1973, p. 43.
Variety. December 13, 1972, p. 20.
The Washington Post. February 14, 1973, p. F1.

HELLO, DOLLY!

Released: 1969
Production: Ernest Lehman for Chenault Productions, Inc.; released by Twentieth Century-Fox
Direction: Gene Kelly
Screenplay: Ernest Lehman; based on the musical play of the same name by Michael Stewart, adapted from *The Matchmaker* by Thornton Wilder
Cinematography: Harry Stradling
Editing: William Reynolds
Production design: John De Cuir (AA)
Art direction: Jack Martin Smith and Herman Allen Blumenthal (AA); set decoration, Walter M. Scott, George Hopkins, and Raphael Bretton (AA)
Special photographic effects: L. B. Abbott and Art Cruickshank
Makeup: Dan Striepeke
Costume design: Irene Sharaff
Choreography: Michael Kidd
Sound: Murray Spivack, Vinton Vernon, Jack Solomon, and Douglas Williams (AA)
Music: Jerry Herman; score, Lennie Hayton and Lionel Newman (AA)
Songs: Jerry Herman
MPAA rating: G
Running time: 168 minutes

Principal characters:
Dolly Levi . . . . Barbra Streisand
Horace Vandergelder . . . . Walter Matthau
Cornelius Hackl . . . . Michael Crawford
Irene Molloy . . . . Marianne McAndrew
Barnaby Tucker . . . . Danny Lockin
Minnie Fay . . . . E. J. Peaker
Ermengarde . . . . Joyce Ames
Ambrose Kemper . . . . Tommy Tune
Orchestra leader . . . . Louis Armstrong
Gussie Granger . . . . Judy Knaiz
Rudolph Reisenweber . . . . David Hurst

When it was released in 1969, *Hello, Dolly!* was rightfully billed as one of the last of the old-fashioned film musicals. Directed and choreographed by two film musical veterans (Gene Kelly and Michael Kidd, respectively), this screen adaptation of the long-running Broadway hit offered a multitude of tuneful songs and spirited dances in a lavish setting but added no particular sophistication or innovation. The motion picture was also the latest—and last—incarnation of a story that began in 1835 as a British play, was adapted by a Viennese playwright in 1842, and then was transformed twice by Thornton Wilder: in 1938 as *The Merchant of Yonkers* and in 1954 as *The Matchmaker*. Filmed under the latter name four years later, it was then adapted as the Broadway musical *Hello, Dolly!* in 1964. As a film, its chief interest for audiences lay in the casting of Barbra Streisand in the title role, only her second screen appearance after her Academy Award–winning debut in *Funny Girl* (1968).

The film opens in New York City in 1890, where matchmaker Dolly Levi (Barbra Streisand) is dispensing business cards to townspeople, actions set to the songs "Call on Dolly," "I Have Always Been a Woman Who Arranges Things," and "Just Leave Everything to Me."

In nearby Yonkers, Horace Vandergelder (Walter Matthau), the wealthy, gruff, no-nonsense owner of a hay and feed store, refuses his tearful niece Ermengarde (Joyce Ames) permission to marry artist Ambrose Kemper (Tommy Tune), because Ambrose cannot support her. Instead, she will be going to New York City, under Dolly's supervision, until she dispels of her foolish notion. He tells his two store clerks, Cornelius Hackl (Michael Crawford) and Barnaby Tucker (Danny Lockin), that he is traveling to New York to march in the Fourteenth Street Parade and propose to a woman named Irene Malloy (Marianne McAndrew). When the inexperienced Cornelius asks why he is marrying, Horace sings "It Takes a Woman," an anthem to the fairer sex's ability to cook, clean, shoe a horse, and shovel ice.

Dolly arrives to fetch Ermengarde. Though clearly attracted to Horace, she covers her dismay at his announcement of impending marriage by telling him that she had arranged a date for him that night with a New York heiress. After he leaves, she muses that she would prefer his store shutters to be painted forest green.

Dolly catches Ermengarde and Ambrose trying to elope and suggests a plan to win Horace's blessing. They are to enter that evening's polka contest at New York's Harmonia Gardens restaurant, where Dolly and her late husband Ephraim had dined weekly. They will win the first-prize money and thereby gain financial support. She also asks Ambrose to tell the headwaiter that she will be there as well.

Tired of never having a day off, Cornelius and Barnaby decide to seek adventure in New York. Overhearing them, Dolly gives them the address of Irene Malloy's millinery shop. Vowing not to return home until they have each kissed a girl, the clerks sing "Put on Your Sunday Clothes." They are joined by Dolly, Ermengarde, Ambrose, and a chorus of singing and dancing townspeople in one of the film's most scintillating production numbers.

In her hat shop, the beautiful Irene Malloy sings "Ribbons down My Back" to her assistant, Minnie Fay (E. J. Peaker), voicing her yearning for romance. Cornelius and Barnaby, flustered at the sight of women, enter the shop. Cornelius and Irene are immediately attracted to each other. The men panic, however, when they see Horace approaching with Dolly, and they hide in the shop. When Irene casually mentions to Horace that she has met fellow Yonkers resident Cornelius Hackl, Dolly tries to convince the disbelieving man that his clerk leads a double life and is actually a wealthy man about town. The two clerks sneeze, giving their presence away, and Horace, believing that Irene has deceived him by dating Cornelius, leaves.

Dolly says that the only way the clerks can rectify the situation is to take the women to dinner, suggesting the Harmonia Gardens and the polka contest. She teaches the men to dance in "Dancing," another buoyant production number.

About to watch the Fourteenth Street Parade, Dolly quietly addresses a locket photograph of her late husband, telling him that she wants to begin living life again and asking for a sign of his approval. She sings of her newfound drive in the rousing "Before the Parade Passes By." At the parade, she sees an out-of-work actress friend, Gussie Granger (Judy Knaiz), and concocts a scheme to have her pose as the heiress Dolly had mentioned to Horace.

That night, Cornelius and Barnaby take Irene and Minnie Fay to the Harmonia Gardens, singing the tongue-in-cheek "Elegance" en route. Meanwhile, Dolly is preparing for her own evening. She sings the ballad "Love Is Only Love," a reflective, down-to-earth view of love.

At the Harmonia Gardens, Horace is less than pleased with the company of the "heiress." Headwaiter Rudolph Reisenweber (David Hurst), delighted at Ambrose's message concerning Dolly's imminent arrival, tells his staff that the service must be doubly efficient in her honor. The brisk "Waiters' Gallop" of cartwheels and other fancy footwork then ensues. Cornelius confesses his true station in life to Irene, who had known from the outset and had planned to pay for the expensive dinner herself; she discovers, though, that her money is at home.

As Dolly had planned, the heiress soon abandons Horace. Dolly makes a show-stopping entrance, and the waiters burst into the high-spirited "Hello, Dolly!" title song. Dolly participates in their lively dance and then scat sings with the restaurant's orchestra leader (Louis Armstrong) before joining an amazed Horace for dinner. When Horace spots his niece and errant clerks in the polka contest, he causes a commotion and fires the men. Outside, Cornelius serenades Irene, telling her that "It Only Takes a Moment" to fall in love. Meanwhile, Horace, realizing that he has begun feeling something for Dolly, nevertheless tells her that he will not marry her. A mastermind of reverse psychology, she replies, in the stinging "So Long, Dearie," that she is leaving him to pursue a better life.

The next morning, Horace finds himself alone in his store until the three couples come to claim their money. Dolly also appears and talks Horace into taking back Cornelius and Barnaby as his partner and chief clerk, respectively.

Horace proposes to Dolly, who demurs, as she has not yet had a sign of Ephraim's approval. That sign for which she has been waiting comes when Horace mentions that he is having his shutters repainted in forest green to give a new painter some business—echoing Dolly's earlier wish about the shutters and her late husband's philosophy about using money for others' benefit. She accepts his proposal, and the two sing a romantic version of "Hello, Dolly!"

Just before the wedding, the cast reprises several musical numbers. The film ends as Dolly and Horace enter the church.

The most impressive aspect of *Hello, Dolly!* is its production values. The budget exceeded twenty million dollars, making it the most expensive musical filmed up to that time, and that expenditure is strikingly evident on screen. The opulent Harmonia Gardens and ornate Fourteenth Street sets, lavish period costumes, and parade logistics—675 marchers, 3,100 extras—fill the screen with eye-pleasing splendor. It is not surprising that the art direction and set decoration teams, headed by production designer John De Cuir, won Academy Awards; Irene Sharaff's costume design received a nomination. Harry Stradling's cinematography, brightly capturing these elements as well as sweeping picturesque views of the Hudson River Valley, was also nominated.

The actors acquit themselves perhaps somewhat more unevenly. Streisand, as talented a performer as she may be, is miscast as Dolly. While she has the character's vitality and a wonderful singing voice which enriches her numbers, she too often seems to be doing a Mae West impression. One does not know, of course, how much of her mugging and mannerisms can be attributed to the direction of Gene Kelly. Matthau fares better as Horace, convincingly moving from a pragmatic curmudgeon to a man willing to take a chance on love and foolishness. Crawford and Lockin make an engaging team as Cornelius and Barnaby; Lockin had played his role for two years on stage. (Sadly, he was murdered several years after the film's release in a domestic dispute.) McAndrew brings beauty and charm to the role of Irene, though Peaker seems simply silly as Minnie Fay. Tune as Ambrose, a standout here mainly for his six-foot-six-inch height, went on to win numerous Tony Awards for his stage projects. The other supporting players well fulfill their roles.

The script by producer Ernest Lehman, whose previous screenplay adaptations include *West Side Story* (1961) and *The Sound of Music* (1965), does not vary greatly from the stage play. The plot and its complications remain thin; eliminated are some of Dolly's speeches to her late husband. In addition to the scenic and choreographic expansion not possible on stage,

Jerry Herman's music was lushly reorchestrated, eliminating two numbers and adding several new ones; Lennie Hayton and Lionel Newman won the Academy Award for score. Michael Kidd's exuberant choreography contributes much to the film, though the "Waiters' Gallop" comes dangerously close to being slapstick.

As director, Gene Kelly keeps the action moving fluidly, especially during the complicated production numbers, though he is short on subtlety and, at times, his camera angles are anything but inobtrusive.

The film received some rave notices, but mixed reviews were the general rule. Critics saluted its opulence, Matthau's performance, and Streisand's singing voice, but questioned her interpretation. Box-office returns were poor. In addition to the aforementioned awards, the film also won the Academy Award for sound as well as nominations for best picture and film editing.

Despite its faults, *Hello, Dolly!* is entertaining, escapist fare. It provides nostalgia on two levels: for its depiction of a bygone, less complicated era, and for its genre, the dazzling film-musical extravaganza, which in itself no longer exists.

Libby Slate

Reviews
America. CXXII, January 31, 1970, p. 113.
Dance Magazine. XLIV, March, 1970, p. 80.
Films and Filming. XVI, February, 1970, p. 51.
Films in Review. XXI, January, 1970, p. 52.
Los Angeles Times. December 22, 1969, Part IV, p. 1.
The New York Times. December 18, 1969, p. 62.
The New Yorker. XLV, January 3, 1970, p. 57.
Saturday Review. LIII, January 10, 1970, p. 57.
Time. XCIV, December 26, 1969, p. 52.
Variety. December 24, 1969, p. 14.
Vogue. CLV, February 15, 1970, p. 44.

HOUSEBOAT

Released: 1958
Production: Jack Rose; released by Paramount Pictures
Direction: Melville Shavelson
Screenplay: Melville Shavelson and Jack Rose
Cinematography: Ray June
Editing: Frank Bracht
Art direction: Hal Pereira and John Goodman; set decoration, Sam Comer
  and Grace Gregory
Makeup: Wally Westmore
Costume design: Edith Head
Music: George Duning
Songs: Jay Livingston and Ray Evans
Running time: 110 minutes

Principal characters:
Cinzia Zaccardi	Sophia Loren
Tom Winston	Cary Grant
Carolyn Winston	Martha Hyer
Angelo Donatello	Harry Guardino
Arturo Zaccardi	Eduardo Ciannelli
Alan Wilson	Murray Hamilton
Elizabeth Winston	Mimi Gibson
David Winston	Paul Petersen
Robert Winston	Charles Herbert

Melville Shavelson's *Houseboat* is at once a 1950's family film about the American obsession with bringing up both children and parents and a romantic comedy about the mating of an apparently mismatched couple (*Bringing Up Baby*, 1938, comes appropriately to mind). Despite the apparent primacy of the romantic plot, the relationship between fathers and children permeates the film, which is concerned with a parent's proper role, the importance of feeling, and the necessity of letting people develop a sense of worth. That this growth occurs on the river and is accompanied by references to Mark Twain's *The Adventures of Huckleberry Finn* is significant, for the film is about initiation and discovering self.

Upon his estranged wife's death, Tom Winston (Cary Grant) returns from Europe to see his three children—Elizabeth (Mimi Gibson), David (Paul Petersen), and Robert (Charles Herbert)—but they are understandably hostile and distant. Robert, the youngest, "hates everybody" and plays his harmonica to communicate his desire not to communicate his feelings. When the camera remains on Robert and his harmonica as the credits are shown, Shavelson suggests that children and communication are his focus. In the sequence following the credits, Tom is removed from his children, who view him from above through the railing. As they watch him, he demonstrates his distance by being unable to make a toy gift work; he is, as he later states, "out of touch," an appropriate phrase because he thinks and speaks rather than feels and acts. Yet when his father-in-law suggests splitting up the children—Elizabeth with her grandparents, the two boys with Carolyn (Martha Hyer), Tom's sister-in-law—he resists the threat to family unity and takes them with him to his cramped Washington, D.C., apartment.

The city is no place for a family; Tom's apartment is a "rabbit hutch." When they all bed down for the night, the problems emerge: David, who "takes things," is also a voyeur; Robert plays his harmonica in the darkness; and Elizabeth fears the dark and the lightning. When Elizabeth exclaims that all the males are at least together, Tom rejoins ironically, "Only in body." His scientific explanations about thunder and lightning do not help, because his daughter needs actions, not words. On the holiday, Tom plays tour guide, not father, as he describes Washington's monuments in terms of when people died and inadvertently upsets his children. At the evening concert, the situation worsens when Robert, who disrupts the concert by playing his harmonica, runs away and is finally returned to a distraught Tom by Cinzia (Sophia Loren), the daughter of Arturo Zaccardi (Eduardo Ciannelli), a touring conductor.

Cinzia, whose Swiss education has been restricted to books, is a young woman her father wants to treat as a child, and she has much in common with the Wilson children: Like Robert, she disrupts the concert; like Robert and David, she runs away; and like David, she is not allowed to grow up. When she counsels Tom, "Be a parent, not a policeman," she is thinking of her own father. David says, "Welcome to our side," and the generational battle lines are drawn. Tom must learn, as Arturo does, that to keep one's children close, one has to let them go.

Because Cinzia is so empathetic with the children, Tom, who mistakenly assumes that she is a poor Italian immigrant seeking a job, engages her as a maid, one whom he discovers is unable to wash clothes or cook. Convinced that he should move his entourage to the country, he buys a house from Carolyn and has Angelo Donatello (Harry Guardino) move it to a new location, but en route the house is destroyed by a train when Angelo's truck stalls on the tracks. Angelo finds a decrepit houseboat for them, and by the time they arrive, Cinzia has taken first place in the children's affections. (During the drive to the country the children join her singing, which comes to represent life and feeling, and ignore Tom's talking, which reinforces her image of him as stuffy and stiff.)

From the time they cross the plank from the shore to the houseboat, the family is on the mend. Because he does not understand that his children need love, not talk, Tom ruefully states that "It will take an act of Congress to get back in this family." He does come to understand, through Cinzia's help, that during a storm Elizabeth needs a hug, not scientific explanations. Elizabeth, who had earlier wanted to shake his hand, gives him his first kiss. While Robert soon abandons his harmonica, David poses more of a problem. He steals things to get attention, to communicate his hurt, and he does not want to be treated as a little boy, a fact his father, who has no confidence in him, does not sense. Tom does not let him attempt to start the stalled vehicle, does not let him tie new mooring lines—the houseboat consequently drifts from its mooring—and attempts to show the more expert David how to fish. Tom demonstrates his love by saving David, who wanted to leave home, from drowning, but he does not, until Cinzia chides him, have the time to talk to David. The talk is futile until Tom lets David show him how to fish and lets David tie up Angelo's boat. Then Tom can use the river to discuss David's nagging questions about death.

While Cinzia has been, as Tom admits, putting the family together again, Carolyn has been moving to end her modern marriage and pursue Tom. Aware, as Tom is not, that Cinzia loves him, Carolyn condescendingly mocks Cinzia's accent and helps Tom buy her an appropriate dress for the Sons of Italy ball. When Cinzia shows her class by revamping the gaudy dress and by donning her mother's pearls, she intimidates Angelo, her date, and he is no longer able treat her as "Italian pastry." After Angelo leaves, Carolyn arrives at the houseboat with Alan Wilson (Murray Hamilton) and his wife. When an inebriated Alan suggests rudely that Cinzia "sleeps in" and then pats her behind, Cinzia throws a drink in his face. Upon learning that Carolyn shares Alan's opinion, Tom sends them away and takes Cinzia to the dance instead. At the country club, Tom logically decides to marry Carolyn, but when he dances with Cinzia he feels that he must marry her. After some ensuing confusion, Tom and Cinzia are united, but not without some further complications.

David, with an adolescent's crush on Cinzia, felt betrayed when she broke her eel-fishing date with him to go dancing with his father, and he is sexually jealous when he sees them kissing in the rowboat. Elizabeth is confused about the prospect of Cinzia being her mother and insists that she is their friend, not their mother. Robert continues to play his harmonica. While the children's reactions to Cinzia's new status are psychologically fairly normal, Cinzia's reaction is not, for she regresses to childhood by returning to her father, leaving her new "education," and vowing, appropriately, "never to jump ship again." When Tom appears, it is her father who insists that they marry, and Cinzia meekly and atypically submits. Tom in turn talks to his children about attending the wedding, but, having been educated on the river, he now asks, "Why do I talk so much?" He and Cinzia are married, and the children do join them at the altar, where Robert plays his harmonica, this time a rendition of "Here Comes the Bride," which Cinzia's father conducts. The musical ending is particularly appropriate, for music in *Houseboat* serves as a harmonizing agent that resolves the discord Cinzia's father mentions at the beginning of the film and reflects Tom's development from his "Stop singing!" response to trouble to his elevation of feeling over thinking. While he has the law on his side when he takes his children from their grandparents, he has his children by his side at the end of the film.

Houseboat is a thoroughly entertaining film which is wholesome in its 1950's emphasis on the nuclear family as the norm, its indictment of modern marriage, and its application of permissive child psychology. Like its counterparts in television's family situation comedies (Petersen appropriately was a member of Donna Reed's television family), *Houseboat* stresses the importance of parents being adults (Tom is urged to grow up) and knowing best and of children being children (Cinzia tells Tom that his problem is that he expects David to be grown up). In 1950's fashion, parent in *Houseboat* means father, because mothers are conspicuous by their absence in the film.

Of course, much of the humor in the film depends on casting Grant, the self-confessed charming and debonair Tom, in a chaotic situation in which his behavior is pretentiously out-of-step, as it often is in the screwball comedies in which he specialized. In *Houseboat*, Grant plays Grant for laughs, yet within a year Alfred Hitchcock's *North by Northwest* appeared and made use of the Grant *persona* in a film about the darker side of the 1950's. For Loren, *Houseboat* was also one of her lesser films, in part because American audiences saw her as another Gina Lollobrigida, a sex symbol with an amusing accent; and it was not until 1961, with her award-winning performance in *Two Women*, that she received full recognition from American audiences. Because it is light fare, a situation comedy that does not fully utilize the acting talents of its costars, *Houseboat* received mixed reviews, but it remains an entertaining account of American family life as it was supposed to be in the 1950's.

Thomas L. Erskine

Reviews

America. C, December 6, 1958, p. 327.
Catholic World. LXIV, October, 1958, p. 64.
Commonweal. LXIX, November 28, 1958, p. 232.
Filmfacts. V, January, 1959, p. 218.
Films and Filming. V, January, 1959, p. 22.
Life. XLV, October 13, 1958, p. 56.
The New York Times. November 14, 1958, II, p. 24.

The New Yorker. XXXIV, November 22, 1958, p. 138.
Newsweek. LII, November 3, 1958, p. 106.
Saturday Review. XLI, December 6, 1958, p. 36.
Time. LXXII, December 1, 1958, p. 82.
Variety. September 10, 1958, p. 6.

THE KILLING OF A CHINESE BOOKIE

Released: 1976 (re-released in an alternate version in 1978)
Production: Al Ruban for Faces International Films, Inc.
Direction: John Cassavetes
Screenplay: John Cassavetes
Cinematography: Al Ruban
Editing: Tom Cornwell
Production design: Sam Shaw
Art direction: Phedon Papamichael; set decoration, Miles Ciletti
Sound: Jack Woods and Buzz Knudson
Music: Bo Harwood
Title design: Richard Upper
MPAA rating: R
Running time: 135 minutes (1976 version)
  108 minutes (1978 version)

Principal characters:
Cosmo Vitelli	Ben Gazzara
Flo	Timothy Agoglia Carey
Mort	Seymour Cassel
Rachel	Azizi Johari
Betty, the mother	Virginia Carrington
Mr. Sophistication	Meade Roberts
Sherry	Alice Friedland
Margo	Donna Gordon
The Chinese bookie	Soto Joe Hugh
Mickey	Miles Ciletti

John Cassavetes is a fiercely independent filmmaker whose films are usually criticized for the roughness of their editing or the improvisational sprawl of their scenes. Yet the most important difference between Cassavetes' work and that of more orthodox Hollywood filmmakers does not have to do with the polish or roughness of the scripting, editing, or sound work, but with the way drama is generated. In a typical Hollywood film the drama is created by presenting characters with a series of problems or conflicts whose origins are more or less outside themselves; in contrast, Cassavetes' films are, in Marianne Moore's phrase, descriptions of wars which are always inward.

While Hollywood offers battles between figures, or between figures and their surroundings, Cassavetes explores inner struggles: chiefly, the struggle of a character to shape a self and to find an adequate expression of himself in the world. The outward action generated by the plot and events in a

Cassavetes film is almost always only a pretext for an inward crisis of self-definition and self-expression through which his characters must work.

John Keats said that we are not born with souls ready-made, but must gradually make them in the course of our lives; in a Cassavetes film, one must forge a self in order to have one at all (unless, in the other sense of the word, one's self is merely "forged"). One's identity cannot be inherited. Even once it is attained, it is in a perpetual state of revision.

This is probably the aspect of Cassavetes' work that has created the most critical confusion. Because his characters are not endowed with fixed or automatic identities and are continuously redefining themselves, they will not be understood in terms of the conventional character-types on which most other films are based. The result is that they can seem cryptic, inconsistent, confusingly unstable, or overwrought to someone looking for the other kind of figure.

Needless to say, insofar as they are unable to recline into stable narrative or worldly roles and functions, and are therefore invariably in states of flux and crisis, Cassavetes' characters are in a far-from-enviable situation. They are figures in an endless quest for figuration. Even at their best and happiest—as with the figure of Lelia in Cassavetes' first film, *Shadows* (1958)—they are in continuous ontological and social jeopardy. At their most tragic—as with the figure of Mabel in his *A Woman Under the Influence* (1974)—they display an anxiety about their definitions of themselves that borders on hysteria and threatens them with psychic self-destruction.

These comments may seem far from the film at hand, but this preface is necessary in order to prevent the potential misunderstanding in which a plot summary of *The Killing of a Chinese Bookie* might otherwise result. Any plot summary necessarily will give the misleading impression that the subject of the film is a series of external confrontations and conflicts, when in fact the external events exist only in order to generate the internal crises of selfhood and expression that Cassavetes is interested in exploring.

With this general caveat then, *The Killing of a Chinese Bookie* is the story of Cosmo Vitelli (Ben Gazzara), the owner of a sleazy Los Angeles strip joint, The Crazy Horse West. Early in the film, on a night of gambling at a mob-run casino, Cosmo gets over his head in debt and is forced to mortgage his club (and ultimately his life) to the mob as collateral for the loan. His life is put on the line subsequently, when, in order to clear the debt, he is ordered to murder a Chinese mob lord (Soto Joe Hugh), the head of a rival criminal empire. (The film's title derives from the fact that the mobsters refer to the man they send Cosmo to kill in code as "a Chinese bookie"—but he is actually what one of the gangsters later calls "the heaviest man on the West Coast.")

Cosmo is mortally wounded in the course of the shoot-out that ensues, and the rest of the film is the narration of his struggle to keep his nightclub going as the life drains out of him, and as the gangsters, afraid that he will implicate them in the murder, now close in around him to attempt to bump him off.

It may sound strange that Cosmo should care so intensely about his Sunset Strip club (more intensely than about his own life), all the more so since it is so tawdry and trashy. Yet The Crazy Horse West is everything that matters in the world for Cosmo. He has put his soul into it. As tacky as it is, it is his attempt at living his dream of doing something in style. Cassavetes goes to considerable lengths to make the viewer aware of what The Crazy Horse West would be without Cosmo and what he would be without it. Sleazy as it is, it is not just another bar or sex joint. (Cassavetes has Cosmo wander into another bar at the beginning of the film in order to remind the viewer how dingy and demeaning such a place can be.) The Crazy Horse West is almost a private repertory theater company with Cosmo its artistic director. The waitresses and barkeepers wear Western gear; the strippers do "artistic" numbers; and Cosmo—who single-handedly writes and choreographs the shows they put on, and who dates the girls he employs—plays the part of padrone to the hilt. As Cassavetes presents it, in its sleazy way, for such as Cosmo and those he hangs out with, The Crazy Horse West is a place of real style and class.

The plot of *The Killing of a Chinese Bookie* affiliates it with *film noir*. Yet a viewer who came into the theater determined to see a gangster film would be bored to tears, long before the film was half over (which is perhaps why the film died completely at the box office). It is Cosmo's personality and his attempt to express himself through his club that interests Cassavetes, not his ability to shoot a gun or kill a gangster.

Cosmo is a character who has identified himself completely with his work and his creation, and who is desperately attempting to hold on to the identity that he thinks they can guarantee him. Yet as all Cassavetes' films demonstrate, such an effort to formulate a fixed and reliable self once and for all, which one can merely hold on to, is a fundamental betrayal both of oneself and of everyone around one. Such a self is, for Cassavetes, a dead end for development, and is as false and unfair to one's own emotional needs as it is to the emotional needs of others.

Cosmo plays the protector and adviser to his strippers, the master of ceremonies for the shows at his club, and the confident, smiling public man to everyone he meets. Yet Cassavetes shows that his masculine poise and self-control is a terrible selling-out of himself and of all the personal relationships into which he enters.

Cosmo struts toward his death in the final hour of the film with an aplomb and assurance that dozens of gangster films have immortalized. From James Cagney, George Raft, and Paul Muni in the 1930's and 1940's, to Sylvester Stallone, Arnold Schwarzenegger, and Clint Eastwood in the

1970's and 1980's, one has seen this he-man maintain his cool under fire as he manhandles the women he lets into the margins of his life. Yet Cassavetes' point is the opposite of the one taken away from a Howard Hawks, Walter Lang, or Eastwood film, in which such coolness and self-possession is celebrated. He shows how far the male project of self-control is a lie about oneself and a betrayal of all the relationships into which one enters. In the second half of the film, as the mob puts ever greater pressure on him, Cosmo puts all of his life in order, as he marches to his doom, but his success is indistinguishable from failure. It is the ultimate cover-up of all of his real needs and desires.

This is a film of relentless cover-ups of true feelings and beliefs by Cosmo and almost everyone around him. The brilliance of Cassavetes' choice of the *film noir* genre is that it is a stylistic realm of personal threats and dangers in which all direct expressions of oneself are hazardous to one's health. Virtually no one is able to speak directly or candidly in this world, where shadows conceal ever-present dangers and lights blind one more often than they illuminate anything. (Much of the film is deliberately shot into either flaring brightness or velvety blackness so that one's eyes can never get accustomed to one or the other. It is as if there were no middle realm of mere daytime fill lighting attainable.) Even the strippers' nakedness becomes a kind of ultimate disguise for them.

Cosmo will not risk letting anyone, even his closest friend and lover—a girl named Rachel (Azizi Johari), one of the strippers in his show, and one of the few characters to attempt to speak intimately and personally to him—get close enough to get past his veneer of mastery and self-possession. His masculine distance and reserve are his attempt to withdraw from the hazards of unconditional, unpredictable relationships in order to remain emotionally invulnerable and controlled.

It is no exaggeration to say that Cosmo Vitelli is the role of Ben Gazzara's career. (The character was written and the film cast with Gazzara explicitly chosen for the part.) Even more than in his previous appearance in Cassavetes' *Husbands* (1970), or his subsequent role in *Opening Night* (1978), the character of Cosmo draws on Gazzara's particular range of expressiveness and his Method acting background to communicate Cosmo's intense inwardness, stoical self-sufficiency, and enigmatic introversion. Cassavetes further uses the quasi-orientalness of Gazzara's features to suggest a profound metaphorical connection between Cosmo and the man he murders.

The dreamlike scene involving Cosmo's stalking and murder of the Chinese Godfather is one of the strangest and most powerful in Cassavetes' work. It is not accidental that there is an uncanny resemblance between the stairways and spaces Cosmo negotiates at the Godfather's house and the backstage corridors of The Crazy Horse West, or that the girl who is present with the Chinese Godfather when Cosmo shoots him looks like one of the strippers at the club. The viewer is made to realize during the course of this scene that the Chinese Godfather is, in a mysterious way, both the father that Cosmo never had and an ego ideal for Cosmo himself as a successful and self-sufficient entrepreneur, lover, and father-figure to his strippers. In his silent and dreamlike passage through the dark hallways of the Chinaman's house (with the only audible sound the disturbing ticking of the clock), Cosmo is confronting an alter ego and then, in proceeding to kill him, in a metaphorical sense is annihilating himself.

Cassavetes' late films increasingly have recourse to dream sequences to represent the imaginations of characters who cannot express their relationships and feelings more directly or personally in the course of their films. Cosmo's dreams can only be expressed in strange and magical rites of passage such as this one. That expressive problem is in fact what *The Killing of a Chinese Bookie* attempts to explore.

All of Cassavetes' work takes the family as the basic metaphor not only for the social interactions of his characters but also for the very process of acting in and directing a film, and one of the themes that recurs in his work is the attempted reconstitution of the family in the face of obstacles to its existence. In this sense, *The Killing of a Chinese Bookie* is a study of Cosmo's effort to build and hold on to a surrogate family made up of himself and his girls at The Crazy Horse West. Yet what Cassavetes wants to show is that the family Cosmo makes through his club is a sham.

Cosmo is like an actor playing a husband, father, or lover who has mastered all the external mannerisms, gestures, and voice tones of his part, but who will not allow himself to be emotionally vulnerable or open enough to become an actual father or lover. Cosmo attempts to use style to replace substance, to camouflage the absence of it. The "family" Cosmo makes with his "girls" is as ersatz as his mimicry of style and class in his chauffeured nights on the town in a rented car, drinking scavenged bottles of Dom Perignon, wearing a clip-on bow tie and a tuxedo shirt a little too long in the sleeves. That suggests how one should understand Cosmo's offer to marry Rachel near the end of the film. He tells her that he is going to give her a diamond ring, but the offer is as merely rhetorical and resoundingly hollow as his final offer to buy drinks for everyone in his club at the end of the film.

The largest issue in this film—just as it is the central issue in most of Cassavetes' other films—is the individual's ability or inability to express himself in the forms of the world, to make his imagination count in practical social and familial forms of relationship. Cosmo is, in his seedy and affectingly awkward way, a man with an extraordinary imagination. Cassavetes contrasts his romantic conception of love with the meanness of the "hot love" represented by his doppelgänger in the film, the strip joint comedian Mr.

Sophistication (played by the distinguished screenwriter and playwright Meade Roberts). "Imagination" is, significantly, the title of one of the sketches Cosmo choreographs, a dance number which is genuinely poetic and evocative. Though it sounds peculiar to say it, Cosmo represents a vision of himself as a self-reliant, self-made man that is almost Emersonian in its grandeur and daring. He is an American dreamer, but one who can never find an adequate expression of his dreams.

In the final account, the problem that Cosmo defines is the predicament of the individual with this capacity of vision who is, for one reason or another, unable to convert it into the currency of life. The touching, painful discrepancy between Cosmo's almost grandiose vision of himself as an artist, a lover, and a friend to his girls, and his paltry, clumsy expressions of himself in his life takes one to the heart of the film's interest. Cosmo's imagination of romance will only be expressed in a strip joint. His Emersonian ideals of self-reliance come into conflict with the mob's decision to make him a fall guy. His fantasies that he is a family man with a girl and a mom, his illusions of style and class, and his faith that he is living the American Dream of success are all ultimately revealed to be bogus.

It is one thing to fool others (as Cosmo does throughout *The Killing of a Chinese Bookie* in denying the seriousness of his gunshot wound), but it seems something different and much worse to fool oneself. Cosmo's romantic imagination is finally only a way of fooling himself, and of attempting to escape from the harder truths and painful vulnerabilities of life. His imagination is a flight from life, not an enrichment of it. He uses his club to wall out danger. Like Robert Harmon in *Lovestreams* (1984) several years later, he attempts to build an imaginative world of his own, a "world elsewhere" in which to live.

Yet, life will not be scripted and choreographed in such ways, Cassavetes says. It will not be turned into a private, one-man show. Life is open and unarrangeable. Cosmo pretends to be his own man, when he is not. By attempting to stage-manage every relationship and every move he makes, Cosmo attempts to avoid the pains of emotional vulnerability and openness. In his retreat from intimacy, in the final scenes of the film, Cosmo has already died to everything that matters in life, even if he does keep on moving in the face of death.

Cosmo is ultimately Cassavetes' ambivalent self-portrait of the artist as a middle-aged man. He is his double reflection on the predicament of the artist who makes his own world to live in imaginatively, and on the situation of the self-made American male, living his dream of self-sufficiency and self-possession. Yet the crucial difference between the character and his creator is that John Cassavetes has none of Cosmo Vitelli's studied coolness, imperturbability, and acceptance of his situation. Where Cosmo offers poise under pressure and bravura acting, Cassavetes offers lurching imbalances, endless vulnerabilities of feeling, and the bewilderment of new experiences. He tells us that we must find our salvation, if at all, in worry, doubt, and disturbance.

Raymond Carney

Reviews
Films in Review. XXVII, April, 1976, p. 243.
Los Angeles Times. February 17, 1976, IV, p. 1.
The Nation. CCXXII, February 28, 1976, p. 254.
New Statesman. XCIX, March 28, 1980, p. 487.
The New York Times. March 7, 1976, II, p. 13.
Newsweek. LXXXVII, March 8, 1976, p. 89.
Saturday Review. III, April 3, 1976, p. 50.
Take One. III, August, 1976, p. 35.
Time. CVII, March 8, 1976, p. 80.
Variety. February 18, 1976, p. 35.

KISS ME, STUPID

Released: 1964
Production: Billy Wilder for the Mirisch Corporation, Phalanx Productions, and Claude Productions; released by Lopert Pictures
Direction: Billy Wilder
Screenplay: Billy Wilder and I. A. L. Diamond; based on the play "L'ora della fantasia," by Anna Bonacci
Cinematography: Joseph LaShelle
Editing: Daniel Mandell
Production design: Alexander Trauner
Art direction: Robert Luthardt; set decoration, Edward G. Boyle
Special effects: Milton Rice
Costume design: Bill Thomas
Choreography: Wally Green
Sound: Robert Martin and Wayne Fury
Music: André Previn
Songs: "Sophia," "I'm a Poached Egg," "All the Livelong Day," by George Gershwin and Ira Gershwin
MPAA rating: no listing
Running time: 126 minutes

Principal characters:
Dino	Dean Martin
Polly, the Pistol	Kim Novak
Orville J. Spooner	Ray Walston
Zelda Spooner	Felicia Farr
Barney Millsap	Cliff Osmond
Big Bertha	Barbara Pepper
Mrs. Pettibone	Doro Merande
Mr. Pettibone	Howard McNear
Milkman	James Ward

Kiss Me, Stupid opened in December, 1964, when director Billy Wilder was at the top of his popularity and critical reputation. After almost two decades of comic and dramatic successes, such as two Best Director Academy Awards—for *The Lost Weekend* (1945) and *The Apartment* (1960)—Wilder was both the creator of major new films and the subject of retrospectives of his past films, such as one held at the Museum of Modern Art in New York concurrent with *Kiss Me, Stupid*'s release. This position, however, was severely shaken by the overwhelmingly negative reception of *Kiss Me, Stupid*, a sincere romantic comedy set in pent-up, small-town America, which seemed to rub everyone the wrong way.

First, the Catholic Legion of Decency gave it a condemned rating and

strongly rebuked the filmmakers for their unflattering critique of current social values and their utilization of a plot that included a straightforward acceptance of adultery. The Motion Picture Association of America (MPAA)
also refused to approve the film, and this caused United Artists, who regularly distributed Mirisch films, to drop *Kiss Me, Stupid* and hand it over to
its subsidiary, Lopert Pictures. Reviewers, primed for the attack, labeled the
film lewd, immoral, and a long dirty joke. The film was held up as an
example of the degeneration of the film industry as it moved away from the
MPAA standards, and, consequently, it was buried under a frenzy of rhetoric.

While the film treats mature sexual themes in a highly comic fashion, it is
far from a succession of off-color jokes and titillating situations. Rather, it is
a carefully constructed comedy, whose characters travel a path from aloof
self-sufficiency to humble vulnerability. The adultery plot is treated with humor and compassion and, moreover, is not the *raison d'être* of the film. As
in Wilder's earlier dissection of American sexual peccadillos, *The Seven Year
Itch* (1955), the central character's lust becomes a sincere emotion, brought
on by a retapping of his true inner desires, which, in the end, is redirected
from the adulterous partner back to wife and family.

Wilder had previously dealt with mature subjects in a more and more
open fashion in *Some Like It Hot* (1959), *The Apartment*, and *Irma La
Douce* (1963), but each of these films was distanced from average American
experience, either through a period setting or, as in *The Apartment*, by
depicting the rarefied world of corporate New York. Yet *Kiss Me, Stupid*,
though nominally set in Nevada, actually depicts an average small town anywhere. Photographed in sharp focus, wide-screen black and white, the film
has a *Life* magazine look. The clean, linear sets by Alexander Trauner
depict the Norman Rockwell model of American simplicity and comfort.

This identification with apple-pie American values is central to Wilder's
comic effect, but it is also provoking. Wilder has turned the labels around.
The town is named Climax. The inhabitants are not relaxed and happy, but
hyperactive and dissatisfied. There is little to do but watch television and
dream of how to get rich (in order to get out of the small town and to the
city). While Wilder's wit is sharp, however, he is not without compassion.
His characters and their dreams, while held up for scrutiny, are not the subject simply of satire. Rather, Wilder uses his mature insight and understanding to bring them into confrontation with the demons that haunt them in
order to cast them out and restore the values he is so often accused of
debunking.

While driving to Los Angeles, Dino (Dean Martin), a Las Vegas singer
known for his heavy drinking and sexual appetite, makes a detour through
the small town Climax, Nevada. Stopped at the local gas station, he is recognized by the owner, Barney Millsap (Cliff Osmond), who quickly alerts

the local piano teacher, Orville J. Spooner (Ray Walston), who is also his song-writing partner. Orville concocts a plan to sabotage Dino's car in order to force him to stay overnight in Climax. This will allow Orville and Barney to attempt to interest Dino in some of their songs.

Their plan works, and Dino reluctantly accepts Orville's invitation to spend the night at his house. Orville, however, jealous about his wife Zelda (Felicia Farr), who is one of Dino's biggest fans, and aware of Dino's womanizing reputation, provokes an argument with her that sends her out of the house in tears. He then replaces her with Polly, the Pistol (Kim Novak), an accommodating waitress from the local bar, The Belly Button. Polly enjoys her new domestic role as Orville's "wife," and Dino wonders at his good luck, especially when Orville encourages him to make advances.

The evening is a success as Polly cooks dinner and Orville performs his material for Dino. Polly plays her role so naturally, however, that gradually Orville begins to identify her as his real wife, and his encouragement of Dino's lust stops and his jealousy emerges. Unable to contain himself, he jumps on Dino and throws the thoroughly confused guest out of his house. Realizing that he has spoiled his chances for success, Orville nevertheless knows that he did the right thing. As he and Polly accept each other as husband and wife for the night, he encourages Polly to leave Climax and pursue a life for herself.

Meanwhile, Dino ends up at The Belly Button for a drink. Needing a room for the night, he is given Polly's trailer, where he discovers Zelda asleep after drinking away her domestic unhappiness. Zelda, learning who he is and why he is in need of a bed, decides to indulge her fantasy, but not before she extracts Dino's promise to make one of Orville's songs a hit.

A few weeks later Orville and Zelda, arm-in-arm in their rekindled love, pass a television in a store window. On the television, Dino is singing one of Orville's songs. When Orville expresses his puzzlement, Zelda whispers for him to shut up and kiss her.

Production of *Kiss Me, Stupid* began with Peter Sellers in the role of Orville, but it had to be stopped a third of the way through when Sellers suffered a severe heart attack. He was replaced by Walston, whose performance was severely criticized. Unlike Sellers, who seemingly would have invented a broad comic personality for the role, Walston gives a completely natural performance that fits perfectly Wilder's direction. Walston makes the scheming, hot-tempered Orville a believable and ultimately vulnerable husband and lover, which is not easy, as Wilder, in typical fashion, initially shows the character in strongly negative terms.

The roles of Dino and Polly are constructed with obvious artifice, but each becomes a fully realized character. Dino is clearly based on the public image of Dean Martin. Wilder contrasts this image, and the efforts of Dino to live up to it, with the private man. This brings an unexpected softening to a role with rather simple outlines. Polly, in turn, reflects the screen image of the beautiful blonde who wants to be a housewife. Novak individualizes the role with great dexterity and adds an extra dimension with her air of resigned fatalism, brought about by recognition of her own sexual needs as well as the desires of the men around her.

Kiss Me, Stupid, along with the later *Avanti!* (1972), is one of Wilder's most complete expressions of his romantic pessimism. During the course of the film, Orville changes from a mean, suspicious, and grasping husband to a feeling and tender lover through his unexpected affection for the put-upon party girl, Polly. When he accepts her as his "wife" after chasing out Dino, it is a sincere love that has changed him. This humanization makes Orville a more understanding man and strengthens his love for his real wife. The experience with Orville also changes Polly, letting her recognize her own desires and giving her the confidence to try and change her life.

The humanization of a hardened, wound-up, mechanical man (or woman) is a theme in many of Wilder's comedies, from *A Foreign Affair* (1948) through *Sabrina* (1954) to *Avanti!* In each film, this theme is expertly integrated with Wilder's terse sense of humor and insightful commentary, creating an appealing and comic setting for the story, which never compromises the emotional base. This special romantic "touch," so in evidence in *Kiss Me, Stupid*, has often been overlooked or misunderstood. It stands at the heart of Wilder's comedies, however, giving them a lasting appeal and a special place in the memory.

Terry Nixon

Reviews

Commonweal. LXXXI, December 18, 1964, p. 421.
Film Quarterly. XVIII, Spring, 1965, p. 60.
Films and Filming. XI, April, 1965, p. 27.
Films in Review. XVI, February, 1965, p. 118.
Life. LVIII, January 15, 1965, p. 51.
Monthly Film Bulletin. March, 1965, p. 34.
The New Republic. CLVI, January 9, 1965, p. 26.
The New York Times. December 23, 1964, II, p. 22.
Newsweek. LXIV, December 28, 1964, p. 53.
Positif. LXXXVII, May, 1965, p. 41.
Saturday Review. XLVIII, January 2, 1965, p. 31.
Sight and Sound. XXXIV, Spring, 1965, p. 95.
Time. LXXXV, January 1, 1965, p. 69.
Variety. December 16, 1964, p. 6.
Vogue. CXLV, March 1, 1965, p. 97.

THE LONG, LONG TRAILER

Released: 1954
Production: Pandro S. Berman for Metro-Goldwyn-Mayer
Direction: Vincente Minnelli
Screenplay: Albert Hackett and Frances Goodrich; based on the novel of
the same name by Clinton Twiss
Cinematography: Robert Surtees
Editing: Ferris Webster
Art direction: Cedric Gibbons and Edward Carfagno
Music: Adolph Deutsch
MPAA rating: no listing
Running time: 103 minutes

Principal characters:

Tacy Collini	Lucille Ball
Nicholas Collini	Desi Arnaz
Mrs. Hittaway	Marjorie Main
Policeman	Keenan Wynn
Mrs. Bolton	Gladys Hurlbut
Mr. Tewitt	Moroni Olsen
Foreman	Bert Freed
Aunt Anatacia	Madge Blake
Uncle Edgar	Walter Baldwin
Mr. Judley	Oliver Blake
Bridesmaid	Perry Sheehan

The Long, Long Trailer brought together three comedic talents (stars Lucille Ball and Desi Arnaz and director Vincente Minnelli) at the height of their powers. The result was a film which delighted audiences in 1954 and which is still funny in the late 1980's.

Ironically, Lucille Ball and Desi Arnaz had not made a motion picture together since *Too Many Girls* (1940), during the filming of which they met and fell in love. That film is memorable for a bizarre final scene in which Arnaz dances around a college victory bonfire pounding a conga drum and singing his theme song, "Babalu," while dressed in a fully padded football uniform. Aside from this surreal sequence and a critically acclaimed death scene in *Bataan* (1943), Arnaz's film career was brief and spotty. In contrast, Ball had been in Hollywood since the early 1930's, progressing from roles as a Busby Berkeley chorine (*The Kid from Spain*, 1932) and a bit-player in Fred Astaire-Ginger Rogers musicals (*Follow the Fleet*, 1936) to featured roles (*The Big Street*, 1942). By the late 1940's, however, despite her designation as "Technicolor Tessie" because of her fiery red hair, her career was also declining. The husband-and-wife team decided to forsake motion pictures and take a chance on a weekly show in the new medium of television.

That show, *I Love Lucy*, was (and is, as it has never stopped appearing in reruns) the most successful program in the history of television. Arnaz was Ricky Ricardo, bandleader and long-suffering husband of Lucy Ricardo, whose plans, frequently sparked by her desire to better herself by getting into show business, were always the focus of the comedic action—and action there was. Audiences loved seeing Lucy clown her way through broad slapstick situations which were underscored by Ricky's frantic and often bombastic reactions. Although the absolute peak of interest in the show was the night in January, 1953, when Ricky Ricardo, Jr., was born on the show on the same night that Desi Arnaz, Jr., was born in real life, *I Love Lucy* was still very popular a year later when *The Long, Long Trailer* was released.

Not surprisingly, the film's plot is a modified version of the kind of marital daffiness featured in *I Love Lucy*. In *The Long, Long Trailer*, Arnaz and Ball play a couple who fall in love and get married early in the film; the rest is the story of their honeymoon, which quickly becomes a disaster. Nicky Collini is a construction engineer whose job requires that he be constantly on the move. As in *I Love Lucy*, the comic situation develops at the instigation of his bride, Tacy, who suggests—almost demands—that they live in a trailer which they can pull from construction site to construction site. They buy the trailer and are immediately beset with every kind of problem which that choice generates. First, the trailer costs much more than they thought it would; then Nicky discovers that because of the weight of the trailer, they will have to buy a more powerful and more expensive car. He also has to learn from painful experience how to drive the huge rig; the trailer must be stopped before the car or it will run over the automobile. He obviously does not take enough lessons, for in trying to leave some visiting relatives, he backs over a garden and destroys a porte cochere.

Tacy's greatest desire is to be the perfect mate for her husband, creating a pleasant home for him in cramped quarters, and most of the film's slapstick scenes stem from these efforts. Tacy tries to prepare dinner while the trailer is moving and winds up as tossed as the salad. When the trailer is parked on a sharp incline, she tries to make dinner and can only serve the wine when the glasses are taped to the table. Later the same night during a rainstorm, she tumbles out the door into a mudhole and emerges spattered and distraught, as at the conclusion of an *I Love Lucy* sketch. Nicky also has his problems, losing a battle with a shower. With pressures such as these on the marriage, Tacy leaves Nicky, but with the help of other trailerites, they are together again at the end of the film.

If this type of action in a trailer sounds predictable, the fact that it is nevertheless funny must be attributed not only to the acting of the stars but also to the direction of Minnelli. Although primarily noted for his work in musicals—*The Long, Long Trailer* was the next film he directed after the highly successful *The Band Wagon* (1953) with Astaire and Jack Buchanan—Minnelli had also shown that he was a fine director of comic dialogue in *Father of the Bride* (1950). His influence is clear in the most hilarious sequence in the film, which involves the couple's attempt to get their trailer home over the Sierra mountains at Yosemite Valley. Tacy has been collecting rocks from every place they have visited, but Nicky orders her to throw them out in order to make the rig as light as possible as they climb the mountains. Tacy cannot bear to give up her precious and romantic rocks, so instead of discarding them she hides them all over the trailer. Both become more and more apprehensive as the car struggles to move the massive trailer up an ever-increasing slope. The humor of the scene is doubled as, while both stare straight ahead, to hide their fright they discuss in detail the plot of a film they have seen. The scene builds because of the skillful use of dialogue, and one cannot imagine it appearing on an episode of *I Love Lucy*, which went for the quick laugh. This sequence is all Minnelli's, and it is reminiscent of other scenes in his films featuring a combination of comedy and fear, such as the "Be a Clown" number in *The Pirate* (1947). Minnelli's directorial skill also coaxes new freshness into the performances of several veteran performers who are doing their standard turns. Marjorie Main plays a battle-ax with a heart of gold, Keenan Wynn has a brief scene as an apoplectic policeman, and Moroni Olsen contributes his usual portrayal of a flustered middle-aged husband.

The first audiences of the film were highly receptive, so it is surprising that Arnaz and Ball never made another film together. Even more surprising was the reaction of the company which made the trailer featured in the film. Although *The Long, Long Trailer* is a record of everything that can possibly go wrong with life in a mobile home, redeemed only by the magnificent scenery through which the couple passes, the trailer company took out a full-page ad in *Variety* urging theater-owners to set up promotional tie-ins designed to help sell their product.

James Baird

Reviews
America. XC, February 27, 1954, p. 582.
American Magazine. CLVII, February, 1954, p. 12.
Commonweal. LIX, March 5, 1954, p. 554.
Films in Review. V, February, 1954, p. 96.
Library Journal. LXXIX, February 15, 1954.

National Parent-Teacher. XLVIII, March, 1954, p. 38.
The New York Times. February 19, 1954, II, p. 24.
Newsweek. XLIII, February 8, 1954, p. 86.
Saturday Review. XXXVII, February 20, 1954, p. 32.
Time. LXIII, February 22, 1954, p. 102.
Variety. January 6, 1954, p. 52.

MYSTERY OF THE WAX MUSEUM

Released: 1933
Production: Henry Blanke; released by Warner Bros.
Direction: Michael Curtiz
Screenplay: Don Mullaly and Carl Erickson; based on a story by Charles S. Belden
Cinematography: Ray Rennahan
Editing: George Amy
Art direction: Anton Grot
Makeup: Perc Westmore
Costume design: Orry-Kelly
Wax figures: L. E. Otis, assisted by H. Clay Campbell
Music: no listing
MPAA rating: no listing
Running time: 78 minutes

Principal characters:
Ivan Igor .... Lionel Atwill
Charlotte Duncan .... Fay Wray
Florence Dempsey .... Glenda Farrell
Jim (the editor)................... Frank McHugh
Ralph Burton...................... Allen Vincent
George Winton.................... Gavin Gordon
Joe Worth .... Edwin Maxwell
Sparrow .... Arthur Edmund Carewe
Otto............................. Matthew Betz

Mystery of the Wax Museum was a lost film for almost twenty-five years, until an original thirty-five millimeter color print was found in Jack Warner's private vault and was subsequently screened at the New York Film Festival in September, 1970. In the years of its absence, its reputation had grown so considerably that its rediscovery was disappointing to those who remembered it fondly, but it remains an accomplished and interesting film—a rare foray into the horror genre by Warner Bros.—the special qualities of which were not fully appreciated when it was released in 1933. The collaboration of art director Anton Grot, director Michael Curtiz, and cinematographer Ray Rennahan (Hollywood's Technicolor expert) provided the film with a rich visual style, including the most imaginative use of color for a horror film prior to the 1960's, when Roger Corman produced his celebrated cycle of films based on stories by Edgar Allan Poe.

The film opens on a rainy London street at night in 1921. Ivan Igor (Lionel Atwill) is visited in his wax museum by a doctor friend and an archaeologist who plan to exhibit his "sculptures" more widely. Their departure is immediately followed by the entrance of Igor's financial backer, Joe Worth (Edwin Maxwell). Showing him an insurance policy, Worth suggests that Igor's severe debt could be repaid by a fire. The two men struggle as Worth torches the display, leaving the unconscious Igor in the inferno surrounded by melting wax models.

The scene then shifts to New York City, New Year's Eve, 1932. Amidst the celebration, the dead body of a socialite, Joan Gale, is carried out of an apartment building as Igor looks on. Soon thereafter, the body is stolen from the morgue by a hideous figure while a female reporter, Florence (Glenda Farrell), is fired from her job by her editor, Jim (Frank McHugh), for partying too much. Florence, however, fascinated by the socialite's alleged suicide on New Year's Eve and the subsequent disappearance of the body, interviews suspect George Winton (Gavin Gordon), a rich acquaintance of the dead woman, in the Tombs (a New York penitentiary), where he is being held for questioning. The mystery is compounded for the audience by the reappearance of Worth, whose inexplicable dealings revolve around a crate similar to that used to transport the victim's body.

Later, Florence accompanies her roommate, Charlotte (Fay Wray), to visit the latter's boyfriend, Ralph (Allen Vincent), who is working on an exhibit for the now-crippled Igor, who is about to open a new wax museum in New York. In wandering around the exhibit, Florence notices that Joan of Arc looks exactly like the dead Joan Gale, and her suspicion leads her to follow another of Igor's assistants, Sparrow (Arthur Edmund Carewe), to Worth's office/residence. There, in the basement, she spies not only the monster that was glimpsed stealing the body but also the crate, and she informs millionaire playboy Winton—whom she is using as her driver—and the police. They open the crate, however, and discover only whiskey. Winton identifies Worth as his bootlegger, and the police then arrest Sparrow and interrogate him: They claim he is a drug addict. Thus, Worth is marked as being a criminal of high proportions—involved in murder, bootlegging, and drug trafficking. Igor has been tracking Worth (through Sparrow) presumably since the fire in 1921, and Worth is next seen as a corpse in the waxworks laboratory beneath the museum, giving the audience another clue about the "sculpting" of the wax figures.

When Florence's friend Charlotte returns after the opening of the museum to look for Ralph, Igor, who had been struck by Charlotte's likeness to Marie Antoinette, the London wax figure he cherished the most, traps her. He rises out of his wheelchair to embrace her, and as she struggles, she cracks the mask he wears over his disfigured face—he is the monster. In the Griffithian climax, Ralph is knocked down while the apparently naked Charlotte is strapped to a carriage beneath a tube-like device of boiling wax. Florence brings Winton and then the police, one of whom shoots Igor, who falls into the central vat of wax. Ralph revives and wheels Charlotte away from the overflowing tube in the nick of time. Surprisingly, after returning to Jim's office in triumph, the wisecracking Florence decides to marry her editor, rejecting her rich, film-long companion, Winton.

Mystery of the Wax Museum was developed as "The Wax Works" and shot as "Wax Museum." Its hybrid nature—part horror, part comedy, part detective, part gangster, part "journalist as hero" film—reflects the studio's lack of faith in the straightforward horror genre. The title changes also reflect this uncertainty, and the contemporary urban setting, the hard-boiled humor, fast-paced dialogue and action, and particularly the newspaper story all move Mystery of the Wax Museum closer to a mainstream Warner Bros. product. Another indication of a shift of perspective away from horror is that Glenda Farrell, who was billed third beneath Atwill and Wray, is actually accorded more screen time than anyone else, far more than Wray, who clearly plays a supporting role as the principal female victim (unlike her role in King Kong, 1933, a film which was shot earlier but released later). More surprisingly, though, Farrell is the main protagonist in Mystery of the Wax Museum, a position usually reserved for the male lead. Though one could argue that her character capitulates at the end of the film, in marrying her editor, even there she seems to be taking the initiative, and all through the film she is at the "intellectual" center. She is privileged with point-of-view and reaction shots throughout, and she makes the most important discovery: that the wax figures (Voltaire as well as Joan of Arc) resemble missing dead people. Other Warner Bros. films of the period featured women reporters—Five Star Final (1931), Blessed Event (1932)—and Glenda Farrell reprised the role often, in Hi, Nellie! (1934) and then as a regular character, Torchy Blane, in a series of films beginning with Smart Blonde in 1937. In fact, Florence in Mystery of the Wax Museum may well have been one of the very "toughest" women characters—in terms of her control over events—in all Hollywood films of the "classical" period, and she is ultimately much more in command here than Rosalind Russell's Hildy is in His Girl Friday (1940).

The police detectives are unsympathetic, even nasty, in Mystery of the Wax Museum: It is suggested that they may have tortured Sparrow. The vicious edge is also carried into the newspaper offices, but there it is balanced by humor. Indeed, Florence is essentially a comic heroine, and her search for clues is punctuated by frightening, yet funny "old house" techniques—from films such as The Cat and the Canary (1927) and The Bat Whispers (1930)—where she is made to jump and recoil from closing doors, moving boxes, and one of Igor's workers wielding a knife over a lifelike wax figure. Also, one of the strengths of the film is its dynamic pacing (a Warner Bros. trademark); here one can detect Curtiz' influence, since the 186 "scenes"— or shots—of the final screenplay were extended to more than eight hundred shots in the finished film, for an average shot length of less than six seconds—a remarkably fast cutting rate for the period. Much dialogue was excised, and there are fully nineteen shots in the opening scene before a word is uttered.

The identity of the monster is withheld from the viewer much longer than in *The Phantom of the Opera* (1925)—a film which was clearly an influence—and a general aura of mystery is cleverly sustained through much of *Mystery of the Wax Museum*. Crosscutting disorients the viewer, keeping him on edge, and it helps to suggest that Worth may be the body snatcher. When Worth is reintroduced in New York, he is viewed from behind for a long period so that his identity is unclear, and the audience is led further astray because Sparrow works for both Igor and Worth. The opening shots of the film set up the theme of concealment with a heavily shadowed, rainy London street hiding the location of the lurking Worth.

Adding to the sense of mystery, the most dangerous places are always downstairs, from the first London wax museum to Worth's basement to the wax-making laboratory in New York, yet knowledge of the actual location of this last set—beneath the wax museum—is withheld until the end. A tracking and panning camera gradually reveals these sets to the audience; such an exposition can also be regarded as belonging generically to the detective film. The vertical depth of the scenes is emphasized by craning camera moves, while other sets have an exaggerated lateral perspective built in by art director Anton Grot to enhance their aura of menace.

The obvious artificiality of the art direction and cinematography may have been partly responsible for *Mystery of the Wax Museum*'s lack of success at the box office, but it now seems to constitute the film's real achievement. In the press book written for the film's release, the director, Curtiz, wrote of deliberately invoking German expressionism as an appropriate style to represent unease, mystery, and horror, and no element functions better than color in this way. Two-color Technicolor cannot present the full color spectrum, and pink/orange and green/brown dominate. It is clear that the filmmakers deliberately exploited the contrast of pink and green in the overall stylistic scheme of *Mystery of the Wax Museum*. As flesh tones can be accurately reproduced in two-color Technicolor and as the film is centrally concerned with the artificial representation of human flesh in wax, the story line invites a play on flesh tones, from their normal appearance to a nauseating green. Igor's monstrous face is made more ugly by being colored brown/green, and when Charlotte makes her way down to the waxworks, she passes the deaf-mute Otto (Matthew Betz)—another of Igor's assistants—hiding amongst green wax heads, is startled by another mad-looking green gargoyle, and is herself observed by human eyes behind a green hood. The boiling vat of wax contains a sickening combination of a green periphery with a bubbling pink core, while the tube of wax intended to entomb Charlotte is toned a garish pink/red as it boils over. Thus, the unease that suffuses the film reaches a peak in the attraction/repulsion dichotomy focused around the "creation" of the wax figures that Igor terms "his children." The viewer is repulsed by Igor's practice yet attracted by his sympathetic nature—his suffering in the fire and his quiet demeanor endear him to the viewer—and fascinated by his lifelike reproductions. Curtiz, Grot, and Rennahan brilliantly understood that the medium of film was also merely a "representation" of life and therefore drew attention to its artifice in their manipulation of the two-color palette.

Peter Rist

Reviews
Film Comment. VII, Spring, 1971, p. 71.
The New York Times. February 18, 1933, II, p. 13.
Variety. February 21, 1933, p. 14.

SALT OF THE EARTH

Released: 1954
Production: Paul Jarrico; presented by Independent Productions Corporation and the International Union of Mine, Mill and Smelter Workers
Direction: Herbert J. Biberman
Screenplay: Michael Wilson
Cinematography: Leonard Stark and Stanley Meredith
Editing: Ed Spiegel and Joan Laird
Art direction: no listing
Sound: Dick Stanton and Harry Smith
Music: Sol Kaplan
MPAA rating: no listing
Running time: 94 minutes

> *Principal characters:*
> Esperanza Quintero . . . . Rosaura Revueltas
> Ramón Quintero . . . . Juan Chacón
> Sheriff. . . . . Will Geer
> Frank Barnes . . . . Clinton Jencks
> Luís Quintero. Frank Talavera
> Barton . . . . David Wolfe
> Alexander . . . . David Sarvis
> Hartwell . . . . Mervin Williams

While nothing should distract the viewer from responding fully and directly to this extraordinary film, the story behind the making of *Salt of the Earth* is nearly as dramatic and educational as the film itself. In the early 1950's, Hollywood—like the rest of America—was in the midst of a serious political crisis: Everyone connected with such a high-visibility industry as filmmaking was being scrutinized to determine if he were sufficiently free from any taint of radicalism or loosely defined "un-American" activities, associations, or beliefs. Sanctions were applied with a heavy hand: An uncooperative appearance before the House Un-American Activities Committee (HUAC) could result in a contempt citation and imprisonment, as it did for Herbert Biberman, one of the so-called Hollywood Ten; and even those considered suspiciously sympathetic to movements for social change, such as producer Paul Jarrico and actor Will Geer, could be blacklisted, illegally but effectively cut off from working in films.

Partially as a means of providing work for themselves and others on the blacklist and partially to create films on topics in which Hollywood showed little interest (for example, racial equality, labor unions), Biberman, Jarrico, the writer Michael Wilson, and others formed Independent Productions

Corporation. Their first, and, as it turns out, only completed effort was *Salt of the Earth*, a semidocumentary story of a strike of zinc miners, which was filmed at Silver City, New Mexico, close by the site of a real strike only a few years earlier. The difficulties of independent production were compounded by direct interference from Hollywood executives, government officials, and conservative unions, who maintained a somewhat hysterical campaign against a film they were certain was dangerous. That the film was completed and released was in itself a major triumph, but, although it opened to generally favorable critical reception, its distribution was restricted and it has never gained the audience nor the place in film history it deserves. A fresh look at *Salt of the Earth* may well confirm that it is a kind of American *Potemkin* (1925): It lacks the brilliant montage sequences and overall rhythm and unity of Sergei Eisenstein's classic, but it is filled, like *Potemkin*, with increasingly dramatic images of the self-education, solidarity, and strength of an ever-growing mass of people.

The film begins with the voice-over narration of Esperanza Quintero (Rosaura Revueltas) and images of her hard at work outdoors. Her bleak situation at least initially belies the hopefulness suggested by her name. Ramón (Juan Chacón), her husband, spends his days with dynamite and darkness, working in a mine run by sneering or otherwise unsympathetic Anglos; her young son Luís (Frank Talavera) is constantly fighting with the white kids who attempt to push him around; and Esperanza's daily struggle in a house without hot water or a bathroom leaves her exhausted, praying only that the child with whom she is pregnant will not be born into such a world. Taken alone, these problems are serious enough—indeed, overwhelming—yet they have the further effect of exacerbating the sexism of the workers. The men are rightly concerned with job safety and equality, but they trivialize the women's demands for sanitation and continually exclude them from serious discussions and decisions. Much of the power of *Salt of the Earth* comes from its simultaneous examination of domestic as well as political problems: The women need to be liberated from the men just as surely as the men need to be liberated from the bosses.

At first, the film focuses on the problems in the mine. The company's insistence that the men work alone—a cost-cutting measure that also symbolizes the owners' basic opposition to the workers' joining one another in any way—is repeatedly discussed and protested by the men, but when one of them is hurt in a preventable accident, the rest call a spontaneous strike. Interestingly, the film emphasizes what one might think of as "undramatic" aspects of the strike. Audiences whose main impression of labor disputes derives from television and newsreel shots of violent confrontations between strikers, police, and scabs may be surprised—and educated—by the film's attention to lengthy, honest discussions of ideas, the slow formulation of policies, and the growing bond among the workers and the women, in the meetings and on the picket line. *Salt of the Earth* contains dramatic episodes, to be sure. For example, Ramón is targeted as one of the union leaders and beaten by two deputies, an incident made particularly memorable because it is rapidly crosscut with shots of Esperanza having her baby: Ramón and Esperanza cry out to each other in their moment of deepest need and pain. The emphasis, though, is on less dramatic but equally important themes, such as the breaking down of boundaries between the Mexican-American workers and the white representative from the International Union, who is sympathetic and democratic but still needs to learn more about the lives and heritage of his brothers (he does not even recognize the portrait of Benito Juárez, the father of modern Mexico).

Similarly, the men have to learn more about their wives, and perhaps the dominant theme of the last two-thirds of the film is the increasing integration of the women into the strike, to the point where they become not only participants but also organizers. The women form a Ladies' Auxiliary to the union, and though they continue to have their own demands for "sanitation not discrimination," they back their husbands' demands fully. They are at first timid, but they soon join the picket line, following the lead of a woman whose husband was killed in a strike a few years earlier. When a Taft-Hartley injunction is served, ordering the men to stop picketing, the women propose that they substitute for the men. They have no vote in union matters, but when the union meeting is reconstituted as a town council, they are allowed to vote and their suggestion is adopted. This widening of the democratic process is by no means painless, and some of the husbands, including Esperanza's, continue to be "backward" and refuse to allow their wives to picket, but ultimately this resistance breaks down: not so much because the husbands are easily educated but because the women prove themselves to be independent, strong, and resourceful. Even when they are thrown in jail, their solidarity is unwavering, and, in one of the few comic moments of the film, they torment their captors with singing and cries for "the formula" to feed Esperanza's child, whom she has refused to leave behind.

With the women more or less in control of the strike and capable of protecting themselves, the men are displaced, relegated to what had formerly been "women's work." Predictably, this gives them new insight into the women's demands for bathrooms and hot water, and Ramón, exhausted from washing and hanging clothes all day and chopping wood for the home fire—woman's work indeed!—concludes that the union's demands from the start should have been more comprehensive. The deeper lesson of the strike, however, is difficult for Ramón to accept. "Sex equality" is as radical a demand to the men as "job equality" is to the owners, in part because it is perceived not so much as true equality but as a complete reversal of roles. Esperanza gains a tremendous amount of vitality as she becomes involved in the union struggle, but Ramón is too depressed by his own displacement from power to realize that Esperanza's newfound authority will ultimately complement rather than threaten his own strength. She finds faith in an all-encompassing friendship between men and women that will enable them to succeed in their common struggle, but he is resentful rather than cooperative. He and the other men pick up their guns to go hunting, a rather ominous male ritual that could prove particularly dangerous in a time of labor conflict and domestic distress.

The final crisis of the film comes when the company orders the eviction of the Quinteros from their company-owned house. As the sheriffs carry out the eviction order, a crowd begins to gather. The men rush back from their hunting party fully armed, and for a moment it seems as though there may be a violent confrontation: Ramón aims his rifle but then puts it down, implicitly realizing that their most effective weapon is not armed violence but the strength and solidarity of the entire community, including the women. Just as quickly as the sheriffs bring out the furnishings of the house, the townspeople return them through another door, and all the while the crowd around the house is increasing, swelled by new arrivals of men and women from nearby towns and other mines. The crowd is never threatening, seeming almost immobile, but its quiet determination and power convince the mine representatives to end not only the eviction but also the strike itself. Ramón thanks the newly solidified community around him, his brothers and sisters, but he thanks Esperanza in particular: He was clinging to the "old ways," resisting the friendship of the women, but he has been won over by their "dignity." Esperanza has the final words in the film, and her closing voice-over narration expresses her great faith that the meaning of the victorious strike lies in the legacy of unity and equality left to the children, the true salt of the earth.

By some standards, _Salt of the Earth_ is a flawed film. Many of the actors are nonprofessional; Juan Chacón, for example, was the real-life leader of the union involved in the strike against the mine owners, and other members of the union appear either in individual roles or simply as part of the all-important crowd. While this adds a great deal of authenticity to the film, much of the acting is, by Hollywood standards, wooden and unconvincing. The story itself is frequently melodramatic and the characters tend to fall into stereotypical groups: the sinister, totally reprehensible owners versus the sincere, sympathetic workers. Partially because of production difficulties, the technical qualities of the film are somewhat primitive: The sound is often badly mixed, there are problems in continuity, and the camera work is static and uninventive. Even those generally sympathetic to radical politics and filmmaking may have serious reservations about the film. While its message was enough to frighten "Red-baiters" and union busters of the 1950's, modern viewers may judge that the film does not go far enough. For example, at one point Ramón overhears the manager of the mine talking about the importance of the strike because of its place in "the big pic-ture"—if the workers win here, they might win elsewhere. Ramón becomes haunted by this phrase, and, to a certain extent, the success of the workers comes only when they adopt their version of "the big picture" and integrate their struggles with those of their wives and other workers. The sympathetic crowd at the end of the film is the embodiment of "the big picture" for them, but, while this is a powerful cinematic image, it stops short of offering a revolutionary vision. In real-life situations, the owners may not always give in so easily, and, even if they do, concessions may not be enough to alter the deep-seated adversarial relationship between owners and workers.

The greatness of *Salt of the Earth*, though, rises above these criticisms. It simply cannot be measured by the Hollywood standards that in so many ways it contests, and the true audience for this film is composed of men and women who care less for finely crafted fantasies than for ruggedly honest films that explore and, to a certain extent, resolve basic problems of life, work, and sexual relations. That such an audience is, at last, growing appre-ciably is evident in the popularity and critical success of such films as *Norma Rae* (1979), featuring Sally Field's Academy Award-winning performance as a strike leader, Barbara Kopple's *Harlan County, U. S. A.*, also an Academy Award winner as Best Documentary of 1976, and Marin Karmitz's *Coup pour coup (Blow for Blow*, 1972), about striking women in a garment fac-tory. *Salt of the Earth* stands behind each of these in a way that is only recently coming to be properly acknowledged.

Sidney Gottlieb

Reviews
Commonweal. LIX, April 2, 1954, p. 651.
Film Culture. Fall, 1970, Number 50, p. 79.
Film Library Quarterly. V, Winter, 1971, p. 51.
Films and Filming. I, November, 1954, p. 20.
Films in Review. V, April, 1954, p. 197.
The Nation. CLXXVIII, April 10, 1954, p. 314.
The New York Times. March 15, 1954, II, p. 20.
Newsweek. XLIII, March 29, 1954, p. 87.
Time. LXIII, March 29, 1954, p. 92.
Variety. March 17, 1954, p. 6.

STAR TREK
The Motion Picture

Released: 1979
Production: Gene Roddenberry; released by Paramount Pictures
Direction: Robert Wise
Screenplay: Harold Livingston; based on a story by Alan Dean Foster and
   on the television series of the same name created by Gene Roddenberry
Cinematography: Richard H. Kline and Richard Yuricich
Editing: Todd Ramsay
Production design: Harold Michelson
Art direction: Joe Jennings, Leon Harris, and John Vallone; set decoration,
   Linda De Scenna
Special photographic effects: Douglas Trumbull, John Dykstra, and Dave
   Stewart
Special animation effects: Robert Swarthe
Special science consultant: Isaac Asimov
Makeup: Fred Phillips, Janna Phillips, and Ve Neill
Costume design: Bob Fletcher
Sound: Tom Overton and Richard Landerson
Music: Jerry Goldsmith
MPAA rating: G
Running time: 132 minutes

Principal characters:
Admiral James T. Kirk . . . . William Shatner
Mr. Spock . . . . Leonard Nimoy
Dr. McCoy ("Bones") . . . . DeForest Kelley
Mr. Scot ("Scotty") . . . . James Doohan
Ilia . . . . Persis Khambatta
Captain Decker . . . . Stephen Collins
Sulu . . . . George Takei
Dr. Chapel . . . . Majel Barrett
Chekov . . . . Walter Koenig
Uhura . . . . Nichelle Nichols

Admiral (no longer Captain) Kirk (William Shatner) is recalled for duty
after two and a half years without logging a single starflight. He does not
understand the sophisticated new designs built into the Federation's refitted
starship *USS Enterprise*. His age and experience count, however; he is
reappointed captain for a crucial mission—"to intercept, investigate, and
take whatever action is necessary" to prevent a mysterious and massive
energy field, emanating from the "most powerful consciousness" of what

proves to be a living machine, from destroying the Earth. As Kirk takes a lengthy tour of the old ship with engineer Scotty (James Doohan) before she is launched, his ample chest expands with sentimental pride. A snazzier and more streamlined uniform kindly makes him look more like his younger, slimmer self.

Almost from its first shots, the viewer can taste the flavor of nostalgia that pervades *Star Trek: The Motion Picture*; even this first of the "Trekkie" movies is a homage to a dead television show (immortalized by a hundred reruns), a return to a past experience and addiction. For it is not merely Kirk who has to be "recalled." As the action begins, only Scotty the engineer is still working on the *Enterprise*. Spock (Leonard Nimoy) is on his home planet of Vulcan, nearing the end of long studies to achieve the state of "kolinahr" or "total logic," when he senses his old shipmates' need and the attraction of "thought patterns of exactingly perfect order" emanating from the "super-intelligence"; graying and gaunter, he catches up with the *Enterprise* in mid-flight. Besides needing to develop such strategies as this to cope with the fact that its leading actors are visibly and irrevocably older, *Star Trek* clings throughout to the belief that nothing essential has really changed: that the past, complete with all its attitudes, great and not-so-great, can be re-created. Thus, for example, as the momentary mouthpiece of this fundamental premise, in response to Spock's cold reception of their greetings, Doctor McCoy (DeForest Kelley) opines: "Spock, you haven't changed a bit—you're just as sociable as ever." The Vulcan Science Officer responds with the near-ritual reply: "Nor have you, Doctor, as your continued predilection for irrelevancy demonstrates."

McCoy himself, one might add, now sports as many wrinkles as a bloodhound; embarking late, in haste, he has had no time yet to change his 1960's hippy outfit. His heavy beard and shoulder-length hair are, again, emblems of the film's nostalgic return to the past, in which one senses the beginnings of the self-conscious parody that was to climax in the fourth film (released in 1987) of the series that this film initiated. Always the purveyor of pithy homespun wisdom, sarcastic bon mots, and psychological catchphrases, the doctor can be relied upon to verbalize self-consciously this aspect of his function in the film (he hates the remodeled sick bay, for example: It is "like working in a damn computer center"), and to summarize conveniently some of the key concepts of this film in particular and the science-fiction genre as a whole. "Why," he complains, this time as mouthpiece for the audience too, "is any object we don't understand always called a 'thing'?"

Dialogue like this also encapsulates the outdated and idealistically positive attitudes allowed expression by the film, as they were by the entire television series. This is perhaps its most nostalgic characteristic. People are seen not as members of a machine-dominated crew but as individuals held together by feelings of friendship and loyalty, with a right to their idiosyncrasies and their outspokenness. Technology, meanwhile, is regarded with some "down-home" suspicion, although overall the new, the unknown, and the technological hold promise of great progress and potential for good. Thus McCoy, for example, is recalled to active service and "beamed up" by his old captain against his wishes but is reconciled to his duty when reminded of old ties and old-fashioned values and told, in pathetic tones, "Bones . . . I _need_ you." More important, the whole thrust of the plot is toward expressing naïve optimism about technology and the future of the human race; as the end title puts it, "The human adventure is just beginning." The film offers an extreme, optimistic, very openly stated, and only mildly lunatic version of contemporary science fiction's half-fearful fascination with the microchip and the machine, and a rose-tinted view of the classic antinomy of the genre: _Star Trek_ invites the viewer to believe in a "living machine" and the possibility of creative union between the human and the nonhuman.

One's initial perception that the "super-intelligence" threatening Earth is a force hostile to man (and Vulcan) is accordingly proved wrong in the course of the film. Suspicions that the force is benevolent are aroused quite early (with concomitant loss of dramatic tension), despite such obviously hostile acts as its frying alive a ship full of Klingons (unpleasant aliens with zipperlike seams up their foreheads, hence expendable) and consigning to nothingness a roomful of Federation employees at home base while they are broadcasting their exciting new findings to the _Enterprise_—one of many clichés of the screen shamelessly reworked in _Star Trek_. It turns out that the force had in fact been trying to communicate and was being ignored. Once it has made contact with and rendered impotent the _Enterprise_, it kidnaps with surprisingly beneficial results one Lieutenant Ilia (Persis Khambatta), a bald beauty from the planet Delta with whom Executive Officer Decker (Stephen Collins)—demoted from his position as captain by the returning Kirk—is in love. Ilia returns to the ship as the cloned and reprogrammed probe of a force calling itself "V-ger," which now states its mission in quasi-Christian terms which cannot but arouse the audience's recognition and sympathy. V-ger is traveling to Earth to "join with the Creator." In short, like the crew of _Enterprise_ themselves in their many questing adventures in alien worlds on the small screen, V-ger is posing questions about life and the universe. For all of its massive intelligence and knowledge, V-ger does not have many answers.

Such a twist of the plot not only enlists the viewer's sympathy for V-ger, the living machine (as a similar twist does for the rebellious and murderous androids in _Bladerunner_, 1982), but also enlists the viewer's sympathies for the human race, for V-ger, one now discovers, is none other than Voyager 6, launched three hundred years before to "learn all that is learnable." V-ger represents, then, the limitations of knowledge and the necessity of faith.

It also causes hearts to warm toward the cold, crusty, and questioning Spock. His fascination with V-ger, the apparent epitome of all he himself would be, leads to enlightening disappointment; his best instinct, it turns out, was to abandon "total logic" and submit to being loved and nagged by his old shipmates. As the heroically fallible Kirk puts it: "What V-ger needs in order to evolve . . . is our capacity to leap beyond logic."

Action is now taken in accordance with this glowing view of human nature and the potential of the machine. V-ger signals its willingness to start transmitting its results to Earth (in other words, to "join with the Creator"), but next burns out its own antenna leads. It wants to transmit, it seems, "in person." Even in outer space—this film's most inadequate and overblown solution of the moment—a good sex life is the solution to one's problems. V-ger achieves transmission and evolution by joining, in the person of its probe, Ilia, in physical union with the expendable former captain Decker, who has been in love with Ilia from the first and seems happily unable to tell a clone from the real McCoy. Uplifted by the wonder they have witnessed, the birth of a new life form, the crew returns to the ship. "Heading, sir?" enquires the helmsman. "Out there," replies Kirk, in an enchanted whisper. Then he recollects himself, and adds, as if he were the Lone Ranger, "Thattaway."

Struggling to the end of such a plot brings several points into sharp focus. First, this is a slim framework to sustain a film that runs well over two hours; *Star Trek*'s sin of cinematic sins is that it spends far too much time drooling over its own gadgetry and graphics, which at the time of release seemed interesting but are no substitute for dramatic meat. The hypnotized gaze of the crew of the *Enterprise* into her huge "viewer," set aft like a window but actually a species of television screen, even suggests the fascination of these misguided filmmakers with the images they provide for the characters' enrapturement and indeed hints at the idea or metaphor of television (medium of the original series) as our window on the wonders of the universe.

Second, this film clearly sets up many conflicts which are never fully developed, or which, perhaps, are developed only to the scale required in a one-hour television program with commercial breaks, that requires a minor climax every ten minutes. The rivalry between Kirk and Decker dwindles into triviality. Decker, a new character, appears to have been provided not only to be sacrificed at the end but also to usurp Kirk's role of romantic lead. Later *Star Trek* films thought better of this innovation. Yet viewers do not have to wait for later films to find abandoned the nascent psychological interest of Kirk's destructive "obsession" with the *Enterprise* that Doctor McCoy proposes. Further, the interplay between, and eventual union of, Decker (human yearning) and Ilia/probe (cold logic) merely restates in different terms (and unfortunately detracts from) the single most interesting

578 Magill's Cinema Annual 1987

and sustained tension of the television series, the infinitely more interesting relationship between logical Mr. Spock and emotional Captain Kirk. Later films in the *Star Trek* series rectified this error, returning Spock to center stage and drawing much more strongly on the symbolic strength of all four major characters: Spock, the mystic scientist-as-priest and logical "head" to the "heart" of Kirk, the risk-taking, emotional individualist; Scotty, the slightly bumbling engineer always working against time to get the job done, getting his hands dirty while Spock supplies the theoretical input; and Mc-Coy, the doctor-as-confessor and outspoken conscience.

Joss Marsh

Reviews

Analog. C, July, 1980, p. 100.
Fantasy and Science Fiction. LVIII, June, 1980, p. 90.
The Nation. CCXXX, January 5, 1980, p. 27.
New Statesman. XCVIII, December 14, 1979, p. 954.
The New York Times. December 8, 1979, II, p. 14.
The New Yorker. LV, December 17, 1979, p. 167.
Newsweek. XCIV, December 17, 1979, p. 110.
Saturday Review. VII, February 2, 1980, p. 28.
Time. CXIV, December 17, 1979, p. 61.
Variety. December 12, 1979, p. 22.

A STOLEN LIFE

Released: 1946
Production: B. D., Inc.; released by Warner Bros. and First National
  Picture
Direction: Curtis Bernhardt
Screenplay: Catherine Turney; adapted by Margaret Buell Wilder from a
  novel by Karel J. Benes
Cinematography: Sol Polito and Ernest Haller
Editing: Rudi Fehr
Art direction: Robert Haas; set decoration, Fred M. MacLean
Special effects: William McGann, E. Roy Davidson, Willard Van Enger, and
  Russell Collings
Makeup: Perc Westmore
Costume design: Orry-Kelly
Sound: Robert B. Lee
Music: Max Steiner
MPAA rating: no listing
Running time: 109 minutes

> *Principal characters:*
> Kate Bosworth.......................Bette Davis
> Patricia "Pat" Bosworth...............Bette Davis
> Bill Emerson ....Glenn Ford
> Karnok ....Dane Clark
> Eben Folger ....Walter Brennan
> Freddie Linley ....Charlie Ruggles
> Jack Talbot ....Bruce Bennett

Dual roles have long been a popular theme in American film and the challenge of playing two parts has attracted Hollywood's biggest stars. Norma Shearer played a socialite and a juvenile delinquent in *Lady of the Night* (1925), Greta Garbo gave a comic interpretation of identical sisters in *Two-Faced Woman* (1941), Olivia de Havilland was convincing as twins under psychoanalysis in *The Dark Mirror* (1946), and Bette Davis won audiences as Kate and Pat Bosworth in the romantic triangle of *A Stolen Life* (1946).

Kate Bosworth is a shy, attractive artist who is visiting her cousin and guardian, Freddie Linley (Charlie Ruggles), at his New England cottage. When she misses the ferry to the island, Kate persuades Bill Emerson (Glenn Ford), an engineer inspecting the bay's lighthouse, to take her as a passenger on his private launch. Kate is immediately drawn to Bill and devises a stratagem to paint a portrait of the crusty lighthouse-keeper, Eben

Folger (Walter Brennan), in order to get to know Bill. One evening, a thick fog makes it impossible for Kate to sail home. She and Bill exchange confidence and discover that they are both lonely people in search of someone with whom they can share their world. As Kate and Bill fall in love, she manages to keep secret the fact that she has a twin sister, Patricia (Bette Davis). They look identical, but Pat's personality is dramatically different. In contrast to Kate's deep sensitivity, Pat is forthright, cynical, and sophisticated.

Bill makes a luncheon date with Kate and accidentally meets Pat, who allows him to mistake her for her sister. They have lunch at Freddie's cottage and he notices a difference in her. He finds "Kate" surprisingly alluring: The cake, as he puts it, now appears "well frosted."

Kate returns to the cottage, and Pat's trick is exposed. Bill is stunned to learn that there are two Miss Bosworths, but he still believes that he is in love with Kate. She, however, is deeply concerned, suspecting that Pat has the power as well as the inclination to take Bill away from her. Her suspicions are soon confirmed. Bill is entrapped by Pat's sex appeal, and, believing that he has found a Kate with "frosting," he asks Pat to marry him.

Alone again, Kate returns to New York and throws herself into her painting. At an exhibition of her work, she meets Karnok (Dane Clark), a Bohemian artist who attacks her style as shallow—the product of a repressed, bourgeois mentality. Kate is stimulated by Karnok's criticism and begins studying with him.

A brief visit from Bill, on his way to a job in Chile, drives Kate back to the New England cottage. To her surprise, Pat is there. Pat explains that she was ill and could not go with Bill. The sisters seem close for the first time and decide to go sailing. While they are out in the bay, a terrible storm comes up. Pat is washed overboard, and, as Kate grasps for her hand, Pat's wedding band slips off her finger. When Kate awakens, she is wearing the ring. She learns that her sister is dead and realizes that everyone assumes she is Pat.

Kate, who has never stopped loving Bill, seizes the opportunity to take Pat's place as Bill's wife. When Bill joins her in New York, she discovers that the couple is on the verge of a divorce, that Pat was never a faithful wife, and that when she died she was in the middle of an affair with a man named Jack Talbot (Bruce Bennett).

Once Kate sees the truth about Pat's life, she knows she cannot possibly continue the masquerade. She leaves Bill and returns to the cottage. Now fully accepting her loneliness and solitude, Kate walks out into the damp New England night to the spot where she and Bill fell in love. Without warning, Bill steps out of the fog, forgives her, begs her to forget the past, and admits that until this moment he was not ready for the true marriage that awaits them.

When *A Stolen Life* was released in 1946, the film's technical achievements represented significant progress in the field of special effects. Cinematographer Sol Polito and his team of assistants abandoned the old-fashioned split-screen as well as the traveling matte process (an in-camera technique) and utilized a newly developed optical method of blending two images. This enabled Polito to achieve a series of impressive shots: Davis crossing the screen in front of herself, lighting a cigarette for her twin, and Kate and Pat walking down a pier side by side. When Polito became ill with appendicitis, Ernest Haller took over and shot the very effective storm sequence.

The picture was the only film released by Bette Davis's own production company, B.D., Inc., which she formed in order to distribute her salary and avoid heavy taxes. Jack Chertok, who had produced her last picture, *The Corn Is Green* (1945), began work on *A Stolen Life* but was soon fired from the studio, and the Warner Bros. executives gave Davis the nominal title of producer. Davis did become deeply involved in the production process but concedes that she shared the job of producer with her director, Curtis Bernhardt. Bernhardt, however, maintains that he was responsible for the day-to-day problems of both directing and producing.

The property was based on *A Stolen Life* (1939), a British film starring Elisabeth Bergner and Michael Redgrave. The adaptation was initially assigned to Margaret Buell Wilder, author of the book *Since You Went Away . . . Letters to a Soldier from His Wife* (1943), who made an important contribution with the character of Karnok but quit the production when personality clashes with Bernhardt made collaboration impossible. She was replaced by screenwriter Catherine Turney, who was faced with structural problems and the major rewriting of the central characters. In the original, the "bad" twin was the intriguing sister, but Turney wanted Kate to be the sympathetic and interesting one.

The prevailing censorship presented some interesting narrative challenges for Turney. Under the Production Code, the assumption was that as the "good girl" Kate would have been a virgin and, therefore, would be faced with certain practical problems when she took over Pat's life. Turney remembers working out the dilemma with Bernhardt. "Curt loved to speculate about things like that. We decided that the night Bill and Kate were out together something happened. But, they never slept together after she comes back as Pat. I remember him saying, 'Bill would find out quick enough if they had!'"

Under the Production Code, the act of adultery often called for the death of the woman, or, at the very least, her relinquishment of the loved one. Since Kate's deception never crossed over into adultery, the censors could not demand that she be severely punished. For them, the emotional suffering of both Kate and Bill served as punishment enough.

Karnok's character, as developed by Turney, was a daring departure for the time. His comparatively unrestrained sexuality, masked in terms of his artistic freedom and his insatiable appetite, does more to open up Kate than one night with Bill. Karnok's direct challenge to Kate's femininity, "I'll bet you're not even a real woman," forces her to explore deeply her painting for the first time. Once she is involved with Karnok, Kate begins to mature and blossom. Although the changes in her personality are subtle, her sexual growth is implied by her acquisition of the classic "bad girl" trait—cigarette smoking.

A Stolen Life raises several questions about female sexuality and male/female relationships. It delves into a young woman's fears about unleashed libido and about the consequences of sexual abandonment. The story shows the audience that only through great emotional pain can Kate integrate her desires to be both a seductress and a nurturing wife/mother. It suggests that she must "kill" her fear of uncontrollable lust and let go of her need to repress her true self before she can be a complete woman. Yet, exactly how she is to accomplish her sexual growth without breaking contemporary social and moral codes is left unresolved.

The film also stretches beyond the usual confines of the "woman's film" and addresses the man's conflicting expectations from romantic love. Bill's struggle between his comfortable relationship with Kate and his sexual attraction to Pat perfectly illustrates Western culture's divided view of woman as the mother and the whore.

In retrospect, Catherine Turney believes that the film's lesson was as much for the men in the audience as it was for the women. Through its narrative, the film not only reveals how Kate comes to terms with her sexuality, expressed and unexpressed, but also successfully demonstrates that before Bill can be a proper husband, he must learn that all frosting and no cake inevitably leads to disaster.

Joanne L. Yeck

Reviews
Commonweal. XLIV, May 17, 1946, p. 119.
Cosmopolitan. CXX, June, 1946, p. 165.
The New York Times. May 2, 1946, II, p. 27.
The New Yorker. XXII, May 4, 1946, p. 46.
Newsweek. XXVII, May 13, 1946, p. 92.
Photoplay. XXIX, August, 1946, p. 4.
Theatre Arts. XXX, June, 1946, p. 346.
Time. XLVII, May 13, 1946, p. 98.
Variety. May 1, 1946, p. 8.
Woman's Home Companion. LXXIII, August, 1946, p. 10.

A TOUCH OF LARCENY

Origin: Great Britain
Released: 1959
Released in U.S.: 1960
Production: Ivan Foxwell; released by Paramount Pictures
Direction: Guy Hamilton
Screenplay: Roger MacDougall, Guy Hamilton, and Ivan Foxwell; based on the novel *The Megstone Plot*, by Andrew Garve
Cinematography: John Wilcox
Editing: Alan Osbiston
Art direction: Elliot Scott
Costume design: Edith Head
Music: Philip Green
Song: "The Nearness of You," by Hoagy Carmichael and Ned Washington
MPAA rating: no listing
Running time: 92 minutes

Principal characters:
Commander Max Easton . . . . James Mason
Virginia Killain . . . . Vera Miles
Charles Holland . . . . George Sanders
Captain Graham . . . . Harry Andrews
Larkin . . . . Robert Flemyng
Sublieutenant Brown . . . . Peter Barkworth
Commander Bates . . . . Ernest Clark
Admiral . . . . John Le Mesurier
Russian officer . . . . Richard Marner
First Special Branch officer . . . . Duncan Lamont
Second Special Branch officer . . . . Gordon Harris
Clare Holland . . . . Rachel Gurney
Nightclub singer . . . . Jimmy Lloyd

A Touch of Larceny manages to be a light romantic comedy while also examining the cynicism and malaise of post-World War II England and satirizing British institutions, Cold War tensions, and the war between the sexes. The film displays the subtlety and economy of director Guy Hamilton's work before he began making such James Bond films as *Goldfinger* (1964), and it also offers James Mason one of the best parts in his long, distinguished career.

In World War II, Max Easton (James Mason) was a heroic submarine commander given the colorful nickname "Rammer." In peacetime, Commander Easton is a desk jockey at the Admiralty, bored with his work, of which he does as little as possible. Easton's life is filled with finding ways to get out of the office and into the arms of beautiful women, none of whom he takes very seriously.

After running into Charles Holland (George Sanders), an old acquaintance from the Foreign Office, Easton is introduced to Holland's fiancée, Virginia Killain (Vera Miles), an American widow living in London. Easton senses almost immediately that she is not like all his easy conquests. Virginia proves him correct by resisting his charms as he pursues her. She is amused by his devious machinations as he steals her glove and ingratiates himself into an evening out with her friends, but Virginia is certain that he is hardly the man for her, no matter how dull Holland may seem in comparison.

Easton takes her sailing and, impressed by her ability to handle his boat, realizes that he loves her. Knowing that he cannot have such a wife without the money to support her in the style to which she has grown accustomed, he unveils a scheme for getting rich quickly. He tells Virginia that he could appear to have given top-secret documents to the Soviets, prove himself innocent after the press brands him a traitor, and sue the newspapers for defamation of character. Although Virginia has fallen in love with him against her will, she says that they can never see each other again.

Resolved to change her mind, Easton pretends to be drunk at a Soviet Embassy reception and makes certain that his superiors see him speaking animatedly to a Soviet officer. Before going on leave the next day, he leaves an ambiguous note crumpled in his desk, sells his car, and goes by his office to drop a top-secret folder behind a file cabinet. He then sails to Liverpool, asks some policemen where the *Karl Marx* is moored, gets into an argument with them, and leads the officers to think that he has boarded the Soviet ship. Arriving at one of the Skerries, a group of tiny, rocky islands off the coast of Scotland, Easton sinks his boat and sets up camp to await the charges against him. Meanwhile, Virginia has told Holland of the plot, which she considers a joke.

When Easton does not return from his leave, the police and the press begin to assemble the case against him, concluding that he has sold atomic-submarine secrets to the Soviets because he is being blackmailed. Virginia talks Holland into not notifying the authorities, and the Admiralty is thrown into chaos. The London newspapers begin running stories with such titles as "I Served with a Traitor" and "Easton Nanny Reveals All."

Hearing on his radio that he has been reportedly seen in Warsaw, Easton decides to return to civilization and submerges his remaining supplies prior to lighting a bonfire, but he falls into the sea, loses his can of gasoline, and is unable to start the fire with wet matches. Now he is truly stranded on the uncomfortable rock as a storm begins.

The police show up a few days later to rescue him. Easton thinks that his scheme has been discovered, but a bottle with a message describing his shipwrecked plight has been planted by Virginia. Easton's boss, Captain Graham (Harry Andrews), is embarrassed to tell him how the press has treated him and suggests that this innocent victim sue for damages.

Holland is angered by Virginia's bottle ploy and informs the police of Easton's deception, omitting his fiancée's participation. Confronted by the police and asked to describe the bottle and message, Easton confesses to having set adrift several bottles with different messages. The police, still suspicious, nevertheless abandon the case gracefully.

Easton goes to see Virginia, who still refuses to give in. As Holland arrives to explain how he has attempted to foil his rival, Virginia calls him a stool pigeon, and their engagement ends. After Holland leaves, Easton explains that he is not going to sue the newspapers but will sell the "true" story of his shipwreck to the highest bidder. Virginia finally tells this "wicked" man that she loves him.

A Touch of Larceny appeared when British cinema was making a transition from the Ealing comedies, Terence Rattigan drawing-room dramas, and World War II adventures of the 1950's to the harder-edged, often angry films of the 1960's. The cynical tone of *A Touch of Larceny* is established in the opening scene, in which Easton and a woman are lying on a couch listening to "Try a Little Tenderness" when her husband comes home unexpectedly. As Easton protests that the woman has not told him that she is married, she points out that he has never asked, making it clear that Easton is a rake who considers all women fair game. The woman wants to know what to tell her husband, and Easton replies, "What do you usually tell him?" The commander's cynicism is only underscored by his dexterity in lying his way out of the situation by claiming to be returning the couple's dog.

A Touch of Larceny is cynical about institutions such as marriage, the press, the military, government, and business. When Easton sells his sports car, the dealer puts a sign on the windscreen announcing that it is on sale for 160 pounds; as soon as Easton leaves the lot, the six becomes a nine. Holland, the film's representative of government and the people in charge of a morally bankrupt society, approves of Easton's plan when Virginia tells him about it because the newspapers deserve to be fooled. Yet when the plot is set in motion, he is appalled that someone has dared to disturb the calm surface of a superficially placid existence. In Holland's view, nothing should be allowed to deviate from its traditional role in what he imagines to be a highly ordered world.

Easton is a cynic because he finds this order boring. A romantic who misses the excitement of war, he carries out his scheme less to make money than to have a challenge to meet for a change. He is attracted to Virginia because he recognizes similar romantic tendencies in her. She finally rejects Holland not only because he is a hypocrite but also because life with him would be too dull. That Virginia and Easton are out of step with their unromantic times is made clear when they are dancing in a nightclub but sit down when the band announces a cha-cha.

Ironically for a film making fun of conceptions of order, *A Touch of Larceny* has a tightly controlled structure. The screenplay by Roger MacDougall, producer Ivan Foxwell, and Hamilton presents the action in three distinct sections: the first and longest carefully building up to Easton's plot, the middle one economically detailing his scam, and the last, shortest, and fastest paced showing the consequences of his acts. The subtlety, control, and good taste shown by the filmmakers may have been considered too conventional when the film first appeared, but, with the decline of simple storytelling skills in the years since its release, these qualities seem to represent a classical competence. Not a single shot in the film is extraneous.

Indicative of the film's subtleties are the series of scenes depicting a day Virginia reluctantly spends with Easton. She wants to maintain a safe distance, but they are forced closer than is comfortable for her by the smallness first of his car and then of his boat. The day ends with their dancing cheek to cheek as a nightclub singer croons "The Nearness of You." The close-ups of Mason and Miles in this last scene are shot in heavy shadows, a style which Hamilton and cinematographer John Wilcox use throughout the film to stress the moral grayness of the society being examined and the emotional confusions of the characters.

As Charles Holland, George Sanders is cast slightly against type, since for most of his career he played rogues like Max Easton. Here he rejects the smirky gestures he usually employs as a scoundrel and underplays the role to make the character believably stuffy rather than a caricature.

Despite appearances in such classic films as John Ford's *The Searchers* (1956) and Alfred Hitchcock's *Psycho* (1960), Vera Miles was a usually bland leading lady during this period. As Virginia Killain, she must be cool, intelligent, sophisticated, and sexy, and she embodies all these qualities convincingly. She is aided somewhat by the clothes designed by Edith Head but is still radiant in simply a sweater and jeans on Easton's boat. Because she is allowed to play a woman of beauty and substance for once, Miles gives perhaps her most effective performance in this film.

A Touch of Larceny belongs, however, to James Mason. Along with the characters in *Odd Man Out* (1947), *The Reckless Moment* (1949), *The Desert Fox* (1951), *A Star Is Born* (1954), *Lolita* (1962), *Georgy Girl* (1966), *The Verdict* (1982), and *The Shooting Party* (1984), this is one of his best roles. Max Easton is second only to *Lolita*'s Humbert Humbert in allowing Mason to show his range as romantic leading man, light comedian, and lovable villain.

The subtlety of Mason's acting style and the comic tone of *A Touch of Larceny* are both captured in the scene in which Easton is pretending to be stranded on his Scottish rock and, with a glass of wine held debonairly in one hand, he waves to a distant ship with the other while slowly whispering, "Help. Help." This scene's deft drolleries epitomize the film's civilized charm.

Michael Adams

Reviews
America. CII, February 27, 1960, p. 659.
Commonweal. LXXI, February 12, 1960, p. 456.
Films and Filming. VI, February, 1960, p. 24.
Films in Review. XI, February, 1960, p. 101.
McCall's. LXXXVII, February, 1960, p. 8.
The New Republic. CXLII, February 29, 1960, p. 20.
The New York Times. March 17, 1960, II, p. 28.
The New Yorker. XXXVI, March 26, 1960, p. 148.
Newsweek. LV, February 1, 1960, p. 81.
Saturday Review. XLIII, January 23, 1960, p. 26.
Variety. January 13, 1960, p. 7.

OBITUARIES

Brian Aherne (May 2, 1902-February 10, 1986). Aherne was a handsome English actor who began his career on the British stage at the age of eight. His first film was *The Eleventh Commandment* (1924). He came to the United States in 1931, where his starring role in Broadway's *The Barretts of Wimpole Street* earned for him a career in Hollywood. His first American film was *Song of Songs* (1933), and thereafter he specialized in playing romantic leads. He was married to actress Joan Fontaine from 1939 to 1945. Aherne appeared in nearly fifty films; after his retirement, he published an autobiography entitled *A Proper Job* (1969) as well as a biography of his colleague, actor George Sanders, *A Dreadful Man* (1979). Other acting credits include *Sylvia Scarlett* (1935), *Juarez* (1939), *My Sister Eileen* (1942), *I Confess* (1953), and *Lancelot and Guinevere* (1963).

John Alcott (1931-July 28, 1986). Alcott was a British cinematographer best known for his work with director Stanley Kubrick. He broke into film in the early 1960's as a focus puller on such British films as *The Singer Not the Song* (1961) and *Whistle Down the Wind* (1961). He helped photograph Kubrick's *2001: A Space Odyssey* (1968) and was director of photography for three other Kubrick films: *A Clockwork Orange* (1971), *Barry Lyndon* (1975), and *The Shining* (1980). His work on *Barry Lyndon* earned for him an Academy Award. In the 1980's, Alcott developed a process known as System 35, which enables films shot in 70 millimeter to be shown on television without visual distortion. Other film credits include *March or Die* (1977), *Fort Apache, the Bronx* (1981), and *Greystoke: The Legend of Tarzan* (1984).

Robert Alda (February 26, 1914-May 3, 1986). Born Alphonso Giuseppe Giovanni Roberto D'Abruzzo in New York, Alda worked in vaudeville and radio before making his first film appearance as the star of *Rhapsody in Blue* (1945), a biography of composer George Gershwin. Although he made more than twenty additional films, his initial role remained his most distinguished. He had a successful Broadway career, winning a Tony Award for his role in the original production of *Guys and Dolls* in 1951. He lived in Italy from 1961 to 1975, acting in several European films before returning to the United States in 1976. He was the father of actor-director Alan Alda. His film-acting credits include *Cinderella Jones* (1946), *Nora Prentiss* (1947), *Imitation of Life* (1959), *The Serpent* (1973), and *I Will I Will . . . for Now* (1976).

Lewis Allan (1903-October 30, 1986). Born Abel Meeropol, Allan was a songwriter who wrote the lyrics to the title song of the Academy Award-winning short subject *The House I Live In* (1945). The film starred Frank Sinatra, and its message was social tolerance, one of Allan's lifelong concerns. His best-known song was "Strange Fruit," an antilynching ballad popularized by Billie Holiday. When Julius and Ethel Rosenberg, convicted Communist spies, were executed in 1953, Allan and his wife adopted the Rosenbergs' two sons.

George Amy (1903-December 18, 1986). Amy was an editor and director who worked in both film and television. He did his best work for Warner Bros., where, between 1927 and 1948, he edited many of the studio's most important films. He was nominated for an Academy Award for his editing of *Yankee Doodle Dandy* (1942) and *Objective Burma* (1945) and won the award for his work on Howard Hawks's

Air Force (1943). He also directed four films: *She Had to Say Yes* (1933; codirected with Busby Berkeley), *Kid Nightingale* (1939), *Gambling on the High Seas* (1940), and *Granny Get Your Gun* (1940). Additional editing credits include *Captain Blood* (1935), *The Green Pastures* (1936), *Kid Galahad* (1937), *The Sea Wolf* (1941), and *Life with Father* (1947).

Heather Angel (February 2, 1909-December 13, 1986). Born in England, Angel was a successful actress in such British films as *The Hound of the Baskervilles* (1931) and *Bill the Conqueror* (1932). She came to the United States in 1933 and, for a time, won leading roles in films that included *Berkeley Square* (1933), *The Mystery of Edwin Drood* (1935), and John Ford's *The Informer* (1935). Her career soon foundered, however, and although she continued to act, appearing in nearly fifty films, her roles were essentially minor ones. She also appeared on Broadway and television. She was married and divorced from actors Ralph Forbes and Henry Wilcoxon; her third husband, director Robert B. Sinclair, was murdered in 1970. Additional film credits include *The Three Musketeers* (1935), *The Last of the Mohicans* (1936), *Bulldog Drummond in Africa* (1938), *Cry Havoc* (1943), *The Saxon Charm* (1948), and *Premature Burial* (1962).

Harold Arlen (February 15, 1905-April 23, 1986). Born Hyman Arluck, Arlen was one of the twentieth century's greatest songwriters. A prolific composer, he wrote more than five hundred songs, often in collaboration with such lyricists as Johnny Mercer, Yip Harburg, Ira Gershwin, and others.

Arlen was the son of a Buffalo, New York, cantor, and he first sang publicly in his father's synagogue. At the age of twenty-two, he moved to New York to pursue a career in music. A year later, in 1928, his "Get Happy" was a hit in the Broadway production *9:15 Revue*, and his compositions were much sought after in musical theater, in film, and by recording artists. Arlen wrote or cowrote such standards as "I Love a Parade," "That Old Black Magic," "Stormy Weather," "Ac-cent-tchu-ate the Positive," and "One for My Baby (and One More for the Road)."

Arlen scored twenty-four films as well as contributing individual songs to many others. His first film score was *Let's Fall in Love* (1934). In 1939, he won an Academy Award for "Over the Rainbow," written with Yip Harburg, which was sung by Judy Garland in *The Wizard of Oz* (1939). In addition, Arlen's film credits include songs or complete scores for *Blues in the Night* (1941), *Star Spangled Rhythm* (1942), *Cabin in the Sky* (1943), *The Sky's the Limit* (1943), *Here Come the Waves* (1944), *My Blue Heaven* (1950), and *A Star Is Born* (1954).

Desi Arnaz (March 2, 1917-December 2, 1986). Born Desiderio Alberto Arnaz y de Acha III, in Cuba, Arnaz moved to Miami as a teenager and became a musician. He was instrumental in popularizing the Conga dance in the 1930's. He appeared on Broadway in *Too Many Girls* in 1939 and in the film version of the play in 1940. One of his costars in the film was Lucille Ball; they were married in 1940, shortly after the completion of the film. Arnaz appeared in several more films but is best known for his role as Ricky Ricardo in the *I Love Lucy* television series. Arnaz played an excitable bandleader married to a scatterbrained housewife played by Ball; the combination resulted in one of the most popular and enduring television programs in the history of the medium. The show's success led to two spin-off films in the mid-1950's: *The Long, Long Trailer* (1954; reviewed in this volume) and *Forever Darling* (1956), both of which were comedies featuring Arnaz and Ball as a married couple. The pair created Desilu Productions, a successful television production company which eventually purchased the RKO studios. Arnaz and Ball were divorced in 1960. In 1976, Arnaz published his autobiography, *A Book*, which ended with his divorce from Lucille Ball. His films include *Four Jacks and a Jill* (1941), *Bataan* (1943), *Cuban Pete* (1946), and *Holiday in Havana* (1949).

Edith Atwater (April 22, 1911-March 14, 1986). Atwater was a character actress whose career spanned four decades. She made her stage debut at the age of fifteen, and her first film was *We Went to College* (1936). Thereafter, she divided her career between film, stage, and television. She married actor Kent Smith in 1962; he died in 1985. Atwater's additional film appearances include *The Body Snatcher* (1945), *Sweet Bird of Youth* (1962), *True Grit* (1969), *The Love Machine* (1971), and *Family Plot* (1976).

Hermione Baddeley (November 13, 1906-August 19, 1986). Baddeley was a British actress who specialized in comic, often bawdy roles on stage and in film. She was a child star in England by the age of sixteen, and two years later she made her first film, *The Guns of Loos* (1928). She made one more film before beginning a family and was absent from the screen for eleven years. Her best-known roles in British cinema were in *Brighton Rock* (1947) and *Room at the Top* (1959), for which she received an Academy Award nomination for Best Supporting Actress. She moved to the United States in 1960 and appeared in such films as *The Unsinkable Molly Brown* (1964) and *Mary Poppins* (1964). She may be best known to contemporary audiences as Mrs. Naugatuck, the irascible maid in the television series *Maud*. Her additional films include *A Christmas Carol* (1951), *The Belles of St. Trinian's* (1954), *Expresso Bongo* (1959), *Harlow* (1965), and *Casino Royale* (1967).

Way Bandy (1941-August 13, 1986). Bandy was a makeup artist who worked with many actresses, including Elizabeth Taylor, Barbra Streisand, Catherine Deneuve, and Raquel Welch; he also worked with First Lady Nancy Reagan.

Elisabeth Bergner (August 22, 1900-May 12, 1986). Bergner was a celebrated actress in the 1920's and 1930's. Born in Poland and educated in Vienna, she made her stage debut at the age of nineteen and her film debut four years later. She made ten films in Germany between 1923 and 1932 before fleeing the country with her husband, director Paul Czinner, when Adolf Hitler came to power. She continued her acting career in England and the United States, earning an Academy Award nomination for her work in *Escape Me Never* (1935), directed by Czinner. Critic Alexander Woollcott called her "probably the ablest actress living." She made only one American film—*Paris Calling* (1942)—but performed successfully on Broadway as well as on the European stage and in European film productions. Her additional acting credits include *Der Evangelimann* (1923), *Der Träumende Mund* (1932), *Catherine the Great* (1934), *As You Like It* (1936), *Cry of the Banshee* (1970), and a cameo appearance in *The Pedestrian* (1974).

Herschel Bernardi (October 30, 1923-May 9, 1986). Bernardi was an actor who performed in a variety of Broadway, film, and television roles. He grew up in New York and studied in the city's Yiddish theater; his first film roles, in *Green Fields* (1937) and *Yankel the Blacksmith* (1939), were Yiddish productions. Bernardi first earned national attention for his Emmy-nominated role as Lieutenant Jacoby in the television series *Peter Gunn* in the late 1950's, and he won further reknown on Broadway starring in *Fiddler on the Roof* and *Zorba the Greek*. His film credits include *Stakeout on Dope Street* (1958), *The George Raft Story* (1961), *Irma La Douce* (1963), *Love with the Proper Stranger* (1964), and *The Front* (1976).

Gunnar Björnstrand (November 13, 1909-May 24, 1986). Best known for his work with Ingmar Bergman, Björnstrand was a Swedish character actor who appeared in more than 150 films. The son of an actor, he made his film debut in *The False Millionaire* (1931). His early roles were frequently comic, and he specialized in playing the humorous villain. He first worked with Bergman in *It Rains on Our Love* (1946), and he also appeared in such important Bergman films as *Smiles of a Summer Night* (1955), *The Seventh Seal* (1957), *Wild Strawberries* (1957), *Persona* (1966), and *Fanny and Alexander* (1982), earning international respect for his performances. Other films include *Panic* (1939), *Torment* (1944), *Sawdust and Tinsel* (1953), *Winter Light* (1963), and *Autumn Sonata* (1978).

Herman Allen Blumenthal (1916-March 30, 1986). Blumenthal was a production designer who won an Academy Award for his work on *Cleopatra* (1963) and *Hello, Dolly!* (1969). He broke into film in 1934 and worked on such films as *The Three Faces of Eve* (1957) and *Journey to the Center of the Earth* (1959), which earned for him his first Academy Award nomination. Other films include *Voyage to the Bottom of the Sea* (1961), *What's Up, Doc?* (1972), and *Zorro, the Gay Blade* (1981).

Harry Brown (April 30, 1917-November 2, 1986). Brown was a novelist and screenwriter who won an Academy Award for his screenplay *A Place in the Sun* (1951). He attended Harvard University and wrote for *Time* and *The New Yorker*, and, while serving in the Army during World War II, he began to write about the war in Europe. His 1944 novel, *A Walk in the Sun*, was made into a film in 1945, for which he wrote the script. Other significant films on which he worked include *Sands of Iwo Jima* (1949), *D-Day the Sixth of June* (1956), and *Ocean's 11* (1960).

Susan Cabot (July 9, 1927-December 10, 1986). Cabot starred in a number of B-movie action films in the 1950's. Her first film was *On the Isle of Samoa* (1950), and she specialized in Westerns and films set in exotic locales until 1957. That year she began working with director Roger Corman, appearing in such films as *Sorority Girl* (1957), *Machine Gun Kelly* (1958), and *The Wasp Woman* (1959). In 1959, at about the same time that gossip began to link her romantically with King Hussein of Jordan, she retired from films. Her death was caused by a severe beating that occurred in her home; her twenty-two-year-old son was charged with the murder. Other film credits include *Flame of Araby* (1951), *Son of Ali Baba* (1952), *Gunsmoke* (1953), *Carnival Rock* (1957), *War of the Satellites* (1958), and *Surrender—Hell!* (1959).

Adolph Caesar (1933-March 16, 1986). Caesar was a veteran black actor whose film performances in the 1980's earned for him increasing respect in the film industry. He began his career on the stage and performed with the Negro Ensemble Company in numerous productions. His first film role was in *Che!* (1969), and he will probably best be remembered for his role as Sergeant Vernon Walters in *A Soldier's Story* (1984), for which he garnered an Academy Award nomination for Best Supporting Actor. Caesar had originally developed and played the role in the stage version of the story, entitled *A Soldier's Play*, which won for him both an Obie Award and a New York Drama Desk Award. Additional film credits include *The Hitter* (1980) and *The Color Purple* (1985).

James Cagney (July 17, 1899-March 30, 1986). The multitalented Cagney was one of American film's greatest actors. Born on New York's Lower East Side, Cagney was the son of an Irish saloonkeeper. He grew up in a tough neighborhood and was a successful amateur boxer as a teenager.

Cagney dropped out of college when his father died and worked odd jobs to help support his family. One of these jobs turned out to be the beginning of his career in show business: He worked for two months as a female impersonator. The following year, he joined the chorus of a Broadway musical. Adept at dancing, Cagney soon found plenty of work on Broadway and in vaudeville. This led to a screen test with Warner Bros., with whom he signed in 1930.

After playing supporting roles in four films, Cagney won the part that made him famous—the hoodlum Tom Powers in *The Public Enemy* (1931). Cagney was a new kind of screen villain—one with wit and flair. The famous scene in which he shoved a grapefruit into costar Mae Clarke's face startled audiences of the day. Cagney brought an intensity to the screen that lifted him out of the ranks of ordinary actors and into stardom.

His next film, made before *The Public Enemy* opened, was *Smart Money* (1931), in which he played a supporting role to Edward G. Robinson. It was to be his last nonstarring film. In *Blonde Crazy* (1931), he proved adept at comedy. After a series of contract disputes with Warner Bros., he appeared in *Footlight Parade* (1933), his first musical. He played a boxer in *The Irish in Us* (1935) and Bottom in William Shakespeare's *A Midsummer Night's Dream* (1935), handling each role with aplomb. By the mid-1930's, Cagney had established himself as the most versatile actor in Hollywood.

Conflicts over his salary and the actor's rancorous relationship with studio head Jack Warner dominated the period between 1936 and 1938. The studio and its star were reconciled, however, and Cagney's role in *Angels with Dirty Faces* (1938; also starring Pat O'Brien, Humphrey Bogart, and the Dead End Kids) earned for him his first Academy Award nomination. *The Strawberry Blonde* (1941), a period comedy set in turn-of-the-century New York, is another fine film from this era.

Cagney's best-known film is *Yankee Doodle Dandy* (1942). His tour-de-force performance as Broadway star George M. Cohan won for him an Academy Award for Best Actor and insured his cinematic immortality. It was also Cagney's own personal favorite among his many outstanding performances.

Cagney's always fragile relationship with the studio deteriorated again in the late 1940's, and he organized his own production company, although he continued to make films for Warner Bros. The best of his late 1940's films is *White Heat* (1949), in which he played a sociopathic criminal. In the 1950's, Cagney's energy flagged perceptibly. His production company expired, and he himself appeared tired. Among the sixteen films he made during the decade, only *Mister Roberts* (1955), *The Seven Little Foys* (1955; in which he again played George M. Cohan), and *Love Me or Leave Me* (1955) stand out.

Cagney turned in another worthy performance in Billy Wilder's comedy *One Two Three* (1961) and then retired for two decades. He returned to the screen for the last time to deliver an outstanding supporting performance in Miloš Forman's *Ragtime* (1981).

In addition to his marvelous acting career, Cagney directed one film, *Short Cut to Hell* (1957). He published his autobiography, *Cagney by Cagney*, in 1976 and collaborated with Doug Warren on *James Cagney: An Authorized Biography* (1983).

In 1974, this great actor received the American Film Institute's Life Achievement Award. Additional acting credits include *Taxi* (1932), *Jimmy the Gent* (1934), *G-Men* (1935), *Ceiling Zero* (1936), *The West Point Story* (1950), *What Price Glory* (1952), *Man of a Thousand Faces* (1957), *Shake Hands with the Devil* (1959), and *The Gallant Hours* (1960).

Mushy Callahan (November 4, 1904-June 14, 1986). Born Vincent Morris Scheer, Callahan was a boxing champion from 1926 to 1930. When he retired from the ring, he joined Warner Bros., where he trained actors for boxing films and choreographed their fight sequences. The stars with whom he worked include James Cagney, Errol Flynn, Burt Lancaster, Ronald Reagan, Kirk Douglas, Elvis Presley, and Steve McQueen. He also appeared in several films, including *Some Like It Hot* (1959), *Elmer Gantry* (1960), *Hello, Dolly!* (1969; reviewed in this volume), and *Julia* (1977).

Yakima Canutt (November 29, 1895-May 24, 1986). Born Enos Edward Canutt, Yakima Canutt was the most famous stuntman in film history. He was a five-time national rodeo champion who lived near Yakima, Washington (thus his nickname), until 1924, when he parlayed his rodeo skills into a career as a Hollywood cowboy. He starred in several fast-paced silent-era Westerns, including *Romance and Rustlers* (1924) and *The Human Tornado* (1925), but his relatively high-pitched voice failed to match his rough-and-tumble screen image, and his acting career foundered for a time with the advent of sound.

Filmmakers were intrigued with Canutt's ability to perform daredevil stunts, however, and he was soon in demand for less prominent roles in action films. He played Indians so frequently and convincingly that many viewers erroneously assumed that he was of Native American descent. He also served as a stand-in for less daring actors, doubling for John Wayne, Clark Gable, Roy Rogers, Gene Autry, Errol Flynn, and Henry Fonda.

By the late 1930's, Canutt was acting as a second unit director. He was recognized as Hollywood's best at action and stunt sequences, including those in *Stagecoach* (1939), *The Dark Command* (1940), *Angel and the Badman* (1947), *Ben-Hur* (1959), *Spartacus* (1960), and *Cat Ballou* (1965).

In 1966, Canutt was given a special Academy Award for his pioneering work. The citation commended him "for creating the profession of stuntman as it exists today and for the development of many safety devices used by stuntmen everywhere." Additional acting credits include *Desert Greed* (1926), *Fighting Texans* (1933), *Westward Ho!* (1935), *Gone with the Wind* (1939), *In Old Oklahoma* (1943), and *The Far Horizon* (1955).

Adolfo Celi (July 27, 1922-February 19, 1986). Celi was an Italian character actor who specialized in playing villains. His first film was *Proibito rubare* (1948), and he appeared in more than thirty films produced in Europe and the United States. His most famous role was that of Emilio Largo, James Bond's nemesis in *Thunderball* (1965). Celi's films include *That Man from Rio* (1964), *Von Ryan's Express* (1965), *King of Hearts* (1966), *Brother Sun, Sister Moon* (1973), and *The Devil Is a Woman* (1975).

Mamo Clark (1914-December 18, 1986). Clark was an actress who specialized in films set in the South Seas. Born in Honolulu, she made her film debut in *Mutiny on the Bounty* (1935), with Clark Gable, in which she was billed only as Mamo. Her additional acting credits include *The Hurricane* (1937), *Hawaii Calls* (1938), *Booloo*

(1938), *Mutiny on the Blackhawk* (1939), *One Million B.C.* (1940), and *Girl from God's Country* (1940).

Jerry Colonna (October 17, 1904-November 21, 1986). Colonna was a wide-eyed, leather-lunged, walrus-mustached comedian best known for his work with Bob Hope. His first film appearance was in *52nd Street* (1937). A year later, he landed a spot on Hope's popular radio show. He continued to split his time between radio and film, and he joined Hope on a series of tours of military bases after the outbreak of World War II. He appeared in three of the Hope-Crosby "Road" pictures, including the first, *The Road to Singapore* (1940), and the last, *The Road to Hong Kong* (1961). Colonna's films include *College Swing* (1938), *Star Spangled Rhythm* (1942), *The Road to Rio* (1947), and *Andy Hardy Comes Home* (1958).

Marguerite Courtot (1897-May 28, 1986). Courtot was an actress during the silent era. Her films include *Rolling Stones* (1916), *Crime and Punishment* (1917), and *Down to the Sea in Ships* (1923).

Broderick Crawford (December 9, 1911-April 26, 1986). Crawford was a veteran actor who achieved success in film, on stage, and in television. His father was a vaudevillian, and his mother, Helen Broderick, was an actress and comedienne. Crawford grew up on the stage, performing in vaudeville and radio before making his theatrical debut in London in 1932. His work as Lenny in the Broadway production *Of Mice and Men* in 1937 won for him critical raves and led to a career in film.

Although he appeared in dozens of films over the next decade, Crawford seemed typecast—typically as a hoodlum—and stuck in minor roles in films such as *Beau Geste* (1939), *Larceny Inc.* (1942), and *Sin Town* (1942). His big break occurred in 1949, when director Robert Rossen decided to use a cast of unknowns in his political drama *All the King's Men* (1949). Crawford won the lead role, and his taut performance earned for him an Academy Award for Best Actor as well as the New York Film Critics Award.

Crawford also impressed audiences and critics with his flair for comedy in *Born Yesterday* (1950), opposite Judy Holliday. Following *The Mob* (1951), a crime drama, his career seemed to stall. He made more than thirty additional films in the United States and Europe during the course of his career, but most were inconsequential. The one exception was *Il bidone* (1955), a comedy directed by Federico Fellini.

In addition to his film work, Crawford was featured in several television programs in the 1950's and 1960's, most notably *Highway Patrol*, which ran from 1955 to 1959. Additional films include *Anna Lucasta* (1949), *New York Confidential* (1955), *Big House USA* (1955), *A House Is Not a Home* (1964), *The Oscar* (1966), and *The Private Files of J. Edgar Hoover* (1978).

Scatman Crothers (October 23, 1910-November 22, 1986). Born Benjamin Sherman Crothers, the black character actor earned the nickname "Scatman" because of his vocal style during his career as a musician during the 1930's. His first film appearance was in *Meet Me at the Fair* (1952); thereafter, his film career flagged until his performance on the popular television show *Chico and the Man* revived interest in his acting abilities. His most prominent film role was that of the telepath in *The Shining* (1980). Crothers' other acting credits include *Hello, Dolly!* (1969), *One Flew over the Cuckoo's Nest* (1975), *The Shootist* (1976), *Bronco Billy* (1980), and *Twilight Zone—The Movie* (1983).

Howard Da Silva (May 4, 1909-February 16, 1986). Born Harold Silverblatt in

Cleveland, Da Silva was an actor of distinction on Broadway and in films. He began acting on the stage in New York in 1928, appearing in Orson Welles's production of *The Cradle Will Rock* and also in *Golden Boy*, *Abe Lincoln in Illinois*, and *Volpone*. His best-known Broadway role was in the play *Oklahoma!*, in which he originated the role of Jud.

Da Silva began making films in 1940, with *Abe Lincoln in Illinois* (1940). Early in his career, he also appeared in *The Sea Wolf* (1941), *Sergeant York* (1941), *The Lost Weekend* (1945), and *The Blue Dahlia* (1946). In films, he tended to be cast as a heavy.

After refusing to testify to the House Un-American Activities Committee in 1951 regarding accusations that he was a member of the Communist Party, Da Silva was blacklisted by Hollywood. The last film in which he appeared for over a decade was Joseph Losey's *M* (1951). His talents continued to be welcomed on Broadway, where he wrote, produced, and directed plays in addition to acting throughout the 1950's and early 1960's.

Da Silva returned to films in *David and Lisa* (1963) and achieved his greatest public recognition in the early 1970's when he starred as Benjamin Franklin in the musical *1776* (1972), a role he had originated three years earlier on Broadway. He also won an Emmy for his role in the television special *Verna: USO Girl* in 1978. His films include *Two Years Before the Mast* (1946), *The Great Gatsby* (1949), *They Live by Night* (1949), *The Outrage* (1964), and *The Great Gatsby* (1974).

Carmen DeRue (1908-September 28, 1986). The daughter of a director, DeRue appeared in nearly two hundred films during the silent era. Her first screen appearance, as "Baby DeRue," was in Cecil B. De Mille's Western epic *The Squaw Man* (1914), in which she played an Indian boy. As a child star, she appeared in many of the Franklin brothers' Triangle kiddie series and Fox kiddie series. As she matured, she was cast as a vamp, appearing in such films as *A Broken Doll* (1921) and *The Flirt* (1922).

Leif Erickson (October 27, 1911-January 29, 1986). Born William Anderson, Erickson was a brawny actor who forged a successful career in film and television over four decades. He married actress Frances Farmer in 1934 and made his own film debut a year later in *Wanderer of the Wasteland* (1935). Divorced from Farmer in 1942, Erickson appeared in more than fifty films, usually as the second lead. From 1967 to 1971, he starred in the television series *High Chaparral*. His film credits include *Conquest* (1937), *The Big Broadcast of 1938* (1938), *Pardon My Sarong* (1942), *The Snake Pit* (1948), *On the Waterfront* (1954), *The Carpetbaggers* (1964), and *Twilight's Last Gleaming* (1977).

Chester Erskine (November 29, 1905-April 7, 1986). Erskine was a director and screenwriter who worked on Broadway as well as in film. In 1930, he directed the Broadway prison drama *The Last Mile*. The play featured Spencer Tracy and later Clark Gable in the lead role; both actors used their work in Erskine's production as a springboard to distinguished film careers. Erskine broke into film as assistant to director Lewis Milestone on *Rain* (1932). In 1934, he produced and directed an early Humphrey Bogart vehicle, *Midnight* (1934). He directed, coproduced, and cowrote *The Egg and I* (1947), and he directed and wrote *A Girl in Every Port* (1952).

Derek Farr (February 7, 1912-March 22, 1986). Farr was a British actor whose career spanned four decades. Specializing in playing men under pressure, he acted on the stage for two years before making his first film, *The Outsider* (1939). He went on to make another twenty-five films through the early 1970's, at which time he began acting in British television. His film credits include *Spellbound* (1940), *Conspiracy in Teheran* (1947), *Front Page Story* (1953), *The Truth About Women* (1958), and *Pope Joan* (1972).

Emilio Fernandez (March 26, 1904-August 6,1986). Actor-director Emilio Fernandez was a monumental figure in Mexican film. The films he made in the 1940's brought the struggling national cinema its first international attention. A colorful character, Fernandez fled Mexico for the United States in 1923 to avoid a prison sentence imposed on him during Mexico's revolution. He found work in the film industry, and when he returned home after a decade in exile, he began working on Mexican films. In 1941, he directed his first film, *La isla de la pasión* (1941), and during the 1940's, he rose to international prominence. *María Candelaria* (1943) was a Grand Prize-winner at Cannes, and *La perla* (1946; from John Steinbeck's *The Pearl*) won the International Prize at the San Sebastian Film Festival. The quality of his work declined in the 1950's, and he returned to acting for a time. In the 1960's, he served as John Huston's assistant director on *The Unforgiven* (1960) and *The Night of the Iguana* (1964). Between 1965 and 1975, he acted in several American films, including *The War Wagon* (1967), *The Wild Bunch* (1969), and *Lucky Lady* (1975). His legal troubles did not end with the Mexican Revolution. He once shot a hostile film critic (who refused to press charges), and in 1976, he killed a laborer in a fight. He was imprisoned for three years, effectively ending his film career, although he continued to act in Mexican television productions. His Mexican directorial credits include *Flor silvestre* (1943), *Pepita Jiménez* (1945), *Enamorada* (1946), *Río escondido* (1947), *Acapulco* (1951), and *Zona roja* (1976).

Pasquale Festa Campanile (July 28, 1927-February 24, 1986). Festa Campanile was an Italian novelist, screenwriter, and director who was active in films from 1950 through 1982. He broke into film as a screenwriter on *Faddija* (1950). He hit his stride in the 1960's with *Rocco and His Brothers* (1960) and *The Leopard* (1963). In 1963 he began to direct his own screenplays and developed into one of Italy's most commercially successful filmmakers. He specialized in sex comedies such as *Adultery Italian Style* (1966), *When Women Had Tails* (1970), and *Il ritorno di Casanova* (1978).

Martin Gabel (June 19, 1912-May 22, 1986). Gabel was a character actor. He made his Broadway debut in 1933 and joined Orson Welles's Mercury Theater in the late 1930's. He broke into film by directing *The Lost Moment* (1947), a drama which featured Robert Cummings and Susan Hayward. He acted in such films as *M* (1951), *Marnie* (1964), *Lady in Cement* (1968), and *The Front Page* (1974). In 1961, he won a Tony Award for his performance in the Broadway play *Big Fish, Little Fish*. He was married to actress Arlene Francis, with whom he made frequent appearances on the television show *What's My Line?* Gabel published a biography of his wife entitled *Arlene Francis: A Memoir* in 1978. His additional film credits include *Deadline USA* (1952), *Tip on a Dead Jockey* (1957), *Lord Love a Duck* (1966), and *Divorce American Style* (1967).

Louise Gibney (1896-September 22, 1986). Born Lillian Harrington, Gibney was an actress in the silent era. A Ziegfeld Follies girl, she moved to Hollywood in 1924, breaking into films as an extra. She was featured in such film as *Tumbleweeds*

(1925), *The Beautiful Cheat* (1926), *My Old Dutch* (1926), and *Mother* (1927). Gibney had a high-pitched voice, and the advent of sound films shortened her acting career, although she did appear in Cecil B. De Mille's *The Sign of the Cross* (1932).

Virginia Gilmore (July 26, 1919-March 28, 1986). Born Sherman Virginia Poole, Gilmore was an actress who appeared in more than forty films from the 1930's to the early 1950's. Her first film was *Winter Carnival* (1939), and both Metro-Goldwyn-Mayer and Twentieth Century-Fox attempted to make a major leading lady out of her in the 1940's. Her best films were *Western Union* (1941) and *Swamp Water* (1941), but her career never took off, and she abandoned film in 1952 for television and theater. From 1944 to 1960, Gilmore was married to actor Yul Brynner. Her film credits include *Pride of the Yankees* (1942), *Orchestra Wives* (1942), *Wonder Man* (1945), and *Walk East on Beacon* (1952).

Benny Goodman (May 30, 1909-June 13, 1986). Goodman was a giant in the jazz world, earning the nickname "The King of Swing" for his pioneering big band sounds in the 1930's and 1940's. Like many bandleaders of that era, he and his band were featured in several Hollywood musicals, including *The Big Broadcast of 1937* (1936), *Hollywood Hotel* (1937), *The Powers Girl* (1942), *Stage Door Canteen* (1943), *Sweet and Lowdown* (1944), and *A Song Is Born* (1948). Goodman became the subject of a cinematic biography in 1955, *The Benny Goodman Story* (1955), starring Steve Allen as Goodman.

Cary Grant (January 18, 1904-November 29, 1986). Born Archibald Alexander Leach in Bristol, England, Grant was Hollywood's prototype leading man—handsome, suave, and sophisticated. He made seventy-two films over the course of a career that lasted thirty-four years.

Grant ran away from his poverty-stricken home at the age of thirteen to join a troupe of itinerant acrobats. Three years later, in 1920, he moved to New York briefly before returning to England to pursue an acting career. He returned to the United States for good in 1927, where his theatrical work earned for him a contract with Paramount Pictures in 1932. It was at this time that he changed his name, selecting "Cary" from one of his stage roles and "Grant" from a list of possibilities supplied by the studio.

Grant made seven films in his first year with the studio. Six found Grant in supporting roles, but he starred opposite Marlene Dietrich in *Blonde Venus* (1932). After Mae West cast him in two of her films the following year—*She Done Him Wrong* (1933; in which West asked Grant to "come up and see me sometime") and *I'm No Angel* (1933)—he was established as a successful romantic lead.

It was not until 1937, however, that Grant found the sort of role that would make him immortal. On loan to Metro-Goldwyn-Mayer, he appeared in *Topper* (1937), his first screwball comedy. His mastery of rapid-fire verbal repartee and his ability to strike romantic sparks with a variety of female leads made him a natural for the genre. He appeared opposite Irene Dunne in *The Awful Truth* (1937), and a year later he and Katharine Hepburn collaborated in Howard Hawks's classic *Bringing Up Baby* (1938).

Grant proved his versatility in the adventure film *Gunga Din* (1939) and in *Only Angels Have Wings* (1939), in which he played a hard-bitten pilot. He returned to comedy for another Howard Hawks classic, *His Girl Friday* (1940), opposite Rosalind Russell. Grant's other memorable performances in the early 1940's include *The*

Philadelphia Story (1941) and *Penny Serenade* (1941), for which he was nominated for an Academy Award.

Also in 1941, Grant made the first of his four films with Alfred Hitchcock. The director's work revealed Grant's talent for portraying the dark side of his characters in *Suspicion* (1941) and *Notorious* (1946). He teamed with Grace Kelly in the glamorous *To Catch a Thief* (1955) and played a bewildered executive pursued across the country by spies and police in *North by Northwest* (1959).

Grant continued his acting career into the 1960's, and his films—especially *That Touch of Mink* (1962) and *Charade* (1963)—were still substantial critical and popular successes. He began to feel frustrated, however, at being cast in romantic leads opposite actresses who by then were often less than half his age. Still at the height of his popularity, he retired abruptly after making *Walk, Don't Run* (1966). He firmly resisted all efforts to coax him back to acting.

In his private life, Grant often had trouble living up to his own screen image. "Everyone wants to be Cary Grant," he said ruefully, "I want to be Cary Grant." He was married five times, and an acrimonious divorce from his fourth wife, actress Dyan Cannon, led to public revelations of Grant's bad temper and his repeated use of LSD to relieve depression.

Whatever his private foibles, however, Cary Grant remains Hollywood's quintessential leading man—the standard to which all who follow him will be compared. In 1970, Grant was given a special Honorary Academy Award "for his unique mastery of the art of screen acting." He died of a stroke while touring with his one-man show "A Conversation with Cary Grant," a compilation of film clips with commentary by Grant. Additional film credits include *Sylvia Scarlett* (1936), *Holiday* (1938), *My Favorite Wife* (1940), *Mr. Lucky* (1943), *Night and Day* (1946), *The Bachelor and the Bobby Soxer* (1947), *Mr. Blandings Builds His Dream House* (1948), *I Was a Male War Bride* (1949), *Houseboat* (1958; reviewed in this volume), *Indiscreet* (1958), *Operation Petticoat* (1959), and *Father Goose* (1964).

Virginia Gregg (1917-September 15, 1986). Gregg was an actress who worked in film, radio, and television, often in association with actor-producer Jack Webb, the creator of the popular radio and television show *Dragnet*. Gregg appeared in the film version of *Dragnet* (1954). In Alfred Hitchcock's *Psycho* (1960), she provided the voice of Norman Bates's mother. Additional film credits include *Body and Soul* (1947), *Love Is a Many Splendored Thing* (1955), *Operation Petticoat* (1959), and *Spencer's Mountain* (1963).

Murray Hamilton (1923-September 1, 1986). Hamilton was a character actor who appeared in dozens of films from the 1950's to the 1980's. *Bright Victory* (1951) marked his first screen appearance. His best-known films are *The Graduate* (1967), in which he played the cuckolded Mr. Robinson, and *Jaws* (1975) and *Jaws 2* (1978), in which he played the mayor. In addition to his film work, Hamilton also acted in numerous television series. His film credits include *The Spirit of St. Louis* (1957), *No Time for Sergeants* (1958), *Anatomy of a Murder* (1959), *The Hustler* (1961), *The Way We Were* (1973), and *1941* (1979).

David Hand (January 23, 1900-October 11, 1986). Hand was an animator who worked with two of film's pioneering cartoonists, Max Fleischer and Walt Disney. After animating *Andy Gump* (1919), Hand joined Fleischer in producing the "Out of the Inkwell" series. He worked with Walt Disney from 1930 through 1943, and he was the animator and director for more than sixty cartoon shorts in the Mickey Mouse and Silly Symphonies series. His best-known work includes *Snow White and the Seven Dwarfs* (1937) and *Bambi* (1942), full-length animated features on which he served as supervising director.

Sterling Hayden (March 26, 1916-May 23, 1986). Born John Hamilton, Hayden was a tall blond leading man of the 1940's and 1950's and a distinguished character actor thereafter. Attracted to seafaring at an early age, Hayden dropped out of high school at sixteen to pursue a life at sea. He was a captain at twenty-two and took up acting to raise money to buy his own ship. His rugged good looks soon landed him a contract with Paramount Pictures in 1940. He made two films (billed as "Stirling" Hayden, "The Most Beautiful Man in the Movies"), *Virginia* (1941) and *Bahama Passage* (1941), before enlisting in the Marine Corps for the duration of the Second World War.

Hayden returned to films in 1947, but it was not until *The Asphalt Jungle* (1950) that his acting ability, rather than his looks, won him attention. Shortly afterward, he was subpoenaed by the House Un-American Activities Committee. Unlike many who refused to testify, Hayden admitted past membership in the Communist Party and also identified several colleagues as Communist sympathizers. Thus he was spared the blacklist, but his decision to inform on his associates was one that Hayden would come to regret.

He continued to act during the 1950's and 1960's, but, perhaps because he was as interested in sailing as he was in acting, many of the roles he chose made little use of his native talent. Exceptions included Nicholas Ray's *Johnny Guitar* (1954) and Stanley Kubrick's *The Killing* (1956).

In 1959, he took his four children on a sailing trip to the South Seas in defiance of a court order obtained by his former wife. He wrote of his love for the sea in a 1963 autobiography entitled *Wanderer*. His second book, a novel, *Voyage: A Novel of 1896* (1976), also concerned sailing.

Hayden will perhaps best be remembered for his roles in Kubrick's *Dr. Strangelove, Or: How I Learned to Stop Worrying and Love the Bomb* (1964), in which he played the crazed General Jack D. Ripper, and Francis Coppola's *The Godfather* (1972), in which he played a corrupt policeman. His additional film credits include *Variety Girl* (1947), *Flaming Feather* (1952), *So Big* (1953), *Zero Hour* (1957), *Hard Contract* (1969), *The Long Goodbye* (1973), and *Winter Kills* (1979).

Roland Hill (February 5, 1895-November 10, 1986). Hill was an art director and set designer who worked on a number of important films. His early credits include *The Jazz Singer* (1927), *Queen Kelly* (1928), and *Captain Blood* (1935). He also worked on three Academy Award-winning short subjects: *I Won't Play* (1944), *Star in the Night* (1945), and *A Boy and His Dog* (1946). He joined Walt Disney in the 1950's and worked on *20,000 Leagues Under the Sea* (1954). A trained architect, Hill also worked with Disney in designing many parts of the Disneyland amusement park.

Phil Karlson (July 2, 1908-December 12, 1986). Born Philip N. Karlstein, Karlson is best known for directing a number of well-made crime films in the 1950's. He broke into film with Universal in the 1930's, working as a prop man and then as an editor until the outbreak of World War II. His first project as a director was *A Wave a Wac and a Marine* (1944) for Monogram. He made more than a dozen low-budget

B-pictures for that studio in the 1940's, including *The Shanghai Cobra* (1945) and *Kilroy Was Here* (1947). His realistically violent *film noir* pictures, shot between 1952 and 1957, are considered his best. These include *Kansas City Confidential* (1952), *The Phenix City Story* (1955), and *The Brothers Rico* (1957), which some critics place among the best American films of the genre. His *The Scarface Mob* (1962), made for television, launched the enormously popular series *The Untouchables*. In the 1960's, Karlson directed two of Dean Martin's Matt Helm espionage thrillers, *The Silencers* (1966) and *The Wrecking Crew* (1968). His most commercially successful film, *Walking Tall* (1973), was one of his last. His additional directing credits include *G.I. Honeymoon* (1945), *Down Memory Lane* (1949), *Lorna Doone* (1951), *Five Against the House* (1955), *Kid Galahad* (1962), and *Framed* (1975).

Frederick Kohner (1905-July 6, 1986). Born in Czechoslovakia and educated in Vienna, Kohner was a novelist, playwright, and screenwriter. He wrote his dissertation on cinema, and when he moved to the United States, he found work in the film industry. In 1938, he won an Academy Award for his screenplay of the film *Mad About Music* (1938). His 1957 novel *Gidget*, which described his daughter and her teenage pals in the surfing scene on Malibu beach, inspired a series of five films and a television series, beginning with the original *Gidget* (1959). Other screenwriting credits include *It's a Date* (1940), *Nancy Goes to Rio* (1950), and *Never Wave at a WAC* (1952).

Elsa Lanchester (October 28, 1902-December 26. 1986). Born Elizabeth Sullivan, Lanchester was an English actress who specialized in eccentric roles and comedy. She was taught dancing as a child by Isadora Duncan and appeared in children's theater at the age of sixteen. She made her first film appearance in *One of the Best* (1927).

In 1929, Lanchester married actor Charles Laughton, whom she met while appearing in the play *I've Danced with the Man Who Danced with the Girl Who Danced with the Prince of Wales*. They appeared together in *The Private Life of Henry VIII* (1933), with Laughton starring as King Henry and Lanchester playing Anne of Cleves. They moved to Hollywood in 1934. Although Lanchester appeared in four more British films between 1936 and 1938, the bulk of her screen acting career was spent in the United States. She and Laughton became United States citizens in 1950. The couple's thirty-three-year marriage ended with Laughton's death in 1962, after which it was revealed that he had been homosexual.

One of Lanchester's most memorable performances was in the title role of James Whale's *The Bride of Frankenstein* (1935). She appeared opposite Laughton in *Rembrandt* (1936) and *The Beachcomber* (1938). She was nominated twice for an Academy Award as Best Supporting Actress—for *Come to the Stable* (1949) and for *Witness for the Prosecution* (1958). She capped a film acting career that spanned five decades with a role in *Murder by Death* (1976). Her additional acting credits include *Potiphar's Wife* (1931), *David Copperfield* (1935), *Lassie Come Home* (1943), *The Spiral Staircase* (1946), *Bell, Book and Candle* (1958), *Mary Poppins* (1964), *Easy Come, Easy Go* (1967), and *Willard* (1971).

Emmet Lavery (1902-January 1, 1986). Lavery was a playwright and screenwriter who was president of the Screen Writers Guild between 1945 and 1947. His play, *The First Legion*, was produced on Broadway in 1934. A year later, he began his film career. Thereafter, he divided his time between the theater and film. Indeed, two of his plays were later produced as films: *The First Legion* (1951) and *The Magnificent Yankee* (1955). Lavery's additional film credits include *Hitler's Children* (1943) and *Behind the Rising Sun* (1943).

Alan Jay Lerner (August 31, 1918-June 14, 1986). Lerner was a gifted lyricist, playwright, and screenwriter who, along with his partner, Frederick Loewe, wrote many of the most memorable musicals of the 1950's and 1960's. Lerner was born in New York, and his father was the founder of the Lerner's clothing-store chain. Lerner was educated at Harvard and broke into show business by writing material for radio shows. His collaboration with Loewe began in 1943; by 1947, they had their first Broadway smash, *Brigadoon*, which was followed by *Paint Your Wagon* (1951), *My Fair Lady* (1956), and *Camelot* (1960). All were later made into films.

Lerner's first film was *Royal Wedding* (1951); he wrote the screenplay as well as the lyrics to the songs, one of which, "Too Late Now," was nominated for an Academy Award. That same year, Lerner won the Oscar for Best Story and Screenplay for *An American in Paris* (1951). He won another Oscar for the screenplay of *Gigi* (1958) and a third, shared with Loewe, for the title song from that film. He was nominated for an Academy Award for his screenplay for *My Fair Lady* (1964) and, along with Loewe, for Best Scoring and Best Song for *The Little Prince* (1974).

In 1978, Lerner wrote his autobiography, entitled *The Street Where I Live*. Additional film credits include *Brigadoon* (1954; screenplay and lyrics), *Camelot* (1967; screenplay and lyrics), *Paint Your Wagon* (1969; production, screenplay, and lyrics), and *On a Clear Day You Can See Forever* (1970; screenplay and lyrics).

Boris Leven (August 13, 1908-October 11, 1986). Born in Moscow, Leven moved to the United States in 1927 and became one of the film industry's most respected art directors. Over the course of a career that spanned five decades, Leven was nominated for eight Academy Awards: *Alexander's Ragtime Band* (1938), *The Shanghai Gesture* (1941), *Giant* (1956), *West Side Story* (1961; for which he won), *The Sound of Music* (1965), *The Sand Pebbles* (1966), *Star!* (1968), and *The Andromeda Strain* (1971). In addition, Leven worked with director Martin Scorsese on such films as *New York, New York* (1977), *The Last Waltz* (1978), *The King of Comedy* (1983), and *The Color of Money* (1986; reviewed in this volume). Additional film credits include *The Silver Chalice* (1955), *Anatomy of a Murder* (1959), and *The Color Purple* (1985).

John Lormer (1905-March 19, 1986). Lormer was a veteran character actor who appeared on the stage and television before breaking into film in *I Want to Live!* (1958). Additional film credits include *Youngblood Hawke* (1964), *The Singing Nun* (1966), *The Sand Pebbles* (1966), *Rooster Cogburn* (1975), and *Creepshow* (1982).

Bessie Love (September 10, 1898-April 26, 1986). Born Juanita Horton, Love was an important leading lady of the silent era. Her film career extended into the early 1980's. Legend has it that she made her film debut as an extra in D. W. Griffith's *The Birth of a Nation* (1915) while still in high school. It is certain that by 1916 her star was rapidly ascending, for she appeared in a major role in *The Aryan* (1916) opposite William S. Hart, in *Reggie Mixes In* (1916) opposite Douglas Fairbanks, and as the Bride of Cana in the Judean sequence of Griffith's *Intolerance* (1916).

Thereafter, Love's career took a variety of turns, as she was cast first in ingenue roles, then in melodramas, and finally in light comedies and musicals. She introduced the Charleston dance step to the nation's film viewers in *The King of Main*

Street (1925). Love adapted well to the advent of sound in film; she was nominated for an Academy Award for her performance in the early musical *The Broadway Melody* (1929). Nevertheless, producers' uncertainties over exactly how to cast Love undoubtedly hurt her career. In 1931, she began a ten-year retirement from film, and in 1935, she moved to England.

Love resumed her film career with *Atlantic Ferry* (1941) and continued to act regularly on the stage, in radio, film, and, later, television. Her more than eighty films include *Nina the Flower Girl* (1917), *Deserted at the Altar* (1922), *Sally of the Scandals* (1928), *Morals for Women* (1931), *The Barefoot Contessa* (1954), *The Loves of Isadora* (1969), *Sunday Bloody Sunday* (1971), and *Ragtime* (1981).

Mary C. McCall, Jr. (1906-April 3, 1986). McCall was a veteran screenwriter who was active in the Writers Guild of America, serving three times as its president in the 1940's and early 1950's. McCall's novels and short stories attracted the attention of Hollywood studios, and her first screenwriting credit was for her work on the adaptation of *A Midsummer Night's Dream* (1935). She became a staff writer at Metro-Goldwyn-Mayer, writing scripts for seven of the ten "Maisie" films which starred Ann Sothern as a scatterbrained blonde. McCall's last film was *Juke Box Rhythm* (1959), after which she began writing for television. Her film credits include *Craig's Wife* (1936), *Maisie* (1939), *Congo Maisie* (1940), *Mr. Belvedere Goes to College* (1949), *Dancing in the Dark* (1949), and *Thunderbirds* (1952).

Frank McCarthy (June 8, 1912-December 1, 1986). McCarthy was a retired brigadier general and former assistant secretary of state who joined Twentieth Century-Fox in 1949 as a producer. His earliest efforts, including *Decision Before Dawn* (1951) and *Sailor of the King* (1953), were war films, as was his most successful production, *Patton* (1970), which won the Academy Award for Best Picture. McCarthy's other productions include *A Guide for the Married Man* (1967) and *MacArthur* (1977).

Tim McIntyre (1945-April 15, 1986). McIntyre was an actor and musician whose best role was that of rock-and-roll disc jockey Alan Freed in *American Hot Wax* (1978). He was also featured in *The Gumball Rally* (1976), *The Choirboys* (1977), and *Brubaker* (1980). He was the voice of the mutant dog Blood in *A Boy and His Dog* (1975), and he wrote and performed the music for *Jeremiah Johnson* (1972). He was the son of actor John McIntire and actress Jeanette Nolan.

Siobhan McKenna (May 24, 1923-November 16, 1986). McKenna was an Irish actress best known for her work on stage in Dublin and London, where she made her reputation in the 1954 production of George Bernard Shaw's *Saint Joan*. Thereafter, she acted on Broadway as well as in Irish and English theatrical productions. Her first film was *Hungry Hill* (1946). She also appeared in *Daughter of Darkness* (1948), *The Lost People* (1949), *King of Kings* (1961), *The Playboy of the Western World* (1962), *Of Human Bondage* (1964), and *Doctor Zhivago* (1965).

Gordon MacRae (March 12, 1921-January 24, 1986). MacRae was a handsome actor and singer who starred in a number of films in the 1950's. He won an amateur singing contest at the 1939 New York World's Fair, which led to a singing career on the stage and in radio. A 1946 Broadway performance in *Three to Make Ready* earned for him a film contract with Warner Bros., and his first film was *The Big Punch* (1948). His voice won for him roles in musicals, and his looks served him in good stead in action films.

Perhaps, MacRae's best-remembered role will be that of Curly, the singing cowboy in the film version of *Oklahoma!* (1955). A year later, he starred in *Carousel* (1956), another musical. MacRae made only one more film after 1956: *The Pilot* (1979). Instead, he concentrated on television and personal appearances, often with his first wife, Sheila MacRae. Their daughter Meredith MacRae is a television and film actress. MacRae's additional film credits include *Look for the Silver Lining* (1949), *The West Point Story* (1950), *The Desert Song* (1953), *Three Sailors and a Girl* (1953), and *The Best Things in Life Are Free* (1956).

Herbert Magidson (1908-January 2, 1986). Magidson was a prolific songwriter who wrote for Broadway musicals and films. He wrote the lyrics to "The Continental," featured in the Fred Astaire-Ginger Rogers vehicle *The Gay Divorcee* (1934); the song won the first Academy Award given for Best Song. Magidson received two other Academy Award nominations: "Say a Prayer for the Boys over There," in *Hers to Hold* (1943), and "I'll Buy That Dream," in *Sing Your Way Home* (1945). Additional film credits include *The Great Ziegfeld* (1936), *The Life of the Party* (1937), *Music for Madame* (1937), *Radio City Revels* (1938), and *Priorities on Parade* (1942).

Norman Maurer (1926-November 23, 1986). Maurer was a cartoonist and producer who worked in film and television. He started out as a comic-book illustrator and helped to invent the first three-dimensional comic book. In 1956, he joined Columbia Pictures as a producer, where he helped resuscitate the Three Stooges' film career with *The Three Stooges Meet Hercules* (1962), *The Three Stooges in Orbit* (1962), and *The Three Stooges Go Around the World in a Daze* (1963). He also married the daughter of chief stooge Moe Howard and managed the group for fifteen years. In 1975, he returned to the cartoon field, working with the Hanna-Barbera studios as a writer-editor and with CBS and ABC as a consultant on their animated television series. Additional production credits include *The Outlaws Is Coming!* (1965) and *Who's Minding the Mint?* (1967).

Una Merkel (December 10, 1903-January 2, 1986). Merkel was a veteran character actress who appeared in more than one hundred films in a career that spanned five decades. As a teenager, her close resemblance to silent film star Lillian Gish resulted in her first on-screen appearances as Gish's stand-in in *Way Down East* (1920) and *The White Rose* (1923). Her first prominent role was in *The Fifth Horseman* (1924), but that film was a box-office failure, and she abandoned cinema for the Broadway stage. Hollywood beckoned again in 1930, and Merkel appeared in a major role in *Abraham Lincoln* (1930). Shortly thereafter, she revealed a gift for comedy that would keep her in demand for decades. Appearing occasionally in lead roles, but more frequently as the heroine's wisecracking friend, Merkel made dozens of films in the 1930's and 1940's. Not all of her roles, however, were comic. One of her finest dramatic performances was in Tennessee Williams' *Summer and Smoke* (1961). In addition to her work in film, Merkel received a Tony Award for her performance in *The Ponder Heart* in 1956. Additional film credits include *The Bat Whispers* (1930), *Daddy Long Legs* (1931), *42nd Street* (1933), *It's in the Air* (1935), *Destry Rides Again* (1939), *The Bank Dick* (1940), *It's a Joke Son* (1947), *The Merry Widow* (1952), *The Parent Trap* (1961), and *Spinout* (1966).

Ray Milland (January 3, 1905-March 10, 1986). Born Reginald Truscott-Jones in

Wales, Milland played light romantic leads in the 1930's and 1940's. Later in his career, which spanned more than five decades and more than 170 films, he specialized in character roles, sometimes in distinguished productions and other times in low-budget horror films.

Milland came to film directly from a career in the British cavalry, and his knowledge of riding and shooting won for him small roles in films such as *The Plaything* (1929) and *The Informer* (1929). At this stage in his career, he called himself Spike Milland; he began using Raymond Milland later that same year in *The Flying Scotsman* (1929).

Early in his career, making films in both England and the United States, Milland got by more on the basis of his looks than on his then-rudimentary acting ability. He applied himself to his craft, however, and his performances improved to the point that he graduated from second leads to lead roles by the mid-1930's. Most of his films were romantic comedies, leavened by an occasional mystery or adventure film. These films included *Bolero* (1934), *Charlie Chan in London* (1934), *Three Smart Girls* (1936), *Bulldog Drummond Escapes* (1937), and *Beau Geste* (1939).

Milland gave his most memorable performance, for which he won an Academy Award, when he was cast against type as an alcoholic writer in Billy Wilder's *The Lost Weekend* (1945). As sometimes happens to Academy Award-winners, Milland had trouble finding roles worthy of his talent. Although he continued to work regularly throughout the next decade, most of his films were unmemorable. Exceptions to this rule include roles in Alfred Hitchcock's *Dial M for Murder* (1954) and *The Girl in the Red Velvet Swing* (1955). Between 1955 and 1967, Milland tried his hand at directing, making five films in which he also starred: *A Man Alone* (1955), *Lisbon* (1956), *The Safecracker* (1958), *Panic in the Year Zero!* (1962), *Hostile Witness* (1967).

Milland began working with horror-exploitationist Roger Corman in the early 1960's, and Corman's *Premature Burial* (1962) and *X—The Man with the X-Ray Eyes* (1963) set the tone for the sort of films in which Milland would appear during the latter stages of his film career, including *Frogs* (1972), *The Thing with Two Heads* (1972), and *Terror in the Wax Museum* (1973). His last noteworthy performances were in *Love Story* (1970) and *Oliver's Story* (1978).

In addition to his film work, Milland appeared frequently on television. He starred in the situation comedy *The Ray Milland Show* from 1953 to 1955, and in *Markham*, a detective series, from 1959 to 1960. He published his autobiography, *Wide-Eyed in Babylon*, in 1974. Additional acting credits include *The Bachelor Father* (1931), *Orders Is Orders* (1933), *I Wanted Wings* (1941), *The Major and the Minor* (1942), *California* (1947), *It Happens Every Spring* (1949), *Jamaica Run* (1953), *Gold* (1974), and *The Last Tycoon* (1976).

Vincente Minnelli (February 28, 1903-July 25, 1986). This award-winning director was best known for his Metro-Goldwyn-Mayer musicals in the 1940's and 1950's. Born in Chicago into a show-business family, Minnelli worked as a costume designer and art director in the New York theater in the 1930's before becoming one of Broadway's top directors. His stage successes led to a contract with Metro-Goldwyn-Mayer in 1940.

Metro-Goldwyn-Mayer gave Minnelli a lengthy and intensive tutorial in the art of filmmaking, gradually assigning him more independent responsibility over a two-year period. This training, in combination with Minnelli's own native ability, made him a success from the outset. His first film, *Cabin in the Sky* (1943), was a musical featuring an all-black cast that showcased Ethel Waters, Lena Horne, and Louis Armstrong. His second project that year was *I Dood It* (1943), a vehicle designed to capitalize on the popularity of radio comic Red Skelton.

A year later, Minnelli made his first in a long string of classic musicals. *Meet Me in St. Louis* (1944), a nostalgic and tuneful look at turn-of-the-century Middle America, was Minnelli's first color film. It starred Judy Garland, whom Minnelli married in 1945.

That marriage lasted from 1945 to 1951, during which time Garland appeared in three more Minnelli films: *The Clock* (1945), a drama, and *Ziegfield Follies* (1946) and *The Pirate* (1948), both musicals. The marriage produced a daughter, singer-actress Liza Minnelli.

Minnelli's professional association with Gene Kelly also began in the mid–1940's. The dancer, actor, and choreographer appeared with Garland in *Ziegfield Follies* and *The Pirate*, and he also starred in *An American in Paris* (1951) and *Brigadoon* (1954). Kelly choreographed the latter two films. *An American in Paris* was nominated for eight Academy Awards and won six, including Best Picture; *Brigadoon* was nominated for three Academy Awards.

In *The Bad and the Beautiful* (1952), Minnelli presented the story of a ruthless Hollywood mogul from the perspective of those around him. The film starred Kirk Douglas and Lana Turner, and it won five Academy Awards. Douglas was also featured in *Lust for Life* (1956), which Minnelli counted as his personal favorite among his own pictures. The film was a thoroughly researched and finely drawn biography of artist Vincent van Gogh. *Lust for Life* garnered three Academy Award nominations, with Anthony Quinn winning for Best Supporting Actor.

Minnelli's most honored film was *Gigi* (1958). The tastefully told story of a young woman's preparation for life as a courtesan was nominated for and won nine Academy Awards, including Best Picture and Best Direction. The film has been called the last of the classic Metro-Goldwyn-Mayer musicals.

Minnelli continued making films into the 1970's, with mixed results. *Some Came Running* (1959) was a good drama which featured Frank Sinatra and Shirley MacLaine, and *Bells Are Ringing* (1960), with Dean Martin and Judy Holliday, was an above-average musical-comedy. *The Four Horsemen of the Apocalypse* (1962), however, was a critical and financial failure, and films such as *The Sandpiper* (1965) failed to enhance Minnelli's reputation.

Minnelli's final two films were the objects of some controversy, as the director charged that postproduction studio interference led to the weakening of both the Barbra Streisand vehicle *On a Clear Day You Can See Forever* (1970) and *A Matter of Time* (1976), which featured Minnelli's daughter, Liza.

At the height of his powers, Minnelli brought a distinctive flair to the Hollywood musical. He was the last great practicioner of the genre. He published his autobiography, *I Remember It Well*, in 1974. Additional film credits include *Madame Bovary* (1949), *Father of the Bride* (1950), *The Band Wagon* (1953), *The Long, Long Trailer* (1954; reviewed in this volume), *Kismet* (1955), *Tea and Sympathy* (1956), *The Courtship of Eddie's Father* (1963), and *Goodbye Charlie* (1964).

Abraham Mirkin (1918-July 28, 1986). Mirkin was a midget who acted in films and television. His most famous role was that of the Munchkins' mayor in *The Wizard of Oz* (1939). His other film credits include *Oil for the Lamps of China* (1935), *Ghost Catchers* (1944), and *Dragon Seed* (1944).

Ray Moyer (1898-February 6, 1986). Moyer was an award-winning set decorator whose career spanned the years 1933 to 1970. He won three Academy Awards: for his work on *Samson and Delilah* (1949), *Sunset Boulevard* (1950), and *Cleopatra* (1963). In addition to these three Academy Awards, Moyer was nominated for the award nine other times, for *Lady in the Dark* (1944), *Love Letters* (1945), *Kitty* (1945), *Sabrina* (1954), *Red Garters* (1954), *The Ten Commandments* (1956), *Funny Face* (1957), *Breakfast at Tiffany's* (1961), and *The Greatest Story Ever Told* (1965).

Ray Nazarro (September 25, 1902-September 8, 1986). Nazarro was a veteran director who spent most of his career making low-budget Westerns and other action films. Early in his career he worked for Columbia Pictures, making his debut with *Outlaws of the Rockies* (1945). He made two more films in 1945 and twelve in 1946. Nazarro's pictures were noted for their nonstop action, and he turned out films at the rate of six per year through 1958. His career went into decline when the market for B-Westerns vanished, although he continued to work in television. He also made two films in Europe in the 1960's. His credits include *Cowboy Blues* (1946), *West of Dodge City* (1947), *Quick on the Trigger* (1949), *The Palomino* (1950), *China Corsair* (1951), *Kansas Pacific* (1953), *The White Squaw* (1956), and *Arrivederci Cowboy* (1967).

Ben Nye, Sr. (1908-February 9, 1986). Nye was a makeup artist who worked on nearly five hundred films for Twentieth Century-Fox and other studios between 1930 and 1968. He was adept at not only conventional makeup work but also challenging special-effects projects such as *The Fly* (1958) and *Planet of the Apes* (1968). Additional film credits include *Gone with the Wind* (1939), *Intermezzo* (1939), *Rebecca* (1940), *All About Eve* (1950), *Oklahoma!* (1955), *The King and I* (1956), *South Pacific* (1958), *Cleopatra* (1963), and *The Sound of Music* (1965).

Joseph D. Oriolo (1914-December 25, 1986). Oriolo was an animator who worked with Max Fleischer on the Popeye and Betty Boop series. He also created Casper the Friendly Ghost and worked on the Felix the Cat cartoons.

Lilli Palmer (May 24, 1914-January 27, 1986). Born Lillie Marie Peiser in Germany, Palmer was the daughter of a physician and an actress. She was known for her sensitive and intelligent performances on the stage and in film. She began her stage career in Berlin but left Germany after Adolf Hitler's rise to power. By 1935, she was making films in England, where her early performances included a role in Alfred Hitchcock's *Secret Agent* (1936).

Between 1937 and 1946, Palmer was an important leading lady in British films, appearing in *Command Performance* (1937), *Thunder Rock* (1942), and *The Gentle Sex* (1943). In 1943, she married actor Rex Harrison, with whom she appeared in *The Rake's Progress* (1945).

In 1946, Palmer and Harrison moved to Hollywood, where both of their careers prospered. Palmer appeared in *Body and Soul* (1947) and thereafter made dozens of films in the United States, England, and Germany. She and Harrison were divorced in 1957, by which time Palmer was an international star. She went on to appear in *Mädchen in Uniform* (1958), *The Amorous Adventures of Moll Flanders* (1965), *Oedipus the King* (1968), and *De Sade* (1969).

By the mid-1970's, Palmer had begun to devote most of her energies to writing, publishing *Change Lobsters and Dance*, her autobiography, in 1975, as well as two novels: *The Red Raven* (1978) and *Night Music* (1982). Additional acting credits include *Crime Unlimited* (1935), *The Door with Seven Locks* (1940), *English Without Tears* (1944), *My Girl Tisa* (1948), *The Four Poster* (1952), *But Not for Me* (1959), *Sebastian* (1968), *Lotte in Weimar* (1975), and *The Boys from Brazil* (1978).

Otto Preminger (December 5, 1906-April 23, 1986). Born in Austria, Preminger was a producer-director-actor whose fierce independence generated considerable controversy throughout his long and successful career. He was educated as a lawyer, but his first love was theater, and he began acting as a teenager. By his mid-twenties, he had given up law and was directing plays for important Viennese theatrical companies. At the age of twenty-five, he also directed his first film, *Die Grosse Liebe* (1931), his only German-language film.

In 1935, Preminger, who was Jewish, fled Europe to avoid the spread of Nazism. He directed plays in New York and signed a contract with Twentieth Century-Fox, for which he directed two low-budget films, *Under Your Spell* (1936) and *Danger— Love at Work* (1937). He quarreled with studio head Darryl Zanuck—the first of many public controversies in which he was to be involved—and was fired, whereupon he returned to New York as a theatrical director. In 1939, he cast himself as the Nazi villain in *Margin for Error*. His shaved head and accent were so convincingly Prussian that he was quickly in demand as an actor in similar roles in Hollywood films. He was grudgingly allowed to direct again when he refused to act in the film version of *Margin for Error* (1943) unless he could direct it as well.

Despite a fragile relationship with Zanuck, Preminger continued to produce and direct for Twentieth Century-Fox through 1950. His biggest hit was *Laura* (1944), for which he was nominated for an Academy Award for Best Director. *Forever Amber* (1947), however, for which the studio had great expectations, was a resounding flop.

In 1951, Preminger became an independent producer. His film version of *The Moon Is Blue* (1953), a seemingly innocuous comedy, created a furor because the screenplay contained the words "virgin" and "pregnant"—then taboo in the industry. Audiences were unaccustomed to such frankness, and the film was banned in many localities until the Supreme Court ruled in the film's favor in 1955. Preminger also filmed *Carmen Jones* (1954), an all-black version of Georges Bizet's *Carmen*. In 1955, he generated more controversy with *The Man with the Golden Arm*. The film, which starred Frank Sinatra, was an unsparing look at the world of a drug addict.

Preminger's best film was probably *Anatomy of a Murder* (1959), which was nominated for six Academy Awards, including Best Picture. In the 1960's, he made *Exodus* (1960), *The Cardinal* (1963; for which he received an Academy Award nomination for Best Director, and which is reviewed in this volume), and *Hurry Sundown* (1967), among other films. He continued making films through the 1970's, but few were financial or critical successes.

Politically, Preminger was an outspoken liberal. His announcement in 1960 that Hollywood Ten member Dalton Trumbo had written the screenplay for *Exodus* is credited with dealing the death blow to the McCarthy era blacklist of writers who had refused to testify before the House Un-American Activities Committee about their ties to the Communist Party. Preminger was married three times, and he announced that striptease artist Gypsy Rose Lee was the mother of one of his children. He published *Preminger: An Autobiography*, in 1977. His additional film credits include *Fallen Angel* (1945), *Daisy Kenyon* (1947), *Stalag 17* (1953; as an actor only), *River of No Return* (1954), *The Court-Martial of Billy Mitchell* (1955), *Saint Joan* (1957), *Bonjour Tristesse* (1958), *Bunny Lake Is Missing* (1965), *Tell Me That You Love Me Junie Moon* (1970), and *The Human Factor* (1980).

Robert Presnell, Jr. (1914-June 14, 1986). Presnell was a screenwriter who worked in film and television. His father, Robert Presnell, Sr., was a producer and screenwriter. Presnell, Jr., wrote radio scripts for Orson Welles and published a novel, *Edgell's Island*, in 1951. His first screen credit was *Man in the Attic* (1953), and he also wrote *The Rawhide Years* (1956), *Screaming Eagles* (1956), *Legend of the Lost* (1957), *Let No Man Write My Epitaph* (1960), and *The Third Day* (1965).

Donna Reed (January 27, 1921-January 14, 1986). Born Donna Belle Mullenger, Reed was a leading lady in films of the 1940's and 1950's before switching to television to star in her own series. Reed grew up on a farm in Iowa and won beauty contests there and in Los Angeles, where she attended college. She attracted the attention of Metro-Goldwyn-Mayer, which signed her to a contract in 1941.

Reed first appeared in "nice girl" roles, billed as Donna Adams, in such films as *Shadow of the Thin Man* (1941) and *The Courtship of Andy Hardy* (1942). She won bigger roles in *The Human Comedy* (1943) and *The Picture of Dorian Gray* (1945). A year later, she played a memorable role as Jimmy Stewart's wife in Frank Capra's *It's a Wonderful Life* (1946).

In 1951, Reed signed with Columbia Pictures where she continued to be cast in wholesome roles. She was cast against type in *From Here to Eternity* (1953), in which she played a prostitute and won an Academy Award for Best Supporting Actress. The award, however, did little to advance her film career. She made nine more films between 1954 and 1958, most of which were unmemorable.

In 1956, Reed moved to television, where her situation comedy, *The Donna Reed Show*, was a hit for eight seasons. She continued to appear on television into the 1980's. Additional acting credits include *Calling Dr. Gillespie* (1942), *See Here Private Hargrove* (1944), *Green Dolphin Street* (1947), and *The Benny Goodman Story* (1956).

Leah Rhodes (1902-October 17, 1986). Rhodes was a costume designer who won an Academy Award for her work on *Adventures of Don Juan* (1949). She spent most of her career with Warner Bros., where she headed the studio's costume department. Additional screen credits include *Old Acquaintance* (1943), *Mission to Moscow* (1943), *Northern Pursuit* (1943), *God Is My Co-Pilot* (1945), and *Confidential Agent* (1945).

Harry Ritz (May 22, 1906-March 29, 1986). Born Harry Joachim, Ritz was the last surviving member of the Ritz Brothers comedy trio. Along with his brothers Al and Jimmy, he perfected his routines in vaudeville and supper clubs. The brothers' first film was *Hotel Anchovy* (1934). Although critics preferred the Marx Brothers, the Ritz Brothers proved popular with the public, and the act appeared in more than a dozen films over the next decade, including *Sing Baby Sing* (1936), *On the Avenue* (1937), *Straight Place and Show* (1938), *The Gorilla* (1939), and *Hi'Ya Chum* (1943). Ritz appeared in three films after the death of his brother Al broke up the group: *Blazing Stewardesses* (1975) and *Won Ton Ton—The Dog Who Saved Hollywood* (1976) with his brother Jimmy, and *Silent Movie* (1976).

Benny Rubin (February 2, 1899-July 15, 1986). Rubin was a comic actor who got his start in vaudeville and burlesque. Specializing in ethnic and dialect humor, he broke into film with *Naughty Baby* (1929) and continued to appear in films over the next four decades. His screen credits include *It's a Great Life* (1929), *Hot Curves* (1930), *Sunny Skies* (1930), *Here Comes Mr. Jordan* (1941), *The Errand Boy* (1961), *Thoroughly Modern Millie* (1967), and *Won Ton Ton—The Dog Who Saved Hollywood* (1976).

Harold Schuster (August 1, 1902-July 19, 1986). Schuster was a director who made thirty-two films from 1937 to 1957. He broke into film in 1927 as an actor, cameraman, and editor, and he made his debut as a director for Twentieth Century-Fox a decade later. His first film, *Wings of the Morning* (1937), was followed by such films as *Dinner at the Ritz* (1937), *Framed* (1940), and *My Friend Flicka* (1943). Although Schuster's early films were well received, his later efforts are widely regarded as lackluster. After making *Portland Expose* (1957), he left film to direct for such television series as *Lassie* and *The Twilight Zone*. Additional film credits include *One Hour to Live* (1939), *Girl Trouble* (1942), *Jack Slade* (1953), and *The Courage of Black Beauty* (1957).

Charles Starrett (March 28, 1903-March 22, 1986). Starrett was an actor best known for his role as the Durango Kid in numerous B-Westerns. He began his film career while in college, appearing as an extra in *The Quarterback* (1926). His first feature was *Fast and Loose* (1930), and he played romantic lead roles until 1936, when he signed with Columbia Pictures and became that studio's most popular cowboy star. He appeared in nine low-budget pictures a year in his heyday and was often paired with comic Smiley Burnette as his sidekick. His acting credits include *Touchdown* (1931), *The Mask of Fu Manchu* (1932), *The Sweetheart of Sigma Chi* (1933), *Stampede* (1936), *Two Gun Law* (1937), *The Durango Kid* (1940), *Pardon My Gun* (1942), and *Rough Tough West* (1952).

Robert Stevenson (March 31, 1905-April 30, 1986). Born in England, Stevenson was one of the most commercially successful filmmakers of all time, directing films in a variety of styles, principally for RKO and Walt Disney. His career spanned forty-four years.

Stevenson saw his first film at the age of twenty-two while working on a research project at Cambridge University, and he immediately vowed to make film his life's work. His first film-related job was as a screenwriter, and he directed his first picture, *Happy Ever After* (1932), at the age of twenty-seven. He made eleven films in England over the next seven years, the best known of which is *King Solomon's Mines* (1937).

In 1939, Stevenson signed a contract with David O. Selznick and Metro-Goldwyn-Mayer. Although under contract to Metro-Goldwyn-Mayer for ten years, Stevenson never made a film for that studio, as Selznick loaned him out to other studios throughout the course of the decade. During this period, he directed such films as *Tom Brown's Schooldays* (1940), *Back Street* (1941), and *Jane Eyre* (1944; for which he also cowrote the screenplay). During World War II, Stevenson also made films for the United States War Department.

In 1949, Howard Hughes of RKO bought Stevenson's contract. Stevenson made five films for RKO, including *I Married a Communist* (1949), which was reputedly assigned by Hughes as a test of Stevenson's patriotism. Stevenson's last film for RKO was *The Las Vegas Story* (1952), after which he worked in television as a director and writer for five years.

In 1956, Stevenson began a twenty-year association with the Disney studios, during which time he directed so many box-office smashes that in 1977 *Variety* named him the most commercially successful filmmaker in the history of cinema (a rank from which he has been since displaced by George Lucas and Steven Spielberg). He directed most of Disney's live-action comedy and adventure films from the late 1950's through the mid-1970's, including *Johnny Tremain* (1957), *Old Yeller* (1957), *The Absent-Minded Professor* (1961), and *The Love Bug* (1969). The quintessential Disney director's films were, for the most part, light, family-oriented fare. His most successful film was *Mary Poppins* (1964), for which he received an Academy Award nomination for Best Director and which won five Academy Awards. His additional films include *Tudor Rose* (1936), *Non-Stop New York* (1937), *Darby O'Gill and the Little People* (1959), *Son of Flubber* (1963), *That Darn Cat* (1965), *Bedknobs and Broomsticks* (1971), *Herbie Rides Again* (1974), and *The Shaggy D.A.* (1976).

Paul Stewart (March 13, 1908-February 17, 1986). Born Paul Sternberg, Stewart joined Orson Welles's Mercury Theater at the age of twenty. He made his film debut in *Citizen Kane* (1941). Frequently cast as a gangster, Stewart carved out a career as a character actor in film and in television. His films credits include *Mr. Lucky* (1943), *Twelve O'Clock High* (1950), *Chicago Syndicate* (1955), *In Cold Blood* (1967), *W. C. Fields and Me* (1976), and *Revenge of the Pink Panther* (1978).

Nigel Stock (1921-June 23, 1986). Born on the island of Malta, Stock moved to England where he began acting in 1931. He was a character actor who appeared in more than forty films, as well as on the stage and in television, during the course of his career. His film credits include *Dam Busters* (1955), *Eye Witness* (1956), *The Lion in Winter* (1968), *Lost Continent* (1968), *Cromwell* (1970), *The Nelson Affair* (1973), and *Russian Roulette* (1975).

Blanche Sweet (June 19, 1895-September 6, 1986). Sweet was an actress who appeared in 121 films in the silent era. Born into a show-business family, she began acting at the age of four and made her first film ten years later: *A Man with Three Wives* (1909). Later that same year, she made *A Corner in Wheat* (1909) for D. W. Griffith and appeared in several of Griffith's early films, including *The Painted Lady* (1912) and *Judith of Bethulia* (1914). The latter film made her a star. Unlike many of her contemporaries, who specialized in playing fragile heroines, Sweet played strong-willed women and even an occasional unsympathetic character. She starred in *Anna Christie* (1923) and *Tess of the D'Urbervilles* (1924)—the latter film directed by her first husband, Marshall Neilan.

Sweet's career ended with the advent of sound; she made three talkies, the last of which was *The Silver Horde* (1930), and retired from film. Her last screen appearance was a cameo in the Danny Kaye film *The Five Pennies* (1959). Additional acting credits include *The Lonedale Operator* (1911), *The Goddess of Sagebrush Gulch* (1912), *Strongheart* (1914), *A Woman of Pleasure* (1919), *The Deadlier Sex* (1920), *Bluebeard's Seven Wives* (1926), and *Show Girl in Hollywood* (1930).

Andrei Tarkovsky (1932-December 29, 1986). Tarkovsky was a Russian director known for the hallucinatory quality of his best films. His first film, *Ivan's Childhood* (1962), won the Golden Lion Award at the Venice Film Festival. His next film, *Andrei Rublev* (1966), about a fifteenth century monk, was banned in the Soviet

Union until after it won a prize at the 1970 Cannes Film Festival. *Solaris* (1972), a science-fiction film, won the Jury Prize at Cannes. His last film, *The Sacrifice* (1985; reviewed in this volume), about nuclear holocaust, won the Special Jury Prize at Cannes in 1986. He also made *Mirror* (1975), which was appreciated in the West but was deemed too avant-garde by Soviet audiences and critics, and *Stalker* (1979), another science-fiction film.

Forrest Tucker (February 12, 1919-October 25, 1986). Tucker was an actor who had numerous leading roles in Westerns and other action films throughout the 1940's and 1950's. Later in his career, which included more than fifty films, he specialized in character roles. Tucker got his acting start in burlesque theater; his first film was *The Westerner* (1940). Tall and husky, Tucker played villains early in his career, but by the 1950's he was playing heroes in such films as *Fighting Coast Guard* (1951), *Montana Belle* (1952), and *The Quiet Gun* (1957). From 1965 to 1967, he had a featured role in television's comedy-Western, *F Troop*. Additional acting credits include *The Yearling* (1946), *Sands of Iwo Jima* (1949), *Oh Susanna!* (1951), *Auntie Mame* (1958), *Chisum* (1970), and *Final Chapter—Walking Tall* (1977).

Lorenzo Tucker (1907-August 19, 1986). Tucker was a black actor known as "the colored Valentino." He was discovered by pioneer black director Oscar Micheaux, who cast him in matinee-idol roles in a series of all-black films beginning in 1928. He appeared in nearly twenty films and also acted in touring theatrical shows in the 1940's and 1950's. He became an authority on early black cinema and served as a consultant to several scholars preparing books or documentaries on the subject. His films include *When Men Betray* (1928), *Wages of Sin* (1929), *A Daughter of the Congo* (1930), *Harlem After Midnight* (1934), *One Round Jones* (1946), and *Reet, Petite and Gone* (1947).

Rudy Vallee (July 28, 1901-July 3, 1986). Born Hubert Pryor Vallee, Vallee rose to fame as a singer. Along with Al Jolson, he was one of America's first pop stars. As the first singer to utilize the crooning style later adopted by performers such as Bing Crosby and Perry Como, Vallee's hits included "My Time Is Your Time" and "The Whiffenpoof Song." He parlayed his musical popularity into a lengthy film career. Indeed, his first film, *The Vagabond Lover* (1929), was named after one of his most popular songs.

His early acting performances were slight, and his films were often little more than songs tied together by a thin plot. As his singing career waned, however, his acting abilities grew. He became adept at light comedy, portraying pompous millionaires in *The Palm Beach Story* (1942) and *Happy Go Lucky* (1943). He occasionally played a straight part—most notably in *The Admiral Was a Lady* (1950)—and, in *The Helen Morgan Story* (1957), he played himself. Nevertheless, comedy remained his forte, and he continued making films through 1980.

One of his best-known performances was in *How to Succeed in Business Without Really Trying* (1967). Vallee's autobiography, *My Time Is Your Time*, was published in 1962, and he also wrote *Let the Chips Fall*, another book of reminiscences, in 1975. Additional acting credits include *International House* (1933), *Too Many Blondes* (1941), *The Bachelor and the Bobby Soxer* (1947), *I Remember Mama* (1948), *Mother Is a Freshman* (1949), *Ricochet Romance* (1954), and *Live a Little Love a Little* (1968).

Willard Van Dyke (December 5, 1906-January 23, 1986). Van Dyke was an important twentieth century photographer who was also a noted documentary filmmaker. In 1922, he helped found f.64, the San Francisco photography group that included Ansel Adams, Edward Weston, and Imogen Cunningham. His first film was Pare Lorenz's *The River* (1937), on which he worked as a cameraman. In 1939, he codirected (with Ralph Steiner) the classic documentary *The City*, which dealt with urban planning and is known for its editing and sound track. He also made *San Francisco* (1945), the United Nations' official documentary concerning its origins. His other films include *The Bridge* (1942), *Skyscraper* (1958), *Harvest* (1962), and *Shape of Films to Come* (1968).

Hal Wallis (September 14, 1899-October 5, 1986). Wallis, a studio executive and producer active in Hollywood for forty-five years, was associated with many popular and critical successes over his long career. Born in Chicago, he moved to Los Angeles in 1922, where he managed one of the city's most important cinema theaters. His success attracted the attention of Warner Bros., which hired him in 1923. By 1928, he was studio manager, and by 1933, after jockeying for power with Darryl Zanuck, Wallis became the studio's executive producer in charge of production.

At Warner Bros., Wallis was responsible for producing the studio's most important films, including *Little Caesar* (1930), *I Am a Fugitive from a Chain Gang* (1932), *Captain Blood* (1935), *High Sierra* (1941), *Sergeant York* (1941), *The Maltese Falcon* (1941), *Yankee Doodle Dandy* (1942), and *Casablanca* (1943). During his tenure at Warner Bros., he was twice (in 1938 and 1943) the recipient of the Irving G. Thalberg Memorial Award, given to producers "whose body of work reflects a consistently high quality of motion picture production."

In 1944, Wallis formed Hal Wallis Productions, an independent production company that released films through Paramount Pictures. His films during this period include *Sorry, Wrong Number* (1948), *My Friend Irma* (1949), *Come Back Little Sheba* (1952), and *The Rose Tattoo* (1955). During this period, he produced several films featuring Elvis Presley, including *Loving You* (1957), *King Creole* (1958), and *G.I. Blues* (1960), as well as a number of Dean Martin-Jerry Lewis comedies, including *That's My Boy* (1951), *Scared Stiff* (1953), and *Artists and Models* (1955).

In 1969, toward the end of his career, Wallis began releasing films through Universal. These films include *True Grit* (1969), *The Nelson Affair* (1973), and *Rooster Cogburn* (1975), his last production.

During the course of his career, Wallis produced some 400 films, which earned 132 Academy Award nominations and won 32 of the awards. He was married twice, to actresses Louise Fazenda and Martha Hyer. Additional production credits include *G-Men* (1935), *Kid Galahad* (1937), *Jezebel* (1938), *Dr. Ehrlich's Magic Bullet* (1940), *Kings Row* (1942), *Gunfight at the O.K. Corral* (1957), *Becket* (1964), *Barefoot in the Park* (1967), and *Anne of the Thousand Days* (1969).

Waldon O. Watson (1907-August 15, 1986). Watson was a sound director, who, in 1967, won a special scientific award for his work in designing Universal's music scoring stage, and in 1974, he won another scientific award for helping to invent the Sensurround system. The films on which he worked include *Flower Drum Song* (1961), *That Touch of Mink* (1962), *Captain Newman, M.D.* (1963), *Father Goose* (1964), *Shenandoah* (1965), *Gambit* (1966), and *Thoroughly Modern Millie* (1967).

Margery Wilson (1898-January 21, 1986). Wilson was an actress and director in the silent era. Her first major film role was that of Brown Eyes in D. W. Griffith's *Intol-*

erance (1916), and she starred opposite William S. Hart in *The Return of Draw Egan* (1916), *The Primal Lure* (1916), and *The Desert Man* (1917). She directed three films: *That Something* (1921; in which she also starred), *Insinuation* (1922), and *The Offenders* (1924). After retiring from film, she wrote books on etiquette and charm for young women. In 1956, she published an autobiography entitled *I Found My Way*. Additional film credits include *Bred in the Bone* (1915), *Mountain Dew* (1917), *The Blooming Angel* (1920), and *Old Loves and New* (1926).

Walter Wottitz (1911-November 1, 1986). Wottitz was a French cinematographer. He began his career at Paramount Pictures' French studios in the 1930's. He is perhaps best known in the United States for his work on *The Longest Day* (1962), for which he won an Academy Award.

Keenan Wynn (July 27, 1916-October 14, 1986). Born Francis Xavier Aloysius James Jeremiah Keenan Wynn, Wynn was a versatile character actor whose film career spanned more than four decades. The son of vaudeville comedian Ed Wynn and actress Hilda Keenan, Wynn began acting on the stage as a teenager and appeared in twenty-one Broadway plays before signing a film contract with Metro-Goldwyn-Mayer (his father's studio) in 1942. His first film was *Northwest Rangers* (1942).

Equally adept at playing comic roles and villains, Wynn worked in 220 films during the course of his career. Perhaps his most famous role was that of Colonel Bat Guano, a deranged paratrooper, in *Dr. Strangelove, Or: How I Learned to Stop Worrying and Love the Bomb* (1964). He published his autobiography, *Ed Wynn's Son*, in 1959. His son Tracy Keenan Wynn is a screenwriter and director. Wynn's acting credits include *For Me and My Gal* (1942), *The Three Musketeers* (1948), *Annie Get Your Gun* (1950), *Kiss Me Kate* (1953), *The Absent-Minded Professor* (1961), *Point Blank* (1967), *Nashville* (1975), and *Best Friends* (1982).

LIST OF AWARDS

Academy Awards
Best Picture: Platoon (Orion Pictures)
Direction: Oliver Stone (*Platoon*)
Actor: Paul Newman (*The Color of Money*)
Actress: Marlee Matlin (*Children of a Lesser God*)
Supporting Actor: Michael Caine (*Hannah and Her Sisters*)
Supporting Actress: Dianne Wiest (*Hannah and Her Sisters*)
Original Screenplay: Woody Allen (*Hannah and Her Sisters*)
Adapted Screenplay: Ruth Prawer Jhabvala (*A Room with a View*)
Cinematography: Chris Menges (*The Mission*)
Editing: Claire Simpson (*Platoon*)
Art Direction: Gianni Quaranta and Brian Ackland-Snow; set decoration, Brian Savegar and Elio Altramura (*A Room with a View*)
Sound Effects Editing: Don Sharpe (*Aliens*)
Special Visual Effects: Robert Skotak, Stan Winston, John Richardson, and Suzanne Benson (*Aliens*)
Sound: John "Doc" Wilkinson, Richard Rogers, Charles "Bud" Grenzbach, and Simon Kaye (*Platoon*)
Makeup: Chris Walas and Stephan Dupuis (*The Fly*)
Costume Design: Jenny Beavan and John Bright (*A Room with a View*)
Original Score: Herbie Hancock (*'Round Midnight*)
Original Song: "Take My Breath Away" (*Top Gun:* music, Giorgio Moroder; lyrics, Tom Whitlock)
Foreign-Language Film: The Assault (The Netherlands)
Short Film, Animated: A Greek Tragedy (CineTe pvba)
Short Film, Live Action: Precious Images (Calliope Films)
Documentary, Feature: Artie Shaw, Time Is All You've Got (Bridge Film) and *Down and Out in America* (Joseph Feury), tie
Documentary, Short Subject: Women—For America, For the World {Educational Film and Video Project)

Directors Guild of America Award
Director: Oliver Stone (*Platoon*)

Writers Guild Awards
Original Screenplay: Woody Allen (*Hannah and Her Sisters*)
Adapted Screnplay: Ruth Prawer Jhabvala (*A Room with a View*)

New York Film Critics Awards
Best Picture: Hannah and Her Sisters (Orion Pictures)
Direction: Woody Allen (*Hannah and Her Sisters*)

Actor: Bob Hoskins (*Mona Lisa*)
Actress: Sissy Spacek (*Crimes of the Heart*)
Supporting Actor: Daniel Day-Lewis (*My Beautiful Laundrette* and *A Room with a View*)
Supporting Actress: Dianne Wiest (*Hannah and Her Sisters*)
Screenplay: Hanif Kureishi (*My Beautiful Laundrette*)
Cinematography: Tony Pierce-Roberts (*A Room with a View*)
Foreign-Language Film: The Decline of the American Empire (Canada)

Los Angeles Film Critics Awards
Best Picture: Hannah and Her Sisters (Orion Pictures)
Direction: David Lynch (*Blue Velvet*)
Actor: Bob Hoskins (*Mona Lisa*)
Actress: Sandrine Bonnaire (*Vagabond*)
Suppporting Actor: Dennis Hopper (*Blue Velvet* and *Hoosiers*)
Supporting Actress: Dianne Wiest (*Hannah and Her Sisters*) and Cathy Tyson (*Mona Lisa*), tie
Screenplay: Woody Allen (*Hannah and Her Sisters*)
Cinematography: Chris Menges (*The Mission*)
Music: Herbie Hancock ('*Round Midnight*)
Foreign Film: Vagabond (France)

National Society of Film Critics Awards
Best Picture: Blue Velvet (De Laurentiis Entertainment Group)
Direction: David Lynch (*Blue Velvet*)
Actor: Bob Hoskins (*Mona Lisa*)
Actress: Chloe Webb (*Sid and Nancy*)
Supporting Actor: Dennis Hopper (*Blue Velvet*)
Supporting Actress: Dianne Wiest (*Hannah and Her Sisters*)
Screenplay: Hanif Kureishi (*My Beautiful Landrette*)
Cinematography: Frederick Elmes (*Blue Velvet*)
Best Documentary: Marlene (Alive Films)

National Board of Review Awards
Best English-Language Film: A Room with a View (Cinecom Pictures)
Direction: Woody Allen (*Hannah and Her Sisters*)
Actor: Paul Newman (*The Color of Money*)
Actress: Kathleen Turner (*Peggy Sue Got Married*)
Supporting Actor: Daniel Day-Lewis (*A Room with a View* and *My Beautiful Laundrette*)
Supporting Actress: Dianne Wiest (*Hannah and Her Sisters*)
Foreign-Language Film: Otello (Italy and the Netherlands)

Golden Globe Awards
Best Picture, Drama: Platoon (Orion Pictures)
Best Picture, Comedy or Musical: Hannah and Her Sisters (Orion Pictures)
Direction: Oliver Stone (*Platoon*)
Actor, Drama: Bob Hoskins (*Mona Lisa*)
Actress, Drama: Marlee Matlin (*Children of a Lesser God*)
Actor, Comedy or Musical: Paul Hogan (*"Crocodile" Dundee*)
Actress, Comedy or Musical: Sissy Spacek (*Crimes of the Heart*)
Supporting Actor: Tom Berenger (*Platoon*)
Supporting Actress: Maggie Smith (*A Room with a View*)
Screenplay: Robert Bolt (*The Mission*)
Original Score: Ennio Morricone (*The Mission*)
Foreign Film: The Assault (The Netherlands)

Golden Palm Awards
Gold Palm: Under the Sun of Satan (Maurice Pialat)
Grand Special Jury Award: Repentance (Tengiz Abuladze)
Actor: Marcello Mastroianni (*Black Eyes*)
Actress: Barbara Hershey (*Shy People*)
Direction: Wim Wenders (*The Sky over Berlin*)
Artistic Contribution: Stanley Myers (*Prick Up Your Ears*)

British Academy Awards
Best Picture: A Room with a View (Cinecom Pictures)
Direction: Woody Allen (*Hannah and Her Sisters*)
Actor: Bob Hoskins (*Mona Lisa*)
Actress: Maggie Smith (*A Room with a View*)
Supporting Actor: Ray McAnnally (*The Mission*)
Supporting Actress: Judi Dench (*A Room with a View*)
Original Screenplay: Woody Allen (*Hannah and Her Sisters*)
Adapted Screenplay: Kurt Luedtke (*Out of Africa*)
Cinematography: David Watkin (*Out of Africa*)
Editing: Jim Clark (*The Mission*)
Production Design: Gianni Quaranta and Brian Ackland-Snow (*A Room with a View*)
Special Visual Effects: Robert Skotak, John Richardson, Suzanne Benson, and Stan Winston (*Aliens*)
Costume Design: Jenny Beavan and John Bright (*A Room with a View*)
Sound: Tom McCarthy, Jr., Peter Handford, and Chris Jenkins (*Out of Africa*)
Original Score: Ennio Morricone (*The Mission*)

MAGILL'S
CINEMA
ANNUAL

TITLE INDEX

TITLE INDEX

DIRECTOR INDEX

DIRECTOR INDEX

DIRECTOR INDEX

629

SCREENWRITER INDEX

631

SCREENWRITER INDEX

SCREENWRITER INDEX

635

SCREENWRITER INDEX

CINEMATOGRAPHER INDEX

641

642

CINEMATOGRAPHER INDEX

CINEMATOGRAPHER INDEX

645

EDITOR INDEX

EDITOR INDEX

GOURSON, JEFF
Flight of the Navigator   487
GOW, JOHN
Gospel According to Vic   490
GREEN, BRUCE
April Fool's Day   477
Friday the Thirteenth, Part VI   488
GREENBERG, JERRY
No Mercy   500
Wise Guys   466
GREENBURY, CHRISTOPHER
Haunted Honeymoon   490
GREENE, DANFORD B.
Head Office   491
GRENVILLE, GEORGE
Iron Eagle   493
GROSS, DAN
Annihilators, The   476
GROSSMAN, MARC
Vamp   514
GROVER, JOHN
Labyrinth   494
GUIDO, ELISABETH
Cage aux folles II, La [1985]   480

HAINES, RICHARD W.
Class of Nuke 'em High   482
Toxic Avenger, The   512
HALLE, TERRY
Imagemaker, The   492
HALSEY, RICHARD
Down and Out in Beverly Hills   171
HAMBLING, GERRY
Absolute Beginners   475
HANEKE, TOM
Mother Teresa   314
HANKINS, DAVID
Transformers, The   513
HANLEY, DANIEL
Armed and Dangerous   477
Gung Ho   220
HARKNESS, RICHARD
On the Edge   501
Signal Seven   508
HARRIS, FRANK
Low Blow   496
HARRIS, RICHARD A.
Golden Child, The   212
Wildcats   516
HAZELL, C. VAUGHN
America   476
HECK, SUSAN
Hard Traveling   490
HEITNER, DAVID
Place of Weeping   503
HERRING, PEM
Legal Eagles   255
HILL, DENNIS M.
UFOria   459
HILL, MICHAEL
Armed and Dangerous   477
Gung Ho   220
HIRSCH, PAUL
Ferris Bueller's Day Off   189

HIRTZ, DAGMAR
Marlene [1983]   278
HOENIG, DOV
Manhunter   497
HOFSTRA, JACK
Band of the Hand   478
Youngblood   517
HOLMES, CHRISTOPHER
Bad Guys   477
HONESS, PETER
Highlander   491
HONEY, MICHAEL
Rebel [1985]   506
HONTHANER, RON
Free Ride   488
HORVITCH, ANDY
Boys Next Door, The   480
Eliminators   185
HUGGETT, DAVID
Fast Talking [1984]   487
HUMPHREYS, NED
Never Too Young to Die   499

JAFFE, GIB
Ruthless People   377
JAFFE, JANE SCHWARTZ
Trick or Treat   513
JAKUBOWICZ, ALAIN
Delta Force, The   158
Invaders from Mars   493
Texas Chainsaw Massacre, Part II, The   511
JENKINS, ERIC
Whoopee Boys, The   516
JYMPSON, JOHN
Little Shop of Horrors   265

KAHN, MICHAEL
Wisdom   516
KAHN, SHELDON
Legal Eagles   255
KARLSON, PHIL
Obituaries   600
KARR, GARY
Playing for Keeps   503
KELLY, LUIS
Doña Herlinda and Her Son [1985]   167
KEMPER, STEVEN
3:15   512
KENNEDY, PATRICIA
Airplane! [1980]   521
KENNEDY, PATRICK
Boy Who Could Fly, The   479
KERAMIDAS, HARRY
"About Last Night . . ."   59
KIKUCHI, JUNNICHI
Crazy Family, The [1984]   483
KNUE, MICHAEL N.
House   492
Night of the Creeps   499
KOOLER, INGRID
Echo Park   181
KRESS, CARL
Rad   505
KUNZE, BARBARA
Angry Harvest [1985]   476

649

EDITOR INDEX

652

EDITOR INDEX

ART DIRECTOR INDEX

ART DIRECTOR INDEX

658

ART DIRECTOR INDEX

ART DIRECTOR INDEX

ART DIRECTOR INDEX

MUSIC INDEX

665

MUSIC INDEX

PERFORMER INDEX

AAMES, WILLIE
  Cut and Run   483
AANENSEN, PETER
  Cactus   480
ABBOTT, DIAHNNE
  Jo Jo Dancer, Your Life is Calling   493
ABDUL-JABAAR, KAREEM
  Airplane! [1980]   521
ABERCROMBIE, IAN
  Firewalker   487
ABRAHAM, F. MURRAY
  Name of the Rose, The   332
ACHESON, JAMES
  P.O.W. the Escape   504
ACKER, IRIS
  Flight of the Navigator   487
ACKLAND, JOSS
  Lady Jane   495
ACKRIDGE, BILL
  Signal Seven   508
ADAMO, SHERRY
  American Justice   476
ADAMS, MASON
  F/X   203
ADLER, MATT
  Flight of the Navigator   487
AGINS, ROBERT
  Color of Money, The   132
AHERNE, BRIAN
  Obituaries   589
AIMÉE, ANOUK
  Man and a Woman, A   496
AKERS, ANDRA
  Desert Hearts   485
ALAIMO, MARK
  Avenging Force   477
ALBANO, CAPTAIN LOU
  Wise Guys   466
ALBERT, EDDIE
  Head Office   491
  Heartbreak Kid, The [1972]   533
ALBERT, EDWARD
  Getting Even   489
ALDA, ALAN
  Sweet Liberty   510
ALDA, ROBERT
  Obituaries   589
ALETTER, FRANK
  Vasectomy   514
ALLAYLIS, TONI
  Fast Talking [1984]   487
ALLDREDGE, MICHAEL
  "About Last Night. . ."   59
ALLEN, BILL
  Rad   505
ALLEN, CHAD
  Terrorvision   511
ALLEN, DEBBIE
  Jo Jo Dancer, Your Life is Calling   493

ALLEN, JO HARVEY
  True Stories   447
ALLEN, JOAN
  Manhunter   497
  Peggy Sue Got Married   349
ALLEN, STEVE
  What Happened to Kerouac?   515
ALLEN, WOODY
  Hannah and Her Sisters   228
ALMAGOR, GILA
  Every Time We Say Goodbye   486
ALMAZ, NOAM
  Caravaggio   480
ALMGREN, SUZIE
  Separate Vacations   507
ALONSO, MARIA CONCHITA
  Fine Mess, A   487
  Touch and Go   512
ALPERSTRE, GIANFRANCO
  Ginger and Fred [1985]   207
ALTERMEN, STEVE
  Big Trouble   478
ALTUNTAS, ALI DEDE
  Wall, The [1983]   515
AMERSON, TAMMY
  My Little Pony   498
AMES, CHRISTOPHER
  Last Resort   495
AMES, JOYCE
  Hello, Dolly! [1969]   539
AMES, LEON
  Jake Speed   493
  Peggy Sue Got Married   349
AMPHOUX, MICHEL
  Mystery of Alexina, The [1985]   499
ANCONINA, RICHARD
  Police [1985]   503
ANDERSON, GORDON
  Ratboy   505
ANDERSON, ISABELLE
  Rebel [1985]   506
ANDERSON, JOHN
  Never Too Young to Die   499
  Scorpion   507
ANDERSON, LAURIE
  Home of the Brave   492
ANDERSON, LOUIE
  Quicksilver   504
  Ratboy   505
ANDERSON, MELODY
  Boy in Blue, The   479
  Firewalker   487
ANDERSON, MILES
  Sky Bandits   509
ANDERSON, MITCHELL
  Spacecamp   509
ANDEW, CHRIS
  Radioactive Dreams   505
ANDREWS, HARRY
  Touch of Larceny, A [1959]   583

PERFORMER INDEX

BETTIN, VAL
Great Mouse Detective, The 215
BETZ, MATTHEW
Mystery of the Wax Museum [1933] 564
BIAFRA, JELLO
Unheard Music, The 513
BIANCO, TOMMASO
Camorra 480
BICKNELL, ANDREW
Lady Jane 495
BIEHN, MICHAEL
Aliens 64
BIGGS, BOB
Unheard Music, The 513
BIGNEY, HUGH
Nutcracker, The 501
BILLERAY, RAOUL
Betty Blue 101
BINGENHEIMER, RODNEY
Unheard Music, The 513
BINNS, EDWARD
Whatever It Takes 515
BIRD, BILLIE
Ratboy 505
BIRKETT, JACK
Caravaggio 480
BISHOP, DEBBY
Sid and Nancy 401
BISHOP, JOEY
Delta Force, The 158
BISLEY, STEVE
Fast Talking [1984] 487
BJÖRNSTRAND, GUNNAR
Obituaries 592
BLACK, KAREN
Cut and Run 483
Invaders from Mars 493
BLACKBURN, DIANA
French Lesson 488
BLACKWOOD, VAS
Arthur's Hallowed Ground [1984] 477
BLAIR, LIONEL
Absolute Beginners 475
BLAKE, ELLEN
Last Resort 495
BLAKE, MADGE
Long, Long Trailer, The [1954] 560
BLAKE, OLIVER
Long, Long Trailer, The [1954] 560
BLAKELY, COLIN
Loophole [1983] 496
BLAKELY, DON
In the Shadow of Kilimanjaro 492
Wired to Kill 516
BLANC, MEL
Heathcliff 491
BLANC, MICHEL
Ménage 287
BLANEY, TIM
Short Circuit 508
BLAU, MARTIN MARIA
Ginger and Fred [1985] 207
BLEE, DEBRA
Hamburger 490

BLESSING, JACK
Hamburger 490
BLOOM, JANE IRA
Home of the Brave 492
BLORE, CATHIANNE
American Tail, An 70
BLOUNT, LISA
Cut and Run 483
Radioactive Dreams 505
BLUM, MARK
"Crocodile" Dundee 143
BOEKE, JIM
In the Shadow of Kilimanjaro 492
BOER, CASPAR DE
Assault, The 80
BOGERT, BILL
Whatever It Takes 515
BOGOSIAN, ERIC
Special Effects 509
BOHT, JEAN
Arthur's Hallowed Ground [1984] 477
BOLGER, JOHN
Parting Glances 344
BOLL, HELEN
Poltergeist II 504
BOLLES, ERIC
Eye of the Tiger 486
BOLTON, HEATHER
Dark of the Night [1985] 484
BONACELLI, PAOLO
Camorra 480
BONDO, ULRIKKE JUUL
Twist and Shout [1985] 456
BONEBRAKE, D. J.
Unheard Music, The 513
BONEBRAKE, DINKY
Unheard Music, The 513
BONNAIRE, SANDRINE
Police [1985] 503
Vagabond [1985] 514
BONO, SONNY
Troll 513
BOOTH, JAMES
Avenging Force 477
Bad Guys 477
BOSCO, PHILIP
Children of a Lesser God 122
Money Pit, The 498
BOTSFORD, SARA
Jumpin' Jack Flash 493
BOTTOMS, TIMOTHY
In the Shadow of Kilimanjaro 492
Invaders from Mars 493
BOUCHERY, CLAUDE
Mystery of Alexina, The [1985] 499
BOUIX, EVELYNE
Man and a Woman, A 496
BOUJENAH, MICHEL
Three Men and a Cradle [1985] 432
BOUKANEF, KADER
Tea in the Harem [1985] 511
BOUSHEL, JOY
Fly, The 198

PERFORMER INDEX

PERFORMER INDEX

PERFORMER INDEX

681

DE BELLEFEUILLE, DAISY
Ninety Days [1985] 500
DEE DEE
Sherman's March 391
DEEZEN, EDDIE
Whoopee Boys, The 516
DEFINA, DON
Signal Seven 508
DE LA PAZ, DANNY
3:15 512
DELAUNÉ, YVETTE
Femmes de personne [1984] 487
DELAUNEY, ANDRE
Belizaire the Cajun 478
DELEVINGNE, PHILIPPE
Sincerely Charlotte 508
DELFOSSE, RAOUL
French Lesson 488
DEL SOL, LAURA
Amor brujo, El 75
DEL TORO, GUADALUPE
Doña Herlinda and Her Son [1985] 167
DELUISE, DOM
American Tail, An 70
Haunted Honeymoon 490
DELUISE, PETER
Free Ride 488
Solarbabies 509
DEMOREST, DANIEL
P.O.W. the Escape 504
DEMOSS, DARCY
Friday the Thirteenth, Part VI 488
Reform School Girls 506
DEMPSTER, CURT
Manhattan Project, The 273
DEMUNN, JEFFREY
Hitcher, The 491
DENCH, JUDI
Room with a View, A 363
DENHAM, MAURICE
Mr. Love 497
DE NIRO, ROBERT
Mission, The 292
DENNEHY, BRIAN
Check Is in the Mail, The 481
F/X 203
Legal Eagles 255
DEPARDIEU, GÉRARD
Ménage 287
Police [1985] 503
DEPP, JOHNNY
Platoon 354
DERN, BRUCE
On the Edge 501
DERN, LAURA
Blue Velvet 110
DERRICKS, CLEAVANT
Off Beat 501
DERUE, CARMEN
Obituaries 596
DE SOTO, ROSANNA
American Justice 476
DE TELIGA, SARAH
Bliss [1985] 106

DEVEAU, ALAN
Loose Screws 496
Recruits 506
DEVITO, DANNY
Head Office 491
My Little Pony 498
Ruthless People 377
Wise Guys 466
DEWAEME, PASCAL
Tea in the Harem [1985] 511
DEWHURST, COLLEEN
Boy Who Could Fly, The 479
DEY, SUSAN
Echo Park 181
DE YOUNG, CLIFF
Flight of the Navigator 487
F/X 203
DIAZ, JUSTINO
Otello 339
DICENZO, GEORGE
"About Last Night. . ." 59
Longshot, The 496
DICKERSON, GEORGE
Blue Velvet 110
DIEFENDORF, DIANE
UFOria 459
DILLON, DENNY
Seven Minutes in Heaven 507
DILLON, KEVIN
Platoon 354
DILLON, MATT
Native Son 499
Rebel [1985] 506
DIMANCHE, JACQUES
Wall, The [1983] 515
DINOME, JERRY
Dangerously Close 483
DIPRIMA, DIANE
What Happened to Kerouac? 515
DISANTI, JOHN
Running Scared 373
DISHY, BOB
Brighton Beach Memoirs 116
DJOLA, BADJA
Lightship, The 495
DOE, JOHN
Unheard Music, The 513
DOMINGO, PLÁCIDO
Otello 339
DONALDSON, TEX
Crossroads 148
DONAT, RICHARD
My American Cousin [1985] 318
DONNELLY, PATRICE
American Anthem 476
DONOHOE, AMANDA
Foreign Body 488
DONOHUE, TROY
Low Blow 496
DONOVAN, MARTIN
Hard Choices 490
DONOVAN, TATE
Spacecamp 509

PERFORMER INDEX

683

PERFORMER INDEX

PERFORMER INDEX

689

MADSEN, VIRGINIA
  Fire with Fire   487
  Modern Girls   498
MAGLIO, MITCH
  Combat Shock   482
MAGOIA, ELENA
  Ginger and Fred [1985]   207
MAHON, JACKIE
  Separate Vacations   507
MAHONEY, JOHN
  Manhattan Project, The   273
MAIDEN, SHARON
  Clockwise   482
MAIN, LAURIE
  My Chauffeur   498
MAIN, MARJORIE
  Long, Long Trailer, The [1954]   560
MAIRESSE, VALÉRIE
  Sacrifice, The   381
MAKEPEACE, CHRIS
  Vamp   514
MAKHENE, RAMOLAO
  Place of Weeping   503
MAKO
  Armed Response   477
  P.O.W. the Escape   504
MALAKOVA, PETRA
  Otello   339
MALCOLM, CHRISTOPHER
  Labyrinth   494
MALL, PAUL
  Flight of the Navigator   487
MALONEY, MICHAEL
  Sharma and Beyond   508
MALONEY, STACEY
  American Anthem   476
MANCHESTER, MELISSA
  Great Mouse Detective, The   215
MANCUSO, NICK
  Death of an Angel   484
MANDEL, HOWIE
  Fine Mess, A   487
MANION, CINDY
  Toxic Avenger, The   512
MANN, DUTCH
  Bad Guys   477
MANN, LEONARD
  Cut and Run   483
MANN, TERRENCE
  Critters   483
MANN, TRACY
  Fast Talking [1984]   487
MANNING, NED
  Dead-end Drive-in   484
MANNIX, PEGGY
  Eliminators   185
MANTEGNA, JOE
  Money Pit, The   498
  Off Beat   501
  Three Amigos   511
MANZAREK, RAY
  Unheard Music, The   513
MANZO, TONY
  Girls School Screamers   489

MARADEN, FRANK
  King Kong Lives   494
MARANDA, ANDREE
  Toxic Avenger, The   512
MARANGOSOFF, JANNA
  Men [1985]   282
MARANO, EZIO
  Ginger and Fred [1985]   207
MARCEAU, SOPHIE
  Police [1985]   503
MARCUS, RICHARD
  Deadly Friend   484
MARDIROSIAN, TOM
  Eat and Run   485
  Power   504
MARENTES, CARLOS
  Death of an Angel   484
MARGOLIN, STUART
  Fine Mess, A   487
MARGULIES, DAVID
  Nine and a Half Weeks   500
MARIANA, MICHELE
  Adventures of Mark Twain, The   475
MARIELLE, JEAN-PIERRE
  Ménage   287
MARIKA, BANDUK
  Cactus   480
MARIN, RICHARD "CHEECH"
  Echo Park   181
MARINI, STEFANIE
  Ginger and Fred [1985]   207
MARKHAM, MONTE
  Jake Speed   493
MARLEY, JOHN
  On the Edge   501
MARLOWE, LINDA
  Mr. Love   497
MARNER, RICHARD
  Touch of Larceny, A [1959]   583
MARONEY, KELLY
  Chopping Mall   481
MARQUEZ, WILLIAM
  Black Moon Rising   479
MARS, KEN
  Adventures of the American Rabbit, The   474
MARSHALL, BRYAN
  Bliss [1985]   106
MARSHALL, E. G.
  My Chauffeur   498
  Power   504
MARSHALL, STEVE
  Night of the Creeps   499
MARSHALL, WILLIAM
  Vasectomy   514
MARSILLACH, CRISTINA
  Every Time We Say Goodbye   486
MARTEL, PAUL
  Seven Minutes in Heaven   507
MARTIN, ANDREA
  Club Paradise   482
MARTIN, DEAN
  Kiss Me, Stupid [1964]   556
MARTIN, JARED
  Quiet Cool   505

MARTIN, PEPPER
Bad Guys 477
MARTIN, REMI
Tea in the Harem [1985] 511
MARTIN, SANDY
Extremities 486
Vendetta 514
MARTIN, STEVE
Little Shop of Horrors 265
Three Amigos 511
MARTINEZ, PATRICE
Three Amigos 511
MARVIN, LEE
Delta Force, The 158
MARX, BRETT
Thrashin' 511
MASINA, GIULIETTA
Ginger and Fred [1985] 207
MASON, JAMES
Touch of Larceny, A [1959] 583
MASON, MARSHA
Heartbreak Ridge 235
MASON, TOM
Crimes of the Heart 138
Whatever It Takes 515
MASSEY, ANNA
Foreign Body 488
MASSEY, WALTER
Boy in Blue, The 479
MASTERS, BEN
Dream Lover 485
MASTERSON, MARY STUART
At Close Range 86
MASTRANTONIO, MARY ELIZABETH
Color of Money, The 132
MASTROIANNI, MARCELLO
Ginger and Fred [1985] 207
MASUR, RICHARD
Head Office 491
Heartburn 240
MATHEWS, THOM
Dangerously Close 483
Friday the Thirteenth, Part VI 488
MATHOU, JACQUES
Betty Blue 101
MATLIN, MARLEE
Children of a Lesser God 122
MATTHAU, WALTER
Hello, Dolly! [1969] 539
Life Achievement Award 3
Pirates 503
MATZ, JERRY
Gig, The 489
MAUCERI, PATRICIA
Saving Grace 507
MAUGHAN, MONICA
Cactus 480
MAXWELL, EDWIN
Mystery of the Wax Museum [1933] 564
MAXWELL, ROBERTA
Psycho III 504
MAYER, JOHN
Adventures of the American Rabbit, The 474
MAYO-CHANDLER, KAREN
Hamburger 490

MEARA, ANNE
Longshot, The 496
MEATLOAF
Out of Bounds 502
MEDFORD, PAUL
Black Joy 479
MEILLON, JOHN
"Crocodile" Dundee 143
MEINRAD, JOSEF
Cardinal, The [1963] 525
MEJDING, BENT
Twist and Shout [1985] 456
MELODY, TONY
Mr. Love 497
MELVILLE, PAULINE
Mona Lisa 297
MENAHEM, DAVID
Delta Force, The 158
MENGATI, JOHN
Knights of the City 494
MENTON, LOREE
Stripper 510
MENZIES, ROBERT
Bliss [1985] 106
Cactus 480
MERANDE, DORO
Kiss Me, Stupid [1964] 556
MERCADO, HECTOR
Nomads 501
MERCIER, LAURENCE
Sincerely Charlotte 508
MEREDITH, BURGESS
Cardinal, The [1963] 525
MERIL, MACHA
Vagabond [1985] 514
MERKEL, UNA
Obituaries 604
MERKINSON, EPATHA
She's Gotta Have It 395
MESCI, AYSE EMEL
Wall, The [1983] 515
MESSICK, DON
Transformers, The 513
MESSING, CAROL
Nothing in Common 501
METCALF, MARK
One Crazy Summer 502
METRANO, ART
Police Academy III 503
MEYER, BESS
One More Saturday 502
MEZA, ARTURO
Doña Herlinda and Her Son [1985] 167
MHLOPHE, GEINA
Place of Weeping 503
MIANO, ROBERT
Hollywood Vice Squad 491
MICHAS, JENNIFER
Boy Who Could Fly, The 479
MICHEL, DOMINIQUE
Decline of the American Empire, The 152
MIDLER, BETTE
Down and Out in Beverly Hills 171
Ruthless People 377

PERFORMER INDEX

701

PERFORMER INDEX

709

WALTON, EMMA
  That's Life! 427
WALTON, LEE-MAX
  Separate Vacations 507
WALTZ, LISA
  Brighton Beach Memoirs 116
WANAMAKER, SAM
  Raw Deal 506
WANG, PETER
  Great Wall, A 490
WANG XIAU
  Great Wall, A 490
WARD, FRED
  UFOria 459
WARD, JAMES
  Kiss Me, Stupid [1964] 556
WARD, LYMAN
  Ferris Bueller's Day Off 189
WARD, MARY B.
  Playing for Keeps 503
WARD, SELA
  Nothing in Common 501
WARFIELD, MARSHA
  Whoopee Boys, The 516
WARNECKE, GORDON
  My Beautiful Laundrette [1985] 323
WARREN, JASON
  Loose Screws 496
WARREN, MARCIA
  Mr. Love 497
WASHINGTON, DENZEL
  Power 504
WASS, TED
  Longshot, The 496
WASSON, CRAIG
  Men's Club, The 497
WATANABE, GEDDE
  Gung Ho 220
  Vamp 514
WATERS, JOHN
  Something Wild 406
WATERSTON, SAM
  Just Between Friends 494
WAY, ANN
  Haunted Honeymoon 490
WEATHERHEAD, CHRIS
  Whatever It Takes 515
WEAVER, FRITZ
  Power 504
WEAVER, SIGOURNEY
  Aliens 64
  Half Moon Street 225
WEBB, CHLOE
  Sid and Nancy 401
WEBB, DANIEL
  Year of the Quiet Sun, A [1984] 470
WECK, PETER
  Cardinal, The [1963] 525
WEDDLE, VERNON
  Short Circuit 508
WEDGEWORTH, ANN
  Men's Club, The 497
WEEKS, MICHELLE
  Little Shop of Horrors 265

WEGENER, SABINE
  Men [1985] 282
WEISMAN, ORIT
  Every Time We Say Goodbye 486
WEISSER, NORBERT
  Radioactive Dreams 505
WEIST, DWIGHT
  Nine and a Half Weeks 500
WELKER, FRANK
  Transformers, The 513
WELLER, ELLY
  Assault, The 80
WELLES, GWEN
  Desert Hearts 485
  Men's Club, The 497
  Nobody's Fool 500
WELLES, ORSON
  Transformers, The 513
WELLS, MARY
  Howard the Duck 492
WENDT, GEORGE
  Gung Ho 220
  House 492
WEST, PAUL
  Dream Lover 485
WESTON, JACK
  Longshot, The 496
  Rad 505
WESTON, STAN
  Torment 512
WHALEY, GEORGE
  Bliss [1985] 106
WHEATON, WIL
  Stand by Me 413
WHINNERY, BARBARA
  Crawlspace 483
  Hamburger 490
WHITAKER, ALBIE
  Flight of the Navigator 487
WHITAKER, CHRISTINA
  Naked Cage, The 499
WHITAKER, FOREST
  Color of Money, The 132
  Platoon 354
WHITE, ANDREW M.
  American Anthem 476
WHITE, CAROLE ITA
  Naked Cage, The 499
WHITECLOUD, JOHN P.
  Poltergeist II 504
WHITEHEAD, PAXTON
  Back to School 92
WHITFORD, PETER
  Dead-end Drive-in 484
WHITLOW, JILL
  Night of the Creeps 499
WHITMORE, JAMES
  Adventures of Mark Twain, The 475
WHITROW, BENJAMIN
  Sharma and Beyond 508
WHITTON, MARGARET
  Best of Times, The 97
  Nine and a Half Weeks 500
WHYLIE, JAMES
  Place of Weeping 503

SUBJECT INDEX

The selection of subject headings combines standard Library of Congress Subject Headings and common usage in order to aid the film researcher. Cross references, listed as *See* and *See also*, are provided when appropriate. While all major themes, locales, and time periods have been indexed, some minor subjects covered in a particular film have not been included.

SUBJECT INDEX

SUBJECT INDEX

SUBJECT INDEX